Rural Social Work

Building and Sustaining

Community Assets

Edited by
T. LAINE SCALES
Baylor University

CALVIN L. STREETER
University of Texas, Austin

THOMSON
BROOKS/COLE

Australia • Canada • Mexico • Singapore • Spain
United Kingdom • United States

THOMSON

BROOKS/COLE

Executive Editor: *Lisa Gebo*
Assistant Editor: *Alma Dea Michelena*
Editorial Assistant: *Sheila Walsh*
Marketing Manager: *Caroline Concilla*
Marketing Assistant: *Mary Ho*
Advertising Project Manager: *Tami Strang*
Signing Representative: *Richard Colangelo*
Project Manager, Editorial Production:
  Rita Jaramillo

Print/Media Buyer: *Judy Inouye*
Permissions Editor: *Sommy Ko*
Production Service: *Mary E. Deeg, Buuji, Inc.*
Copy Editor: *Alan DeNiro, Buuji, Inc.*
Cover Designer: *Larry Didona*
Cover Photo: *Clark Baker*
Cover Printer: *Webcom*
Compositor: *Buuji, Inc.*
Printer: *Webcom*

Printed in Canada
1 2 3 4 5 6 7 07 06 05 04 03

For more information about our products,
contact us at:
Thomson Learning Academic Resource Center
1-800-423-0563

For permission to use material from this text,
contact us by:
Phone: 1-800-730-2214   Fax: 1-800-730-2215
Web: http://www.thomsonrights.com

Library of Congress Control Number:
2003104292

ISBN 0-534-462163-5

Brooks/Cole/Thomson Learning
10 Davis Drive
Belmont, CA 94002
USA

Asia
Thomson Learning
5 Shenton Way #01-01
UIC Building
Singapore 068808

Australia/New Zealand
Thomson Learning
102 Dodds Street
Southbank, Victoria 3006
Australia

Canada
Nelson
1120 Birchmount Road
Toronto, Ontario M1K 5G4
Canada

Europe/Middle East/Africa
Thomson Learning
High Holborn House
50/51 Bedford Row
London WC1R 4LR
United Kingdom

Latin America
Thomson Learning
Seneca, 53
Colonia Polanco
11560 Mexico D.F.
Mexico

Spain
Paraninfo
Calle/Magallanes, 25
28015 Madrid
Spain

✳

In tribute to the courage and commitment of
Elisabeth Kenny, MSW (1936–2003),
asset builder with rural children and families

Contents

✳
Preface

The idea for this book grew out of our involvement with the National Institute on Social Work and Human Services in Rural Areas held in May 2001 at the University of Texas at Austin. The theme of our conference was asset building, which suggests that social workers identify, utilize, and build upon individual and community assets and strengths to improve quality of life. Although asset building has become a significant catchphrase in recent years, social work has a long tradition of professional practice focused on client and community strengths. We believe the asset-building theme of this book will contribute to a further development of a practice framework based on assets and strengths, rather than pathologies and deficiencies.

As social work educators facing the challenges of integrating rural content into our courses, we understand the necessity of current and classroom-friendly readings with discussion questions and assignments to facilitate study of the material at both the BSW and MSW levels. We hope that students, teachers, and practitioners will find this book a useful resource to help them think about rural social work in new ways.

ACKNOWLEDGMENTS

We have many people to thank, beginning with the lead teachers and contributors who worked diligently to prepare and revise their work. We also thank Lisa Gebo and Sheila Walsh of Brooks/Cole, who have been so efficient and pleasant. We especially appreciate Jeanie Fitzpatrick, and Jennifer Nelson for their careful attention to detail in the manuscript preparation.

In addition, we are grateful to the following reviewers who gave us helpful feedback: Robert Vernon, IUPUI School of Social Work; Rasby Marlene Powell, University of North Carolina–Pembroke; Susan Sarnoff, Ohio University-Athens; Robert Blundo, University of North Carolina–Wilmington; Naurine D. Lennox, Saint Olaf College; Barbara J. Nowak, Florida A&M University.

Many people have inspired, guided, and influenced our professional and personal development. We call those people asset builders. I (Laine) would like to acknowledge my dad, Charlie Scales, who along with my mom, provided my first learning about rural communities. Growing up in rural Kentucky and North Carolina, I watched (and helped) my parents as they tirelessly gave their time and energy building natural helping networks to sustain our small communities. I am also indebted to Donoso Escobar, teacher and friend who first taught me that rurality is not just a matter of where we are located geographically, but an important cultural study; and that social workers can (and need to) do this essential work. My deepest gratitude goes to my husband, Dr. Glenn Blalock, who reminds me how important good writing, reading, and critical discussion are for the learning process, and supports me faithfully in our life and work together.

I (Cal) was influenced by countless asset builders, many of whom didn't know they influenced me, who have shaped who I am today. I would like to thank all those who have helped me along the way. In particular I want to acknowledge my parents, Lloyd and Delores Streeter. My earliest memories of rural community life center around my parents' active participation in the life of their small farming community in central Nebraska. Working together with neighbors, sharing their dreams and aspirations, influencing one another's opinions, and supporting and encouraging one another during difficult times was a normal and natural part of their life. They were and continue to be asset builders for many, young and old. I would also like to express my gratitude to my wife, Diane, and my children, Brian and Aaron, who remind me daily of the importance of family in our ongoing journey through life.

ABOUT THE EDITORS

T. Laine Scales, Ph.D., is an assistant professor of social work at Baylor University, Waco, Texas. She earned her MSW at Carver School of Church Social Work and completed her Ph.D. at the University of Kentucky. She served as the associate director of a project to place social work interns in rural churches in Kentucky and Indiana and wrote and produced a training video, *Church Social Work in Rural America* (1992). Dr. Scales taught classes in rural social work at Stephen F. Austin State University, Nacogdoches, Texas. In addition to her interest in rural social work, she has published in the areas of social welfare history and spirituality and religion in social work. She is the author of

All That Fits a Woman: Training Southern Baptist Women for Charity and Mission, 1907–1926 (Mercer University Press, 2000). Other publications include *Spirituality and Religion in Social Work Practice: Decision Cases with Teaching Notes* (coeditor) and *Christianity and Social Work: Readings on the Integration of Christian Faith and Social Work Practice, 2nd edition* (coeditor). Dr. Scales is a member of the Rural Social Work Caucus and has held leadership positions in the National Association of Social Workers, Texas Chapter.

Calvin L. Streeter, Ph.D., is the Meadows Foundation Centennial Professor in the Quality of Life in the Rural Environment and the director of the Ph.D. program in social work at The University of Texas at Austin. He earned his BSW from the University of Nebraska at Kearney and his MSW and Ph.D. from Washington University in St. Louis. Dr. Streeter teaches in the areas of macro practice and research. In addition to his interest in rural social work, his recent research has focused on school reform and school-based services. He recently completed an evaluation of the Safe School/Healthy Students Initiative in Georgetown, Texas. He is currently part of a team evaluating the long-term benefits of an innovative solution-focused school model called Solution-focused Alternatives for Education (SAFED). He is also a member of the Rural Social Work Caucus and has been on the national board of the Association for Community Organization and Social Administration. Finally, he is active in many local causes and has served on numerous nonprofit boards and taskforces.

ABOUT THE CONTRIBUTORS

Lead Teachers

Freddie L. Avant, MSW, is an associate professor and the director of the BSW program at Stephen F. Austin State University, Nacogdoches, Texas. He is a doctorate student at Jackson State University, Jackson, Mississippi. His practice background and research interests include mental health, mental retardation, rural social work practice, medical social work, social work administration, and school social work.

Judith A. Davenport, Ph.D., is a professor and the former director of the School of Social Work, University of Missouri–Columbia. She has an MSSW from the University of Tennessee and a Ph.D. from the University of Wyoming. She has more than 30 years' experience as a social worker, teacher, and researcher in the area of rural human services. Her current research interests include the social impacts of the corporatization of agriculture, social issues related to Hispanic/Latino immigration to rural communities, and international social work.

Barry L. Locke, Ph.D., is an associate professor in the Division of Social Work, School of Applied Social Sciences, West Virginia University. He has an

MSW from Virginia Commonwealth University and an Ed.D. from West Virginia University. He teaches both BSW and MSW courses in rural social work practice and he is well known for his research and writing in the area of rural human services. His current research focuses on welfare reform in West Virginia, with specific focus on the impact of welfare reform on small communities. He is former president and secretary of the National Rural Social Work Caucus. Additionally, he currently serves as a City Council member in Shinnston, West Virginia, where he is active in rural community and economic development.

Susan Murty, Ph.D., is an associate professor at the University of Iowa School of Social Work and coordinator of the MSW program. She has an MSW from the University of California at Berkeley and a Ph.D. from Washington University in St. Louis. She has more than 25 years of experience in rural mental health and human services and her current research is focused on rural family violence and rural end-of-life and bereavement services. She is a past president of the Rural Social Work Caucus and a former editor of *Human Services in the Rural Environment.*

Dennis L. Poole, Ph.D., received his MSW from West Virginia University and his Ph.D. from Brandeis University. He is a professor at the University of Texas School of Social Work and chair of the Administration and Planning Concentration in the MSSW program. He has many years of practice experience in rural human service settings and has written extensively in the area of community planning and development, management of nonprofit agencies, and outcome-based evaluation. He has served as editor-in-chief of the *Journal of Health and Social Work.*

ADDITIONAL CONTRIBUTORS

Roger Aker, MSW, MDiv, MA, is the director of Love in the Name of Christ of Nacogdoches, Texas, a community clearinghouse that assists people by referring those in need to church volunteers. Previous experience includes 20 years of direct and indirect service to children and families.

Bernard Albaugh, MSW, is a licensed social worker with a clinical specialty. He also has a master's degree in political science. He has 25 years' experience as a USPHS Indian Health Service Clinical/Medical Social Worker, director of Behavioral Health, and director of Outpatient Clinics. He is the director of The Center for Human Behavior Studies. He has written 57 funded health/mental health/research grants and numerous refereed journal publications. Albaugh is a recognized expert in alcohol/drug treatment and the cross-cultural diagnosis of mental disorders.

Patricia Albaugh, MSW, is licensed with a clinical specialty. She has been on the faculty of Southwestern Oklahoma State University for the past 25 years and is the founding director of the nationally accredited Baccalaureate Social

Work program at that university. She has numerous journal publications and is recognized for her work in international social work. With a particular focus on traditional societies and social change, she has directed a series of international cultural study tours.

Tosha Apodaca, MSW, is a school social worker in rural Wyoming. After completing her BSW, Ms. Apodaca worked in a community center serving children and families for five years prior to completing her MSW. She has extensive experience with the child welfare system.

Dale A. Barron, MSW, is the development director at World Hunger Relief, Inc., in Elm Mott, Texas. He serves as a adjunct faculty and field instructor at Baylor University's School of Social Work in Waco, Texas. His previous experience includes clinical and administrative work in cancer treatment and residential child-care facilities.

Jay Bishop, Ph.D., is an associate professor and coordinator of the Dual Degree Program in Sociology and Social Work at the University of Maryland Eastern Shore. He has taught social work and sociology for more than 23 years in undergraduate and graduate programs. He has received numerous grants from federal, state, and other sources on HIV/AIDS prevention, alcohol and drug abuse prevention, and dislocated workers. He has been published in books on group work and is on the board of directors of the Association for the Advancement of Social Work with Groups.

Sean M. Borzea, BSW, is a graduate research assistant at Arizona State University, where he is pursuing a master's degree in public administration. He is also a management intern with the town manager of Queen Creek, Arizona. As an undergraduate at the University of Wyoming, he studied and researched rural child welfare issues. His interests now focus on the policy process of government.

Fran Cissna Butler, MSW, is a direct service provider with several years of social work practice experience serving children and families in rural communities in central and southern Oklahoma. She has taught social work at East Central University, Ada, Oklahoma and Murray State College, Tishomingo, Oklahoma as adjunct faculty. She has experience in legislative advocacy, program development, establishment of collaborations with Native American governments, and directing services focusing on family and child welfare. She has engaged in research on welfare reform's impact on rural public transportation in conjunction with the University of Oklahoma.

Sarah Chard, Ph.D., is a project director at the National Association of Local Boards of Health. As a medical anthropologist, her research interests include women's health issues, social networks, and access to care.

Pat Conway, Ph.D., is a professor at the University of Wyoming. She has also taught in social work programs at the University of Texas at Austin, the University of South Carolina, and the University of Arkansas at Little Rock.

She has worked in the areas of child welfare, mental health, disabilities, AIDS, and domestic violence. Currently, she is collaborating with child welfare agencies in two rural, sparsely populated states to conduct research and training.

H. Stephen Cooper, MSW, is the director of the Community Field Unit, School of Social Work, Stephen F. Austin State University. Nacogdoches, Texas. He previously served as the clinical director for Hope Center Therapeutic Wilderness Programs. His work experience includes child and adolescent mental health treatment and law enforcement. His research interests include child and adolescent mental health, juvenile delinquency, family violence, rural social work, and social work field education.

Wilma Cordova, MSW, is a lecturer at the School of Social Work, Stephen F. Austin State University, Nacogdoches, Texas. Prior to moving to Texas, she was an adjunct faculty member with the School of Social Work, New Mexico State University, Las Cruces, New Mexico. She had a private practice for 10 years in New Mexico where she worked in rural communities. She is currently involved with the development of a resource center for the Hispanic community in Nacogdoches, Texas.

Jami Curley, MSW, is a Ph.D. student at the Gerorge Warren Brown School of Social Work at Washington University, St. Louis. She is a research associate at the Center for Social Development at Washington University. She has previously published on child welfare policy and asset-building. Her research interests include antipoverty policy, asset-building, and child welfare issues.

Michael R. Daley, Ph.D., is a professor at the School of Social Work, Stephen F. Austin State University, Nacogdoches, Texas. He has served in educational administration for 16 years and has been an active member of the Rural Social Work Caucus for the same length of time. He has both written and presented in the area of rural social work and has held numerous leadership positions in NASW.

Tamara S. Davis, MSSW, is a doctoral candidate and research associate at the School of Social Work, University of Texas at Austin. She has conducted research on systems of care, wraparound, and cultural competence in two rural and three urban communities across Texas. She has published and provided consultation on program evaluation to numerous human service organizations. Her practice experience includes community development, evaluation, and direct work with children and families involved with multiple public service systems.

Robin L. Ersing, Ph.D., is an assistant professor in the College of Social Work, University of Kentucky, Lexington, Kentucky. She teaches social policy and community practice courses in the undergraduate and graduate programs. She has more than 17 years' experience delivering housing and human services to residents and families living in distressed neighborhoods. Research interests include looking at the effects of residential environments on the development of children and families.

Michal Grinstein-Weiss, MSW, is a doctoral candidate in the George Warren Brown School of Social Work at Washington University in St. Louis. Currently, she is a research associate at the Center of Social Development at Washington University. Grinstein-Weiss's work is concentrated on the evaluation of individual development accounts as an antipoverty policy. Throughout her studies and research, she received many scholarships and fellowships, coauthored several articles and reports, and presented at several national conferences.

Shirley M. Haulotte, MSSW, is a member of the clinical faculty at the School of Social Work, University of Texas at Austin. She has a background in rural medical social work and currently teaches courses in cultural diversity, social work methods, and gerontology. While at the School of Social Work, Haulotte has developed a number of classroom exercises, field experiences, and field placements in rural social work.

Samuel A. Hickman, MSW, has been the executive director of the National Association of Social Workers, West Virginia Chapter, since 1985. He also has experience serving rural areas as a disaster mental health administrator, hospital social work director, and community health program coordinator. A member of the Rural Social Work Caucus since 1980, Hickman helped draft the Rural Social Work professional policy statement approved by the 2002 NASW Delegate Assembly and published in *Social Work Speaks* in January 2003.

William King, Ph.D., is a professor of criminal justice at Bowling Green State University in Ohio. He received his Ph.D. in criminal justice from the University of Cincinnati in 1998. Although his primary area of teaching and research concerns the quantitative study of police organizations, he has also published in the areas of Afrocentric community corrections, combating domestic violence in rural areas, and police interactions with the mentally ill.

Alan B. Kirk, Ph.D., is a professor and chair of the Human Services Department at Kennesaw State University in Georgia. His professional practice background includes service with the U.S. Air Force and the Veteran's Administration, and full-time private practice in the Miami/Fort Lauderdale metropolitan area. His writings and research are published in several books and national journals, including *Social Work*, the *Journal of Gerontological Social Work*, and *AdultSpan*. Dr. Kirk has written several training programs that have been implemented by federal and state governmental organizations.

Steven Lab, Ph.D., is a professor of criminal justice and chair of the Department of Human Services at Bowling Green State University in Ohio. He is the author of *Victimology* (with W. G. Doerner; Anderson Pub.), *Crime Prevention* (Anderson Pub.), and *Juvenile Justice: An Introduction* (with J. T. Whitehead; Anderson Pub.), as well as the editor of two books and more than three dozen articles and book chapters. His primary research interests include victimology, crime prevention, and crime in schools.

Liddell L. Madden, DSW, is an associate professor and the coordinator of the Dual Degree Program in Social Work and Sociology, Salisbury University, University System of Maryland. Her professional practice background includes public social services, child welfare, and work with special populations, such as newer immigrants of color and migrants and seasonal farmworkers. She has served as director of several undergraduate social work programs. Her writings and research are published in books and journals, including *Lippincott's Case Management* and *Child and Adolescent Social Work Journal*.

Dario Menanteau-Horta, Ph.D., is a professor and the director of the Center of Rural Sociology and Community Analysis, University of Minnesota. He has conducted research in the United States and Latin America and published several monographs, book chapters, and more than 100 papers in English and Spanish. He was awarded the title of "Extraordinary Professor" by the University Austral of Chile. His research interests include social organization, efficiency of social systems, rural social change, income inequality, and sustainable development.

Lynda Mitchell, MSW, is a counselor at Trinity Counseling Associates of East Texas in Tyler, Texas. Her practice centers on families with children in rural communities and social work in school settings.

Linda Morales, Ph.D., is an assistant professor at the School of Social Work, Stephen F. Austin State University, Nacogdoches, Texas. She has been teaching in the BSW program for 14 years, and also has taught courses in the master's program. She is an advanced clinical practitioner, with many years' experience in the delivery of mental health services.

Susannah More, B.S., is a doctoral student in the School Psychology Program, Department of Educational Psychology, University of Texas at Austin. Her interests include meeting the educational needs of rural students and of children with disabilities.

Kristen Nyman, MSSW, is starting a statewide microenterprise association in Texas to support both rural and urban microenterprise programs. In March 2002, she provided public testimony on comprehensive asset development strategies to the Texas House Committee on Human Services. She was formerly a planner with the Texas Workforce Commission and assisted in the implementation of the agency's asset development program. Nyman is a doctoral candidate in the School of Social Work at the University of Texas at Austin. She is writing her dissertation on asset development strategic bridging collaborations.

Jackie L. Olaveson, MSW, is a core indicator project assistant with the Wyoming Institute for Disabilities. She began this project as her MSW research project. Ms. Olaveson has lived in Wyoming for 32 years, and prior to that lived in rural areas in Kansas and Nebraska. She is an advisor for the local and state chapters of People First.

Suzanne Oliver, MSSW, is an assistant director of social services for Girling Health Care, Inc. She oversees the delivery of social work services to homebound Medicare patients in seven states and directs corporate social service interventions to aged and disabled recipients of the Medicaid Community Care Program in Texas and Oklahoma. She has extensive experience in rural field practice and with the development of social service programs that coordinate direct interventions with community resources.

Melanie D. Otis, Ph.D., is an assistant professor and the director of undergraduate studies in the College of Social Work, University of Kentucky, Lexington, Kentucky. She has taught social work at the University of Kentucky for six years in both the graduate and undergraduate programs. She does consultation and program evaluation for agencies and organizations working to develop social capital and community assets.

Lucinda A. Potter, MSW, MPA, is a doctoral candidate in the political science program at West Virginia University in Morgantown, West Virginia. She has worked in child welfare, family services, regional economic development, and higher education administration. Her research interests include rural economic development, state and local government bureaucracies, employment in rural areas, and poverty studies.

Ruben Rodriguez, MSW, is the program manager for Buckner Fragile Families, an outreach program for young fathers in Lufkin, Texas. He has worked as a school social worker for the Nacogdoches Independent School District. His community work has allowed him to participate in numerous projects in East Texas. He was honored by NASW in 1998 as Social Worker of the Year, Texas Chapter.

F. Matthew Schobert, Jr., MDiv, MSW, is the interim associate director of the Center for Christian Ethics at Baylor University in Waco, Texas. His professional experience includes administrative work at World Hunger Relief, Inc., and clinical practice in acute psychiatry and chaplaincy services.

Chad Shaver, BA, is currently an MSW student at the University of Wyoming. He is interested in child welfare, especially interventions with adolescents and their outcomes.

Glenn Shields, DSW, is the director of the social work program in the Department of Human Services, Bowling Green State University in Ohio. He has taught undergraduate social work for 12 years and is active in practice with individuals and families. He served 20 years as a U.S. Army social worker in the Medical Service Corp and retired in 1990. His publications and research have been in the areas of families and delinquency, personal safety issues for human service workers in rural community agencies, and program evaluation.

Paul H. Stuart, Ph.D., is a professor in the School of Social Work, University of Alabama, Tuscaloosa, Alabama, where he has served as a member of the faculty since 1987. Previously, he taught social work at the baccalaureate, master's, and doctoral levels in Missouri, South Dakota, and Wisconsin, and served as a social worker with the Indian Health Service in South Dakota. His research has focused on the history of social welfare and the social work profession.

Sharon B. Templeman, Ph.D., is an assistant professor in the School of Social Work, Stephen F. Austin State University, Nacogdoches, Texas. Her research interests are in the areas of child and family well-being, rural social work, and international social work.

Leela Thomas, Ph.D., is an assistant professor at the School of Social Work, University of Oklahoma. She received her MSW in both India and the United States. She has taught courses on research methods, statistics, and health care policy in both the graduate and undergraduate programs. Her publications and presentations have been in the areas of health/mental health, managed care plans, and scale construction.

Nancy L. Todd, MSW, is a therapist with the adult mental health team at Southeast Wyoming Mental Health Center in Cheyenne, Wyoming. She is co-editor of two special issues of the *Journal of Family Therapy*. Her interests include grief and loss issues, working with children in foster care, and play therapy.

Ted R. Watkins, DSW, is a professor of social work and the director of the BSW program at Southwest Texas State University, San Marcos, Texas. His practice background is in mental health, substance abuse, residential treatment of adolescents, and family counseling. His research and writing are in the areas of mental health, substance abuse, dual diagnosis, and juvenile gangs and delinquency. He teaches human behavior in the social environment, research, and practice at the graduate and undergraduate levels.

Kenneth R. Wedel, Ph.D., is a professor at the School of Social Work, University of Oklahoma. He is the chair for the Administration and Community Practice concentration in the MSW program. His teaching areas include social program administration and social policy. He has been principal investigator for several research grants on rural transportation and welfare reform. He is also evaluator for a grant funded to establish community coalitions for youth violence prevention in Cleveland and McClain counties, Oklahoma.

Marion Williams, Ph.D., is an assistant professor of criminal justice at Bowling Green State University in Ohio. She has taught classes on the criminal courts, criminal procedure, drug use, and race/gender/diversity issues. Her research interests include criminal law, sentencing, capital punishment, and social justice. In addition, she has worked funded projects covering such topics as domestic violence, capital punishment, and public defenders.

Jim Winship, DPA, is an associate professor of social work at the University of Wisconsin–Whitewater. A former chair of the Rural Social Work Caucus, he has written on case management for and evaluation of programs serving those experiencing homelessness. He is active in advocacy issues around homelessness/housing on the local, state, and national levels.

Introduction

Asset Building to Sustain Rural Communities

T. LAINE SCALES

CALVIN L. STREETER

Imagine you have just returned home from a brisk walk through the countryside on a warm and sunny spring day. You are hot, tired, and very thirsty. As you enter your home you see a glass of cool refreshing water sitting on the kitchen table. The glass is filled to the halfway mark. How do you see the glass? Is it half-full or is it half-empty?

If you are thirsty, you probably focus on the glass as half-full and you are grateful that someone has left it for you to drink. On the other hand, if the water in the glass isn't enough to quench your thirst, you may focus on the glass as half-empty. In this case, whether you view the glass as half-full or half-empty probably doesn't matter. But how one answers the age-old question, "Is the glass half-empty or half-full?" may suggest how one perceives the world.

It has been said that perception is reality. What we believe to be true often becomes the center of our thoughts so much that it really becomes true. When we view the glass as half-empty, we focus on the negative aspects of life and we can become consumed with negativity and overcome with despair. But when we see the glass as half-full, we focus on the positive elements in our life and the world around us.

John Kretzmann and John McKnight (1993), in their book *Building Community From the Inside Out*, challenged us to view the glass as half-full rather than half-empty. They contend that our focus on the half-empty glass leads us to see only the deficiencies and problems facing our communities. In rural areas this often means we

see communities where few opportunities exist to retain young people, where we are too spread out to afford hard-surface roads, Internet access, or cable television for everyone; where residents must leave town to acquire many goods and services; and where farms and local businesses are controlled by big corporations from afar.

By viewing the glass as half-full, we begin to see the depth of the human spirit and the richness of the creative potential that exists in rural communities. We see people who are talented and experienced in a variety of areas. We see strong social networks and associations. We see that with rural services the lines are short, the hassles are few, and our business is easy to take care of. We see beautiful landscapes where we can easily enjoy nature. We see people getting things done that need to be done by using what is available. In other words, we see the strengths and assets rather than the problems and deficiencies.

As social workers, it is easy to become overwhelmed with a sense of despair because of the serious personal problems and societal conditions we are called upon to address. We see the child who has been verbally and physically abused. We witness the terrible toll that alcohol and drug abuse can take on a family. Daily we confront the reality of poverty, prejudice, and oppression in our society. Because our professional lives are wrapped up in the misery and trauma of the less advantaged in our community, it is no wonder that social workers are sometimes accused of seeing the glass as half-empty. For social workers in rural communities where resources are scarce, it may be even more difficult to view the glass as half-full.

The asset-building framework, however, allows helping professionals to see people as citizens of the community, not just as clients. Every citizen has capacities that can be tapped to make life in the community better. Rural communities contain a wide range of assets and strengths, such as voluntary associations and close personal relationships between people, local institutions, histories and traditions, and land and property. Models of professional practice that focus on asset building can empower rural people to use their resources in innovative ways to create new assets. It can help them determine their own direction, set their own priorities, and leverage both internal and external resources in ways that make sense for their community.

Of course, social work has a long tradition of practice focused on strengths and assets. For example, Dennis Saleebey and his colleagues at the University of Kansas School of Social Welfare have spent much of the last 2 decades developing, testing, and promoting a strengths perspective for social work practice (1997). Drawing on the profession's commitment to building on people's strengths, rather than focusing on their deficiencies, problems, or disabilities, the strengths-based perspective provides an orientation to practice that seeks to uncover and reaffirm people's abilities, talents, survivor skills, and aspirations. It assumes that a clear and unyielding focus on the strengths found in individuals, families, neighborhoods, groups, and communities will increase the likelihood that people will reach the goals they set for themselves.

THREE STREAMS
OF THOUGHT
ON ASSET BUILDING

In addition to the work at the University of Kansas, there are at least three significant streams of work during the last decade that have helped shift our focus from deficiencies to assets.

Although somewhat different in their approach to asset building, they share a common theme. All three embrace and celebrate the strengths and capacities of individuals and communities.

The first of these is the work of Kretzmann and McKnight (1993), mentioned previously. Their book *Building Community From the Inside Out* provides a conceptual framework for asset-based community development. In their book, Kretzmann and McKnight outline a set of tools for asset-based community practice that can be used to map assets and build capacities in our communities. At the heart of their asset model is relationships. From their perspective, asset mapping and capacity building are about identifying resources and fostering relationships in the community.

More recently, Kretzmann and McKnight have established the Asset-Based Community Development Institute at Northwestern University to provide resources and technical support for people seeking to "build community from the inside out." Challenging the traditional approach to solving community problems, which focuses service providers and funding agencies on the needs and deficiencies of people and their communities, the ABCD Institute demonstrates that community assets are key building blocks in sustainable rural community revitalization efforts (Snow, 2001). These community assets include the skills of local residents, the power of local associations, the resources of public, private and non-profit institutions, and the physical and economic resources of local places. Central to their approach is the premise that every single person has capacities, abilities and gifts. The key is to identify and embrace those assets. To facilitate this process, the Institute has developed a "Capacity Inventory," designed to identify the capacities of members of the community. The Institute now has over 30 highly skilled practitioner/trainers who work with communities all across the country to promote asset-based community development.

A second stream of work focused on asset building is located at the Search Institute in Minneapolis, Minnesota. In an effort to identify the elements of a strength-based approach to healthy youth development, the Search Institute devised a framework of developmental assets for children and youth. This framework identified 40 critical factors for young people's growth and development.

The assets are divided into external and internal assets. The external assets focus on positive experiences that young people receive from the people and institutions in their lives and include a supportive environment, evidence that the community values youth and their contribution to community life, clearly stated boundaries and expectations, and opportunities for constructive use of time. However, a community's responsibility for its young people does not end with the provision of external assets. There needs to be a similar commitment to nurturing the internal qualities that guide choices and create a sense of centeredness, purpose, and focus. These assets focus on helping young people develop a commitment to learning, positive values to guide their choices, social competencies to build relationships, and a strong sense of their own power, purpose, worth, and promise.

When drawn together, the assets offer a set of benchmarks for positive child and adolescent development (Benson, 1997). The developmental assets framework clearly shows the important roles that families, schools, congregations, neighborhoods, youth organizations, and others in the community play in shaping young people's lives.

The Search Institute's framework of developmental assets for children and youth has caught on all across the country with asset-building initiatives flourishing in small towns and rural communities throughout the United States. For example, in Kearney, Nebraska, a grassroots coalition called the Nebraska Asset Building Coalition is working to assist communities across the state in developing their own asset-building initiatives. In Manchester, New Hampshire, Making It Happen has helped the community view all young people as "at promise," not "at risk" by promoting healthy choices and reducing risky behaviors while building developmental assets in children and youth. In Annandale, Minnesota, *Youth First* is a grassroots initiative to inspire and challenge the entire community to become asset-builders for youth in the community. In Georgetown, Texas, The Georgetown Project is devoted to the framework of developmental assets as a means to build a healthy community where all children and youth can grow into capable, caring, and resilient adults. And in countless other communities across the country, the developmental assets framework provides the foundation for youth development initiatives that emphasizes the positive contribution that children and youth make in the life of the community.

The work of Mike Sherraden and his colleagues in the Center for Social Development at the George Warren Brown School of Social Work at Washington University in St. Louis represents a third exciting area of work focused on the asset-building framework. With a focus on developing economic resources for poor families, Sherraden (1991) outlined his ideas about asset-based welfare policy in his seminal book published in 1991 titled *Assets and the Poor: A New American Welfare Policy*.

Challenging our traditional models of public assistance for low-income families, Sherraden has proposed asset building as an antipoverty strategy. He argues that existing consumption-based welfare policies make it impossible for people to get out of poverty because they penalize families for accumulating personal economic assets. From his perspective, the way to move people out of poverty is to encourage them to accumulate assets, which they can then leverage to purchase a home, capitalize a small business, or pay for an education for their children. The mechanism for doing this is something called Individual Development Accounts (IDAs).

Sherraden and his colleagues lead a national demonstration project on asset building using individual development accounts (IDAs). The Downpayment on the American Dream Demonstration (ADD) is the first large-scale test of the efficacy of (IDAs) as a route to economic independence for low-income Americans. Thirteen community-based organizations from around the country operate IDA programs as part of the ADD demonstration, including three rural sites in Kentucky, New York, and Wisconsin (Schreiner et al., 2001). When the project is completed, these organizations will have established at least 2,000 IDA programs in low-income and asset-poor communities. More importantly, the ADD demonstration will be a catalyst for connecting a rapidly growing field of community-based IDA programs around the country.

EXPLORING ASSET BUILDING IN RURAL COMMUNITIES

We believe that practice models that keep us focused on the strengths, assets, and capacities of people are critical for social work practice in rural communities. That belief leads us to create this resource for the classroom. It is designed to assist social work students and teachers as they integrate themes of asset building and social work practice in the rural context.

The idea for this book grew out of our involvement with the National Institute on Social Work and Human Services in Rural Areas held in May 2001 at the University of Texas. About half of the articles included in this collection began as workshops at the conference. The remaining articles were written by authors who were invited to address particular topics. The theme of the conference was asset building and as we participated in the conference dialogue we identified several issues important to rural social workers that had been neglected in existing literature. In conversation with other social work educators, we made a list of issues that had particular relevance when viewing rural social practice using asset-building frameworks.

Since we are both educators involved in the day-to-day challenge of integrating rural content into our courses with few current and classroom-friendly readings, we began to discuss with other educators what type of new resource would be useful. The ideal resource would be more than a mere collection of readings. It would be interesting and accessible for students

at the BSW and MSW levels and provide discussion questions and assignments to facilitate study of the material.

We envisioned this book as a valuable educational resource on contemporary issues in rural social work practice and as a forum where scholars, students, and practitioners can share their current research and practice experience in rural communities. We reviewed other rural resources for social workers and found several ways in which we wanted this resource to be distinctive.

First, in contrast to other resources for students, these readings consistently integrate asset-building themes, applying one of the newer, most talked-about theoretical foundations for social work. We have emphasized the depth of the human spirit and the richness of the creative potential that exists in rural communities. We introduce new research tools, such as asset mapping; and new theoretical models, like asset-based community development. The readings highlight the tremendous resources that exist in rural communities and demonstrate ways to integrate them into contemporary social work practice.

We also address the globalization of social work and the international context of social work practice in the 21st century. We include such topics as the impact of globalization on rural communities throughout the world, practice with immigrants bringing their assets to the United States, borderland issues in the Southwest United States, and asset-based community development as a strategy for global rural development.

Finally, we address some of the most current policy issues, particularly around the areas of welfare reform and faith-based initiatives. These and other contemporary policy issues are very important to social workers, but have not been addressed thoroughly in other resources on rural social work. In addition to discussions of policy, we engaged authors to address the newest strategies for economic development, such as Individual Development Accounts (IDAs) as a strategy for building self-sufficiency, and micro-enterprise as a method of rural development.

The intent of *Rural Social Work: Building and Sustaining Community Assets* is to provide material for readers that are in the process of learning to use asset-building frameworks and at the same time, suggest ways for social workers to participate in sustaining rural communities. We expect that our readers will have a wide variety of experiences with rurality. Some of our readers may live and work in rural communities and may have read widely on rural social work. Many readers may live rural lifestyles, but have not had an opportunity to reflect upon their own cultures and how the rural environment impacts social work practice. Others may be destined for social work in urban areas and they are preparing themselves to work with clients that have migrated to their city from rural areas. For all of these readers, our hope is that these articles, discussion questions, and assignments stimulate meaningful dialogue about how asset-building frameworks can enhance practice with rural populations.

GETTING THE MOST FROM THIS BOOK

Following this introduction on asset-building perspectives and their application to community building in rural contexts, we have 27 articles written by social work scholars, students, and practitioners. Each article includes three elements: an article that integrates the themes of asset building and rural social work, discussion questions that facilitate critical thinking around the article, and suggested activities and assignments to provide opportunities for practical application of the concepts presented in the article.

The articles are organized into five parts with an organizing framework following curriculum areas often used by programs accredited by the Council on Social Work Education. The parts are:

1. Introduction to Rural Social Work
2. Human Behavior and Rural Environments
3. Practice Issues in Rural Contexts
4. Policy Issues Affecting Rural Populations

5. Using Research to Evaluate Practice in Rural Settings

This framework for organizing will assist teachers who wish to integrate a few readings on rural issues into each course. Students may buy the book early in their program and instructors may use this book to supplement other textbooks that often carry an urban focus. The work will also be useful in introductory courses in both MSW and BSW programs, as it introduces new social work students to a variety of curriculum areas they will be studying and encourages students to consider these areas within a rural context. Finally, we expect the book will be particularly well-suited for the growing number of specialized courses in rural social work.

Experienced instructors of rural social work courses have written brief introductions that explore the connections between the readings and the curriculum area covered in that part. These veteran teachers and scholars have prepared students and teachers for the part of readings as if they were preparing their own students for a new unit in their classes. We intend for these introductory parts to invite readers to anticipate particular themes and connections as they work through the articles.

The discussion questions and assignments are designed to provide maximum autonomy for student learners. We believe that students should be at the center of their own learning, so we designed the activities to be used with as little or as much guidance as the teacher believes his or her particular class will need. Teachers are encouraged to adapt these assignments as they want and to create their own questions and assignments to fit their unique contexts.

No matter how students, teachers, and practitioners might choose to use this resource, we are confident that they will find good readings, discussion questions, and assignments to help them think about rural social work in new ways. We have learned a great deal from reading and editing the work of these well-informed and experienced contributors. We hope others' experience with this resource will be equally enjoyable and stimulating.

REFERENCES

Benson, P. L. (1997). *All kids are our kids: What communities must do to raise caring and responsible children and adolescents.* San Francisco: Jossey-Bass.

Kretzmann, J. P., and McKnight, J. L. (1993). *Building communities from the inside out: A path toward finding and mobilizing a community's assets.* Chicago: ACTA Publications.

Saleebey, D. (Ed.). (1997). *The strengths perspective in social work practice* (2nd ed.). New York: Longman.

Schreiner, M., Sherraden, M., Clancy, M., Johnson, L., Curley, J., Grinstein-Weiss, M., Zhan, M., & Beverly, S. (2001). *Savings and Asset Accumulation in Individual Development Accounts,* research report. St. Louis: Center for Social Development, Washington University.

Sherraden, M. (1991). *Assets and the poor: A new American welfare policy.* Armonk, NY: M. E. Sharpe.

Snow, L. K. (2001). *The organization of hope: A workbook for rural asset-based community development.* Chicago: ACTA Publications.

INFOTRAC® COLLEGE EDITION

asset mapping
capacity building
developmental assets

rural communities
rural social work practice
strengths perspective

PART I

✳

Introduction to Rural Social Work

FREDDIE L. AVANT

The development of rural social work has been an evolutionary process. For many years, rural social work was explored and practiced from a "deficits" perspective. Thus, the primary focus was on identifying problems and generating solutions. Social workers emphasized working with people in rural areas, but gave little attention to their environment. Over the years, the literature on rural social work has been enriched as authors have examined definitions of rurality and researchers have explored environments in relation to rural populations.

Current findings support a new paradigm, indicating a shift of fundamental views of rural social work. For example, social work literature points to the need for building assets in rural communities and with rural people. Rural people and rural areas face significant challenges in attempting to meet their needs. To achieve their desires and aspirations, an asset-building approach provides increased opportunities for positive change. Social work has a specific commitment to understanding empowerment and human strength at both the personal and community levels. Therefore, rural social work assumes that people are most likely to be able to grow and develop when their strengths, rather than their problems, receive recognition and support.

The articles in this part introduce readers to rural social work, by defining rurality, providing an historical overview of rural social work, and describing professional organizations for rural social workers. In the first article, Olaveson, Conway, and Shaver provide a review of definitions used in rural social work and stress the importance of rural communities' diverse assets. They begin with a critique of concepts related to rural social work and the issues surrounding the rural/urban continuum. They point to the significance of operationalizing rural definitions. The lack of clarity creates inconsistency in identifying rural areas and assets for rural populations. The authors conclude with a proposed method of defining levels of rurality.

Stuart provides an historical analysis of the development of social welfare services in rural areas. He points to a chronology of events that contribute to the transition of social welfare services from rural to urban areas. Stuart addresses the significance of land to the lifestyle of rural people and discusses many of the changes that have propelled a reexamination of rural social work. This history illustrates the transitioning of social welfare services from rural to urban areas.

Daley and Avant examine the framework for rural social work practice and propose that rural social work should be viewed on a continuum where rural cultural lifestyles supersede all other geographical characteristics. They also advocate for the development and application of a theoretical framework for rural social work based on a strengths perspective. Daley and Avant further emphasize the importance of building on assets of rural people by acknowledging and appreciating their cultural lifestyles in diverse environments.

Finally, Hickman discusses the origin of the Rural Social Work Caucus, the importance of the National Institute on Social Work and Human Services in Rural Areas, and the most recent National Association of Social Workers (NASW) Professional Policy Statement on Rural Social Work. Each of these has had a major impact on the evolutionary process of rural social work. The Rural Social Work Caucus has served as the vehicle of creation and dissemination of rural social work knowledge. The National Institute on Social Work and Human Services in Rural Areas is the annual conference for rural social work practitioners and educators. Their efforts have brought about a greater awareness, understanding, acknowledgment, and appreciation for rural people and their environments. The creation of a new NASW Professional Policy Statement for Rural Social Work is an excellent example of the combined efforts of the two groups. The text of the policy statement can be reviewed in Appendix A.

1

Defining *Rural* for Social Work Practice and Research

JACKIE OLAVESON
PAT CONWAY
CHAD SHAVER

Whether or not rural and urban areas are different has been debated by social work experts (Edwards & Hopps, 1995; Locke, 1991; Lusk & Mason, 1992) and experts in other fields, such as economics, sociology, geography, and agriculture (Cleland, 1995; Deavers, 1992; Dewey, 1960; Fuguitt, Brown, & Beale, 1989; Pahl, 1966; York, Denton, & Moran, 1989). Some objective measures, such as health indicators, do vary by degree of urbanization (Urban and Rural Health Chartbook, 2001); for instance, "residents of the most rural counties fare worst on some measures and residents of the most urban counties fare worst on others" (p. 2). Rural areas have higher death rates for children and young adults. Urban areas have higher rates of homicide.

Learning more about the specific characteristics of regions under examination is essential in order to accurately identify community assets and compare those assets across different areas. Assets in a bush community in Alaska might be very different from those in a heavily populated but agrarian community in southeastern Arkansas. Researchers have disagreed about whether or not needs and services vary by rural and urban designation areas (Hoggart, 1990). Morris (1995) reported that nonmetropolitan (rural) areas have higher rates of poverty, due to economic restructuring, changing national policies, and historical patterns of oppression and inequality, especially for rural communities with a higher percentage of persons who are of African American, Native American, or Hispanic origin.

York, Denton, and Moran (1989) examined how social work practice differed between rural and urban communities, through a survey of a random sample of social workers who were members of the National Association of Social Workers, North Carolina Article. Twenty-five percent (*n* = 295) returned the survey, primarily from more highly populated counties. York, Denton, and Moran created a measure of the degree of rurality, using population, population density, and number of family farms in the county in which the respondent was employed as the benchmarks. When analyzing the data from social workers and considering their roles, level of specialization, use of informal helping networks, and presenting problems of their clients, the researchers found no significant difference between social workers in rural and urban areas. York concluded that the lack of difference may result from the fact that no difference really exists, or from the unique sample, the lack of sensitivity to measuring differences in practice, the potential diversity between rural communities, and the possibility that schools of social work do not prepare social workers to vary their practice depending on the particular needs of a particular community. The varying and contradictory results found by researchers examining the similarities and differences between rural and urban regions may result from different ways of operationalizing the terms (Cleland, 1995; Willits & Bealer, 1967; Willits, Bealer, & Crider, 1986).

Determining how to consistently and easily measure the degree of rurality would allow researchers to better identify similarities and differences within populations and communities in different regions. This has implications for identifying assets in social work practice. If characteristics of some areas designated as rural are different than other rural areas—and different than the characteristics of areas designated as urban—perhaps social work practice would need to be adjusted or enhanced to meet the particular needs of the population of the area being served. Any definition of rural would need to be as value-free as possible, allowing the precise assessment of a rural community's assets and areas of need (Cromartie & Swanson, 1996; Flora, Flora, Spears, & Swanson, 1995; Hardcastle, Wenocur, & Powers, 1997; Kretzmann & McKnight, 1993).

Defining the concept of community (Flora, Flora, Spears, & Swanson, 1995) is also important when considering rural communities. Flora and coauthors (1995) define community as a "place or location" (p. 15), although they recognize that community is sometimes defined by more qualitative characteristics, such as level of support and shared values. When assessing a community's capacity, knowing a community's degree of rurality will allow researchers to determine interactions between degree of rurality, community resources, and scarcity of services (Kretzmann & Green, 1998; Simons, Johnson, Conger, & Lorenz, 1997; Wyoming Department of Health, 2000). Even the designation of an area affects the allocation of resources. For instance, De la Torre, Fickenscher, and Luft (1991) argue that health resources for rural areas are negatively affected by imprecise definitions of rurality. Simons, Johnson, Conger, and Lorenz (1997) argue that the quality of a community impacts the lives of individuals and families living in it. They examined stresses impacting single parent families in Iowa, including the characteristic of the participant's neighborhood, as measured by the proportion of families in poverty, adult males underemployed, persons receiving public assistance, and adults

with less than a high school education. Simons and coauthors concluded that disorganized communities contributed to poorer parenting by single parent females, especially through the connection between community disorganization and depression. By using a numerical measure of degree of rurality, the authors would be able to test their hypothesis that, regardless of location, a socially disorganized community negatively impacts families.

This article describes a variety of definitions of rural and proposes a method to operationally define degree of rurality.

COMMON GOVERNMENTAL ENTITIES' METHODS FOR DEFINING RURAL

The U.S. Census Bureau and the Office of Management and Budget (OMB) provide the two most widely used definitions of rural and urban. The two methods operationalize rural differently; therefore, their reported numbers of people in rural and urban areas vary. Using the OMB definition, 19.8% of the population in 1996 was rural or nonmetropolitan (Ricketts, Johnson-Webb, & Taylor, 1998). According to the 1990 Census Bureau, 24.8% of the population was rural.

The Census Bureau

The most widely used definition for urban-rural is the Census Bureau's, which is used both for the decennial census and for all research related to the census data (Ricketts, Johnson-Webb, & Taylor, 1998). Census data provides the basis for determining voting areas, shapes funding packages for different regions, and myriad other uses. The definition of urban-rural used by the Census Bureau has changed over time, influenced by the dramatic changes in population and economy (Deavers, 1992). The Census Bureau has conducted population counts every decade for the last 127 years, providing a longitudinal method for documenting characteristics of rural regions and populations. In 1874, the Bureau of Census first identified rural counties. In 1910, the Census Bureau changed the population threshold from 8,000 to 2,500 for defining rural. By 1980, the Census Bureau had introduced the concept of nonmetropolitan counties and, in the 1990 census, revised the rural definition again (Ricketts, Johnson-Webb, & Taylor, 1998). In 1990, urban was considered to be all territories, populations, and housing units in urbanized areas and all places of 2,500 or more inhabitants outside of urbanized areas. An urbanized areas (UA) was defined as a continuously built-up area with a population of 50,000 or more, with a central place and adjacent densely settled areas, and a population density of 1,000 persons per square mile. Everything else was considered rural. "Territories outside of urbanized areas and urban places are designated rural, and can have population densities as high as 999 per square mile and as low as 1 or 2 per square mile" (Ricketts, Johnson-Webb, & Taylor, 1998, p. 3). This definition considered population density, relationship to cities, and population size.

The 2000 census is based on a different and more detailed definition of rural. Consistent with the recommendation of Cromartie and Swanson (1996), it uses census tracts instead of counties as the measure for density. According to Cromartie and Swanson, census tracts are a desirable geographic boundary, because they are comparable across regions and can be "aggregated to form county-degree statistical areas when needed" (p. 32). Differences between rural regions become visible, due to the differences in size of census tracts and the relationship between large population concentrations and more sparsely populated areas. Cromartie and Swanson recommend placing census tracts into five categories: (1) metro core, (2) metro outlying, (3) non-metro adjacent, (4) nonmetro nonadjacent with city, and (5) non-metro nonadjacent no city.

The 2000 census calculates density based on the land area of a census tract. It defines urban areas and urban clusters, based on population and relationship between census tracts. The Census Bureau has available maps of any area in the United States by census tract. This operationaliza-

tion of urban and rural is much more objective and less political than previous census definitions and will probably increase the percentage of persons identified as urban and decrease the percentage of land defined as urban.

Through the 1990 census, the percentage of the rural population considered "farm population" was reported, but this was dropped for the 2000 census, due to the low count in this category (1.9% of the total population in 1990; Ricketts, Johnson-Webb, & Taylor, 1998, p. 4). This change has ramifications for agrarian communities across the country and signals a change in perceptions of the country.

Office of Management and Budget

The Office of Management and Budget (OMB) provides definitions for metropolitan and nonmetropolitan areas. A metropolitan area is either a county with a "place with a minimum population of 50,000, or a 1990 Census Bureau–defined urbanized area with a total Metropolitan Area (MA) population of at least 100,000 (75,000 in New England)" (Rural Policy Research Institute, 1999). Adjacent counties are included in a metropolitan area if 50% or more are in the urbanized area or a high proportion commute to the central city. The definition means that a county's designation constantly changes. "Non-metropolitan" counties are all of those counties not defined as metropolitan. The OMB routinely updates a map designating metropolitan areas, and by default, nonmetropolitan areas.

United States Department of Agriculture

The USDA has modified the Census Bureau and OMB definitions to create a continuum of rural to urban, named the Urban Influence Codes (Ricketts, Johnson-Webb, & Taylor, 1998). This definition incorporates the concepts of density and whether or not the area is adjacent to large metropolitan areas. This is based on the OMB definition of a metropolitan area, using counties as the measure. A second USDA definition, based on 10 categories, four categories of metropolitan counties and six categories of nonmetropolitan counties, has also been created. The first method is more helpful for health and human services policy and program development, because it provides a picture of regional care areas. The codes are available through the USDA Web site http://www.ers.usda.gov/briefing/rurality/UrbanInf/

The USDA also developed a classification of counties by economic activity and policy traits (Cook & Mizer, 1994; Deavers, 1992; Ricketts, Johnson-Webb, & Taylor, 1998). Economic types are farming-dependent, mining-dependent, manufacturing-dependent, government-dependent, services-dependent, and nonspecialized. The policy types are retirement-destination, federal lands, commuting, persistent poverty, and transfer-dependent (more than 25% of the population receives public funds). What is transfer dependent? The USDA definition provides guidance for funding in agrarian areas, and for the development of services, especially services through extension offices.

Other Definitions of Rural

Keller, Zimbelman, Murray, and Feil (1980) defined a continuum of rural to urban areas: "less than 100–200, 200–300, 300–400, and 400–500 persons per square mile" (p. 16). Smith, Anderson, Bradham, and Longino (1995) defined as rural "small towns of fewer than 2,500 population" (p. 277), loosely based on the Census Bureau's definition. Goldsmith (1993) stated that rural was having "45% of the work force commute 30 minutes or more to work" (p. 1). Cleland (1995) created a rurality index, based on physical access (commuting patterns as measured by access to metropolitan areas via interstate) and population density; three institutional measures (education ratio, employment in retail services, and employment in professional services); political power, as measured by number of people employed in public positions; and financial resources (median family income, level and persistence of poverty, and whether or not the area had a local newspaper). He then applied this index to each state, awarding them a rating from 0 (least rural) to 19 (most rural).

The varying definitions are created for practical and political purposes. "Governments and organizations create definitions for a variety of purposes: to define those who should be served by a particular program, to identify those who should be exempt from specific policy, to make their job more manageable, or to target resources" (Flora, Flora, Spears, & Swanson, 1995, p. 7). The varying definitions do not allow for comparability across studies, examining the characteristics of communities for the purpose of community development.

To better describe very sparsely populated areas, the concept of frontier was developed (Popper, 1984). Fewer than six people per square mile, county, or census tract is considered a frontier area (Rural Policy Context, Frontier Areas, n.d.). Almost all frontier areas are in the Western portion of the United States (including Alaska). People in such sparsely populated areas view relationships and resources in a very different manner than people in urban areas, but measuring the view of relationship and resources is difficult without a more accurate definition of degree of rurality.

De la Torre, Fickenscher, and Luft (1991) built on Popper's (1984) definition of frontier by proposing that density be measured by zip codes in order to determine rurality. The measure identified less than 6 people per square mile as frontier, 6–15 people per square mile as rural, 16–30 people per square mile as semirural, and more than 30 people per square mile as urban. They proposed using density by zip code instead of county, in order to better refine the quality of rurality.

COMMON FACTORS USED TO CREATE DEFINITIONS OF RURAL

Seven factors are commonly used to define rural:

1. Population by measure (square mile, hectare, zip code)
2. Population by political boundary (town, county)

3. Political boundary (town, county, state)
4. Commuting patterns
5. Economy
6. Open country
7. Outside Standard Metropolitan Statistical Areas

Population by Measure

Population by measure defines degree of rurality by the number of people in an area, for instance 75 or 100 people per square mile (Beaulieu & Berry, 1994; Center for Rural Pennsylvania, 1991; Imhoff, 2000; Keller, Zimbelman, Murray, & Feil, 1980; Morris, 1984; Williams, Lethbridge, & Chambers, 1997; Willits & Bealer, 1967). One article used satellite imaging to determine population density by hectare. The measure of density using people per square mile is common, although the number of people considered to be rural varied by author. For example, Keller, Zimbelman, Murray, and Feil (1980) created a continuum of "100–200, 200–300, 300–400, 400–500 people per square mile" (p. 18). Morris (1984) considered a rural area to be "less than 1,000 persons per square mile" (p. 16). Imhoff considered an urban area to be a "density of at least 10 people per hectare" (p. 155). De la Torre and coauthors (1991) proposed measuring density by zip code.

Population by Political Boundary

Most definitions of density based on political boundary used town or county as the political boundary (Edmondson, 1997). Although several authors defined a rural area as less than 2,500 persons per political boundary, based on the U.S. Census Bureau definition, there was a wide range of figures used in the literature from less than 2,500 to 200,000 (Buse & Driscoll, 1992; Center for Rural Pennsylvania, 1991; Denton, York, & Morgan, 1988; Flora, Flora, Spears, & Swanson, 1995; Foster & McBeth, 1996; Fugitt, Brown, & Beale, 1989; Galston & Baehler, 1995; Marsden, Lowe, & Whatmore, 1990; McNellie, 2001; Miler & Ray, 1990; Morrison, 1990; Nooe & Bolitho, 1982; Ray & Murty, 1990; Ricketts, Johnson-

Webb, & Taylor, 1998; Smith, Anderson, Bradham, & Longino, 1995; Toomey, First, Greenlee, & Cummins, 1993; United States Fire Administration, 1998; Wagner, Menke, & Ciccone, 1994).

Political Boundary

Most studies using a political boundary to define rurality were based on an entire state; for instance Utah, West Virginia, Wyoming and the Southern region states of Alabama, Arkansas, Florida, Georgia, Kentucky, Louisiana, Mississippi, Missouri, Oklahoma, South Carolina, Tennessee, and Texas (Davis, 1988; Gordon & Blakely, 1995; Kusimo, 1999; Wagner, Menke, & Ciccone, 1994). For example Davis stated that "The state of Wyoming [was defined as rural because it had a] low population per square mile; ranks 49th in the nation by population density and there are no counties that are Standard Metropolitan Statistical Areas" (p. 13). Morris (1984) defined "the western States of Alaska, Idaho, South Dakota, Montana and Wyoming [as rural, because] virtually all of the rural population is located outside metropolitan areas" (p. 11).

Commuting Pattern

Although many authors used commuting distance to an urban area to measure degree of rurality, a wide variation in commuting patterns has been used (Beach, 1997; Goldsmith, 1993; Luloff & Swanson, 1990; Ray & Murty, 1990; Ricketts, Johnson-Webb, & Taylor, 1998; Smith, Anderson, Bradham, & Longino, 1995; Willits & Bealer, 1967). Some authors assumed that "rural areas experience higher cost of services due to greater distances" (Spence, 1992, p. 16). Smith, Anderson, Bradham, and Logino (1995) defined rural residence as a place located in open country, or in a "small town of fewer than 2,500 in population, that is some distance away from a large population concentration" (p. 277). The most common measure was the use of the thirty-minute measure connecting a rural area to an urban area. For example, Luloff and Swanson (1990) gave the measure as "45% of the work force commut[ing] 30 minutes or more to work" (p. 77).

Economy

The most striking point that emerged when reviewing ways in which the economy helped to measure the degree of rurality was the diversity in the definitions, including the variety of economic factors identified as characteristic of a rural area, such as extraction of natural resources, family farms, fishing, logging, mining, scarcity or lack of services, and telecommunications (Denton, York, & Morgan, 1988; Flora, Flora, Spears, & Swanson, 1995; Galston & Baehler, 1995; Gilbert, 1982; McNellie, 2001; Offner, Seekins, & Clark, 1992; Ricketts, Johnson-Webb, & Taylor, 1998). The most comprehensive definition comes from the USDA's measure of the type of economy, discussed earlier.

Open Country

The term "open country," adapted by some authors from the Census Bureau definition, has been used to mean wide-open spaces without inhabitants, as well as sparsely populated areas outside an incorporated area (Beaulieu & Berry, 1994; Buse & Driscoll, 1992; Flora, Flora, Spears, & Swanson, 1995; Smith, Anderson, Brandham, & Longino, 1995). For instance, Flora, Flora, Spears, and Swanson (1995) use the term to mean "those living in open country side that lay outside urbanized areas" (pp. 6–7).

Outside Standard Metropolitan Statistical Areas

Many studies used the OMB's definition of "outside Standard Metropolitan Statistical Areas" to define rural (Beaulieu & Berry, 1994; Flora, Flora, Spears, & Swanson, 1995; Fugitt, Brown, & Beale, 1989; Nooe & Cunningham, 1992; Ricketts, Johnson-Webb, & Taylor, 1998; Smith, Anderson, Brandham, & Longino, 1995; Toomey, First, Greenlee, & Cummins, 1993; United States Fire Administration, 1998; Williams, Lethbridge, & Chambers, 1997; Young & Martin, 1989).

SUMMARY AND RECOMMENDATIONS

Complications of Existing Definitions of Rural

Current definitions of rural have evolved over time to better understand the population at a specific point in time, to better describe and serve specific populations, and to guide the provision of specific services throughout the United States (Ricketts, Johnson-Webb, & Taylor, 1998). For instance, the "Urbanized Area" portion of the Census Bureau definition has been used by health agencies to define rural because the OMB definition incorrectly identified some rural areas as metropolitan (Ricketts, Johnson-Webb, & Taylor, 1998). The fluctuating definition creates complications in conducting research, comparing results of research, and policy and program planning.

Complications with existing definitions include a lack of detail, lack of complexity, lack of capacity to measure "shades" of rurality, and the inclusion of rural areas in urban definitions. Some definitions do not apply to all areas; for instance, using density by zip codes precludes the translation of that information to density by county, since zip codes sometimes cut across county lines. The OMB definition includes rural areas within regions defined as metropolitan (Smith, Anderson, Bradham, & Longino, 1995). "The Office of Management and Budget (OMB) points out that extensive, highly rural areas are misclassified as metropolitan. This problem occurs all across the nation, but particularly in very large counties in the Western region of the United States" (Taylor, 1998, p. 244).

Earlier versions of the Census Bureau definition of urban, urbanized areas, and rural were complicated by lack of comparison across areas and political considerations that influenced definitions. Commuting distance to another urban area and economic differences are not reflected in this definition. For instance, an urban area of 50,000 people in the middle of a sparsely populated state that is at least 125 miles from any other urban area might have very different resources and needs than another urban area of the same size that is contiguous to urban areas with hundreds of thousands of people. A frontier area that is several hours' drive to the nearest hospital may engender a different sense of isolation than a community that has no roads connecting it to the rest of the state. The uniqueness added to an area by its economic base is lost in this definition. An area dependent on a single economic source such as mining would be different from an area dependent on farming, manufacturing, and service.

Utilizing commuting patterns to define rural can be imprecise and can vary from one town to an entire state. Furthermore, commuting patterns are not absolute predictors of rurality, even though it is noted that traveling vast distances in open areas is a consistent theme most often associated with a rural environment.

Deavers (1992) argues that the use of economy no longer adequately defines what areas are rural because of the drop in the percentage of the economy related to natural resource–based activities (farming and mining, fishing, and forest products industries) and the increase in manufacturing and service industries in traditionally rural areas. It seems like a valuable way to measure differences between rural areas and between rural and urban areas.

Finding one definition that is comparable across regions and adequately describes something so complex as "economy" is complicated. Numerous discrepancies occur when rural areas are measured or defined by being equated with open country. For example, in states such as Virginia, which has open country adjacent to urban areas, the open country cannot be accurately identified as either urban or rural.

Defining an entire state as rural is too extensive and limits the possibility for individually defining other areas within the state as either urban or rural. For instance, some areas in Texas are heavily urban, such as Houston and San Antonio, but the western region of Texas is very

sparsely populated. Considering the population of an entire state to determine rurality is complicated for other reasons. What measure is a valid representation of rural? When the number of people who live in rural areas is considered for an entire state, Pennsylvania, Texas, and North Carolina are considered the most rural states (Ricketts, Johnson-Webb, & Taylor, 1998). When the proportion of the population that is rural is considered, Vermont, West Virginia, and Maine are the top three rural states. Wyoming, Vermont, and Alaska have the smallest total state populations of all states (U.S. Census Bureau, 2001). The most sparsely populated states, calculated by total number of persons per square mile, are Alaska, Wyoming, North Dakota, and South Dakota. De la Torre, Fickenscher, and Luft (1991) note similar complications: "Over 99% of the California population is concentrated in urban areas. Thus, California, as compared to a more rural state such as North Dakota, cannot be classified as a predominately rural state. However, the total rural population in California is considerably larger than the rural population in North Dakota" (pp. 258–9). Cleland's (1995) method of scoring rural areas, although complicated, does allow a more detailed measure of degree of rurality. His index rates rurality on 11 items, such as income and access to an interstate highway. The scale ranges from 0 (less rural) to 19 (more rural). When applied to each state, it creates an unusual measure of degree of rurality for some states. For instance, Wyoming, the most sparsely populated state, scores a 3, which indicates a less rural area. Finally, the measures include the use of services and resources as part of the definition of rurality.

The Need for a Consistent Definition of Rural

The varying definitions of rural have led to contradictions in research findings regarding rural areas. A common definition of what is rural, and a common way to measure degree of rurality, is needed to better assess the strengths of rural communities and identify areas that require attention. Deavers (1992) argues for the need to differentiate between rural and urban areas, and between different types of rural areas. Supporting the need to move from a dichotomous definition, the *Health, United States, 2001 With Urban and Rural Health Chartbook* (October, 2001) reports that health outcomes are better for persons living in suburban areas, rather than more urban or rural areas. Using only the categories of rural or urban blurs these types of differences. Ricketts (1992) proposed that a single definition of rural is neither feasible nor desirable, but recommended that significant rural data be organized in a continuum, so that different definitions and typologies can be constructed to define rural (p. 47). Beaulieu and Berry (1994) began developing a continuum by proposing four levels of rurality instead of using the rural/urban dichotomy. The levels they proposed are adjacent rural areas, urbanized rural areas, frontier areas, and countryside rural areas.

Toward a New Way of Defining Degree of Rurality

Creating common ways to measure degrees of rurality is becoming easier with the caliber of current technological developments. For example, a thermal imaging system provided by computer-enhanced photographic satellites allows for precise measurement of density, using people per hectares, census tract, or square mile. In addition to density per geographic area (hectare, census tract, or square mile), understanding the economic base for a particular area enhances the measurement of degree of rurality. The USDA's measure of economic and political categories, added to a measure of density per geographic area, creates a more comprehensive picture of degree of rurality. The USDA measure does not include services such as health and education, but could use degree of rurality to assess those services by their availability, appropriateness, and quality. The use of the Census Bureau's revised definitions of urban, urban areas, and rural are a way to measure the

impact of proximity to a central, populated area, a crude measure of commuting.

The resulting measure of degree of rurality would include density by census tract, a measure of economy, and a measure of proximity to densely populated areas. Individuals and organizations could layer political and social needs for any area in the continental United States over the measure of degree of density, economy, and proximity to describe any area they wish. This definition would meet Halfacree's (1993) recommendation for a "compound definition, for example a combination of two or more elements of rural which would attempt to capture the multiple meanings of the word" (p. 34). The components of the proposed model for identifying degree of rurality are:

1. The use of census tracts, which are comparable across areas and agreed upon nationally, thus standardizing the measure of density. Census tracts can be translated into county measures, for comparison with other measures.

2. The use of the USDA's components of economy and policy.

3. The Census Bureau's definition, which measures distance from an urban area: urban, urban areas, and rural.

The definition of rural and its operational definition, measuring degree of rurality, would automatically be updated as the nation changes both demographically and economically. This is recommended by the OMB (1998), which urges that the "definition of rural needs to be frequently updated" (p. 63). Because this definition is based on the most current national measures of population and economics, it would be constantly changing. Researchers and policy makers would need to be mindful of the fact that comparing information from different cohorts would be inappropriate, because the measure changes over time.

When using this measure of degree of rurality for research, respondents to surveys could easily identify their area of residence or work place on a map of census tracts, thus allowing researchers and policy makers to create comparable measures across geographic regions. For instance, the similarities and differences between rural areas, such as more densely populated Southern rural areas and sparsely populated Western rural areas, could be measured using population density, economics, and commuting patterns. The assumption that rural is different in northwest Nebraska than in southern South Carolina could be tested by creating a constant measure for degree of rurality as a backdrop for examining cultural similarities and differences.

Further research is needed to validate the use of multiple measures to create a measure of degree of rurality. Additional issues to consider are qualitative opinions people have of what is rural (Flora, Flora, Spears, & Swanson, 1995), what Halfacree calls a social representation of rural. Asking people for their opinions about what is rural, and comparing those with the more quantitative operational definitions of rural, would be one way to determine their similarities and differences. Using this more objective measure of degree of rurality then allows the assessment of assets and strengths and allows community planning that builds on these assets (Daley & Avant, 1999; White & Marks, 1999).

DISCUSSION QUESTIONS

1. How did the Census Bureau define areas that were urban in 2000?

2. What are some complications that may occur when comparing results of the 1990 Census with the 2000 census (geographical area, measurement of farming, ethnicity)?

3. What are the advantages and disadvantages of considering economy when defining degree of rurality? What about when considering distance from urban areas?

4. If degree of rurality is assessed using a continuum from most rural to most urban, how might this method of measurement be useful when identifying assets in a community?

5. How would you recommend that the culture of different rural areas be assessed? How might the presence of differing cultures impact identification of assets in a community?

CLASSROOM ASSIGNMENTS
AND ACTIVITIES

1. Describe the community in which you lived when you were six years old.

   • Town (or community), county, state.

   • Estimated number of people in your county.

   • Size of school, and the distance between your home and school. Did you ride a bus? If yes, for how long?

   • Distance from your home to your physician. The local hospital.

   • Primary source of income (i.e., farming, manufacturing, services, mining).

   • What were the most important strengths in your community?

   • On a continuum from most rural to most urban, how would you describe your community?

2. Create a population map of the county in which you currently live.

- Find and print out your county's map and the census tracts within your county on the Census Bureau web page.
- What is the density by census tract for your county?
- How is your county rated (urban, urban area, and rural)?

- What is the primary economy of your county, based on the Department of Agriculture measure?
- Describe the population map of your county, including its density, distance from urban area, and primary economy. How rural is your county?

REFERENCES

Beach, B. (1997). *Perspectives on rural childcare.* Charleston, WV: Clearing-house on Rural Education and Small Schools.

Beaulieu, J., & Berry, D. (Eds.). (1994). *Rural health services: A management perspective.* Ann Arbor, MI: AUPHA Press/Health Administration Press.

Buse, R., & Driscoll, J. (1992). *Rural information systems: New directions in data collection and retrieval* (1st ed.). Ames: Iowa State University Press.

Center for Rural Pennsylvania. (1991). *Do rural counties have adequate information and referral services?* Harrisburg, PA: Author.

Cleland, C. (1995). Measuring rurality. *Human Services in the Rural Environment, 18,* 13–18.

Cook, P. J., & Mizer, L. L. (1994). The revised ERS county typology, *Rural Development Research Report,* Number 89, Economic Research Service, U.S. Department of Agriculture.

Cromartie, J. B., & Swanson, L. L. (1996). Census tract more precisely define rural populations and areas. *Rural Development Perspectives, 11*(3), 31–39.

Daley, M., & Avant, F. (1999). Attracting and retaining professionals for social work practice in rural areas: An example from East Texas. In I. B. Carlton-LaNey, R. L. Edwards, & P. N. Reid (Eds.), *Preserving and strengthening small towns and rural communities* (pp. 335–345). Washington, DC: National Association of Social Workers Press.

Davis, L. (1988). Rural attitudes towards public welfare allocation. *Human Services in the Rural Environment, 12,* 11–18.

De la Torre, A., Fickenscher, K., & Luft, H. (1991). The zip (postal) code difference: Methods to improve identification of rural subgroups. *Agricultural Economics Journal, 3*(3), 253–262.

Deavers, K. (1992). What is rural? *Policy Studies Journal, 20*(2), 184–189.

Denton, R., York, R., & Morgan, J. (1988). The social workers view of the rural community: An empirical examination. *Human Services in the Rural Environment, 11,* 14–21.

Dewey, R. (1960). The rural-urban continuum: Real but relatively unimportant. *The American Journal of Sociology, 66*(1), 59–66.

Edmonson, B. (1997). A new era for rural America. *American Demographics.* Retrieved December 3, 2001, from http://www.demographics.com/Publications/AD97_ad/9709_ad//ad97-96.

Edwards, R., & Hopps, J. (1995). *Encyclopedia of social work* (19th ed., Vols. 1–3). Washington DC: National Association of Social Work Press.

Flora, C., Flora, J., Spears, J., & Swanson, L. (Eds.). (1995). *Rural communities: Legacy and change.* Boulder, CO: Westview Press.

Foster, R., & McBeth, M. (1996). Urban-rural influences in U.S. environmental and economic development policy. *Journal of Rural Studies, 12,* 387–396.

Fuguitt, G., Brown, D., & Beale, C. (1989). *Rural and small town America.* New York: Russell Sage Foundation.

Galston, W., & Baehler, H. (1995). *Rural development in the United States: Connecting theory, practice, and possibilities* (1st ed.). Washington, DC: Island Press.

Gilbert, J. (1982). Rural theory: The grounding of rural sociology. *Rural Sociology, 47,* 608–629.

Goldsmith, H. (1993). *Isolated rural areas.* Retrieved September 7, 2000, from http://www.rupri.org/policyres/context/ira.html

Gordon, E., & Blakely, E. (1995). Progress toward compliance with Americans with Disabilities Act: A statewide survey of rural social service agencies. *Human Services in the Rural Environment, 18,* 11–15.

Halfacree, K. (1993). Locality and social representation: Space, discourse, and alternative definitions of the rural. *Journal of Rural Studies, 9,* 23–34.

Hardcastle, D. A., Wenocur, S., & Powers, P. R. (1997). *Community practice: Theories and skills for social workers.* New York: Oxford University Press.

Hoggart, K. (1990). Let's do away with rural. *Journal of Rural Studies, 6,* 245–255.

Imhoff, D. (2000). The rural inhabitants of America. *Human Services and the Rural Environment, 23,* 155–157.

Keller, P., Zimbelman, K., Murray, D., & Feil, R. (1980). Geographic distribution of psychologist in the Northeastern United States. *Journal of Rural Community Psychology, 1,* 18–24.

Kretzmann, J. P., & Green, M. B. (1998). *Building the bridge from client to citizen: A community toolbox for welfare reform.* Chicago: ABCD Institute.

Kretzmann, J. P., & McKnight, J. L. (1993). *Building communities from the inside out.* Chicago: ACTA Publications.

Kusimo, P. (1999). *Rural African Americans and education: The legacy of the Brown decision.* Charleston, WV: Clearinghouse on Rural Education and Small Schools. (ERIC Document Reproduction Service No. ED346082).

Locke, B. L. (1991). Research and social work in rural areas: Are we asking the "right" questions? *Human Services in the Rural Environment, 15*(2), 12–15.

Luloff, A., & Swanson, L. (Eds.). (1990). *American rural communities.* Boulder, CO: Westview Press.

Lusk, M., & Mason, D. (1992). Development theory for rural practice. *Human Services in the Rural Environment, 16,* 5–9.

Marsden, T., Lowe, P., & Whatmore, S. (1990). *Rural restructuring: Global processes and their responses.* London: Fulton.

McNellie, B. (2001). The advanced rural generalist. *The New Social Worker, 2,* 16–17.

Morris, C. (1984). Population in rural communities: An analysis of 1980 census data. *Human Services in the Rural Environment, 9,* 10–16.

Morris, L. C. (1995). Rural poverty. In L. Beebe, N. A. Winchester, F. Pflieger, & S. Lowman (Eds.), *Encyclopedia of Social Work* (19th ed.) (pp. 2068–2075). Washington, DC: National Association of Social Work Press.

Morrison, P. (1990). *A taste of the country: A collection of Calvin Beal's writings* (1st ed.). University Park: The Pennsylvania State University Press.

Nooe, R., & Bolitho, F. (1982). An examination of rural social work literature. *Human Services in the Rural Environment, 7,* 11–18.

Nooe, R., & Cunningham, M. (1992). Rural dimensions of homelessness: A rural-urban comparison. *Human Services in the Rural Environment, 15,* 5–9.

Office of Management and Budget. (1998). Alternative approaches to defining metropolitan and non-metropolitan areas: Notice OMB. *Federal Register, 63,* 244.

Offner, R., Seekins, T., & Frank, C. (1992). Disability and rural independent living: Setting an agenda for rural rehabilitation. *Human Services in the Rural Environment, 15,* 6–8.

Pahl, R. (1966). The rural urban continuum. *Sociological Ruralista, 5,* 299–324.

Popper, F. (1984). Survival of the American frontier. *Resources, 77,* 1–4.

Ray, J., & Murty, S. (1990). Rural child sexual abuse prevention and treatment. *Human Services in the Rural Environment, 13,* 24–29.

Ricketts, T., Johnson-Webb, K., & Taylor, P. (1998). *Definitions of rural: A handbook for health policy makers and researchers* (HRSA 93-857 (P)). Chapel Hill, NC: Office of Rural Health Policy Clearinghouse.

Rural Policy Context (n.d.). "Frontier areas: Definitions from the Frontier Education Center." Retrieved May 12, 2003, from http://www.rupri.org/policyres/context/fa.html.

Rural Policy Research Institute. (1999, July 24). *Metropolitan and non-metropolitan counties: Definitions from the U.S. Office of Management and Budget.* Retrieved November 10, 2001, from http://www.rupri.org/policyres/context/omb.html.

Simons, R. L., Johnson, C., Conger, R. D., & Lorenz, F. O. (1997). Linking community context to quality of parenting: A study of rural families. *Rural Sociology, 62*(2), 207–230.

Smith, H., Anderson, R., Bradham, D., & Longino, C. (1995). Rural and urban differences in mortality among Americans 55 years and older: Analysis of the national longitudinal mortality study. *The Journal of Rural Health, 11,* 274–285.

Spence, S. (1992). Use of community-based social services by older rural and urban blacks: An exploratory study. *Human Services in the Rural Environment, 15,* 16–19.

Taylor, P. (1998). Change in federal definition of rural areas? *Federal Register, 63,* 244–250.

Toomey, B., First, R., Greenlee, R., & Cummins, L. (1993). Counting the rural homeless population:

Methodological dilemmas. *Social Work Research & Abstracts, 29,* 23–27.

United States Fire Administration. (1998). *A profile of the rural fire problem in the United States.* (Report No. FA-181). Washington DC: Author.

Urban and Rural Health Chartbook. National Center for Health Statistics. (2001). *Urban and rural health highlights.* Retrieved July 15, 2002, from http://www.cdc.gov /nchs/products/pubs/pubd/hus/urbrural.pdf

U.S. Census Bureau. (2001). *Urban and rural definitions.* Retrieved July 15, 2002, from http://www.census .gov/population/censusdata/urdef.txt.

Wagner, J. D., Menke, E. D., & Ciccone, J. K. (1994). The health of rural homeless women with young children. *The Journal of Rural Health 10*(1), 49–57.

White, C., & Marks, K. (1999). A strengths-based approach to rural sustainable development. In I. B. Carlton-LaNey, R. L. Edwards, and P. N. Reid (Eds.), *Preserving and strengthening small towns and rural communities* (pp. 27–42). Washington, DC: National Association of Social Workers Press.

Williams, R., Lethbridge, D., & Chambers, W. (1997). Development of a health promotion inventory for poor rural women. *Family and Community Health, 2,* 13–23.

Willits, F., & Bealer, R. (1967). An evaluation of a composite definition of "rurality." *Rural Sociology, 32,* 164–177.

Willits, F. K., Bealer, R. C., & Crider, D. M. (1986). Persistence of rural/urban differences. In D. A. Dillman & D. J. Hobbs (Eds.), *Rural society in the US: Issues for the 1980s* (pp. 69–76). Boulder, CO: Westview Press.

Wyoming Department of Health Office of Rural Health and Primary Care. (2000). *Primary care: Undeserved areas report Wyoming 2000.* Cheyenne, WY: Author.

York, R. O., Denton, R. T., & Moran, J. R. (1989). Rural and urban social work practice: Is there a difference? *Social Casework, 70*(4), 201–209.

Young, C., & Martin, L. (1989). Social services in rural and urban primary care projects. *Human Services in the Rural Environment, 13,* 30–35.

INTERNET RESOURCES

Link to Census Tract Outline Map State Folders
http://ftp2.census.gov/plmap/pl_trt/

Census Bureau Home
http://www.census.gov/main/www/cen2000
.html

Census Economic facts by county
http://quickfacts.census.gov/qfd/index.html

 INFOTRAC COLLEGE EDITION

assets
community development
frontier

research
rural
U.S. Census Bureau

2

Social Welfare and Rural People

From the Colonial Era to the Present

PAUL H. STUART

The history of rural social welfare is in part a story of the transfer of the location and control of social welfare services from rural areas to metropolitan areas. From the establishment of the first European settlements in North America early in the seventeenth century to the American Revolution, most people lived in rural areas. The proportion of Americans living in urban areas increased steadily during the nineteenth and twentieth centuries, however. By the first decades of the twentieth century, over half of the American population lived in urban places. State governments and the federal government provided an increasing array of social services. More importantly, the state and federal governments funded and regulated many of the services delivered to rural people at the local level.

A parallel history involves the social development of rural areas. Abundant land and its rapid development characterized North America from the time of the European invasions of the sixteenth and seventeenth centuries until the early twentieth century. The historian Frederick Jackson Turner (1893), concluded that "the existence of an area of free land, its continuous recession, and the advance of American settlement westward, explain American development" (p. 1). The land had been taken from Native American groups, sometimes by purchase but often as a result of warfare, deceptive dealings, or simple dispossession. The Constitution gave the federal government plenary power to deal with the Indian tribes; lands alienated from Indian owner-ship became part of the public domain. Congress followed a social investment strategy during the nineteenth century, characterized by human and social capital investments and the development of individual and community assets (Midgley, 1999). The strategy rested on a liberal land policy, which resulted in the rapid development of the West. That liberal strategy, some have suggested, has provided a model for the developing world in the twenty-first century (de Soto, 2000).

Thus, two themes were important in the interaction of social welfare services and rural people. The financing and control of social services shifted as the population shifted from rural to urban areas, in a process that some social scientists have called modernization. The novelist Norman Mailer, in his examination of the real-life execution of Gary Gilmore, referred to "Eastern" (or urban) and "Western" (or rural) voices to capture this transition (Mailer, 1979). Rural areas lost control of social welfare service delivery during the nineteenth and twentieth centuries. At the same time, the economic and communal development of rural areas was an objective of national policy. Development implied the transfer of assets to prospective settlers and investment by the state or federal government in education, transportation, and community development. Thus, asset-building and social investment to meet the needs of emigrating native-born white and immigrant families dominated American social policy before 1900, often to the detriment of indigenous populations.

COLONIAL PERIOD

The British colonies in North America faced chronic labor shortages. Colonial landowners depended on the involuntary labor of slaves, convict laborers, and indentured servants. Land policy in many of the British North American colonies, however, was liberal. The availability of land on terms that made landowning feasible for ordinary people made British North America "the best poor man's country"—at least for Europeans—during the eighteenth century (Lemon, 1972). Thus, access to assets and asset accumulation explained much about the appeal of America to potential immigrants from Europe, even before independence.

Native Americans successfully frustrated attempts to enslave them, and colonial authorities turned to a variety of types of bound labor to counteract chronic labor shortages during the seventeenth and eighteenth centuries. "Bound" laborers were obligated to work for a master, either for a term of years or for life, in the case of African slaves. In addition to slaves, bound laborers included convict laborers, paupers from the streets of English cities, and indentured workers from the British Isles and the continent of Europe, who worked for a term of years to repay the cost of their passage from Europe to North America. Bound workers provided the labor that cut the trees, planted and harvested the crops, loaded the ships, and performed a variety of other jobs in the New World.

Competition for laborers with other European colonies around the world induced the colonial elite to create incentives to European settlement, including religious toleration and ready access to land (Baseler, 1998). Contracts for indentured service in the middle colonies often provided for land ownership at the conclusion of the period of indentured service. The prospect of land ownership provided a major incentive for prospective immigrants. According to a student of colonial era migration, "Throughout the eighteenth century . . . European emigrants could choose from a variety of destinations for future settlement—America was far from the only

choice. When prospects at home looked dim, the 'pull' factors for selecting a particular destination tended to mirror the problems they sought to escape. Land, employment, and trading opportunities were strong lures, for they promised a decent living for colonists and their families" (Wokeck, 1999, p. 224). Religious freedom, coupled with a land policy that made it relatively easy for recent immigrants to acquire land, created a powerful magnet for immigration.

In a study of the social and economic structure of the colonies, Jackson Turner Main (1965) found four phases in the development of the Northern colonies: a frontier phase, subsistence farming, commercial farming, and urbanization. Land was easy to obtain in the frontier stage: "Land prices . . . were low enough so that poor men could become farmers almost at once . . . [and] better land, which was of course more valuable, could always be obtained on credit" (p. 9). The Southern colonies were more varied, and the institution of slavery contributed to greater inequalities in wealth. However, in subsistence-farming regions there was substantial equality. "Southerners had a disorderly way of settling without a land title" and many subsistence farmers evaded land taxes (p. 48).

A locality's level of development affected its social welfare programs. Following English practice, local rather than provincial governments provided the social and institutional services that existed. The Elizabethan Poor Law made poor relief a local responsibility. Colonial towns and counties devised programs for the poor and deviant appropriate for their level of social and economic development. In many rural areas, poor relief arrangements were informal. Often, local authorities used households to deliver services by boarding the dependent poor (Guest, 1989).

Main (1965) found few differences in wealth or status among the pioneers during the frontier phase. Before the development of such institutions as poorhouses, jails, and hospitals, rural township or county authorities handled problems of poverty, frailty, and deviant behavior informally. As a region moved from subsistence farming to commercial farming and towns began to develop, local governments developed some services in order to provide for more efficient handling of the increasing numbers of the poor that accompanied economic development. Town or county governments opened poorhouses, jails, and in some cases schools and hospitals.

EARLY NATIONAL PERIOD

Congress invested in internal improvements and followed a liberal land policy that promoted settlement after the American Revolution (Young, 1969). A land-rich and cash-poor federal government used public land sales to finance a variety of public projects, subsumed under the summary appellation "internal improvements" (Larson, 2001). These included transportation—roads, canals, and later railroads—and schools, including common schools and state universities. Even before the Constitution, the Continental Congress laid out plans for developing the territory west of the Allegheny Mountains. The Land Ordinance of 1785 provided for surveying the public domain into six-mile square townships. One square-mile section in each township was to be reserved for the support of the common schools. The Northwest Ordinance of 1787 provided for the organization of territories and their eventual progression to statehood, as did a similar ordinance enacted in 1790 for the territory south of the Ohio River. States admitted to the union after 1800 received grants of land to support state universities and other state services.

American pioneers created new social institutions on the frontier that were similar to those with which they were familiar. Thus, American frontier society and institutions resembled those found in the East (Berkhofer, 1964). The four phases of frontier society identified by Main (1965)—frontier, subsistence agriculture, commercial agriculture, and in some cases urbanization—were to be repeated, with variations, as the new nation expanded westward.

During the first half of the nineteenth century, Congress repeatedly liberalized land policies to make it easier for individuals to acquire and work the land. A Jeffersonian ideal that emphasized the superiority of the yeoman farmer and the benefits of the family farm provided the basis for a liberal land policy. Although land sales provided a major revenue source for the federal government, the pressure for liberal terms for land ownership proved irresistible. A series of land laws made land more accessible to ordinary people. In 1841, Congress enacted the Preemption Act, providing that squatters on the public land could claim their land after 14 months of residence. Payment of as little as $1.25 an acre secured their ownership. The Graduation Act of 1854 reduced the price per acre for land that had been unsold for a period of time. Land that had been on the market for a decade sold for one dollar per acre. After 15 years, the price dropped to 75 cents per acre, after 20 years to 50 cents per acre, and so on. Land that remained unsold for 30 years sold for 12 1/2 cents per acre (Hibbard, 1924).

Congress provided free land for soldiers who fought in the Revolutionary War, the War of 1812, and the Mexican War. The benefit was often provided in scrip that could be exchanged for land, and many veterans sold the scrip to speculators who held the land for increased prices. These veterans' measures began a tradition of generous benefits for veterans that continued with the Civil War pensions and, in the twentieth century, the programs for veterans of World Wars I and II and the conflicts in Korea, Viet Nam, and the Persian Gulf.

A more liberal land policy, often combined with provisions for internal improvements, facilitated the settlement and development of the Middle West. Between 1800 and the 1850s, settlers poured into the Ohio and Mississippi River valleys, the Great Lakes region, and the old Southwest. Substantial federal investment supported this expansion. The federal government purchased land from Native Americans, fought wars against them, and ultimately removed them from lands soon to be occupied by white settlers. The system of frontier military outposts often provided the first markets for Western farmers (Prucha, 1967). Appropriations for internal improvements supported the construction of roads, canals, and eventually railroads to facilitate the movement of settlers westward and the transportation of crops to market.

Towns and counties continued to provide basic social welfare services—support for the dependent, increasingly in small institutions such as almshouses and poor farms. However, the campaigns of Dorothea Dix and others to expand state services, usually institutional care, for specific categories of poor people—the insane, the retarded, children, and criminals—increased the power and prominence of state government in the provision of social welfare services. Indeed, as social welfare provisions became more specialized and more targeted upon persons with identifiable physical, emotional, cognitive, or moral impairments, states began to expand their social welfare activities. Although county and town services continued to be important as a first line of care for the "undifferentiated poor," some state leaders argued the superiority of state services as opposed to the backward, often corrupt town or county services. Reformers charged that county officials awarded contracts to supporters and engaged in patronage, rewarding supporters and relatives with jobs. The theme of local government incompetence and corruption would become increasingly important after the Civil War.

THE CIVIL WAR
AND AFTER

A half-century of agitation for a more liberal land policy culminated in the successful passage of four "Western Measures"—the Homestead Act, the Morrill Land Grant College Act, the Department of Agriculture Act, and the Pacific Railroad Act—by the first Civil War Congress in 1862. Different coalitions within the newly ascendant Republican Party supported the measures and no one at the time thought of them as constituting a program for Western development. However, the four measures determined the subsequent development of the Western United States to a much larger extent than anyone anticipated in 1862.

The Republican Party's 1860 platform pledged support for two of the measures—the Homestead Act and the Pacific Railroad Act. President Lincoln endorsed the Department of Agriculture and the land grant college bill at the behest of Eastern Congressmen concerned about problems of soil exhaustion in their states.

The four Western measures were the culmination of an increasingly liberal land policy but promoted an aggressive program of internal improvements as well. They embodied a social investment approach to the development of the Western United States (Midgley, 1999). The federal government distributed assets in the form of land to settlers and invested in research, education, and a transportation infrastructure through direct appropriations and land grants to states and railroads. The Homestead Act of 1862 was an important part of the Congress' late 18th-century Western policy. Between 1863 and 1912, the federal government distributed over 239 million acres of free land to homesteaders (although settlers claimed final title to only 150 million acres). Homesteaders were not the only recipients of public land, however. The states received nearly 100 million acres in land grants for agricultural and mechanical colleges, and railroad companies received nearly 350 million acres (Morrill Act of 1862, Pacific Railroad Act of 1862). Some have criticized the inconsistency of Congress in opening some lands to free settlement while granting other lands to be sold to support internal improvements (Gates, 1936). However, the four laws, as modified by subsequent legislation, were to provide the basic structure for the development of the Western United States (Bogue, 1969; White, 1991).

Congress created the Department of Agriculture in 1862 "to acquire and to diffuse among the people of the United States useful information on subjects connected with agriculture . . . and to procure, propagate, and distribute among the people new and valuable seeds and plants" (p. 387). The department was to become a large agricultural research agency where new farming techniques, seeds, and fertilizers could be developed and tested. Initially the agency's chief, the

Commissioner of Agriculture, was not a member of the President's cabinet, but Congress raised the agency to cabinet status in 1889. However, scientific research lagged until President McKinley appointed James "Tama Jim" Wilson Secretary of Agriculture in 1897. A graduate of Grinnell College and former professor of agriculture at Iowa State College, Wilson remained in office until 1913, serving Presidents McKinley, Roosevelt, and Taft. During his tenure, in cooperation with the land grant colleges, he expanded the department's scientific research, including experiment stations and laboratories, and its extension work.

Initially, land grant colleges were to provide agricultural instruction to future farmers and the children of farmers. In some states, farmers objected to the fact that many faculty members preferred a traditional liberal arts curriculum. They feared that this preference would impede the goal of teaching "such branches of learning as are related to agriculture and the mechanic arts" (Cumo, 1998; Douglass, 1992). However, the lasting contribution of the land grant colleges was their introduction of "useful knowledge" into the higher education curriculum, to accompany the classical studies (Geiger, 1998). At some of the agricultural colleges, faculty began to provide information to farmers in brief institutes held in rural areas. Faculty members at many of these colleges began to conduct agricultural research. In 1887, Congress passed the Hatch Act, to "aid in acquiring and diffusing among the people of the United States useful and practical information on subjects connected with agriculture, and to promote scientific investigation and experiment respecting the principles and applications of agricultural science" (p. 440). The Hatch Act provided funding to support agricultural experiment stations operated by the agricultural colleges (Kerr, 1981).

In 1890, a second Morrill Act authorized an annual cash appropriation (initially from the proceeds of land sales) to support the agricultural colleges. This infusion of cash "contributed to the rapid development of land-grant colleges . . . [most of which] received a total of $48,000 within 12 to 18 months" (Williams, R. L., 1998,

p. 76). The second Morrill Act also authorized payments to separate institutions for African Americans in states that maintained segregated educational systems; the funds were to be "equitably divided" between white and African American institutions (Morrill Act of 1890, p. 418). Thus, Congress provided for "separate but equal" institutions six years before the Plessy v. Ferguson Supreme Court decision of 1896. The second Morrill Act resulted in the creation of the "1890 schools," historically African-American institutions whose missions were similar to the white land-grant institutions. The Department of Agriculture failed to enforce the requirement that funds be "equitably divided," and the 1890 institutions continue to struggle with inadequate appropriations (Schuck, 1972; Williams, F., 1998).

The Homestead Act succeeded in distributing large amounts of land to settlers, who could claim 160 acres of free land upon payment of a small filing fee. Full ownership would be granted if the settler improved the land and lived on it for five years. The act extended homesteading to unmarried women and widows, African Americans, Native Americans who abandoned tribal membership, and to immigrants who declared an intention to become citizens. By 1897, over 525,000 farms totaling over 67 million acres had been created as a result of the act, making it the most significant asset distribution program in American history (Gates, 1968). While the half million farms were home to over two million people, the American population had increased by over 32 million people during the same period (White, 1991), with the largest increases in urban areas.

Railroads were a necessary part of development in the late nineteenth century. The railroads carried the settlers west and delivered the farmers' agricultural products to market. The United States provided land grants to encourage railroads to construct lines, creating the Union Pacific Railroad in the Pacific Railroad Act of 1862. During the late-nineteenth century, the federal government distributed much more land to railroads—either directly or through state grants for internal improvements—than it gave to settlers under the Homestead Act. Railroad corporations received over 223 million acres of land, although they had to forfeit 35 million acres because of delays in completing the lines (White, 1991).

States began to centralize social welfare and correctional services during the late-nineteenth century. Following Massachusetts' lead in 1863, many states created boards of charities and correction to organize state institutions on a businesslike basis. State social welfare provision expanded as state boards examined outcomes of institutionalization. Specialized mental health services, correctional services, and a variety of other institutional services were provided under state auspice, rather than by towns or counties. Services administered by state governments were believed to be less patronage-ridden and corrupt than local services. The widely imitated New York State Care Act of 1890 gave the state responsibility for providing care to all of the insane poor (Dowbiggin, 1992; Trattner, 1999). In some states, commissioners visited township and county institutions and recommended improvements in local programs. Wisconsin went even further, mandating that counties provide care for chronically mentally ill residents in county institutions (Ebert & Trattner, 1990).

THE PROGRESSIVE ERA

By the twentieth century, the United States had become an urban nation. Urban population, only a quarter of the total in 1880, increased to 40% in 1900 and to half of the population in 1920 (see Table 2.1). Even with increased urbanization, the years between 1901 and 1913 represented the heyday of homesteading, as an average of 78,000 persons per year claimed homesteads, compared to 37,000 a year between 1863 and 1900 (Nugent, 1999). Despite agricultural expansion, rural areas began to be seen as problem areas. In comparison to cities, rural areas had fewer specialized services and less economic opportunity. Following European precedent, in 1908 President Theodore Roosevelt organized a Country Life Commission. The Commission celebrated rural life, but criticized the "self-defeating individual-

Table 2.1 U.S. Population, 1800–1920

Year	Urban (%)
1800	6.1
1830	8.8
1860	19.8
1880	26.3
1900	40.2
1920	51.4

SOURCE: Bureau of the Census (1975), Series A 57–72

ism of the farmers themselves" (Rodgers, 1998, p. 334). It called for the development of cooperative enterprises and focused attention on the problems of farm wives and the difficulty of keeping children on the farm. The Country Life Movement, a national effort to reform the rural family and the rural community, resulted. The new discipline of rural sociology arose to describe rural family and community life (Martinez-Brawley, 1981; Rodgers, 1998).

Although social reformers focused primarily on urban problems, they had discordant ideas about rural life. Two distinctly different themes characterized thinking about rural communities in the early-twentieth century. For many, the rural community provided the image of ideal community life. In this view, strong bonds of friendship and even stronger family relationships resulted in an ethic of mutual assistance that softened the difficulties of rural life. These reformers viewed rural life as the solution to urban social problems. Introducing mutual support and self-reliance, they believed, would help to resolve urban social ills (Mills, 1943). The "orphan train" movement, which placed New York City "street urchins" on Midwestern farms between 1853 and the eve of the Great Depression, provides an example of this view of rural life (Holt, 1992).

Other social reformers viewed rural communities themselves as problem areas. More poverty-stricken and backward than urban areas, excessively individualistic, and lacking adequate remedial services, rural areas were themselves "in crisis." In the eyes of these social reformers, rural communities, especially in the South, were themselves a significant social problem (Sealander, 1997). For some, presumed rural backwardness was an inherent part of the nature of rural communities. Others believed that urban development had resulted in the deflection of rural resources to cities.

Although reformers could cite evidence for both contradictory impressions of rural community life, neither described the reality of life in the rural United States. One view idealized the rural community, while the other was too pejorative. Yet the varying ideas about rural communities had implications for how and when reformers got involved in providing services in rural areas. Were rural areas models for the cities? Had they been "underdeveloped" as a result of urbanization? Or were their problems the result of inherent rural backwardness and a lack of resources?

Some reformers wanted to make farms more efficient. They speculated that rural decline resulted from the inefficiencies of the family farm. This group of reformers promoted farm demonstrations and agricultural extension programs. In addition, they believed that improved health and education services would help to eradicate both disease and ignorance from the countryside. Philanthropic foundations, including the Rosenwald Fund and the Rockefeller Foundation, supported the extension of education and health services to rural populations, especially to underserved rural African Americans in the Southeast.

In 1914, Congress enacted the Smith-Lever Act, which authorized appropriations to support agricultural extension work carried out by the land grant colleges. States that had segregated land grant colleges established by the second Morrill Act were free to allocate resources as they saw fit between the white and African-American institutions. The result was to perpetuate segregated and unequal services, as Southern states created dual extension services for African American and white farmers (Schuck, 1972).

A major agenda of the progressive era was the expansion of state regulation and state social welfare services. Social workers campaigned for the children's code, a codification and expansion of state laws that included mothers' pensions and juvenile courts, as well as child labor restrictions, compulsory school attendance laws, and other state social welfare measures (Clopper, 1921). However, the reforms were often limited to urban areas. For example, Missouri's mothers pension law, the first in the nation, applied only to St. Louis and Kansas City when enacted in 1911. State social welfare legislation had the potential to influence rural areas by establishing standards for children and families, but often it was only potential. Problems of funding, inadequate resources, and rural resis-tance frustrated reform efforts in rural America.

WORLD WARS, PROSPERITY, DEPRESSION, AND PROSPERITY AGAIN

American farm population peaked at 32.5 million in 1916 and began a decline that continued through the twentieth century. Mechanization, farm tenancy, expanding opportunity in the cities, and drought took their toll even before the agricultural depression of the 1920s that preceded the Great Depression of the 1930s. New homestead filings had peaked in 1913, but during the 1920s, homesteading dwindled. In 1934, the Taylor Grazing Act closed most of the public domain to homesteading (Nugent, 1999).

During World War I, the American Red Cross organized the Home Service, a national social service program. Red Cross workers attempted to link servicemen, many of whom were away from home for the first time, with their families on the home front (Black, 1991). For the first time, social workers attempted to organize services in rural areas as well as in cities. Several social workers that were to be associated with rural services in the 1920s and 1930s, notably Josephine C. Brown, began their professional careers in the program (Davenport & Davenport, 1984; Martinez-Brawley, 1981).

Drought and agricultural depression in the 1920s accelerated the move to the cities that began during World War I. The war ended large-scale immigration as the buildup of wartime industry created new demands for workers. Immigration legislation in 1924 severely limited immigration from Eastern and Southern Europe, creating new industrial employment opportunities for domestic migrants displaced by the agricultural depression or fleeing rural poverty. Rural states in the Great Plains lost population as homesteaders abandoned their claims and sought wage work. African Americans and poor whites left the South, moving to Eastern and Midwestern cities in search of economic opportunity.

For social workers, public welfare seemed to have come of age during the 1920s. As one social work executive put it, they had witnessed a "transition from charities and correction to public welfare" beginning in 1910 (Kelso, 1923, p. 21). In 1929, social work educator Porter Lee declared that social work, once "a Cause . . . a movement directed toward the elimination of an [e]ntrenched evil," had become "a Function of well-organized community life" (p. 3). The children's code movement succeeded in state after state, and state child welfare laws extended social services into even the most isolated rural areas. States from Alabama to Minnesota established county child welfare boards to enforce child labor and school attendance laws, to establish juvenile courts and juvenile probation services, and to provide support to dependent children (Hodson, 1921; Burson, 2001).

During the Great Depression of the 1930s, rural areas, already hit hard by the agricultural depression of the 1920s, suffered even more than the cities. New Deal planners addressed rural problems. A Division of Rural Rehabilitation within the Federal Emergency Relief Administration encouraged community gardens and other self-help measures, while the Agricultural Adjustment Administration sought to support the prices of agricultural products. New Deal power-generating projects, including the Tennessee Valley Authority, Boulder Dam, and projects on the Missouri and Columbia Rivers, provided electric power to rural Americans organized by the Rural Electrification Administration (Schlesinger, 1958). The Social Security Act of 1935 addressed rural problems in two ways. First, the law established three public assistance programs, Old Age Assistance, Aid to Dependent Children, and Aid to the Blind, and required states to provide them to persons living in all political subdivisions of the state, not merely in urban areas. The Act also established a number of social service programs, such as Child Welfare Services and Crippled Children's Services. Congress required states to target children living in rural areas when planning services provided under these programs.

World War II resulted in a resumption of large-scale migration from rural areas to cities, as the defense buildup created a demand for workers who had previously been excluded from the industrial labor force—women and rural people, including African Americans, whites, Hispanics, and Native Americans. After the war, the GI Bill provided opportunities for vocational and higher education to veterans from rural as well as urban backgrounds, providing many with entrée to the middle class. The homeownership provisions of the GI Bill, combined with the improvement of road systems, facilitated the development of suburbs surrounding central cities. The postwar arms race with the Soviet Union provided continuing employment for defense workers, including many returning veterans. Postwar prosperity fueled an industrial expansion that stimulated continued urban growth.

Rural areas seemed less isolated as an interstate highway system replaced the railroad as the major linkage between farmers and markets and between the countryside and cities in general. The Hill-Burton Act of 1946 stimulated the construction of hospitals in rural areas, increasing the availability of health services. Advances in communication, radio, and most importantly television, seemingly reduced the isolation of rural areas even while replacing homemade recreation with mass entertainment. By the end of the twentieth century, the computer and the World Wide Web brought information and entertainment to rural schools, libraries, and homes. Advances in marketing, the franchise fast food restaurant, and the retail super center made a wider range of products available to rural people, even as they threatened to homogenize rural life.

RECENT DEVELOPMENTS

By century's end, rural areas had higher rates of poverty than urban areas; the nation experienced "a rural crisis of severe proportions" during the 1980s that continued into the next decade (Martinez-Brawley, 1988, p. 251). The highest concentrations of poor Americans were in rural areas in the Southeast and the Southwest; notably the Southeastern "black belt," the Appalachian mountain region, the Rio Grande Valley and the Texas Gulf Coast, and the Southwest's Native American reservations. An absence of jobs for all seeking employment, a lack of high-paying jobs, inadequate health and social services, and inferior schools often exacerbated rural poverty (Flynt, 1996).

Contemporary observers, like those of the Progressive Era, noted a relative lack of general resources and inadequate and inaccessible community agencies in rural communities. Consolidation of social service agencies left many rural people without nearby services. Others noted a tendency for urban areas to drain resources from rural areas. The result for social service providers included large caseloads and insufficient staff and resources (Ray & Murty, 1990). For example, in a survey of 61 rural child welfare workers, Ray & Murty (1988) found that "over 80% of all clinicians surveyed perceived a lack of trained counselors or resources to deal with the problem of child sexual abuse. Only 48% of those providing services thought child sexual abuse victims were receiving good services. The rating of problems by agency staffs showed a pattern of staff shortages, lack of resources, and increasing caseloads among all three types of rural agencies. Other problems included poor interagency coordination, lack of community support,

and problems stemming from societal denial of sexual abuse" (p. 1).

Privatization compounded the problems of rural social welfare. Reimbursement systems often favored urban service providers. Egan & Kadushin (1997) found that "the prospective payment system [used to reimburse health care providers] . . . differentially reimburses rural facilities at lower rates than urban facilities" (p. 1). This results in severe cost constraints. Rural communities also had relatively fewer aftercare resources than urban areas. Yet certain resources not easily available in urban areas were found in rural areas. Rural practitioners made use of natural helping networks, including extended kinship systems, lodges, and churches (Sundet & Mermelstein, 1984; Patterson, Memmott, & Germain, 1995). Distinctive cultural aspects of rural areas were also relevant to rural practitioners. Jones (1981) found that "social workers in rural midwestern areas such as Iowa must consider distinctive characteristics of the poor in those areas to help clients within the framework of family and community." These important characteristics included "the presence of father in family, residence in small towns with a single industry, presence of high numbers of female elderly, community skepticism of social welfare programs and denial of poverty conditions, independence and rugged individualism as societal values, distant or nonexistent social services, intolerance of difference, predominance of primary or kin relationships, lack of anonymity, less mobility, [and] more stigmatization" (p. 1).

Jones (1981) also emphasized the importance of a "generalist, autonomous, and self-directed" social worker who "needs to be creative in developing resources, and must provide a very personal type of service" (p. 13). Religion was important in many rural communities. Johnson (1997) found that "spirituality and religion are very important components in the rural community, providing strength, support, and simultaneous integration for the individual to the collective population" (p. 58).

Despite the relative prosperity of the 1990s, many rural areas lagged behind or even deteriorated economically *vis-à-vis* metropolitan areas (Wimberley & Morris, 1997). Although some rural areas became popular vacation and retirement centers, not all rural residents benefited from this demographic change. The influx of "new residents" sometimes caused the dislocation of less affluent rural residents. Other areas have continued to lose population, as the continuing mechanization of agriculture results in demands for fewer and fewer workers and alternative ways of earning a living have been slow to emerge. While federal programs from the New Deal to the present expanded the supply of health and social services in rural areas, present-day trends toward privatization, mergers, and consolidations in private and semi-public social service providers threaten to drain rural areas of available services.

At the start of the twenty-first century, the transfer of the location and control of social welfare services from rural areas to metropolitan areas seemed complete. Ironically, the devolution of social welfare services to states and private entities seemed to accelerate this trend rather than reverse

it. Block grants, including the TANF Block Grant of 1996, shifted power from the federal government to the states, but states have not generally empowered local governments in rural or urban areas. Privatization has often meant consolidation as private and semiprivate contractors sought to maximize economies of scale.

As the proportion of Americans living in urban areas has increased, nostalgia about rural areas has grown. Much of the appeal of suburban and exurban areas derives from this nostalgia, but ignores the challenges faced by many rural Americans. A contemporary equivalent of the "Western measures" of 1862 to develop rural communities has not as yet been developed. Such a social investment approach would combine asset building and job creation with investments in education, research, and transportation. Developing such an approach may be the key to revitalizing rural communities in the twenty-first century.

DISCUSSION QUESTIONS

1. Local governments controlled and financed social welfare services during the Colonial and Early National periods of American history. The growing importance and wealth of urban areas resulted in a shift of financing and control from local governments to state and federal governments. As Norman Mailer might say, Eastern voices became more prominent than Western voices. Is it possible to envision another scenario, one in which rural areas maintained control of social welfare services? Would the results have been beneficial for rural communities and for the consumers of social welfare services? Why or why not?

2. Rural areas presented a dilemma for social reformers during the progressive era, one that is not unfamiliar today. On the one hand, rural areas provided a model of the good society; of cooperation, strong family ties, and community integration. On the

other hand, rural areas were viewed as corrupt and patronage-ridden, characterized by a paucity of services and an abundance of social problems. In the bleakest view, urban growth had drained the best and the brightest members of rural society, leaving a residue of unproductive people and intractable problems. Which view or combination of views about rural society is the most accurate? What are the implications of the varying views for crafting solutions to social problems in rural areas?

3. Recent years have seen the devolution of power from the federal government to the states, as Congress has "returned" authority for many decisions about social welfare services to the states (often reducing federal budget commitments in exchange for greater flexibility). However, states have not in turn devolved power and authority to local governments. Would such devolution

be desirable or not? What would the consequences be for rural communities and for the consumers of social welfare services? Why?

4. A contemporary equivalent of the "Western measures" of 1862 may be required to revitalize rural communities in the twenty-first century. Such a social investment approach would combine asset building with investments in education, research, and transportation. How might such an approach be developed today?

CLASSROOM ACTIVITIES
AND ASSIGNMENTS

1. Investigate the patterns of early land acquisition in your area. When was the county or region first occupied or organized by European Americans? How did the first occupiers of the land secure title to their lands after the region was organized as a colony, territory, state, or reservation? What assistance did early residents receive? Was the distribution of wealth relatively equal or unequal? Sources for your investigation might include published local and state histories, the local or state historical society, a local public library, and the university archives (if it collects information on local history).

2. Describe one aspect of late-nineteenth century social investment in rural areas. Take either homesteading, collegiate education in agriculture, agricultural extension services, agricultural research, or investment in transportation and show how and to what extent the activity contributed to the development of rural communities and the welfare of rural people. What lessons does the experience provide for contemporary efforts to revitalize rural communities? Sources for your investigation might include contemporary reports of relevant government

agencies, accounts of beneficiaries of the programs, other contemporary comment, and academic research that attempts to assess the contribution of the program.

Today's "new federalism" represents an attempt to "return" authority for decision making about social welfare services to the states and local communities where it was originally lodged (at least in common belief). Investigate the implications for rural areas of the devolution of power from the federal government to the states using at least two of the following Web sites:

Assessing the New Federalism (The Urban Institute)
http://www.urban.org/Content/Research/NewFederalism/AboutANF/AboutANF.htm

Association for Community Organization and Social Administration
http://www.acosa.org/

Influencing State Policy
http://www.statepolicy.org/

Rural Social Work Caucus
http://www.uncp.edu/sw/rural/

The Policy Action Network
http://www.movingideas.org/

REFERENCES

Baseler, M. C. (1998). *Asylum for mankind: America, 1607–1800*. Ithaca, NY: Cornell University Press.

Berkhofer, R. F., Jr. (1964). Space, time, culture, and the new frontier. *Agricultural History 38*(1), 21–30.

Black, W. G., Jr. (1991). Social work in World War I: A method lost. *Social Service Review, 65*(3), 379–402.

Bogue, A. G. (1969). Senators, sectionalism, and the "Western" measures of the Republican Party. In

D. M. Ellis (Ed.), *The Frontier in American Development: Essays in Honor of Paul Wallace Gates* (pp. 20–46). Ithaca, NY: Cornell University Press.

Bureau of the Census. (1975). *Historical statistics of the United States: Colonial times to 1970.* Washington, D.C.: Government Printing Office.

Burson, H. I. (2001). *Alabama's mothers' pension statute: Identification and analysis of institutional determinants.* Ph.D. Dissertation, University of Alabama.

Clopper, E. N. (1921). The development of the children's code. *Annals of the American Academy of Political and Social Science, 98,* 154–159.

Cumo, C. (1998). The rise of publicly funded agricultural experimentation in Ohio, 1864–1882. *The Historian, 60*(3), 543–560.

Davenport, J., III, & Davenport, J. A. (1984). Josephine Brown's classic book still guides rural social work. *Social Casework, 65*(7), 413–419.

de Soto, H. (2000). *The mystery of capital: Why capitalism triumphs in the west and fails everywhere else.* New York: Basic Books.

Douglass, J. A. (1992). Creating a fourth branch of state government: The University of California and the constitutional convention of 1879. *History of Education Quarterly, 32*(1), 31–72.

Dowbiggin, I. (1992). Midnight clerks and daily drudges: Hospital psychiatry in New York State, 1890–1905. *Journal of the History of Medicine and Allied Sciences, 47*(2), 130–152.

Ebert, T., & Trattner, W. I. (1990). The county mental institution: Did it do what it was designed to do? *Social Science Quarterly, 71*(4), 835–847.

Egan, M., & Kadushin, G. (1997). Rural hospital social work: Views of physicians and social workers. *Social Work in Health Care, 26*(1), 1–23.

Flynt, Wayne (1996). Rural poverty in America. *National Forum, 76*(3), 32–35.

Gates, P. W. (1968). *History of public land law development.* Washington, D.C.: Public Land Law Review Commission.

Gates, P. W. (1936). The Homestead Law in an incongruous land system. *American Historical Review, 41,* 652–681.

Geiger, R. L. (1998). The rise and fall of useful knowledge: Higher education for science, agriculture & the mechanics arts, 1850–1875. *History of Higher Education Annual, 18,* 47–65.

Guest, G. (1989). The boarding of the dependent poor in Colonial America. *Social Service Review, 63*(1), 92–112.

Hatch Act, approved March 2, 1887, 24 Stat. 440.

Hibbard, B. H. (1924). *A history of the public land policies.* New York: Macmillan.

Hodson, W. (1921). A state program for child welfare. *Annals of the American Academy of Political and Social Science, 98,* 159–167.

Holt, M. I. (1992). *The orphan trains: Placing out in America.* Lincoln: University of Nebraska Press.

Homestead Act of 1862, 12 Stat. 392 (approved May 20, 1862).

Johnson, S. K. (1997). Does spirituality have a place in rural social work? *Social Work and Christianity, 24*(1), 58–66.

Jones, L. P. (1981, July). *Distinctive features of mid-west rural poverty: Implications for social work practice.* Paper presented at the 6th National Institute on Social Work in Rural Areas, Beaufort County, SC. (Eric Document Reproduction Service No. ED346082)

Kelso, R. W. (1923). The transition from charities and correction to public welfare. *Annals of the American Academy of Political and Social Science, 105,* 21–25.

Kerr, N. A. (1981). Troubled years of progress: The Alabama agricultural experiment station, 1887–1896. *Alabama Review, 34*(3), 184–201.

Larson, J. L. (2001). *Internal improvements: National public works and the promise of popular government in the early United States.* Chapel Hill: University of North Carolina Press.

Lee, P. (1929). Social work: Cause and function. *National Conference of Social Work Proceedings, 1929,* 3–20.

Lemon, J. T. (1972). *The best poor man's country: A geographical study of early southeastern Pennsylvania.* Baltimore: The Johns Hopkins Press.

Mailer, N. (1979). *The executioner's song.* Boston: Little, Brown.

Main, J. T. (1965). *The social structure of revolutionary America.* Princeton, NJ: Princeton University Press.

Martinez-Brawley, E. E. (1981). *Seven decades of rural social work: From country life commission to rural caucus.* New York: Praeger.

Martinez-Brawley, E. E. (1988). Social work and the rural crisis: Is education responding? *Journal of Social Work Education, 24*(3), 251–65.

Midgley, J. (1999). Growth, redistribution, and welfare: Toward social investment. *Social Service Review, 73*(1), 3–21.

Mills, C. W. (1943). The professional ideology of social pathologists. *American Journal of Sociology, 49*(2), 165–180.

Morrill Act of 1862, 12 Stat. 503 (approved July 2, 1862).

Morrill Act of 1890, 26 Stat. 417 (approved August 30, 1890).

Nugent, W. (1999). *Into the west: The story of its people.* New York: Knopf.

Pacific Railroad Act of 1862, 12 Stat. 489 (approved July 1, 1862).

Patterson, S. L., Memmott, J. L., Germain, C. B. (1995). Old wine in new bottles: Utilizing gender-specific natural helping capacities in rural social work. *Human Services in the Rural Environment, 19*(1), 42–47.

Prucha, F. P. (1967). *Broadax and bayonet: The role of the United States Army in the development of the northwest, 1815–1860.* Lincoln: University of Nebraska Press.

Ray, J., & Murty, S. A. (1990). Rural child sexual abuse prevention and treatment. *Human Services in the Rural Environment, 13*(4), 24–29.

Ray, J., & Murty, S. A. (1988, July). *Child sexual abuse prevention and treatment service delivery: Problems and solutions in rural areas of Washington State.* Paper presented to the 13th Annual National Institute of Social Work and Human Services in Rural Areas, Fort Collins, CO. (Eric Document Reproduction Services No. ED261816)

Rodgers, D. T. (1998). *Atlantic crossings: Social politics in a progressive age.* Cambridge, MA: Harvard University Press.

Schlesinger, A. M., Jr. (1958). *The coming of the new deal.* Boston: Houghton Mifflin.

Schuck, P. H. (1972). Black land-grant colleges: Discrimination as public policy. Reprinted in E. E. Martinez-Brawley (1981) (pp. 190–95). *Seven decades of rural social work: From country life commission to rural caucus.* New York: Praeger.

Sealander, J. (1997). *Private wealth and public life: Foundation philanthropy and the reshaping of American social policy from the progressive era to the new deal.* Baltimore: The Johns Hopkins University Press.

Smith-Lever Act, approved May 8, 1914, 38 Stat. 372.

Sundet, P. A., & Mermelstein, J. (1984). Rural crisis intervention. *Human services in the rural environment, 9*(2), 8–14.

Trattner, W. I. (1999). *From poor law to welfare state: A history of social welfare in America* (6th ed.). New York: Free Press.

Turner, F. J. (1893). The frontier in American history. In *The frontier in American history* (1920), pp. 1–38. New York: Henry Holt.

U.S. Department of Agriculture Act of 1862, 12 stat. 387 (approved May 15, 1862).

White, R. (1991). *It's your misfortune and none of my own: A history of the American west.* Norman: University of Oklahoma Press.

Williams, F. (1998). The second Morrill Act and Jim Crow politics: Land-grant education at Arkansas AM&N College, 1890–1927. *History of Higher Education Annual, 18,* 81–92.

Williams, R. L. (1998). Justin S. Morrill and George W. Atherton: A quarter century collaboration to advance the land-grant colleges. *History of Higher Education Annual, 18,* 67–80.

Wimberley, R. C., & Morris, L. V. (1997). *The southern black belt: A national perspective.* Lexington, KY: TVA Rural Studies.

Wokeck, M. S. (1999). *Trade in strangers: The beginnings of mass migration to North America.* University Park: Pennsylvania State University Press.

Young, M. (1969). Congress looks west: Liberal ideology and public land policy in the nineteenth century. In D. M. Ellis (Ed.), *The Frontier in American development: Essays in honor of Paul Wallace Gates* (pp. 74–112). Ithaca, IL: Cornell University Press.

INFOTRAC COLLEGE EDITION

agricultural extension

asset building

Homestead Law

immigration

land-grant college

settlement

social investment

3

Rural Social Work

Reconceptualizing the Framework for Practice

MICHAEL R. DALEY
FREDDIE L. AVANT

Historically, social work developed from urban roots and paid relatively little attention to the issues and concerns related to rural populations (NASW, 1997). Traditionally, even authors who dealt with rural social work practice have tended to view rural social work from a community-based deficit perspective (York, Denton, & Moran, 1998; Martinez-Brawley, 1990; Ginsberg, 1998; Southern Regional Education Board, 1998; Barker, 1999). The predominant view is that rural social work occurs in areas of low population density, and that the problems of rural people stem from the physical environment or geographic location where resources are sparse.

Although this perspective has been helpful in directing the attention to the service needs of long neglected rural communities and the people who live in them, it has been somewhat limiting in advancing both the education and practice skills of rural social workers. Specifically, this approach has primarily examined rural community deficits and has not focused either on identifying the assets and strengths in rural communities or in using them in the helping process. For example, rural communities are rich in traditions that promote the values of independence and hard work and strong links to family, the land, and social institutions such as the church. Often these strengths are overlooked.

In addition, the development of literature regarding social work with rural individuals, families, groups, and organizations has lagged far behind the community-based rural literature. Rural social work should be viewed as work with rural people as well as practice in and with rural communities. This perspective maintains both the person in environment and the multi-system focus that is so critical for rural social work practice. In the past, by concentrating on the rural community aspects of practice, we tended to overlook the interaction between the rural environment and other systems that influence behavior. Indeed, the cultural or lifestyle issues relating to rural populations in terms of individuals, families, groups, and organizations translate into behavior that may be as important as the community environment in understanding the problems of and in shaping social work practice with rural people. Understanding the strengths inherent in rural cultural or lifestyle issues should be an important part of the social work helping process.

The purpose of this article is to reexamine the framework for rural social work practice and to suggest ways in which it can be broadened in order to strengthen this important field of practice. The article will first look at traditional definitions of rural communities and rural social work. Then ways in which these traditional definitions can be broadened to enhance the framework for rural social work will be presented. Finally, the implications for this expanded framework will be discussed.

TRADITIONAL DEFINITIONS OF RURAL COMMUNITIES

Rurality, or the presence of rural characteristics, is clearly the context for rural social work, just as mental health, health care, families and children, education, and corrections provide the context for other fields of social work practice. However, what is not so clear is what defines a context for practice as rural or not rural. In part, this lack of clarity has arisen because of differing definitions of rurality that exist. Thus, the term *rural* is not always consistent in its usage, unless specifically defined.

The traditional definition of rurality is based both on geography and population density. The Bureau of the Census defines this method and it has many attractive features. The Census definitions are in wide use, and they are appealing because they are absolute in that they unambiguously and clearly classify a region as either rural or nonrural. All except the most recent definition of rurality classify rural as part of a rural-urban dichotomy. Perhaps the most traditional definition of rurality is that used by the Census Bureau prior to 1991. In this definition, a rural community was one with a population of less than 2,500 living in either incorporated or unincorporated areas. Communities of 2,500 or larger were classified as urban. This was a long standing definition dating from the period when the country was primarily rural, and a definition that had become somewhat outdated with the growth in the country's population.

In 1991, the Census Bureau developed a more functional definition for rurality. This definition moved away from the dichotomous rural-urban approach and viewed communities on a rural-urban continuum. *Metropolitan* and *non-metropolitan* became preferred terms as opposed to *rural* and *urban*. Metropolitan communities were those that had a central city population of

50,000 or more. Metropolitan statistical areas (MSA) were communities formed by this core city and the county in which this central city was located. Non-metropolitan or rural communities consisted of everything lying outside of the MSAs (Davenport & Davenport, 1995; Ginsberg, 1998).

The 2000 Census brought further changes to rural and urban definitions (United States Census Bureau, 2000). Under the new criteria, there are additional classifications for urbanized areas (UA) and urban clusters (UC). Urbanized areas (UAs) consist of a densely settled core of census block groups along with surrounding census blocks that encompass a population of at least 50,000 people. Urban clusters (UCs) consist of a densely settled core of census blocks along with adjacent densely settled census blocks that have a population of at least 2,500 but fewer than 50,000 people. Rural populations are classified as those not residing in either UAs or UCs. The latter definition is helpful because it avoids the rural-urban dichotomy by adding a third classification of the urban cluster (UC) to demarcate small to medium-sized communities. Yet the existence of three "official" definitions for rurality that could be employed opens the door for confusion in the literature as to which definition of rurality is being used.

Based on any of these definitions, the rural population of the United States is considerable, although clearly a minority. Using the metropolitan–nonmetropolitan definition, U.S. Census figures indicate that nonmetropolitan population is 22.5% of the population, while the metropolitan population is 77.5%. In other words, over 55 million people in the United States reside in rural areas (Ginsberg, 1998). This is a substantial population that needs the services social workers deliver. The percentage of the population that is rural varies considerably by state and by region. In some states, such as North Dakota, the majority of the population lives in rural areas. High concentrations of rural people may also be found in regions such as the West and the South. Even in states such as Texas, where about 75% of the population lives in metropolitan areas, approximately 25% of the population and 70% of the land area is nonmetropolitan.

TRADITIONAL DEFINITIONS OF RURALITY AS DETERMINANTS OF SOCIAL WORK PRACTICE

Given these traditional definitions of rurality, the question arises as to how they assist or hinder us in understanding rural communities and rural people in a way that furthers social work practice in this context. Traditional definitions of rurality that focus on geographic population density offer some strengths in terms of being able to clearly demarcate rural from nonrural communities. The separation of communities into rural and urban offers clear comparisons between the two types of communities and social work practice in those contexts.

The exclusive focus on rurality as an arbitrary function of geographic boundaries and population density leads one to naturally focus on the characteristics of the community as the primary basis of difference between rural and urban environments. While it is undeniable that there are clear differences between rural and urban communities, from a social work perspective, this tends to ignore major differences that exist between other important systems that influence social problems, behaviors, and the responses to them. In other words, definitions of rurality that focus primarily on community characteristics lead us to an environmental perspective, as opposed to a person-in-environment perspective. While the environmental perspective is a useful one, the person-in-environment approach is more appropriate as the basis for social work practice.

Community focus in defining rurality has shaped the rural social work literature in its discussion of the nature of practice in this context.

Thus, in attempting to identify the salient characteristics that define rural social work, the focus has been on community characteristics such as poverty, lack of transportation, nondiversified economies, poor housing, inadequate education and health care systems, shortage of professionals, and lack of services. Although these are all important problems in the rural United States, they are all deficits. Too little attention has been focused on the community assets that may be used in addressing these problems and in developing a strengths perspective from which rural social workers can practice. In addition, the concept of a rural-urban dichotomy limits the development of a framework for rural practice. The concept of a rural-urban dichotomy leads to the conclusion that there are clear differences between rural and urban communities.

Using this logic, one might argue that rural social work practice should differ sharply from urban social work practice. Neither conclusion is entirely correct. It is perhaps easiest to point out the differences between communities in the extremes; say, between a city of 1 million persons and a small town of 800 persons. But where does this leave us when assessing the differences between a city of 55,000 and a town of 30,000? The differences in these cases are not so clear.

Rather, it is probably more accurate to conceptualize rural and urban differences as part of a continuum ranging from very large cities to very small communities. If we conceptualize rurality as part of a continuum, then specific community factors such as population density, distance from metropolitan areas, and total population become important in classifying a community (Ginsberg, 1998). However, even given this shift in viewpoint to a continuum, we are still left with the problem of the community or environment as the crucial factor in defining rurality. Given these limitations, how might we view rurality in a light that is more productive in building a framework for rural social work practice? Perhaps shifting our point of view from a community perspective to a cultural or lifestyle perspective may be helpful. Indeed, cultural or lifestyle issues may be even more important than the physical environment in understanding the problems of rural populations and in shaping rural social work practice. Thus, we should examine human behavior and problems in the rural environment from a person-in-environment perspective and consider the social problems of rural populations as stemming from both a physical environment and from a sociocultural or rural lifestyle perspective (Farley, et al., 1982).

RECONCEPTUALIZING THE FRAMEWORK FOR RURAL SOCIAL WORK

The authors believe that a more useful framework for rural social work practice is one in which the nature of the social interactions both within and between systems are integral components. The framework examines behavior from a strengths perspective, rather than a deficit approach. It focuses on the nature of social interaction as the basis for explaining and evaluating the behavior of rural people. Figure 3.1 displays a model for the new framework for rural social work proposed in this article.

Each corner of the triangle represents a key element or concept in the practice of rural social work. The first element of this model is the multisystem and person-in-environment perspective. These concepts are critical because rural people are deeply enmeshed in their environment and the social systems that comprise that environment. For example, it is common for rural people dealing with an organization to have some relationship such as friend, neighbor, or relative with the organization's representative. Often this relationship with the organization's representative either positively or negatively affects how the organization responds. Thus, any assessment or intervention with rural people must take into account the fact that behavior reflects the interaction with multiple systems, often simultaneously.

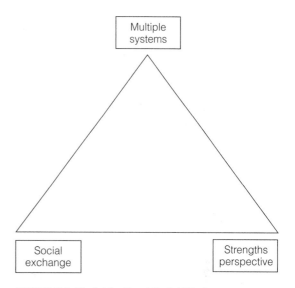

FIGURE 3.1 Model for Rural Social Work

The interactions between social systems are crucial for understanding the origin of problems and in devising strategies for addressing them. We should understand that the exchanges between these systems are based on principles of social exchange, and these exchanges are key to understanding how to work effectively with rural people and in rural communities. We know that in rural communities, the nature of social exchange tends to be informal or personal, as opposed to the formal exchanges and relationships that exist in urban communities (Ginsberg, 1998). These informal relationships are, in fact, strengths because they represent affirmative coping skills in rural communities where formal agencies and services often either do not exist or are difficult to access.

The second element of the triangle is the concept of social exchange. Because rural people are so enmeshed in a network of social systems, the nature of the exchange between people and systems is extremely important in assessing problems and designing interventions to address these problems. One of the key ways in which rural people differ from those in other contexts is the informal and personal relationships that they develop with the systems that comprise their environment. Understanding this and the dynamics of these informal relationships is extremely important to effective rural social work practice. Social exchange theory from social psychology helps us to understand the rural behavior in the environmental context that is so critical to social work practice.

Social exchange theory is based on a central premise, that the exchange of social and material resources is a fundamental form of human interaction. The social exchange is based on the idea that relationships between people are centered on the perception that certain positive outcomes may ensue as a result of the relationships. The strongest relationships are likely to be established with those from whom the benefit or potential is likely to be greatest. Social exchange theory deals with both the ties that bind people together and the effects of interactions between people (Collins, 1988).

Martinez-Brawley (2000) has suggested that the classic sociological concepts of *Gemeinschaft* and *Gesellschaft* are useful in explaining differences between rural and urban communities. *Gemeinschaft* communities are those closely identified with small towns and rural areas in which human relationships are personal, lasting, and based on where a person stands in society. Thus, social relationships are clear and based upon who a person is rather than what he or she has done. In addition, *Gemeinshaft* communities tend to be relatively homogeneous in which the church and family are strong sources of norms and values. In contrast, *Gesellschaft* is more closely identified with urban communities in which impersonal and contractual relationships are more important.

The *Gemeinschaft* and *Gesellschaft* paradigms conceptualize communities according to the nature of the social interactions among members, rather than according to population density, size, or geography. Since social work practitioners are primarily concerned with the nature of both functional and problematic social relationships, these theoretical constructs help us to identify important factors to consider in developing a framework for rural social work.

The concept of *Gemeinschaft* is particularly useful in this regard. *Gemeinschaft* communities are those in which family, place, and friendship are key elements. Thus, the relationships with one's family, connection with the land or locality, and social relationships define who a person is and are key factors in understanding behavior in small towns and rural communities. Small towns and rural communities may also be characterized as traditional, as opposed to rational–legal in their authority structure (Martinez-Brawley, 2000).

The third element of the triangle is the strengths perspective. Typical characterizations of the rural environment and rural people focus on the lack of formal resources. In social work with rural communities and people, it is important to understand the strengths both systems have which enable them to use informal means of providing needed resources, whether formal resources are available or not. Failure to recognize and identify the considerable strengths and resources of rural people and communities can constitute a barrier to effective social work.

From a social work perspective, social exchange in rural communities may be seen as a positive form of adaptation to the environment; in other words, these relationships are community assets. As many authors have suggested, social welfare needs may not be easily met in a rural area for several reasons. First, income to meet basic needs may be limited. In addition, formal helping resources such as social agencies may be scarce or nonexistent. Finally, helping professionals may not be readily available (Daley & Avant, 1999; Ginsberg 1998; National Association of Social Workers, 1997). Therefore, instead of relying heavily on the formal social welfare system, rural people are more likely to find assistance by establishing personal relationships that may offer them help in meeting their social welfare needs. By using personal relationships to substitute for a formal social welfare system, individuals in effect create an informal service system that is more likely to meet their needs. This is a very functional and utilitarian adaptation to a rural environment. In addition, because of the personal nature of relationships in rural communities, relationships based on exchange may extend beyond interactions with individuals and connect them to family, groups, organizations, and the community.

For example, social exchange in a rural context begins with a focus on "who the person is" as opposed to what the person's accomplishments might be or the formal position he or she holds. Further, the social exchange focus is not limited to person-to-person interactions, but affects exchanges with other systems such as families, groups, organizations, and the community as well. Thus, the personalized nature of relationships is a key element in explaining and changing behavior in rural communities and small towns, and it is critical for social workers to understand these relationships.

The concept of using social relationships and exchange as a central principle in rural social work logically leads us from a deficit- to a strengths-based perspective for practice. As Saleebey (1992) states, the strengths perspective ". . . depicts the natural world of living. . . . [It] is a relative of other terms that express normalcy, assertiveness, proactiveness, and integrity." Social relationships and exchanges are used as effective mechanisms for coping with the day-to-day challenges of living in a rural environment.

Therefore, we can either look at the glass as half-empty or half-full. We can look at rural practice as occurring in a context where many important things like transportation, health care, formal services, and social service professionals are in short supply; or we can look at the positive adaptive behaviors of rural people who effectively develop and use informal resources to meet their needs.

Clearly, the former is a deficit-based perspective, while the latter focuses on assets and strengths-based criteria. By using a strengths-based approach, social workers are more likely to identify the problem-solving abilities routinely used by rural people and operate in a culturally competent context. Furthermore, by employing a strengths-based approach, it is less likely that social workers who work with rural people will be viewed as either backward or lacking in coping skills.

Implications for Rural Social Work Practice

In the rural social work literature, it has been axiomatic that the generalist method of social work is the practice approach best suited to rural communities (Brown, 1980; Daley & Avant, 1999; Davenport & Davenport, 1998; Ginsberg, 1998; Southern Regional Education Board, 1998; York et al., 1998). It has been suggested that the generalist method is most appropriate because rural social workers are generalists as opposed to specialists. Although this point of view is widely accepted, it is somewhat at variance with the literature, which tends to focus most heavily on the community aspects of practice. The framework identified in this article is entirely consistent with the generalist method of practice. The rural social worker is a generalist because he or she works with all social systems, including families, groups, individuals, organizations, and communities. The person-in-environment and strengths perspectives are also important parts of the generalist method. Thus, the framework for rural social work identified here clearly indicates that the generalist method is the most appropriate method.

We do not mean to suggest that social workers in rural areas do not have or need advanced or specialized skills in working with these systems. Rural social workers, because of the nature of their communities, have to deal with a broad spectrum of social problems and issues. Often they may be the only resource to deal with a problem, and therefore need an ability to work with all systems. In these situations they must be adept at using existing strengths and assets as part of the helping process. However, rural communities face the same types of problems that their urban counterparts face, so there is a clear need for advanced skills to work with the more complex and difficult problems related to these systems.

Obviously, not all rural communities have the same traditions, values, and norms. Rural Arkansas may be very different than rural Wyoming. However, since personal (informal) relationships are key to living and coping in small towns and rural communities, maintaining some kind of social order is essential for individual and community survival. Rural people rely on others—friends, relatives, clergy, the beautician, or even the mail carrier—much more extensively for information than they rely on formal resources such as agencies. Rural populations depend heavily on the use of natural helping networks such as family, church, and friends to resolve problems. The visibility of individuals in rural communities often leads to a reluctance to seek help from formal agencies. Seeking help through family, friends, and church may be no more private, but is generally considered more acceptable than seeking help from a trained professional.

To outsiders, the rural way of coping may seem strange, conservative, and resistant to change. It may also appear that outsiders are not trusted and that diversity and change are not tolerated. These appearances can easily be interpreted as deficits or some form of social pathology infecting the rural community. Rather, these are real strengths for the rural community because they provide mechanisms for community survival by defining expectations for behavior in the community. Unfortunately, when rural people move to an urban environment, these personalized (informal) coping mechanisms that they have learned may not be as functional, and problems may develop. All too often, social workers in urban environments are surprised to find themselves working with rural individuals, families, and even communities inside of a metropolitan area. These are populations with whom urban educated and urban oriented social workers are ill prepared to deal (NASW, 1997). Urban social workers "have difficulty applying their knowledge to rural practice and must adapt their practice model significantly to do a credible job in rural areas" (NASW, 1997, p. 293). Thus, urban social workers are not well-prepared to assist clients from rural areas who have moved to the city.

In order to work effectively with rural people in any setting, it is important for social workers to understand the cultural context in which they were socialized. Social workers must be sensitive to the cultural differences that characterize rural communities and be ready to question many of the existing myths and stereotypes about rurality (Southern Regional Education Board, 1998). Indeed, rurality has its own, often invisible culture that must be considered as part of any effective work with this population. Culture in this sense represents "the customs, habits, skills, technology, arts, values, ideology, science, and religious and political behavior of a group of people in a specific time period" (Barker, 1999, p. 114). Rural people are socialized into a culture that has its own values, norms, beliefs, and even languages that help them adapt to their environment. As social workers we must be culturally sensitive to these issues. Unfortunately, educational preparation in working with rural people and communities does not tend to be strong. Locke (1991), in a review of five studies of educational preparation for social work practice, concluded that schools of social work needed to better prepare social workers for practice in small towns and rural areas. Weber (1980) suggests that the commitment of social work to rural communities is not adequate and that attention to rural issues in most social work educational programs is superficial.

We should aspire to prepare rural social workers as "well-trained, creative professionals who can work in relative isolation with limited additional resources" (Barker, 1999, p. 421). However, in order to do so, we must address rural issues and content in a stronger and more meaningful way. Hopefully, by looking at some of the basic premises that have provided the foundation for rural social work, we can build upon, expand, and refine these concepts, and reconceptualize rural social work. Then we can provide the basis for development of theory and research that will continue to make rural social work a vital and important area of professional practice.

DISCUSSION QUESTIONS

1. What are the strengths and assets of rural communities? Identify at least five strengths and how these assets might be of use in social work practice. For example, you might look at traditional music such as folk, blues, or country music to identify important themes related to rural life. Take a look at issues related to family, values, socio-economic status, ethnicity, or religion, and how rural people view coping with problems. Other examples might include analyzing language or a piece of fiction, nonfiction, or a movie.

2. How have the definitions of rural and urban changed over the twenty-five years? Why is it important for social workers to have common understandings of rural definitions?

3. According to the authors, why is the generalist method of practice the most appropriate for rural social work?

4. How does shifting our view from a community to a cultural or lifestyle perspective affect the way we view the rural–urban continuum?

CLASSROOM ASSIGNMENTS AND ACTIVITIES

1. Visit a rural community (not your own) and identify ways in which life in this community is different than that in your home community. What are some of the differences in language, values, and norms that you can identify?

2. Use pieces of music, literature, nonfiction, or film to identify at least seven rural idioms or phrases. First, define these idioms or phrases and then use these definitions to explain what they tell you about the rural culture they represent.

3. List at least ten characteristics that you would associate with rural living. Then list at least ten characteristics that you would associate with urban life. Compare and contrast the rural and urban characteristics you have identified in terms of the following: positive or negative, progressive or conservative, and strengths or weaknesses. Based on your comparison, which environment seems more appealing to you and why?

REFERENCES

Barker, R. L. (1999). *The social work dictionary.* Washington, DC: National Association of Social Work Press.

Brown, P. (1980). Our rural past: May 11, 1935, the new deal lights up seven million farms. In H. W. Johnson (Ed.), *Rural human services: A book of readings* (pp. 140–148). Itasca, IL: F. E. Peacock.

Collins, R. (1988). *Theoretical sociology.* Washington, DC: Harcourt Brace Jovanovich.

Daley, M., & Avant, F. (1999). Attracting and retaining professionals for social work practice in rural areas: An example from East Texas. In I. B. Carlton-LaNey, R. L. Edwards, & P. N. Reid (Eds.), *Preserving and strengthening small towns and rural* communities (pp. 335–345). Washington, DC: National Association of Social Work Press.

Davenport, J., III, & Davenport, J. A. (1998). Rural communities in transition. In L. H. Ginsberg (Ed.), *Social work in rural communities* (pp. 39–54). Alexandria, VA: Council Social Work Education.

Farley, O. W., Griffiths, K. A., Skidmore, R. A., & Thackeray, M. G. (1982). *Rural social work practice.* New York: Free Press.

Ginsberg, L. H. (1998). *Social work in rural communities* (3rd ed.). Alexandria, VA: Council Social Work Education.

Locke, B. L. (1991). Research and social work in rural areas: Are we asking the right questions? *Human Services in the Rural Environment, 15*(2), 13.

Martinez-Brawley, E. E. (1990). *Perspective on the small community: Humanistic views for practitioners.* Washington, DC: NASW Press.

Martinez-Brawley, E. E. (2000). *Close to home: Human services and the small community.* Washington, DC: National Association of Social Work Press.

National Association of Social Workers. (1997). *Social work speaks: National association of social workers policy statements.* Washington, DC: National Association of Social Work Press.

Saleebey, D. (1992). Introduction: Power in the people. In D. Saleebey (Ed.), *The strengths perspective in social work practice* (pp. 3–17). New York: Longman.

Southern Regional Education Board. (1998). Educational assumptions for rural social work. In L. H. Ginsberg (Ed.), *Social work in rural communities* (pp. 23–26). Alexandria, VA: Council Social Work Education.

United States Census Bureau. (2000). Urban and rural classification census 2000: Urban and rural criteria. Retrieved March 12, 2002 from http://www.census.gov/geo/www/ua/ua_2k.html

Weber, G. (1980). Preparing social workers for practice in rural social systems. In H. W. Johnson (Ed.), *Rural human services: A book of readings* (pp. 203–214). Itasca, IL: Peacock Publishers.

York, R. O., Denton, R. T., Moran, J. R. (1998). Rural and urban social work practice: Is there a difference? In L. H. Ginsberg (Ed.), *Social work in rural communities* (pp. 83–97). Alexandria, VA: Council Social Work Education.

INFOTRAC COLLEGE EDITION

Gemeinschaft
Gesellschaft

rural
social exchange

4

Rural Is Real

Supporting Professional Practice through the Rural Social Work Caucus and the NASW Professional Policy Statement for Rural Social Work

SAMUEL A. HICKMAN

In the mid-1970s, social work practitioners and educators serving rural areas formed a loose organization that continues to this day. Known as the Rural Social Work Caucus, its members are joined by a common interest in and appreciation for rural cultures and people, and a desire to use and enhance social work skills to support and improve them. Caucus members coined the phrase *Rural Is Real* to impress upon their social work colleagues across the nation that rural life and rural social work practice are thriving in the vast areas located beyond urban and suburban centers, and to raise awareness that urban sprawl and similar influences can threaten to homogenize or overcome desirable aspects of rural culture.

Twenty-five percent of the population of the United States resides on 83% of its landmass (U.S. Department of Commerce, 1998). Let this fact settle in for a moment. Tens of millions of people reside in small communities and remote areas, on reservations, or in narrow valleys not far from town. They are separated by time and distance but strongly connected by family, culture, and sense of place. They share the same hopes and dreams as their urban and suburban neighbors. A smaller population and economic base, however, can limit the availability and quality of public and private services in rural areas—not only in terms of access to health care and social services, but also to libraries, cultural activities, and public services such as transportation, infrastructure, and education. For the professional social worker, several

questions may immediately spring to mind, including how to provide reliable services to a widespread population. How do we assess varying needs from community to community? Who is available to help advocate, raise money, or provide volunteer services? And where should one begin?

Rural social work practice is rewarding and satisfying (Williams, 2002; in Stoesen, 2002). Human relationships tend to be more genuine among rural people (Martinez-Brawley, 2000). The potential is great for a small group of committed individuals to achieve something of lasting impact or meaningful change (Yevuta, 1999). Although the term *generalist* is often applied to preparation for rural social work practice, the term should not be confused with *generic*, implying a smattering of rudimentary skills (Ginsberg, 1977, 1993). Effective rural practitioners must command a wide variety of specialized social work skills and interventions (Carlton-LaNey, Edwards, & Reid, 1999). Their work often requires them to combine multiple aspects of direct practice, advocacy, needs assessment, and research, with an understanding of human behavior, social systems, and interactions. Managing confidentiality issues and professional-client relationships in rural areas requires a highly tuned understanding of the NASW Code of Ethics.

Although the challenges of rural practice are real, professional social workers have values and skills uniquely suited to assessing needs, providing effective services, and building mechanisms and organizations that enhance or improve rural communities and the lives of rural people and families.

A romantic notion portrays rural America as made up of pristine, sedate, unchanging pockets of nostalgia (Carlton-LaNey, Edwards, & Reid, 1999). In reality, rural communities are dynamic and rapidly changing. They can differ more widely from each other than urban areas. Although many rural communities are economically diverse, prosperous and thriving, 195 of the 200 most impoverished counties in the United States are located in rural areas of the Southwest, the Appalachian Mountains, and central valleys of California (RUPRI, 1995; U.S. Department of Commerce, 1998). Immigration has dramatically changed the cultural mixture of small cities and towns, bringing the United States face-to-face with the rest of the world (Stoesen, 2002). Suburban sprawl has claimed what was once rural land, bringing new residents who have differing expectations and values. Sometimes property taxes are increased to the point that poor rural residents find it difficult to keep their land. Vast tracts of rural lands are owned or controlled by government, corporations that extract natural resources and minerals, and large agribusiness interests. Outside ownership of land can restrict the ability of rural residents to influence laws and policies on taxation and land use in favor of local development initiatives.

THE NATIONAL INSTITUTE ON SOCIAL WORK AND HUMAN SERVICES IN RURAL AREAS

The Rural Social Work Caucus was formed in the mid-1970s to focus attention on and encourage scholarly study of social and professional issues unique to rural social work practice, rural people, and rural client populations. Although relatively few in numbers, committed members of the Caucus have made a significant impact on professional social work education and practice, social policy development, and on the activities of professional associations.

The primary vehicle for encouraging scholarship and collaboration among rural social workers is the annual National Institute on Social Work and Human Services in Rural Areas. Each year since 1976, rural social workers have gathered in various locales of the United States to experience this unique three-day professional conference. The Institute cultivates an inclusive and supportive environment where social work students, practitioners, and faculty meet and explore common interests. They present professional papers and listen to speakers who discuss timely local, regional, national and even international topics about rural issues and initiatives. The annual business meeting of the Rural Social Work Caucus also takes place at the conference. Organized outings, tours, concerts, and cultural immersion activities are sometimes the most powerful memories of a particular Institute, leading to recollections like, "I remember we had to get out and push the bus out of the mud at the county fair," or "Which was the real Appalachia . . . the living farm museum or the young musicians continuing the old time music tradition?"

In some ways as much a homecoming as a professional conference, the annual Institute on Social Work and Human Services in Rural Areas attracts a variety of participants, including stalwart annual attendees (and often their families) and social workers from the host area (Stoesen, 2002). After hours, social workers continue with impromptu discussions, music, and singing. A theme song written by caucus members declares ". . . *words like change, community are drifting through the trees,*" and *"as long as people feel at home . . . this travelin' rural road show will pop up again somewhere"* (Winship & Hickman, 1992).

The Caucus exerts minimal control over the planning of the Institute. There are sometimes well-intentioned efforts to alter the structure, but as one frequent attendee put it, "I always thought it was a bigger challenge to try to be different—to hold the institute in places that were hard to get to; to include stories, humor, music, and traditions of the populations in the area; to include families of the participants in all the events so that they were cross-generational" (N. Lennox, personal communication, September 15, 2002).

Social work educators and students at the University of Wisconsin and the University of Tennessee, Knoxville were instrumental in establishing the Caucus and the annual Institute, with the first Institute held in Knoxville in 1976. Subsequent Institutes have attracted social work educators and students from every geographic region of the country. Interprofessional collaborations between agricultural extension agents and organizations such as the Rural Mental Health Association and Rural Health Association have sometimes occurred. When held near international borders, social workers from neighboring countries are invited to participate. Use of the Internet to publicize the institute has resulted in participation by social workers from as far away as Israel, Korea, and Australia.

Activities of the Rural
Social Work Caucus

A meeting of the Rural Social Work Caucus can be an interesting and refreshing affair. It is often proudly referred to as an *organization by rumor.* Caucus members share a profound, common excitement for and interest in rural people and rural social work, as well as for preserving the strengths of rural people in a constantly changing world. They quickly pool their knowledge and resources to identify the best ways to have a positive impact on rural communities and social work practice. All Institute participants are welcome at Caucus meetings, and those present are considered equal voting members. A scant leadership structure of elected officers facilitates the agenda to get things started. Regional representatives are sometimes identified to provide input from different areas of the country. The most contentious Caucus meetings have occurred over the question of whether to establish a more structured organization. Additional Caucus meetings are frequently included on the agendas of the Annual Program Meeting (APM) of the Council of Social Work Education (CSWE) and Baccalaureate Program

Directors (BPD) meetings, and at National Association of Social Workers (NASW) national and state conferences and meetings.

An "organization by rumor" has certain advantages. Hierarchy is minimized so that every participant feels free to contribute at meetings. The organization can adapt quickly to change and be opportunistic in its approach to planned intervention. Although the Rural Social Work Caucus represents the interests of a significant number of practitioners and educators, its actual membership and size can be a moving target. Left to the imagination, an appearance of influence can be cultivated that is sometimes beyond that of the actual power base, enhancing effectiveness. Members of the Caucus have always been encouraged to use the name of the Caucus to enhance activities that support rural policies and people. What is perhaps most significant about this is the members' self-restraint, professionalism, and commitment to rural causes that have prevented abuses of the privilege.

Another important function of the Caucus has been to advance the professional development and academic careers of its members. A significant group of social work educators has supported one another through the completion of their doctoral degrees. Their dissertations have often focused on rural social work and how best to prepare students for rural practice. Many of these doctoral students have become deans and senior faculty whose research on rural social work is well-respected.

Achievements of the
Rural Social Work Caucus

Informal or not, the Rural Social Work Caucus has achieved a great deal. It has successfully fostered the annual Institute every year since 1976. It produced two successful NASW professional policy statements on the nature of rural social work practice. Its members have evoked the name of the Caucus to create coalitions and enact policies that support rural people and practice. A scholarly journal called *Human Services in the Rural Environment* (HSITRE) was created to further enhance scholarly writings and research and provide a much-needed publishing outlet for social work educators having trouble convincing their urban colleagues of the differences between rural and urban/suburban social work. Over the years, articles, books, and research papers published in HSITRE have helped establish and define these differences. Not currently in print, HSITRE may eventually evolve into an online professional journal.

In the mid-1970s, Caucus members supported the National Association of Social Workers' move to a statewide chapter system from the previous metropolitan-based structure. This change provided a home article for NASW members living in less populated areas, giving them reasons to be more active in professional advocacy. It also placed NASW in a better position to influence the actions of senators from every state. Caucus members supported the creation of a special chapter development fund within NASW to support the operating costs of NASW state chapters with fewer than 1,000 members. At present, 29 of 56 NASW chapters are in this category. These strategies have helped make NASW more effective in changing social and health care policies, and have increased the influence and effectiveness of the social work profession. In addition, NASW briefly provided funding for rural social work interests and policy development, and Caucus members crafted the original professional policy statement on Social Work in Rural Areas approved by the 1990 NASW Delegate Assembly and published in *Social Work Speaks* until 1999.

A GENERALIST APPROACH

Much of the effort to define an educational model for rural social work practice came to be known as a "generalist" approach. Arguably, the greatest impact of this discussion has been at the MSW level of social work education. Practice specialization had heretofore been a hallmark of urban and suburban institutions offering the MSW degree. Rural social workers helped the profession evolve in its understanding of the term

generalist. The NASW Professional Policy Statement on Rural Social Work submitted to the 2002 NASW Delegate Assembly argues that the rural generalist needs well-developed practice skills and a thorough knowledge of the NASW Code of Ethics in order to be most effective. Why? Rural communities often have fewer resources and services available. This requires the social worker to use a variety of practice skills to best serve the population. For example, clients may experience conditions for which no appropriate referral resources are available. In order to respond to such needs, the rural social worker may find it necessary to advocate for the development of a new service or program.

Life in small towns and rural areas offers frequent challenges in maintaining client confidentiality and distinct client-practitioner relationships. A thorough understanding of the dual or multiple relationships provisions of the NASW Code of Ethics is necessary. Dual or multiple relationships are those that potentially place the professional in conflict with the best interests of the client. These provisions are sometimes misinterpreted to mean that such relationships should always be avoided. In actuality, the social worker must evaluate whether the relationship could exert a harmful effect on the client. Dual relationships can be more difficult to avoid in rural practice. For example, the social worker may have to decide whether to shop at a store where a client works. Urban areas may offer several shopping alternatives, thereby solving the problem. Rural areas typically have fewer options.

Including Rural Social Work in Educational Curricula

The professional policy statement on Rural Social Work approved by the 2002 NASW Delegate Assembly encourages all social work educational programs—whether rural, suburban, or urban—to offer instruction on the unique characteristics of social work practice with rural populations. This is encouraged in part as an issue of cultural competence in social work that mandates social workers to work effectively with individuals, families, groups, and communities of different cultural backgrounds, norms, and influences.

There are two additional reasons for including rural issues in the social work education curricula. Rural people have a long history of relocating to urban and suburban centers for gainful employment. Close-knit rural groups have sometimes gathered in distinct neighborhoods or ghettos where assimilation into their new culture is slow. At other times, they have scattered to the winds as it were, cut off entirely from their social support systems. In any case, the urban and suburban social worker with knowledge of rural cultures is better equipped to work effectively with displaced rural people.

Also, the 2000 Census shows that rural and inner-city people have reasons to work together to meet local needs. Congressional redistricting due to a population shift to suburban areas continues to diminish the number of seats in Congress that represent either rural or inner-city people and interests (RUPRI, 1995). Both rural and urban areas tend to experience similar challenges, such as a lack of adequate health care and human services, and lack of a tax base that is sufficient for meeting local needs. Public schools, libraries and infrastructure suffer as a result. Job opportunities and economic growth are limited. Social workers could be instrumental in creating new coalitions among rural and urban people to facilitate a congressional voting block that could redefine how Congress reacts to both rural and inner-city problems.

A BRIEF HISTORY OF THE RURAL SOCIAL WORK PROFESSIONAL POLICY STATEMENT

Members of the Rural Social Work Caucus have developed and advocated for professional policies that increase the social work profession's awareness of and support for rural issues, and that define elements of preparation for rural practice.

These improvements have been achieved through participation in two primary professional groups: the National Association of Social Workers (NASW) and the Council on Social Work Education (CSWE). NASW is the largest professional membership organization for Social Workers, while CSWE reviews and accredits social work education programs at colleges and universities, and also standardizes the components for the BSW and MSW degrees.

NASW uses the democratic process to identify, analyze, and approve professional and social policy statements. Chapter representatives elected to the Delegate Assembly, held every three years, consider, amend, and vote on the statements in much the same way a legislative body deliberates over a bill that is to become law. The decisions of the Delegate Assembly are binding upon the association and its state chapters. The finalized professional and social policy statements are published by NASW in *Social Work Speaks* and widely disseminated. They influence the public image of the social work profession and help define the message to the public and nation about a wide variety of social, health, and public issues, ranging from adoption to welfare reform. Professional policy statements provide direction to social work practitioners and educators on a variety of practice issues. For example, there are statements to guide social workers working with special client groups such as the elderly, children and families, and indigenous populations.

At the 1981 NASW Delegate Assembly, Caucus members created a vision and applied their energies to the achievement of a specific goal: adoption of the first professional policy statement on Social Work in Rural Areas. The Caucus drafted and presented a statement to the Delegate Assembly for consideration. As discussions were held about the proposed statement, Caucus members positioned supporters at the various microphones to see that favorable comments were frequently heard and the statement was adopted. Primarily an educational tool for urban and suburban social workers, the 1981 professional policy statement encouraged NASW to advocate for rural human services issues, such as health care, diversity, poverty, and the environment, in its legislative and social policy agenda efforts.

THE 2002 RURAL SOCIAL WORK PROFESSIONAL POLICY STATEMENT*

Asset-Based Approaches

The professional policy statement adopted by the 1981 NASW Delegate Assembly endured for 18 years. At the 1999 NASW Delegate Assembly, it was recommended for elimination as outdated and in need of revision. The statement's elimination from *Social Work Speaks* served as a call to action for Caucus members. The Caucus mounted an immediate effort to draft a new Professional Policy Statement on Rural Social Work.

In a meeting at the University of Texas during the 2001 Institute, Caucus members formed a working group to draft a new professional policy statement and submit it for consideration at the 2002 NASW Delegate Assembly. The new statement differed from its predecessor in that it concentrated on professional social worker roles and functions in rural practice, as well as the need to include rural practice issues in all social

work education programs. In addition, it addressed unique ethical practice issues, cultural competency, and the need to use a strengths or asset-based approach when working with rural populations.

The new statement made a case for viewing generalist social work practice in rural areas as requiring a combination of highly developed skills and applications, rather than as a grouping of core competencies. Regarding dual or multiple relationships as addressed in the NASW *Code of Ethics*, the authors of the new statement noted that, because of special difficulties in managing client contacts and relationships in rural areas, an advanced understanding of the Code was required for effective rural practice. Education and practice competence for multicultural awareness, now commonly referred to as developing cultural competency, was also addressed. Finally, the statement encouraged taking a strengths or asset-based approach to rural social work. In this approach, social workers identify and build on the natural assets of people and systems to help them achieve positive changes or outcomes. Focusing on assets requires that the social worker be highly observant and acutely aware of the unique cultural norms and values of rural people, their culture and their social institutions.

DISCUSSION QUESTIONS

1. The Rural Social Work Caucus encourages the belief that rural practice differs from urban practice, and that all students of social work should be taught skills that help prepare them to work effectively with rural people. Discuss whether you agree that there are differences between rural and urban social work practice. Support your argument with examples of similarities or differences.

2. Ethical standard 1.06(c) of the NASW *Code of Ethics* describes dual or multiple relationships as occurring "when social workers relate to clients in more than one relationship, whether professional, social, or business." It is assumed that avoiding dual or multiple relationships is more challenging in rural areas. Discuss whether you agree with this assumption. Provide at least two reasons to support your argument.

---

* The Rural Social Work professional policy statement adopted by the 2002 NASW Delegate Assembly is included in the Appendix to this book.

3. The Rural Social Work Caucus is sometimes called an organization by rumor. Discuss the advantages and disadvantages of this type of organization.

4. The 2002 NASW Delegate Assembly approved the Rural Social Work professional policy statement. This action was the successful culmination of a year-long effort by the Rural Social Work Caucus. During that time Caucus members wrote and reviewed drafts, met deadlines, and developed support among professional colleagues. Discuss what Caucus members might have had to do differently if they had instead been attempting to convince Congress to enact a law requiring all human service workers in rural areas to earn a BSW or MSW degree.

CLASSROOM ASSIGNMENTS AND ACTIVITIES

1. List two ways you would change the social work education curriculum to better prepare yourself for rural practice. Elaborate by adding at least two sentences of explanation for each item. For example, how would your way help you feel better prepared for rural practice? Why would it improve your effectiveness in working with rural people?

2. Pretend you are a rural social worker who helps place abused or neglected children into the homes of qualified foster parents. Describe a hypothetical dual or multiple relationship in which you could find yourself with a client or clients. How would you go about setting clear, appropriate, and culturally sensitive boundaries to manage the situation effectively?

3. You work in a county with a high rate of poverty. The state offers a free health care program for low-income children, called Children's Health Insurance Program (CHIP), but only a small percentage of the children who are eligible have enrolled in spite of a glitzy advertising campaign on television, radio and in newspapers. List three reasons why the advertising campaign might not have resulted in higher enrollment. Then list three things you would do to get the campaign on track and encourage parents to enroll their children in the free health insurance program.

REFERENCES

Carlton-LaNey, I. B., Edwards, R. L., & Reid, P. N. (1999). From romantic notions to harsh realities. In I. B. Carlton-LaNey, R. L. Edwards, & P. N. Reid (Eds.), *Preserving and strengthening small towns and rural communities* (pp. 5–12). Washington, DC: National Association of Social Work Press.

Ginsberg, L. (1977). Rural social work. In J. Turner (Ed.), *Encyclopedia of social work 17 (2)* (pp. 1228–1234). Washington, DC: National Association of Social Work Press.

Ginsberg, L. (1993). *Social work in rural communities*. Alexandria, VA: Council on Social Work Education.

Martinez-Brawley, E. (2000). *Close to home: Human services in the small community*. Washington, DC: National Association of Social Work Press.

Rural Policy Research Institute (RUPRI). (1995). *Opportunities for rural policy reform: Lessons learned from recent farm bills*. Retrieved October 18, 2002 from http://www.rupri.org/archive/old/rupolicy P95-2.html.

Stoesen, L. (2002). Reconnecting to a historical foundation: Rural social workers embrace challenge. *NASW News, 47*(9), 3.

U.S. Department of Commerce (1998, September). *Poverty in the United States: 1997, U.S. Bureau of the Census, Current Population Reports*. Washington, DC: Author.

Winship, J., & Hickman, S. (1992). Rural Social Work Caucus Theme Song (folk process).

Yevuta, M. A. (1999). Nitpicking in rural West Virginia. In I. B. Carlton-LaNey, R. L. Edwards, & P. N. Reid (Eds.), *Preserving and strengthening small towns and rural communities* (pp. 315–325). Washington DC: National Association of Social Work Press.

INTERNET RESOURCES

Association of Social Work Boards
http://www.ASWB.org

Council on Social Work Education
http://www.CSWE.org

National Association of Social Workers
http://www.socialworkers.org

Rural Policy Research Institute
http://www.RUPRI.org

Rural Social Work Caucus
http://www.uncp.edu/sw/rural/

INFOTRAC COLLEGE EDITION

Delegate Assembly
NASW Code of Ethics

National Association of Social Workers
Rural Social Work Caucus

PART II

✳

Human Behavior
and Rural Environments

JUDITH A. DAVENPORT

The literature on rural life in the United States indicates that rural communities possess extensive social capital. This social capital has contributed to a strong sense of community, with residents often developing solid social ties and reciprocal helping behaviors. The study of the interplay between human behavior and the rural social environment is essential for utilizing assets in work with individuals, families, groups, communities, or organizations. This part provides information that is vital in appreciating the benefits of asset building and recognizing how these benefits enable us to support or intervene at the appropriate time and with the appropriate client systems.

The first two articles in this part, written by Menanteau-Horta and Watkins, reflect traditional rural communities' abilities to adapt to change and the strengths they possess to accomplish this task. Rural communities have suffered from lack of economic vitality and out-migration to metropolitan areas. Although strong natural helping networks and cooperative human services delivery have been touted in rural areas, these have not worked as well as their potentials would indicate. These authors stress the need for community members to work more efficiently and effectively to achieve fundamental change for community survival.

Rural communities in the United States have traditionally been described as homogeneous. Outside of the rural South, California, and Southwestern border states, rural communities have typically been populated by whites, many of whom originated from the same country or region of Europe. This is changing rapidly for many rural communities with the in-migration of persons from Latin and South America, the Caribbean, the Middle East, Asia, and Africa.

The last articles by Avant, Cordova, and by Madden, Bishop, and Kirk discuss three distinct population groups in rural areas of the United States. African Americans, Hispanics, and Haitian immigrants and refugees possess distinctive attitudes, beliefs, and behaviors, with each group developing its own set of assets. These three articles provide information on the relationship between ethnicity, culture, and the development of assets and social capital over the life span of individuals, families, groups, communities, and organizations. They discuss vulnerable and at-risk populations that have moved to communities where the local population has also been perceived as vulnerable. Resiliency factors are identified and the authors stress the importance of recognizing and appreciating the assets that different racial and ethnic group cultures provide for their members and for the larger communities in which they reside. Previously homogeneous communities can enhance and borrow from the assets that newcomers bring.

African Americans have been a large part of the rural landscape in the United States, especially in the southern parts of our nation. Through the generations they have developed tremendous assets for survival and growth that have provided them with self-esteem and resilience. During the last two centuries, a large number migrated to cities, primarily in the North, in search of greater opportunities. There still remain rural areas, mostly in the Southeast, where African Americans are the majority population.

Freddie Avant presents various theoretical perspectives related to the nature of African-American culture but emphasizes the value of seriously considering the use of the Afrocentric perspective in working with rural as well as urban African Americans. He presents various aspects of the Afrocentric theoretical perspective as a mechanism for understanding strength in rural African-American culture and notes the importance of cultural values and how to appreciate them in relation to the Afrocentric point of view.

Hispanics, mostly Mexicans or Mexican Americans, have been in the United States for centuries; however, the sheer numbers and the locales in which they live have changed drastically in recent years. Hispanics are now considered the largest minority group and have moved beyond the Southwestern and Western border states and big cities to the rural Deep South and Midwest. The article "Life in a *Colonia*: Identifying Community Assets" deals with aspects of rural Hispanic life and culture. Although there is reason for much despair related to the conditions in which these Hispanics live, author Wilma Cordova discusses how the asset of resiliency is used effectively to overcome the many obstacles inherent in these communities.

Haitians are not new to our country, either, although their numbers and demographic diversity do not match those of African Americans or Hispanics. Also, many have refugee status, which can involve issues related to trauma and the knowledge that they may never be able to return to their home country. Therefore, the possibilities for this population group to become more vulnerable and be at greater risk are evident. The need for recognition and nourishment of assets within this population becomes especially vital in helping them to achieve success both as individuals and as a community.

Each of these articles presents compelling arguments for identifying and building assets exhibited by individuals and their environments and the relationship between the two. Authors provide examples to illustrate how using the principles of asset and social capital building can have positive benefits. When reading the articles, it is important to consider ways in which the assets of micro, macro, and mezzo systems help individuals, families, groups, communities, and organizations adapt and cope through the life span. We must understand the special considerations of ethnicity and culture in relation to their impact on the ethnic or racial group, as well as the community at large. If we can successfully use the knowledge gained in the use of asset building, we can help various client systems in rural areas thrive and prosper.

5

Strategies of Cooperation and Delivery of Human Services in Rural Areas

Sharing Community Assets

DARÍO MENANTEAU-HORTA

THE CHALLENGE FOR RURAL COMMUNITIES

The survival of many rural communities in the United States is at risk. Over the last three decades, the nation has witnessed a dramatic decline in the ability of rural areas and small government units to provide human and social services needed by their local populations. Current economic and demographic changes affecting rural areas in the United States are clear indicators that more services will be necessary in the future to meet the needs of a growing older population, keep and expand the number of jobs, and improve education and technology required by an information society.

Survival and development of social systems have been historically related to the processes of adaptation and enhancement of systems' functions. The key element of sustainability of a society is, therefore, the capacity to create and maintain an adaptive and dynamic form of social organization. As rural social systems and local communities lose population and political power, the design of new forms of organization for administering diminishing resources becomes urgent.

Many rural communities in the United States struggle to adapt to a changing social, political, and economic landscape. Their ability to retain their populations, keep and create new job opportunities, and provide human and social services in the future will be largely determined by new strategies of cooperation among rural communities. Research reveals that county collaboration and cooperative efforts enhance community asset-building, encourage democratic planning, and improve the delivery of services in rural areas. This study deals with the following questions:

1. *What are some of the most prominent patterns of change affecting rural communities and limiting their abilities to provide human services?*

Technological advances, urban growth, decline of farming, demographic shifts, and the new economy of global markets represent a few factors with important implications in the functioning of rural social systems. The 1997 Census of Agriculture shows that the number of full-time farmers continued declining during the last decades. It has been estimated that since 1935, the United States has lost more than 4.5 million farms, and the most affected by this decline have been the family farm enterprises. According to Cochrane (2000), of the over 6.5 million farms that existed 65 years ago only 2 million farm units remain. However, the 2 million figure is not entirely accurate, "because 1.3 million 'farms' (or about 63% of the total) are limited-resource, residential, or retirement farms—leaving approximately 700,000 actively managed farms in the nation" (p. 2).

As the number of farmers diminishes, small towns and rural communities keep losing their human and social capital, entrepreneurial capacity, and political power.

2. *What are the impacts of rural social organization, county structures, and local government units upon the service delivery process?*

   Nationally, there are almost 55,000 rural local governmental entities of all types with more than 318,000 elected officials dealing with shrinking resources and increasing social needs.

3. *To what extent might a collaborative mode of public policy development and service implementation prove to be more efficient in the delivery of social services?*

   As economist David Freshwater (2000) points out, "At the turn of the 21st century, one thing is clear: rural areas will not return to the way they were. If rural people and places are to benefit from ongoing changes, rural advocates must build coalitions, gain urban support, and promote sound policies" (p. 2).

This article reports on collaborative experiences as organizational examples of adaptation of rural areas. Results of two models for provision of services studied in the state of Minnesota are presented and discussed: (1) an autonomous-isolated model, and (2) a collaborative model of policy development and service implementation.

Collaboration for Development

Recent sociological literature, as well as many popular descriptions about rural social life in the United States, has focused attention upon two opposite views. One is a strong sense of individualism and independence that nourished pioneers, early settlers, and farmers throughout the land. The other is a genuine concern for "thy neighbor" that is deeply rooted in values of solidarity, mutual assistance, and community sharing. These perspectives may appear to signal contradictory characteristics of individuals. However, the fact that they are integral parts of the cultural

legacy of rural America implies that they also have important consequences for social organization, and therefore constitute fundamental assets for community life.

Warren (1972) defines the community as "that combination of social units and systems which perform the major social functions having locality relevance" (p. 9).

Implicit in this definition are the assets of the community that facilitate basic social functions to sustain and enhance life in society. The following are among the main functions universally recognized in the organization of communities:

1. Economic activities and adequate utilization of resources are necessary elements to satisfy individual and social needs. These include the production, distribution, and consumption of goods and services as well as the proper stewardship of the natural environment.

2. Socialization is a key process in every society for the transmission of values and cultural assets. Every community participates in the socialization tasks carried out by social institutions such as the family, schools, churches, and other organizations.

3. Communities exercise social control through a variety of mechanisms that guide private and public behavior of their members. These mechanisms usually range from informal mores and traditions accepted by the majority of individuals to formal norms, written laws, and ordinances that regulate social behavior and preserve community assets.

4. Social participation is an essential function for the development of community life. It ensures the possibility of direct democracy and involvement of all members in community affairs. Citizen participation not only has important implications for a genuine democracy, but it also generates a sense of belonging to the community and gives ownership of the community to all members.

5. Social solidarity, including mutual help in times of need, is the function that distinguishes

the community as an active social network from other forms of more distant social arrangements. Solidarity, rather than competition and conflict, is what permits individuals to maintain and expand community assets by sharing common values, goals, and institutions. The ability of community members to engage in mutually supportive relationships is critical to maximize community assets and increase what Coleman (1988) calls social capital.

Bernstein (2002) defines social capital as "the norms and networks of civil society that lubricate cooperative action among both citizens and their institutions" (p. 19). The truly sustainable community, Bernstein notes, must utilize cooperation: "Without adequate supplies of social capital—that is, without civic engagement, healthy community institutions, norms of reciprocity and trust—social institutions fail" (p. 19).

Discussing the importance of linkages between structural arrangements and the social-psychological perspective of rural places, Donohue (1993) remarks, "For individuals, the community is really the source of identity. It gives you anchorage when you are interacting with others or when you feel some sense of loss of affiliation. Your community is part of your identity, and your occupation and status give you some anchorage within the community" (p. 6).

This sense of belonging and participation in the community provides a first step in understanding and solving local problems. This type of locality identity and social commitment is particularly visible when the origins of the problems are predominantly internal to the community.

Identity, however, needs to expand to larger units. This is especially the case when problems respond to external constraints and local resources are limited and insufficient. When one considers the magnitude and complexity of today's rural problems, urban demands, and global conditions, the notion of community reaches the county, region, and state.

To face this new reality, rural communities need to build new organizational forms of collab-

oration by expanding their identity and functional boundaries. According to Donohue (1993), "The critical catalyst is organization. Rural areas are so individualistic that they cannot really achieve a level of organization for dealing with the larger urban structure, which have far greater organizational power among special interest groups than rural areas" (p. 8). He concludes, "The most effective innovation imaginable for rural areas is a new form of organization that can mobilize the resources they have" (p. 8).

The losses of political and economic power, the reduction of local autonomy, and the diminishing strengths of rural communities are alarming, and reinforce the opinions of those who call for new organizational and institutional responses for rural areas of the United States. The need for citizen participation in problem evaluations, strategy designs, and action programs appears to be critical in any new form of social organization.

A similar view is expressed by Freshwater (2000) when he states, "Rural groups will need to develop a new paradigm that allows them to see that their individual interests are best served by working to develop mutual interests. Unfortunately," he adds, "rural residents generally lack the skills and experience necessary for organizing such partnerships and the rural ethos of independence as self-reliance is an impediment" (p. 5).

In an analysis of some past experiences of multicounty collaboration, Borich and Cantrell (1992) consider school consolidation, regional planning and development programs, and the 1980s multicounty clusters initiative of the Minnesota Extension Service as prime examples of collaboration between rural communities. These clusters of counties were organized to share expertise and programs of the University of Minnesota in an effort to maximize community resources. According to these authors, "Cooperation between communities has historically been seen as a logical adaptive strategy for rural regions facing declining populations and diminishing resources. Shared services, institutional consolidations and joint planning can return some of the advantages of scale to regions in decline, and for this reason have often been encouraged, and in some cases mandated by development organizations and government agencies" (p. 5). In addition to being an adaptive strategy, intercommunity cooperation functions as a powerful force to enhance community assets and capacity building.

The issue of cooperation by mandate, however, is not always well-accepted by local groups who may perceive those mandates as another imposed mechanism from outside. This is perhaps one among other reasons that some of the cooperative programs launched in the 1970s and 1980s may not have survived the test of time. Although the geographical and political scope of citizens' participation may be initially based at the immediate local community, the maintenance and survival of programs require expanding services imposed on larger communities at county and multicounty levels.

If world sustainability is now defined in terms of a global society, the imperatives for rural communities seem to be connected to developmental collaborations. It is through cooperation based upon shared values and common goals that communities may generate and expand three key categories of assets required for sustainable development: their natural and human resources, functional skills, and strong social commitment of their members. This seems to be especially urgent in many communities as a result of ongoing changes in the agricultural structure of rural regions.

Changes in Agriculture

Over the last decades, the nation has experienced a major shift in the traditional sources of labor, income, and resources. Although farming used to be the main pillar of the rural economy and fundamental support of rural communities, current trends lead toward a substantially reduced farm sector. Freshwater (2000) summarizes the nature of these changes affecting rural places: "The last 100 years have ushered in major change to the countryside. Once a majority, rural people are now a minority, while farmers have become a minority even in rural areas. Mines have opened and closed, creating and eliminating communities.

Forests have been harvested and restored. And in some rural regions, a wave of manufacturing has swept in and then largely disappeared" (p. 2).

Rural communities have become passive observers of unprecedented changes in the economic, technological, and institutional structures of American agriculture. As the number of full-time farmers continues fading away, the family farm is at risk and local communities lose ground.

A quick glimpse of some of the changes reported by the United States Department of Agriculture (USDA) in recent years reveals the following main trends and outcomes:

1. Today, less than 10% of the rural population lives on farms. Throughout the years, the wide demographic base that has constituted one of the most vital assets of rural communities in terms of human resources and political power has been dwindling.

2. During the last 20 years, the proportion of the rural labor force involved directly in farming dropped from 14 to 8% (Whitener, 2000, p. 32). The creation of new agricultural-industries and "structural changes in the farm sector have reduced farming's importance and altered traditional perceptions of farm" (Gale, 2000).

3. In comparison with the past, the number of counties and local communities that now depend on farming for the majority of their income has been substantially reduced (Kassel & Carlin, 2000).

4. Today, over 80% of the farm household income comes from off-farm sources, mostly from wages and salaries (Whitener, 2000, p. 32).

5. Rural communities have sought to offset shrinking employment in the farm sector by adding value to farm products (Gale, 2000).

The future of farming and rural communities is critically related to the capacity of rural counties and local places to keep and expand their assets, improve their human resources, generate employment, and offer services for the well-being of their population.

THE COUNTY STRUCTURE

Concentration of social, economic, and political resources in large urban centers has resulted in an increasing inequality between these centers and rural areas. One consequence is a dramatic decline in the ability of rural communities and small government units to provide services for the basic needs of their populations.

The origin of counties goes back to the English shire at the beginning of the last millennium. Early settlers of the eastern coast of North America brought with them the structural forms of shires. After the formation of the U.S. government, the Constitution left issues of local administration to the states, leaving counties as subdivisions of the state governments. The role of local governments grew rapidly, especially since World War I, as a result of population growth, suburban development, and government reform movements. Today, they play a central role in the provision of health, education, and welfare services (Berman, 1993).

There are 3,035 counties in 48 of the 50 states. Two states, Connecticut and Rhode Island, have counties without active governments. Delaware, Hawaii, and Massachusetts have the fewest number of counties. The states with the largest number of counties are Texas (254), Georgia (156), Kentucky (119), Missouri (114), and Kansas (104). There are 31 city-county governments such as Denver, New York, and San Francisco, in addition to the 3,035 counties.

About three-fourths of all counties have populations of 50,000 or less, and about a quarter of them have less than 10,000 people (1999 Census). Los Angeles County in California is the largest county with over 9.2 million residents, while Loving County, Texas, is the least populated with only 140 residents. In terms of geographical size, Arlington County in Virginia is the smallest county with a surface of 67 sq. km, while North Slope County in Alaska is the largest with a total of 227,559 sq. km.

The diversity of counties in terms of population, revenue sources, and other assets is remarkable. Among the 10 largest counties with populations over 3 million are Los Angeles, CA (9,213,533), Cook County, IL (5,189,689), and Harris, TX (3,206,063). The demographic reality of these counties is exceptional considering that the majority of counties nationwide are smaller and are less populated. Over half of all counties (52%) have less than 25,000 inhabitants, and only 79 counties (2.6%) have populations of 500,000 or larger. Table 5.1 shows the vast demographic range found in various population categories of counties, the number of those units, and the percentage in each category.

Counties raise revenue in the United States through property taxes, sales taxes, and fees. Table 5.2 lists the leading sources of revenue for the largest counties.

The Economic Research Service of the USDA classifies nonmetropolitan counties according to their dominant economic activity into mutually exclusive groups. According to this classification, counties fall into either farming, mining, manufacturing, government, or services-dependent categories, or the nonspecialized county category. Farming-dependent counties are those counties that earned 20% or more of their weighted annual average total labor and proprietor income from farming from 1987 to 1989.

Rural counties, particularly farming-dependent counties, are mostly found in the Midwest. Mining-dependent counties are found in the West and South, and manufacturing-dependent counties are mostly found in the Southeast. Other types of counties are scattered throughout the country. Table 5.3 gives the number of counties in the United States and in Minnesota according to their main economic functions. As mentioned in the introduction of the article, this study draws upon data from the state of Minnesota and for this reason, Tables 5.3 and 5.4 illustrate some general comparisons between types of counties in the United States and Minnesota.

Counties are also classified according to "policy types." Retirement counties are counties that have 15% or more of their population aged 60 or above. Federal land counties are those that are dominated by land that belongs to the federal government. Likewise, commuting counties are

Table 5.1 Counties by Population

Population Range (%)	Number	Percentage
Less than 9,999	731	24.1
10,000–24,999	908	29.9
25,000–49,999	612	20.1
50,000–99,999	375	12.4
100,000–249,999	239	7.9
250,000–499,999	91	3.0
500,000 and more	79	2.6
Total	3,035	100.0

Table 5.2 Sources of Revenue of Largest Counties in the U.S.

Source (%)	Amount ($)	Percentage
State aid	$20,217,806,000	45.8%
Charges/fee	$ 9,511,532,000	21.5%
Property tax	$ 9,338,753,000	21.1%
Interest	$ 2,073,449,000	4.7%
Sales tax	$ 1,753,247,000	4.0%
Federal aid	$ 1,273,111,000	2.9%

Table 5.3 Dominant Economic Activity of Counties in the U.S. and Minnesota

Type of county	U.S.	Minnesota
Farming	556	29
Mining	46	0
Manufacturing	506	10
Government	244	6
Services	323	7
Nonspecialized	484	17

Table 5.4 Classification of Counties According to Policy Types in the United States and the State of Minnesota

Type of county	U.S.	Minnesota
Retirement	190	1
Federal lands	270	2
Commuting	381	4
Persistent poverty	535	2
Transfer-dependent	381	10

so named because a considerable percentage (40% in 1990) commute to jobs outside the counties in which they reside. Those classified as poverty counties are those that had 20% or more of their population below the poverty level in 1960, 1970, 1980, and 1990. Finally, transfer-dependent counties relied on unearned income transfers from government.

The large number of counties and the diversity of their functions have been a major issue of political discussion. Policy makers and elected officials have to deal with increasing needs for services with fewer resources.

Demographic and economic changes in rural areas suggest that more ser-vices will be necessary in the future to meet the needs of a growing senior population. Providing jobs to a larger number of workers in the labor force, and expanding education and technology required by an information society will also be needed.

In Minnesota, economic growth and availability of resources and services tend to favor urban and suburban metro counties over the rural areas. Urban counties control key resources such as population, industries, employment, and educational facilities. By contrast, rural counties show lower income levels, higher unemployment, a larger proportion of families in poverty, and higher income inequality than urban counties. These conditions create severe constraints for development and delivery of services (Menanteau-Horta, 1993, 2000).

Minnesota has 87 counties and, according to the 2000 population census, 4,919,179 residents. A total population of 2,798,642 (57%) lives in the 11-county metropolitan area (Anoka, Carver, Chisago, Dakota, Hennepin, Isanti, Ramsey, Scott, Sherburne, Washington, and Wright). Out of these, Hennepin County is the largest with 1,116,200 residents, followed by Ramsey County with a population of 511,035. With 31,287 residents, Isanti County is the least populated among the metropolitan counties. Nineteen counties are rural or with less than 2,500 urban population.

Each of the 87 Minnesota counties represents a self-governing unit established by the state legislature to provide essential services such as health care, education, social assistance, transportation facilities, and infrastructure investments. Counties are more than simple geographical and demographic units; they constitute active forms of local government and communities of administration and public service.

Organization of Services

Rural sociological research suggests that development and quality of services are largely dependent on: (1) the amount and quality of natural and human *resources*, (2) access to and exercise of political *power*, and (3) creative and just *social organization*. As rural communities and small counties lose population and power, the design of new forms of organization for administering shrinking resources becomes urgent.

Intercounty collaboration and cooperative efforts among local communities are frequently mentioned as dynamic organizational forms that may help to achieve more efficient coordination, planning, and delivery of social services. Recent research suggests that linkages between the community, county, state, and federal governments can help to maintain and improve community assets, facilities, and services at the local level. Generally, more differentiation of opportunities and services occurs in areas where linkages are strong. Although communities may give up autonomy in some areas, leaders having more relationships and involvement with external units tend to take more initiative for development.

In Minnesota, county linkages and collaborative activities among local agencies have been facilitated by three mechanisms. One is the Joint Powers Act of the state legislature, requiring county initiative for its implementation. The second consists of a few rarely imposed state mandates. The third is the intercounty arrangement based on mutual needs and local initiative. According to a recent rural sociology survey of Minnesota county commissioners, about 57% of county linkages originated under the Joint Powers Act, 41% from local initiatives, and 2% were initiated by state mandates (Menanteau-Horta & Guang, 1995).

With intercounty linkages, collaboration between units may contribute to expansion of traditional community boundaries. Such linkages show the extent to which cooperation between units is more effective than competition in delivering social services and maximizing assets.

Research Results

The research results are based on a study comparing the collaborative efforts among four Minnesota counties with delivery of services provided by a single county. Three of the four collaborating counties have population sizes and income per capita levels similar to the single county. In combination, however, the cluster has a larger population base (51,839 people), higher income levels, a larger pool of individuals with high school and college education, and a larger, fully employed population than the single county, which has a larger share of its population living in poverty.

1. The Autonomous Mode:
The Single County

The planning of social services was done by a single county agency governed by a welfare board of seven members, of which five were county commissioners. Lack of funding hindered planning and development. Services to youth at risk and their out-of-home placement were sometimes avoided because of limited resources. Despite increasing needs, the county was under tax levy limits imposed by the state legislature and was "boxed in" regarding money for social services.

Service planning was centralized, leaving the social services director responsible for 13 different plans annually, with much of the planning mandated by the statute. Lacking a formal, comprehensive planning body, the county's agency relied on staff members to gain citizen participation. Numerous citizen and provider groups, specializing in narrow fields of interest, added outside input.

These groups may or may not review plans before they are sent to the Welfare Board for approval. To illustrate, the Mental Health Plan mandates citizen review of service objectives by the Coordinating Committee, but other plans such as Community Social Services or day care proposals do not mandate citizen input or review.

This county had joined three other counties to attain grant eligibility under the State Community Health Services program. Nevertheless, most of the planning was still done along individual county lines. With the exception of the Community Health Services grant meetings, there were no meetings for planning or service development.

2. The Collaborative Mode

A collaborative health and welfare arrangement of four counties in southern Minnesota offers a different type of organization.

The intercounty Community Health Services Agency was organized by county commissioners and social services directors shortly after 1978 and is governed by a Board of Commissioners from the four counties. Smaller counties have one member on the Board, while the larger county has two. Also, each of the four counties has a consumer/provider on the Board. These counties have also become one agency for providing health services via a Joint Powers Resolution.

Planning was done in a two-year cycle. The citizen group providing input into service development was an advisory committee of 20 members that included county commissioners, consumers, and providers. The county commissioners appointed constituents from their districts to fill the advisory committee. This group agreed to meet at least quarterly but in fact met monthly with strong participation.

Social services were also collaborative in a multicounty welfare agency organized since 1974 under a Joint Powers Agreement. Joint Powers were considered for two reasons. First, the less populated counties experienced difficulties in obtaining adequate county levies to absorb larger social service costs. Second, small counties had difficulty attracting and maintaining directors of social services. By combining agencies, they could provide better services with lower administrative costs.

The agency had a 12-member advisory committee that met monthly, with four members from each county appointed by the region's welfare board. All were lay citizens, and despite making few recommendations, they reviewed programs and reported to the board monthly. The committee's major role was public education.

Building Community Capacity

This study emphasizes the importance of social organization and intercommunity cooperation for achieving more efficient and effective delivery of social services. Findings generally support the conclusion that intercounty cooperative arrangements facilitate a more pluralistic decision-making process with important cost savings by sharing human resources, administration, and financial resources. Collaborative work in a cluster of counties leads to more democratic planning and better delivery of services than in a single autonomous county organization.

While the consolidation of counties within the state remains a sensitive political issue, the needs for services and solutions to local problems demand urgent and creative efforts. Intercounty collaboration is a good alternative that places people above traditional geopolitical boundaries.

Sharing institutional services may help to integrate different localities and strengthen rural communities. Sharing assets and common values may lead community members to what Warren (1972) describes as "a level of participation on which people come together in significant relationships for the provision of certain necessary living functions" (p. 32).

Fellin (1987) refers to the notion of "the competent community" as that network of social relations and institutions characterized by an efficient and fair utilization of community assets. A competent community is more likely to enter in collaboration with other communities to increase the assets to benefit all its members. According to Cottrell (1983), a competent community represents a type of social organization that "can achieve a working consensus on goals and priorities; can agree on ways and means to implement the agreed-upon goals; and can collaborate effectively in the required actions" (p. 403).

Community vitality and sustainability requires, therefore, an active collective effort to preserve and improve the assets available to the community. This process is what Mayer (1994) defines as community capacity composed by local resources, population skills, and community commitment. According to this author, these commu-

nity assets "can be deployed to build on community strength and address community problems" (p. 3).

Implicit in the concept of community capacity is a developmental perspective that involves the processes of creating and expanding the assets necessary to build community. This is the challenge to individuals, groups, and institutions to improve the quality of life for all community members.

NOTE

Minnesota's rural counties of Big Stone, Fillmore, Grant, Kittson, Lac Qui Parle, Lincoln, Mahnomen, Murray, Norman, Red Lake, Sibley, and Traverse were also classified as "farming-dependent" counties. Big Stone County was categorized as a "transfer" county in addition to being a rural farming county; while another, Mahnomen County, was categorized as a "poverty" and "transfer" county. Other counties that are in the "transfer" category are Aitkin, Cass, Clearwater, Hubbard, Koochiching, Lake, Pine, and Wadena.

DISCUSSION QUESTIONS

1. Rural communities interested in forming partnerships will have to find shared values or needs on which to base them. What characteristics should be considered, and what are the limitations of each; for example, if counties or communities collaborate based on similarity of current population needs/ values, and that population is rapidly shifting, what predictions can be made about the utility of this basis for cooperation 10 years down the line? Are there more viable shared characteristics? Is there a shared environment? How about shared needs? What is the extent of external pressures?

2. What measures can be used to determine the overall performance of rural communities

and/or counties in relation to access of social services, quality of life, and sustainability of rural communities?

3. Some members of rural communities may not be easily "heard" within the current political and economic system. What populations are becoming, or have become, invisible to the system? What does this mean for asset building and shared community resources?

4. What external pressures are acting on the rural population, and what is the level of awareness of these pressures? What are some viable strategies of cooperation to improve human and social services in rural communities?

CLASSROOM ASSIGNMENTS
AND ACTIVITIES

Strategies of Intercounty Collaboration and Community Assets in the United States and/or Your State

1. Seek the cooperation of two or three of your classmates and proceed, as a group, to develop an inventory of community assets that can be observed and measured in your community. Include specific assets that constitute resources (natural and human), skills, and community commitment.

2. Identify the main problems for achieving agreement and/or consensus for collaboration between counties and/or rural communities.

3. In a class presentation, define and describe the following concepts presented in this article: community assets; social capital; strategies of cooperation; community capacity; and "the competent community."

Comparison of Selected Counties/Communities

Select two rural counties or communities in your area and address the following:

1. Develop a general description of the selected communities. Include demographic characteristics, economic resources, occupational structure, and social institutions.

2. Develop a general description of social needs and community social problems.

3. Describe the relevant available social services—or the lack of them in the communities.

4. What advantages and disadvantages can be seen for intercommunity collaboration?

5. Develop a vision and strategy for collaborative delivery of social services—include some aspects of shared identity.

Developing a Research Design for Sharing Resources

1. Assemble and present data on changes in land use, economic resources, farming, social institutions, education, and social services for the last 20 years across two or three counties in your area.

2. Assemble and present data on changes in population, occupational activities, income levels, and poverty rates for the same time period.

3. Assemble and present data on local government structures, patterns of leadership and political participation of members of selected communities.

4. After assembling these baseline data, try to identify major trends. Determine what areas of human services and what target populations may show the greatest needs, according to your data. What services are currently provided by each county? Which type of resources could be shared? What kind of problems limit intercounty cooperation? Identify and discuss the potential benefits of cooperative arrangements in the delivery of social services in the rural communities of your study.

REFERENCES

Berman, D. R. (Ed.). (1993). *County governments in an era of change*. Westport, CT: Greenwood Press.

Bernstein, S. (2002). Using the hidden assets of America's communities and regions to ensure sustainable communities. *Center for Neighborhood Technology*. Retrieved January 10, 2002, from http://www.cnt.org/hiddenassets/pt2e.html.

Borich, P. J., & Cantrell, R. (1992). Multi-county collaboration and rural development. *Sociology of Rural Life, 12*, 3.

Cochrane, W. W. (2000). American agriculture in an uncertain global economy. *Minnesota Agricultural Economist, 700*, 1–4.

Coleman, J. S. (1988). Social capital in the creation of human capital. *American Journal of Sociology, 94*, 95–119.

Cottrell, L. S. (1983). The competent community. In R. Warren & L. Lyon (Eds.), *New perspectives on the American community* (pp. 401–412). Homewood, IL: The Dorsey Press.

Donohue, G. (1993). What is the future of rural communities? *Sociology of Rural Life, 13*, 1.

Fellin, P. (1987). *The community and the social worker*. Itasca, IL: Peacock Publishers.

Freshwater, D. (2000). Rural America at the turn of the century. *Rural America, 15*, 3.

Gale, F. (2000). Nonfarm growth and structural change alter farming's role in rural economy. *ERS Information, 10*, 2–6.

Kassel, K. & Carlin, T. A. (2000). Economic growth in farming areas lags the rest of rural America. *Rural Conditions and Trends, 10*, 2.

Mayer, S. E. (1994). *Building community capacity*. Minneapolis, MN: Rainbow Research.

Menanteau-Horta, D. (1993). *Social well-being and development in Minnesota counties*. St. Paul, MN: University of Minnesota Center for Rural Social Development.

Menanteau-Horta, D. (2000). Indicators of social performance in the heartland of the United States. In F. Parra-Luna (Ed.), *The performance of social systems* (pp. 277–292). New York: Kluwer Academic/Plenum Publishers.

Menanteau-Horta, D., & Guang, L. (1995). State and county relations: A vital partnership. *Sociology of Rural Life, 14*(3), 5–8.

Warren, R. L. (1972). *The community in America*. Chicago: Rand McNally & Company.

Whitener, L. A. (2000). Developing a safety net for farm households. *Rural America, 15*, 3.

INFOTRAC COLLEGE EDITION

community assets
community collaboration
delivery of social services

rural development
social organization

6

Natural Helping Networks

Assets for Rural Communities

TED R. WATKINS

Within the last 150 years, cities have come to dominate U.S. culture. Social conditions created by urbanization led to the development of social service agencies and to the very profession of social work. Social welfare programs are now generally designed to meet the needs of the urban rather than the rural environment, even though approximately one-quarter of the population still lives in rural areas (Foster, 1997). Although there have been relatively few studies of services in rural areas (Booth & McLaughlin, 2000), it is generally believed that the rural population is often ill-served by programs and policies designed for urbanites, due to inappropriate administrative, legal, and regulatory systems (Dunbar, 1999). However, rural services can be greatly improved by focusing on the strengths and assets of rural communities (Johnson, 2001).

RURAL COMMUNITIES

By definition, "communities are composed of people who have relationships that are systematic, interactive, and interdependent" (Smith, 1997, p. 14). Rural communities are characterized by multiple primary relationships and interdependence. Citizens are likely to have gone to school together, attended the same church and community activities, and shared the same doctors and other professional and service persons. In many cases there are extended family connections and fictive kin, people who share significant relationship but are not related by birth or marriage

(Carlton-LaNey, Edwards, & Reid, 1999). Within such small populations, interaction is intensified and there is a greater sense of mutuality and involvement with one another (Wodarski, Giordano, & Bagarozzi, 1981). "Rural communities are seen as more supportive than their urban counterparts, as members of rural locales frequently are more aware of the details of neighbors' lives" (Lindhorst, 1997, p. 4). Martinez-Brawley (2000) implies that a sense of mutuality may be particularly strong in rural communities of African Americans and Latinos.

A conservative lifestyle is still typical (Ginsberg, 1993). Local values and beliefs often are not open to diversity or social differences (Smith, 1997). "In rural areas, more than any other geographic setting, conformity is strongly urged, if not demanded. Deviation from the 'traditional way of living' is strongly discouraged" (Foster, 1997, p. 24). This has positive and negative consequences. Well-established behavioral norms provide clear guidelines in many areas of life and reduce the incidence of deviant behaviors, such as alcohol abuse. On the other hand, those individuals who are "different" may be stigmatized more than in diverse urban environments. Unfortunately, racism, sexism, and homophobia may be tolerated in this conservative context (Smith & Mancoske, 1997). For example, gay, lesbian, bisexual, or transgendered persons may be extremely hesitant to come out in a rural community for fear of ostracism or even violence. However, over time, communities tend to "find a niche" for such persons, as can be seen in creating "work" for developmentally disabled adults or acceptance of an eccentric crossdresser ("That's just the way he is, you know").

Residents of rural communities stress the value of taking care of their own through informal mechanisms (Fekete, Bond, McDonel, Salyers, Chen, & Miller, 1998; McCoy, McCoy, Lai, Weatherly, & Messiah, 1999). Consequently, there is a reluctance to utilize professional mental health or other social services (Foster, 1997; Jacob, Willits, & Jensen, 1996).

Strong religious faith and affiliation with conservative churches generally support the overall conservatism of rural areas. In communities with few highly educated persons, ministers hold high status, and their influence increases by the fact that they often reinforce messages handed down by tradition, rather than introducing new ideas as mental health professionals or other well-educated newcomers are likely to do. Lindhorst (1997) illustrates the influence of religiosity on sexual minority groups: "The church is the center of the rural community, and may serve to reinforce beliefs that support homophobia" (p. 3). On the other hand, ministers and compassionate parishioners can become major catalysts in instituting changes in attitudes and behaviors toward those who do not fit community expectations.

These characteristics provide the sociocultural context within which the human services worker must function in order to meet the needs of persons with a variety of problems in living. There is a need for structuring services to create the best fit for this context and a need for individual workers to tap into the strengths and assets that rural communities provide in the form of natural helping networks.

TRADITIONAL
HELPING NETWORKS

All of the characteristics of rurality noted previously can be seen as residual from earlier times, when survival on the frontier depended on mutual assistance. The lore and literature of early North America is replete with anecdotes involving the efforts of individuals and families to help each other out during hard times. Examples include the folklore of Abraham Lincoln's borrowing of books from neighbors to read in childhood; assistance to the immigrant family in *My Antonia* (Cather, 1918); numerous stories of barn-raisings; joining together to defend in battles against intruders; and taking in orphaned children (Brace, 1976).

Although historically rural areas were populated by persons who desired "breathing room" and privacy, there was nevertheless a premium on "neighborliness." Shortages of money and supplies encouraged the sharing of equipment. If Farmer Brown owned a planter and Farmer Garber owned a harvester, by sharing equipment they were able to reduce the costs of production. There was seldom any formalized *quid pro quo,* but rather an open sharing of resources that acknowledged that cooperation was in everyone's best interest. Some might have had more goods than others, but there was a partnership in building productive farms or businesses in the context of limited resources.

Many of the helping functions now provided by agencies such as child welfare agencies—shelters for battered women, temporary employment agencies, and even medical services—were provided on an informal basis. My parents provided a home for a teenage boy who needed respite from a troubled family, took him into the family and nurtured him until he completed school and could live on his own. They also gave shelter as needed to a neighbor whose drug-addicted husband was sometimes violent. A neighboring farm family prevented the institutionalization of a man with serious intellectual challenges by housing him on their property and keeping him supplied with basic goods in exchange for his help with farm chores.

Helping across racial barriers also occurred. Historically, rural women served as midwives for one another regardless of race or economic status. My father, a white tenant farmer, was hospitalized with appendicitis just as his crops were ready for harvest. He asked his teenage son to hire a nearby family of black farm laborers to harvest the crop. When he later went to pay the family, they refused to take the money: "We couldn't take money for helping a neighbor in trouble!" was their response.

THE INSTITUTIONALIZATION OF SOCIAL SERVICES

Urbanization brought dramatic changes in the way people interacted with each other. Individuals moved away from extended family and other primary relationships to cities where primary relationships were replaced by more role-based interactions. Population density and crowding were accompanied by emotional distancing to preserve a sense of privacy and individuality. In low-income neighborhoods, needs overwhelmed the resources of neighbors. Many persons in need were new to the cities and had no support networks. Formalized or institutionalized social services were a rational response to the peculiar social patterns and needs of these urban residents. Services funded privately could be tailored to specific community needs. However, when federal, state, and local governments increased their role in providing services, the programs were no longer tailored for a specific community. In efforts to increase efficiency and fairness, services became more bureaucratic and standardized. The new model of service delivery that developed preferred secondary, "professional" relationships and interactions that were rule- and role-based rather than those that were more personal. Needy individuals were depersonalized into "clients." The "helping hand" came from outside the community (O'Looney, 1993). Personal relationships between client and social worker were not only unlikely in the urban environment, they were actively discouraged as illustrated in the National Association of Social Workers Code of Ethics, which warns against "dual relationships" (Reamer, 1998).

This process of professionalization of social services included a new emphasis on confidentiality. Social workers were instructed not to give the "client's" friends, family, or neighbors any information about the client's needs. Supportive family and friends were discouraged from becoming involved in clients' affairs, lest they interfere with the service plan.

Although this developing institutional or industrial model (O'Looney, 1993) of service delivery was an effective adaptation for urban settings, bureaucratic mandates universalized its use. On the one hand, institutionalization of services, especially those funded through governmental agencies, brought increasing financial support to social services in rural areas. But there was a tendency for the new services to replace, rather than augment, existing informal helping networks. Agency policies were administered inflexibly; local cultures, mores, and social networks were ignored. The result was that in many rural settings voluntary and personalized help was replaced by a system of universalized, but less culturally acceptable services. O'Looney (1993) states: "The advantages of a rural service delivery model are those that are represented by the archetype of traditional rural services and community practices—not by the existing reality that has admittedly veered away from this model during the last few decades" (p. 23).

Figure 6.1 contrasts the helping network resources of rural and urban settings. The interconnectedness of rural resources provides a helping environment very different from the formality of the urban network.

There is clearly a need for social workers to combine the strengths of the two models of service delivery discussed—the personal concern and individualization of the natural helping networks, and the entitlements (and financial resources) inherent in the more universal formal delivery systems. The following suggestions and examples indicate how the rural social worker can function within both the organizational structure of a traditional agency and the natural helping networks of the small community.

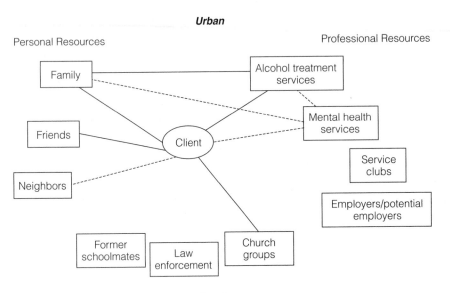

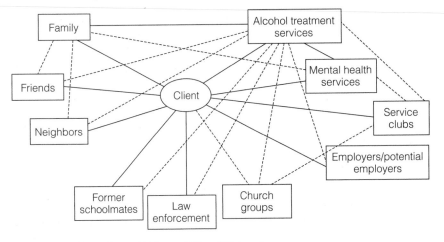

FIGURE 6.1 Comparison of Urban and Rural Network

RECONSIDERING ORGANIZATIONAL STRUCTURE

Eugen Pusic (1970) spoke of the need for development of "post-bureaucratic organizations," which he described as consisting of modules that have little hierarchy in terms of status and power, are task-specific, and are fluid in composition. As these task groups achieve their objectives, they reorganize themselves around new tasks. Without bureaucratic structural constraints and the inefficiency of a hierarchical structure, more effort can go into addressing the job at hand. The role of the minimalist administration of such organizations is to coordinate and loosely oversee the work being done. This is consistent with O'Looney's recommendations for shifting the power alignments among workers, consumers, managers, and organizations (O'Looney, 1993). This model has applicability to many rural social service needs. The professional social worker, typically overworked and with too few resources, becomes the coordinator of services, many of which are supplied by families and neighbors of the service recipient. "Social work services in rural communities are often more indirect, relying on professional consultation, referrals to informal helping networks and use of service extenders (voluntary helping persons who are not trained as social workers)" (Lindhorst, 1997, p. 7).

There are specific tensions inherent in developing such a system. Agency rules and community rules often are at odds with each other.

Confidentiality The Code of Ethics of the National Association of Social Workers states "social workers should respect clients' right to privacy" (Reamer, 1998, p. 270), and the training and education of social workers generally gives considerable attention to the prohibition of discussing client material that is confidential in nature.

Natural helping network methods, on the other hand, are dependent on friends and neighbors knowing the service recipient's business. If Aunt Jane is abusing her prescription medication, neighbors will observe that she is staggering and incoherent at times, which will lead to the "prying" that identifies the substance abuse problem. This in turn leads to a call to the doctor, where the overuse of the prescribed medication is reported. The physician agrees to more carefully monitor Jane's "nerve medicine." Through discussion among friends and relatives, an intervention of sorts takes place. Members of the informal network take turns calling Aunt Jane, driving her to town on errands, stopping by to see her, and otherwise keeping her busy and involved in the life of the community. Her problem, while widely known, diminishes as a result of actions taken by persons who care enough to interfere in her life. In situations in which clients' problems are already public knowledge, social workers can use that knowledge in constructive ways (Martinez-Brawley, 2000).

Stakeholder Input Professional social work generally identifies the client and immediate family as legitimate stakeholders in service to the client. Occasionally others, such as employers or landlords (Faketa, et al., 1998), are included as part of the information input and decision-making team. The decision concerning who is a legitimate stakeholder in a case relates closely to the issue of confidentiality discussed previously. The professional worker is generally cautious in identifying persons who have a right to know the client's business, and therefore who can be a part of the helping process. In the rural community the intensity of interpersonal relationships and multiple intersections of the lives of neighbors broadens the scope of those who might need to know the client's concerns. Depending on the size of the community, the entire village (or a significant part of it) may have lives so intertwined with that of the client that they can be considered legitimate stakeholders, providing information, suggestions, and services. A method of using large natural helping networks was described by Attneave, who applied her Native American tribal methods of networking to other populations (Speck & Attneave, 1973). The tribal custom was to call together everyone in the village to address problems of inappropriate behavior of members of the community. An example of the method in an urban setting was when a teenager's acting out behavior led to the parents' calling the mental health agency for help. Attneave's team pulled together as many stakeholders in the teen's life as they could locate, for a series of large group meetings. These family members, neighbors, and friends of the teen and family were asked to identify issues that might be contributing to the teen's problems, share ideas about what ought to be done, and volunteer to participate in restructuring a social environment that would be more supportive of healthy functioning. This method seems particularly appropriate for use in rural communities. The whole network participated in "treating" the acting-out teen.

Religious Values It is well documented that rural residents tend to place greater emphasis on religion and conservative views of morality than urban residents. The churches are major sources of help for those in need (Spence, 1994). Often helping a needy family becomes a special project of a Sunday School class or other church group. Ministers are called into situations to coordinate helping services in much the same way as case managers. A family's problems may be the focus of a Wednesday night prayer meeting. Moralizing or evangelizing may or may not be a part of the helping package.

Although there is a recent movement in social work education to acknowledge spiritual dimensions of helping, many social work practitioners are still cautious about the influence of religious groups. Judgment and discrimination may sometimes be a part of involving religious organizations in the helping process. The rural practitioner, especially if not a native of the area, may have a hard time finding the community acceptance that is necessary for effective practice if he or she appears to be antireligious. The dissonance between the potential for negative judgment and the need to utilize community volunteer helpers is a dilemma that must be confronted if the natural and professional helping networks are to be merged into a responsive rural model.

Dual Relationships A fourth problem, more related to rurality than to the structure of services, is tension over the concept of "dual relationships." The rural social worker may have long-time relationships, or even kinship, with clients (Scales & Cooper, 1999). The Code of Ethics of the National Association of Social Workers states that "[s]ocial workers should not engage in dual or multiple relationships with clients or former clients in which there is a risk of exploitation or potential harm to the client" (National Association of Social Workers, 1996, Standard 1.06(c)). Coale (1998) refers to the controversy over dual roles as a red herring. "Some experts go so far as to support that practitioners engaging in dual roles *of any kind,* should lose their licenses and professional association memberships. . . . They [relationships] in fact, can be useful treatment resources when used appropri-

ately" (pp. 101–102). The rural professional is foremost a member of the community and secondarily a professional. "In any small community, dual roles are inevitable" (Coale, 1998, p. 105). The sparse population density of rural communities "places professional helpers in a fishbowl situation. Things they say or do are heard or observed by the larger community. . . . They come into contact with their consumers, agency staff, and community leaders on a regular basis" (Foster, 1997, p. 26). The National Rural Social Work Caucus, recognizing the inevitability of dual relationships in rural practice, advocated for softer language in the NASW Code of Ethics, and was able to change the wording from prohibiting to discouraging dual relationships (Miller, 1994). Borys and Pope (1989) provide guidelines that seem more appropriate than blanket condemnation of dual relationships. They suggest, above all, do no harm; practice only with competence; do not exploit; treat people with respect for their dignity as human beings; protect confidentiality; act, except in the more extreme instances, only after obtaining informal consent; practice, insofar as possible, within the framework of social equity and justice. Miller (1994) summarizes her conclusions: "Dual relationships may at times be a natural part of social work practice in rural communities. Practitioners may need to learn how to experience and sometimes even embrace the second relationship, particularly if it arises out of the essentials of the culture" (p. 7).

ILLUSTRATIVE CASES

The differences between formal and informal helping processes present a major challenge to the rural social service professional. The following examples illustrate efforts to create a model of helping that has the flexibility to adapt service delivery to the rural environment.

Case Example 1 centers around a rural village's response to a young man with the dual disorders of schizophrenia and alcohol abuse. It has often been reported that rural areas are disadvantaged with regard to services for treatment of both mental illness and substance abuse disorders. Contrary to that belief, the assets of the rural setting can be used advantageously in the treatment of dually disordered individuals. There are many stakeholders in the life of the rural mentally ill substance abuser. The paucity of formal services should lead us to more effectively utilize the assets that are available, such as families, neighbors, clergy and church congregations, childhood schoolmates, fraternal organizations, family physicians, and law enforcement. With the permission of the client, the social worker may tap into many relationships and bring many social resources to bear on the client's problems.

In small communities, informal relationships override bureaucratic role restrictions. Citizens perceive that individuals are the ones to provide services, not bureaucracies, and individuals are generally less rigid than bureaucracies. In the rural community, the personal relationships among agency employees often bypass formal referral procedures and agency policy guidelines. Bureaucratic red tape is conveniently ignored for the benefit of the client and of future working relationships between the agencies' employees. By their very nature, rural settings are more conducive to interdisciplinary and collaborative practice due to the scarcity of service providers (Morris, 1997).

CASE EXAMPLE 1 *

Mobilizing Rural Community Resources on Behalf of a Mentally Ill Substance Abuser

Ray, age 38, has lived his entire life in Cave City, Tennessee. He has had several brief hospitalizations in the regional state mental hospital where he was given a diagnosis of schizophrenia. In the two years since his last hospitalization, Ray has not held a job and has become something of a nuisance, as he is often under the influence of alcohol and has been arrested numerous times

for disturbing the peace. The village residents are tolerant of his behavior up to a point, but wish that someone would do something about the situation. After his fourth episode of drunken disruptive behavior in a month, the sheriff, in exasperation, called the local outreach worker (Barbara Quinn, MSW) for the tricounty Mental Health/Mental Retardation (MHMR) agency and asked her if she could do something for Ray. She said she hoped that she could help, but asked if she could stop by the sheriff's office to discuss the situation. He said he was in and out of the office too much to meet with her there, but maybe they could talk over bowls of chili at Mae's Café at about 12:30. Ms. Quinn had no trouble identifying the sheriff when she arrived at Mae's and the sheriff excused himself from the table of local men with whom he had been talking and got a table in the most isolated corner of the café for himself and the social worker.

In the ensuing conversation the sheriff acknowledged that he knew the MHMR center had deployed a worker to the local community, but he had never before called the agency because he knew the worker "wasn't from around here" and he was not sure just what services might be available. After briefly explaining the agency's services, Ms. Quinn asked about Ray's history, his family, and the identity of any other local residents who might be interested in Ray's welfare. She also gently suggested that the sheriff might want to have around-the-clock observation of Ray for the first two or three days after an arrest, as a precaution against possible harm from delirium tremens or other alcohol-related health risks. The sheriff was impressed by her insight into the problems of incarceration of inebriated persons and his natural concerns about the safety of persons held in his custody. Before they parted, Ms. Quinn thanked the sheriff for his help and agreed to talk with Ray at the jail as soon as he was sober. The sheriff assured her that he would be glad to help in any way he could as the case progressed.

---

* Names and places have been disguised to protect the privacy of persons involved in the case examples.

The next morning Ms. Quinn received a call from the sheriff reporting that Ray had "sobered up enough" for her to interview him. Ray was cooperative in the interview, open and matter-of-fact but emotionally flat. His first hospitalization had occurred in eleventh grade and he never returned to school to complete his high school education. He had taken several psychotropic medications through the years, but disliked the side effects and thought that taking medicine made him different from other people. Consequently, his compliance had been spotty. He considered his several periods of employment in the local community to be the high points of his life. His jobs included loading merchandise for the feed store, stocking parts at the John Deere dealership, and janitorial work at the First Baptist Church. Each job lasted a shorter time than the previous one, and in each case he had been fired for being drunk on the job. He said that he would really like to have a job again. Ms. Quinn asked Ray if he could think of anything that he could have done differently to keep from being fired, and the only thing he could think of was to hide his drinking better. Ms. Quinn asked if he would have any interest in working with her to see if he could improve his chances of getting and holding another job. He said he certainly would, and would do anything to be able to work again. She told him that he would probably be let out of jail later in the day, and asked if he would promise to refrain from drinking any alcohol until she could talk with him again the next day, and he agreed to do so.

Over the next six weeks Ms. Quinn met frequently with Ray and, with his permission, consulted with several community residents to enlist their help in providing the structure and guidance that he needed to refrain from drinking and to get back on his prescribed medication. A neighbor, who had a history of bringing "extra" dinner from her family's meals to Ray, agreed to stop in each morning to see that he took his medication. Frank, a man who had gone to school with Ray, stopped by after work every day to make sure that Ray had something planned for the evening that did not involve drinking. Two evenings a week they went to Alcoholics Anonymous meetings together. Sometimes they watched sports events on TV with Frank's family. Other nights Ray stayed at his own place with the understanding that if he got restless or got the urge to drink, he would call Frank who would come to "kill time with him" until he had overcome the desire for alcohol. Ms. Quinn worked with Ray to help him begin to recognize that his drinking and his lack of medication compliance had a great effect on his ability to keep a job and remain out of the hospital. She also impressed on the community helpers how important it was for them to reinforce the message that staying sober and staying on medication were essential to Ray's community adjustment. With Ray's permission, Ms. Quinn met with his physician to discuss the fragility of Ray's community adjustment and to inquire whether any relapses that might occur could be treated at the nearby general hospital rather than at the more distant state psychiatric hospital. The physician was hesitant to take on the responsibility of treatment of a "mental case" because of his limited knowledge of antipsychotic medications, but Ms. Quinn assured him that the medical director of the MHMR agency would offer assistance if asked, as would the state hospital physicians. She stressed the importance of Ray's remaining connected with his community helpers.

Ray became restless about not having a job and applied for a position as nightwatchman at the local paper box factory. Frank was concerned that the long nights alone on the job would not be conducive to Ray's continued sobriety, so he talked with his minister at the First Baptist Church about hiring Ray to do the seasonal lawn maintenance for the next few months. Ray thought this second option would be more interesting than the night job, and hoped that it might eventually lead to his getting back his janitorial job at the church. Ms. Quinn met with the minister, who coincidentally was her own pastor, to discuss the confusion that mentally ill persons with histories of religious ideation may have when in religious settings. With careful monitoring by friends and by the minister, Ray was successful in his new position. With continued sobriety and medication compliance, Ray was making a better adjustment than he had in years. Ms. Quinn phased out her involvement in the case but made it clear to Ray and his community helpers that she would be available if needed in the future. The several neighbors and friends of Ray, who laughingly referred to themselves as the "Committee on Ray" asked her to let them know if there were other "cases" that needed their help.

Rural social work requires both clinical and community practice skills, but offers the opportunity to impact dimensions of the client's life that are inaccessible to workers in urban settings. This broadened impact greatly increases the chances of success with the most difficult clients—those with both serious mental illness and substance abuse problems.

CASE EXAMPLE 2

"Stone Soup"

The Young Adults' Sunday School class of Cornwall United Methodist Church sought a way to demonstrate their faith through a community improvement project. One member of the class, Ross Lowrie, MSW, worked as a therapist in a local residential treatment program for adolescents. He was aware of the lack of quick-response emergency assistant resources in the rural county, and suggested that the class could develop a plan to institute such services. Another class member, Jeannie, brought to the group an article she had read in a magazine about a volunteer-staffed emergency service in a rural area in Australia. The class voted to use the Australian program, FISH, as a model for their own efforts.

Led by Lowrie, the class brainstormed to identify specific needs, both goods and services, that might be met through volunteers. They developed a form that listed numerous items that might be donated and several services that could be provided on an emergency basis. They first spoke to their own church congregation and asked that members identify on the form what they would be willing to contribute to the pro-

gram. They then visited other churches in the county, explained their plan for an emergency assistance program, and solicited more pledges of assistance. The results were astonishing. One church donated a small apartment for short-term use of families made homeless by fire or other disasters. Another church volunteered to collect used clothing for the project, and another offered to create a food pantry. Individuals offered a wide variety of services as needed, including babysitting, taking hot meals to families in need, and home repair services to elderly persons. Many families offered unused furniture that they had stored in their attics.

The social worker, Lowrie, trained a core of response team leaders in communication skills and problem identification. The Sunday School class subscribed to the only answering service in the county and publicized a telephone number for persons seeking assistance. When a call came in, the answering service forwarded the call to the volunteer on duty (initially, always a member of the class), who would identify the need, thumb through the card file of volunteered services and goods, and line up the appropriate resources. In the first weeks of service, an elderly widow had a window pane replaced after a falling tree limb broke it; a young couple with a medical crisis had their children cared for in their own home for several hours until family could arrive from another community; a family from out-of-state who were involved in a serious automobile wreck were given shelter in the donated apartment until their hospitalized member could return home with them; and a frightened 9-year-old boy called for reassurance when left at home unattended.

Persons whose services or goods were used generally became advocates for the service. Individuals from outside the original Sunday School class asked to be trained as response team leaders. The owner of the telephone answering service offered to contribute her service without charge after the first two months. At the end of the first year of service, volunteers were representative of many different church and civic groups. The project had grown well beyond the initial Sunday

School class. Although Lowrie and the originators of the project remained involved, the project now belonged to the community at large. After the second year of service, the United Way picked up the cost of a full-time BSW-level coordinator for the program. Lowrie eventually moved to a job in another state, but his influence is still felt in the rural county where he spearheaded the development of a community improvement project through recognizing and using the religious community as a rural cultural asset.

CONCLUSION

Rural social work is integrally tied into the total fabric of the community. The role of the professional cannot be entirely separated from the personal life of the worker. The process of helping an individual client can build strength in natural helping networks. In rural areas, a lone social work professional can become a catalyst for community change. A single project to address a specific need can establish the infrastructure needed for more broadly based change.

It is imperative that efforts be redirected from trying to make rural communities more like urban areas to investing in the assets inherent in the rural social environment. New strength in the rural setting can be developed through the combination of financial and organizational support that government-funded bureaucratic organizations provide, and the natural helping networks that historically have been used to meet needs of rural residents. This third way of service delivery will require that bureaucracies and professional organizations become more flexible and responsive to local conditions, and that natural helpers accept a necessary degree of structure and accountability imposed by the funding agency.

DISCUSSION QUESTIONS

1. Social work practice often involves competing values. For example, we value family, but sometimes intrude into families in order to protect children, whose safety and well-being we also value. How do rural environments challenge and shape our view of social work values such as confidentiality, the worth and dignity of the individual, and self-determination? What other professional social work values may take on different nuances in the rural setting?

2. How may the rural setting enhance the quality of family life of the rural social worker? How may it be detrimental to the worker's family life?

3. Churches are often the most viable organizations in very small communities and often nurture natural helping networks. Yet rivalries between members of different congregations sometimes create divisions in the community. How can the rural social worker utilize churches in building community assets?

4. One of the social workers depicted in this article, Ms. Quinn, used some techniques that are not standard practice in urban settings. What is your opinion of their use in this rural case?

CLASSROOM ASSIGNMENTS
AND ACTIVITIES

1. Analyze several articles in the current issue of a major social work journal. Look for content relevant to rural settings. How often is there specific reference to rural implications? Is there content on theories and practices that you think might be irrelevant

or inappropriate for use in rural communities? What signs do you find of an urban bias? Are there signs of a rural bias? What implications does this have for professional and nonprofessional helping?

2. Interview (in person, by telephone, or by e-mail) an individual who is a member of a sexual minority group (gay, lesbian, bisexual, or transsexual) about the advantages or disadvantages of life in rural settings. Are their opinions based on personal experience, the experience of acquaintances, hearsay, or conjecture? Do they have suggestions about what social workers can do to improve the quality of life for sexual minorities in rural communities?

3. Similarly, interview a person with a severe physical disability to get similar feedback about the strengths and deficiencies of rural life for the disabled.

4. Contact rural units of Alcoholics Anonymous and inquire how they handle issues of anonymity, stigma, social control, and professional treatment resources in rural communities. These contacts can be located through the AA Web site http://www .alcoholics-anonymous.org. Some rural units have e-mail addresses; others have toll-free telephone numbers.

REFERENCES

Booth, B. M., & McLaughlin, Y. S. (2000). Barriers to and need for alcohol services for women in rural populations. *Alcoholism: Clinical and Experimental Research, 24*(8), 1267–1275.

Borys, D. S., & Pope, K. S. (1989). Dual relationships between therapist and client: A national study of psychologists, psychiatrists, and social workers. *Professional Psychology: Research and Practice, 20*(5), 283–293.

Brace, E. (1976). *Life of Charles Loring Brace chiefly told in his own letters.* Manchester, NH: Ayer Company Printers.

Carlton-LaNey, I. B., Edwards, R. L., & Reid, P. N. (Eds.). (1999). *Preserving and strengthening small towns and rural communities.* Washington, DC: National Association of Social Work Press.

Cather, W. (1918). *My Antonia.* New York: Houghton-Mifflin.

Coale, H. W. (1998). *The vulnerable therapist: Practicing psychotherapy in an age of anxiety.* New York: Haworth.

Dunbar, E. R. (1999). Strengthening services in rural communities through blended funding. In E. B. Carlton-LaNey, R. L. Edwards, & P. N. Reid (Eds.), *Preserving and strengthening small towns and rural communities* (pp. 15–26). Washington, DC: National Association of Social Work Press.

Fekete, D. M., Bond, G. R., McDonel, E. C., Salyers, M., Chen, A., & Miller, L. (1998). Rural assertive community treatment: A field experiment. *Psychiatric Rehabilitation Journal, 21,* 371–379.

Foster, S. J. (1997). Rural lesbians and gays: Public perceptions, worker perceptions, and service delivery. In J. D. Smith, R. J. Mancoske, and J. Ronald (Eds.), *Rural gays and lesbians: Building on the strengths of communities* (pp. 23–35). New York: Haworth.

Ginsberg, L. (1993). *Social work in rural communities* (2nd ed.). Alexandria, VA: Council on Social Work Education.

Jacob, S., Willits, F. K., & Jensen, L. (1996). Residualism and rural America: A decade later. *Journal of Sociology and Social Welfare, 23*(3), 151–162.

Johnson, M. (2001). Meeting health care needs of a vulnerable population: Perceived barriers. *Journal of Community Health Nursing, 18,* 35–52.

Lindhorst, T. (1997). Lesbians and gay men in the country: Practice implications for rural social workers. In J. D. Smith, R. J. Mancoske, and J. Ronald (Eds.), *Rural gays and lesbians: Building on the strengths of communities* (pp. 1–11). New York: Haworth.

Martinez-Brawley, E. (2000). *Close to home: Human services and the small community.* Washington, DC: National Association of Social Work Press.

McCoy, V., McCoy, C. B., Lai, S., Weatherly, N. L., & Messiah, S. (1999). Behavior change among crack-using rural and urban women. *Substance Use and Misuse, 34,* 667–684.

Miller, P. (1994). Dual relationships in rural practice: A dilemma of ethics and culture. *Human Services in the Rural Environment, 18*(2), 4–8.

Morris, J. A. (Ed.). (1997). *Practicing psychology in rural settings: Hospital privileges and collaborative care.* Washington, DC: American Psychological Association.

National Association of Social Workers. (1996). *NASW Code of Ethics.* Washington, DC: Author.

O'Looney, J. (1993). Organizing services in rural communities: Moving toward service integration and flexible specialization Part I: Models for organizing service delivery. *Human Services in the Rural Environment, 16*(4), 22–29.

Pusic, E. (1970). Lecture material, Doctoral seminar in social policy, University of Pennsylvania. Spring semester, 1970.

Reamer, F. (1998). *Ethical standards in social work: A critical review of the NASW Code of Ethics.* Washington, DC: National Association of Social Work Press.

Scales, T. L., & Cooper, H. S. (1999). Family violence in rural areas: Law enforcement and social workers working together for change. In I. B. Carlton-LeNey, R. L. Edwards, & P. N. Reid (Eds.), *Preserving and strengthening small towns and rural communities* (pp. 104–116). Washington, DC: National Association of Social Work Press.

Smith, J. D. (1997). Working with larger systems: Rural lesbians and gays. In J. D. Smith, R. J. Mancoske, and & J. Ronald (Eds.), *Rural gays and lesbians: Building on the strengths of communities* (pp. 13–21). New York: Haworth.

Smith, J. D., & Mancoske, R. J. (Eds.). (1997). *Rural gays and lesbians: Building on the strengths of communities.* New York: Haworth.

Speck, R. V., & Attneave, C. L. (1973). *Family networks.* New York: Vintage Books.

Spence, S. (1994). Informal assistance for older rural African Americans: A study of the relationship between perceived need and extent of support. *Human Services in the Rural Environment, 18*(2), 8–11.

Wodarski, J., Giordano, J., & Bagarozzi, D. (1981). Training for competent community mental health practice: Implications for rural social work. *Arete 6*(4), 45–62.

INFOTRAC COLLEGE EDITION

assets
helping
mutuality

natural helping
networks
rural

7

African Americans in Rural Areas

Building on Assets from an Afrocentric Perspective

FREDDIE L. AVANT

African Americans in rural areas have consistently been disadvantaged compared to urban African Americans and other ethnic groups living in rural areas. Unemployment among rural African Americans is twice as high as other groups in rural areas. Rural African Americans often live in distinct communities with high poverty, a lack of opportunity, and limited economic benefits derived from more education and training (Economic Research Service (USDA), 2002).

Although the socioeconomic conditions of rural areas were more favorable at the end of the 1990s, in this decade rural areas still lag behind urban areas in earnings and income levels, as well as experience higher poverty rates. Rural areas have seen a growth in the African American population. With historically higher rates of poverty and unemployment and lower levels of education, African Americans represent a disproportionate share of the disadvantaged segment of the rural population. Now, as in the past, many African Americans growing up in these areas who develop the skills to succeed must use them elsewhere, leaving behind an even poorer community (Economic Research Service (USDA), 2002). The current U.S. Census data reveal that people of color make up over 30 percent of the total U.S. population, and are projected to become greater than 50 percent in the year 2060 (U.S. Bureau of the Census, 2000). African Americans are one of the largest ethnic groups living in rural areas. According to U.S. Census 2000, over 56 million people are living in rural areas, with over 6 million being African Americans. Geographically,

53.6% of African Americans live in the South, 18.8% live in the Midwest, 18% live in the Northeast, and 9.6% live in the West (U.S. Bureau of the Census, 2000). There has been a reverse migration of African Americans to the South as part of a quest to reestablish roots and improve their economic situation (Miller & Jonsson, 2001). The 2000 Census reveals that for the first time this century, the South's African-American population grew faster than that of any other region in the 1990s. Many African Americans have returned to the South because of an expanding economy, history, the climate, the pull of tradition, and the overall comfort level of being around family (Miller & Jonsson, 2001). African Americans can serve as vital resources for rural communities. For example, Miller & Jonsson indicate African Americans returning to the South are becoming more politically active and assuming various leadership positions in their communities. By combining the skills of returning African Americans and those lifelong community leaders, social workers can help build assets for rural communities.

Demographic data suggest that within a professional "lifetime" of practice, a social worker most likely will come into contact with persons from cultural backgrounds other than her or his own. Thus, social work practitioners should be prepared to work competently with African Americans in rural areas.

Nastasi, Varjas, Bernstein, and Jayasena (2000) suggest that effective practice is based on four areas. First, there must be knowledge and understanding of the diversity of populations we serve. Second, we must be able to work with individuals from a multitude of cultures different from our own. Third, we must be able to conduct assessments that are nondiscriminatory and have high treatment validity. Finally, we must be able to develop interventions that can address all of the diverse needs of the population we serve.

Social work has a specific commitment to understanding diversity and human strength at both the personal and political levels (Hartman, 1993; Saleebey, 1992). Therefore, it is imperative to examine and apply theories that build upon human strengths. As a way to understand and meet the diverse needs of populations, different theories of cultural styles have been proposed.

A considerable amount of the social work literature has been directed at addressing the concerns of people of color. The social work practice models most frequently discussed are ethnic-sensitive (Devore & Schlesinger, 1981; Lum, 1992), cross-cultural (Greene & Ephross, 1991; Chau, 1992), and the black experience-based framework (Martin & Martin, 1995). In social work practice, these models are adapted to serve people of color, with special attention given to racism (Pinderhughes, 1989; Schiele, 1996). Although these approaches stress the need for cultural awareness and sensitivity, they do not emphasize the importance of cultural values of people of color as a theoretical base for understanding and addressing problems. Moreover, practice models that are not based on the cultural values of people of color can be viewed as ethnocentric; that is, based on the belief that one set of values is the only set that can explain behavior, and should be the basis for solving people's problems (Schiele, 1996).

Consequently, few practice models are based on theoretical foundations that mirror the diversity of cultural values and worldviews found in the U.S. society, which includes people of color. Because people of color, especially African Americans, experience greater poverty and have fewer material resources than the general population (U.S. Bureau of the Census, 1994), it is important that cultural values be considered in the development of practice models. Social work educators and practitioners should begin to affirm and integrate cultural values and worldviews of African Americans in the development of practice models, scholarship, and professional practice.

In addition, it is imperative to build on the assets of people of color to strengthen their involvement in the social work process. Building assets is about establishing positive, sustained relationships that are so critical to working with people of color in rural areas. Working with African Americans from this perspective will allow their talents, interests, and values to develop in ways that help them reach personal goals and contribute to society. The Afrocentric perspective is an approach to working with African Americans that identifies and builds on their assets as a way to resolve problems (Schiele, 1996).

The purpose of this article will be to examine the Afrocentric perspective and apply it to practice with African Americans in rural areas. This perspective supports the asset-building framework by emphasizing the human capacity for resiliency, strength in the face of adversity, and the right of individuals to form their own aspirations and definitions of their situations.

AFROCENTRIC PERSPECTIVE

Theoretical foundations are necessary for understanding and creating shared realities. The Afrocentric perspective illustrates how developing knowledge of another culture from the viewpoint of that culture can transform social work practice (Swigonski, 1996). The development of knowledge from this perspective conveys a powerful means of empowerment for clients. The Afrocentric perspective describes the ethos and values of Africans and African Americans (Everett, Chipungu, & Leashore, 1991). This perspective proposes a frame of reference in which African history, culture, and worldviews become the context for understanding Africans and African Americans (Asante, 1988).

According to Barker (1999), Afrocentric theory is an orientation or social philosophy that uses cultural values, history, and shared experiences of people of African descent as a framework to explain social phenomena and to solve human problems. It is in direct opposition to deficit models that focus exclusively on weaknesses and problems in the behaviors of people of color. This perspective provides a viewpoint from which to develop a proactive stance and emphasize assets (Swigonski, 1996). The construction of models of human behavior from an Afrocentric perspective portrays African Americans in ways that are free from ethnocentrism.

The birth of the Afrocentric perspective paralleled the movement to redefine blacks as African Americans, a people with their own history and culture. This new way of viewing African Americans was pioneered by Molefi Kete Asante, a professor of African-American studies. The Afrocentric perspective originated from an African-centered philosophy that was called Afrocentrism. The development of Afrocentrism was viewed as being much broader than merely understanding African-American culture (Asante, 1990). It advanced a strengths-based approach and countered the perception of inferiority and the political disempowerment of African Americans by affirming identities and ethnic national pride. It further validated the experiences and worldviews of African Americans.

Although the literature suggests the importance of understanding African Americans using an Afrocentric perspective, it is just as important to recognize and respect differences within groups as it is to acknowledge differences between groups. Moreover, understanding African Americans within their context at least begins the operationalization of the maxim in social work practice that states "start where the client is." This is such an important principle for both beginning and experienced social work practitioners. Coupled with this principle, the Afrocentric perspective can be a guiding post for all social workers who work with African American populations. The Afrocentric perspective affirms three major assumptions about human beings that will be explained in more detail in this section: (1) human identity is a collective identity, (2) the spiritual or nonmaterial component of human beings is just as important and valid as the material component, and (3) the affective approach to knowledge is epistemologically valid (Akbar, 1984; Asante, 1988; Kambon, 1992; Schiele, 1990).

Individual Identity
as Collective Identity

A noteworthy characteristic central to the Afrocentric perspective is that the group is much more important than the individual. Human identity as a collective identity emphasizes the significance of culture within the social group (Baldwin & Hopkins, 1990; Asante, 1988; Schiele, 1997b). This validates the common experiences, beliefs and values of African Americans. Most African Americans share a common history of slavery that greatly influences their lives. This history is very important and must be taken into consideration to properly understand the Afrocentric worldview (Swigonski, 1996; Schiele, 1990). Cooperation, interdependence, the collective responsibility of the individual to the group, and the commonality of individuals are highly stressed in the Afrocentric worldview. Thus, the Afrocentric perspective conceives the individual identity as a fluid and interconnected way of uniquely expressing a collective or group ethos.

This perspective does not discard the uniqueness of the individual but it does reject the idea that the individual can be understood separately from others in his or her social group (Akbar, 1984). The focus on collectivity in the Afrocentric perspective also encourages an emphasis on sharing, cooperation, and social responsibility (Martin & Martin, 1985; Kambon, 1992). The African-American family is seen as a cohesive unit. The family should not be equated with nuclear family but should, instead, include the nuclear family plus kin and other persons, blood-related or not, who share in the family group experience.

Spiritual Nature of Human Beings

The Afrocentric perspective recognizes the importance of spirituality or the nonmaterial aspects of human beings. From an Afrocentric perspective, spirituality is concerned with the ability, through our attitudes and actions, to relate to others, to ourselves, and to a Creator or a Supreme Being (Schiele, 1994). The term *spiritual* also refers to practices, insights, states of being and frames of references most influenced by forces beyond, and inclusive of, the individual and his or her personal, interpersonal, and suprapersonal (or transcendent) experiences.

In traditional African philosophy, God, or the generative spirit, is thought to be reflected in all elements of the universe and is thus seen as the connective link between humanity and the universe (Zahan, 1979). In the Afrocentric perspective, the soul is considered just as much a legitimate source of study as the mind and body. In addition, the soul, mind, and body are considered interdependent and interrelated phenomena (Schiele, 1994; Lee, 2002). While specific teachings and beliefs vary among African Americans, there is an almost universal belief in the importance of spirituality and the influence of spiritual forces in the balance of one's life. Health and well-being are believed to be the result of the complex interplay between the physical world (i.e., our bodies), our mental processes (our thoughts and emotions), our environment (our family, culture, etc.), and the spiritual forces outside of us and the learned spiritual practices that become part of us.

From the Afrocentric perspective, spirituality is viewed very broadly. It is more than religion. It is the complex and often conflicting nature of spiritual teachings, a sense of purpose and being, of the future, and of a higher power guiding and shaping our existence. It includes religion and religious teachings from every conceivable point of view. The mind, body, and soul are believed to have equal weight and must be balanced to achieve a state of well-being. In the African-American community spirituality is viewed as an important factor in the mental well-being of children and families (Zahan, 1979; Lee, 2002; Martin & Martin, 1985).

Affective Knowledge

In the Afrocentric perspective, affect (feeling or emotions) is viewed as a valid source of knowing. In this perspective reasoning or thoughts do not occur in a vacuum but are filtered through the maze of people's emotions and values (Kambon, 1992; Schiele, 1996). Thus, thoughts do not occur independently of feelings, and feelings do not occur independently of thoughts. A major principle of Afrocentricity is that emotions are the most direct experience of self (Akbar, 1984).

The Afrocentric perspective begins to build on the strengths and assets of African Americans. It is considered a social science paradigm predicated on the philosophical concepts of contemporary African Americans and traditional Africa (Akbar, 1984; Schiele, 1996). Several authors believe that the social isolation of African Americans created by slavery and racial segregation, in addition to sustaining the desire to maintain tradition, helped preserve traditional African philosophical assumptions among African Americans (Akbar, 1979; Martin & Martin, 1985). Researchers who have advanced the Afrocentric perspective acknowledge a variation in the degree of internalization of traditional African values among African Americans. However, the literature suggests that traditional African culture has survived to the point where it can support a distinct cultural and ethnic group. Therefore, the application of Eurocentric theories of human behavior to explain the behavior and ethos of African Americans is inappropriate (Akbar, 1979, 1984; Baldwin & Hopkins, 1990; Kambon, 1992).

Using an Afrocentric Perspective to Build Assets

Historically, African Americans have struggled in our society with social and economic policies and practices that have been extremely exclusionary. From the beginning of slavery to the present, concern for issues of social equality and justice remain part of their lifestyle. For years, African Americans have shouldered the blame for their own oppression, as family instability, drug use, and welfare dependency were said to be the chief sources of their plight (Solomon, 1976). The Afrocentric perspective gives African Americans an identity and a sense of pride.

One important factor that is valuable in understanding how to work with African Americans in rural areas is the type of lens or worldview through which they perceive their experiences. Montgomery, Fine, and Jaer-Myers (1990) define "worldview" as a structure of philosophical assumptions, values, and principles upon which one may perceive the world. According to Kambon (1992) the worldview orientation is the index of functioning of people of color, especially African Americans. An Afrocentric worldview is described as a holistic perspective, assuming a spiritual/material unity and the interconnectedness of all things (Myers, 1988). It is centered in a spiritual and kinship connection to African culture (Asante, 1990). Examples of values inherent in the Afrocentric worldview include cooperativeness, cohesiveness, oneness with nature, spirituality, positive interpersonal relationships, and flexible time orientation (Kambon, 1992; Myers, 1988). It is well-known in the African-American community that time does not control the nature and extent of the social events of the day. Many authors writing about the Afrocentric perspective suggest that those who embrace the worldview orientation to understanding African Americans build on their strengths and not their weaknesses.

This approach encourages practitioners to take an asset-building perspective when problem-solving with African Americans. Incorporating African Americans' own perceptions of their problems and solutions into the problem-solving process validates their view of their situation. This is very important in assessing and choosing appropriate intervention strategies. Many times, African Americans are denied the right to define themselves in their own terms or to define their experiences within their own contexts and meanings

(Swigonski, 1996). When working with African Americans, using an Afrocentric perspective to understanding problems is a more culturally competent approach than applying a Eurocentric perspective. The chosen theoretical orientation will determine the view of the presenting problems and the practical solutions. In other words, meeting the needs of the individual without regard to the collective group will not address the problems.

Myers (1988) sees the Afrocentic and Eurocentric worldviews as contradicting and conflicting with one another. For example, he argues that from the Eurocentric worldview, one's self-worth is contingent upon individualism and material acquisition. The Afrocentric worldview stresses cooperation, group connectedness, and kinship bonding.

The lifestyle of rural African Americans is very traditional (Solomon, 1976; Baldwin & Hopkins, 1990). Relationships are defined by the people you know and the shared experiences that have strengthened relationships between people living in the rural communities. For rural African Americans, kinships and friendships are based on interpersonal and social experiences (Martinez-Brawley, 1990, 2000).

Using the Afrocentric perspective, the considerable strengths of African-American families become visible. Rather than placing primary focus on the nuclear family, this perspective emphasizes the significance of the extended family in African American culture. The Afrocentric perspective redirects social work practice to address family problems by developing support and resources that include collective efforts, self-help, and mutual aid (Everett, Chipungu, & Leashore, 1991). Developing resources through social, civic, fraternal, and religious groups explicitly emerges from the African value of collective work and responsibility (Everett, Chipungu, & Leashore, 1991). Social work practice from an Afrocentric perspective challenges the social work profession to examine other practical approaches to working with clients. Social work practitioners must develop alternative social structures that both empower and confront the oppression and injustice of existing systems and structures (Solomon, 1976; Asante, 1988; Schiele, 1997a). Competency-based practice must include placing the culture of African Americans at the center of the practice model. This requires a theoretical framework for social work practice that is asset-based, which builds on the strengths and assets of African Americans.

AFRICAN AMERICANS IN RURAL AREAS

According to Census 2000, definitions of rural areas must give attention to classifications of urbanized areas (UA) and urban clusters (UC). Urbanized areas (UAs) consist of a densely settled core of census block groups, along with surrounding census blocks that encompass a population of at least 50,000 people. Urban clusters (UCs) consist of a densely settled core of census blocks along with adjacent densely settled census blocks that have a population of at least 2,500 but fewer than 50,000 people. Rural populations are classified as those not residing in either UAs or UCs. Based on this definition, there exists a significant rural population.

Census data show that the United States population is 281.4 million (U.S. Bureau of the Census, 2000). For the first time since the beginning of census reports, respondents could self-identify. This means individual and families could choose their own racial background. The census data collected on race can be separated into two categories: those who self-identify with one race and those who choose to self-identify with multiple racial groups. Of the total U.S. population, 36.4 million people, or 12.9%, self-identified as having a black or African-American racial background. This number includes 34.7 million people, or 12.3%, who reported only black, in addition to 1.8 million people, or .06%, who reported black as well as one or more other racial group. One way to define the African-American population is to combine those respondents who

reported only "black" with those who reported black as well as one or more racial group. Another way is to define the African-American population by counting those who chose to identify themselves as African American only. The author chooses the former definition to discuss the African-American population in rural areas. Using this definition, census data report 21.5% growth in the African-American population (U.S. Bureau of the Census, 2000). This definition more clearly reflects the growth of the African-American population and provides a more accurate representation of the biracial composition of African Americans living in rural areas. Historically, racial categories have limited the extent that persons of color could identify their own ethnicity. This definition supports an asset-building perspective by allowing African Americans to recognize and value their own diversity.

Across the nation rural communities differ drastically from one another. No single set of prescriptions could possibly apply to all rural communities of African Americans. However, there are some common characteristics of rural communities that make them similar. Thus, in attempting to identify the salient characteristics that define rural lifestyle, the focus has been on community deficits such as poverty, the need for transportation, poor housing, inadequate education and health care systems, lack of employment opportunities, and shortage of professionals.

The lifestyles of African Americans are significantly affected by these problems. For example, the poverty rate for rural African Americans (20.7%) is higher than for any other group (Economic Research Service (USDA), 1996). Rural poverty rates for African Americans are also higher in the South and West, which is where most are living (Economic Research Service (USDA), 1996).

Education is a strong predictor of income. In rural areas of the United States, level-of-education differences account for 24 percent of the difference in poverty rates between African Americans and people of European descent. The differences in household structure also result in higher poverty rates for African Americans in rural areas. Thirty percent of African American households are female-headed families. Education and household structure only partially explain the nature and extent of poverty rates of rural African Americans. Even for persons with similar education in households of the same type, poverty rates for African Americans remain high. Likely explanations of these differences include discrimination in employment and wages, and concentrations of African Americans in areas that are unable to attract high-wage employers (Economic Research Service (USDA), 1996).

Much of this discussion has focused on the problems of rural areas. Unfortunately, the literature itself tends to present rural lifestyle from a deficit perspective. However, rural communities and rural lifestyles have many assets and strengths that should be used to work with African Americans. For example, rural communities have strong natural helping networks. They are rich in traditions that promote the values of independence and hard work, strong links to family and the land, and social institutions such as the church. African Americans have a strong connection to traditions, extended family, and spirituality. Understanding the strengths inherent in rural communities and lifestyles is important for the social work helping process when working with African Americans (Martinez-Brawley, 1990, 2000).

Understanding Human Behavior of African Americans in Rural Environments

The Afrocentric perspective can be used as a foundation for understanding the behaviors of African Americans and for implementing rural practice models that are effective. Most current theories of human behavior and practice models are Eurocentric models that have been adapted to work with people of color. The Afrocentric perspective is more applicable for understanding and working with African Americans. Many authors stress the importance of culturally sensitive practice by combining appropriate theoretical frameworks with practice models. An Afrocentric perspective includes features that are based on African and African-American assumptions that support a practical approach for understanding and addressing the needs of African Americans in rural areas. Rural social work practice is defined as the many social work related activities that involve working with and for people in and from rural areas to bring about change in their social functioning. It is important to work with rural African Americans from a cultural or lifestyle perspective, as well as considering the geographical perspective (Daley & Avant, 1999). As African Americans migrate to rural areas, they may need services but could also serve as valuable resources for social work practitioners. The cultural or lifestyle perspective for defining rurality is also appropriate and applicable to working with rural African Americans who must travel to urban areas to receive services.

The Afrocentric perspective will assist social work practitioners in engaging rural African Americans in the helping process. Traditions are very strong for rural African Americans, and many traditional gatherings are held by families and communities in rural areas. The rural church continues to serve as the center of both spiritual development and social activities. Rural churches also function as community centers for youth and adults, serving as places where African Americans gather to meet, mingle, eat, and create social relationships. Many African-American churches have created rural community family life centers. They serve as resources for spiritual enhancement and community outreach for addressing many of the social and economical issues being faced by African Americans (Martin & Martin, 1985; Martinez-Brawley, 2000). Church members also create a natural support system to help one another. Pastors or spiritual leaders are primary leaders in rural communities and many community and personal decisions are influenced by spiritual leaders. It is important that social workers include spiritual leaders, local civic groups, women's and men's clubs, and fraternities as resources.

CONCLUSION

The Afrocentric perspective provides a culturally specific approach for serving African Americans in rural areas. Although currently used primarily by African-American social workers, the Afrocentric perspective and practice are tools that all social workers can use. Cheatham, Tomilinson, and Ward (1990) emphasize that embracing one's ethnic heritage is an essential part of the developmental process of African Americans. Schiele (1994) suggests that a positive African American identity can help foster resistance to a number of life problems such as drug addiction, violence, and social injustices. The Afrocentric perspective can serve as a theoretical foundation for building assets with African Americans in rural areas.

DISCUSSION QUESTIONS

1. It is important for social workers to understand the lifestyles of their clients to effectively assess and intervene when necessary. Discuss the significance of the application of the Afrocentric perspective and the implications for practice with African Americans.

2. The author proposes the Afrocentric perspective as a way to begin understanding the lifestyles of African Americans in rural areas. In your opinion, is this perspective appropriate for rural social work practice? What are some strengths and limitations of this perspective?

3. What is the racial or ethnic make up of the population in your area? Is your area ethnically segregated or more integrated? What are the histories of different ethnic groups in the area? How might the histories of different groups affect the community today?

CLASSROOM ASSIGNMENTS
AND ACTIVITIES

1. Interview someone who is considered a "spiritual leader" for African-American people in your area. Keep in mind that spiritual leaders come from a variety of different religious traditions. Share what you learned from the interview with your class. Discuss together how that spiritual tradition may serve as an asset to African Americans.

2. Observe the lifestyles of people of color in your area. Are they visible in the community? Where do they live and work? How are their lifestyles different from others living in the area?

3. The 2000 Census data gave people of color a new outlook. Individuals were able for the first time to self-identify one or multiple ethnic categories. Using Census data for your area, research how this change affected the demographics of the population. What are some strengths as well as limitations of this new approach?

REFERENCES

Akbar, N. (1979). African roots of black personality. In W. D. Smith, H. Kathleen, M. H. Burlew, & W. M. Whitney (Eds.), *Reflections on black psychology* (pp. 79–87). Washington, DC: University Press of America.

Akbar, N. (1984). Africentric social sciences for human liberation. *Journal of Black Studies, 14,* 395–414.

Asante, M. K. (1988). *Afrocentricity: The theory of social change.* Trenton, NJ: Africa World Press.

Asante, M. K. (1990). *Kemet, afrocentricity, and knowledge.* Trenton, NJ: Africa World Press.

Baldwin, J., & Hopkins, R. (1990). African-American and European-American cultural differences as assessed by the worldviews paradigm: An empirical analysis. *Western Journal of Black Studies, 14,* 38–52.

Barker, R. L. (1999). *The social work dictionary* (4th ed.). Washington, DC: National Association of Social Work Press.

Chau, K. L. (1992). Educating for effective group work practice in multicultural environments of 1990s. *Journal of Multicultural Social Work, 1*(4), 1–15.

Cheatham, H. E., Tomilinson, S. M., & Ward, T. J. (1990). The African self-consciousness construct and African American students. *Journal of College Student Development, 31,* 6, 492–499.

Daley, M., & Avant, F. (1999). Attracting and retaining professionals for social work practice in rural areas: An example from East Texas. In I. B. Carlton-LaNey, R. L. Richards, & P. N. Reid (Eds.), *Preserving and strengthening small towns and rural communities* (pp. 335–345). Washington, DC: National Association of Social Work Press.

Devore, W., & Schlesinger, E. G. (1981). *Ethnic sensitive social work practice.* St. Louis, MO: Mosby.

Economic Research Service (USDA). (1996). *Rural Conditions and Trends, 9 (*2), 81–90.

Economic Research Service (USDA). (2002). *Rural population and migration: Rural Population Change, 11*(2), 1–5.

Everett, J. E., Chipungu, S. S., & Leashore, B. B. (Eds.). (1991). *Child welfare: An Africentric perspective.* New Brunswick, NJ: Rutgers University Press.

Greene, R. R., & Ephross, P. H. (1991). *Human behavior theory and social work practice.* New York: Aldine de Gruyter.

Hartman, A. (1993). The professional is political. *Social Work, 38*(4), 365–368.

Kambon, K. (1992). *The African personality in America: An African-centered framework.* Tallahassee, FL: Nubian Nation Publication.

Lee, G. (2002). *Religion and spirituality: Coping mechanisms for African American women living in poverty* (Dissertation Proposal). Jackson State University (Mississippi) School of Social Work.

Lum, D. (1992). *Social work practice & people of color: A process-stage approach.* Pacific Grove, CA: Brooks/Cole.

Martin, E. P., & Martin, J. M. (1985). *The helping traditions in the black family and community.* Silver Spring, MD: National Association of Social Workers.

Martin, E. P., & Martin, J. M. (1995). *Social work and the black experience.* Washington, DC: National Association of Social Workers.

Martinez-Brawley, E. E. (1990). *Perspective on the small community: Humanistic views for practitioners.* Washington, DC: National Association of Social Work Press.

Martinez-Brawley, E. E. (2000). *Close to home: Human services and the small community.* Washington, DC: National Association of Social Work Press.

Miller, S. B., & Jonsson, P. (2001). For African Americans, trend is back to the south. *Christian Science Monitor, 93,* 143, 1–4.

Montgomery, D. E., Fine, M. A., & Jaer-Myers, L. (1990). The development and validation of an instrument to assess an optimal afrocentric world view. *Journal of Black Psychology, 17,* 37–54.

Myers, L. J. (1988). *Understanding an afrocentric world view: Introduction to an optimal psychology.* Dubuque, IA: Kendall/Hunt.

Nastasi, B. K., Varjas, K., Bernstein, R., & Jayasena, A. (2000). Conducting participator culture-specific consultation: A global perspective on multicultural consultation. *School Psychology Review, 29,* 401–413.

Pinderhughes, E. (1989). *Understanding race, ethnicity and power.* New York: Free Press.

Saleebey, D. (Ed.). (1992). *The strengths perspective in social work practice.* New York: Longman.

Schiele, J. H. (1990). Organization theory from an afrocentric perspective. *Journal of Black Studies, 21,* 2, 145–161.

Schiele, J. H. (1994). Afrocentricity as an alternative world view for equality. *Journal of Progressive Human Services, 5,* 1, 5–25.

Schiele, J. H. (1996). Afrocentricity: An emerging paradigm in social work practice. *Social Work, 41*(3), 284–294.

Schiele, J. H. (1997a). An afrocentric perspective on social welfare philosophy and policy. *Journal of Sociology and Social Welfare, 24*(2), 21–39.

Schiele, J. H. (1997b). The contour and meaning of afrocentric social work. *Journal of Black Studies, 27*(6), 800–819.

Solomon, B. B. (1976). *Black empowerment: Social work in oppressed communities.* New York: Columbia University Press.

Swigonski, M. E. (1996). Challenging privilege through africentric social work practice. *Social Work, 41,* 2, 153–161.

U.S. Bureau of the Census. (1994). Statistical abstract of the United States. Washington, DC: U.S. Government Printing Office.

U.S. Bureau of the Census. (2000). Urban and rural classification census 2000: Urban and rural criteria. Retrieved March 28, 2002, from http://www.census .gov/geo/www/ua/ua_2k.html.

Zahan, D. (1979). *The religion, spirituality, and thought of traditional Africa.* Chicago: Univeristy of Chicago Press.

INFOTRAC COLLEGE EDITION

African Americans
African culture
Afrocentric
oppression

religion
rurality
spirituality

8

Life in a *Colonia*

Identifying Community Assets

WILMA CORDOVA

Understanding and identifying assets is essential to implementing successful changes within communities. Assets can be defined as "individual, association and organizational skills, talents, gifts, resources and strengths that are shared with the community" (Connecticut Assets Network, 1999, p. 1). Traditional methods of asset identification have been needs-driven, but Kretzmann and McKnight (1993) recommend an "alternative path" in which communities are viewed from a "capacity-focused development" process (p. 5). This alternative path indicates a more positive approach by identifying those community assets already in place. In this article, a capacity-focused process will be used to identify existing assets within a *colonia*.

Asset building, from a financial perspective, involves the process in which one increases economic gains. Asset building is much the same process in communities. Those who live in *colonias*, within a rural community, experience a unique and challenging way of life. One issue is high unemployment rates, causing those who live in *colonias* to struggle with poverty, lack of concrete services, and lack of tangible resources. Research is limited in regard to how residents of *colonias* develop and maintain their own formal and informal support systems. Another challenge for those living in rural *colonias* is the struggle to be valued and accepted as part of the community at large. People of the *colonias* learn to establish their own sense of belonging and empowerment to maintain an identity within a rural community.

In this article a rural *colonia* will be discussed as well as how, despite many barriers to a more convenient way of life, people of *colonias* rally together to support one another and implement their own process of community development. Understanding those who live in *colonias* and their way of life, including their customs and beliefs, contributes to the social worker's knowledge base. My aim in writing this article is to inform social workers and stimulate further research. The community to be examined is in East Texas and although it would not be included in the most narrow geographic definitions of a *colonia,* its struggles are the same as other *colonias.*

WHAT IS A *COLONIA* AND WHO LIVES THERE?

Colonia, in the Spanish language, means "neighborhood or community." According to one definition, Texas *colonias* are similar in that they share the same struggles as developing countries. The hardships include coping with lack of running water, proper drainage of sewage, and the lack of other services such as street lighting, paved roads, and electricity (Ward, 1999). Several authors have limited the definitions of *colonias* to those communities along the U.S.-Mexican border. However, with the large influx of Mexican immigrants into the United States, these neighborhoods appear to be forming as far away as 500 miles from the border areas. Such is the case with the *colonias* in Nacogdoches (pronounced Nack-a-doe-chez), Texas, in which the residents of *colonias* come from countries other than Mexico, including Nicaragua and El Salvador, who travel 1,500 miles and more to settle in rural and remote communities (J. H. Montoya, personal communication, September 14, 2001). Some geographical definitions are more specific, defining *colonias* as rural communities and neighborhoods located within 150 miles of the U.S.-Mexican border and lacking adequate infrastructures and other services (U.S. Department of Housing, 2000).

Colonias in the United States are believed to have existed since the 1950s (Dabir, 2001), but were not acknowledged until the 1980s, when there was the possibility of an epidemic of cholera. During this time, the state of Texas was embarrassed politically because of its "Third World" conditions (Ward, 1999). According to Ward, it was not until the late 1980s and early 1990s that Texas legislators attempted to convince Congress of the need for federal funds to improve conditions. Though these areas continue to struggle with health issues because of the lack of adequate infrastructure, services are available through the local clinics. Ward also notes that serious health issues are evident along the U.S.–Mexico border *colonias,* where diseases such as shigellosis and hepatitis are contracted at twice the U.S. rate. Some of these conditions continue today as *colonias* continue to exist.

Little is known about health issues in the neighborhoods of Mexicans living in "Third World" conditions in the rural community of Nacogdoches. As Fitchen (1998) explains, the rural poor are invisible because they live in places where few others live or travel. The geographical isolation of the various Nacogdoches *colonias* and the poor road conditions within them deter outsiders from coming in. Plus, the residents appear to prefer remaining invisible, or to some degree inconspicuous. Children are unable to get to health services and at times families are unwilling to seek services.

In order to discuss how *colonias* in East Texas sustain their own support systems, it is important to understand the difference between a settlement and a community. Ward (1999) compares Mexican *colonias* and U.S. *colonias*, noting that Mexican *colonias* maintain a greater sense of community versus settlement. A settlement is defined by spatial and demographic terms that do not identify a particular social infrastructure of governance. In contrast, communities have shared goals and values that govern social behavior and organization. Settlements depend on "supra-local" decision making for project initiatives and programs to be implemented, whereas communities tend to be more proactive, seeking links with external agents and identifying their own needs (Ward, 1999). The *colonias* in Nacogdoches are settlements that lack the cohesion to advocate. As a result, there have been isolated incidents of exploitation, though residents of each *colonia* attempt to protect one another.

A *COLONIA* IN RURAL EAST TEXAS: *"LA SELVA"*

Nacogdoches County is located in the piney woods of East Texas, about 100 miles from a metropolitan area. It has a land area of 947 square miles and a population of 58,874 (U.S. Bureau of the Census, 2001). Nacogdoches struggles with its own challenges regarding lack of resources and services for an increasing population of Mexican and other Latin American migrants. The current U.S. Census data indicates that 11.2% of Nacogdoches County is of Hispanic or Latino origin (these terms are used interchangeably by the U.S. Census Bureau.) The 1990 Census information estimated only 4%, which indicates that the Hispanic/Latino population in the county has more than doubled in the last decade.

Three areas within Nacogdoches have been identified by county regulatory officials as lacking basic services, including city utilities. One is the *colonia* of Briar Forest, known as *La Selva* by the people living in the neighborhood. *La Selva* means "the jungle" in Spanish. One of the concerns brought to the attention of city officials is the lack of infrastructure within this particular neighborhood, which is due in part to the refusal of the city or county to take responsibility for *La Selva*. If a *colonia* falls beyond the discretionary Extra Territorial Jurisdiction (ETJ), the area often lacks basic services such as running water, drainage, street lighting, paving, and electricity (Ward, 1999). Other concerns are that the responsibilities of the city are nebulous, and there is no incentive to maintain the *colonia,* due to the lack of voter constituency there.

According to Ward (1999), *colonia* homes are comprised of a mixture of trailers and self-built constructions that may eventually become brick-built dwellings. Such is the case in *La Selva*. The area was initially settled by local residents who, in the late 1980s to early 1990s, were joined by migrants from Mexico and other countries. Often when Mexican families move to a new country, one family moves into a home and eventually other extended family members are brought to live in the same home until they can make arrangements to acquire their own residence. As these families migrate into the area, other close family friends, known as *compadres,* move in with the family. The neighborhood of *La Selva* is home to 170–180 families, mostly of Mexican descent (J. H. Montoya, personal communication, September 14, 2001). I initiated an opportunity to observe and converse with people in *La Selva* while a new home was being constructed. During the weekend and after work hours, family members and neighbors came together to assist with the process. Although the men constructed the home, the women involved themselves with various other tasks, such as preparing meals and caring for the children. The home was completed with the help of close friends, neighbors, and family. This is a good example of how these families complete a goal and work together using their own resources.

IDENTIFYING ASSETS
IN A *COLONIA*

Community Traditions as Assets

The people of *La Selva* tend to be culturally focused and continue practicing their customs and beliefs. Typically, those living in *La Selva* socialize only with family and friends, but they celebrate birthdays and weddings to which the entire community is invited by word of mouth. As the entire neighborhood offers food, decorations, or gifts, the residents have an opportunity to fellowship with those residents outside of their normal social circle. Children's birthdays, *cumpleaños*, are celebrated despite financial hardships. A family will save money to celebrate, especially, the coming of age for female adolescents, known as a *quincinera*. Godparents are often responsible for costs and play an important role. Unhappy times are also acknowledged by community members in *La Selva,* and people come together to offer moral support. Sharing in common celebrations of good times and bad is important in *La Selva*, as many residents experience isolation from the larger community.

Natural Helping

La Selva is physically laid out in a semicircle with a radius of about one mile. The road and driveways to the homes are unpaved and wash out during heavy rain. As a result, the road cannot be traveled without a 4-wheel-drive vehicle. School buses do not even travel into the community because of the condition of the road, and children are dropped off at the corner where they are met by parents and caretakers to complete their journey to and from school and home. On occasion the men in the community have come together to grade the road and make it somewhat passable.

Because of the close proximity of homes, those without electricity run an electrical extension cord to their neighbor's outlets, and although this presents a safety issue and a possible health hazard, this is one manner in which the families of *La Selva* support one another in providing services and help a family get a step ahead. An unspoken exchange system exists between these families that is repaid in a service, or food, if the family is unable to pay for the utility with cash. The service might be in child care or transportation, as well as meeting other tangible or intangible needs.

Employment is obtained by word of mouth, and most adults are employed at a local poultry processing plant. Men also gather early in the morning in labor pools to await community people to pick them up and transport them either to their personal homes or other places of business to work for the day. The men protect one another by informing each other regarding exploitation by potential employers.

The Church as a Resource

Churches are usually one of the first places the people go for assistance. For the most part, the people of *La Selva* continue many of their religious traditions, leaving the *colonia* to attend mass in one of the two Catholic churches in Nacogdoches. Both Catholic churches, as well as some Baptist and Methodist churches, offer services in Spanish. One Christian church sits in *La Selva* by the main roadway; its minister lives in the community and is available any time. As is quite common in rural communities, churches play a major role in offering moral support, as well as in assisting with daily living necessities. They serve as counseling resources for family concerns, including crisis situations, and provide special services.

In 2000, when Immigration and Naturalization Services sanctioned amnesty for residents and their family members to apply for legal residency, Catholic churches played an important role. Because application for amnesty can be quite complicated and confusing, one of the Catholic churches organized two full-day workshops to assist Nacogdoches residents with the paperwork. A lawyer specializing in immigra-

tion and naturalization trained volunteers—members and nonmembers of the church—and assisted with the process. The church offered facilities, recruited volunteers, and announced the event during worship services.

Integration into the Larger Community

Although there does appear to be some social detachment from the community as a whole, there are small attempts at integration within Nacogdoches. One of the local churches sponsors a multicultural event in the downtown area for families to experience and celebrate a variety of cultures. Specific businesses sell traditional Mexican/Hispanic food, artifacts, and clothing, especially for religious celebrations.

Community members, including elected officials and Hispanic leaders, have attempted to make changes in neighborhoods where Hispanics reside. Some changes include assuring safe housing, passable roads, and accessibility to needed health care. As conditions improve and Hispanic leaders emerge, Nacogdoches could potentially become home to a diverse population.

The manner in which the people of *La Selva* sustain their existence and meet their needs is through informal social infrastructure. According to Ward (1999), this refers to the networks of communication and habitual contacts between individuals and the interaction to meet their needs. One good example of this is when a group of non-Catholic residents of the community expressed the need for a Pentecostal church providing Spanish-speaking services. Eventually a Pentecostal church was established within the community. This is also a good example of both horizontal and vertical integration. This phenomenon is explained by Ward (1999) as the amount of interactions at a local level and number of contacts between the community and organizations outside the community. Horizontal integration is communication at the local level and the interactions that take place among individuals to access resources. Vertical integration is the interaction with the organization and power figures outside the area (i.e., city, state, region, and federal).

The tangible needs of the people of *La Selva* have been identified within the social institutions such as public schools, health clinics, churches, and other public entities. Other entities such as the local university have groups organizing drives for clothing, food, and blankets.

In situations where there is a need for governmental intervention, leaders within a community are often identified by the amount of resources they have. This does not appear to be the case among the people of *La Selva*. At *La Selva,* leaders emerge based on the specific circumstances and situation. For example, the men of *La Selva* joined together to improve the road condition for children to get to school. They did not wait for city or county officials to determine who had jurisdiction.

How Can Social Workers Build on Assets?

To work with the people in *colonias,* one must not assume to know their needs. Social workers must respond with the highest sincerity and practice much patience. One school social worker in *La Selva* waits for people to come to him for assistance or advice. He lives among the people, and families come to his home in the evening to address what they consider emergencies when working with the school system. He states that they approach his home with respect, wait in their vehicles for him to come to them, and sincerely apologize for disturbing him at home. He states that this is a rare occurrence and is quite customary of traditional culture, in which people living in rural areas do not communicate by telephone but prefer face-to-face contact to assure sincerity and respect (J. H. Montoya, personal communication, September 14, 2001). Trust is a process in itself, because of the lack of trust in institutions, with the exception of the Church. Populations such as Hispanic immigrants and First Nations (Native American) people

may not easily trust the government for various reasons, including their history with oppressive governments (Clews, 1999).

Characteristics of Hispanic culture include the importance placed on family and personal interactions. For social workers, home visits and working with the entire family is not only important but an absolute necessity. Social workers should use caution when considering attendance of community celebrations. Unless invited, attendance may be regarded as an invasion.

To begin to build relationships with a community such as *La Selva* one must be willing to take risks. Attend public gatherings and events in the larger community where this population might be present. Volunteering at various community agencies or services such as Church bazaars, fiestas, and any programs geared toward children like Big Brother/Big Sister will provide opportunities to foster relationships. Introduce yourself as you become familiar with some of the individuals. You may have opportunities to begin to advocate for families and individuals in the workplace. For example, a bilingual school social worker hosted a Spanish program for the Nacogdoches Independent School District on their local television station. The program, entitled *La Conexion Hispaña,* featured various guests from community agencies and businesses.

The safety and care of children is important to the community; neighbors and extended family watch over them. Because of the lack of infrastructure, concerned parents have placed homemade signs along the road to warn drivers of school bus stops. Social workers might involve volunteers in service projects to post needed signs, providing opportunities for getting to know this community.

Churches are the most trusted institutions for those living in *La Selva* and need to be approached. This means a face-to-face contact with priests and ministers. Clergy may allow social workers to meet with churchgoers during Spanish services for the purpose of providing information about resources and their right to vote if they have citizenship. By participating and joining in community one can begin to identify respected leaders in a community like *La Selva*. Social workers can facilitate the process of effective asset building by allowing natural community leaders to serve as mobilizers and advocates.

LOBBYING FOR
LEGISLATIVE ACTION

At this time, there are several programs mandated by the Department of Housing and Urban Development, Department of Health, Department of Agriculture's Rural Development, and other government agencies to provide services and assistance to *colonias* along the U.S.–Mexico border. Most of this federal assistance is concentrated in a geographical location that does not meet the needs of *La Selva*. Those living in *colonias* away from the borderlands must sustain their communities the best way they can with or without financial resources. Ward (1999) compares *colonias* in the United States and Mexico, noting that Texas *colonias* have less of a sense of community than do Mexican colonias. However, Ward is only addressing those *colonias* along the border areas, so it is not known if this is also true for *colonias* outside the borderlands.

Policy issues that must be considered include drawing clear parameters between city and county government, especially in regard to areas outside city limits, referred to as Extra Territorial Jurisdiction (ETJ). This is a concern for *La Selva* as noted above. The policies I have reviewed on *colonias* all pertained to U.S.–Mexico border *colonias*. The definition of *colonia* must include areas outside the borderlands. This is especially true with the large influx of Mexican and other Latino people in areas beyond the border.

Making Changes
from the Inside Out

Building assets within the *colonia* of *La Selva* requires social workers to develop cultural competence in regard to Mexican and other Hispanic cultures and in identifying the assets already in place. Educating community leaders about deplorable conditions, as well as the assets that can be used to address those conditions, is advantageous in building partnerships for change and breaking the system of barriers, such as those in vertical and horizontal power struggles. Integrating diverse populations into the community is a process in itself and requires the social worker to be active in two separate communities. Awareness of policies that affect these communities and advocating for policy changes will also make a difference. Most importantly, understanding the lives of those who live in *colonias* and making changes from the inside out will be the best way to assure success.

DISCUSSION QUESTIONS

1. Taking into consideration rural behavior, what would be important to know about *colonia* living and about Hispanic migration to assure cultural competence?

2. It has been suggested that some of the most common theories of development (Freud, Erickson, Piaget, and others) may not apply to minority populations. After learning about

La Selva, why do you think that might be true?

3. How do you think the environment of a *colonia* contributes to a child's positive self-image?

4. How does the behavior of organizations and the larger community impact *La Selva?*

CLASSROOM ASSIGNMENTS
AND ACTIVITIES

1. Take a field trip in the community to various *colonia*-like neighborhoods, or other disadvantaged communities. Report back to your class regarding the location and the general makeup of the community. Using Ward's definition of settlements and communities, how would you identify the place you visited?

2. Research one *colonia* in the community by interviewing a social worker, community leader, student, or resident. Are the residents of the *colonia* or the community American born, or are they immigrants?

3. View the PBS video *Beyond the Border: Mas Alla de la Frontera* (available for purchase from Dos Vatos Productions; http://www.dosvatos .com. E-mail: erenmcginnis@hotmail.com). *Beyond the Border* is the story of four Mexican brothers who settle in the United States away from the borderlands. Although they do not live in a *colonia,* they encounter many of the issues described in this article. Further information about the Ayala family and their story is available from http://pbs.org/itvs/ beyondtheborder/. Identify assets of this Mexican family. Which assets do you believe are unique to this family? Which assets are common for many Mexican families in the United States? How might these assets be used to address this family's challenges?

REFERENCES

Clews, R. A. (1999). Antiracist social work curriculum development for preserving and strengthening indigenous communities in rural New Brunswick, Canada. In I. B. Carlton-LaNey, R. L. Edwards, P. N. Reid (Eds.), *Preserving and strengthening small towns and rural communities* (pp. 249–267). Washington, DC: National Association of Social Work Press.

Connecticut Assets Network Glossary of Terms (1999). Retrieved April 5, 2002, from http://www.ctassets .org/library/glossary.cfm.

Dabir, S. (2001). Hardship and hope in the border *colonias. Journal of Housing Community Development, 58*(5), 31–34.

Fitchen, J. M. (1998). Rural poverty and rural social work. In L.H. Ginsberg (Ed.), *Social work in rural communities* (3rd ed., pp. 115–133). Alexandria, VA: Council on Social Work Education.

Kretzmann, J., & McKnight, J. (1993). *Building communities from the inside out: A path toward finding and mobi-lizing a community's assets.* Evanston, IL: Institute for Policy Research.

McGinnis, E. I. (Producer), & Palos, A. L. (Director and Producer). (2001). *Beyond the Border: Mas Alla de la Frontera.* [Motion picture.] Available from Dos Vatos Productions, http://www.dosvatos.com or http://www. pbs.org/itvs/beyondtheborder/.

U.S. Bureau of the Census. (2001). *State and county quickfacts.* Retrieved August 1, 2002, from http:// quickfacts.census.gov/qfd /stated/48/48347.html.

U.S. Department of Housing and Urban Development (2000). *Community development block grant colonias.* Retrieved December 30, 2001, from http://www .hud.gov/offices/cpd/communitydevelopment/ programs/colonias/cdbgcolonias.cfm.

Ward, P. M. (1999). *Colonias and public policy in Texas and Mexico.* Austin: University of Texas Press.

INFOTRAC COLLEGE EDITION

asset building
colonias
community building

Hispanics/Latinos/Mexicans
immigrants

9

Asset Building
with Rural Haitian Immigrants

A Psychoeducational Group Intervention

LIDDELL L. MADDEN
JAY BISHOP
ALAN B. KIRK

The Haitian refugee experience has been particularly chaotic and negative (Bastien, 1995). Recent research indicates that trauma from such refugee experiences creates both posttraumatic stress and social adaptation problems. Although healthy assimilation requires coping skills associated with social and personal adaptation, these mechanisms have been postponed for many Haitians because of trauma in flight, rejection, or detention while awaiting asylum in the new country. Barriers to successful social work interventions include the prejudice and discrimination experienced by this marginalized, vulnerable rural population. Worthwhile to note is the need to use the terms *immigrant* and *refugee* in the appropriate context as they relate to Haitian populations in the United States. We will use the term *immigrant* to categorize the Haitian who has entered the United States legally and intends to reside permanently in the new host country, and is an alien registration recipient. We will use the term *refugee* to categorize the Haitian who is seeking safety from religious, ethnic, or political persecution experienced in Haiti. Also, the term *refugee* implies asylum-seeking, sometimes detention, and in the case of the Haitian, almost always a lengthy wait before an asylum hearing takes place (Barker, 1995).

Research indicates that, because their immigration experience has been particularly chaotic

and negative, Haitian immigrants have yet to find strength in their ethnic identity, social networks, and existing resources. Portes, Kyle, and Eaton (1992) conclude that Haitians have been underserved by health and mental health systems in the United States. Furthermore, assimilation patterns of coping and adaptation and use of existing individual and community assets are not alternatives for many Haitians because of their experiences with detention camps while awaiting asylum hearings (Silove, 1999). To facilitate asset building within this population, we propose a model of social work practice for use with newer immigrants that entails a psychoeducational group process.

PSYCHOEDUCATIONAL GROUPS FOR IMMIGRANTS

This article presents a culturally relevant psychoeducational group work model as an appropriate intervention for rural Haitian immigrants. The model is a systematic intervention that facilitates both identity redefinition and subsequent client empowerment. The article pays particular attention to certain realities inherent in social work with isolated groups who have been displaced and do not have a history of membership in the local community (Ahern, 2000; Saleebey, 1997). Group sessions are built around conceptual processes, which include coping and adaptation, redefining self as a marginalized group member, and combating oppression through development of proactive behavior patterns. Discussions focus on the strengths and assets, not problems and deficiencies, of this rural immigrant population. Implications for practice include empowerment of the at-risk rural client and developing coping skills essential for oppressive situations. Implications for research include measurement of group treatment effects in terms of coping skills and self-esteem (Saleebey, 1997).

Psychoeducational groups are ones in which a planned process is used to teach skills in a structured format within a specified timeframe. Recent literature supports the perspective that groups with a structured, time limited agenda focusing on homogenous concerns are more effective than groups with less structure and a more diffuse focus (Schulman, 1992; Schwartz, 1971). The proposed psychoeducational group work model is beneficial for such marginalized at-risk, rural populations who seek acceptance, belonging, a feeling of membership through strong associations, and a process of receiving mutual aid (Queralt, 1996).

The model—adapted from Toseland and Rivas (1998), Van Voorhis (1998), and Barlow, Blythe, and Edmonds (1999)—is a systematic intervention that facilitates identity redefinition, use of existing talents, and subsequent empowerment of the rural Haitian immigrant. Group sessions capitalize on strengthening self-image, survivor skills, strong associations, and relationships with the oppressor. Additional topics include redefining self as a marginalized group member, facilitating rural asset building, overcoming feelings of alienation, and combating oppression through development of proactive behavior patterns. Each group session has a unique focus and transitions into the next session.

Haitian Immigration

According to Parillo (1994), Haitians have come to the United States in three waves, beginning in the 1950s. The first wave consisted of the well-educated upper class fleeing from the brutality of President Francois Duvialier. The next decade brought a group of approximately 35,000 Haitians who were primarily middle class. The third wave began fleeing Haiti in the 1970s and included both undereducated farm workers and the "boat people" (Parillo, 1994, p. 439). Thousands of undocumented Haitians fled to the United States in the 1980s and the 1990s. These newcomers often encounter lengthy periods of detention in refugee camps and delayed asylum hearings (Drachman, 1995).

Federal policy as created by the INS has denied refugee status to Haitians. Many have seen this as an effort to discourage their entry into the United States. Those who do enter illegally are immediately deported (Parillo, 1994). A small percentage of Haitians are legal and naturalized citizens. In spite of these constraints, the Haitian community in the United States is experiencing profound growth. Balgopal (2000) maintains that one million Haitians reside in the United States. This group includes legal residents, naturalized citizens, and illegal residents (denied political asylum). Some Haitians have settled in rural areas. States with rural ethnic Haitian enclaves include New York, New Jersey, Delaware, Maryland, Virginia, and Florida (U.S. Bureau of the Census, 2000).

The Haitian refugee experience has been traumatic. Many Americans resent these newcomers and have created increasing political pressure to restrict Haitian immigration. Haitians arrived by the thousands, mainly through South Florida, during the confusion of the 1980 Cuban boatlift, and after the United States had spent several years resettling 350,000 Asian refugees. Apart from concern over the sheer number of refugees, rioting in the refugee resettlement camps in Arkansas, Florida, and elsewhere added to the general impression that these newest arrivals were extremely undesirable. Negative stereotyping of Haitians increased because of fears that this group would form a new poverty class composed of persons of color who were unable to speak English and had a high incidence of physical disease, mental disorder, and criminal behavior (Liebkind & Jasinskaja-Lahti, 2000; Portes & Stepick, 1985; Santana & Dancy, 2000).

Timberlake and Cook (1984) posit that there are some common aspects to the experiences of all refugees and immigrants. According to Moos (1974), uprooting "is indicative of the Haitian refugee experience and profound change in an ongoing life pattern . . . the occurrence of which usually evokes or is associated with, some adaptive or coping behavior on the part of the involved individual" (p. 358). In spite of the fact that Haitian immigrants have undergone a more traumatic experience than other newcomers to the United States, their desires for a successful life for themselves and for their children are universal (Center for Applied Linguistics, 1983).

There has been little research on Haitian coping patterns during the processes of uprooting and subsequent resettlement in the United States. One obvious problem is that Haitian resettlement has, to a great extent, consisted of detention in camps and centers in both rural and urban areas, primarily in the Eastern United States. Thus, along with the lengthy legal processing of those who are detained, most Haitians are prevented from the beginning to go through normal stages of social adaptation leading to self-determination. These stages include securing basic resources such as employment and education, as well as developing coping skills necessary for successful social networking. Survivor skills include communication through language, management of stress in a positive way, and the fulfillment and betterment of self by developing personal strengths and assets. Equally important is cultural integration, in which immigrants maintain the original cultural tradition and history while adjusting to the new culture (Center for Applied Linguistics, 1983; Omidian, 2000).

The effects of detention and prolonged uncertainty about status in a new homeland can be devastating to the individual. Research indicates that refugees staying for any length of time in holding camps and centers lack the survival skills needed to cope with initial months of resettlement, and instead feel dependent, worthless, and disoriented (Ahern, 2000). To counter these feelings, helping the rural Haitian community to recognize existing assets and creative talents would strengthen and empower the group as a whole.

Rural Haitian Immigrants and Their Assets

Language problems, fear of deportation, and educational level of Haitian immigrants make information gathering problematic; it is therefore difficult to determine exact numbers of immigrants living in rural communities (Alperin & Richie, 2001). However, the U.S. Census provides labor statistics that give some indication of how immigrants survive. Occupational category statistics report the following labor force participation for Haitian immigrants: service (33.1%); farming, forestry, and fishing (2.8%); production, craft, and repair (7.8%); and operators, fabricators, and laborers (20.1%). These groupings describe an unskilled labor force of 63.8% for all Haitians reportedly employed in the United States (U. S. Bureau of the Census, 2000).

There are several ethnic enclaves of rural Haitian immigrants in areas such as Caroline County on Maryland's Eastern Shore. Major occupations include seasonal farm work and entry-level poultry plant work (e. g., chicken catcher). Community life focuses on the rural church and public school. Rural Haitian adults often have strong family values, a belief in academic achievement, and are very spiritual. These assets remain in place in spite of a traumatic immigration experience. Poverty often accompanies this lifestyle and brings with it a sense of disempowerment and isolation from the greater community.

The most common assets of rural people include their voluntary associations, close personal relationships, local institutions, histories and traditions, and land inherited from family. The displaced, essentially rootless population of rural Haitian immigrants presents a challenge to standard concepts of asset building in rural communities. Kretzmann and McKnight (1993) describe a useful tool called the Capacity Inventory. Clearly, this inventory does not emphasize needs, but instead could be used with immigrants to help them reframe their circumstances in such a way that they could recognize and value their strengths and assets.

To enact an empowerment agenda with rural Haitian immigrants would require a focus on their unique assets. These include: strong associations with groups such as the Haitian American Community Association and Center for Haitian Studies, ethnic enclaves, and affectionate, close family relationships. Additionally, rural Haitian immigrants bring with them a culture that values academic achievement (Portes & Macleod, 1996) and family in spite of an interrupted family system attributed to a disruptive immigration experience.

THE PSYCHOEDUCATIONAL GROUP MODEL

There is a need for development and testing of culturally competent group interventions for use with distressed immigrant groups such as Haitians (Timberlake & Cook, 1984). Psychoeducational groups are used to teach skills necessary to enhance processes of coping and adaptation that are vital to successful resettlement. This adaptation of psychoeducational group treatment is a systematic asset-building intervention that facilitates client identity redefinition, release of individual and group capacities, and subsequent empowerment (Bachay, 1998; Kretzmann & McKnight, 1993). Also, group sessions center around redefining self as a marginalized group member, combating oppression, and

strengthening the rural ethnic enclave (Van Voorhis, 1998).

How can the model be used? Here are two examples:

1. Working through individual church pastors, the social worker—perhaps representing the community mental health system—would solicit voluntary participants for the group. Members would join the group for the purpose of strengthening the rural community and improving the quality of their lives.

2. In rural Palm Beach County, Florida, the social worker—perhaps representing the Haitian American Community Council, or the Haitian Center for Family Service—would work with principals in the elementary schools to reach rural Haitian immigrant parents who could benefit from psychoeducational group membership (Alperin & Richie, 2001). Because 47% of Haitian immigrants do not speak English "very well" (U.S. Bureau of the Census, 2000), a willing member from each group volunteers to facilitate any needed translations from Creole to English. Each group could choose a different "translator" for one of the group sessions. Of course, should the social worker be fluent in both Creole and French, a translator would not be needed unless such a plan would further indigenous leadership.

The following six sessions serve as a suggested group work model for use with newer immigrants; in particular, Haitian populations.

Session 1:
Guiding Group Focus and Interaction

Haitian group members would be asked to assess their own self-image and their connection to their culture. The group leader could provide the members with helpful insights for strengthening self-image by focusing on the creative talents of each member as well as the extraordinary survivor skills demonstrated during the processes of resettlement. Then the group might break into dyads to share their thoughts about how they can contribute to the new culture and their ideas about their level of personal power. Members would be encouraged to examine the similarities and differences between themselves and how this relates to their perceptions of the new dominant culture. The group members can discuss how to improve their self-image and how to integrate this perspective into their daily lives. Each member would be asked to state two relevant tasks to complete in the coming week. Such tasks could include sharing personal feelings of pride based on a rich cultural heritage, and discussing the reasons why Haitian individuals often conceal their ethnic identity.

Another assignment might be to build on the group's strong belief in academic achievement by seeking out further education or perhaps job training. Members would brainstorm ideas for these self-help tasks and may choose one that seems appropriate or interesting. The social worker should remind the participants that the next session begins with brief reports from the members about the outcome of the tasks.

Session 2: Reframing and Redefining Personal Boundaries

After the first session and in all subsequent sessions, the leader might begin each meeting with members reporting how they have attempted to apply the previous session's material to their lives. Members will be encouraged by the leader to openly discuss their ideas, offer suggestions, and provide encouragement and support to each other. In the second session group members would learn through discussions involving self-disclosure and group feedback how they could examine their personal boundaries and their perspectives.

The group facilitator may begin the group discussion by explaining how understanding differing patterns of self-disclosure and self-containment would enable new immigrants of color to understand how they are perceived by the host society (Barlow, Blythe, & Edmonds, 1999). This

insight gained through small group discussion, would enable group members to become more flexible in coping with and adapting to the mainstream. Only by reframing cultural perspectives would the Haitian immigrants be able to solve problems and tackle difficult situations. Examples of difficult situations encountered by the Haitian newcomer could include dilemmas with child welfare and law enforcement, because of child rearing practices of Haitian families that conflict with values of the host community (Stepick & Portes, 1986). Also, Haitian parents experience value-based conflicts between their children and themselves. These conflicts escalate because of the interrupted extended family system caused by the immigration process. The leader would instruct the members about useful communications skills and techniques that would assist them in overcoming these obstacles.

The group leader would provide the group with information on how to be open and honest as group members and how to disclose personal information in a proactive and nondefensive manner. The group would work in triads and take turns in practicing self-disclosure and giving feedback. Members would then discuss how they felt about the experience and lessons learned. The members would help each other in determining how they can use the group experience to empower themselves outside the group. The group leader would provide the group with information on useful coping skills and how others have used these skills in adapting to difficult situations. The group members would then work in small groups to develop lists of their perceptions of difficult situations in daily life and how utilizing personal strengths could effectively solve them. Session 2 ends with a brief discussion of self-improvement tasks for the upcoming week.

Session 3: Modeling, Role Playing, Rehearsing, and Coaching

Session 3 focuses on the need to re-connect with other members of the Haitian American community. Members think of one personal experience that illustrates a need to reestablish connection to their cultural community and the effects that experience had on their lives. The group leader might facilitate this discussion by providing a case example that illustrates the challenges discussed in this session. One case example could involve the frustration experienced by the Haitian individual or family seeking help from a practitioner who is neither linguistically nor culturally prepared to work with Haitians. This may prove to be a frustrating and disempowering experience. Another possible example might involve institutional invisibility experienced within the social welfare delivery system. The illustration might highlight how Haitians often feel isolated and overwhelmed when trying to solve problems and seek help.

Group members would then discuss the scenarios in dyads for approximately 10 minutes. The leader would then reassemble the group to allow each dyad to share their ideas. Following this, members state two lessons learned from this session and relate how these lessons apply in the coming week.

Session 4: Giving Suggestions and Providing Resources

Session 4 focuses on relationships with significant others and how these relationships affect important aspects of one's life. The group leader would emphasize the value of an extended family system, close affectionate primary relationships and the positive power of religious tradition. Intergenerational primary relationships, for example, can experience heightened conflict during times of resettlement. The group leader would discuss with the group how others have had difficulties with personal relationships and how these relationships can improve. After this brief introduction, the leader would break the group into two subgroups. Each subgroup reviews a written case scenario with questions for later discussion with the entire group. The leader should have prepared these written scenarios in advance. The scenarios should focus on family relationships as a source of strength during times of stress or crisis. The leader should be careful to

create scenarios that are realistic. Any case studies based on actual events should protect anonymity of the case subjects. The two subgroups take approximately 15 minutes to discuss their scenario and develop a response to the discussion questions about the scenario.

After each group makes its report, the leader would facilitate a discussion focusing on how to use the case examples and the information learned to empower themselves and their children. These discussions may mark the reemergence of identity and cultural pride, essential assets for Haitians. Only after identity and cultural pride emerge can the social worker guide the group toward actual identity and cultural synthesis. Once the group is pleased with its identity and cultural pride and sees ways in which interactions are possible with members of one's own group, members may be comfortable with confronting members of the oppressor group. As in previous sessions, the group members would close the session by committing to a self-help activity for the upcoming week. The social worker could refer group members to one or more of the following resources: the Center for Haitian Studies (http://www.haitianstudies.org), Haitian Times (http://www.thehaitiantimes.com), and Haiti Globe (http://www.haitiglobe.com).

Session 5: Clarifying Content and Making Processes Explicit

Haitian group members would learn through group discussions involving self-disclosure and group feedback how they could assess personal and group strengths, resources, and assets. This is particularly important for developing coping and adaptation skills and for redefining themselves in a positive way. The social worker introduces how both discrimination and disenfranchisement can block successful coping, adaptation, and adjustment. Examples could include individual experiences with detention, with the police, with employment and promotion, with educational opportunities, or with other experiences involving governmental organizations. The group facilitator would remind members that the

termination process has begun and would conclude in Session 6.

Session 6: Involving Group Members

Session 6, the final session, begins with reviewing and applying the previous week's strategies,
moving to a summary and application of lessons
learned through this group experience. The
group leader begins this discussion by providing
a few examples of how others have successfully
dealt with oppression and resolved their feelings
of oppression by focusing on personal and group
assets. This task is of particular importance in
developing a more functional relationship with
those perceived as mainstream oppressors. It is at
this juncture that the social worker, using a
strengths perspective, focuses on the group's abilities, assets, and skills. The group leader presents
strategies to manage accumulated stress. These
strategies are: the development of coping skills,
behavioral rehearsal, seeking social support within the community, and help-seeking efforts that
protect an individual from the effects of internal
and external stress. Feelings of alienation
decrease as members work in triads to develop
useful personal strategies. Members would meet
as a whole group and discuss which of the strategies are best for them in their situations.
Members would work in dyads and practice
reviewing personal situations that produced feelings of isolation and how they successfully
resolved these situations. Members would meet
and share their insights with the group. The
group would prioritize these suggestions and discuss how they could integrate them into their
lives. Suggestions may include how to utilize
local institutions for community asset building,
the contacting of Haitian organizations that
would empower them to work with local associations, and how to provide support for asset-
based community development and planning.
Community residents are a major source of
knowledge of informal helping networks

(Dunbar & Morris, 1997, p. 179). Through participating in planning, Haitian community members contribute vital information, essential to
empowering their rural community to use assets
and foster self-determination.

Termination

During the fifth session the leader reminded
Haitian group members that there would be only
one more meeting. The termination process might
be difficult because rural Haitians traditionally
develop strong emotional bonds with each other.
An appropriate topic of discussion at this meeting
would be how they feel about the ending of the
group. The leader needs to keep the members
focused on how they have learned to better cope
with their individual challenges. During the termination phase of the group, the members may try
to renegotiate the initial understanding and have
the group continue meeting for an unlimited
number of sessions. This is a common problem
when members are facing the group's termination.
The leader needs to remain firm and hold the
members to the original number of sessions by
reminding them that they can continue being
friends and support each other after the group
ends (Johnson & Johnson, 1997).

During the final meeting (sixth session), it is
important to have a celebration to clearly mark the
end of the group and to note the transition of the
members to other efforts (Cox, Erlich, Rothman,
& Garvin, 1997). Suggestions for the ceremony
include a final reward, such as a certificate from the
leader to each member. This is also an excellent
opportunity for each member to share final senti-
ments and last words with the entire group. Many
groups also have a group photograph taken.
Members may also want to exchange phone numbers and addresses in order to keep in touch. Many
groups enjoy sharing a meal.

It is important for group members and the
social worker to acknowledge that the environment of the host society remains, at times,

unsympathetic and discriminating (Toseland & Rivas, 1998). The social worker praises the power of each individual's coping skills and problem-solving abilities as empowering assets.

ADDRESSING PSYCHOSOCIAL NEEDS OF RURAL HAITIAN IMMIGRANTS

Psychoeducational group practice is an empowering intervention appropriate to address the psychosocial needs of the rural Haitian immigrant population. The model is suited to marginalized, vulnerable populations who seek acceptance, belonging, a feeling of membership, and mutual aid. It is both timed-limited and structured.

It is important to listen to clients' stories, assess the psychosocial effects of oppression, intervene to enhance identity, and empower the client to change oppressive social conditions. With rural Haitian populations, the social worker would expect to encounter feelings of alienation from self and others, denial of marginalized group status, and delayed development of primary coping patterns especially after a period of detention. Also, Haitian refugees have demonstrated an aversion to seeking help (Portes, Kyle, & Eaton, 1992). Additionally, the arrival of the Haitians was sudden and overwhelming, and their reception has been nonwelcoming. Using culturally relevant interventions, social workers can prompt clients to redefine self, develop pride in identity, overcome feelings of alienation, and develop partnerships based on personal assets. Psychoeducational groups can empower Haitian immigrants to change oppressive conditions.

DISCUSSION QUESTIONS

1. Discuss the relationship between "survivor skills" and successful cultural assimilation among Haitian immigrants.

2. Compare and contrast the immigration experiences of Haitians with Latino immigrants or another group of color.

3. Name and discuss strengths (assets) within the Haitian community that facilitate successful assimilation into mainstream American culture.

4. How can rural Haitian immigrants utilize local institutions to improve their membership status in the community?

CLASSROOM ASSIGNMENTS AND ACTIVITIES

1. List five positive aspects of your own cultural heritage. Describe how these assets have a positive effect on daily living.

2. Access the Center for Haitian Studies on the Internet (http://www.haitianstudies.org/menu.htm). Summarize available services that might enhance asset building within a rural Haitian community.

3. Write a brief paper presenting a comparison and contrast of the Haitian immigrant experience with another new immigrant group of color.

REFERENCES

Ahearn, F. L., Jr. (Ed.). (2000). *Psychosocial wellness of refugees: Issues in qualitative and quantitative research.* Herndon, VA: Berghahn Books.

Alperin, D. E., & Richie, N. D. (2001). *Human services and the marginal client.* Springfield, IL: Charles C. Thomas.

Bachay, J. (1998, April). Ethnic identity development and urban Haitian adolescents. *Journal of Multi-cultural Counseling and Development, 26*(2), 96–110.

Balgopal, P. R. (Ed.). (2000). *Social work practice with immigrants and refugees.* New York: Columbia University Press.

Barker, R. L. (1995). *The social work dictionary* (3rd ed.). Washington, DC: National Association of Social Workers Press.

Barlow, C., Blythe, J., & Edmonds, M. (1999). *A handbook of interactive exercises for groups.* Boston: Allyn & Bacon.

Bastien, M. (1995). Haitian Americans. In R. L. Edwards (Ed.), *Encyclopedia of social work, Vol. 2* (19th ed., pp. 1145–1155). Washington, DC: National Association of Social Workers Press.

Center for Haitian Studies. (2002). Retrieved November 15, 2002, from http://www.haitianstudies.org.

Center for Applied Linguistics/Language and Orientation Resource Center. (1983). *Social adaptation of refugees: A guide for service providers.* Washington, DC: Author.

Cox, F. M., Erlich, J. L., Rothman, J., & Garvin, J. (1997). *Contemporary group work* (3rd ed.). Needham Heights, MA: Allyn & Bacon.

Drachman, D. (1995). Immigration statuses and their influence on service provision, access and use. *Social Work, 40,* 188–197.

Dunbar, E. R., & Morris, L. C. (1983). Building rural community participation in the planning process: Is it possible? In F. M. Cox, J. L. Erlich, J. A. Rothman, and J. E. Tropman (2nd ed., pp. 174–184). Itasca, IL: Peacock Publishers.

Haiti Globe. (2002). Retrieved November 15, 2002, from http://www.haitiglobe .com.

Haitian Times. (2002). Retrieved November 15, 2002, from http://www .haitiantimes.com.

Johnson, D., & Johnson, F. (1997). *Joining together: Group theory and group skills.* (6th ed.). Needham Heights, MA: Allyn & Bacon.

Kretzmann, J. P., & McKnight, J. L. (1993). *Building communities from the inside out: A path toward finding and mobilizing a community's assets.* Chicago: ACTA Publications.

Liebkind, K., & Jasinskaja-Lahti, I. (2000, January/February). The influence of experiences of discrimination on psychological stress: A comparison of seven immigrant groups. *Journal of Community and Applied Psychology, 10*(1), 1–16.

Moos, R. H. (1974). Psychological techniques in the assessment of adaptive behavior. In G. V. Coelho, D. A. Hamburg, & J. E. Adams (Eds.), *Coping and adaptation* (p. 358). New York: Basic Books.

Omidian, P. (2000). Qualitative measures and refugee research: The case of Afghan refugees. In F. L. Ahearn, Jr. (Ed.), *Psychosocial wellness of refugees: Issues in qualitative and quantitative Research* (pp. 41–66). New York: Berghan Books.

Parillo, V. N. (1994). *Strangers to these shores, race and ethnic relations in the United States* (4th ed.). New York: Macmillian.

Portes, A., Kyle, D., & Eaton, W. E. (1992, December). Mental illness and help-seeking behavior among Mariel Cuban and Haitian refugees in South Florida. *Journal of Health and Social Behavior, 33,* 283–298.

Portes, A., & Macleod, D. (1996, October). Educational progress of children of immigrants: The roles of class, ethnicity and school context. *Sociology of Education, 69*(4), 255–275.

Portes, A., & Stepick, A. (1985). Unwelcome immigrants: The labor market experiences of 1980 Mariel Cuban and Haitian refugees in South Florida. *American Sociological Review, 50,* 493–514.

Queralt, M. (1996). *The social environment and human behavior, a diversity perspective.* Boston: Allyn & Bacon.

Saleebey, D. (Ed.). (1997). *The strengths perspective in social work practice* (2nd ed.). New York: Longman.

Santana, M., & Dancy, B. L. (2000, April/May). The stigma of being named a Haitian-American women. *Health Care for Women International, 21*(3), 161–172.

Schulman, L. (1992). *The skills of helping individuals, families and groups* (3rd ed.). Itasca, IL: Peacock Publishers.

Schwartz, W. (1971). On the use of groups in social work practice. In W. Schwartz & S. Zalba (Eds.), *The practice of group work* (pp. 3–24). New York: Columbia University Press.

Silove, D. (1999). The psychosocial effects of torture, mass human rights violations, and refugee trauma: Toward an integrated conceptual framework. *Journal of Nervous and Mental Disease, 187*(4), 200–207.

Stepick, A., & Portes, A. (1986). Flight into despair: A profile of recent Haitian refugees in South Florida. *International Migration Review, 20,* 329–350.

Timberlake, E. M., & Cook, K. O. (1984). Social work and the Vietnamese refugee. *Social Work, 29,* 108–113.

Toseland, R., & Rivas, R. (1998). *An introduction to group work practice* (3rd ed.). Boston: Allyn & Bacon.

U.S. Bureau of the Census. (2000). Supplementary survey, http://www.census.gov/population.html.

Van Voorhis, R. (1998). Culturally relevant practice: A framework for teaching the psychosocial dynamics of oppression. *Journal of Social Work Education, 34*(1), 121–133.

INFOTRAC COLLEGE EDITION

group process
Haitian
immigrants

psychoeducational groups
refugees

PART III

⁜

Practice Issues
in Rural Contexts

SUSAN A. MURTY

Effective rural social workers build on community assets. These workers have a wide range of highly developed social work skills. They are very good at assessment with individuals and families, and they are also able to identify the assets of the local community and build on them. Rather than trying to do everything themselves, they are good at mobilizing members of the community to make things happen. They develop new programs, obtain funding for services, foster community support, recruit volunteers, train boards, and initiate community efforts. They are effective at working with individuals and families and groups, but also with community organizations, service providers, and informal support systems. They are also highly skilled at accessing resources from outside the local community to supplement and enhance the strengths that exist locally. Finally, they are excellent advocates for their rural communities and are willing to work to change policies to improve access to resources and services for rural communities. All of these highly developed skills are essential for effective work in the rural environment.

Rural social work challenges and demands those who practice it. Rural social workers are versatile, creative, and flexible. They are good at thinking on their feet! They solve new problems constantly because they always encounter situations that are unique and individual. They cannot afford to limit themselves to a narrow set of methods or to restrict themselves to working only with specific populations. Effective rural social workers are true generalist social workers who stimulate change at many levels including change in organizations, in neighborhoods and communities, and in policy. They are able to develop new programs to meet new challenges. They can intervene in multiple ways.

Although the challenges of this type of work may sound overwhelming, keep in mind that rural social work is also infinitely rewarding. Effective rural social workers know that they have made a difference. They get the satisfaction of seeing that the results of their hard work have an impact on peoples' lives and on the communities they serve. The articles in this part present examples of effective rural social work. Together they will inspire and motivate you as you prepare to enter the fascinating and challenging field of social work practice.

The first article by Haulotte and Oliver will show you how to assess the assets and strengths of rural communities. These assets and strengths are not always immediately obvious; it takes time and effort and commitment to locate them. This chapter shows you step by step how to search them out and build on them. These steps form the foundation of any effective rural service and program. No matter what kind of rural social work you become involved with, you need to learn the methods covered in this first chapter.

The remaining articles provide examples of effective rural social work programs of various kinds. Each one assesses the assets of a particular rural community or a set of rural communities and then builds on these assets to develop local community support. Each one accesses resources both inside and outside the community. Each program is individualized for the particular community and its leaders, assets, and challenges. These are not "cookie cutter" programs. Rather than imposing a standard approach, these authors encourage social workers to individualize programs to match individual communities and their residents. Even if you plan to practice with different programs or populations, you can learn how to develop individualized and creative rural programs from these articles.

As you will see, the articles in this part deal with a wide range of practice situations and programs. Rodriguez, Cooper, and Morales introduce you to the world of the *colonias* in rural Texas. They show how social workers can improve services for the residents of these communities and how they can mobilize change to integrate the *colonias* better into the larger community. Davis presents wraparound services as a creative way to deliver individualized services to rural families with seriously emotionally disturbed children. Poole and More present ways to improve the participation of rural youth in higher education. Ersing and Otis write about an approach to improving rural public health and community well-being through community development and building local community capacity. Finally, Schobert and Barron add an international perspective on impoverished rural communities in developing countries with their chapter on community and economic development based on sustainable agriculture.

You have a treat in store as you read these articles. You will see such a wealth of varied examples of effective rural social work practice, which will stimulate you to develop additional ideas on your own. You will be inspired to become a creative rural social worker in your own career!

10

A Strategy for Uncovering, Accessing, and Maximizing Assets and Strengths in Rural Area Social Services

SHIRLEY M. HAULOTTE
SUZANNE OLIVER

Training social workers to practice in rural settings presents a number of challenges, since many are unfamiliar with rural regions and have little idea how to begin to practice in nonurban environments. In a typical cohort of undergraduate or graduate social work students, some may come from rural areas but few have experience in accessing rural community resources. Only a handful of programs address the needs of workers new to the field of rural social work and often workers begin to provide services in a haphazard fashion. In the best of cases, the worker gains competence through trial and error. In the worst, the worker feels inadequate and ineffective, and subsequently abandons the rural arena of social work practice.

A PROPOSED STRATEGY

A strategy to uncover, access, and maximize assets in rural social services addresses this dearth of experience and training. The strategy assists students in gaining a foundation for social work practice in rural communities and is based upon a strengths perspective, identification of assets, and basic principles of community analysis.

The strengths perspective first gained eminence in the mid-1980s and is a prevalent theoretical framework of social work practice as evidenced by prominent authors of current social

work textbooks (O'Looney, 1996; Locke, Garrison, & Winship, 1998; Derezotes, 2000; Kirst-Ashman & Hull, 1999; Poulin, 2000). Prior to this time, emphasis was placed upon a deficit model or pathology perspective of social work at the micro, mezzo, and macro levels (Becker, 1963; Rosenhan, 1973; Scheff, 1984). Problem-based assessments are still the norm in much of social work practice; at the community level, problem language continues as evidenced by the following statement from a recently published textbook on community social work practice: "Community practice involves building solutions to three kinds of community problems broadly conceived . . . problem of cohesion . . . problem of capability . . . problem of competence" (Rothman, Erlich, & Tropman, 2001, pp. 3–4).

Dennis Saleebey (1992), one of the major proponents of strengths-based practice uses different language to put forth a positive view of the community:

No matter how a harsh environment tests the mettle of inhabitants, it can also be understood as a lush topography of resources and possibilities. In every environment there are individuals and institutions who have something to give, something that others may desperately need; knowledge, succor, an actual resource, or simply time and place. Usually these individuals and institutions exist outside the usual panoply of social and public services. And, for the most part, they are untapped and unsolicited. (p. 7)

The language we use not only affects the way we view our work with clients at all levels of practice, but also how clients view themselves. This is not a new concept. Michel Foucault (1972) and Paulo Freire (1973) addressed the issue of internalized oppression wherein individuals and groups subjugate their own experience and knowledge to the group in position of power and privilege. Thus, it is important for social workers to have a preconceived plan to uncover rural community assets rather than community deficits. With this attitude, the richness of information, resources, and assistance can be brought into the forefront to deal with challenges as they occur.

The strengths perspective is the initial point in the strategy for uncovering, accessing, and maximizing rural resources. With this perspective in place, the social worker can explore a particular rural community in a manner similar to unwrapping a valuable package to disclose the contents. Asset mapping is a strengths-based technique that is "capacity-focused" (Kretzmann & McKnight, 1993) and focuses on the strengths and capacities of communities in the collection of data (O'Looney, 1996). Community analysis techniques give us further tools to unwrap the package of resources in a rural community. Si Kahn (1994) stresses the importance of community analysis as a preliminary step in empowerment:

> It is the (social worker's) responsibility, even before she enters a community, to analyze it as well as she can. This analysis helps her put the work she will be trying to do there into perspective and to understand some of the problems she will have to confront. Without a good analysis of the area, there is danger that, at best, the work she does will be fragmentary and irrelevant to the actual problems of people in the community. At worst, the (social worker) may actually reinforce the conditions that make and keep people poor and helpless. (p. 10)

Mark Homan (1999), in his work on promoting community change, uses a similar language of empowerment. He suggests that when needs are not met in a community, it does not necessarily mean there are no resources. Instead, workers should be aware of the ways in which resources may be misallocated and be able to recognize potential in underutilized, seldom-used, or unidentified resources.

The combination of a strengths-based, asset-seeking perspective of the community and the community analysis framework supports the strategy of learning about a rural community and its resources. The next phase of the strategy is pragmatic and is comprised of concrete actions using readily available materials. These tools become the knowledge base for a preliminary understanding of how a community functions and how it meets the needs of individuals and groups.

Tools to Launch the Strategy

Census Bureau data provide information on populations according to age and race, income levels, and employment groups. This information is valuable in conceptualizing the community demographically. The degree of diversity or homogeneity in income, age, and ethnicity will likely affect the amount and types of services and opportunities in the area. For example, the size of certain age groups yields fruitful information. A large older adult population may mean the community has a number of services designed for elders. It may also indicate that elders may be an untapped resource. Rediscovering seniors as assets within the community can lead to uncovering economic, cultural, historical, and experiential resources (Kretzmann & McKnight, 1993, p. 52).

County Extension Agents may provide information regarding the geographic areas that residents consider to be their local community. However, official county level data may not provide detailed information specific to the areas considered communities in rural areas.

Road maps that detail each county in the United States are published by the U.S.

Department of Commerce in cooperation with state highway departments. The maps provide specific information for rural areas and include notations on individual farms, houses, stores, schools, churches, post offices, state police barracks, prisons, filling stations, motels, factories, sawmills, radio stations, golf courses, and gravel pits. Simply noting the number and location of various buildings, agencies, and organizations helps construct a visual image of the area. It is important to obtain the most current maps available to ensure accuracy. If an up-to-date map is unavailable, it is advised to consult with a local resident to determine any inaccuracies.

Telephone directories are a quick reference for data gathering and are available at the local telephone company or at the public library. Looking through the phone book and noting the last names may provide information about the ethnic makeup of the community; however, be aware that last names do not always indicate ethnic background. The commercial and Yellow Pages sections give an overview of the businesses and services available and indicate those that dominate this format for advertising and name recognition. Noting the businesses from nearby population centers gives an idea of the relationship between the community and its regional trade and service centers. Service clubs and ethnic organizations also may be listed in the local directory, but be aware some active organizations may not be listed.

Local newspapers may be published weekly or biweekly. Although they may provide little in the way of national or state news, they provide a wealth of information about what is going on in the local community on a daily basis. Articles on church socials, weddings, sports teams, school events, recreational activities, new businesses, local politics, meetings of clubs, groups, and civic organizations, and other activities give a glimpse into the everyday life of the population and help to identify active organizations and community leaders.

Regional magazines and papers usually are published monthly and contain news, activities, and business advertising for a multicounty area. Observations from a regional perspective help place the specific community in the context of the surrounding counties.

Travel or tourism pamphlets or brochures provide excellent (although perhaps somewhat inflated) descriptions of various points of interest. They usually contain information about businesses, natural resources, historical information, artists and artisans, parks, and recreational facilities.

Bulletin boards provide information on events that reveal the types of activities that residents are likely to attend. Often the ethnic or cultural interests of the community are articulated in the flyer. A brats and sauerkraut supper tells you something about the people as does a blessing of the watercraft. Community bulletin boards are often found in grocery stores, laundromats, banks, and other businesses.

Locations to Find Information

The public library has much of the information cited previously. In addition, most librarians are eager to share their expertise in information retrieval.

City Hall offices house written materials about the area. Oftentimes, a clerk or city official will provide anecdotal information about the population.

Hospitals and clinics give a picture of the health services available in the area. The admissions and intake personnel provide information about the in-house services and typically give referral information for other medical services. If the community does not have a hospital or clinic, a visit to the local nursing home may provide similar information.

Grocery stores carry items most used by their customers and provide clues to the food choices made by individuals. A large ethnic food section gives an indication of the culture of the community. If no alcoholic beverages are for sale, this may indicate that the sale of alcohol is prohibited entirely or that certain groups control the sales in that area. Signs indicating that stores are closed or that certain items cannot be sold on Sundays may suggest the influence and power of certain religious groups and the existence of blue laws. Sales and promotion of recreational and activity licenses indicate the interests of the residents and recreational visitors.

Visitors Bureau or Chamber of Commerce personnel are friendly, informative, and eager to answer inquiries. Usually printed material is abundant. Tourism is an important element of the economy in many rural areas and is useful to assess.

Restaurants and diners are generally small in size and provide a microcosm of life in the community. Waitpersons often greet local customers by name and engage in discussions ranging from the weather to family events. Spending time in a booth or on a counter stool yields insight into everyday life. An added bonus is that the food is usually quite good. These places often serve as community gathering places where groups of local residents may meet at a certain time daily or weekly to talk.

Funeral home directors know their communities well and are savvy about the values and customs of the residents. Since they are in a consumer-driven industry, the directors are usually personable and helpful.

Religious institutions are frequently the center of interaction among individuals and groups and are significant social service providers in the rural community. The clergy and office staff are often eager to talk about how their congregation cares for people in their area. Lists of local churches can be found in the local newspaper and phone directory.

Depending upon the culture of the community, other informal resources may include taverns, barbers, hairstylists, hardware stores, and feed stores.

THE FIRST SIX STEPS

The social worker or service provider enters a rural community with certain goals; for example, to make assessments, to link needs to resources, or to provide for basic care. To achieve these goals, the worker must first gain personal access to the population being served and ultimately must ensure the client's access to the community at large. The most critical step in this process is making a preliminary effort to enter the client's community with relevant knowledge about the community and a high potential for accessing the people and services. Demonstrating creative insight into the existing and potential service opportunities, both unique and universal, facilitates the development of trust and partnership. This preparation, prior to initiating interventions, will more likely result in real and durable solutions.

To maximize the function and outcome of home visits, eligibility studies, biopsychosocial assessments, and other planned interventions, the worker must first conduct a study and assessment of the region, the culture, the climate, and the habitation of the community and people being served. Based on our own practice experiences, we recommend six steps which will equip the worker for uncovering, accessing, and maximizing strengths and assets in rural areas.

Step One: Know the Geographic Area
Obtain and review detailed maps of the local area. Study those with county roads and easements identified. Learn the names and sizes of local and surrounding counties and the location of county seats. Observe the location and concentration of transportation routes and the proximity to urban areas. Note large, undeveloped areas that may indicate public, private, or commercial ownership and learn the existing and planned land use.

Conduct a *windshield sweep,* driving around the area to make a physical assessment of the overall environment of the community. Observe the geography, housing, agriculture, and industry. You will likely find a range of environments and construction conditions. Note the locations and proximities of new, clean, and well-maintained constructions as well as buildings that are old, dirty, dilapidated, or abandoned. Identify the location of mobile home parks—often neighborhoods where low income, immigrant, and transient families live. Read the signs on fences, gates, street corners, and billboards to learn about local affiliations, cultural mores, and political campaigns. Notice any changes in road conditions and properties when crossing county or precinct lines. Identify natural resources such as waterways and mineral deposits, electrical power sources such as reservoirs and power plants, and natural features including both geographic and historic landmarks.

The history of settlement, development, and community adaptation to the area can provide the worker with significant information regarding attitudes toward government, public agencies, private groups, corporations, and the concept of community services. One also learns motivations, strengths, and opportunities that currently exist in the community.

The process of gathering information for this first step leads directly on to the next five steps. Driving through and learning the geographic area not only provides a mechanism for studying the demographics, culture, and resources of the community, it also provides the context within which the remaining five steps can be applied.

Step Two: Know the Demographics Social workers must know the population characteristics of the specific community. Census data for the area can provide statistics regarding the age, race, gender, occupational groups, income levels, and sources of income for people of that area. Visual observations can provide clues to issues of financial and racial segregation, integration, and the proportional relationships of various groups.

Identify the employment base, industry, and labor options in the community. Consider the opportunities provided and the dynamics inherent to the existing and potential employment choices. What are the employment and unemployment rates and average wages? Are unemployed people employable in the current environment? Have wage levels fluctuated in the recent past? What is the community's capacity to attract new industry? What percentage of the population could be classified as working poor?

Additions or closures of schools, hospitals, clinics, stores, or other enterprises can impact the local population both psychologically and economically. Demographic and economic changes may be welcomed, despised, viewed as a mixed blessing, or perceived as a necessary evil. Viewed from an asset-building perspective and with an eye for opportunity, the changes may increase the capacities and coping strategies of that community. The gross and subtle adaptation to changes in the community can affect the attitudes toward current conditions and future potential. What skills do residents have because of previous enterprises located there? Can the community rely on some of these skills for continued self-sufficiency and community development?

Step Three: Know the Culture The initial drive through the community provides the first glimpse of the local culture. Observe the housing styles, color choices, gardens, livestock, common automobiles, and implements. Visit the county seat and the surrounding smaller towns. Walk through the town, stop and visit with people at the café and hardware store. Talk to the gas station attendant. Make note of what is sold, what services are provided, the customers, and the conversations among those present. Read the informal notices posted on community bulletin boards and identify what items and services are both offered and requested. Observe the culture of relationships and norms among various groups, considering gender, ethnicity, and socioeconomic status.

Identify the local political groups and religious affiliations, noting the predominance of any one group over another. Are there any activities where the entire community gathers, such as sporting events or cultural celebrations? What are the gathering places for the community events? Are civic groups (e.g., Chamber of Commerce, service organizations, parent teacher associations) present and are there signs of recognition and awards functions or public service opportunities? Identify what appear to be community assets and any evidence of subcommunities. Consider the historic means for employment or self-sufficiency and its social status; note the challenge or ease of changing images and personal styles.

Step Four: Know the Formal Resources
Identify the existence, location, and access to the services provided by the federal, state, and local authorities and organizations. Go to the offices that provide these resources. Know for whom these resources are intended and who in the community does and does not have access to them. Distinguish entitlement programs from those with eligibility requirements. Learn what the eligibility requirements are. How do the community members access these resources? What is the proximity of agency offices to community residents and what are the transportation and scheduling needs for access? Note that some will be in the county seat or in a nearby population center rather than in the local community itself.

Typical formal resources might include:

Federal
- Social Security Administration
- Medicare
- Supplemental Security Income

State
- Health Department
- Department of Human Services
- Area Agency on Aging
- Medicaid programs for children and the aged and disabled
- Protective and Regulatory Services
- mental health services, community care programs

County
- hospitals
- clinics
- nursing homes
- subsidized housing
- public works

- extension services
- court systems
- local judges
- the county commissioners' office
- sheriffs' office

Community
- political councils
- fire departments
- clinics
- assistance programs for housing, food, and utilities
- libraries
- schools
- prescription medication assistance
- distance learning programs

Organizational
- industry associations
- labor unions
- hospice
- employer-based services such as banks, credit unions, health services, employee assistance programs, child and adult day care, and family support programs

Step Five: Know the Informal Resources As with the formal resources, identify the intention, location, and eligibility requirements of each informal resource. Informal resources may not be as obvious or as easily identifiable as the formal resources. Many informal resources do not have offices, staff, or even addresses or phones. An informal resource may be as limited as the availability of neighbors, friends, and family members.

Identify the religious organizations and places of worship. Are there social and community services offered by churches, synagogues, mosques, or temples? What faith-based associations are present, such as St. Vincent de Paul, Lutheran Social Services, or Jewish Family Services? Is there a ministerial association of congregations in the community? If so, what does it do? Visit with the staff members on duty and inquire as to the status and ratio of paid or volunteer workers, and hours of operation. Inquire about any recent increase or decrease in resources and services offered and the relative increase or decrease in community utilization.

Determine the local organizations which are active in the community (e.g., Kiwanis, Rotary, Lions, Optimist clubs, Shriners, and Masons). What services and support do they offer? Do support groups exist and for what issues? Where do they meet? Do volunteer groups exist and is there a history of support groups that are not currently active? Where are the nearest recreation and community centers? How do potential participants learn about the available programs?

Step Six: Practice Ethically   Analysis and decision making are required when workers face ethically ambiguous situations. According to Linzer (1999), an ethical dilemma is a choice between two actions that are based on a conflict in values. Both values are morally correct and professionally grounded but are in conflict with each other in the situation.

Frank Lowenberg and Ralph Dolgoff (1996) propose a system for dealing with ethical dilemmas called the Ethical Principles Screen (EPS). If the professional code of ethics does not answer an ethical question directly, then the authors suggest utilizing a set of rank-ordered principles to arrive at a decision. The higher ordered principles take precedence over the satisfaction of lower ordered ones.

Ethical Principles Screen (EPS)

ETHICAL PRINCIPLE 1
Protection of life

ETHICAL PRINCIPLE 2
Equality and inequality

ETHICAL PRINCIPLE 3
Autonomy and freedom

ETHICAL PRINCIPLE 4
Least harm

ETHICAL PRINCIPLE 5
Quality of life

ETHICAL PRINCIPLE 6
Privacy and confidentiality

ETHICAL PRINCIPLE 7
Truthfulness and full disclosure

The following are examples of ethical dilemmas in rural social work practice. Each example is accompanied by the numbers of the ethical principles from the Ethical Principles Screen. Although the ethical dilemmas presented by the authors are not limited to rural practice, they highlight typical areas of concern.

Cost of Services versus Needs of Individuals
Some clients are chronic users of resources or have a history of requiring high levels of service from agencies. For public, nonprofit, and for-profit agencies, this provides a dilemma regarding accountability for funds. Does the agency provide intensive care for a few clients or some care for many clients? (Ethical Principles 2, 4, and 5)

Safety of the Individual versus Self-Determination   When clients choose to make decisions that are not necessarily in their best interest (e.g., noncompliance with a medical diet) a concern is raised about the client's right to make that decision. (Ethical Principles 1, 3, 5)

Family Values versus Societal Values   Housing conditions, personal hygiene, family dynamics, and relationships between what the client chooses and what the worker chooses may be dramatically different. What may look like a dirty dump to one person may be seen as home to another. (Ethical Principles 3, 5)

Ethics and Values versus Legal Issues   When a client chooses to remain home in conditions that are considered unsafe for the client or potentially litigious to agencies, workers must be able to give consideration to client self-determination while maintaining compliance with regulatory and licensure requirements, as well as agency risk management guidelines. (Ethical Principles 1, 3, 4, 5, 6)

Some Cautions

Providing services in rural communities typically requires large amounts of driving time and increased need for advance preparation and efficiency. If adequate preparation is done, any additional needs for resource linkage and even health monitoring and crisis intervention can be conducted over the telephone. For this to be possible, the worker must be equipped with in-depth knowledge of, and access to, the client's community. A number of pitfalls may be encountered when working in rural environments but the most common can be avoided by following these guidelines for advance preparation prior to intervention. Along with the recommendations of what they might do, workers are advised to take some precautions:

1. It is best not to attempt provision of services before following the first six steps outlined previously.

2. Be careful not to assume that formal resources are available. Frequently age, income, physical capacity, legal status, and isolation can prevent persons from being eligible for formal resources. Often there are service needs that are not provided for by formal organizations; if they are, they may not be accessible to rural residents. This has been true historically and remains a concern today. This means that service providers must be creative problem solvers. The successful social worker possesses the ability and willingness to face any situation with the attitude that assets can be found or developed to enhance the situation. Without this attitude, many cases would be viewed as hopeless. The worker should take the opportunity to recognize how much is provided and how common needs are met by informal means. It is the worker's job to ensure a client's access to entitled services, and to assist the client and the community in developing new resources as needs arise.

3. It is best not to assume that formal resources are always appropriate. Primarily, workers must be knowledgeable of the eligibility requirements and the limitations of the federal, state, and local services. Sometimes individuals choose to decline the most obvious formal resources. This may happen for a variety of reasons: the fear of legal jeopardy or repercussions, an undesirable stigma associated with the source of assistance, the application and maintenance requirements that are so cumbersome that the client views them as not worth the trouble, or the resource that is simply unpalatable to the client.

4. Avoid confusing value differences with moral edicts. Lifestyle and value differences between clients and social workers can present obstacles to accurate identification of strengths and assets. Keen awareness of one's personal values and focused attention to the client's goals are essential; otherwise initial suggestions and comments might alienate clients from service workers and community resources. For example, a client may live in an environment that the worker may consider dirty and unsafe. The worker may advocate for changes while the client is content with the home and does not want any changes made. Another example may be the client who chooses to invite individuals to live in the home who are not considered appropriate by the worker. If the worker allows his or her values to dominate, the worker may falsely assume that exploitation has occured.

5. Don't give up too quickly. You may be able to find services or create them yourself. Options and potential assets must be fully explored in order to uncover resources. The brainstorming process can be helpful in generating multiple options for consideration. The task of the worker is to be a creative force working in collaboration with the clients and the community to discover workable alternatives to situations. Have confidence that people in the community will help you. Have the courage to ask for help. Most community residents want and need to be part of any positive change.

SUMMARY

Social workers new to rural settings may be somewhat perplexed by a community that may seem at first like a confusing labyrinth with scarce resources and assets. However, by walking a systematic path through the landscape of a rural community, the worker can begin to uncover not only the obvious resources of social service agencies, but also the numerous assets and strengths that often go untapped. Furthermore, by discovering the assets and strengths in a community, the worker may creatively combine formal and informal resources to meet client needs.

DISCUSSION QUESTIONS

1. What do you know about the rural areas in your geographic region? What community strengths and assets do you assume currently exist and are utilized? What assets exist that are not commonly viewed as such?

2. Who or what do you see as the best source of information about additional community assets? Why?

3. What community resources might be available through local schools or religious organizations?

CLASSROOM ASSIGNMENTS AND ACTIVITIES

Take a Moment to Discover: An Exercise to Train Social Workers to Look for Clues in a Community

Examine your own home and neighborhood. Look through the eyes of an "outsider" or someone who doesn't know you. First, walk slowly around and through your home. Make note of each item and arrangement that is a clue to who you are, what your culture is, what your affinities are, and what your means of personal expression is.

Now expand your walk to the area immediately surrounding your home. Again, notice all clues that help you understand more about the residents in this area.

From both inside your home and the immediate community surroundings, notice what could help you answer the following questions about the residents of this community:

1. What inconveniences do they take for granted or apparently have adjusted to?
2. What do they or don't they enjoy doing?

3. What values do they hold?
4. How do they communicate information?
5. Who does what work and what work isn't done?
6. How do they generate income?
7. What new technology do they use or have access to?
8. What forms of transportation are used and available for use?
9. What opportunities exist for education, social interactions, and community support?
10. How fluid or adaptable to change are the residents here?

In this inventory, list the strengths and assets.

Community Wisdom

The purpose of this exercise is to uncover the assets and strengths in the community through interviewing two adults. Conduct one interview with an older adult who has been a lifelong resident of a rural community. Then conduct an interview with a young adult in the same community.

Compare and contrast the responses. Use the following questions as a guide for your interviews.

1. How long have you lived here?

2. Tell me the history of this area.

3. What are the main changes you have seen while living here?

4. What are the good points of living here?

5. What are the bad points of living here?

6. Who are the important leaders in the community?

7. If I needed a place to stay, who would I talk to?

8. If I didn't have any money and I was hungry where would I go?

9. If I were sick where would I go?

10. If I needed a job who would I see?

11. Who are the chronic gripers in this area? What is their common complaint?

12. What's the most important thing you want me to know about this place?

REFERENCES

Becker, H. (1963). *Outsiders: Studies in the sociology of deviance.* New York: Free Press.

Derezotes, D. S. (2000). *Advanced generalist practice.* Thousand Oaks, CA: Sage.

Foucault, M. (1972). *The archaeology of knowledge and the discourse on language.* New York: Pantheon.

Friere, P. (1973). *Education for critical consciousness.* New York: Seabury.

Homan, M. S. (1999). *Promoting community change* (2nd ed). Pacific Grove: Brooks/Cole.

Kahn, S. (1994). *How people get power* (Revised ed.). Washington, DC: National Association of Social Work Press.

Kirst-Ashman, K. K., & Hull, G. H., Jr. (1999). *Understanding generalist practice* (2nd ed.). Chicago: Nelson Hall.

Kretzmann, J. R., & McKnight, J. L. (1993). *Building communities from the inside out: A path toward finding and mobilizing a community's assets.* Chicago: ACTA Publications.

Linzer, N. (1999). *Resolving ethical dilemmas in social work practice.* Boston: Allyn & Bacon.

Locke, R., Garrison, R., & Winship, J. (1998). *Generalist social work practice: Context, story, and partnerships.* Pacific Grove, CA: Brooks/Cole.

Lowenberg, F. M., & Dolgoff, R. (1996). *Ethical decisions for social work practice* (5th ed.). Itasca, IL: Peacock Publishers.

O'Looney, J. (1996). *Redesigning the work of human services.* Westport, CT: Quorum.

Poulin, J. (2000). *Collaborative social work: Strengths-based generalist practice.* Itasca, IL: Peacock Publishers.

Rosenhan, D. L. (1973). On being sane in an insane place. *Science, 179,* 250–258.

Rothman, J., Erlich, J. L., & Tropman, J. E. (2001). *Strategies of community intervention* (6th ed.). Itasca, IL: Peacock Publishers.

Saleebey, D. (1992). *The strengths perspective in social work practice.* New York: Longman Publishing Group.

Scheff, T. (1984). *Being mentally ill: A sociological theory* (2nd ed.). New York: Aldine.

INFOTRAC COLLEGE EDITION

asset mapping
community analysis
data collection

ethics and values
strengths perspective

11

Working with Mexican Immigrants in Rural East Texas

RUBEN RODRIGUEZ

H. STEPHEN COOPER

LINDA MORALES

On January 7th, 2002, fire spread quickly through a manufactured home occupied by a Mexican immigrant family in a *colonia* outside the city limits. The intensity of the heat was enough to ignite several nearby cars. As with most fires, numerous calls were placed to 911, concerned citizens began to gather, and everyone speculated about what had happened. But something was missing. There wasn't a big red fire truck to supply water to the firefighters. There were no firefighters to deal with the fire and assist those that lived in the home. Law enforcement personnel did not come to provide traffic control and to ask questions. When the firefighters finally arrived, the fire, having consumed everything within its reach, had satisfied its hunger and was dying. Fortunately, no lives were lost in this fire; however, the tragedy extends beyond those irreplaceable memories that were destroyed. Although this incident surprised many members of the community at large, it did not surprise the neighborhood residents.

Most citizens have expectations of what is *supposed* to happen when there is a fire. Someone dials 911 and a dispatcher sends out professional responders who are prepared to assist in quelling the crisis. So what went wrong? The fire brought to light a number of issues created by the attempts of a rural town to accommodate growth. The town has been in the process of centralizing the 911 dispatch system, which should prevent such an occurrence. Without the centralized system, a dispatcher receives a call and then must contact other dispatchers, who either dispatch the appropriate agency or contact an additional dispatcher to send the respondents. Centralization of the 911 system was a concern for 10 years in this community.

Another issue lies with the neighborhood itself. Over the last 5 years, the predominately Mexican immigrant *colonia* has received attention for its dilapidated housing and road conditions, as well as poor drainage and lack of sewer services.

The incident has brought some positive results. For example, people are asking questions such as: How is it that life can go on like this? How can a community be satisfied with the *status quo?* Is "that's how things have *always* been done around here" an acceptable answer? Or must this community wait for a life to be lost? And if the lives lost are of illegal immigrant laborers, would it minimize the loss itself? These questions and their answers have brought a resurgence of concern for a population that is, at best, invisible. Before the fire the Mexican immigrants tended to be viewed from one perspective, as providers of quality labor at minimal cost. Although most people understand the importance of the immigrant to the poultry, timber, and agriculture-related businesses, there seems to be little concern for their well-being. However, this fire has served as a wake up call to community members, including city and county officials. The message is clear: the time has come for the community to fulfill its obligation to provide this population with fair and equal treatment, as well as protection. For this community it is another test of their solidarity and loyalty to each other. Their lack of services and dilapidated living conditions are substandard and offensive to all that live on the outside looking in. This community has not requested help, nor do they expect it. They manage to care for each other with limited intrusions and have been successful in putting out the small fires by coming together and working as a true community.

HISPANIC POPULATIONS IN NACOGDOCHES

As noted previously in Article 8, the City of Nacogdoches (pronounced Nack-a-doe-chez) has a population of 32,260 and is the seat of Nacogdoches County (population 59,203) located in northeast Texas. Currently, Hispanics make up 11.2% of the county's population (U.S. Bureau of the Census, 2000), which is a result of steady growth over the past 20 years. The growth includes a boom in 1989 and approximately a 120% increase in Hispanic population in the last 10 years. The majority of this population consists of families that have immigrated from Mexico, as well as a small number of immigrants who are from other Latin American countries. The immigration process is one that is typical throughout the United States, wherein large groups of people immigrate from the same geographical regions to the same areas in the United States. Such a pattern promotes regional unity among the "older" or more established immigrants. The other portion of the group consists of descendants of the founders of Texas, who are either of Spanish or Mexican ancestry. The two groups vary from one another in that the descendent Hispanic families are well-established and integrated into the community, and the immigrant families live in *colonias*, the majority of which are located in the less settled areas of the county. The term *colonia* typical-

ly refers to neighborhoods or communities located in close proximity to the U.S.–Mexico border that are characterized by high poverty rates, poor roads and drainage systems, lack of treated water and waste water systems, dilapidated housing, and a lack of formal governance. The *colonias* of Nacogdoches County meet all of the criteria except the specification of proximity to the border, a criterion that has been debated in the Texas Legislation. The Nacogdoches *colonias* exist mainly on private land developed for mobile home sites. The only commonality among these neighborhoods is that they are each located near a poultry hatchery or poultry plant. In normal circumstances, these developing neighborhoods would be regulated by the county. However, in almost all instances, the *colonias* are on privately owned land, and it is therefore up to each owner of the land to implement sewer, drainage, and so on. The living conditions are not uniform among the different *colonias*. Ponderosa is clear of trees and plotted evenly with paved roads and street lights and maintained by the county; whereas, Briar Forest, nicknamed *La Selva* (the jungle) for the thick forestation surrounding it, is on private land. Its roads are not paved nor maintained, and sewer and drainage is in the process of being completed.

Research revealed barriers common to Hispanic migrant workers, consisting of geographical isolation, transportation, language, and lack of time for leisure and family activities (Slesinger & Cautley, 1981).

All of these barriers except language are common to rural areas in general. However, some of these barriers can be reframed as assets, and the Hispanic community, like other rural populations, has other valuable strengths that help it to adapt and maintain functioning. For example, Hispanics within the community are valued for their strong work ethic and recognized for their strong family and religious foundations. Also, helping professionals working with these families recognize a rare sense of unity, both in community and family. Finally, even though ties with the greater community are weak, there are many strong informal helping networks within the *colonias* that are capable of responding to member needs. Since Spanish is the primary language of most households and a significant number of adults have not mastered English, language is a significant barrier. The language barrier is compounded by limited media in Spanish (television, radio, and print) and lack of representation in community businesses and organizations.

Furthermore, the educational system may not adequately meet the language needs of bilingual students. For example, Hispanics comprise 22% of Nacogdoches Independent School District's (NISD) student body (Texas Education Agency, 2000). According to the Academic Excellence Indicator Report, NISD has 658 students of Limited English Proficiency (LEP) currently enrolled in its schools (Texas Education Agency, 2000). These LEP students are present in every grade from prekindergarten to 6th grade in bilingual education programs, moving into English as a Second Language (ESL) Education from 7th to 12th, constituting 11% of the district student body (Texas Education Agency, 2000). Thus, 50% of NISD's Hispanic population does not participate in mainstream education, which limits access to additional opportunities to develop English proficiency and integrate into the English-speaking community. Limited English Proficiency students have limited contact with mainstreamed students. The younger students commingle between groups at lunch and during recess, although during lunch they sit by classrooms. The older ESL students commingle in the mornings after the bus drops them off, during lunch, and in the afternoons on their way home. In high school, the students will have physical education together. Very little contact is made during academic periods and during periods of free time (dropped off from bus or waiting for the bus in the afternoon). The groups are clearly divided; however, it is expected that cliques exist in junior high and high school students. One of the assets regarding the language barrier, however, is that these children *will* learn English and will one day

be bilingual, a marketable skill to have in this area. In addition, the fact that they don't know English solidifies ties within the small communities that does not distinguish what country or region they came from. The people depend on each other for information, current events, and orientation to their new location, bringing neighbors closer together.

As in most rural areas, geographic isolation interferes with access to stores, schools, and other community resources (see Figure 11.1). Six of the seven *colonias* are located in the county and are 6–10 miles from the downtown area of Nacogdoches. The seventh *colonia* is located in Nacogdoches and is approximately 2 miles south of the downtown area. Families and individuals without access to private transportation must either walk or utilize the public transportation system. However, accessing public transportation is difficult because bus services end at Loop 224, a highway that circles the city, located 1 to 7 miles from the six county *colonias*. This isolation, however, is an asset for some of the residents as they prefer to live on their own, under their own terms. This isolation has created a strong connection between a community of residents that have similar needs and expectations. Provisions of transportation for one's neighbor has built and strengthened relationships; for example, churches use their vans to transport members or parishioners to local markets to do their shopping. This becomes an enticing perk to join a church body.

Lack of time for community involvement can be a barrier to this population. For example, there tends to be a low rate of unemployment in these communities, with many of the men holding more than one job. The amount of time dedicated to employment, in conjunction with varying work schedules and long hours, has inhibited involvement in school activities and access to community-based resources. In addition, geographical isolation and transportation issues may also limit time. Thus, lack of time is a barrier when it prevents families from engaging in leisure activities, attending social functions, and seeking preventative services, and children from engaging

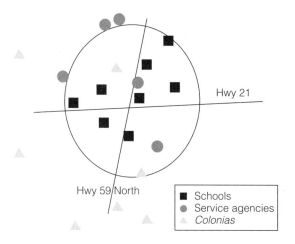

FIGURE 11.1 Nacogdoches, Texas

in extracurricular activities. Although "free time" is often scarce, the families manage to dedicate whatever precious time is available to family activities, such as church, weddings, and other social activities. In essence, the limited time available becomes an asset when it is dedicated to family bonding and strengthening events.

PROMOTING INTEGRATION OF A *COLONIA*

How does a social worker respond when a *colonia* becomes further isolated from the larger community?

In August 1997, Southwest Student Transportation, the local school bus company, decided to stop serving a *colonia* located approximately 4 miles south of Nacogdoches, because of the dreadful road conditions. Specifically, no school buses, including special education/special needs buses, would enter the area. The problem was exacerbated by the location of the neighborhood on private land, which placed the responsibility for road maintenance on the landowner instead of the county and state agencies. Furthermore, the school district claimed they did not have the power to overturn the decision because of their contractual relationship with

Southwest Student Transportation. The decision forced neighborhood children to walk up to 1 mile (one way) to and from the nearest school bus stop located on FM 2836, a two-lane paved state road. Among these students was a young man with pulmonary telangiectasia, a rare lung disease that prevented him from breathing without the use of oxygen; he was also required to walk or find another way to the bus stop.

It was this young man that prompted my involvement. I, Ruben Rodriguez, was employed as a social worker for Nacogdoches Independent School District (NISD). I realized that the residents of the *colonia* did not have someone who could effectively advocate for them. As the social worker for the bilingual education program, I perceived my role as one of education and advocacy, rather than just providing educational services to children who arrived at the school. Specifically, I felt it was important to inform the family of their rights regarding transportation and accommodations to meet special student needs, as well as assist them in exercising their rights. In response to the situation, I organized a meeting of individuals who worked directly with the *colonia* residents and others with positions of influence in the community.

Representatives from Spanish-speaking churches, the Department of Health, the Department of Human Services, healthcare services, law enforcement, education, and the media attended the meeting. Within a week of the meeting, the group had organized a work crew composed of *colonia* residents, community members, and county jail inmates. The work crew improved the road using materials and equipment donated by members of the community. Although the road was not completely repaired, the improvements allowed the buses to restart services.

The fellowship provided by this opportunity had a lasting effect and led to the formation of HACER (Hispanic Alliance for Community EnRichment). HACER was founded in 1997 as a 501c(3) nonprofit organization with the mission of promoting the development and welfare of the local Spanish-speaking community. *Hacer* is the Spanish word for "to do" or "to cause." The formation of HACER brought the realization that knowledge about the Mexican immigrant and Spanish-speaking community was limited. Growing up as an immigrant myself, I had an idea of the community's mannerisms, values, and behaviors based on culture and tradition; yet as a social worker with a community as a client system, I could not make assumptions about what they needed and wanted. I helped organize and lead a team of people that would facilitate service delivery, but I needed an in-depth assessment of how much help was needed. The paradox that warranted caution was that families expressed a willingness and desire for their children to learn the language of the land to facilitate assimilation and acculturation. However, the families would also express a disdain for an "Americanized" child who would talk back, find activities more important than the family, and other behaviors learned at school that pulled children away from traditional mores and respectful behavior. Devore and Schlesinger (1999) suggest that ethnicity can be both a source of cohesion and of conflict and strife. They suggest the use of the strengths perspective (Saleebey, 1999) and empowerment models (Lee, 1994) as the most congruent social work theories for use with ethnic minority groups. By recognizing traits that were once viewed as limitations—or even, by some, as pathologies—as assets and strengths of an immigrant group, the community practitioner can gain a strong vantage point to begin building assets within the immigrant community. For example, practitioners may view the adherence to rituals, celebrations, and language of the country of origin not as a limitation but as an asset by which members of ethnic minorities maintain cohesion and solidarity among the members of the new community. The strengths-based community practitioner will promote maintenance of the old language and cultural traditions rather than total assimilation and loss of cultural traits. At the same time, the worker will recognize the need for acquisition of new language skills and the necessity for adaptation to the host environment for mere survival. Rather than "trashing" the old customs and traditions, the community social work-

er builds on these attributes, so that the immigrant eventually experiences gain and enrichment rather than the devastation of loss of old ways, traditions, and language.

Utilizing this strengths perspective, the community practitioner who ventures into an immigrant community such as the *colonia* will assess assets, cultural strengths, and sources of cohesion; as well as deficits and limitations. Often even the deficits can be reframed as strengths or assets.

The community practitioner with the strengths perspective thus will not promote total assimilation but will assist in the complicated process of helping the immigrant recieve necessary coping and adaptive skills for attaining "the good life," which the immigrant has journeyed to the United States to gain while retaining the deep richness of the old traditions. It is entirely possible for Latinos to achieve that delicate balance between sustenance of the old and accommodation to the new culture.

By pulling back from who I am into a professional helping role, I discovered that it would be a fine line to balance service honoring self-determination and educating without making condescending assumptions. I decided to formulate a survey in Spanish that would allow me to collect information about a population that I knew in a general sense, but didn't know in this particular environment.

CREATING A PROFILE USING A SURVEY INSTRUMENT

I designed a survey instrument to identify specific characteristics, assets, and concerns of the Mexican immigrant population, including: (1) general demographics, (2) safety and security, (3) health issues, (4) socioeconomic issues, and (5) educational concerns, needs, and attitudes. The survey was developed by gathering feedback from ten families, who assessed the overall readability of the instrument. The final instrument consisted of 60 questions in Spanish, which were divided into three sections. The first section contained general demographic questions about the respondent, including an attempt to ascertain residency status. The second and third sections consisted of true–false and yes–no questions (respectively) designed to assess various strengths and needs. The instrument also included two open-ended questions that allowed respondents to identify services they would like to see offered by NISD and/or a community center for Spanish-speaking families. The final instrument was tested with 10 Spanish-speaking families attending a community English class to provide feedback on the register of Spanish used in the survey.

The sample consisted of 55 Mexican immigrant families residing in the rural East Texas County of Nacogdoches. All of the respondents were parents of children attending bilingual prekindergarten and kindergarten classes at Brooks-Quinn-Jones Early Learning Center, which is the largest campus with Limited English Proficient (LEP) population in Nacogdoches ISD. The campus selection was based on the number of LEP students, which was 147. The bilingual teachers pinned a survey to the clothing of each bilingual student prior to being sent home. "Pinning" is a common practice at the Brooks-Quinn-Jones campus, and is a fairly effective method of disseminating information to parents. Of the 147 surveys distributed, 60 were returned, 55 of which were completed, yielding a response rate of 37%. I later discovered that two of the teachers did not pin the survey to their students, which may have affected the return rate. Out of these two classes, only five surveys were returned, clearly a lower response rate than the classes that pinned them to the students.

What the Social Worker Learned

Demographics As expected, the majority of the respondents (94%) were Mexican immigrants; 52.7% were female. The median age range for respondents was 26–33 years of age (38.9% of the respondents), with 23.9% in the range of 18–25, and 28.3% in the range of 34–50 years of age. Almost half (43.4%) had less than a 6th grade

education. The majority of the respondents (85%) made less than $400 per week and 41% made less than $250 per week. The average number of children per household was three. Forty-two percent responded as a multiple family household *on occasion, sometimes, or always.* The results were not surprising, except for the large group in the 34–50 years of age group, because they seem extraordinarily old to have children in prekindergarten and kindergarten. Everything else was foreseen, as the families did not have gainful employment, the parents were undereducated, and it was not uncommon to host other families that needed assistance. See Table 11.1 for a visual elaboration of these demographics.

Socioeconomic Situation According to the Federal Poverty Guidelines (see Table 11.2), approximately 73% of the respondents live in poverty (U.S. Department of Health and Human Services, 2001). Additional analysis of the data reveals that even households with more than one family fell under the poverty guidelines, and that 36% of them depended on one income. The prominence of poverty is significant when considering that 47.3% of the respondents either own or are purchasing their residence. Unfortunately, as the authors have witnessed firsthand, some of those homes owned are passed down mobile homes with minimal protection from the elements. This could be one of the reasons why many chose to live outside the city limits where home restrictions are nonexistent. Those with lower incomes tended to be anxious about their economic situation, were prone to transportation problems (43.4%), and were unable to budget money for food (28%). It is interesting that 31.5% do not have heat in their homes, but 85% had phone service. The high number of phones could be due to the value placed on communication with family members, especially those who remain in Mexico.

The survey also measured other aspects of socioeconomic well-being, such as public assistance and transportation. As expected, many reported that they did not know how to access programs offering financial assistance (62%).

Table 11.1 Income per Multifamily Household

| Responses | Income/ Week ($) | "MORE THAN ONE FAMILY LIVES AT MY HOME." | | | | | | |
		1–2 People	3–4 People	5–6 People	7–8 People	9–10 People	11+ People	Total
Never	0–150			2				2
	151–250		4	4	1	1	2	12
	251–400	1	3	5	2			11
	401–500		1					1
	500+		1	1				2
	Total	1	9	12	3	1	2	28
On occasion	151–250			2				2
	251–400		1		1	1		3
	401–500		1		1			2
	Total		2	2	2	1		7
Sometimes	151–250		2		1			3
	251–400		1	4	3			8
	Total		3	4	4			11
Always	151–250			2				2
	251–400		1	1				2
	500+				1			1
	Total		1	3	1			5

However, 58% receive some sort of public assistance, with Women with Infant Children (WIC) being the most utilized. As for transportation, 71% report difficulty with transportation and 67.8% depend on someone else for transportation.

Family and Social Activities Responses tended to confirm the strong sense of family connectedness that is often attributed to the Hispanic culture. Specifically, 94% reported eating dinner as a family at least "sometimes" or "always." Also, 93% report that they engage in social activities as a family. These responses, coupled with 98% of the respondents attending church at least occasionally (if not sometimes or always), indicate a strong social structure within the *colonias*. To gain insight regarding who respondents would seek out as a "first response" for assistance, the survey asked them if their pastor played that role; 51% of the respondents did not view their pastor as the first line of assistance. Because information to explain this response was not solicited, interpretation is purely based on speculation. A logical assumption and a definite strength of this community may be that family members, church members, and/or community members provide an informal helping network that is effective in addressing issues before they reach the pastor.

Education One of the most exciting pieces of information I found was that, regardless of the parents' level of education, all of the parents felt that education was the most important asset for their children. For example, 98.1% of the parents

Table 11.2 2001 HHS Poverty Guidelines

Size of Family Unit	48 Contiguous States and DC	Alaska	Hawaii
1	$ 8,590	$10,730	$ 9,890
2	11,610	14,510	13,360
3	14,630	18,290	16,830
4	17,650	22,070	20,300
5	20,670	25,850	23,770
6	23,690	29,630	27,240
7	26,710	33,410	30,710
8	29,730	37,190	34,180
For each additional person, add	$ 3,020	$ 3,780	$ 3,470

SOURCE: *Federal Register*, Vol. 66, No. 33, February 16, 2001, pp. 10695–10697.

are strongly supportive of bilingual education and 84% also want the school to help the children to perfect their Spanish language abilities. These responses are congruent with the basis of the LEP program, that instructors will assist students with their native tongue initially as the students gradually begin to develop their English language abilities. It is also important that 96.2% of the respondents expressed interest in the school district providing English classes for parents. Although 82% of the parents report that they attend school functions "sometimes" or "always," 67.3% indicated a lack of understanding regarding the school system. Another significant finding is that 72.6% of the parents felt that their level of education impedes their ability to assist their children with homework.

Sense of Security Responses indicate general feelings of apprehension when venturing outside of the home, which appear to be related to several different factors. For example, 84.3% of the respondents felt uncomfortable (with various levels of frequency) when they were unable to comprehend a conversation, which is supported by the 90% that feel uncomfortable when there is not a bilingual individual present. Furthermore, 96% leave their homes with caution and 88%

reported having been a victim of crime. Further analysis demonstrated a significant relationship between caution and victimization. Another surprise was that even though 92.6% of the respondents felt safest in their current home, 77.4% would move if their economic situation improved. We can only wonder if they would move to another *colonia*.

Medical and Health Services When considering the percentages of households functioning in poverty and those who were unsure how to access financial assistance, it is reassuring that over half of the respondents reported that their children had health insurance. Furthermore, they reported that they were treated well at *La Clinica* (East Texas Community Health, Inc.). It is encouraging that 71% of the parents whose children had insurance also had social security numbers, an indicator of legal employment, protected by labor laws, that provides benefits, insurance, and at least a minimum wage. Although Texas has a state program for health insurance, those that cannot prove legal residency are not eligible. Other heartening news was that 96% of the respondents knew where to go for medical attention and 64% had annual dentist visits. Also, the data collected indicated that a fairly high percentage of the population was able to access at least basic community resources such as health care. The local health community has heeded the call of necessity in these impoverished communities by writing and receiving grants that allow practitioners to open the doors to service or to bring practitioners out to these communities, by having bilingual staff and by providing minimal documentation.

Legal Status One of the most important issues among the Mexican immigrant population is that of legal status. Although status is usually irrelevant to helping professionals due to the obligation to serve those in need, it is still an issue for the client. Furthermore, the issue of legal status makes it difficult to assess the number of undocumented aliens. Thirty-seven percent of the respondents indicated they did not have a social security number, which indicates the legal status of an undocumented alien. However, if the individuals who did not answer this question (social security number) are also assumed to be undocumented, the percentage of undocumented respondents rises to 50%. Employment based on these numbers is irrelevant. Factories and plants require legal documentation but some do not feel the need to verify the authenticity of those documents. Day labor, that requires minimal documentation if any, is popular, visible, and utilized heavily in this community.

Placing the Profile in Context

As expected, the results contain common themes that are either directly or indirectly related to lack of time, geography, transportation, and language. The first three factors are easily explained by the characteristics of a rural environment, but the question is, do they present greater difficulty for Mexican immigrants? Or are they merely rendered more extreme by the language barrier? It may be helpful to approach these questions from the framework of acculturation, which is "the process of conditioning an individual or group to the social patterns, behaviors, values, and mores of others" (Barker, 1999, p. 3). The importance of acculturation is that it determines to what degree the group will integrate into the community and society at large. Studies demonstrate that acculturation depends on both individual circumstances and characteristics of the surrounding community (Portes & Zhou, 1993; Sherraden & Barrera, 1997). For example, if there are limited opportunities for the two cultures to learn about one another, then acculturation will occur at a slower rate, or not at all. Thus, the question is: what is the effect of the barriers upon the process of acculturation?

Although these barriers encourage the development of strong ties within the *colonia,* they may also interfere with the process of acculturation. For example, geographical isolation combined with transportation issues may prevent children from participating in extracurricular activities

(such as band, choir, and sports) and academic activities (such as tutorials). Since such activities are an important part of academics and socialization, limited access may impede development. Furthermore, activities that build self-esteem and social skills help children avoid delinquent activities such as truancy, substance abuse, and gang involvement. Isolation also limits the ability of the family members to participate in community activities and government. For example, the study found that 95.9% of the respondents could not identify their community leaders, and more than half stated they did not know their rights as residents. On the other hand, it should be mentioned that community and civic leaders would not be able to identify Hispanic community leaders either. It appears that isolation eventually becomes insulation. In other words, items and services needed for daily living move into the *colonia.* They are readily available to the residents, so the *colonia* becomes insulated. The drawback is that insulation further interferes with acculturation by limiting interactions with the larger community, which may explain the reports regarding safety and security. Although insulation can be viewed as self-sufficiency, in extreme cases insulation would result in a closed community, one that does not welcome nor solicit interaction with the environment.

Acculturation may also be affected by the stress of daily living. For a mother, the additional stress may result from trying to manage a household when access to transportation and resources is limited or when negotiating an unfamiliar and complicated educational system. For a father, it could be the stress of working long hours everyday to support the household, while wondering if ends will meet. For the adolescent daughter it could be the stress of trying to fulfill the role expectations set by peers, family, culture, and mainstream society. Although all adolescents go through this process, she also must adjust to a new culture with different expectations. In other words, acculturation increases the difficulty of finding a balance between peers and parents. Cultural differences also interfere with the parents' ability to balance their expectations and the wants and needs of their children. When one combines all of these variables and examines the family situation, what would be the effect on family functioning? What family strengths would assist with coping?

The stress created by acculturation may also be enhanced by problems of residency status. Salcido (1979) examined the relationship between stress and the residency status of Mexican families. Results indicated the levels of stress differed between documented and undocumented families. Among the documented aliens, only 20% reported high levels of stress, whereas 52% of the undocumented aliens reported high levels of stress. It is possible that the difference is related to Salcido's (1979) finding that undocumented aliens have less economic resources and education. Although some attribute this to underutilization of formal services, it is more likely a result of legislation. For example, Gelfand and Bialik-Gilad (1989) document the scarcity of resources available for undocumented aliens who were not affected by the Immigration Reform and Control Act (IRCA) of 1986. The act allowed for the "legalization" of approximately 3 million alien residents who could demonstrate entrance into the United States prior to January 1, 1982. This allowed up to one million temporary agricultural workers to obtain residency (Longres, 2000). Furthermore, the act sought to prevent future entrance of undocumented aliens through a variety of sanctions and policies (Longres, 2000). Gelfand and Bialik-Gilad went on to state that unless the majority of the immigrants returned to their native countries, attempts by helping professionals to assist with resource acquisition would be futile. They predicted that the policy would prevent undocumented aliens from attaining adequate living conditions, and that health care needs and homelessness would be on the increase.

At this point, it is clear that acculturation is a difficult process for this population. But is it impossible? A number of cultural attributes or strengths are helpful assets in reducing accultura-

tive stress. The Hispanic culture places a high value on friendship and social relationships. Relationships are based on *simpatica* or the need for behaviors that promote smooth social relationships, friendships, loyalty, and reciprocity. Another cultural strength is allocentrism, which is an orientation to the family or group instead of the individual. The focus is on the meeting of family needs, and individual sacrifices are made for the good of the collective. Allocentrism is directly related to familialism, or the placement of the family first, even before friendships. Familialism includes a focus on extended family members and fictive kin, who play a role similar to that of godparents. The fictive kin or *comadre* and *compadre* (coparents) take an active role in the family and often assist with meeting family needs.

Looking back to the survey results, evidence clearly exists to support the presence of *simpatica,* allocentrism, and familialism. The pooling of resources such as housing, food, utilities, and transportation, as well as the holding of multiple jobs to support the household, are common practices. The importance of family is also demonstrated through emphasis on family activities despite time constraints. Furthermore, the parents tend to be active in the education of their children and possess a desire to further their own education. The survey responses also demonstrate resourcefulness in spite of the barriers. For example, many of the respondents have accessed public assistance programs, medical and dental services, and other community resources. The most impressive task has been the formation of *colonias* that exemplify allocentrism at a community level, with people of a common language living near each other, close to employment or transportation to employment. Also, the members want to be involved with the community at large, at least within the realm of education of their children. Since the population appears, at least to some degree, to possess the desire and ability to integrate with the community, the question becomes: is the greater community ready for integration?

There is evidence to support the larger community's willingness to move toward integration.

For instance, some community stores are making a noticeable effort to cater to the Spanish-speaking population by actively seeking bilingual employees and stocking culturally related food products (beyond food products of the Mexican genre that mainstream would buy, such as taco shells or *picante* sauce). Such efforts have resulted in the majority of the respondents reporting that the community grocery stores treat them well. Other attempts to extend services can be seen in the healthcare community, law enforcement, and community mental health. In fact, the City of Nacogdoches has formed a committee that is charged with examining the needs of the Hispanic population and making formal recommendations for interventions to address those needs. Thus, it seems that at least those community entities that value the consumer aspect of these individuals appear to be taking positive steps toward integrating the Hispanic population.

Using the Profile to Improve Community Practice

In order to be an effective social work practitioner, one must possess a comprehensive understanding of the client population, their needs, and their perception of the issues. Most social workers will agree that this is often a difficult task, especially when additional barriers, such as language and culture, are present. However, failure to obtain such information may result in a failed intervention, unpleasant experiences, and/or damaged relationships. An inherent risk is the assumption of a client system based solely on academic knowledge, theory, and a multicultural class. In the case of the young man with the lung disease, this young man's plight and a father's request for assistance led to community mobilization and exposure of an invisible community. Requests for assistance came to organizers, and politicos jumped on the bandwagon of compassion, only to find that the residents wanted more help in organizing and resource allocation than hands-on assistance. They felt that they could raise their own funds and fix the road themselves. Was this an instance of the *colonias* distancing themselves

from the outside community out of fear or pride or culture? A lesson taken by this, regardless of reason, was for HACER to adopt a different approach for helping this community. It was clear from this experience and others that assistance would come in the form of education, information, and role modeling. This approach may appear to be a passive way to mobilize a community, but it is the most effective with the least amount of harm done. The hope is that members of the *colonias* could integrate as individuals first, if they were armed with the right information, made aware of laws, and educated about social norms and local customs.

HACER has utilized this information to establish itself as a beacon for the Spanish-speaking segment of this community. The organization provides information to the residents of the *colonias* regarding important legislation and available services through informal community meetings that are scheduled to meet individual time constraints. Meetings are often held in the *colonias,* and members from the various *colonias* attend and take the information back to the others. The participants are encouraged to provide input and feedback. These meetings have assisted HACER with opening communication between the *colonias* and the community. Furthermore, Nacogdoches community members often utilize HACER as a resource for identifying leaders in the Hispanic community for organizational board appointments and other positions. HACER often provides representatives for special committees and task groups that are addressing community issues. All of these activities have resulted in HACER gaining the respect from the Mexican immigrant and Hispanic population. It is HACER's intent to use this respect as a foundation for future involvement, moving toward the establishment of a community center to serve as a clearinghouse for information and an orientation center for new immigrants. Such a center would also provide cultural events and educational opportunities for the entire community in order to facilitate integration.

The Mexican immigrant population of Nacogdoches County possesses a number of assets, such as kinship ties, strong work ethic, and family values that have assisted them with the formation of *colonias*. Although the internal ties are strong, development of external links to the community has been slow, which can be attributed to the barriers of geographical isolation, transportation, time, and language. All of these barriers serve to isolate the *colonias* from the community at large and can eventually exacerbate life problems, such as the ones exemplified by the previously mentioned case examples. However, it is reasonable to assume that interventions that focus on these barriers, as well as on the *colonias* and the community at large, will lead to successful integration. The end result of using this information is not for assimilation but to ensure a smooth acculturative process by reducing the chances for added stress to the families. The survey results provide information

pertinent to the development of a community center that will provide the entire community with an opportunity for cultural enrichment. After all, knowledge and understanding are prerequisites for respect and tolerance. It's ironic that a serious illness of a little boy could mobilize an entire community to assist. That young man now possesses new lungs donated by relatives and has made good progress. Meanwhile life in *La Selva* goes on. There is a new (used) trailer on the lot where one had burned. The residents and HACER are penning a letter to the school bus system, as school is about to begin, asking them to assess the progress that has been made to the road by the residents, hoping the buses will come round again. And the community leaders breathe a little easier with a centralized 911 system, as the twenty-first century comes to East Texas.

NOTE

Ruben Rodriguez, the "I" in the article, was the school social worker who completed the needs assessment survey and implemented the change efforts. H. Stephen Cooper assisted with statistical analysis and community practice.

Linda Morales was the professor who guided the initial research efforts. The authors would like to thank Tara Etter, LSW, for assistance with the initial data collection and analysis.

DISCUSSION QUESTIONS

1. How does a social worker who works with an immigrant community best demonstrate respect for the values of a community at large (i.e., maintaining confidentiality, managing dual relationships among family members that respect informal relationships, etc.)?

2. What does a social worker do when he or she encounters families who are undocumented aliens? Does he or she have an obligation to report this? Why or why not?

3. Should school systems work on accomplishing assimilation to the host culture of migrant children, or should they work on building on ethnic pride while gradually acculturating children? What are the pros and

cons of each approach? Which is the preferred approach? How might the preferred approach be implemented?

4. If a social work researcher wants to complete a needs assessment in a *colonia* or other immi-grant community, what steps must he or she go through to engage the community before data can be gathered? In other words, what is the best way to gain entrance into that community for data collection?

5. If a school system fails to meet specific needs of migrant children, what might a community social worker do to initiate change?

CLASSROOM ASSIGNMENTS
AND ACTIVITIES

1. Define acculturation, assimilation, cultural pluralism, and biculturalism. Compare and contrast them. Be sure to clearly identify the goals and purpose of each. Which of these concepts best describe the processes experienced by residents of the *colonias* in this article?

2. Define "acculturative stress." What indicators of this type of stress has this article described? What else could indicate the presence of acculturative stress? How could "acculturative stress" be reframed as a strength or asset? As a social worker, how would you assess a client for acculturative stress?

3. Call a social worker for your local school system, or another official, such as a principal or school counselor (if there is not a social worker), and find out if the district has a Hispanic immigrant or migrant worker population. If so, how does the school district address acculturative stress? In what ways does the school system meet the special needs of the population? What strengths or assets exist among the immigrant population in your area? What needs are not adequately met and why?

4. Define and contrast these three models of community practice: Social Planning Model, Social Action Model, and Empowerment Model of Community Building.

5. The community social worker in this article primarily utilized the Empowerment Model, but used some principles and tactics from all three approaches. From the discussion in this article, identify five tactics or methods that the social worker utilized in his efforts to gain access to the community.

6. Which of the three models of community practice work best with the assets-building approach. Why?

REFERENCES

Barker, R. L. (1999). *The social work dictionary* (4th ed.). Washington, DC: National Association of Social Workers Press.

Devore, W., & Schlesinger, E. (1999). *Ethnic-sensitive social work practice* (4th ed.). Needham Heights, MA: Allyn & Bacon.

Gelfand, D. E., & Bialik-Gilad, R. (1989). Immigration reform and social work. *Social Work, 34,* 23–27.

Lee, J. A. B. (1994). *The empowerment approach to social work practice.* New York: Columbia University Press.

Longres, J. F. (2000). *Human behavior in the social environment* (3rd ed.). Itasca, IL: Peacock Publishers.

Portes, A., & Zhou, M. (1993). The second generation: Segmented assimilation and its variants. *Annals of the American Academy of Political and Social Science, 530,* 74–96.

Salcido, R. M. (1979). Undocumented aliens: A study of Mexican families. *Social Work, 24,* 306–311.

Saleebey, D. (1999). The strengths perspective: Principles and practices. In B. R. Compton & B. Galaway (Eds.). *Social work processes* (6th ed., pp. 14–27). Pacific Grove, CA: Brooks/Cole.

Sherraden, M. S., & Barrera, R. E. (1997). Family support and birth outcomes among second-generation Mexican immigrants. *Social Service Review, 71,* 607–633.

Slesinger, D. P., & Cautley, E. (1981). Medical utilization patterns of Hispanic migrant farm workers in Wisconsin. *Public Health Reports, 96,* 255–263.

Texas Education Agency. (2000). *Academic excellence indicator report, 1999–2000.* Retrieved April 12, 2001, from http://www.tea.state.tx.us.

U.S. Bureau of the Census. (2000). *Census 2000.* Retrieved December 12, 2001, from http://quickfacts.census.gov/qfd/states/48/48347.html.

U.S. Department of Health and Human Services. (2001). *2001 Department of Health and Human Services poverty guidelines.* Retrieved April 1, 2001, from http://aspe.hhs.gov/poverty/00poverty.htm.

INFOTRAC COLLEGE EDITION

acculturation

acculturative stress

assimilation

biculturalism

cultural pluralism

Mexican immigrants

rural populations

12

Using Wraparound to Build Rural Communities of Care for Children with Serious Emotional Disturbance and Their Families

TAMARA S. DAVIS

Imagine yourself as a social worker employed by the local rural community mental health center. You just received a referral from the local junior high school for a 13-year-old male named Colby who physically assaulted another youth at school. You know this is not Colby's first time in trouble because you worked with him and his mother a year ago, when he was charged with vandalizing his neighbor's car. His mother, who works almost 12 hours a day at two jobs to make ends meet, tells you she is just about to give up on Colby. She has two other kids at home to think about, and she is afraid he might follow through on his threats to hurt one of them while she is not at home. Colby's mother thinks she might need to find someplace else to send him.

If you have seen situations like this too many times before, you know the outcome is rarely a happy ending. Kids like Colby need special services from multiple systems, and you are only one person. The lack of resources in your community for children and youth who have serious mental health issues means they are often sent to residential care 150 miles away. Your hopes for this young man and his family might begin to fade. But what if you were to learn about a process that has worked with seriously emotionally disturbed children and their families all across the country? What if you knew there was a way to utilize the assets and the resources of Colby, his family, and

the community to increase his chances of successfully remaining in his own community? And what if you knew this process was generally compatible with the values of rural communities? You would jump on it, no doubt! This article introduces you to such a promising practice increasingly used for delivering services to families who have a child with serious emotional disturbance. The name of the practice is *wraparound*. "Wraparound is a philosophy of care that includes a definable planning process involving the child and family that results in a unique set of community services and natural supports individualized for that child and family to achieve a positive set of outcomes" (Burns, Goldman, Faw & Burchard, 1999, p. 13).

Although the term *wraparound* emerged in the 1980s to describe a service delivery approach advocated in children's mental health, the ideas behind its philosophy are neither new nor exclusive to mental health. Indeed, social work has a long tradition of family-centered practice focusing on the family's contextual interface with one another and the larger environment (Hartman & Laird, 1983). Numerous variations of practice models valuing strengths-based partnerships with families and communities are evolving. "Patch" and "Family Group Decision Making" (Adams & Krauth, 1995; American Humane Association, 1997) are two examples from child welfare, and Adams and Nelson (1995) highlight other models implemented in schools and social service programs.

A community development model offered by Kretzmann and McKnight (1993) provides clear guidelines on how a community can build on its assets rather than its deficits. This model was highlighted in the Surgeon General's Report on Mental Health (U.S. Department of Health & Human Services (USDHHS), 1999) with its recommendation for the development of culturally appropriate mental health programs in local communities. In a similar vein, Benson (1997) and colleagues at the Search Institute launched the Healthy Communities–Healthy Youth Initiative. They designed their developmental assets model to use the assets and strengths of youth and their communities to help them navigate positive and healthy development into adulthood. Wraparound within a system of care combines elements of all these models. The assets or strengths of seriously emotionally disturbed children and their families are combined with the assets or resources of the community in an effort to ensure that children can remain in the care of their families within their home community.

Before learning about the specific practice of wraparound in children's mental health, it is important to understand some related issues. The article begins with a brief history of the growing children's mental health movement in the United States. This leads into a brief discussion on the status of mental health prevalence, risk factors, barriers, and strengths of related service delivery issues in rural communities. Finally, the wraparound process is described in detail as it is currently used within systems of care to serve children, youth, and their families struggling with serious emotional disturbance. You will learn about the values and principles guiding these processes and how wraparound is different from traditional mental health practice. You will see that wraparound is a parallel development to strengths-based social work (Saleebey, 2002), strengths-based case management (Kisthardt, 1997), and other assets-based models previously noted. Through this discussion, you will discern how "generalist" social work

training prepares you to become a social work "specialist" through individualized wraparound care for children, youth, and families within their own communities.

THE CHILDREN'S MENTAL HEALTH MOVEMENT

There is increasing recognition of the need to develop more effective mental health systems for children with serious emotional disturbance and their families in the United States. Current national data indicate that one out of every five children will need mental health services at some point before reaching adulthood, and the Surgeon General's Report (USDHHS, 1999) indicated that approximately 9 to 13 percent of all children suffer with serious emotional disturbances. Considering U.S. Census 2000 estimates that 11.6 million children under the age of 18 live in rural areas of the country, we can estimate that 1 to 1.5 million children in rural communities experience significant functional mental impairments.

Building on three decades of momentum, the United States is zealously moving toward addressing the needs of children and families struggling with mental illness. The Joint Commission on Mental Illness and Health found in 1961 that mental health needs of children and youth were going unmet. Noting a lack of community resources and uncoordinated mental health programs, the report cited specific recommendations to "shape community mental health programs around local needs" (p. 122). In 1969, the Joint Commission on the Mental Health of Children recommended building *systems of care* for children with serious emotional disturbance and their families (Lourie, Katz-Leavy, DeCarolis, & Quinlan, 1996). Nearly 30 years later, a landmark study by the Children's Defense Fund found that mental health services to children remained fragmented, uncoordinated, and sometimes inappropriate (Knitzer, 1982).

Subsequent to these studies, the National Institute of Mental Health launched the Child and Adolescent Service System Program (CASSP) in 1984 to assist states in developing coordinated systems of care for children and adolescents with serious emotional disturbances and their families. The CASSP effort resulted in the seminal publication, *A System of Care for Severely Emotionally Disturbed Children and Youth* (Stroul & Friedman, 1986), providing a conceptual framework for implementing systems of care that value community-based, child and family-centered, and culturally competent care. Structuring case management functions—including mobilizing, coordinating, and maintaining an array of services and resources that meet the child and family's needs over time (Evans & Armstrong, 2002)—around the systems of care values base was recommended. The chosen case management model became known as wraparound.

MENTAL HEALTH PREVALENCE AND RISK FACTORS OF RURAL CHILDREN AND YOUTH

What Do the Prevalence Data Indicate?

Recent data indicate that the 9–13 percent estimate reported by the Surgeon General may be somewhat low. Costello, Keeler, and Angold (2001) completed a study in 1998 that included a representative sample of 541 rural "black" and 379 rural "white" children ages 9–17. Looking specifically at the effects of poverty on psychiatric prevalence, an overall three-month prevalence rate of 20 percent was found for major psychiatric disorders. Although differences between urban and rural mental health prevalence rates have been debated for years (Wagenfeld, 1982; Keller & Murray, 1982), more recent reports indicate little difference in overall prevalence rates between urban and rural youth. However, Cutrona,

Halvorson, and Russell (1996) reported increasing use of substances by rural youth, noting higher prevalence rates for use of alcohol and smokeless tobacco by youth in some rural areas than is found nationally. They also reported that loneliness due to geographic isolation from friends is a problem for rural youth and suggested loneliness may contribute to higher rates of suicide for rural youth.

Although rural life is more commonly associated with tight-knit communities where "everyone knows everyone else," Benson (1997) and colleagues' research on youth developmental assets found the quality of socialization for rural youth essentially the same as the quality of socialization for youth in large cities. In fact, they found a great lack in the quality of socialization (for example, relationship-building, social experiences, and interaction) for all youth across geographic boundaries.

What Are the Mental Health Risk Factors for Children and Youth?

Mental health risk factors for children and youth living in rural communities remain consistent over time. Risk factors frequently identified include poverty, unemployment, family history of psychopathology, transitory housing, child abuse, and poor parenting skills (Costello, et al., 2001; Cutrona, et al., 1996; Wodarski, 1983). Some of these risk factors are unavoidable, as they are often characteristic of living in rural areas. For example, rural communities suffer from high rates of poverty; there simply are not enough jobs for everyone. The numbers of jobs available for well-educated people and in local industry are limited. This issue has only increased as the number of rural independent farms has diminished over the years (Ginsberg, 1998).

In rural and urban communities alike, unemployment is tied to other risk factors, such as transitory housing and lack of health insurance and health care. When caregivers are without means to pay for general physical healthcare, they are more likely to avoid seeking assistance for mental health care. Similarly, the stress associated with the inability to provide for one's family can lead a caregiver to resort to inappropriate disciplinary action, potentially resulting in child physical abuse. Costello and colleagues (2001) noted the most significant risk factors for children in their study included family history of mental illness, poor parenting, multiple moves, lack of parental warmth, a lack of parental supervision, and harsh punishment by parents.

Mental Health Service Delivery to Children, Youth, and Families in Rural Communities

Think back to the example presented at the beginning of the article. Colby is involved with several different public systems: education, juvenile justice, and mental health. If you were working with Colby, where would you focus your intervention? Since you are the mental health professional, you may decide that you can offer him counseling or therapy. You know there are no school social workers within 50 miles of your community. You also know that the folks at juvenile probation may not be an appropriate resource because Colby has already completed his retribution and probation period from last year's incident. You are it!

This family probably sounds a little overwhelming to a new social work practitioner. And it can be overwhelming for experienced social workers when many barriers are preventing families from obtaining services. The next section discusses routine challenges for rural social workers. It further examines strengths of rural communities, which make them an ideal context for using wraparound approaches with families.

What Are the Challenges and Barriers for Rural Communities?

Rural communities face a different set of challenges and barriers to mental health service provision than do inner-city communities. These barriers are not to be taken lightly, as they have proven pervasive over time. Key issues for the rural mental health social worker to consider include the community's external environment

(geography, transportation, communication), its social and cultural environment (values, beliefs, social structures), and resource availability (Ginsberg, 1998; Keller & Murray, 1982).

External Environment Geography is one of the greatest barriers to accessing mental health services in rural areas. Over half of rural residents live in areas designated as having a shortage of psychiatric services (Cutrona, et al., 1996). Thus, families must travel long distances to receive whatever mental health services are available to them, and this distance adds challenges to even securing adequate transportation for families. Because availability of public transportation is limited, rural residents must depend on a privately owned vehicle to get from place to place. Factoring in the issue of poverty, the expense of maintaining a vehicle may be too inhibitive for families, leaving them dependent on others to provide transportation (Ginsberg, 1998).

Geography also impacts the ability of the social worker to provide the amount of services needed within a geographic region. If great distances must be traveled to meet with families in their homes, the number of families on a social worker's caseload will be affected. Likewise, communication is impacted by geography. Some families live too far away from town for a phone line, while others may be unable to afford phone service. Yet with continuing media advances, rural residents watch the larger society changing around them. All of these external factors contribute to physical and emotional isolation of rural residents from the rest of the world.

Social and Cultural Environment All rural communities possess unique values and beliefs that keep them operating as a unit. The agricultural community culture initially shaped these systems; everyone knew their roles within the community. However, industrialization brought many changes to rural communities, leaving them struggling with how to reshape community structures and resident roles (Keller & Murray, 1982). The value often held by rural communities to "take care of their own" and not talk to outsiders, creates challenges for the mental health social worker. This value, in particular, feeds into the wider issue of stigma associated with mental health problems. The power of the fear associated with stigma often keeps families from accessing professional mental health services. Families may first seek other resources they feel are more trustworthy, such as medical health professionals or clergy (Cutrona, et al., 1996; Ginsberg, 1998). Since everyone generally knows everyone else in a rural community, it is extremely difficult to maintain confidentiality. Mental health social workers must not simply gain work familiarity with the community, but must consider how to personally become a part of the community. This aspect of rural life presents interesting ethical dilemmas for social workers requiring thoughtful resolution on an individual basis.

Resource Availability As is probably apparent from the discussion so far, the availability of mental health resources in rural areas is limited. Once social workers are professionally trained in a metropolitan area, it becomes more difficult to recruit them into rural communities. If recruited, retaining or providing them with adequate ongoing training in the mental health field presents challenges, which ultimately leads to a shortage of qualified mental health providers in rural communities (Cutrona, et al., 1996; Keller & Murray, 1982). This is especially true for providers of crisis services.

Lack of resources is also related to systemic issues. Mental health services in rural communities are long noted as fragmented, uncoordinated, or duplicative across systems. In addition, policies related to federally funded mental health centers place many regulations on accessing and using the funds. Federal monies obtained specifically for Community Mental Health Centers are restricted to purchasing traditional categorized mental health services. Keller and Murray (1982) called for more flexibility in governmental regulations and more community involvement in planning mental health programs that would allow rural communities to use their dollars more beneficially. Traditional clinical approaches may be necessary at times, but existing resources and natural support systems within communities should be

targeted for enhanced development. For example, a wraparound team in one of our rural research communities created an innovative solution to the lack of available respite care. Once a month, families provided supervision to one another's children as a means of obtaining short periods of respite. Development of natural supports is a particular focus for wraparound plan development.

What Are the Assets and Strengths of Rural Communities?

Some of the challenges of mental health service provision in rural communities can be reciprocally viewed as assets or strengths. The very character of rural communities lends itself to the innovative assets and strengths-based approaches to community and youth development presented in this book. Indeed, rural communities have found themselves well-prepared to develop systems of care to support wraparound service delivery processes. The following study description speaks to a number of strengths commonly found in some variation throughout rural communities, providing potential ground for mental health services development.

During the 1990s a longitudinal study was conducted with over 400 youth and families living on farms in Iowa over a 6-year period. (See Elder & Conger, 2000, for a complete description of the study and its findings.) A number of prominent characteristics of these rural farm communities emerged as keys to success for youth in the study. Youth and families placed specific value on family life, generational continuity, intergenerational relationships, and a parental network of social ties achieved through their involvement with the local schools, a religious affiliation, and civic activities. Parents with strong community ties demonstrated increased resourcefulness. They were better educated, had stronger relationships in the community, and had stronger ties to the land over generations. Parents with weak community ties had a lack of social resources. Common values among the sample included hard work, self-reliance, a sense of responsibility, commitment to family life, social trust, the ability to work together, resourcefulness, nonmaterialism, community ties, and involvement in leadership for the common good. Resilience of youth in these farm communities was linked to "doing well academically, participation in a religious community, and feelings of self-confidence" (Elder & Conger, 2000, p. 207). Youth with ties to the land were more successful in all life domains than rural youth without such ties.

The values espoused by the successful youth and families in Elder and Conger's (2000) study are also embedded in Benson's (1997) developmental assets model. Benson's model describes 30–40 youth assets associated with positive youth development and healthy communities. In Elder and Conger's study these assets were related to the families' connectedness with the community. Similarly, a study by Scales and colleagues (2001) found that adults' increased investment in their local community was associated with adult involvement with young people. Related adult values and actions in this study included adults living in their neighborhoods for long periods of time, adult attendance at religious services, adult volunteering, and adult participation in neighborhood/community meetings.

Although many of the previously noted challenges are unavoidable realities for many living in rural areas, needed mental health services can be provided through innovative and creative problem solving using the identified assets and strengths of the community. Residents of rural, urban, and suburban communities all address similar needs, but the solutions they develop must address the unique characteristics of their communities.

WRAPAROUND SERVICE DELIVERY IN SYSTEMS OF CARE

Now that the need and models for mental health services in rural communities are established, wraparound will be more fully explored as it is used in systems of care for seriously emotionally disturbed children and their families. Refer once more to the example with which the article opened. Recall that Colby is involved with multiple service systems, a common situation for families with children who are seriously emotionally disturbed. Research indicates an extremely high prevalence rate of psychiatric disorders in youth served in public systems, including child welfare, juvenile justice, mental health, public school services, and alcohol and drug services (Garland, et al., 2001). Given the multiple issues and systems impacting the child and family, their needs cannot be met through the mental health system alone. Rather, a broad array of comprehensive services and supports is necessary to meet the families' needs (Stroul & Friedman, 1986). As previously noted, this lack of services is a well-documented area of need for rural communities. However, studies have found that systems of care models are successful in developing such an array within urban and rural communities.

What Are the Values and Principles of Wraparound and Systems of Care?

Discussing wraparound as it is used in children's mental health is difficult without also talking about systems of care. Thus, one can describe systems of care philosophy first to provide the "bigger picture" of how wraparound fits within a whole system. Stroul and Friedman (1986) define a system of care as "a comprehensive spectrum of mental health and other necessary services which are organized into a coordinated network to meet the multiple and changing needs of children and adolescents with severe emotional disturbances and their families" (p. xx). Core values maintain that systems of care must be community-based, child-centered, family-focused, and culturally competent. These guiding principles embody many of the concepts underpinning family-centered social work practice, assets-based community development, and youth developmental assets models. Systems of care values and principles must be operationalized at practice, community, and policy levels to address the strengths and challenges of providing mental health services in rural communities. There is a great deal of compatibility between the principles and values guiding the systems of care framework and those underlying wraparound. Figures 12.1 and 12.2 illustrate how the values and essential elements of wraparound fit within the values and guiding principles of systems of care. As stated earlier, a wraparound approach involves the child and family in planning services that are individualized to the specific strengths and needs of the family (Burns et al., 1999).

Although wraparound may appear to focus solely on the practice level, this view does not consider what is needed at other levels of the system to support the wraparound process. For example, systems of care guiding principles 2, 4, and 7 reflect access to an integrated, coordinated, and comprehensive array of services with varying levels of restrictive environments. Ensuring the availability of a service array is extremely valuable for implementation of wraparound, yet such an array is largely developed through administrative ranks where policies regulate how agencies work together. Essential wraparound elements 1, 4, 5, 6, and 7 illustrate this point. Without the system pieces in place, it is difficult to develop a truly individualized and flexible plan of care for a family.

As another example, systems of care guiding principles 1 and 6 reflect a requirement to respect everyone's individuality and plan services according to individual need. The related wraparound essential elements, numbers 1 and 8, depend on system policies supporting these practices. Wraparound workers feel much more confident in their ability to plan and follow through on the promise of individualized services when this value of culturally responsive care is also demonstrated at the administrative and policy levels. Though it is possible to provide wraparound without a system structure supporting flexible processes, it is difficult to sustain such efforts without systemic support.

What Exactly Is the Wraparound Approach?

Pulling needed services together requires service coordinators who can successfully navigate the multiple service systems while individualizing work with children and families. This specialized way of working with families requires the knowledge expected of a generalist social worker to understand many levels of service implementation. This generalist knowledge must then be conceptualized within the context of specific family situations. By engaging families in a team process of truly individualizing service plans to match families' strengths and needs, the "generalist" social worker learns to function as a "specialist" for each individual child and family. Wraparound defines the process (policies, practices, and steps) of providing such individualized services and supports (VanDenBerg & Grealish, 1996). The wraparound planning process differs from traditional mental health service planning because it:

1. Requires an interdisciplinary child and family team to partner with the family in planning for care and setting outcome-oriented goals;

2. Focuses on the family as a whole;

3. Focuses on the strengths and uniqueness of the child and family, including the natural supports of the family;

4. Includes flexibility in providing the services needed for an individual family rather than fitting the family into a specific program, while striving to keep the child in the community; and

5. Emphasizes cultural competence as central to effective practice. (Goldman, 1999; Koroloff, Friesen, Reilly, & Rinkin, 1996; VanDenBerg, 1993; VanDenBerg & Grealish, 1996).

Wraparound is one of the most promising practices in children's mental health service delivery, and a vast amount of research is underway to

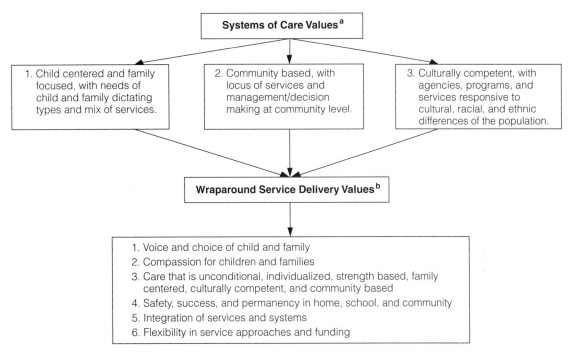

FIGURE 12.1 Wraparound Values within a Systems of Care Framework

[a]Stroul and Friedman, 1986, p. xxiv.
[b]Goldman, 1999, pp. 29–31; VanDenBerg and Grealish, 1996, p. 9.

more clearly define its impact on functional outcomes (Burchard, Bruns, & Burchard, 2002; Burns et al., 1999).

Child and Family Teams that Focus on the Family Perhaps one of the greatest challenges for systems of care and wraparound is partnering with families (Stroul & Friedman, 1986), yet families are increasingly considered a vital resource for their children. Although the value of family input is long recognized in rural communities where resources are limited, this concept challenged traditional mental health services, which placed primary value on the expertise of the provider. Although full partnership is still evolving and growing in acceptance (Friesen & Stephens, 1998), the mental health field increasingly acknowledges the need to partner with parents in planning and delivering services for their

children (Burns, Hoagwood, & Mrazek, 1999; Worthington, Hernandez, Friedman, & Uzzell, 2001) and in planning and overseeing services at the system level (Friesen & Stephens, 1998; Koroloff, et al., 1996; USDHHS, 1999). Empowering youth and families to help develop the service model is akin to the kind of empowerment recommended in the youth developmental assets model. In fact, Benson (1997) includes four developmental assets related to empowering youth within a community. In the wraparound context, youth become empowered to participate in their communities of mental health care.

In addition to the wraparound service coordinator and the family, the family also identifies wraparound team members they consider critical to the child's success (VanDenBerg & Grealish, 1996). For example, members may include professionals from the multiple service systems in which

---

Systems of Care Guiding Principles[a]

1. Individualized services in accordance with the unique needs and potentials of each child.
2. Access to comprehensive array of services that address child's physical, emotional, social, and educational needs.
3. Families as full participants in all aspects of the planning and delivery of services.
4. Integrated services with linkages between child-serving agencies and programs and mechanisms for planning, developing, and coordinating services.
5. Case management to ensure multiple services are delivered in a coordinated and therapeutic manner.
6. Receipt of services without discrimination; services are sensitive and responsive to cultural differences and special needs.
7. Least restrictive, most normative environment that is clinically appropriate.
8. Early identification and intervention is promoted to enhance likelihood of positive outcomes.
9. Smooth transitions of children into adult service system as they reach maturity.
10. Children's rights protected and effective advocacy efforts promoted.

Wraparound Essential Elements[b]

1. Individualized services and supports built on strengths; meet needs of children and families across life domains to promote success, safety, and permanency in home, school, and community.
2. Wraparound efforts based in community.
3. Families are full and active partners in every level of the wraparound process.
4. Care plan developed and implemented based on interagency, community collaborative process.
5. Team-driven process involving family, child, natural supports, agencies, and community services working together to develop, implement, and evaluate the individualized service plan.
6. Wraparound teams have flexible approaches with adequate flexible funding to develop care plans.
7. Wraparound plan has a balance of formal services and informal community and family resources.
8. Culturally competent process.
9. Unconditional commitment of comminity agencies and wraparound teams to serve children and families.
10. Outcomes are set and measured for each goal established with the child and family.

FIGURE 12.2 Wraparound Essential Elements within a Systems of Care Framework

[a]Stroul and Friedman, 1986, p. xxiv.
[b]Goldman, 1999, pp. 29–31; VanDenBerg and Grealish, 1996, p. 9.

the family is involved, or it may include a neighbor or the best friend of the child or caregiver that provides an important supportive role for the family. This team-building process is part of building a community of care around a family. An integral element of the team's planning process is setting goals and writing them into the care plan. These goals should include both short- and long-term outcomes the family hopes to achieve. Progress toward goals is assessed and tracked during regular team meetings. As barriers to the care plan arise, the team addresses the issues and the plan of care is revised accordingly. The members of the team hold each other accountable for following through on assigned tasks.

Feedback from rural service providers with whom our research team has worked indicates that agency collaboration and the need to work together comes naturally for them. Such coordination is found to be a major factor in the survival of their programs, thus their interagency relationships are already well established. Engaging families in the wraparound process is viewed as the next step in their practice, reflecting a good fit with how they believe they have always done business. However, rural communities have run into a few system-level challenges. One challenge is engaging families on a system level, as families in services are not used to being asked to participate in changing the system, and systems are not familiar with families sitting at the decision-making table. Agency folks are finding that strong relationships do not necessarily translate into policy changes.

Strengths-Based Planning Key to individualized wraparound processes is the assessment of the child and family team's strengths and matching these strengths with the service plan. If existing resources in the community do not match the strengths and needs described in the plan of care, then flexible resources are identified or developed. Wraparound trainers call this process of assessing and matching strengths a *strengths discovery* (VanDenBerg & Grealish, 1996). A similar strategy is suggested in the assets-based community development framework. That is, recognize first the capacities of the individuals and organizations present in the community and build capacity from within (Kretzmann & McKnight, 1993).

In a strengths discovery, the wraparound service coordinator engages in a conversation with the child, family, and other team members guided by extensive questions to facilitate the strengths identification process (Burchard, Bruns, & Burchard, 2002; VanDenBerg & Grealish, 1996). In some instances, it may be beneficial to ask other people in the family's life to identify child and family strengths. For example, questions may pertain to identifying friends of the family, values and traditions of the family, perceptions of individual and family qualities, or skills and hobbies of family members. It is important to recognize that strengths are not used in wraparound to the exclusion of child and family needs. Needs are addressed by using strengths to set goals rather than to solve problems (Early & Poertner, 1995).

The processes described for strengths-based work with families in mental health have been developed and written about in social work over many years. Saleebey (2002) describes processes for determining strengths and the elements of strengths-based social work practice. In an earlier version of this same text (Saleebey, 1997), Kisthardt (1997) describes the strengths-based case management model, whereby the primary helping functions are very similar to those described within the essential elements of wraparound.

Flexible-Service Planning As noted previously, a critical component of wraparound is the availability of flexible resources for use with families when individual family needs extend beyond the services available. This generally means a pool of money for use by wraparound service coordinators to obtain out-of-the-ordinary services (Goldman, 1999; Lourie, Katz-Leavy, & Stroul, 1996). For example, in one of our rural research communities, flexible dollars were used as seed money to employ youth in community businesses. If the employment arrangement was successful, the employer took over payment of wages. Although securing these resources often presents a challenge, systems of care across the country have found innovative ways to increase the amount of flexible dollars. The ability to build strong interagency collaborations that support the availability and creation of flexible resources for wraparound is key to successful systems of care development (Hodges, Nesman, & Hernandez, 1999; Koyanagi & Feres-Merchant, 2000).

Cultural Competence As illustrated in Figure 12.1, working with children and families in a culturally competent manner is essential to wraparound and systems of care at all levels. As our society becomes more ethnically diverse, individuals and organizations must be prepared to provide services to meet the needs of a wide variety of ethnic and non-ethnic cultural groups.

Likewise, Benson (1997) found cultural competence key to positive development for youth and included it in his revised list of social competency developmental assets. He recommended that communities affirm the heritage of their youth and encourage them to become culturally competent individuals.

Addressing cultural competence in children's mental health is especially critical, as research indicates a history of unsatisfactory performance by mental health service systems in serving children with diverse backgrounds (Hernandez & Isaacs, 1998; Knitzer, 1982; Roizner, 1996). There are high rates of poverty in rural areas; poverty (especially for minority children) is often associated with unmet mental health needs (Hernandez, Isaacs, Nesman, & Burns, 1998). Recognizing the importance of diversity issues, a model of cultural competence was developed for children's mental health service systems (Mason, Benjamin, & Lewis, 1996). Within this model, the following definition of cultural competence serves as a guide for developing culturally competent systems of care: "Cultural competence is a set of congruent behaviors, attitudes, and policies that come together in a system, agency, or among professionals and enable that system, agency, or those professionals to work effectively in cross-cultural situations" (Cross, Bazron, Dennis, & Isaacs, 1989, p. 13).

Cultural competence is an issue of specific importance for services in rural communities, as residents often include various populations of ethnic groups (Keller & Murray, 1982). Social work in particular recognizes the need to address needs of special populations in rural communities. (See Ginsberg, 1998, where an entire section of the book is devoted to special rural populations.) Although issues of cultural competence generally target the practitioner, systems of care value cultural competence at all levels of the system. A factor in current organizational assessment is whether the ethnic diversity of an agency's consumers is reflected among agency personnel. The importance of this factor manifests itself in the organization's ability to be culturally responsive to all community members in need of services.

Ultimately, the general lack of ethnic persons of color among the decision-making bodies of agencies in rural communities will need to be addressed before disparities in care to ethnic persons of color are truly challenged.

USING ASSETS TO BUILD COMMUNITIES OF CARE FOR CHILDREN AND FAMILIES

The United States has experienced exciting movement toward addressing the mental health needs of children and youth with serious emotional disturbance and their families. Systems of care and wraparound service delivery processes offer assets-based models for structuring and providing mental health services in communities. These models value children and families and place their needs at the center of the work.

Rural communities bring unique challenges to ensuring the meeting of mental health needs for children and families. Rural communities also have special assets that make them viable places to implement innovative and creative strategies for collaborating across agencies and with families. The most important of these assets are the people of the community. As Kretzmann and McKnight (1993) so aptly state, "the raw material for community-building is the capacity of its individual members" (p. 13), and "youth can be essential contributors to the well-being and vitality of the community" (p. 29). Using the models discussed in this article, children and families identify their unique capacities and contributions to the community.

A well-conducted wraparound process models for others how family-focused collaboration can help a community transcend its mental health services challenges and come together to meet the needs of all its citizens (Behar, 1986). The "generalist" social work practitioner learns to function as a "family specialist" through individualized wraparound planning for each child and family. Working with families from a strengths perspective offers rewards for all members of a community that reach far beyond interaction solely between families and practitioners. An assets approach fosters commitment from an entire community to care for all of its children and families.

DISCUSSION QUESTIONS

1. How does the systems of care approach to children's mental health differ from traditional mental health service delivery systems? Discuss how the differences found at the "system" (macro) level and the "practice" (micro) level might impact mental health social work practice in rural communities. What are some potential barriers to systems of care development in rural communities? What advantages does a system of care approach offer a rural community over a traditional mental health service system?

2. What assets are often found in rural communities that can be used to build a system of care for children with serious emotional disturbance and their families? How can these assets be applied to a wraparound service delivery approach? How might a rural community implement the wraparound process without first developing the infrastructure necessary to support wraparound?

3. Describe how rural communities and urban communities might differ in their planning and implementation of systems of care and wraparound approaches. Discuss how typical characteristics of each type of community could impact the planning and implementation processes.

CLASSROOM ASSIGNMENTS
AND ACTIVITIES

1. Compare and contrast wraparound processes first with traditional social work case management models and then with Saleebey's Strengths-Based Case Management model. For each of these case management models, develop separate three-month service plans for the family described at the beginning of the article based on the assumption that you and the family reside in a rural community. Feel free to embellish the details of the family, but be certain to describe how these same details are handled in each of your service plans. Discuss which model you would prefer to use and the reasons for your preference.

2. Identify the local public mental health provider authority in one rural community. Using a "case vignette" (prepared by yourself or your instructor) interview an administrator in this public service system asking her or him to describe in detail how the agency would typically engage with this youth and family. Identify what specific methods the agency uses to evaluate the progress of children and families.

3. As a class, develop a case vignette of a child with serious emotional disturbance and his or her family. Invite a guest from a local rural community mental health provider agency to visit the class and discuss how that agency would work with this child and family. After the discussion with the provider, organize yourselves into groups of 3–4 and brainstorm about how work with this child and family

might be different if services were provided through a systems-of-care approach.

4. Read the following case vignette:

Yvonne is a 29-year-old single, Mexican-American mother of three. Yvonne has three children: an 11-year old son, Raul, a 7-year-old son, Luis, and an 8-year-old daughter, Gloria. The family lives in a rural community 50 miles away from the nearest metropolitan area. Yvonne works part-time as a cashier in a Dollar General store and attends the local community college full-time in hopes of getting an associate's degree in bookkeeping. The family is very involved in their church, and all three children enjoy participating in the church's youth activities. Raul seems to have a good relationship with the youth minister. Raul wants to go to church camp in a few months, but his attendance will depend on how he is managing his behavior.

Yvonne's parents are supportive, but live in metropolis. Yvonne's neighbor watches the children when they get home from school, but has said she can no longer keep Raul due to his behavior. Raul was diagnosed with bipolar disorder two years ago and is on several medications, which he sometimes refuses to take. Raul's intelligence test indicates he has an IQ of 110; however, he refuses to do his schoolwork. He does, however, like art class, and his art teacher sees a lot of talent in Raul's drawings. Raul

generally has poor relations with his peers and was recently in a physical altercation with another student at school. The police were called and took Raul to juvenile detention. This was Raul's first experience with the juvenile justice system. As a result, Raul has been suspended from school for one week.

The other two children are doing well in school. However, they have begun to express fear of Raul because of his explosive behavior. Yvonne was referred to wraparound services by the juvenile probation officer.

Group Assignment: Arrange yourselves in a group of 3–4 persons and work as a group to simulate the following tasks of a wraparound process. Identify a recorder to keep notes for the group to:

a. Report its discussion results back to the rest of the class;

b. Identify potential wraparound team members;

c. Identify potential strengths and assets of the family, other wraparound team members, and the community (remember to think outside the box);

d. Link the identified strengths and assets to possible service plan activities and goals to be achieved; and

e. Share your group's ideas with the rest of the class.

REFERENCES

Adams, P., & Krauth, K. (1995). Working with families and communities: The Patch approach. In P. Adams and K. Nelson (Eds.), *Reinventing human services: Community-and-family centered practice.* (pp. 87–108). New York: Walter de Gruyter.

Adams, P., & Nelson, K. (Eds.). (1995). *Reinventing human services: Community-and family-centered practice.* New York: Walter de Gruyter.

American Humane Association. (1997). *Innovations for children's services for the 21st century: Family group decision making and Patch.* Englewood, CO: Author.

Behar, L. (1986, May–June). A state model for child mental health services: The North Carolina experience. *Children Today,* 16–21.

Benson, P. L. (1997). *All kids are our kids.* San Francisco: Jossey-Bass.

Burchard, J. D., Bruns, E. J., & Burchard, S. N. (2002). The wraparound process. In B. J. Burns, K. Hoagwood, & M. English (Eds.), *Community-based interventions for youth* (pp. 69–90). Oxford: Oxford University Press.

Burns, B. J., Goldman, S. K., Faw, L., & Burchard, J. (1999). The wraparound evidence base. In B. J. Burns & S. K. Goldman (Eds.), *Promising practices in wraparound for children with serious emotional disturbance and their families. Systems of care: Promising practices in children's mental health, 1998 series: Vol. 4* (pp. 95–118). Washington, DC: Center for Effective Collaboration and Practice, American Institutes for Research.

Burns, B. J., Hoagwood, K., & Mrazek, P. J. (1999). Effective treatment for mental disorders in children and adolescents. *Clinical Child and Family Psychology Review, 2*(4), 199–254.

Costello, E. J., Keeler, G. P., & Angold, A. (2001). Poverty, race/ethnicity, and psychiatric disorder: A study of rural children. *American Journal of Public Health, 91*(9), 1494–1498.

Cross, T. L., Bazron, B. J., Dennis, K. W., & Isaacs, M. R. (1989). *Towards a culturally competent system of care* (Vol. 1). Washington, DC: National Technical Assistance Center for Children's Mental Health, Georgetown University Child Development Center.

Cutrona, C. E., Halvorson, M. B. J., & Russell, D. W. (1996). Mental health services for rural children, youth, and their families. In C. A. Heflinger and C. T. Nixon (Eds.), *Families and the mental health system for children and adolescents: Policy, services, and research* (pp. 217–237). Thousand Oaks, CA: Sage.

Early, T. J., & Poertner, J. (1995). Examining current approaches to case management for families with children who have serious emotional disorders. In B. J. Friesen and J. Poertner (Eds.), *From case management to service coordination for children with emotional, behavioral, or mental disorders: Building on family strengths* (pp. 37–59). Baltimore: Brookes.

Elder, G. H., & Conger, R. D. (2000). *Children of the land*. Chicago: University of Chicago Press.

Evans, M. E., & Armstrong, M. I. (2002). What is case management? In B. J. Burns and K. Hoagwood (Eds.), *Community treatment for youth: Evidence-based interventions for severe emotional and behavioral disorders* (pp. 41–68). New York: Oxford University Press.

Friesen, B. J., & Stephens, B. (1998). Expanding family roles in the system of care: Research and practice. In M. H. Epstein, K. Kutash, and A. J. Duchnowski (Eds.), *Outcomes for children and youth with emotional and behavioral disorders and their families* (pp. 231–259). Austin, TX: PRO-ED.

Garland, A. F., Hough, R. L., McCabe, K. M., Yeh, M., Wood, P. A., & Aarons, G. A. (2001). Prevalence of psychiatric disorders in youths across five sectors of care. *Journal of American Academy of Child and Adolescent Psychiatry, 40*(4), 409–418.

Ginsberg, L. H. (1998). Introduction: An overview of rural social work. In L. H. Ginsberg (Ed.), *Social work in rural communities* (3rd ed., pp. 3–22). Alexandria, VA: Council on Social Work Education.

Goldman, S. (1999). The conceptual framework for wraparound: Definition, values, essential elements, and requirements for practice. In B. J. Burns & S. K. Goldman (Eds.), *Promising practices in wraparound for children with serious emotional disturbance and their families. Systems of care: Promising practices in children's mental health, 1998 series: Vol. 4* (pp. 27–34). Washington, DC: Center for Effective Collaboration and Practice, American Institutes for Research.

Hartman, A., & Laird, J. (1983). Family-centered social work practice. New York: Free Press.

Hernandez, M., & Isaacs, M. R. (1998). *Promoting cultural competence in children's mental health services*. Baltimore: Brookes.

Hernandez, M., Isaacs, M. R., Nesman, T., & Burns, D. (1998). Perspectives on culturally competent systems of care. In M. Hernandez & M. R. Isaacs, *Promoting cultural competence in children's mental health services* (pp. 1–25). Baltimore: Brookes.

Hodges, S., Nesman, T., & Hernandez, M. (1999). *Promising practices: Building collaboration in systems of care. Systems of care: Promising practices in children's mental health, 1998 series: Vol. VI*. Washington, DC: Center for Effective Collaboration and Practice, American Institutes for Research.

Joint Commission on Mental Illness & Health. (1961). *Action for mental health: Final report of the Joint Commission on Mental Illness and Health*. New York: Basic Books.

Keller, P. A., & Murray, J. D. (1982). Rural mental health: An overview of the issues. In P. A. Keller & J. D. Murray (Eds.), *Handbook of rural community mental health* (pp. 3–19). New York: Human Sciences Press.

Kisthardt, W. (1997). The strengths model of case management: Principles and helping functions. In D. Saleebey (Ed.), *The strengths perspective in social work practice* (2nd ed., pp. 97–113). White Plains, NY: Longman.

Knitzer, J. (1982). *Unclaimed children*. Washington, DC: Children's Defense Fund.

Koroloff, N. M., Friesen, B. J., Reilly, L., & Rinkin, J. (1996). The role of family members in systems of care. In B. A. Stroul (Ed.), *Children's mental health: Creating systems of care in a changing society* (pp. 409–426). Baltimore: Brookes.

Koyanagi, C., & Feres-Merchant, D. (2000). *For the long haul: Maintaining systems of care beyond the federal investment. Systems of care: Promising practices in children's mental health, 2000 series: Vol. III*. Washington, DC: Center for Effective Collaboration and Practice, American Institutes for Research.

Kretzmann, J. P., & McKnight, J. L. (1993). *Building communities from the inside out: A path toward finding and mobilizing a community's assets*. Chicago: ACTA Publications.

Lourie, I. S., Katz-Leavy, J., & Stroul, B. (1996). Individualized services in a system of care. In B. A. Stroul (Ed.), *Children's mental health: Creating systems of care in a changing society* (pp. 429–452). Baltimore: Brookes.

Lourie, I. S., Katz-Leavy, J., DeCarolis, G., & Quinlan, W. A., Jr. (1996). The role of the federal government. In B. A. Stroul (Ed.), *Children's mental health: Creating systems of care in a changing society* (pp. 99–114). Baltimore: Brookes.

Mason, J., Benjamin, M. P., & Lewis, S. A. (1996). The cultural competence model: Implications for child and family mental health services. In C. A. Heflinger and C. T. Nixon (Eds.), *Families and the mental health system for children and adolescents: Policy, services, and research* (pp. 165–190). Thousand Oaks, CA: Sage.

Roizner, M. (1996). *A practical guide for the assessment of cultural competence in children's mental health organizations*. Boston: Judge Baker Children's Center.

Saleebey, D. (1997). The strengths approach to practice. In D. Saleebey (Ed.), *The strengths perspective in social work practice* (2nd ed., pp. 80–94). White Plains, NY: Longman.

Saleebey, D. (2002). The strengths approach to practice. In D. Saleebey (Ed.), *The strengths perspective in social work practice* (3rd ed., pp. 80–94). Boston: Allyn & Bacon.

Scales, P. C., Benson, P. L., Roehlkepartain, E. C., Hintz, N. R., Sullivan, T. K., and Mannes, M. (2001). The role of neighborhood and community in building developmental assets for children and youth: A national study of social norms among American adults. *Journal of Community Psychology, 29*(6), 703–727.

Stroul, B. A., & Friedman, R. M. (1986). *A system of care for children and youth with severe emotional disturbances*

(Rev. Ed.). Washington, DC: Georgetown University Child Development Center, CASSP Technical Assistance Center.

U.S. Department of Health & Human Services (USDHHS) (1999). *Mental health: A Report of the Surgeon General*. Rockville, MD: U.S. Department of Health and Human Services, Substance Abuse and Mental Health Services Administration, Center for Mental Health Services, National Institutes of Health, National Institute of Mental Health.

U.S. Department of Health and Human Services. (2000). *Report of the Surgeon General's Conference on Children's Mental Health: A national action agenda*. Rockville, MD: U.S. Public Health Service. Washington, DC: National Institute of Mental Health.

VanDenBerg, J. E. (1993). Integration of individualized mental health services into the system of care for children and adolescents. *Administration and Policy in Mental Health, 20*(4), 247–257.

VanDenBerg, J. E., & Grealish, E. M. (1996). Individualized services and supports through the wraparound process: Philosophy and procedures. *Journal of Child and Family Studies, 5*(1), 7–21.

Wagenfeld, M. O. (1982). Organization and delivery of mental health services to adolescents and children with persistent and serious mental illness in frontier areas. *Letter to the field 16*. Frontier Mental Health Services Resource Network. Retrieved March 13, 2002, from http://www.wiche.edu/MentalHealth/Frontier.

Wodarski, J. S. (1983). *Rural community mental health practice*. Baltimore: University Park Press.

Worthington, J. E., Hernandez, M., Friedman, B., & Uzzell, D. (2001). Learning from families: *Identifying service strategies for success. Systems of care: Promising practices in children's mental health, 2001 series: Vol. II*. Washington, DC: Center for Effective Collaboration and Practice, American Institutes for Research.

INFOTRAC COLLEGE EDITION

assets
children's mental health
rural social work

systems of care
wraparound

13

The Use of Asset-Based Community Development to Increase Rural Youth Participation in Higher Education*

DENNIS L. POOLE

SUSANNAH MORE

One key to building healthy, sustainable rural communities is to develop an educated pool of workers with the knowledge and skills necessary to compete in an increasingly complex and technologically sophisticated work environment (Judy & D'Amico, 1997). This is difficult to accomplish when rural youth are half as likely to obtain a college degree as their peers in urban and suburban communities. The situation is worse for rural African Americans and Hispanics, only 4% of whom graduate from college (U.S. Bureau of the Census, 1999). Low-paying production jobs tend to concentrate in areas where educational attainment, income levels, and job-related skills of the labor force are marginal (Gibbs, 1995; Jensen & McLaughlin, 1995). Educational inequality also creates cleavages that affect the quality of social interactions between socioeconomic groups; between those that have knowledge and skills to compete in the workplace and those that do not (Luloff & Swanson, 1995).

Recent policy debates on educational advancement and workforce development have focused largely on the need for major improvements in our nation's public schools. President George W. Bush's plan (2001), for example, calls for more federal spending on rewards to states, school districts, and local schools to ensure "no child is left behind" in primary or secondary education. This plan does not include, however, strategies to ensure these same children are not left behind their peers in the transition to higher education. Nor does it adequately recognize that schools alone cannot solve the problem of underachievement. Entire communities must be mobilized to build support systems around youth to prepare them for higher education—and a career in tomorrow's workplace (Israel, Beaulieu, & Hartless, 2001).

This article addresses the challenge of mobilizing resources to facilitate the transition of rural youth from secondary school to higher education. Social workers in schools, human service agencies, and workforce development centers that help youth negotiate pathways into the workplace can help rural communities meet this challenge. To contribute, social workers must understand the constellation of factors that influence rural participation in higher education. They also need to know asset-based strategies to achieve goals in this area. Especially important are "best practice" models that create a positive community milieu for academic advancement and higher education.

The study was funded by a grant from Texas Rural Communities, Inc., a nonprofit organization involved in rural economic development, loan, grant, and educational programs.

FACTORS AFFECTING RURAL YOUTH PARTICIPATION IN HIGHER EDUCATION

Although much has been written about the issue, little has been done to analyze the problem and find possible solutions. Our systematic survey of journal articles, books, and documents over the past twenty years uncovered a myriad of factors that affect rural youth participation in higher education (Poole & More, 2001). These factors resist neat classification. It is difficult to determine where some begin—conceptually—and others end. Relationships between the factors are intricate, and solutions to the problem of low participation are complex.

One schema of classification that fits fairly well is Kretzmann and McKnight's (1993) asset-based community development model. Significant community development "takes place only when local community people are committed to investing themselves and their resources in the effort" (p. 5). The first step in the process is to map all available resources and to assess their individual capacities to be mobilized for development purposes. The mapping tool offered by Kretzmann and McKnight focuses on the assets of local institutions, associations, and individuals. Our findings call for a slightly different map, one that focuses on the role of institutional, community, family, and individual factors on participation in higher education.

Institutional Factors

Local school systems and other educational institutions can facilitate or impede rural youth participation in higher education. The four factors most frequently cited in the literature relate to academic preparation, teacher attitudes, college and career information, and cost of higher education.

Academic Preparation As a group, rural youth tend to be less academically prepared for college than their peers in urban school systems. Rural students generally have lower achievement scores on standardized tests and less access to advanced preparatory courses, which deter them from attending college. Rural youth that attend college frequently report that high school courses did not adequately prepare them for college (Knisley, 1993). High school faculty and guidance counselors in rural school systems voice similar concerns (Herzog, 1996).

Teacher Attitudes Teacher attitudes are powerful predictors of the academic performance and growth of youth during secondary education. Lee and Croninger's study of six high schools (2001) reports that students gain access to social capital through teachers (e.g., teacher-to-teacher or teacher-to-parent relationships). Supportive, collaborative relationships build trust and facilitate flow of information, which correlate positively with academic development and advancement. Similarly, Muller's analysis (2001) of national longitudinal data suggests that teachers may serve as gatekeepers to knowledge. Students are more likely to put forth effort when they feel their teachers show interest, expect them to succeed, listen, and praise them for their efforts.

College and Career Information Rural youth frequently do not have good access to information on college and career options through higher education (Hodes, 1995). The Appalachian Access and Success Project conducted a survey of school personnel in Ohio to identify barriers to higher education for rural youth. Teachers and guidance counselors reported that they do not receive adequate and timely materials to inform students about college and career opportunities (Institute for Local Government Administration & Rural Development, 1992). Being informed of these opportunities helps rural youth plan for college (Conroy, 1997).

Cost of Higher Education Youth living in rural regions with distressed economies often find higher education unaffordable. The Institute for

Local Government Administration and Rural Development (1992) found that although 80% of rural high school seniors wanted to attend college, only 30% actually went. Parents cited lack of financial aid as the single most important factor that deterred their children from college. Rural youth who attend college often leave for financial reasons before obtaining a degree. Many must work while going to college, making it more difficult for them to succeed academically (Haas, 1992). Moreover, some predominantly rural states only contribute a small amount of state grant aid to low-income students, compared to other states in the nation (National Center for Public Policy & Higher Education, 2000).

Community Factors

Community factors also influence rural youth participation in higher education. Those most frequently cited in the literature are college-educated role models, community attitudes, geographic location, and career opportunities.

College-Educated Role Models Youth encouraged by college-educated members of their community to attend college are more likely to pursue higher education. Since relatively few jobs in rural communities require a college education, rural youth are less likely than youth in urban areas to come in contact with college-educated role models (Gibbs, 1995; Smith, Beaulieu, & Seraphine, 1995; Swift, 1988).

Community Attitudes Community members without a college degree sometimes do not recognize the benefits of higher education. As a result, they may not encourage youth to seek a college degree. Other community members are reluctant to encourage rural high school students to attend college because they might leave the community to pursue jobs elsewhere rather than stay in the local economy (Gibbs, 1995). Rural youth who pursue higher education report that encouragement from community members had a positive influence on their decision to attend college (Beaulieu & Israel, 1997; Knisley, 1993). Individuals that decide to go to college usually have friends with similar plans. Conversely, rural youth with close friends who do not plan to attend college are less likely to pursue higher education (Yang, 1981).

Geographic Location Youth in rural communities face greater geographic barriers to higher education than urban youth. Half of rural high school students in the United States live in counties without colleges. The presence of a two-year or four-year college near home increases the likelihood that youth will pursue higher education (Gibbs, 1995).

Career Opportunities Because relatively few jobs in rural communities require a college degree, rural youth often do not associate an economic benefit with higher education (Smith, Beaulieu, & Seraphine, 1995). Better-paying, higher-skilled jobs that require a college education are more available in metropolitan areas. Thus, for many rural youth, the decision to pursue higher education requires permanent relocation from family and friends.

Family Factors

Families play an important role in higher education. Parental expectations and education, access to information, and financial planning for higher education all influence the decision to attend college.

Parent Expectations Some experts argue that the most influential factor in youth decision-making for higher education is parental expectation (Esterman & Hedlund, 1995; Smith, Beaulieu, & Seraphine, 1995). Parents that perceive higher education as beneficial usually encourage their children to attend college. Parental encouragement has a positive influence, even where students live in a poor economic area, or have no college-educated role models (Gibbs, 1995; Grant, Heggoy, & Battle, 1995). Encouragement from grandparents can have a positive influence on the educational aspirations of rural youth as well (Mekos & Elder, 1996).

Parent Education Rural youth are less likely to have college-educated parents than youth in urban areas (Smith, Beaulieu, & Seraphine, 1995). High school students with college-educated parents, especially college-educated mothers, are likely to attend college (Yang, 1981). In a survey of factors that influenced the educational plans of rural youth in Vermont, students indicated that their college aspirations had been influenced mainly by encouragement from college-educated parents (Knisley, 1993). Another survey found that rural students in North Carolina felt no pressure to attend college when parent levels of education were low. Study participants whose parents did not attend college reported that their parents did not understand the benefits that higher education would have for their children (Herzog, 1996).

Access to Information Rural parents often lack information about available resources for college (Institute for Local Government Administration & Rural Development, 1992). They also are often confused about the process of applying to college. Giving parents information about college encourages them to support their children's plans for higher education (Hodes, 1995).

Financial Resources A disproportionate share of U.S. families with incomes below the poverty line reside in rural areas (Lichter, Beaulieu, Findeis, & Teixeira, 1993). Financial resources possessed by parents often influence the academic aspirations of their children (Weidman & Friedmann, 1984). Rural parents and students also frequently do not know the actual costs of higher education, or how to budget for college. They frequently overestimate the cost of tuition and conclude that college is not affordable. In addition, rural students usually have little knowledge of their family's income and savings, and assume their parents cannot help them pay for college (Institute for Local Government

Administration & Higher Education, 1992). Rural students and parents need information to plan and save for college as well as to apply for scholarships and financial aid (Hodes, 1995).

Individual Factors

Participation in higher education depends on individual factors as well. Those most frequently cited in the literature relate to self-confidence, career aspirations, gender, ethnicity, and culture.

Self-Confidence Many rural youth are not confident that they can compete successfully in a college environment. Smith, Beaulieu, and Seraphine (1995) report that rural students have less confidence than urban students in their ability to succeed in college. A similar study by the Institute for Local Government Administration and Rural Development (1992) reports that 26% of rural students rate themselves as not being intelligent enough for college. Noncollegiate "tracking" during high school contributes to the problem. Alford (1997) argues that tracking downplays the importance of academic achievement, imparts the message to students that they are not intelligent enough to take advanced courses, and discourages them from applying to college. Similarly, Yang (1981) reports that rural youth who feel confident in their ability to succeed in college usually pursue higher education.

Career Aspirations Rural students often have low educational and occupational aspirations. These aspirations attribute partly to socioeconomic status. Rural students in low-income families tend to have lower educational aspirations than their economically advantaged peers (Haas, 1992). A study of occupational goals among rural adolescents found that students of upper socioeconomic status aspire toward careers with higher pay and more prestige than do students of lower socioeconomic status. Many rural students also have unrealistic career aspirations because they are unaware of educational requirements for different careers and of current job market realities. Their salary expectations are usually much higher than the amounts workers actually earn in specific careers (Conroy, 1997).

Gender Issues Educational achievement levels are low among rural females (Smith, Beaulieu, & Seraphine, 1995). Women in rural areas tend to marry earlier and are less likely to attend college than urban women. The decision to marry early and forego college correlates directly with low parental expectations and socioeconomic status (McLaughlin, Lichter, & Johnston, 1993). College-educated parents and parents of higher socioeconomic status usually expect their daughters to attend college (Knisley, 1993). Women whose parents do not expect them to attend college are more likely to marry early after high school rather than pursue a career. Gifted female college students in rural Georgia report that parent expectations strongly influence their career plans (Grant, Heggoy, & Battle, 1995).

Socioeconomically disadvantaged females sometimes marry early for financial reasons. Economic opportunities for rural women are often limited. Marriage can be economically advantageous, especially in the short-run. Not having a college degree, however, usually limits their earning potential to low-paying jobs, and increases their long-term dependency on men for financial support (McLaughlin, Lichter, & Johnston, 1993).

Ethnicity There is a strong relationship between ethnicity and college participation. Only 4% of African American youth and 4% of Hispanic youth in rural areas get a college degree, compared to 11% of white youth and 26% of Asian/Pacific Islanders (U.S. Bureau of the Census, 1999). These discrepancies are partly related to high school "tracking." African-American and Hispanic students with the same test scores are less likely than white students to be placed in advanced courses (Alford, 1997), even though their parents rank college as a higher priority than white parents (Immerwahr, 2000).

Culture Rural youth usually prefer to live close to home after high school, but recognize they must leave family and friends for higher education in distant communities (Howley, 1997). When they attend college, many of them experience "culture shock," overwhelmed by the size and culture of the college (Roe, 1997). Feelings of alienation and homesickness are common, reducing the likelihood that they will complete college (Swift, 1988). Leaving home, making new friends, and adjusting to college life are difficult for many youth from small, close-knit, rural communities (Hemmings, Hills, & Ray, 1997; Herzog, 1996). Their desire for educational achievement conflicts with their attachments to family, friends, and place (Donaldson, 1986).

ASSET-BASED STRATEGIES TO INCREASE PARTICIPATION IN HIGHER EDUCATION

We now turn to asset-based strategies that can increase participation in higher education. We call them "asset-based" to counter the tendency in professional circles to view this challenge from the perspective of deficiencies and problems. Asset-based community development focuses on capacities, skills, and resources. Social workers and other community builders can utilize the asset-based strategies presented next to increase rural youth participation in higher education. Similar to the previous section, we classify them as institutional, community, family, and individual strategies.

Institutional Factors

Institutional strategies vary greatly. Typically they involve the mobilization of school and other institutional assets in the areas of academic preparation, student access to college and career information, workshops for school personnel, and scholarships and financial aid.

Academic Preparation Rural students need to be academically prepared for college (Mehan, 1992). The Early Academic Outreach Program in California targets students from groups under-represented in colleges and enrolls them in preparatory courses. The program also engages students in activities that teach them to prepare for college and to take advantage of college opportunities. The Advancement Via Individual Determination (AVID) Program moves students "tracked" in low-level curricula into advanced preparatory classes with college-bound peers (California State Postsecondary Education Commission, 1996).

Increasing Student Access to College and Career Information Rural students need timely access to information on college and career opportunities. The Gulf County College Counseling Project established centers in high schools for this purpose (Dalton & Erdmann, 1990). Saginaw Valley State College in Michigan sends representatives to high schools to share information about financial aid, admission, housing, course selection, and adjustment to college life (Abel, et al., 1994). The California Student Opportunity and Access Program provides information to high school students on academic preparation needed to pursue different careers through higher education (California State Postsecondary Education Commission, 1996).

Workshops for School Personnel Rural school personnel need timely and accurate information as well. The Gulf County College Counseling Project organizes workshops for high school teachers, counselors, and other personnel to teach them how to encourage rural students to attend college. The project creates college information centers, teaches SAT preparation, and organizes campus visits for students (Dalton & Erdmann, 1990). The Title IV TRIO Program of the Rural Community College Initiative works with high school principals and counselors to encourage rural students to pursue higher education (Eller, et al., 1998).

Scholarships and Financial Aid Youth in low-income families need scholarships and financial aid to afford higher education. Several projects address this need. "I Have a Dream" (IHAD) program provides scholarships to students for college tuition. Scholarships usually do not exceed $5,000, but awards vary depending on student needs. Wealthy donors sponsor disadvantaged students, promising scholarships if they complete high school and attend college (Kahne & Bailey, 1999). The Quantum Opportunities Program (QOP) funded by the Ford Foundation offers financial incentives as well. Students earn stipends and bonuses that are invested into an account to pay for college or advanced training (Hahn, 1995).

Community Factors

Asset-based strategies intervene at the community level as well. Those most frequently cited in the literature involve mentoring, outposting, video conferencing, and business involvement.

Mentoring Mentoring provides college-educated role models for youth. The Southeast Scholars Program at Southeast Community College in Kentucky matches eighth grade students with mentors. Community members introduce the students to college programs, help them identify career options, and encourage them to prepare for college (Eller, et al., 1998). Similarly, the Preparation of Minority Educators provides middle school and high school students with mentors in the teaching profession. Mentors make a commitment to work with students until they complete college (Gutknecht, 1992).

Outposting School districts in New York form partnerships with local colleges to offer advanced placement courses to rural high school students. Some rural school districts hire adjunct professors from local colleges to teach advanced courses in high schools, offering college credits and encouraging students to continue education after high school (New York State Legislative Commission on Rural Resources, 1995).

Video Conferencing To improve access to college courses, the Rural Community College Initiative at Southwest Texas Community College uses video conferencing to make courses available to rural youth at regional learning centers. Texas A&M University uses similar technology to deliver graduate courses to students in remote communities (Eller, et al., 1998).

Business Involvement The business community can have a positive influence on college participation as well. The Faculty Alliance for Education in Newark links high school students with local businesses. Companies sponsor internships for students and offer them savings bonds as an incentive for college (McGrath & Van Buskirk, 1997). The Mathematics, Engineering, and Science Achievement Program of California involves the business community in a more specialized way. Owners and employees of local businesses help students identify career options in math and science and encourage them to attend college (California State Postsecondary Education Commission, 1996).

Family Strategies

Asset-based strategies at the family level focus primarily on parent involvement, improving access to college information, and financial planning.

Parent Involvement Involvement helps parents understand the value of and create a positive home environment for higher education (Israel, Beaulieu, & Hartless, 2001). Parents who want to enroll their children in the AVID Program in California must sign a contract agreeing to actively support their children's participation (California State Postsecondary Education Commission, 1996). Project Choice in Kansas provides workshops and meetings to strengthen parent skills in communication and decision making (Sims, 1997). Similarly, college faculty and students in the On-Track Program at Edinboro University of Pennsylvania involve parents in set-

ting long-term goals for their children, including higher education (Cowher, 1994).

Improving Access to College Information Rural parents need information about college programs and application processes. The "I Have a Dream" program conducts seminars to provide information to parents on programs of study at different colleges. Parents also learn the challenges their children may face during the transition from high school to college (Kahne & Bailey, 1999). The Gulf County College Counseling Project invites representatives from area colleges to speak to parents about college preparation and the application process (Dalton & Erdmann, 1990).

Financial Planning The Gulf County College Counseling Project deploys financial aid staff from Florida State University and the local community college to teach high school parents how to finance a college education. Parents receive financial aid information and learn to complete application forms (Dalton & Erdmann, 1990). The California Student Opportunity and Access Program—a collaborative effort between California State University campuses, area colleges, and local school districts—teaches school counselors to advise parents and students about financial aid in higher education (California State Postsecondary Education Commission, 1996).

Individual Strategies

The fourth level of intervention focuses on the assets of individual youth. Strategies typically include confidence building, student support services, untracking, college exposure, and transitional support services.

Building Confidence Rural students need self-confidence to attend college. The Rural Education Advisory Committee of New York found that students are more confident in their abilities when adults in college systems provide encouragement. State college representatives participate in activities to help rural students recognize that they can succeed in college. The Upward Bound Program targets eighth and ninth graders who would be the first members in their families to attend college. Staff from local colleges work with these students two or three days each week to build self-confidence (New York State Legislative Commission on Rural Resources, 1995).

Student Support Services Rural youth frequently need individual support services to prepare for college. In California, the Alliance for Collaborative Change in Education in School Systems provides tutoring, academic advising, SAT preparation, and problem-solving to improve students' chances of being admitted into college and doing well academically (California State Postsecondary Education Commission, 1996). The Gulf County College Counseling Project offers similar services to students at two high schools in Florida.

Untracking The Advancement Via Individual Determination Program in California encourages ethnic minority students to succeed in high school and pursue a college education. Students are removed from lower-level classes and placed in higher-level classes with college-bound peers. Students also receive tutoring from college students who assist them with the college admission process (California State Postsecondary Education Commission, 1996).

College Exposure College exposure also can remove an individual's cultural barriers to higher education. Many innovative programs use campus visits to familiarize students with college life. The College Reach-Out Program in Florida organizes a two-week program of student visits to local colleges (Medina & Drummond, 1993). Northern Kentucky University sponsors campus visits for junior high and high school students to explain the importance of college preparation. College students share information with visiting students about campus life, class schedules, and financial aid (Stewart, Griffin, & McDaniel, 1993). Project Choice provides a three-week enrichment program to students entering tenth grade. Students

live in dorms at Kansas State University, take college classes, and discuss college life (Sims, 1997). Tenth through twelfth grade students in the On-Track Program visit Edinboro University in Pennsylvania on weekends and for one week in the summer. They receive college orientation sessions on career development, study skills, and extracurricular activities (Cowher, 1994).

Transitional Support Services Disadvantaged youth often need help adjusting to college life. Students in the College Posse Scholarship Program arrive at Vanderbilt University one week before fall classes to become familiar with the campus. They meet regularly with faculty and students to form a cohesive support network as well as participate in campus activities to feel "connected" to the university (Innes, Cunningham, & Sanders, 1993). The North Carolina State University Transition Program (UTP) is also designed to help rural students make a smooth transition from high school to college. Course sections in mathematics and English are restricted to UTP students. Staff members provide career counseling and academic advising during the first six months of college. Students also attend Personal Development Seminars and meet regularly with graduate assistants in the Counselor Education Program to discuss personal issues and concerns (Lee, 1997).

BEST PRACTICE MODELS

The key to asset-based community development is not only locating and utilizing available resources, but "connecting them with one another in ways that multiply their power and effectiveness" (Kretzmann & McKnight, 1993, p. 5). Community social capital for higher education increases when resources are consolidated for collective action (Israel, Beaulieu, & Hartless, 2001; Luloff & Swanson, 1995). Here we present two "best practice" models for mobilizing assets and creating a positive rural community milieu for higher education. These models have proven outcomes; students who participate in them are much more likely to attend college than those who do not.

The Rural Community College Initiative

The Rural Community College Initiative (RCCI) is designed to increase rural student participation in higher education and to promote economic development in rural areas (Eller, et al., 1998). Local school districts, nine community colleges, local businesses, diverse community organizations, and the Ford Foundation participate in the project.

Institutional strategies include scholarships to make college affordable and workshops for school personnel to encourage rural students to pursue higher education. Interventions at the community level match local mentors with students to provide information about college programs and career opportunities, as well as to encourage them to succeed in high school. Video conferencing between distant college campuses and regional learning centers allows rural students to take advanced preparatory courses in proximity to their home communities. Family-level strategies seek to improve access to information and financial planning for higher education, chiefly through workshops with parents on college opportunities, application processes, scholarships, and financial aid. Interventions at the individual level provide support services to help rural youth gain self-confidence, overcome academic deficiencies, and obtain timely access to information about college and career opportunities.

Gulf County College Counseling Project

The Gulf County College Counseling Project in Florida raises educational expectations of rural students and encourages them to pursue higher education (Dalton & Erdmann, 1990). Two high schools collaborate with local business owners, colleges and state universities, and the DuPont Fund as partners in the project.

At the institutional level, college scholarships reward students for school attendance, academic performance, and achievement on standardized tests. Workshops involve teachers in the college counseling process and in preparing students for standardized tests. Family-level strategies are designed to increase parent involvement. College counselors provide information to parents on preparing their children for higher education, and financial aid directors teach them how to finance a college education. At the individual level, the project involves high school students in college centers, where they explore educational and career opportunities in higher education, learn the importance of standardized tests, and develop test-taking skills. The program organizes trips for students to visit college campuses, and later provides services to help them adjust to college life.

SUMMARY

Rural youth often fall behind urban youth during the transition to higher education. This reduces their opportunities to attain educational and career goals, and undermines the long-term economic and social viability of the communities where they live. Social workers in schools and other community settings can increase the sustainability of rural communities by enabling youth to advance from secondary school to higher education. They must understand the myriad of factors that affect participation in higher education, as well as asset-based strategies that mobilize institutional, community, family, and individual resources to achieve community goals in this area. Best practice models, such as the Rural Community College Initiative and the Gulf County College Counseling Project, approach the challenge of higher education through asset-based community development. They consolidate available resources in ways to multiply their power and effectiveness in creating a positive community milieu for higher education.

DISCUSSION QUESTIONS

1. Consider the relationship between higher education and sustainable rural communities. How would your conceptualization of the relationship differ using a deficit versus an asset model?

2. Why are rural youth half as likely to make the transition to higher education than urban youth?

3. How do asset–based development models create a positive community milieu for higher education? Do they "fit" well with the strengths perspective in social work?

CLASSROOM ASSIGNMENTS
AND ACTIVITIES

1. Divide the class into students who graduated from a rural high school and those who graduated from an urban/suburban high school. Using the mapping tool in this article, each group member identifies the major factors that influenced their decision to attend college, as well as their perceived barriers to higher education. Compare and contrast the responses of the two groups. How are these responses similar or different at the institutional, community, family, and individual level?

2. Numerous projects have been developed to increase rural youth participation in higher education. Select three projects from the list of references that follows. Identify the strengths and weaknesses of the evaluation designs used to assess the outcomes of these projects.

Cowher, S. (1994). Rural education initiatives: Preparation for a changing workforce. *Human Services in the Rural Environment 18*, 18-20.

Dalton, H., & Erdmann, D. (1990). *The chance to dream: A community success story.* New York, NY: Plan for Social Excellence, Inc. (ERIC Document Reproduction Service No. ED 353 921)

Eller, R., Martinez, R., Pace, C., Pavel, M., Garza, H., & Barnett, L. (1998). *Rural community college initiative: Removing barriers to participation* (Report No. AACC-PB-98-1). Washington DC: American Association of Community Colleges.

Innes, R., Cunningham, A., & Sanders, N. (1993). The College Posse Scholarship Program: An agent for change. *The College Board Review, 167,* 28-34.

Lee, W. (1997). *Transitioning from high school to college: Surviving a clash of educational cultures.* Paper presented at the Annual Meeting of the Association for the Study of Higher Education. Albuquerque, NM. (ERIC Document Reproduction Service No. ED 346 082)

Mehan, H. (1992). *Untracking and college enrollment, Research reports: 4.* Washington, DC: Office of Educational Research and Improvement. (ERIC Document Reproduction Service No. ED 351 403)

New York State Legislative Commission on Rural Resources. (1995). *Raising aspirations of New York state's rural youth: A resource book of successful programs and strategies for rural school districts.* Albany, NY: Metis Associates.

3. Using 2000 Census data, each student should examine variations in college graduation rates (e.g., ethnicity, gender, and socioeconomic status) in their home community. Interview the school superintendent, a high school principal, and a youth social worker to determine what, if any, programs have been developed to increase participation rates in higher education. What additional programs, if any, should be developed? Conceptualize how social workers could participate in asset-based community development to increase rural youth participation in higher education in that particular community.

REFERENCES

Abel, F., Easton, S., Edwards, P., Herbster, D., & Sparapani, E. (1994). *Serving under-represented diverse populations.* Paper presented at the Annual Meeting of the Association of Teacher Educators, Atlanta, GA. (ERIC Document Reproduction Service No. ED 367 604)

Alford, B. (1997). *Leadership for increasing the participation and success of students in high school advanced courses: Implications for rural educational settings* (Report No. RC-021-244). Paper presented at the Annual NREA Convention, Tucson, AZ.

Beaulieu, L. J., & Israel, G. D. (1997). Strengthening social capital: The challenge for rural community sustainability. In I. Audirac (Ed.), *Rural sustainable development in America* (pp. 191–223). New York: Wiley.

Bush, G. W. (2001). *No child left behind.* Washington, DC: The White House.

California State Postsecondary Education Commission. (1996, December). *Progress report on the effectiveness of collaborative student academic development programs.* Sacramento, CA: Author.

Conroy, C. (1997). *Predictors of occupational choice among rural youth: Implications for career education and development programming* (Report No. RC-021-036). Paper presented at the Annual Meeting of the American Educational Research Association, Chicago, IL.

Cowher, S. (1994). Rural education initiatives: Preparation for a changing workforce. *Human Services in the Rural Environment 18,* 18–20.

Dalton, H., & Erdmann, D. (1990). *The chance to dream: A community success story.* New York: Plan for Social Excellence, Inc. (ERIC Document Reproduction Service No. ED 353 921)

Donaldson, G. A. (1986). Do you need to leave home to grow up? The rural adolescent's dilemma. *Research on Rural Education, 3,* 121–125.

Eller, R., Martinez, R., Pace, C., Pavel, M., Garza, H., & Barnett, L. (1998). *Rural community college initiative: Removing barriers to participation* (Report No. AACC-PB-98-1). Washington, DC: American Association of Community Colleges.

Esterman, K., & Hedlund, D. (1995). Comparing rural adolescents from farm and nonfarm families. *Journal of Research in Rural Education 11,* 84–91.

Gibbs, R. (1995). Going away to college and wider urban job opportunities take highly educated youth away from rural areas. *Rural Development Perspectives 10,* 35–43.

Grant, D., Heggoy, S., & Battle, D. (1995). *Cases of rural gifted college females: Socialization barriers and career choices.* Paper presented at the National Career Development Association Conference, San Francisco, CA. (ERIC Document Reproduction Services No. ED 387 730)

Gutknecht, B. (1992). *Preparation of minority educators (PREMIER).* Paper presented at the Annual Meeting of the Association of Teacher Educators, Orlando, FL. (ERIC Document Reproduction Services No. ED 346 049).

Haas, T. (1992). *What can I become?: Educational aspirations of students in rural America* (Report No. EDO-RC-91-11). Washington, DC: Office of Educational Research & Improvement.

Hahn, A. (1995). *Quantum opportunities program: A brief on the QOP pilot program.* Waltham, MA: Brandeis University, Center for Human Resources. (ERIC Documentation Reproduction Service No. ED 420 735)

Hemmings, B., Hills, D., & Ray, D. (1997). *First year university in retrospect: The voices of rural students* (Report No. RC-021-946). Adelaide, South Australia, Australia: Society for Provision of Education in Rural Australia.

Herzog, M. (1996). *Conditions, attitudes and concerns in rural education: An examination of the Appalachian counties of North Carolina.* Paper presented at the Annual Meeting of the National Rural Education Association, San Antonio, TX. (ERIC Document Reproduction Service No. ED 411 104)

Hodes, C. (1995). *Interest levels of participants from two intervention programs: A comparison of "at-risk" youth.* Paper presented at the Annual Meeting of the Global Awareness Society International, Shanghai, China. (ERIC Document Reproduction Service No. ED 380 523)

Howley, C. (1997). *Rural scholars or bright rednecks? Aspirations for a sense of place among rural youth in Appalachia* (Report No. RC-020-898). Charleston, WV: Appalachia Educational Lab.

Immerwahr, J. (2000). *Great expectations: How the public and parents—White, African American, and Hispanic—view Higher Education.* Washington, DC: National Center for Public Policy and Higher Education.

Innes, R., Cunningham, A., & Sanders, N. (1993). The College Posse Scholarship Program: An agent for change. *The College Board Review, 167,* 28–34.

Institute for Local Government Administration & Rural Development. (1992). *Appalachian access and success: Research update* (Report No. RC-019-343). Athens, OH: Author.

Israel, G. D., Beaulieu, L., & Hartless, G. (2001). The influence of family and community social capital on educational achievement. *Rural Sociology, 66,* 43–68.

Jensen, L., & McLaughlin, D. K. (1995). Human capital and nonmetropolitan poverty. In L. J. Beaulieu & D. Mulkey (Eds.), *Investing in people: The human capital needs of rural America* (pp. 111–138). Boulder, CO: Westview.

Judy, R. W., & D'Amico, C. (1997). *Workforce 2000: Work and workers in the 21st century.* Indianapolis, IN: Hudson Institute.

Kahne, J., & Bailey, K. (1999). The role of social capital in youth development programs. *Educational Evaluation & Policy Analysis, 21,* 321–343.

Knisley, C. (1993). *Factors influencing rural Vermont public high school seniors to aspire or not to aspire to a four year college education.* Paper presented at the Annual Conference of the National Rural Education Association, Burlington, VT. (ERIC Document Reproduction Service No. ED 364 377)

Kretzmann, J. P., & McKnight, J. L. (1993). *Building communities from the inside out.* Chicago, IL: ACTA Publications.

Lee, W. (1997). *Transitioning from high school to college: Surviving a clash of educational cultures.* Paper presented at the Annual Meeting of the Association for the Study of Higher Education. Albuquerque, NM. (ERIC Document Reproduction Service No. ED 346 082)

Lee, V. E., & Croninger, R. C. (2001). The elements of social capital in the context of six high schools. *Journal of Socio-Economics, 30,* 165–167.

Lichter, D. T., Beaulieu, L. J., Findeis, J. J., & Teixeira, R. A. (1993). Human capital, labor supply, and poverty in rural America. In Rural Sociological Task Force on Persistent Rural Poverty (Ed.), *Persistent poverty in rural America* (pp. 39–67). Boulder, CO: Westview.

Luloff, A. E., & Swanson, L. A. (1995). Community agency and disaffection: Enhancing collective resources. In L. J. Beaulieu & D. Mulkey (Eds.), *Investing in people: The human capital needs of rural America* (pp. 351–372). Boulder, CO: Westview.

McGrath, D., & Van Buskirk, W. (1997). *Start with the faculty.* New York, NY: National Center for Urban Partnerships. (ERIC Documentation Reproduction Service No. ED 416 282)

McLaughlin, D., Lichter, D., & Johnston, G. (1993). Some women marry young: Transitions to first marriage in metropolitan and nonmetropolitan areas. *Journal of Marriage & Family, 55,* 827–838.

Medina, V., & Drummond, R. (1993). Profile of rural college reach-out students. *Journal of Employment Counseling, 30,* 15–24.

Mehan, H. (1992). *Untracking and college enrollment, Research reports: 4.* Washington, DC: Office of Educational Research and Improvement. (ERIC Document Reproduction Service No. ED 351 403)

Mekos, D., & Elder, G. H. (1996, March). *Community ties and the development of competence in rural youth.* Paper presented at the biennial meeting of the Society for Research in Adolescence, Boston, MA.

Muller, C. (2001). The role of caring in the teacher-student relationship for at-risk students. *Sociological Inquiry, 71,* 241–255.

National Center for Public Policy & Higher Education. (2000). *Measuring up 2000: The state by state report card on higher education.* Washington, DC: Author.

New York State Legislative Commission on Rural Resources. (1995). *Raising aspirations of New York state's rural youth: A resource book of successful programs and strategies for rural school districts.* Albany, NY: Metis Associates.

Poole, D. L., & More, S. (2001, June). *Participation of rural youth in higher education.* Paper presented at the 26th National Institute on Human Services in Rural Areas, Asset Building to Sustain Rural Communities and Rural Resources. Austin: School of Social Work, The University of Texas.

Roe, J. (1997). *Identification of barriers that confront rural students entering the university system* (Report No. RC-021-953). Adelaide, South Australia: Society of the Provision of Education in Rural Australia.

Sims, A. (1997). *Project Choice: Lessons learned in dropout prevention.* Kansas City, MO: Ewing Marion Kauffman Foundation. (ERIC Document Reproduction Service No. ED 416 283)

Smith, M., Beaulieu, L., & Seraphine, A. (1995). Social capital, place or residence, and college attendance. *Rural Sociology, 60,* 363–380.

Stewart, G., Griffin, A., & McDaniel, G. (1993). How to involve African-American students in recruiting others. *The Journal of College Admission,* 17–22.

Swift, D. (1988). *Preparing rural students for an urban environment* (Report No. EDO-RC-88-08). Washington, DC: Office of Educational Research & Improvement.

U.S. Bureau of the Census. (1999). *Educational attainment in the United States, March 1999, detailed tables for current population report* (Report No. P20-513). Washington, DC: U.S. Department of Commerce.

Weidman, J. C., & Friedmann, R. R. (1984). The school-to-work transition for high school dropouts. *Urban Review, 16,* 25–42.

Yang, S. (1981). *Rural youths' decisions to attend college: Aspirations and realizations.* Paper presented at the Annual Meeting of the Rural Sociological Society, Guelph, Ontario, Canada.

INFOTRAC COLLEGE EDITION

college

community development

high school

higher education

rural youth

14

An Asset-Based Approach to Promoting Community Well-Being in a Rural County

Obstacles and Opportunities

ROBIN L. ERSING

MELANIE D. OTIS

Community is a concept that takes different shapes, depending on who you ask and the goals of the questioning. A basic description of one's community may take the form of visual images of buildings, parks, and neighborhoods—the physical environment that wraps around lives. Although the physical safety, aesthetic appeal, and sense of welcoming that structures bring are important aspects of community, today our vision of community has moved beyond mere structures. "Tell me about your community." "Oh, I live in Buffalo." "I live in Tyler." "I live in Mount Sterling. It's a great town . . . there's a movie theatre on Main Street . . . a new Wal-Mart on the by-pass." "No, tell me about the community." "Well, it's a very friendly town. People care about their neighbors and are willing to work hard to make the local government work . . . the schools better. I can't imagine living somewhere else . . . it's home." It's in these responses that we find the real information on community assets and needs, and come to better understand how to improve community well-being.

For more than a century, improving the public health and well-being of the community has been a central focus of local health departments. In pursuit of this mission, provision of public health services has been closely intertwined with social work practice to promote community development and local capacity-building. This article provides an overview of a collaborative project between the University of Kentucky College of Social Work and a rural county health department located in east-central Kentucky. An asset-based assessment model is constructed to support the short-term goal of providing data on indicators that measure both the current quality of life and well-being of the overall community, and the long-term goal of measuring the sustainability of the county. The model also considers a variety of social, economic, and environmental resources to better inform policy decisions, enhance community planning, develop collaborative partnerships, and build community capacity, while addressing countywide issues and promoting well-being.

COMMUNITY WELL-BEING AND THE SIGNIFICANCE OF PLACE

The context of place; that is, the social and physical environment found within a spatially defined area, is an important component in shaping our identity as individuals and as members of a community. Where we live and work can influence our social ties, choices, and everyday behaviors. Researchers interested in formulating a place-based theory for promoting well-being continue to examine the association between the local residential environment and the health status of individuals living there (Fitzpatrick & LaGory, 2000). Studies in this area suggest that disinvestment in a neighborhood or geographic community can lead to an increased number of hazardous conditions that ultimately can impact negatively on the health status of residents. Such conditions include the presence of abandoned or deteriorated housing (Coulton, et al., 1995; Figueira-McDonough, 1993), a lack of home-ownership (Coulton, Korbin, Su, & Chow, 1995), criminal activity, especially violent crime (Skogan, 1990; Wilson, 1987), and accumulated trash and vandalism (Sampson & Groves, 1989). Residential environments experiencing such circumstances can constrain quality of life. They can also place individuals at greater risk for various physical and mental health symptoms, including higher mortality rates (McCord & Freeman, 1990), increased rates of child maltreatment (Gabarino & Kostelny, 1992), and more babies born with low birth weights (Pearl, Braveman, & Abrams, 2001).

Although many of the risks mentioned above are often associated with urban environments, rural communities must also contend with issues that threaten quality of life for residents. In many cases, small towns and rural communities are sensitive to changes in migration trends. During economic downturns, the well-being and sustainability of the community is in jeopardy as residents migrate out of the area in search of employment opportunities or training programs to develop more marketable skills. The resulting population loss makes it more difficult for other businesses and service providers, including health-care workers, to remain intact (Smith-Mello, 1996).

In contrast, a significant in-migration of new residents during more prosperous times can help to sustain local development while simultaneously presenting a new set of challenges to community well-being (Johnson & Beale, 1995). In this situation, rural towns are faced with increased demands to stretch local resources, including roads and water and sewer systems. Rapid growth often brings with it new issues, including increases in noise, traffic, and various pollutants, as well as the loss of green space as the demand for housing and retail business escalates.

Although the literature suggests that exposure to unhealthy places can negatively affect quality of life and well-being, environments that espouse protective factors and provide residents access to social, economic, and environmental resources to promote capacity building are viewed as healthy and sustainable communities. This ecological perspective is central to social work's interest in understanding the impact of social environmental forces on human behavior (Gitterman & Germain, 1980).

HEALTHY AND SUSTAINABLE COMMUNITIES

The Healthy Community Movement (HCM) is a place-based initiative embedded in the tradition of public health service and health promotion. The movement began in Europe with support from the World Health Organization and eventually gained attention during the 1980s as a way to improve quality of life and well-being in towns and cities across the United States (Hancock, 1993).

The HCM endorses a broad definition of "health" that extends beyond the traditional medical notion of the absence of disease. Under the HCM, health encompasses lifestyle and behavior choices, as well as a person's social, economic, cultural, and physical environment (Norris & Pittman, 2000). Ultimately, a healthy community rests upon the choices that individuals within the community make. The movement promotes the ideas of sustainability by encouraging the identification of local assets and community-based resources that can be employed to develop innovative strategies as interventions to improve community well-being (Sharpe, Greaney, Lee, & Royce, 2000). This component of the movement aligns itself with the discipline of community development to build stronger, healthier, and more sustainable communities. Table 14.1 presents some of the core principles of the Healthy Community Movement discussed by Norris and Pittman (2000).

The Healthy Community Movement provides a holistic perspective of community well-being that fits the mission of social work. Social workers have practiced in public health settings for well over a century, directing their attention to the skills of community-building to enhance the capacity of community members to support goals related to social, emotional, and physical well-being (Leukefeld, 1989; Mosley, 1998). Social work's perspective of community well-being shares the broad view of a "healthy community" by considering the presence of local resources; the quality of housing, education, transportation, and recreation; public safety; and the provision of preventive and supportive services. By incorporating these ideas into an assessment model to promote community well-being, social workers are rejecting the "cookie cutter" approach. Instead, the healthy community perspective leads to a new model that reflects the unique character and shared vision of the local community.

its impact on individual and family well-being, as well as the relationship between asset building and community well-being (Green & Haines, 2002).

The link between individual asset building and community sustainability is created and strengthened, in part, by public participation in civic and community life (Green & Haines, 2002). Research suggests that individual asset building in the form of physical and mental well-being and financial growth increases the likelihood of involvement in public life through increased personal resources and investment in place (Page-Adams & Sherraden, 1997). Collectively, asset building on the individual and community levels provides the foundation for sustainability.

In recent years, a number of community-based indicator projects have begun to examine the extent to which the assumptions of the asset-building model holds true. In 1995 the Urban Institute established the National Neighborhood Indicators Project (NNIP) with the key purpose being to "build the capacities of institutions and residents in distressed urban neighborhoods" (Kingsley, 1999, p. 2). Since that time, the use of indicators to measure sustainability outcomes and support policymaking efforts to improve quality of life in communities has expanded beyond the inner city to include small towns and rural areas across the country.

ASSESSING SUSTAINABILITY AND COMMUNITY WELL-BEING

Over the past decade, asset-based models of community development have moved to accommodate both individual-level factors and community-level factors. Building on the strengths-based social work practice model (Saleebey, 2001), asset-based models for development of sustainable communities explore the reciprocal relationship between asset building and

ASSESSING COMMUNITY WELL-BEING: THE CASE OF MONTGOMERY COUNTY, KY

Montgomery County is one of 120 counties that comprise the Commonwealth of Kentucky. Located in east-central Kentucky, on the fringe of the Appalachian region "where the bluegrass meets the mountains," Montgomery county is situated approximately 30 miles east of the city of

Table 14.1 Six Principles of the Healthy Community Movement

1. Shared vision from community values

    A community's vision expresses the story of its desired future, reflecting the core values of its diverse members. It is a living expression of shared accountability to priorities.

2. Improved quality of life for everyone

    Healthy communities strive to ensure that the basic emotional, physical, and spiritual needs of everyone in the community are addressed.

3. Diverse citizen participation and widespread community ownership

    In healthy communities, all people take active and ongoing responsibility for themselves, their families, their property, and their community. A leader's work is to find common ground among all participants, so that everyone is empowered to take direct action for health and influence community directions.

4. Focus on "systems change"

    The Healthy Community Movement contemplates a different vision for the way people live and work together, how community services are delivered, how information is shared, how local government operates, and how business is conducted. It demands that resource allocation and decision making be spread throughout the community.

5. Development of local assets and resources

    Healthy communities identify and build on a community's strengths and successes and then invest in the enhancement of a community's civic infrastructure. The idea is that, by developing an infrastructure that encourages health, fewer resources will need to be spent on "back end" services that attempt to fix the problems resulting from a weak infrastructure.

6. Benchmarks and measures of progress and outcomes

    Healthy communities use performance measures and community indicators to help expand the flow of information and accountability to all citizens, and to reveal whether residents are heading toward or away from their stated goals. Timely, accurate information is vital to sustaining long-term community improvement.

Source: Adapted from Norris, T. and Pittman, M. (2000). The healthy communities movement and the coalition for healthier cities and communities. *Public Health Reports (2000, March–June),* 118–130. Reprinted by permission of the Association of Schools of Public Health.

Lexington, which is the second largest metropolitan area in the state. According to the latest census information (U.S. Census Bureau, 2002a), Montgomery County has a total population of 22,554. The county seat is Mount Sterling, a city with a population of 5,859. Mount Sterling serves as the hub for much of the shopping, recreation, and political activity of the area. The cities of Camargo and Jeffersonville, with a combined population less than 3,000 persons, are the other most recognized geographical areas in the county. In contrast to the more urban setting of Mount Sterling, both Camargo and Jeffersonville are located in less densely populated rural communities where farming is recognized as an important industry for some families.

The Census Bureau has divided Montgomery County into five census tracts. A census tract is a geographic unit that generally contains between 1,500 and 8,000 individuals, with an average size of 4,000 people (U.S. Census Bureau, 1999). The spatial size of census tracts can vary widely depending upon the density of the population. In other words, tracts in urban areas tend to be smaller geographically compared to those in rural areas where the population is generally less dense. The main purpose of a census tract is to serve as a relatively stable spatial unit of analysis for the presentation of data pertaining to the social and economic characteristics of the people living in that area. The 2000 decennial census marks the first time that the entire United States has been geographically subdivided into census tracts.

Figure 14.1 shows a map of Montgomery County and the geographic breakdown of the area by census tract (U.S. Census Bureau, 2002b).

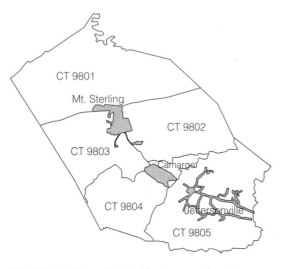

FIGURE 14.1 Census Tracts, Montgomery County, Kentucky

U.S. Census Bureau

Tracts 9801, 9802, and 9803 all contain part of the city of Mount Sterling. Tract 9804 contains nearly all of Camargo, and tract 9805 includes all of Jeffersonville. Based on data from the 2000 decennial census (U.S. Census Bureau, 2002a), Table 14.2 compares the five census tracts, revealing some social and economic disparities found within the county.

For example, Tracts 9804 and 9805, which include the communities of Camargo and Jeffersonville respectively, had poverty rates in 1999 of nearly 20%. The poverty rate measures the number of persons in a census tract living below the federal poverty line as a percent of all persons living in the tract. In comparison, tracts 9802 and 9803 had poverty rates of 11.5% and 15.5% respectively. The lowest reported poverty rate in the county was found in tract 9801 with slightly more than 10% of the persons in that area living below the poverty line. The rate of unemployed persons 16–64 years of age in the county ranges from 1.4% in tract 9801, to rates greater than 5.0% in tracts 9803 and 9805. The Jeffersonville tract (tract 9805) also reports the lowest median household income level at slightly

less than $29,000 compared to the other four tracts in Montgomery County.

An analysis of resident population change in Kentucky counties compiled by the Kentucky State Data Center (2001), using decennial census data for 1970 through 2000, reveals that Montgomery County has experienced migration trends similar to those found in nonmetropolitan areas across the country. Data from the 1980 census indicate a residential population for Montgomery County of 20,046 persons, a net gain of 30.5% over the 1970 figure. Similarly, 2000 census data for the county shows a population of 22,554, a net gain of 15.3% over the 1990 census count. Johnson and Fuguitt (2000) refer to the net migration population gains in rural areas and small towns during the 1970s and 1990s as a "non-metropolitan turnaround" and a "rural rebound," respectively (pp. 28, 29). These demographic trends are thought to be related to advances in transportation and communication technology that have altered the employment sector, through such innovations as telecommuting and the growth of home offices. Currently, community leaders in Montgomery County look upon the expansion of the residential base as a "rural renaissance" (Frey, 1987, p. 240), providing a climate of opportunity to develop sustainability and enhance quality of life. Local stakeholders have a commitment to build a sustainable community in order to effectively address the added strain on resources and infrastructure that rapid growth brings with it. Many view sustainability as a key factor in helping this rural county avoid becoming a stagnant bedroom community to the nearest metropolitan area, and as a way to avoid the loss of shared values and strong sense of community.

The ability to identify and assess the physical, social, economic, and environmental resources of a location provides a solid foundation to formulate strategies that promote the development of a sustainable community. The assessment model developed in this project is grounded in the work of Kretzman and McKnight (1993), and uses an assets-based approach to gauge the health and

**Table 14.2 1990 Census Tract Data for Selected
Social and Economic Characteristics of Montgomery County, KY**

Census Indicator	Tract 9801	Tract 9802	Tract 9803	Tract 9804	Tract 9805
Poverty rate	10.2%	11.5%	15.5%	19.7%	19.5%
Unemployed labor force (Persons 16–64 years)	1.4%	3.1%	5.4%	4.3%	5.1%
Dropout rate (Persons 25 years and over)	20.4%	27.4%	25.3%	37.1%	41.3%
Median household income	$45,029	$32,224	$33.037	$29,100	$28,885

Source: U.S. Census Bureau. (2002a). *Census 2000 Summary File 3 (SF3) sample data.*

well-being of the community. The appeal of such an approach is the ability to avoid a "cookie cutter" design, and instead incorporate the participation of community members in developing a model that truly promotes the uniqueness of the local environment as well as the residents, businesses, and organizations contained within.

The model has two components tailored to the community. The first involves developing a shared vision of the community. This is done through personal interviews with local stakeholders and residents to determine their conceptualization of community well-being, and to determine their perceptions of both local assets and challenges important to quality of life in their community. The second component involves the selection of community indicators to be used for the short-term purpose of creating a baseline depicting how the community is faring socially, economically, and environmentally. After the collection of baseline data, a series of benchmarks will be established to measure long-term progress toward achieving community sustainability.

The development of the assets-based model for promoting community well-being in Montgomery County is discussed below. The project is broken into four phases: setting the ground work, developing a shared vision, selecting the indicators, and promoting community

ownership for future decision making. The key aspects of each phase are presented.

Phase 1: Setting the Ground Work

The purpose of the Montgomery County Model (MCM) is to establish a set of indicators that can be used to collect and analyze data in order to understand current conditions and trends in the county, identify and preserve local community assets, and promote change strategies that resolve problem conditions and maximize new opportunities for sustainability. The MCM will also serve as a source for prioritizing which problem areas should be addressed first, and for partnering with others in the community to take advantage of new opportunities and generate new assets. The most significant objective of the project, however, is the ability to use this assessment model to build local community capacity and active participation of residents in shared decision-making efforts and in the promotion of community well-being.

Initial conversations that gave birth to this project began with leaders from the local health department who wanted to move their efforts beyond traditional public health interventions and into the community development realm. These individuals carried forth a vision of the health department that would make it a single point of entry for collecting and managing data relevant to the immediate goal of developing a healthy community and the long-term goal of achieving sustainability. In order to gain a broad level of support for the project, local leaders attended a town meeting where they discussed the concepts behind the project and gathered insightful feedback from all participants to incorporate into the plan.

Phase 2: Developing a Shared Vision

Leaders from the health department, in consultation with various community members, identified twenty key stakeholders to be interviewed face to face. The stakeholders represented a diverse cross section of the community, including government, human services, education, farming, banking, law enforcement, religion, retail business, and civic organizations. The stakeholders also captured a range of ages, both the employed and the retired, and those who work directly with youth, families, and the aging.

The interview format followed a series of predetermined, open-ended questions. Interviews lasted an average of one hour. The first several questions posed to respondents focused on identifying the types of community-level data that were currently being collected through their work, and determining what types of community-indicator data they would find most useful. The three remaining interview questions were designed as a way to develop a shared vision of the community.

"What Makes Montgomery County a Good Place to Live?" Responses to this question helped develop a shared vision of the perceived assets and resources available in the Montgomery County community. Six distinct asset areas emerged, each containing a variety of local resources valuable to the well-being of the community. The six asset areas include: people, leadership, systems and organizations, public safety, geographic location, and local growth. The first asset area focused on the perceived quality of the people residing within the community. Local residents were described as friendly, possessing a positive attitude and a "spirit of cooperation." Fellow residents were also characterized as willing to pull together as a group during difficult times. The elders in the community were described as important resources for their knowledge and ability to mentor youth, and to serve as volunteers within various organizations.

The second asset identified was leadership within the community. This encompasses both elected leaders from the city and county governments, as well as indigenous grassroots leaders serving on civic boards and committees such as the local board of education or the Chamber of Commerce. Individuals holding leadership positions within the community were described as cooperative and working in the best interests of the local residents. Many respondents believed that community participation was encouraged as part of the decision-making process in the town. There appeared to be two elements at work here. The first involved the attitude of elected officials that allowed them to work cooperatively toward better social and economic outcomes on behalf of the residents of the community. These elected leaders were viewed as "hardworking" individuals, capable of collaborating without getting caught up in a political game of "one upsmanship." The second element involved the recognition of indigenous leadership, with local residents willing to step forward to serve the community and provide a sense of vision. This seemed to occur in the context of recognizing that no single person has all the answers, and therefore it becomes necessary to pull together, pooling resources and ideas in order to achieve a common goal. Overall, respondents believed that the best interests of residents were well-represented and considered as part of the decision-making process. For example, during elections, a program was organized for residents to meet individuals running for various elected positions in the community, and engage in open discussion around local issues of concern. A second example was the establishment of a community "think tank" where ideas could be formulated and passed along to other community entities to plan and eventually implement.

The third asset area that emerged involved the role of the local civic organizations and institutions within the community. The school system in particular was identified as having a very positive relationship with both the city and county governments and was known to engage in partnership activities with numerous community-based organizations in order to enhance the resources available to students and families. The school system was also viewed as a strong asset because of its reputation for providing a quality education and its recent efforts working in conjunction with the business sector to address local workforce issues.

In this same vein, local community organizations were identified as having healthy relationships working jointly toward improving social conditions in the county. Civic, religious, and human service organizations were all recognized for their support and involvement in addressing community issues such as working to improve transportation options to help consumers reach the services they need. Another example of involvement, not uncommon to small towns and rural communities, was the collaboration of organizations in order to maintain access to quality health care services despite economic challenges that threaten their operation.

The business sector was also viewed as a strong asset because of the willingness of local retailers to support the work of the civic organizations to improve quality of life for residents. The area Chamber of Commerce was thought to be an important asset, working to build the image of the community and to attract more businesses, residents, and visitors to the area.

Public safety was the fourth asset area for this community. The local sheriff's department and city police force were both acknowledged for their use of resources that keep crime from being a serious problem in the community. An interesting collaboration between law enforcement and the health department resulted in a successful grant application to purchase a police dog trained in detecting narcotics. This new resource will now be available for crime awareness presentations in the community. The fire department also was identified as a strong public safety asset because of its professionalism and the additional resources that it has brought to the community. Seven fire stations are currently available to service the population. Some respondents perceived fire protection in Montgomery County to be far superior to surrounding areas. "We really worked hard to get fire protection for the people. There's a lot of difference between the price you pay on insurance . . . about a 35% reduction on insurance." Quick response time from ambulance service was also cited as an asset.

The fifth asset area involved proximity of the county to other resources that positively impact quality of life. "Location, location, location" was a repeated theme from those interviewed. Since Montgomery County is strategically located off the interstate for easy access to nearby sites, residents can enjoy the lifestyle of a small town while still having access to events that come from a larger metropolitan venue, including sports, concerts, creative arts, upscale dining, and mall shopping. This arrangement allows residents to avoid taking on the problems that come with life in a larger city, including crime, traffic, and noise.

Although a number of settings exist for fun and relaxation within the county, including tennis, golf, bowling, movies, and various restaurants, respondents identified several additional resources found just outside the local community that enhanced quality of life without having to travel too far from home. These included recreational activities found at two nearby state parks that offer hiking, camping, and fishing; and access to postsecondary schools, including a top research university and a highly respected state college.

Finally, the sixth asset area centered on the community's growth during the past decade. Expansion of the community was viewed as a resource that could be used as a catalyst to attract new business and industry. In this vein, growth brought a new energy to the local community, filled with potential from the assets and skills of new residents. The relatively new bypass in the county near the interstate exchange is a good example of this rapid growth. This area now serves as a hub for new retail business with miniplazas, an array of fast food and family restaurants, and a Wal-Mart.

This last asset however can prove to be a double-edged sword by showing exciting signs of prosperity while bringing with it a host of new challenges. Some of these issues are discussed in the next section, which reflects the second question posed to stakeholders about the well-being of the community.

"What are the Three Biggest Challenges Facing Montgomery County over the Next Five Years?" Responses to this question were used to develop a shared vision of the challenges and barriers that could potentially harm the sense of well-being in the community. Three core themes emerged around issues of local growth, business development, and the aging of the resident population. Feedback from respondents is summarized for each of these core areas.

Growth and Infrastructure This challenge recognizes that uncontrolled or unplanned growth can destroy the very assets that make this community a pleasant place to live and work. The rapid pace of growth has forced the county into a position of having to "catch up" to the issues brought on by increased demands for services and resources. Areas that need particular attention include increased traffic volume, dangerous intersections, traffic patterns that constrain access, new roadways to relieve congestion (especially near the interstate), and wear and tear on the roadways.

The strain on space was another growth-related challenge. During the past several years, the community built three new elementary schools that filled to capacity. As a result, preschool classes are held at a school that was formerly closed. According to one respondent, "So now we got

preschools where we had mothballed a school before . . . well if it was old enough to need to be replaced to begin with, now we got the most impressionable bunch of kids in the whole district in this old building."

Another space strain is finding a way to balance friendly green space in the community with the need for new development such as retail business and housing. Some respondents commented that the time had arrived to begin imposing zoning laws to restrict certain types of development and to ensure systematic code enforcement of new structures.

Stakeholders shared the view that increased demands on the current infrastructure, such as the water and sewer treatment systems, posed significant challenges to the community. The cost of these upgrades are substantial, yet cannot be put off. The concern expressed centered on the burden to taxpayers and the desire to maintain the quality of services. For example, residents wondered whether the increased demand for utility services would result in rate increases for water or electricity.

This same issue pertained to increased demand for police and fire protection as new housing developments become established and new shopping venues emerge. As mentioned previously, a prime example of this new demand is the bypass area near the interstate comprised of numerous fast food restaurants, retail shopping including grocery, and midsized department stores. The key challenge in this area seems to be finding a way to grow smartly in order to accommodate the business needs while continuing to provide a good quality of life for residents. As one respondent put it: ". . . we have a uniqueness and a charm of a small community, and I don't want to relinquish that, and that is our greatest asset we have to sell, we can't reproduce it, so the character of the community is something I want to see stay intact if we can."

Business and Workforce Development The challenge in this area is two-pronged, with a focus on bringing in new job diversity to meet the range of needs from the lower-skilled worker to the professional; and finding ways to keep younger workers from leaving the county in search of better employment opportunities.

New jobs in industry are needed to replace those lost during a recent economic downturn. This also includes the loss of the tobacco industry that served as a prime source of income for many local farming families. As a result, farming now serves as a secondary source of income for many since the work no longer can be counted on to provide a sustainable living for a family. Respondents recognized that in order to bring in new jobs, the community must use its local assets to attract more manufacturing positions, a strategy that previously has been successful in this county. In the twenty-first century, new job development also means tapping into the technology industry and employment opportunities that provide a comfortable living to raise a family. Respondents agreed that any new job development strategy needed to include a step system to allow for employee advancement and maintain the local workforce.

Workforce challenges revolve around the loss of young adult labor as workers are tempted away with opportunities available in locations close enough to make the commute worthwhile, and the need to retool current workers to be able to handle new employment opportunities in technology. As one respondent put it, "We're seeing a large shift of jobs out of this area . . . we have to attack this problem with the training of the workforce. I think of the movie *Field of Dreams,* you know, 'You build it and they will come,' well I think what we have to build here is the workforce." Stakeholders seemed to agree that an important asset in this area is the continued partnership between the local school system and the industry sector, in order to identify the skills that need to be developed based upon the jobs being attracted to the area. Such an approach would remedy both a skills mismatch and a spatial mismatch, with qualified workers being available to fill open positions within their own residential community.

Along with retention of the workforce, another challenge involves luring back individuals who left the county to attend college or to pursue vocational training. The creation of new jobs is only part of the equation. In order to promote community well-being, employment opportunities need to pay a living wage that can help families enjoy a good quality of life, including the ability to purchase a home. According to one resident, "We've got to find ways that these people will grow roots inside a community and hopefully continue to put things back in." Stakeholders agreed that addressing this challenge would be necessary to promote stability in the county and avoid the threat of becoming a bedroom community. In other words, for those who go on to college, the county needs jobs that will lure them back home, and for those who go directly into the workforce, the county must find ways for them to stay here and feel good about their choice.

Aging in Place This challenge centers on the growing elderly population in the county and the implications this will have for the local community, particularly with regard to health care, housing, and transportation. Currently, the local hospital has forty beds available to meet the need for long-term care. A number of stakeholders were concerned about the unstable political climate surrounding Medicare and Medicaid policies and what impact a change in state or federal legislation might have on local resources. Aging in place can also pose economic challenges to the community in terms of the cost to a single hospital to meet the demand for more long-term care services. The addition of beds and other necessary facilities including assisted living and specialized care such as Alzheimer units, can present significant expenditures. The dilemma involves the possibility of having to turn away lifelong residents, forcing them to seek health care services outside the county.

A similar challenge applies to the availability of affordable housing. As residents choose to age in place, a greater demand is usually made for smaller and more efficient housing units. The cost for such housing, however, may exceed the funds available through a fixed income, forcing the retired and aging populations to migrate out of the community.

The need for transportation services is a third obstacle to be overcome by individuals aging in place. Reliable and affordable transportation is a lifeline for elderly residents. Access to this service is vital for socialization as elderly residents continue to participate actively in community events. As stated previously, many stakeholders viewed the aging population as a genuine asset to the local community.

"How Do You Define 'Community Well-Being'?" This question was used to develop an understanding for how members of the community conceptualize well-being on a large scale. Although this question invoked much initial silence as respondents reflected on the term, some common threads in their responses emerged. In general, community well-being was perceived as extending beyond the more traditional aspects of physical and mental health, and instead encompassed social, emotional, and economic factors. Vague terms such as "community participation," "community attitude," and "community personality" were suggested as being important to quality of life in the residential environment. Probably the most attention in defining community well-being centered on the availability and quality of local services. The words "cooperation" and "collaboration" were frequently used as respondents discussed the need for equal access to services, the ability of service providers to openly communicate with each other, and ensuring that resources were well-known throughout the community.

Phase 3:
Selecting of Community Indicators

The next major component of the assessment model is the development of social, economic, and environmental indicators that can be used to measure progress on promoting community well-being. Indicators help reveal the past, present, and future for the community. Indicator data collected through the assessment model can be transformed into a web-based database to be accessed by community members. The idea is to encourage the use of data to support collaborative initiatives among service providers, elected officials, civic groups, and others in addressing local challenges within the county. Based upon data collected from stakeholders and local residents, ten domain areas were identified that reflect the unique assets and challenges of Montgomery County. Each domain area was comprised of multiple indicators to measure that particular area. The first round of data collection resulted in the development of a baseline for the county to determine their current level of well-being in each domain. These data were then used to set community benchmarks, or reference points, to further promote the quality of life in Montgomery County. Finally, a process was put in place for ongoing community involvement in analyzing the status of well-being in the community and determining future indicators and benchmarks.

The Role of Community Indicators The term *indicator* has been defined simply as "a number intended to measure some characteristic of people, organizations, or the community" (Tatian, 2000, p. 2). Indicators provide a picture of conditions or problems present in a community. They can be used in the short term to determine if a problem exists and to what extent (e.g., percent of high school drop outs, unemployment rate), or to address quality of life issues. Many indicators are constructed with a spatial element in mind so comparisons can be made across counties, regions, or states. Other types of indicators can be used for long-term situations, such as measuring progress toward achieving an established goal or to hold some entity accountable for their progress. Indicators used for the long term can also relate to issues of sustainability, attempting to provide evidence of a linkage between various issues in a community (Besleme & Mullin, 1997; Green & Haines, 2002). In this case, sustainability indicators often involve stakeholders and other forms of community participation in order to formulate a shared vision for the future.

The selection of indicators often reveals what is of importance to a community, especially in terms of their shared values or a vision they have developed. Indicators often provide a consistent pattern of measurement so data can be compared over time. This process generally involves setting agreed upon benchmarks that serve as a reference point or target for comparing trends in data collected longitudinally (Tatian, 2000). Bench-marking selected indicators is a useful way to measure progress toward a community goal. For example, a community might adopt the goal of improving child health. One indicator of this goal might be access to health insurance, measured as the percent of children with health care coverage. A second indicator linked to the goal of improving child health might be increasing the immunization rate of children. In both cases the benchmark set by the community might be a 20% improvement on both indicators over a twelve-month period. Data could be collected quarterly, with a final comparison being made at the end of twelve months to determine how close the community has come to achieving the overall goal of a 20% improvement in the status of child health. Examining trends over time helps to raise awareness and to develop interventions to address a concern. These types of long-range indicators are useful for gauging sustainability in a community.

Selecting indicators that are valid and reliable measures of sustainability is an important aspect for developing a healthier community. To be considered valid, an indicator should be closely linked with the objective it is supposed to measure, and that measure should produce consistent results over time (Blair, 2000). Indicators should also be relevant to measuring the goals set forth through a shared community vision. Green and Haines (2002) suggest choosing indicators that are meaningful to stakeholders, contain a spatial or geographical context, and are results-oriented. Similarly, Kingsley (1998) suggests indicators be chosen which promote change rather than simply monitoring trends in outcomes. Initial outcome data from a set of indicators is useful for documenting a particular social, economic, or environmental concern and increasing awareness among community members (Miringoff & Miringoff, 1999). Beyond that, data analyzed from an indicator should be used to build the local community's capacity to articulate both short- and long-term strategies for improving, reducing, or eradicating a targeted condition. These community building strategies define various change goals to be monitored over time.

A final consideration in the selection of indicators is the availability of data that can be collected on that measure. In addition to the use of original surveys that can be distributed across a community, a number of existing data sources are available. For example, Tatian (2000) suggests the use of products from the U.S. Census Bureau including the decennial census, the Survey of Income and Program Participation (SIPP), and the Current Population Survey (CPS). Vital statistics records are another popular data source where information can be obtained from birth certificates, death certificates, and marriage licenses. In most communities the Property Assessor's office maintains records considered within the public domain that can be used as a data collection source (Coulton & Hollister, 1999). Information on rental property, vacant land, and housing values can often be found in these records. Aside from sources available in the immediate community, a search of the Internet should also produce a wide range of secondary or existing data sources that can be accessed to measure various indicators. For example, the Annie E. Casey Foundation (2001) provides access to Kids Count data, an annual collection of social and economic indicators for children and families across the United States. Kids Count data monitors longitudinal trends at the national, state, and county levels. In addition to a series of outcome measures on such indicators as child poverty, prenatal care, and juvenile crime, state rankings are provided as a national comparison.

The assessment model for Montgomery County incorporates a set of ten domains of community well-being: health, economy, education, public safety, environment, housing and neighborhoods, transportation, social welfare, community involvement, and demographics. A domain-based approach is one method to organize community indicators. A domain is a collection of related indicators. For example, the Cleveland Community Building Initiative, a member of the Urban Institute's National Neighborhood Indicators Partnership (NNIP) collected data on the domain of "economic opportunity." The purpose of this domain was to measure such benchmark outcomes as household income, household assets, resident employment, job accessibility, and support for human capital (Kingsley, 1998; Milligan, Nario-Redmond, & Coulton, 1997). Examples of specific indicators used to collect data for this domain include percentage of families below poverty line, median household income, homeownership, unemployment rate, labor force participation rate, residents' perceptions of job accessibility and quality, education attainment of adults, and high school graduation rates.

As mentioned previously, the domain approach is also used in the Montgomery County Model (MCM). A set of ten domains were selected based on the stakeholders vision of a healthy community. A series of indicators were then chosen as measures for each domain. Table 14.3 provides a sample list of the domains along with their indicators to promote community well-being in Montgomery County.

Phase 4:
Promoting Community Ownership
for Future Decision Making

The Montgomery County Model (MCM) to assess community well-being was developed to support the short-term goal of measuring the health and welfare of the local area, and the long-term goal of building community capacity to enhance the planning and policy-making process to improve quality of life for residents and others tied to the area. An important aspect of this project is the involvement of community members in the ongoing collection of data, and the dissemi-

nation of results to promote local ownership. A number of methods have been used, including geo-mapping, visioning, Internet technology, and town meetings, to achieve these goals and ensure the dissemination of information.

Advances in technology have resulted in desktop versions of Geographic Information System (GIS) software that can be used for mapping and spatial analysis of data. Programs such as TIGER (Topologically Integrated Geographic Encoding and Referencing) from the U.S. Census Bureau (2002c), and ArcView (Environmental Systems Research Institute, 1996) allow researchers to map data and examine relationships among various indicators. For example, you might want to examine the spatial relationship between neighborhood poverty rates and the presence of vacant or abandoned housing. In this case you would be looking for a pattern to determine whether neighborhoods with higher rates of poverty also contain a greater number of vacant housing units. Similarly, you might be interested in mapping the unemployment rate of young males between 16 and 25 years of age, and the frequency of police arrests for gang-related activity such as the illegal use of drugs or alcohol, loitering, vandalism, or assault. GIS technology is an important tool for mapping patterns of indicator data, as well as for mapping local assets to more effectively utilize resources in resolving social problems.

A second method important to the dissemination of assessment outcomes is the use of visioning and ongoing training in the collection of data. Stakeholders representing the interests of Montgomery County will participate in annual visioning sessions to support long-range planning for the well-being of the community. These sessions will benefit from the ongoing collection of data by members of the health department as this agency becomes the central entry point for promoting community well-being in the county. Visioning sessions can be useful for determining whether goals for improving the quality of life in the county have been achieved, and to what extent benchmarks need to be adjusted for the future. Supporting this effort will be an opportunity for university students to participate through

Table 14.3 Sample Indicators of Community Well-Being for Montgomery County, KY

Domains	Indicators
1. Demographics	Age, race, sex of population Persons per square mile
2. Health	Percentage of children age 6 and under immunized Percentage of people who report currently using tobacco
3. Economy	Number of women-owned businesses Percentage of population with Social Security income
4. Education	Percentage of high school graduates Average daily attendance rate
5. Public Safety	Number of incidents of crimes against residential property Number of alcohol related juvenile offenses
6. Environment	Percentage of participation in recycling program Number of days air pollutants exceed healthful levels
7. Transportation	Number of accidents reported along interstate bypass Number of households with no vehicle available
8. Social Welfare	Percentage of families living below federal poverty line Rate of substantiated reports of child neglect
9. Community Involvement	Number of community events to support local organizations Percentage of registered voters voting in 2000 election
10. Housing and Neighborhoods	Number of housing code violations Percentage of owner-occupied housing

internships or service learning placements in analyzing data pertinent to community well-being and in mapping local assets.

Linked to the visioning process for stakeholders is the use of town meetings to engage residents and others with an interest in the well-being of the community. Semiannual town gatherings to report on the health and quality of life of the community are an important way to maintain a shared vision for future progress. Town meetings also provide an opportunity to discuss problems or issues that need attention. This forum is also a way to continue identifying and building upon the local assets and resources available from residents, organizations, and other entities.

The final method used in disseminating outcomes was the creation of a community well-being Web site operated by the county health department. Internet technology was used to develop a Web site containing the ten domain areas for Montgomery County, along with the indicators supporting each category. This Web site is accessible to residents, organizations, and others interested in the healthy development of the community. The well-being Web site is useful to those looking to share data for grant writing purposes and to engage in creative collaborations with other groups. The Internet makes it easy for partnerships to develop both within the community and beyond. This use of technology can connect Montgomery County at the regional, state, national, and international levels. The potential for exchanging information and thinking beyond the backyard is limitless.

OPPORTUNITIES AND OBSTACLES FOR PROMOTING COMMUNITY WELL-BEING

Several implications from the Montgomery County Model (MCM) appear relevant to the issue of sustaining rural communities. First, the model provides an opportunity for empowering local individuals to become active participants in defining quality of life in their community. The level of participation in the pilot project and the in-depth quality of responses suggests that a commitment has already been made to the community. Thus, projects such as this tap into that existing commitment, while also providing the collective information to strengthen the community. From a social work perspective, this enhanced capacity among residents translates into an active voice for decision making and asset building.

Second, the MCM provides an opportunity to engage in meaningful systems change. Organizational dynamics that constrain the development of human and social capital must be addressed to fully promote community well-being. Many of the respondents in the pilot project underscored the significant role of organizations and institutions in their community, and clearly identified them as important assets. Although this bodes well for working relationships, it may also mean greater expectations in terms of responses to identified community challenges. Among the most frequently identified challenges were coming to terms with growth and the development of an infrastructure that could support such growth; business and workforce development; and addressing the needs of an aging community population. Interviewees indicated that the community had been success-ful in addressing growth and business-related issues in the past.

Finally, the success of the MCM lies in the ability of the community to develop a shared vision that effectively integrates the social, economic, and physical diversity of local residents. This shared vision will prove instrumental in forging partnerships to develop new resources and to creatively resolve community challenges. The initial responses from the pilot project suggest that a working relationship already exists between local community organizations and the public. Further, the shared sense of these organizations and institutions as positive factors in the community increases the likelihood that the public will be able to work effectively toward shared goals.

With increased growth, however, often comes increased diversity. Although respondents seem to welcome much of this growth, new community members may challenge existing views of what constitutes "community personality" or "community attitude." Participants suggest that efforts to guide and control physical growth are important to the positive development of their community. In addition to these structural factors, sustainable social and civic organizations and institutions will be those that are able to welcome and make positive use of new and diverse community assets.

DISCUSSION QUESTIONS

1. A variety of factors contributing to involvement in community life have been addressed. If you were called upon to work with community leaders on developing a plan for increasing community well-being, what would you do? Where would you begin and why? Would the size of the community change your approach? Why or why not?

2. What are some assets of your local community? In what ways might your list differ from the list of other community members?

3. American society is highly mobile. Many people, particularly in large cities, live far away from their place of birth. What impact does this have on the development of a sense of place? How does this affect community well-being? What challenges do communities with large nonindigenous populations face as a result? How might these challenges be different for rural versus urban communities?

CLASSROOM ACTIVITIES
AND ASSIGNMENTS

What Is Community? Understanding Multiple Perspectives on the Significance of Place

1. Research indicates that a variety of factors contribute to individual differences in feelings of attachment to place. This activity is designed to help you explore ways in which demographics and personal history (e.g., length of residency) contribute to individual perspectives on the social, cultural, and spatial definition of one's community. For this activity you will conduct an exploratory, qualitative study of residents in a single community. You will need to do a purposive sample of community residents to assure variation in age, gender, and length of residency. In your interviews you will be seeking to learn more about how residents view their community and the significance of place in their lives. You should address each of the questions identified below, as well as others you may find relevant.

   a. How do your respondents identify the spatial (geographic) parameters of their community? Is it the city? Their neighborhood? An area of the city (the north side, downtown, etc.)?

   b. How are your respondents involved in the community? Do they vote in local elections? Participate in campaigning? Attend local council meetings? Are they involved in neighborhood groups?

   c. What do your respondents consider the most important issues in the community? Why?

   d. Who do your respondents consider the most important/influential community members? Why?

   e. What makes the community special? What are the strengths of the community? What do they feel could be improved?

   f. Why do they choose to live there?

   Based on your completed interviews, write a narrative identifying common themes that emerged. Did cetain views/perspectives differ based on gender, race, ethnicity, age, length of residence, or some other factor? What unique views/thoughts did you hear? After you have synthesized the information from your interviews, discuss the implications of this information in terms of community development and sustainability.

2. Identifying Community/Neighborhood Quality of Life Indicators

   The purpose of this assignment is to help you identify and interpret indicators of a healthy, sustainable community. A number of short-term and long-term indicators of community well-being have been previously discussed. For this assignment you should identify several indicators of community assets/resources related to social and civic life. These may include such things as employment data, health care availability and coverage, level of participation in local government, level of participation in education, and level of involvement in community planning/development. Whenever possible, you should identify information from more than one year to get a sense of how these things may be changing.

   a. Use available census data to describe the community (population, population changes in last decade, demographics of population, etc.).

b. Identify the indicator and the source of data.

c. For each indicator, explain how you feel it gives a sense of the community's well-

being. Is it an indicator of economic well-being? Equity and social justice? Environmental well-being?

REFERENCES

Annie E. Casey Foundation. (2001). *Kids count data book: State profiles of child well-being.* Baltimore: Author.

Besleme, K., & Mullin, M. (1997). Community indicators and healthy communities. *National Civic Review, 86,* 43–53.

Blair, J. (2000). Evaluating goal-based community indicator programs. *Urban Quality Indicators, 19,* 1–7.

Coulton, C., & Hollister, R. (1999). *Measuring comprehensive community initiative outcomes using data available for small areas.* New York: Aspen Roundtable.

Coulton, C. J., Korbin, J. E., Su, M., & Chow, J. (1995). Community level factors and child maltreatment rates. *Child Development, 66,* 1262–1276.

Environmental Systems Research Institute. (1996). *Using ArcView GIS.* Redlands, CA: ESRI.

Figueira-McDonough, J. (1993). Residence, dropping out, and delinquency rates. *Deviant Behavior: An Interdisciplinary Journal, 14,* 109–132.

Fitzpatrick, K., & LaGory, M. (2000). *Unhealthy places: The ecology of risk in the urban landscape.* New York: Routledge.

Frey, W. H. (1987). Migration and depopulation of the metropolis: Regional restructuring or rural renaissance? *American Sociological Review, 52*(2), 240–257.

Garbarino, J., & Kostelny, K. (1992). Child maltreatment as a community problem. *Child Abuse and Neglect, 16,* 455–464.

Gitterman, A., & Germain, C. B. (1980). *The life model of social work practice.* New York: Columbia University Press.

Green, G. P., & Haines, A. (2002). *Asset building and community development.* New York: Sage.

Hancock, T. (1993). The evolution, impact, and significance of the healthy cities/healthy communities movement. *Journal of Public Health Policy, 14,* 5–18.

Johnson, K. M., & Beale, C. L. (1995). *The rural rebound. American Demographics, 17*(7), 46–53.

Johnson, K. M., & Fuguitt, G. V. (2000). Continuity and change in rural migration patterns, 1950–1995. *Rural Sociology, 65*(1), 27–49.

Kentucky State Data Center. (2001). *Resident Population of Kentucky and Counties 1970 through 2000.*

Louisville, KY: University of Louisville, Urban Studies Institute.

Kingsley, G. T. (1998). *Neighborhood indicators: Taking advantage of the new potential.* Washington, DC: The Urban Institute.

Kingsley, G. T. (1999). *Building and operating neighborhood indicator systems: A guidebook.* Washington, DC: The Urban Institute.

Kretzman, J. P., & McKnight, J.L. (1993). *Building communities from the inside out: A path toward finding and mobilizing a community's assets.* Chicago: ACTA Publications.

Leukefeld, C. G. (1989). Social workers celebrate the centennial of the U.S. Public Health Service. *Health and Social Work, 14*(3), 153–157.

McCord, C. & Freeman, H. (1990). Excess mortality in Harlem. *New England Journal of Medicine, 322,* 173–177.

Milligan, S. E., Nario-Redmond, M. R., & Coulton, C. J. (1997). *The 1995–1996 Cleveland community building initiative: Baseline progress report.* Cleveland, OH: Center on Urban Poverty and Social Change, Case Western Reserve University.

Miringoff, M., & Miringoff, M. L. (1999). *The social health of the nation: How America is really doing.* New York: Oxford University Press.

Mosley, A. M. (1998). Community partnerships in neighborhood-based health care: A response to diminishing resources. *Health and Social Work, 23*(3), 231–236.

Norris, T., & Pittman, M. (2000, March–June). The health communities movement and the coalition for healthier cities and communities. *Public Health Reports, 118–130.*

Page-Adams, D., & Sherraden, M. (1997). Asset building as a community revitalization strategy. *Social Work 42*(5), 423–435.

Pearl, M., Braveman, P., & Abrams, B. (2001). The relationship of neighborhood socioeconomic characteristics to birthweight among five ethnic groups in California. *American Journal of Public Health, 91*(11), 1808–1815.

Saleebey, D. (2001). *The strengths perspective in social work practice* (3rd ed.). New York: Allyn and Bacon.

Sampson, R. J., & Groves, W. B. (1989). Community structure and crime: Testing social disorganization theory. *American Journal of Sociology, 94,* 774–802.

Sharpe, P. A., Greaney, M. L., Lee, P. R., & Royce, S. W. (2000, March–June). Assets-oriented community assessment. *Public Health Reports,* 205–212.

Skogan, W. G. (1990). *Disorder and decline: Crime and the spiral of decay in American neighborhoods.* New York: Free Press.

Smith-Mello, M. (1996). *Reclaiming community, reckoning with change: Rural development in the global context.* Frankfort, KY: Kentucky Long-Term Policy Research Center.

Tatian, P. A. (2000). *Indispensable information: Data collection and information management for healthier communities.* Washington, DC: The Urban Institute.

U.S. Census Bureau. (1999). *Decennial Management Division glossary.* Washington, DC: Bureau of the Census.

U.S. Census Bureau. (2002a). *Census 2000 Summary File 3 (SF3) sample data.* Retrieved November 16, 2002, from http://factfinder.census.gov.

U.S. Census Bureau (2002b). *Census 2000 Summary TIGER/Line Data.* Retrieved November 12, 2002, from http://esri.com/data/download /census 2000_tigerline/index.html.

U.S. Census Bureau. (2002c). *Topologically integrated geographic encoding and referencing system (TIGER).* Retrieved April 14, 2002, from http://www.census .gov/geo/www/tiger/index.html.

Wilson, W. J. (1987). *The truly disadvantaged: The inner-city, the underclass, and public policy.* Chicago: University of Chicago Press.

INFOTRAC COLLEGE EDITION

community assets
community building
Healthy Community Movement

neighborhood indicators
rural community development

15

Community Development in an International Setting*

The Role of Sustainable Agriculture in Social Work Practice

F. MATTHEW SCHOBERT, JR.
DALE A. BARRON

Some experiences are difficult to grasp and even more difficult to make sense of. For a group of middle-class, educated European Americans, witnessing life in Haiti is such an experience. How do you respond to a hungry, malnourished, eight-year-old boy who begs to carry your luggage, even though it nearly outweighs him, just so he can earn a handful of coins for "helping you"? How can you employ, feed, clothe, and educate scores of people who have lovingly befriended you over the course of two weeks, not for what you can give to them, but for simply being interested in them and their community? What do you do when two small boys begging for money offer to comfort you because you have nothing else to give? Members of World Hunger Relief, Inc. encountered these and other overwhelming experiences on a trip to World Hunger Relief, Haiti, an autonomous, indigenous, sister-agency located in the rural community of Ferrier, Haiti.

Part of laboring in international settings entails confronting such unsettling experiences, experiences which compel us toward understanding, solidarity, and service. The four objectives of this article are directed toward these ends.

They include: (1) introducing the practice of and the context for international social work, (2) reviewing social work literature on sustainability and community development programs, (3) discussing NASW policy statements that provide a rationale for understanding agriculture as integral to rural social work practice, and (4) identifying implications of agriculturally informed social work practice.

INTERNATIONAL SOCIAL WORK

What Is International Social Work?

International social work is a rapidly evolving field in the profession of social work. The body of literature on this topic has grown, expanded, and diversified significantly, particularly within the past ten years. In spite of this, international social work is not found in the *Encyclopedia of Social Work* (Edwards, 1995) and is defined only briefly in *The Social Work Dictionary* (Barker, 1995). This incongruity between current literature and recent

---

*Matthew Schobert dedicates this article in honor and loving memory of Paul G. McCormick (1909–2001). Grandfather, mentor, and friend, who modeled loving God, giving to one's community, and caring for the land.

reference work is attributable to two factors. First, international social work is a highly flexible content area that incorporates a considerable diversity of topics and subjects. Practitioners and scholars, therefore, still wrestle with defining this field of practice. Second, a considerable degree of ambiguity abounds around numerous related terms and concepts; for example, comparative social work, international social welfare, and comparative social welfare. (For discussions of these terms see Hokenstad, Khinduka, and Midgley (1992); Edwards (1995); and Friedlander (1975).)

Although it is often unrecognized by many within the profession, international social work enjoys a long, rich history as a distinct area of practice. According to Lynne Healy's historical review, the term *international social work* was initially used in 1928 at the First International Conference of Social Work; articles on international social work began appearing in the *Social Work Yearbook* in 1937 (Healy, 2001). Dating back to this period, debate as to what constitutes international social work has revolved around adopting either a broad or a narrow definition. Stein, a member of the 1956 Council on Social Work Education, which was commissioned to craft a definition of international social work, limits international social work "to programs of social work of international scope, such as those carried on by intergovernmental agencies, chiefly those of the UN; governmental; or non-governmental agencies with international programs" (Healy, 2001, p. 6). Many practitioners, academics, and writers, however, opt for a broader definition. They conceive of international social work incorporating the practice of social work skills, the application of social work knowledge, and the actions of social work professionals in the following venues: working in international settings, working with agencies providing international social services, addressing concerns of an international scope, and exchanging professional skills and knowledge across these venues (Healy, 2001; Hokenstad, Khinduka, & Midgley, 1992; Barker, 1995). Settings for practice include international

intergovernmental organizations (IGOs; e.g., the United Nations and its affiliate agencies), international nongovernmental organizations (NGOs; e.g., Amnesty International), national governmental agencies (e.g., USAID Peace Corps), nongovernmental-based agencies (e.g., International Red Cross), university-affiliated programs (e.g., Inter-University Consortium on International Social Work), foundation programs, religious organizations (e.g., Catholic Relief Services), and even corporate agencies (Barker, 1995; Edwards, 1995; Hokenstad, Khinduka, & Midgley, 1992). These diverse settings represent the variety of social work roles, functions, sanctions, skills, knowledge, methodologies, and challenges found within international social work. In this article, we adopt a broad definition of international social work.

The International Scene for Social Work Practice

Despite the breadth and diversity of practice settings, international social work identifies a number of critical issues of particular concern. These topics include: enhancing international forms of social welfare, alleviating chronic hunger and chronic poverty, promoting social and economic development, providing preventive and basic health care services, protecting the environment and reversing environmental destruction, resettling refugees, advocating for human rights, improving and protecting the status of women and children, and seeking peaceful solutions and alternatives to war and violent conflict (Hokenstad, Khinduka, & Midgley, 1992; Harris, 1990; Kendall, 1978; Lusk & Stoesz, 1994; Midgley, 1990; Segal, 1993). Although each of these subjects is of concern for all countries, including wealthy and industrialized nations, these issues are particularly critical for poorer, developing countries.

Extreme poverty and threats to physical and mental health, especially chronic hunger, top the list of social problems afflicting developing countries. According to the World Bank (2001a), during the decade of the 1990s, extreme poverty, defined as living on less than $1US a day, declined slightly from 28% in 1987 to 23% in 1998. The *World Development Report 2000/2001: Attacking Poverty* reflects these findings, reporting that 2.8 billion of the world's 6 billion people live on less than $2US a day, and that 1.2 billion live on less than $1US a day (World Bank, 2001b). Data on chronic hunger reveals similarly dire circumstances for much of the world's population. The United Nations Department of Economic and Social Affairs (2000) reports that 826 million people in developing countries do not have enough food and that "11 million children under five die every year from starvation and disease." The harsh reality painted by these statistics becomes even more poignant when considering life in the poorest of the developing countries. These countries are located largely in sub-Saharan Africa and in Central and South Asia. Not all of them, however, are far removed from the United States. In fact, just 600 miles southeast of the Florida coastline of the wealthiest nation in the world lays one of the poorest countries in the world.

A Rural Community in a Developing Country: Ferrier, Haiti

Haiti, located on the western one-third of the island of Hispaniola, is an exceptionally noteworthy country in a number of respects. In 1804, at the height of Napoleon's power, Haiti won its independence from France after a successful slave uprising. Haiti became the second nation in the Western hemisphere to gain independence from Europe and remains the only nation in the world that achieved its independence as the result of a successful slave rebellion. Despite this remarkable beginning, political instability, civil unrest, violence, racial oppression, economic chaos, environmental devastation, and repeated foreign military interventions mar Haiti's 200-year history.

Today, Haiti is one of the poorest countries in the world and is the poorest country in the Western hemisphere. Unemployment exceeds 70%; 80% of the population lives in absolute poverty, earning less than $150US per year (Central Intelligence Agency, 2001; World Food Programme, 2002). Small-scale, subsistence farming represents the largest employment sector in Haiti's economy, employing roughly two-thirds of the entire workforce (CIA, 2001). Haiti's impoverished economic health parallels the poor state of its population's physical and mental health. The leading causes of death in Haiti are attributable to chronic malnourishment, preventable infectious diseases, poor sanitation, and a lack of access to basic health-care services and providers (Pan American Health Organization, 1999). With a total land mass of 27,750 square kilometers, slightly smaller than the state of Maryland, and with a population of over eight million people, Haiti is also the most densely populated country in the Western hemisphere. A significant majority of this population (67%) lives in small, rural villages dotting the rugged landscape of Haiti's countryside (CIA, 2001). Ferrier is one such community.

Ferrier is located in the northeastern corner of the country and lies only a few kilometers west of the Dominican Republic. This small village is home to approximately 4,000 people and is ringed by 17 smaller villages. The total population of this geographic area approaches 11,000–12,000 people. Life in Ferrier and the surrounding villages dramatically reflects the portrait painted by the aforementioned statistics. Throughout our time in Ferrier, we toured several farms and orchards, observing the people's dependence upon subsistence agriculture; we witnessed the devastating effects of malnourishment in the frail bodies and discolored hair of many children; and I (Schobert) learned firsthand, from talking with, interviewing, and listening to scores of people, the plight they endured as a consequence of the burden of chronic hunger and chronic poverty.

These twin problems, common throughout the developing world, are intricately interwoven and markedly multifaceted. For these reasons, they defy simple, short-term, solution-focused interventions, and demand long-term commitments by practitioners, agencies, and governments. Reflecting upon my (Schobert's) professional and social interactions and encounters with the people of Ferrier, I noticed how chronic hunger and chronic poverty shaped the reality of life for my Haitian friends in powerful ways by cultivating two predominant modes of thinking, perceiving, and functioning in their world: survival and immediacy. Functioning in survival mode compels people to live in the immediate present, thus reducing their ability to make short-term sacrifices for greater gain or opportunity in the future. In Haiti, as in other impoverished countries, the majority of people make decisions based on their immediate and short-term needs for survival; to do otherwise could seriously jeopardize their or their dependents' health and life. For example, a mango tree that will produce a seasonal food source and aid in the reforestation of the landscape often becomes, instead, charcoal to sell, fuel for cooking, or lumber for building. Chronic hunger and chronic poverty, therefore, produce a vicious cycle of economic, social, and environmental catastrophe for the Haitian people and their country.

In Haiti, as well as in other developing countries, chronic hunger and chronic poverty arise from multiple causes, including economic, educational, political, and sociocultural factors. Economically, hunger and poverty result from a lack of opportunity, particularly attributable to unemployment, underemployment, and subsistence employment. Most workers who lack sufficient economic opportunities also lack the formal education or technical skills necessary to acquire, keep, and excel in vocations that provide livable incomes. Another consequence of lacking an appropriate educational foundation is the absence of knowledge about what governmental, legal, commercial, and social service resources exist to provide aid and assistance to people in need, not to mention the absence of knowledge about how to navigate these systems. Political factors also play a significant role in causing, maintaining, and exacerbating chronic hunger and chronic poverty. Corrupt and repressive governments foster social and political environments inimical to the creation of stable economies and

vibrant societies. Inevitably, political instability, civil unrest, and violence result. Aspects of a society's culture can also contribute to hunger and poverty. These aspects may include sociocultural resistance to the introduction of new practices, beliefs, and methodologies; culturally conditioned beliefs about gender and race; particular sociocultural or religious beliefs; and an atmosphere of hopelessness, learned helplessness, and disempowerment that pervades communities, societies, and countries blighted by chronic hunger and chronic poverty. During my (Schobert's) field research in Haiti, each of these four contributing factors repeatedly confronted me in the state of the country's infrastructure, the living conditions of its people, and the stories of those to whom I listened. The challenge in this community and in rural communities like it around the world is to identify and mobilize a community's strengths and resources in order to effect positive, developmental change in the face of such pervasive and seemingly intractable social problems.

COMMUNITY DEVELOPMENT: PROGRAMS IN SUSTAINABILITY

As we examine rural communities and consider the means to assist them and their members to improve their quality of life, we must answer the question, "How can social workers effectively pursue community development in these settings?" Throughout the history of our profession, social workers have been leaders in advocating for meeting the needs and improving the overall health of urban, suburban, and rural communities,. This section provides an overview of social and economic development with a focus on the concept of sustainability. It reviews the diversity of programs in sustainable development and concludes by discussing the example of World Hunger Relief's programs in sustainable agriculture.

Social Work Literature and Sustainable Development

Social and economic development aims to alleviate a host of basic social problems, including poverty, unemployment, housing, and sanitation. Development refers to processes whereby people and communities engage in intentional efforts to change their circumstances in order to improve their quality of life. This is most often assessed economically. Unfortunately, conceptualizing and articulating social and economic development in this manner deceives practitioners, policy makers, and clients into focusing on short-term economic and material gratifications at the risk of long-term, potentially ruinous social and environmental consequences.

Throughout most of the nineteenth and twentieth centuries, social and economic development was regarded principally as economic growth measured by gross domestic product (GDP) and gross national product (GNP). During the 1960s and 1970s, this prevailing notion of development came under increasingly intense scrutiny and criticism. In 1972, as awareness grew of the finite limit and carrying capacity of the planet and its natural resources and the rapid expansion of human consumption and the degradation of the natural environment through pollution, deforestation, and erosion, the United Nations held the Conference on the Human Environment. One of the most significant contributions of this conference was the articulation of a new concept of development—sustainability. The Conference recognized the interdependence of human beings and the natural environment, linked economic and social development with environmental protection, and called for the creation of a global vision and set of common principles reflecting these viewpoints (Commissioner of the Environment and Sustainable Development, 2001).

The next major step in the evolution of the concept of sustainable development occurred in 1987 at the World Commission on Environment

and Development, more commonly known as the Brundtland Commission. The Brundtlant Commission's published report, *Our Common Future*, defined sustainable development as "development that meets the needs of the present without compromising the ability of future generations to meet their own needs" (World Commission on Environment and Development, 1987, p. 43). Elaborating on these themes, they concluded that the essence of sustainable development is "a process of change in which the exploitation of resources, the direction of investments, the orientation of technological development, and institutional change are all in harmony and enhance both current and future potential to meet human needs and aspirations" (p. 46). The 1990s witnessed the widening acceptance of this understanding of sustainable development across academic disciplines, including social work.

Recent social work literature reflects an awareness of this emerging topic and its considerable practical and theoretical implications. In writing about sustainable development, David Brown, president of the Institute for Development Research at Boston University, identifies four distinct dimensions of development: ecological, economic, political, and cultural (Estes, 1992). Although the spectrum of programs in sustainable development includes financial development programs (Vermaak, 2001), rural and urban community development programs (Fordham, 1993; Hall, 1996; Lack & Gamble, 1998; Weinberg, 2000; Wint, 2000), environmental development programs (Lammerink, 1998; Pandey, 1993), and agricultural development programs (Berger, 1995; Mills, 1994), each incorporates all four dimensions and operates from the premise that contemporary and future development requires concern for the well-being of future generations and the environment. Although some authors address sustainable development in the context of industrialized countries, especially the United States (Fordham, 1993; Lack & Gamble, 1998; Weinberg, 2000), others represent an international focus (Gamble

& Varma, 1999; Hall, 1996; Kramer & Johnson, 1996; Lammerink, 1998; Mok & Lau, 1998; Pandey, 1998;Vermaak, 2001;Wint, 2000).

After reviewing current international and national development policies, Kramer and Johnson diagnose the present system as "convenient, excessive, highly dependent on fossil energy and non-sustainable" (1996, p. 78). They call for a radical reorientation in the dominant concepts and programs of development. The only viable alternatives, they argue, must take into account sustainable development as outlined by the Brundtland Commission. Moving toward sustainable development requires the use of macroinitiatives and microskills. Kramer and Johnson cite a number of macrolevel policy strategies designed to shift our current, nonsustainable system toward greater sustainability; for example, by substituting the Genuine Progress Indicator (GPI) for GDP reports. Gamble and Varma (1999), who share this theoretical and conceptual framework, discuss micro- and mezzopractice skills needed to implement sustainable development programs; for example, by networking, organizing, and political participation.

Rural and Urban Community Development Programs Hall (1996) and Wint (2000) describe community development programs premised on sustainability in Amazonia, Brazil and Kingston, Jamaica, respectively. Although the cultural settings differ between these two locations, both communities successfully initiated and perpetuated community development programs in extremely blighted communities. In both instances, the initial stage of community development depended upon successful joining strategies practiced by outside professionals, in order to partner with community leaders and to mobilize community resources. Because experiences of long-term disempowerment pervaded both communities, educational and consciousness-raising activities characterized the second stage of community development. During this phase, professionals also conducted community needs

assessments. This paved the way for wider community organizing and mobilization, with an emphasis on political advocacy to government and business sectors for resources and assistance in a variety of development projects. These projects included economic, educational, technical, and health programs that targeted specific community needs as determined by the needs assessments. Both communities eventually reached a level of political organization and empowerment that enabled them to continue their communitywide revitalization efforts with drastically reduced assistance from outside professionals and agencies. In other words, the programs demonstrated sustainability rooted in the political dimension.

Financial Development Programs Vermaak (2001) focuses on the economic dimension of sustainability. As stated previously, traditional views of development are tied closely to economic growth. Vermaak argues that, in addition to economic indicators, financial development programs must consider and incorporate noneconomic factors to guarantee continued economic success. Thus, for financial schemes to contribute to sustainable community development, they must diversify their areas of focus and incorporate more qualitative indicators of development, such as political, social, and health indices. Vermaak substantiates his argument by citing sustainable financial development programs in West Africa, South Africa, and parts of Asia that employ this expanded understanding of development.

Environmental Development Programs Lammerink (1998) and Pandey (1998) approach community development through environmental stewardship programs. Lammerink reports on community managed rural water supplies in six developing countries, and Pandey describes a reforestation/forest management program in Nepal. Although their focus is environmental, both authors underscore the political dimension for successful, environmentally based sustainable development programs. In this sense, based on outside professional and local community collaboration, they bear striking resemblance to Hall's and Wint's work. In each case, development followed the model outlined above: joining strategies, education and consciousness-raising, empowerment, community organizing, and collective action.

Agricultural Development Programs
Within the current social work literature, few articles address sustainable agriculture. Berger (1995) mentions, in passing, sustainable agriculture as a solution to a throng of social and environmental problems, including hunger, pollution, deforestation, and erosion. The American Society of Agronomy defines sustainable agriculture as that which, "over the long term, enhances environmental quality and the resource base on which agriculture depends; provides for basic human food and fiber needs; is economically viable; and enhances the quality of life for farmers and society as a whole" (Norman, Janke, Freyenberger, Schurle, & Kok, 1997). This definition recognizes the ecological, economic, and social-cultural dimensions of sustainability, but not the political dimension. Perhaps this omission is attributable to the U.S. context in which it was conceived, a context in which political power and participation by society's membership are assumed. Because this is not the case throughout much of the developing world, it is important to keep in mind the essential role that the political dimension plays, even when considering agriculture.

Just as a variety of sustainable development programs exist, so too a variety of sustainable agricultural interventions exist. Mills (1994) describes research on one model of sustainable agriculture. He addresses the development of appropriate agricultural technologies, cultural acceptance, and food security strategies in the sub–Saharan country of Malawi. One of the new agricultural technologies introduced in this region, following a devastating drought in 1992 that decimated traditional agricultural production, was aquaculture (fish farming). Mills's research findings indicate that small-scale agricultural projects that account for the culture of local communities and correctly assess for the use of appropriate technologies possess incredible potential for attaining sustainable development.

Sustainable Development and Community Development Despite this variety of programs in sustainable development, they all share theoretical and practical commonalities. Whether the development strategies are oriented around community, economic, environmental, or agricultural interventions, each program reflects Brown's four dimensions of sustainable development and relies on the basic skills of community development. This literature review indicates that the skills of joining, networking, assessing, educating, organizing, and advocating are necessary for programs premised on sustainability to succeed.

Practicing and Promoting
Sustainable Development:
World Hunger Relief, Inc.

World Hunger Relief, Inc. (WHRI) is a faith-based, nonprofit organization located in central Texas. It has more than 25 years of experience working to fight poverty, reduce hunger, and promote development in developing countries. WHRI researches, develops, practices, models, promotes, and teaches interventions in sustainable development, particularly sustainable agriculture. The purpose of these projects is to reduce the global problems of chronic hunger and chronic poverty. WHRI pursues this mission through "[t]raining in intensive, natural, sustainable farming techniques; [e]ducation in methods of conserving and sharing resources; and [o]n-site training and assistance in sustainable development in specific locations around the world" (World Hunger Relief, Inc., 2002, p. 2).

WHRI's training and education in sustainable agriculture consists largely of small-scale, integrated farm management systems. These systems consist of crop production, both fruits and vegetables, and small animal husbandry; for example, rabbits, sheep, chickens, and goats. By supplementing local diets through small-scale, sustainable agriculture, WHRI works to overcome the problems of hunger, malnutrition, and hunger-related disease and death. An accompanying goal to the alleviation of hunger is the stimulation of local economies through the production and marketing of surplus agricultural products. This is the long-term goal of sustainable agriculture; once families or local communities meet their own food consumption and nutritional needs, they can expand their small-scale farming systems into a variety of agriculturally based, income-generating projects. Whether from bountiful harvests of fruits and vegetables from their gardens and orchards, or ample breeding from their herds and flocks, families and communities can gradually transition beyond resolving their hunger and health crises to overcoming abject poverty through successful microbusiness enterprises.

Their Work in Ferrier, Haiti Since 1980, WHRI has engaged in agricultural development work in Haiti, particularly in the rural community of Ferrier. WHRI's agricultural development work in Ferrier flowered in the late 1980s and early 1990s. In 1988, WHRI, World Hunger Relief, Haiti (WHRH), the Florida Article of Rotary International, and The Children of Maribao, an agricultural cooperative in Ferrier launched Project T.R.E.E.S. (Training. Reforestation. Education. Extension. Self-Help.). Project T.R.E.E.S. was a multisector collaborative program based on the principles of agroforestry (the integration of agriculture and forestry) and sustainable agriculture. It involved 100 to 150 Haitian families. The program combined reforestation, staple foodstuffs, and cash crops. For three years the program moved toward success and economic sustainability, most notably when the cooperative signed a cash crop contract with a U.S.-based food company to provide peppers for hot sauces. Then, in 1991, because of national political unrest, riots, a military coup, and an international economic embargo on Haiti, Project T.R.E.E.S. suffered huge financial losses. The project continued to produce basic food-

stuffs for local consumption by members of the cooperative, as well as tropical trees for reforestation, food, and building materials; but, without the ability to export its cash crops to the United States, the project could not perpetuate itself financially. For the next four years, although Project T.R.E.E.S. continued to produce limited quantities of foodstuffs, the cash crops rotted in the fields and the Project struggled to survive economically and organizationally. In 1995, over the objections of the Project's organizers, members of the cooperative chose to fell the trees to supply much-needed firewood, lumber, and charcoal. Despite the Project's eventual demise, WHRI continued to work in Ferrier with and through its sister-agency, WHRH, to serve the needs of this community through a wide variety of development efforts, including agricultural, educational, vocational, and environmental projects. For example, WHRI continues to provide educational and technical assistance and support to people and partners engaged in agricultural work, to collaborate with and support WHRH's 22-acre training center and school, and to collaborate and assist with local and regional farming, reforestation, and water well drilling projects.

THE CONNECTION BETWEEN AGRICULTURE AND SOCIAL WORK PRACTICE

Thus far we have looked at international social work and sustainable development programs. Case examples of the rural community of Ferrier, Haiti and the nonprofit organization World Hunger Relief, Inc. served to make these discussions more concrete. This section will explore the connection between agriculture and social work practice by providing theoretical and practical rationale for viewing sustainable agriculture as consistent with and reflecting social work practice and values. Policy statements from the

National Association of Social Workers provide the general framework for this claim and the policy statements regarding Rural Social Work, Community Development, and Environmental Policy substantiate this argument.

NASW Policy Statements

As products of our profession's "most systematic approach to policy development," NASW's policy statements assist social workers in formulating individual and collective responses to important social issues (NASW, 2000, p. ix). Although NASW's policy statements focus on the context of the United States, social workers committed to international issues and service can easily apply them to their particular setting and area of practice. On this basis, the following policy statements are relevant when considering the connections between agriculture and social work practice.

Rural Social Work The majority of the world's population lives in rural environments and, through subsistence farming, depends directly upon the land for their livelihood. The NASW Professional Policy Statement on Rural Social Work (see Appendix) notes that, despite suffering "lower income levels, higher unemployment, and higher poverty rates," rural communities remain woefully underserved and lacking in basic social service infrastructure (see Appendix). But just as rural communities face formidable challenges, they also enjoy unique resources. In terms of strengths and assets, the policy statement notes that rural communities retain "a sense of community, individual character, an awareness of place, and a sense of family and tradition" that fosters "a strong informal helping system" (see Appendix). The truthfulness of these comments about rural communities in the United States becomes even more apparent when observing rural communities in developing countries. In these settings, these very strengths, often fostered by people's mutual dependence and collective work on the land, hold several keys to effective

practice and attaining successful "locality-based community development" (NASW, 2002).

Community Development "The development of strong communities is a basic goal of the social work profession" (NASW, 2000, p. 45). In pursuing this goal from a strengths perspective and with an eye toward a community's assets, practitioners engaged in international social work in rural communities would quickly acknowledge the role that agriculture plays in the life of these communities. In these settings, as illustrated by the example of life in Haiti, a large majority of the population derives their livelihood from small-scale, subsistence farming. Because agriculture constitutes such an integral piece of rural communities' culture, and forms one of the key employment sectors of local and regional economies, education and training in methods of sustainable agriculture become an important means for community development.

WHRI's methods of education, training, and on-site assistance reflect grassroots, bottom-up, interactive approaches to community development. In the face of the profound threats of chronic hunger and chronic poverty posed to the life of international rural communities and their populations, interventions at the grassroots level work toward the achievement of the first policy initiative cited by NASW, "the right of citizens to contribute significantly to the destiny of their local communities. Social workers who assist communities in gaining access to information and resources, develop local and participatory organizational mechanisms, and help citizens make socially responsible decisions can encourage these contributions" (2000, p. 47). By introducing rural citizens to educational and vocational training in their major employment sector, by providing on-site training and assistance, and by supporting and working with local cooperatives, WHRI's methodology in teaching and promoting techniques of sustainable agriculture fulfills this policy initiative.

Environmental Policy Of these three policy statements, the statement on environmental policy speaks most clearly to the merit of sustainable agriculture, to its contribution as an invaluable social work intervention, and to the importance of macrolevel social work and political advocacy. This policy statement links the health and well-being of the natural environment with social work's unique person-in-environment perspective. This distinct perspective directs our attention to humans' impact upon the environment and the reciprocal impact of environmental damage to human health. Undue reliance and excessive use of nonrenewable resources and hazardous chemicals that pollute, contaminate, despoil, and degrade both human health and the natural environment are eventually self-destructive. As Raymond Berger (1995) points out, these practices of "habitat destruction syndrome" form a collective, societal mental illness (p. 441).

Development, however, can be practiced sustainably. As this policy statement affirms, "sustainable development, simply defined, means improving community economic and environmental conditions and simultaneously improving social equity for current and future generations. Protecting people and the natural environment through sustainable development is arguably the fullest realization of the person-in-environment perspective. The compatibility of sustainable development and the person-in-environment perspective is a firm theoretical foundation from which to apply macrolevel social work practice to person–natural environment problems" (NASW, 2000, p. 105). As Mills (1994) and the work of organizations like WHRI demonstrate, agricultural development programs can be designed and implemented that function sustainably, do not rely on hazardous chemical inputs, and promote the health and well-being of both people and their natural and social environments. These programs, therefore, prove the possibility of securing "affordable food systems free of toxic chemicals" (NASW, 2000, p. 106).

These three policy statements clearly suggest several theoretical social work frameworks (e.g., person-in-environment perspective, ecological theory, systems theory, group theory, and community organizing strategies) and practical social work skills and roles (e.g., educator, broker, social change agent, community organizer, and advocate) that can be brought to bear upon rural community development in international settings through interventions based on sustainable agricultural development. Clearly, agriculturally informed social work practice holds merit and potential in our efforts to serve underserved rural communities and to spur locality-based community development that is attuned to the needs of current and future generations.

Implications and Directions for Social Work Practice

In spite of these and other connections between agriculture and social work, there is a noticeable lack of current social work literature on this topic. Much of social work's fund of knowledge related to agriculture and rural practice originated during the 1930s. Following this period, however, there is a puzzling absence of literature about agriculture and rural communities. A combination of factors, including urbanization, industrialization, and a professional shift in interest to the study of individual psychosocial development and pathology diverted social work's attention from these fields of study and practice. Not until the early 1980s did interest in these topics renew (Martinez-Brawley, 1980). Therefore, exploring and developing these content areas promise new directions for social work practice.

Social Work Practice with Agricultural Organizations

Because social workers are not agriculturalists with degrees, training, or education in agronomy and the natural sciences, can social workers realistically consider work in agricultural settings and with agricultural organizations? One of the distinguishing strengths of the social work profession is its generalist foundation that forms the basis for educational methodology and professional practice. As far back as 1933, Josephine

Brown recognized that this characteristic addressed the fundamental social problems of both rural and urban communities (Brown, 1933). Social workers can utilize this strength in ways that enable creative and effective practice in agricultural settings and with agricultural organizations. For example, in agricultural settings, social workers can effectively employ interpersonal and group skills to identify problems, to mobilize strengths and assets, and to forge collaborative alliances to empower communities. In the context of agricultural organizations, social worker's skills in organizational development, program development and evaluation, volunteer recruitment, fund development, and interagency collaboration can serve to strengthen and enhance organizational efforts to support local community development. Research skills are also applicable in both settings and, if used effectively, yield incredible benefits for rural communities and agencies. Quantitative research supplies the necessary data to evaluate the impact of a community's actions and an agency's interventions, while qualitative research gives voice to the people and their stories.

As a discipline, social work must continue to expand and deepen its understanding of rural communities and practice in rural settings. This includes developing an understanding of agriculture's unique role in these contexts, especially with regard to international social work with rural communities, communities which are highly dependent upon small-scale agriculture. One of the best ways to learn about and work within rural communities in developing countries is for social work researchers and practitioners to remain open to learning from people living in these settings; in other words, respecting clients as experts and teachers. The unique culture, history, values, and practices of a particular rural community are too complex to be understood quickly, especially when these communities and professionals do not share a common culture. Because many characteristics of rural life are not obvious to professional outsiders, no matter how keen or well trained, the competent practitioner will draw upon the strengths of a community's knowledge, skills, and experiences when confronting social problems. In this sense, professionals must learn before they can teach and must cultivate trusting relationships that will allow for successful joining with rural communities.

THE WAY FORWARD

As social workers, we are committed to developing strong communities by mobilizing their inherent strengths and assets. Because rural communities, especially in developing countries, are connected to the land and agriculture in powerful ways, it behooves educators and practitioners to take advantage of the significant contribution that agriculturally informed social work practice offers to "heal the earth, and heal men" (Berry, 1985, p. 128).

> AWAKE AT NIGHT
>
> What the world could be
> is my good dream
> and my agony, when dreaming it. . . .
>
> WENDELL BERRY

DISCUSSION QUESTIONS

1. Rural communities potentially provide an idealistic model of a society in which cooperation, mutual assistance, and connection with the land and the environment are normative. Are these characteristics reflected in rural communities in the United States? In developing countries? What accounts for the differences?

2. What does the term *joining* mean? What skills do social workers use to join with clients? Do these skills differ when joining with a community? Describe effective joining strategies for a rural community in the United States. Would these differ with a rural community in a developing country?

3. What is international social work? What are the strengths, challenges, and assets of rural communities in developing countries? How can social workers effectively promote community development in these settings? What role does agriculture play for these communities? What relevance does agriculture have for the profession and practice of social work? What are some of the implications for social work practice with agriculturally dependent rural communities in developing countries?

4. What relevance does agriculture have for the profession and practice of social work? What are some of the implications for social work practice with agriculturally dependent rural communities in industrialized and in developing countries?

CLASSROOM ACTIVITIES AND ASSIGNMENTS

1. Research the history of Haiti. What events have contributed to the current political, environmental, and social conditions? Which of these events could have been avoided with an intact network of social services? How would you propose to establish those services in the midst of the current state of affairs?

   Investigate the policies of the United States toward Haiti. How has U.S. foreign policy impacted Haiti? Outline steps social workers in the United States can take to influence U.S. policy.

2. Divide the class into two groups—one group representing an industrialized country and the other representing a developing country. Each group is to select a country and prepare a country profile, paying particular attention to economic, social, and health indicators. (Suggest that students select countries sharing a significant past or present relationship; i.e., colonialism, trading partners, etc.) Have students compare and contrast the profiles and explore the significant dimensions of the relationship between the countries.

3. How do rural and urban communities differ in assets, strengths, and challenges? How are they similar? What practice implications can you identify for social workers in each of these settings?

REFERENCES

Barker, R. L. (Ed.). (1995). *The social work dictionary* (3rd ed.). Washington DC: NASW Press.

Berger, R. M. (1995). Habitat destruction syndrome. *Social Work, 40*(4), 441–443.

Berry, W. (1985). *Collected Poems: 1957–1982.* San Francisco, CA: North Point Press.

Brown, J. C. (1933). *The rural community and social case work.* New York: Family Welfare Association of America.

Central Intelligence Agency. (2001). *The world factbook: Haiti.* Retrieved August 12, 2002, from http://www.odci.gov/cia/publications/factbook/geos/ha.html.

Commissioner of the Environment and Sustainable Development. (2001). What is sustainable development? Retrieved August 12, 2002, from http://www.oagbvg.gc.ca/domino/cesd_cedd.nsf/html/menu6_e.html.

Edwards, R. L. (Ed.). (1995). *Encyclopedia of social work* (19th ed.). Washington, DC: NASW Press.

Estes, R. J. (Ed.). (1992). *Internationalizing social work education: A guide to resources for a new century.* Philadelphia: University of Pennsylvania School of Social Work.

Fordham, G. (1993). Sustaining local involvement. *Community Development Journal, 28*(4), 299–304.

Friedlander, W. A. (1975). *International social welfare.* Englewood Cliffs, NJ: Prentice-Hall.

Gamble, D. N., & Varma, S. (1999). International women doing development work define needed skills for sustainable development. *Social Development Issues, 21*(1), 47–56.

Hall, A. (1996). Social work or working for change? Action for grassroots sustainable development in Amazonia. *International Social Work, 39*(1), 27–39.

Harris, R. (1990). Beyond rhetoric: A challenge for international social work. *International Social Work, 33,* 203–212.

Healy, L. M. (2001). *International social work: Professional action in an interdependent world.* New York: Oxford University Press.

Hokenstad, M. C., Khinduka, S. K., & Midgley, J. (Eds.). (1992). *Profiles in international social work.* Washington, DC: NASW Press.

Kendall, K. A. (1978). *Reflections on social work education 1950–1978.* New York: International Association of Schools of Social Work.

Kramer, J. M., & Johnson, C. D. (1996). Sustainable development and social development: Necessary partners for the future in the reality of the new global economy. *Journal of Sociology and Social Welfare, 23*(1), 75–91.

Lack, E., & Gamble, D. N. (1998). Southeastern women's involvement in sustainable development efforts: Their roles and concerns. *Journal of Community Practice, 5*(1/2), 85–101.

Lammerink, M. P. (1998). Community managed rural water supply: Experiences from participatory action research in Kenya, Cameroon, Nepal, Pakistan, Guatemala, and Colombia. *Community Development Journal, 33*(4), 342–352.

Lusk, M. W., & Stoesz, D. (1994). International social work in a global economy. *Journal of Multicultural Social Work, 3,* 101–113.

Martinez-Brawley, E. E. (Ed.). (1980). *Pioneer efforts in rural social welfare: Firsthand views since 1908.* University Park: Pennsylvania State University Press.

Midgley, J. (1990). International social work: Learning from the third world. *Social Work, 35,* 295–301.

Mills, G. G. (1994). Community development and fish farming in Malawi. *Community Development Journal, 29*(3), 215–221.

Mok, K., & Lau, K. M. (1998). A reflection of social development in Hong Kong. *Social Development Issues, 20*(3), 17–33.

National Association of Social Workers. (2000). *Social work speaks: National Association of Social Workers policy statements 2000–2003.* Washington, DC: NASW Press.

National Association of Social Workers. (2002). *Professional policy statement on rural social work.* Approved by NASW Delegate Assembly, August 17, 2002, Crystal City, VA.

Norman, D., Janke, R., Freyenberger, S., Schurle, B., & Kok, H. (1997). *Defining and implementing sustainable agriculture: Kansas Sustainable Agriculture Series.* Retrieved August 12, 2002, from http://www.oznet.ksu.edu/kcsaac/Pubs_kcsaac/ksas1.htm.

Pan American Health Organization. (1999). *Haiti: Basic country health profiles for the Americas: Summaries, 1999.* Retrieved August 12, 2002, from http://www.paho.org/English/SHA/prflHAI.htm.

Pandey, S. (1998). Women, environment, and sustainable development. *International Social Work, 41*(3), 339–355.

Segal, U. A. (1993). Cross-cultural values, social work students and personality. *International Social Work, 36,* 61–73.

United Nations Department of Economic and Social Affairs. (2000). *Highlights of the millennium country profiles.* Retrieved August 12, 2002, from http://unstats.un.org/unsd/mi/mi_highlights.asp.

Vermaak, N. J. (2001). Rural financial schemes' contribution to community development. *Community Development Journal, 36*(1), 42–52.

Weinberg, A. S. (2000). Sustainable economic development in rural America. *The Annals of The American Academy of Political and Social Science, 570,* 173–185.

Wint, E. (2000). Factors encouraging the growth of sustainable communities: A Jamaican study. *Journal of Sociology and Social Welfare, 27*(3), 119–133.

World Bank. (2001a). *Income poverty.* Retrieved August 12, 2002, from http://www.worldbank.org/poverty/data/trends/income.htm.

World Bank. (2001b). *World development report 2000/2001: Attacking poverty.* New York: Oxford University Press.

World Commission on Environment and Development. (1987). *Our common future.* Oxford, UK: Oxford University Press.

World Food Programme. (2002). *Country brief: Haiti.* Retrieved August 12, 2002, from http://www.wfp.org/country_brief/index.asp?continent=4.

World Hunger Relief, Inc. (1983). *Backyard food production system.* Elm Mott, TX: World Hunger Relief.

World Hunger Relief, Inc. (2002). *Mission statement.* Brochure. Elm Mott, TX: World Hunger Relief.

INFOTRAC COLLEGE EDITION

agriculture

Haiti

international social work

rural community development

sustainable development

World Hunger Relief, Inc.

PART IV

✳

Policy Issues Affecting Rural Populations

BARRY L. LOCKE

I n its formative years social work practice was influenced by two main roots, one grounded in the Charity Organization Societies and the other in the Settlement House Movement. Asset building as a paradigm through which social welfare policy may be developed is in part a re-discovery of an older view of social work practice most fully expressed in the Settlement House Movement. Building as it does on the notion of strengths, the asset-based approach is designed to empower at the local level and seek a range of external relationships that can bring added value and resources to local issues and concerns.

There has been some controversy within the social work profession about how social welfare policy can be used to support asset-based thinking (Sherraden & Midgley, 1994). A key contribution of asset-based thinking is the acknowledgement that individuals and communities possess assets that in the rural vernacular may be called the "seed corn" for change. Related to this understanding is the recognition that there are significant limitations to the traditional "needs-driven" approach to change at the individual and community levels. These limitations can lead to a deficit view of social issues as expressions of individual failure. Failure is often associated with choices made or not made by the persons experiencing them.

Social welfare policy, to a large degree, has been shaped by this focus on a deficit orientation to policy thinking and program development. This is especially true at the federal level, where the majority of modern social welfare programs have been funded through a specialized categorical approach. This approach has fostered one-size-fits-all thinking and policies designed to reshape client behavior in ways designed to fit the policy makers' views about what is personally responsible behavior in the larger societal context.

Such thinking has created challenges for the delivery of social welfare services in rural communities. The one-size-fits-all view does not respect or reflect the diverse contexts and realities of rural life (nor urban life either). Of equal concern is the idea that policies and delivery models designed to address issues and concerns often associated with social issues in urban areas work equally well in rural areas. The fallacy here is that the operating assumptions underlying the policy often do not match rural reality. For instance the work first policy of welfare reform assumes the availability of work and many rural areas are economically vulnerable.

In this part we find a number of articles that address assets and the rural context in ways that are helpful to thinking about social welfare policy. We begin with the work of Templeman and Mitchell who report on a qualitative effort to identify the assets of rural communities and families in Texas and how social workers may partner with them. After a review of the asset-based approach, they describe a structured focus group process used to identify the existing assets as known by the focus group participants. What emerges from this effort, besides the expected outcome of the importance of professional social work for rural communities, is the need to educate state and federal legislators about the assets of rural families and communities. Through such education it may become more possible to adopt "rural friendly" policies that support further development of local assets within the family and community.

Often local assets and issues, once named by the community, need external partnerships to be addressed or further developed. Nyman addresses one model for facilitating and supporting needed partnerships, the Strategic Bridging Collaboration. This model, which operates at the macro level, facilitates the networking often necessary for rural community and economic development. Using the border region of Texas and Mexico as an illustration, Nyman demonstrates how local asset development can be successfully linked at the macro level with social policies that support the building of networks and encourage economic sustainability within the local community.

Rural areas face compelling issues like institutional development, or redevelopment, homelessness, and transportation. Aker and Scales take a look at the new policy of Charitable Choice and the rural church as an asset, Winship reviews the challenges and opportunities needed by rural homeless families, and Wedel and Butler share their research on the effectiveness of rural transit systems.

Charitable Choice is the policy that supports the use of the church as a social welfare asset. Aker and Scales take a careful look at the potential of this asset for rural contexts, as well as a critical look at the strengths and limitations of the Charitable Choice strategy. This policy has raised an important debate regarding the nature of church and state relations. Aker and Scales consider this debate in light of the rural context and conclude that the church remains an important resource for rural communities and social workers who practice there.

Winship provides a thoughtful review of the nature and challenges facing those individuals and families who become homeless in rural contexts. He reminds us of the assets many homeless families may still have even as they struggle. In responding to homelessness, housing policy becomes an important consideration. Winship reviews these issues and the range of programs that exist to support housing access and provides an excellent example of the use of the church as a resource in the sense that Aker and Scales raised in their article.

A central feature of the welfare reform debate in rural areas has been transportation access. Wedel and Butler report about their research on the effectiveness of rural transit systems in Oklahoma. Such systems are critical to supporting work for TANF clients as many low-income persons lack access to a vehicle. As with most programs, funding does not appear sufficient. One potentially interesting finding is the expanded opportunity for social networking provided by these daily commutes, as well as the resource brokerage roles some of the transit drivers assumed in their local community.

This part concludes with the work of Locke and Potter. They report on TANF research designed to bring the voice of the client into the policy arena. Asset-based development assumes that the best place for the work to begin is with clients most directly affected by the issue. Locke and Potter share the voices of current and ex-TANF recipients highlighting the policy issues associated with their views of TANF and welfare reform in one of the most rural of states in the United States. Their work reminds us just how important the helping relationship is for the client. Additionally, many ex-clients appear to not want to use other public programs once they have exited the TANF program.

REFERENCE

Sherraden, M. & Midgley, J. (1994). Can an asset-based welfare policy really help the poor? In H. J. Karger & J. Midgley (Eds.), Controversial issues in social policy (pp. 276-290). Boston: Allyn and Bacon.

16

Utilizing an Asset-Building Framework
to Improve Policies for Rural Communities
One Size Does Not Fit All Families

SHARON B. TEMPLEMAN
LYNDA MITCHELL

Growing up in the United States, where one in five children is poor, one in six has no health insurance, and one in eight is a high school dropout, is a risky process. At even greater risk are the 14.9 million children growing up in rural areas of the United States (Sherman, 1992), where statistics are even more bleak. This is especially true when service delivery for rural families is fashioned after urban models. Yet models of service delivery for rural families are generally based on urban models, as well as on deficits (Hobbs & Chang, 1996; Morris, 1995), as if one model is universal, or fits all families and communities.

When urban or deficit models of service delivery to families are inappropriately applied to rural communities, the strengths and assets of communities and families are often overlooked or underutilized. This article presents the results of a statewide focus group of social workers and social work students that revealed implications for policy, practice, research, and education, which utilize an asset-based framework to promote well-being and create opportunities in rural areas.

ASSET-BASED DEVELOPMENT

Kretzmann and McKnight (1993) and others (Benson, Leffert, Scales, & Blyth, 1998; Leffert, Benson, Scales, Sharma, Drake, & Blyth, 1998;

Melaville, Blank, & Asayesh, 1993; Mourad & Ways, 1998; White & Marks, 1999) argue convincingly that the traditional deficit or needs model of social intervention may prove more harmful than helpful to rural communities and families. Referring to the needs-driven model as a dead end, Kretzmann and McKnight (1993) warn that a deficiency orientation overlooks strengths, which results in people accepting themselves as fundamentally deficient victims who are incapable of taking charge of their future. This in turn leads to fragmented efforts to provide solutions. Furthermore, the authors argue that, when funded efforts are targeted toward deficits, more of the funding goes to service providers than to residents; while reinforcing the perception that only outside experts, who do not understand the community from the inside, can provide solutions.

In rural communities, needs-based interventions are especially futile. Where tradition, independence, and strong relationships hold special value, solutions to problems often are based on urban models. Such models stress numbers of people affected, translate programs into local activities that teach people the nature and extent of their problems, and develop new services as the answer to the problem (Kretzmann & McKnight, 1993; Templeman, McCall, Mitchell, & Nerren, 1999).

Asset-based development, as an alternative to a problem focus, has captured the interest of successful community leaders who recognize that true effectiveness occurs when people invest themselves and their own resources in the efforts. Koliscz (n.d.) defines an asset as "a protective factor that is put into place when risk factors exist." Examples of the protective assets, or desirable or valuable resources, include good will, active and responsible citizens, safe streets, productive employment, exemplary schools, and healthy children. Fundamental to asset-based development is the belief that individuals, families, and communities each possess "a unique combination of assets upon which to build [their] future. A thorough map of those assets would begin with an inventory of the gifts, skills, and capacities of the community's residents. Household by household, building by building, block by block, the capacity mapmakers will discover a vast and often surprising array of individual talents and productive skills, few of which are being mobilized for community-building purposes" (Kretzmann & McKnight, 1993, p. 3).

Supporters of an asset-building framework (Benson, et al., 1998; Leffert, et al., 1998; Kretzmann & McKnight, 1993; Melaville, Blank, & Asayesh, 1993) suggest that this model leads to the development of policies, activities, skills, and capacities of communities and families that generate success rather than dependence, inadequacy, and hopelessness. As articulated by the Search Institute (1998), the emphasis is on unleashing the capacity of people and organizations to bring about positive change rather than bringing new programs that introduce new professionals. Key themes in asset building include positive relationships, the nurturing of young people in the community, a shared vision, continuous diligence and sustained effort, consistent messages, and a recognition of repetition and duplication of efforts that are valuable.

Asset-building interventions do not, however, deny demographics or imply that many communities and families are not troubled or that they do not need outside resources. Families, especially, cannot succeed alone. They require support and encouragement from neighbors, friends, schools, congregations, organizations, employers, and other influences (Michigan Center Public Schools, 1999). Indeed, economic, political, and social changes over recent decades have brought opportunities for some people, while eliminating opportunities for others, particularly in rural areas. Some of these issues are identified as challenges in the following section. Other sections include elaboration on the process by which strengths and assets of rural communities in Texas were identified, recommendations for change, and implications for rural policy as well as for rural practice and social work education.

THE CHALLENGES OF RURAL LIVING

The breadth and depth of the problems of rural families will not surprise many Americans. "Rural children and families in need are largely ignored, but when they are noticed, they are viewed as poor and part of minority culture" (Baker, 1992, p. 213). They do not fit our stereotypes of needy and at-risk children. Demographically, in their racial and ethnic make-up and family structure, rural families resemble well-off suburban children. But economically, socially, and on health indicators, they are more like children in our inner cities, where children's problems are often worst of all (Rural Policy Research Institute, 1997; Sherman, 1992). Poverty is higher in rural communities (22.7%) than in urban communities (19.2%). Although persistent poverty has a strong impact on cognitive and behavioral development of children, in comparison, children in rural families are more likely to stay poor than urban children. Compared to urban poor, rural poor families are more likely employed and still embedded in poverty.

Child poverty is more pervasive in the rural South than in other regions of the United States, with over half of the poor rural children in America living in the South (Rogers, 2001).

Despite economic expansion in the 1990s, this number remains large, especially for racial and ethnic minorities. In 1998, for example, the poverty rates for African-American children (41%) and Latino children (38%) in the South substantially exceeded the 21% poverty rate of white rural children (Rogers, 2001).

According to the U.S. Census Bureau (as cited in Center for Public Policy Priorities, 2001), children in the South account for almost 75% of all rural children. Although 94% of African American and 48% of Latino rural children are in the South, white rural children are more evenly distributed than in other areas of the country. According to Flynt (1996), the highest concentration of American poverty is not in cities or suburbs, but the Rio Grande Valley, Texas Gulf Coast, rural Appalachia, the Southern cotton belt, and the Native American Reservations of the Southwest. Of the 28 poorest counties in the United States, the common factors are that they are rural and have low education rates. Two of the 28 poorest counties are in Texas along the Mexican border. Child poverty rates there exceed 50%. One of these counties is 97% Latino; the other is 22% Latino.

In Texas, almost one in four (23.6%) children lived in poverty in 2001 and disproportionately large numbers are minorities. Also, families living in poverty are the fastest growing segment of the total population (Children's Defense Fund, 2001). Texas's rate of working poor families is more than 4% higher than the national rate. In this category, Texas rates forty-ninth in the nation. Meanwhile, welfare and food stamp benefits fell 67% in value between 1970 and 1993, placing Texas last in percent of change of benefit value in the nation. Over 25% of children in Texas have no health insurance coverage, compared to the national average of 14.1%. The high school completion rate in Texas is 79.2%, over 6% lower than the national average.

Too often, the challenges of rural families are highlighted, while their strengths and assets are overlooked or ignored. Rural families are viewed as resistant to accepting outside resources. Greater underemployment; lower education levels; lower wages; longer distances between home, childcare, and work sites; and less access to health insurance are met with condemnation of the individuals facing these challenges. In reality they should be linked to factors such as lower population density, which lead to fewer specialized services, lack of a full range of services, and increased costs for consumers (Rural Policy Research Institute, 1999).

SEARCHING FOR STRENGTHS AND ASSETS

The annual conference of the National Association of Social Workers in Texas provided a venue for gathering information regarding the strengths and assets of rural communities to meet the needs of families with children. The authors, both social workers in rural Texas, designed the workshop as a focus group, from which information could be used to lobby for policy change. In using this format, the term *focus group* is loosely applied. No effort was made to meet the strictest definition of the term *focus group* as researchers (Sherman & Reid, 1994) relate it to a specific methodology in qualitative research. For example, information was collected in the form of summary notes rather than data being collected from verbatim transcriptions. Additionally, those interested in social work with rural families could: (1) discuss the unique needs of rural families, (2) identify strengths and assets which exist among rural families and communities in Texas to address these needs, (3) identify barriers to success for families in rural Texas, (4) develop a proposed agenda for change that would utilize these strengths and assets, and (5) advocate for this agenda by submitting the findings to state NASW leaders and state legislators. Together, these efforts were specifically designed to highlight barriers to success for rural families, educate leaders about the practice and futility of inappropriately transferring urban service delivery models to rural communities, and to suggest alternatives.

The focus group included approximately 50 social workers, social work students, and allied helping professionals who, through their participation in the workshop, demonstrated interest in rural families. The following five questions were asked:

1. Are there differences in the needs for services between urban and rural children and families?

2. What are some of the assets in Texas rural communities?

3. What are some of the barriers to success for rural families?

4. In what ways can social workers affect the success of rural families through an asset-building framework?

5. What should professional and legislative leaders know about the strengths and assets of rural families and communities that will promote success?

Responses of Rural Social Workers

Focus group members were active in the discussion and brainstorming experience. Participants were eager to be heard and, through their own participation, to represent the voices of their consumers. They were enthused that their experiences and recommendations would become the substance of advocacy when the findings were eventually conveyed to policymakers.

In the eyes of these social workers, all politics are local and everyone is a politician. Because citizens of rural communities have critical information about rural environments and connections with the families, participants proposed that all state task forces, policy departments, and child welfare boards must include rural representation.

In order to influence local political leaders to advocate for more realistic Temporary Assistance for Needy Families (TANF) benefits, participants suggested that local residents should be informed and stress to their leaders that the current, unrealistic TANF benefits perpetuate poverty. Similarly, because distance is a deterrent to access-ing medical care for many rural residents, Medicaid transportation for healthcare should be expanded to include all recipients. These social workers encouraged the empowerment of local families to pressure local and state leaders for basic services such as water, sewer, and electricity in every rural community.

Members of this focus group argued that the principles of family preservation, which promote community-based planning for individualized intervention and flexible funding, should find serious and full implementation in Texas. Families within the community (whether rural or urban) are better prepared to make decisions about programs and services than are strangers with little stake in the community.

Participants proposed the expansion of the wealth of resources within rural schools by establishing family resource and referral centers. Suggestions to actively utilize the assets of information space, activities, relationships, and expertise offered by the ready-made communities of family within the rural schools resonated within this group.

Although some state loan forgiveness programs and income incentives to recruit qualified professionals to practice in rural communities do exist, participants believed that these should be more widely advertised, streamlined in terms of cumbersome application processes, and extended to retain those with experience once they have come into a community. The advantages of rural living should be made evident to applicants.

In response to the question regarding the existence of differences in the needs for services between urban and rural children and families, the group resolved that there are basic needs that are common to every family, regardless of locale. In some instances the difference lies in the extent or intensity of the need when rural and nonrural families are compared; the need is magnified by the rural context. There are distinct needs, however, such as mechanisms to minimize isolation and increased access to specialized services that are unique to rural families and that do not exist, or exist marginally, for urban families.

The participants acknowledged that, while each community is unique, some common assets are evident across rural communities in Texas, many of which have been identified by researchers (Ginsberg, 1998; Martinez-Brawley 1990; White & Marks, 1999). Among these are strong family values, voluntary helping networks, faith-based organizations, intergenerational thinking, family-friendly business policies, resourcefulness, resilience, and an internal versus external focus (which some refer to as "independence" and often by others with a deficit perspective as "resistance"). In agreement with the World Resources Institute (1995, as cited in White & Marks, 1999), participants recognized that "traditional music, crafts, art, and stories live today because rural residents stayed put and passed on their culture to their children and grandchildren, and most of the nation's natural areas still exist because these generations of local residents have taken good care of the land" (p. 28).

According to this focus group, families in rural communities were viewed as interdependent—they can depend on neighbors and family members for assistance and are, therefore, likely to look inward for solutions and resources before looking outward. Rural people have a sense of pride, as well as a stake in the well-being of their community, as many have claimed the area as home for generations. Rural communities in Texas were also viewed as having stronger boundaries than in nonrural areas, stemming from a network of relationships. In such tightly woven, small-community environments, it is simply more difficult for aberrant behavior to go unnoticed.

Barriers to success for rural families, the third issue examined by the group, dynamically impacted each other in a cyclical fashion. A foundational barrier to success for rural families is the lack of economic opportunity. Lack of economic opportunity impacts, and is impacted by, other factors. The lack of technology and skills, childcare, transportation, healthcare, and housing, in turn, limits economic opportunity. One barrier unique to rural families is isolation, which leads to incomplete knowledge of available resources, low utilization rates, inadequate response time in emergencies, isolation of professionals, and difficulty in attracting and retaining qualified professionals.

Another barrier that is unique to families in rural communities is low population density, which generates high per-unit cost for service, lack of specialized services, limited range of services, lack of market competition, and low quality of services. With outside funding sources frequently committed to a large quantity of consumers served as a primary outcome, scarcity of grants or other funding results in inadequately funded services, often with obsolete technology and support systems—or no services at all. Restricted mobility, another barrier to success identified by participants for rural families, results in inaccessibility of services, limited public transportation, lack of coordination of services, limited hours of service, and increased mileage costs. All of these barriers lead to understaffing, burnout of providers, and lower quality services. The absence of ancillary services leads to the inappropriate transfer of urban models to rural areas.

Participants voiced strong belief, in regards to the fourth question posed by the authors in mind, that using the asset of strong relationships to build collaborative community coalitions with equal representation by consumers, professionals, business leaders, and political representatives would be essential. Through community collaboration, families and neighborhoods discover there is strength in numbers. Goals should be citizen driven and directly related to family well-being. Such collaboration promotes unity, lends legitimacy, builds trust, decreases competition and turf issues, and influences policy. In instances where the focus of funding sources is needs-based—and therefore focused on numbers to demonstrate impact—these relationship capacities can evolve into partnerships with neighboring communities.

Often, in isolated areas, families are unaware of services that already exist. To overcome this barrier, the assets of strong informal helping networks, faith-based organizations, and formal institutions must be paired with community leadership to develop information and referral programs, which would operate out of the local school or Head Start program, in every rural area.

Participants encouraged the engagement of technologically literate people in communities to promote and train families to use technology such as e-mail and the Internet. This will decrease isolation, use the expertise and experience of people with disabilities or who are otherwise homebound, encourage telecommuting to develop higher paying jobs, and make families aware of resources, while bringing additional resources to the community.

Recognizing that existing social workers often hold the trust and respect of community residents as leaders and serve as positive examples of the profession, participants suggested rallying them to educate communities about the value and advantages of school social work and the availability of funding for school social work programs. They also recommended the employment of social workers in all rural schools.

In order to utilize the expertise of community residents with grant-writing skills, and to take advantage of outside funding when it is available and desirable, participants proposed the development of a community grant-writing panel within each area that will be ready to take action when opportunities arise.

Given that many rural families and communities engage an extraordinarily informal style of disseminating information, participants recommended that this process increase public awareness about children and families in the state of Texas. Texas's poor ratings among factors of child and family well-being were viewed by these participants as an embarrassment for a prosperous state.

Finally, participants stressed that service providers and communities should celebrate the resourcefulness, creativity, and resilience of rural poor families. Much can be learned from those who struggle to meet the basic needs of their families.

IMPLICATIONS FOR RURAL POLICY

Policy implications include the development of a model of service delivery that informs legislators about the strengths, assets, and unique attributes that exist within rural families and communities, and the importance of a rural, rather than urban, focus where planning and funding are concerned. Policymakers must be made aware that rural families face barriers—for example, less economic opportunity, greater difficulty accessing technology, isolation, and unavailability of specialized services—that are not necessarily common in nonrural areas. Policymakers must be encouraged to also promote incentives for quality providers to locate in rural communities. Local residents must also be encouraged to use their knowledge and skills as policymakers and to advocate for representation on state level political committees and boards. Social workers must advocate for the establishment of school social work positions in every community.

The model of policy that is suggested here is one that emphasizes the rural community as replete with opportunities for self-empowerment and development. It recognizes the variations in community attitudes, behaviors, and attributes. This model recommends policy changes that focus on community development and prevention by expanding opportunities and providing assistance through collective action. Federal, state, and local policymakers are challenged to work together through continuous horizontal communication and common efforts to develop shared social-political policies in relation to recognizable problems. Policymakers must restate these problems into clear and coherent policy goals that easily translate into operational terms, which are supported by federal funding that considers the local environment. In developing a framework for direct implementation, a multilevel collaboration is necessary to solve the inequity inherent with administrative requirements of federal policies in program development and local service delivery.

This model of policy development helps policymakers to refocus their efforts upon children and families as individuals and systems with unique needs, and to view services as a means to adopt unequivocal standards for child welfare.

In an effort to understand the unique assets and barriers in individual communities, it is imperative to seek input from those closest to the problems: local citizens and service providers. Active participation of informed rural citizens gives policymakers the knowledge and facts they need to develop sociopolitical policies that remove causes and prevent the same thing from happening in future generations. On the basis of local needs and service patterns, local service providers must develop program specifics.

The provision of adequate services to children and families requires the availability of trained and qualified professionals. Policymakers must encourage this by promoting rural incentive programs for service providers. Such incentives include educational grants to encourage rural social work professionals to obtain training for needed skills, recruitment of undergraduate students to work in rural areas, and salary grants to supplement professionals in rural practices, where the volume does not allow for high earnings or paid overtime. Other incentives include relocation grants for professionals who move to selected isolated rural areas, and support grants to universities and institutions of higher education that embrace social work education for and in rural communities as a necessary component of the curricula.

Finally, as a profession that trains practitioners in both service delivery and systems change, social work is an ideal profession to take the lead in advocating and developing collaborative programs that address the needs of rural children and families. School social work positions are needed in every community to encourage schools and community agencies to coordinate and integrate their services to families and children. School social workers can help communities to overcome turf issues by encouraging multidisciplinary relationship building and networking.

Additional Implications for Rural Practice and Social Work Education

More than any profession, social work operates from a strengths perspective. But efforts to assist families and communities are still too often driven by a deficit perspective, where deficiencies and problems gain first attention. This statewide focus group was challenged to consider interventions for rural families that look first at strengths. Participants used an asset-building perspective that allows one to view the glass as half-full rather than half-empty. Such an outlook assumes that even the poorest families and neighborhoods in rural Texas possess a pool of assets (skills, resources, businesses, and institutions) that can be better linked and utilized to maximize success, promote well-being, and create success.

Numerous suggestions emerged for social work practitioners in rural areas. These include taking advantage of the abundant natural support networks to minimize isolation by linking natural support networks into interdependent, neighbor-to-neighbor, collaborative, helping coalitions; as opposed to developing new programs with outsiders as the experts. Because faith-based organizations and institutions are prevalent and viewed as less intimidating, rural social workers might consider developing a coalition or clearinghouse among these organizations to reduce duplication of services and maximize the use of existing resources. Social workers are encouraged to recognize and honor the independence of rural residents who value self-sufficiency. Also, social workers are advised to reinforce and strengthen the healthy boundaries and bonds created by families watching out for other families—neighbors looking out for the safety and well-being of all children in the neighborhood, not just their own or their friends' children. Social workers are encouraged to maximize the role and resources of the school, making it a hub for information, activities, and support. Similarly they are in a position to link the technologically literate in the community with those who are not familiar with the Internet and the opportunities that are unleashed by this technology.

Finally, the information from this forum builds on the work of other researchers, such as Hobbs and Chang (1996) and Morris (1995) who recognize that urban models of intervention are inappropriate for rural communities and that the use of such models minimizes, rather than maximizes, the assets of rural families. These findings can encourage other researchers to carry out similar focus group discussions when social workers gather for area, regional, or statewide meetings. This knowledge can also be integrated into social work education curricula, not only to prepare students for eventual practice with rural families, but also to increase cultural competence in those who practice in any arena.

WHAT THIS STUDY DOES NOT TELL US

Because the information drawn from this focus group is from participants in a single state and who chose to take part in this investigation, it may not be representative of other geographical areas. Similarly, the information was gathered from a small sample of professionals and students in preparation for professional social work. The results would likely be different if the sample size were increased and if consumers were intentionally included in the group. It is believed, however, that the recommendations made by this group of professionals and students who have a strong interest in the well-being of rural families have valuable implications for rural social work.

DISCUSSION QUESTIONS

1. Compare and contrast asset-based assessment with needs-based assessment.

2. Identify ways in which the use of a "one size fits all" perspective is or is not supported by the NASW Code of Ethics.

3. Identify steps that social workers can take to influence policy changes from an asset focus

within various social work settings. In doing so, consider various settings where social work is the primary focus, such as child protection; and others where social work is secondary, such as medical or school social work.

CLASSROOM ACTIVITIES AND ASSIGNMENTS

1. Divide into several small groups of four or five students. Identify and discuss assets that exist within your own families and communities, and the impact these characteristics had on your own well-being as you developed.

2. The following activity is designed to assist you in understanding how problems can be reframed as assets, or, how the glass can be viewed as half-full rather than half-empty.

First, brainstorm problems and needs within your community. Record these in a list on the far-left side of a sheet of paper. Next, identify strengths/assets within the community. Record these in a list on the far right side of your paper. Finally, identify in a list in the center of your page, characteristics of the community that can be viewed as either an asset or problem, depending on your paradigm.

3. Imagine that you are on the funding panel of a grant foundation responsible for awarding funding to communities for initiatives to improve family and community well-being. Identify what asset-based criteria should be included in the funding policy guidelines.

REFERENCES

Baker, C. (1992). Child welfare in the rural setting. In Neil Cohen (Ed.), *Child Welfare: A Multicultural Focus* (pp. 212–240). Boston: Allyn and Bacon.

Benson, P., Leffert, N., Scales, P., & Blyth, D. (1998). Beyond the "village" rhetoric: Creating healthy communities for children and adolescents. *Applied Developmental Science, 2*(3), 138–159.

Center for Public Policy Priorities (2001). Data on and from http://www.cpmcnet.columbia.edu/dept/nccp /ecp1text.html.

Children's Defense Fund. (2001). *Children in the states— 2001: Texas.* Retreived January 3, 2001, from http://www.childrensdefensefund.org/states /profile-tx.pdf.

Flynt, W. (1996). Rural poverty in America. *National Forum, 76*(3), 32–35.

Ginsberg, L. (Ed.). (1998). *Social work in rural xommunities* (3rd ed.). Alexandria, VA: Council on Social Work Education.

Hobbs, B., & Chang, J. (1996). Identifying and meeting the school-age childcare needs of rural families. *Journal of Family and Consumer Sciences, 88*(4), 13–16, 24.

Koliscz, S. (n.d.). University of Rhode Island Cooperative Extension. *Community asset building.* Retrieved January 4, 2002, from http://www.uri.edu/ce/faceit/cd3.html.

Kretzmann, J., & McKnight, J. (1993). *Building communities from the inside out: A path toward finding and mobilizing a community's assets.* Evanston, IL: Institute for Policy Research.

Leffert, N., Benson, P., Scales, P., Sharma, A., Drake, D., & Blyth, D. (1998). Developmental assets: Measurement and prediction of risk behaviors among adolescents. *Applied Developmental Science, 2*(4), 209–230.

Martinez-Brawley, E. (1990). *Perspectives on the small community: Humanistic views for practitioners.* Washington, DC: National Association of Social Workers.

Melaville, A., Blank, M., & Asayesh, G. (1993). *Together we can: A guide for crafting a profamily system of educa-tion and human services.* Washington, DC: U.S. Government Printing Office.

Michigan Center Public Schools (1999). *Asset building for a better life.* Retrieved January 4, 2002, from http://www.mcps.k12.mi.us~assets.

Morris, L. (1995). Rural poverty. In R. L. Edwards (Ed.), *Encyclopedia of social work, vol. 3* (19th ed., pp. 2068–2075). Washington, DC: NASW Press.

Mourad, M., & Ways, H. (1998). *Comprehensive community revitalization: Strategies for asset building.* Retrieved June 1, 2003, from http://www.asu.edu/caed /proceedings98/Mourad/mourad.html.

Rogers, C. (2001). Factors affecting high child poverty in the rural south [Electronic version]. *Rural America, 15,* 50–58.

Rural Policy Research Institute. (1999). *Rural America and welfare reform: An overview assessment.* Columbia, MO: Author.

Rural Policy Research Institute, Rural Policy Panel. (1997). *Rural community implications of the 1996 Farm Bill: Toward a community policy.* Columbia, MO: Author.

Search Institute (1998). Healthy communities—healthy youth. Retrieved January 4, 2002, from http:// www.searchinstitute.org/archives/hchy/1.htm.

Sherman, A. (1992). *Falling by the wayside: Children in rural America.* Washington, DC: Children's Defense Fund.

Sherman, E., & Reid, W. (Eds.). (1994). *Qualitative research in social work.* New York: Columbia University Press.

Templeman, S., McCall, D., Mitchell, L., & Nerren, C. (1999). *One size does not fit all children.* Presentation at the NASW/Texas 23rd Annual State Conference, Houston, TX.

White, C., & Marks, K. (1999). A strengths-based approach to rural sustainable development. In I. B. Carlton-LaNey, R. L. Edwards, & P. N. Reid (Eds.), *Preserving and strengthening small towns and rural communities* (pp. 27–42). Washington, DC: NASW Press.

INFOTRAC COLLEGE EDITION

asset building
community
families

policy
rural

17

The Complex Challenges of Building Assets in Rural Communities and Strategic Bridging Solutions

KRISTEN NYMAN

We generally see asset development occur in low-income communities in two ways. The first approach is to help low-income individuals and families build their own personal assets, such as through low-income homeownership programs, financial education, or small business capitalization. This type of approach usually deals with the specific needs of the individual or family that is taking part in the program. The second type of asset development occurs on a community level. *Community asset development* affects groups of individuals and families living within a neighborhood, town, or county. Community assets include a county or town's infrastructure; for example, its roads or schools, as well as the development of organizations such as banks and businesses. A community that has few of these kinds of assets is a *disinvested community*, and we can find such communities in poor rural counties throughout the United States.

The purpose of this article is to show how rural social workers can use individual asset development programs (and other individual- and family-based social work) as part of a greater community asset-building strategy. More importantly, this article provides a framework to build a strengths-focused relationship between community-building strategies and policymaking. This framework reveals the mutual influence of public policies that govern rural economic development and the organizations and infrastructure that support community asset-building in rural areas. Through *strategic bridging collaborations,* asset development programs can participate in local economic development approaches. The article shows how a larger economic development perspective can lead organizations to work collaboratively to address asset disinvestment in rural areas.

The first two sections introduce Individual Development Account (IDA) programs and other rural economic development strategies. Next, the article explains how to view a community institutionally. Finally, using asset development programs in the Texas-Mexico border region as examples, the article describes strategic bridging collaboration as a method for local economic development.

BUILDING COMMUNITY ASSETS FAMILY-BY-FAMILY

It is the opening day of the Azteca Community Loan Fund's asset development program. Families from the neighboring *colonias* along the Texas-Mexico border have come to the United Farm Workers Union building in San Juan, Texas to hear about a new savings account program offered through Proyecto Azteca's nonprofit community loan fund. The financial education trainer begins the orientation with *Relizar Sus Sueños* (To Realize Your Dreams). The participants learn about how to identify what they need (*cosas que necesito*) and what they want (*cosas que quiero*), and learn that saving money requires a longer-term perspective. The program will help them to prepare for any problems that can occur and that might reduce their ability to save. The participants learn how to complete a deposit slip and how to get to a participating bank. They are told that the savings program will help them to save for a home or for home improvement. The majority of *colonias* residents in Texas own their own homes (Center for Housing and Urban Development, 1998), which they have built from available materials on lots they purchase from land developers for $20–40 a month. However, these *colonias* lack the basic infrastructure that makes a community viable for economic development, such as paved roads, sufficient water systems, and adequate wastewater systems.

Azteca Community Loan Fund (ACLF) works with the Housing Assistance Council and local banks to provide this program to very low-income residents of the 868 *colonias* in Hidalgo County (Federal Reserve Bank of Dallas, 1996). ACLF has assisted residents of Hidalgo County *colonias* since December 2000 when the Board of Directors of Proyecto Azteca set up the nonprofit community loan fund to provide low-cost loan products to *colonias* residents. Proyecto Azteca began providing self-help homeownership services to *colonias* residents nearly a decade earlier in 1991. Over 200 residents are on a waiting list for ACLF's homeownership program (J. Segura, personal communication, November 19, 2002), which provides small loans to Proyecto Azteca home-building professionals to build basic building structures (Cisneros, 2001; Texas C-Bar, 2001). These homes, built at a Proyecto Azteca site, are sold to families at $15,000 per a ninety-percent-completed structure and then moved to the families' *colonias* lots. Participants put 15% down, receive zero-interest, (up to) twenty-year loans, and make payments of $50 to $100 a month while building "sweat equity" through finishing interior details such as sheetrock and painting. The savings program provides a means to save for the down payment on the home loan.

There is a clear economic development benefit ("Azteca" is an acronym for *Asemblea de Zonas de Trabajadores con Equalidad para Casas con Amistad* or "Assembly of Zones of Workers Working in Friendship for Equality in Housing") for these *colonia* residents despite the one-on-one approach to the program. *Colonias* are poor, unincorporated rural areas throughout the U.S-Mexico border region and other rural areas of Texas, Arizona, New Mexico, and California. Most areas lack basic infrastructure, such as paved streets and sidewalks, adequate water supplies, and sewage systems. The residents of the Hidalgo County *colonias* who participate in ACLF's program build houses one at a time, and develop neighborhoods and political power. As these neighborhoods expand, the area's investment potential and tax base grows as well (Center for Housing and Urban Development, 1998).

ASSET CREATION IS MORE THAN TANGIBLE ASSETS

For individuals, assets provide the means to create long-term goals, beyond the short-term consumption needs fulfilled by income alone (Sherraden, 1991). Assets are equally powerful for communities, which can develop assets such as infrastructure, organizational capacity, and social networks or social capital (Putnam, 2000).

Asset generation also relates to information creation. For banks and other financial intermediaries, information assets reduce the risk that they undertake in their day-to-day transactions. For example, banks base much of their loan decisions on the quality and quantity of information that they can obtain about a particular borrower. Understandably, if the information reveals a high risk to the financial institution, then the bank may deny a loan. However, a lack of information poses an even greater risk to the financial intermediary.

This same principle applies to the individual level wherein the information gained by individuals can reduce their risk and uncertainty, and provide the means for long-term goals. Individual Development Account (IDA) programs, such as ACLF's Colonias IDA Program, introduce this idea to their participants, who save between $10–$30 per month in matched savings accounts for home ownership and home improvement. For individuals and families who live in isolated, rural areas, as do many of the participants of the ACLF IDA program, this education may be the first experience that they have with the formal financial sector.

In subsequent financial education classes, such as those offered through the U.S. Department of Labor and the Federal Deposit Insurance Corporation's *Money Smart* program, these participants will receive more detailed information and training, such as credit counseling and money management techniques, consumer rights, and debt management (FDIC, 2002). Furthermore, there is a range of savings goals in IDA programs. Practitioners term these goals as the "Big Three": homeownership, higher education, and small business capitalization. IDA programs typically offer additional courses to participants to assist them in their home purchases, small business development, and pursuit of higher education (Flacke, et al., 1999).

Although IDA programs are a relatively new antipoverty approach (first proposed by Sherraden, 1991), early results of a six-year national demonstration project, the Downpayment on the American Dream Demonstration, show that asset development combined with financial education can successfully bring low-income populations into the formalized economy (Schreiner, et al., 2001). Another national demonstration, the Assets for Independence (AFI) program sponsored by the U.S. Department of Health and Human Services, is evaluating over 125 federally funded demonstration projects in at least 40 states and the District of Columbia over a five-year period (USDHHS, 2002). Other research on financial education has identified a positive relationship between savings patterns and financial education (e.g., Bernheim & Scholtz, 1996 in Sherraden, Shreiner, & Beverly, 2002).

Before the development of IDA programs, financial education was a primary component for microenterprise programs, which assist entrepreneurs in developing a business plan, gaining understanding of economic markets, and providing access to business capital. For many microenterprise practitioners, the benefits of financial education and business development training address more than the participants' self-employment goals. Anecdotal evidence from practitioners and participants, as well as formal research, shows that financial education provides program participants with skills that they can transfer to the workplace, regardless of whether they start their own business (Servon, 1998).

In addition to access to financial assets, IDA programs and microenterprise development strategies include these information-building components as part of a comprehensive approach to asset development. However, as single programs, neither is a sufficient strategy to bring about real asset development for rural communities. In the case of IDA programs, the successful purchase of a home can be hampered by the lack of affordable housing in an area that has developed more through urban/suburban sprawl than through sustainable affordable housing initiatives (Chen, 2001). Therefore, the success of the Colonias IDA Program hinges on the self-help housing components, which offer participants low-cost housing structures and access to zero-interest mortgages. Similarly, small business development may not be a practical strategy for low-income persons who are experiencing severe disinvestments in their community. Each approach must be seen as part of a more comprehensive economic development effort (Rakodi, 1999). The Colonias IDA Program uses this comprehensive development approach through linkages to self-help housing initiatives, loan subsidies, workforce development, microenterprise programs, and community infrastructure development initiatives through the Border Low Income Housing Coalition, an ad hoc collaboration of hundreds of housing organizations, policymakers, and residents (see more information at http://www.bordercoalition.org).

Comprehensive Economic Development in Rural Areas

Rural economic development strategies have been an important public policy focus since the nineteenth century. Early rural economic development programs were created with the First Morrill Act of 1862, which established land-grant institutions in each state to educate, perform research, and disseminate information to local communities on agriculture, home economics, mechanics, and other professions (CSREES, 2000a). The Second Morrill Act of 1890 established land grants for an additional seventeen historically African-American institutions in the South (these are known today as the "1890 Institutions"). In 1994, these land grants were expanded to include Tribal Colleges (CSREES, 2002a).

The Hatch Act of 1887 and subsequent amendments and legislation added the Cooperative Extension System to the existing land-granted university system. The Act authorized the U.S. Department of Agriculture (USDA) to provide land grant universities and other eligible entities with matching grants for agricultural experiment stations to research and improve the agricultural economy and to address the well-being of rural citizens (CSREES, 2002b). Today, the Cooperative Extension System includes federal and state land-granted universities, state departments of economic development, nonprofit organizations, local economic development entities, and other community-based organizations. Hundreds of economic development projects throughout the rural United States are launched through this multi-institutional system.

Other economic development strategies recognize the integral role in comprehensive development for those persons who are most affected by community disinvestment. Many of the agencies that currently participate in local economic development strategies originated during the War on Poverty in the 1960s. During that time, local Community Action Agencies (CAAs) received federal funds to coordinate antipoverty programs and services in conjunction with community-identified needs (Davidson, 1969). Following the original mandate of the 1964 Economic Opportunity Act, which required the "maximum feasible participation" of the low-income community (Naples, 1998), at least one-third of the current CAA Boards of Directors seats are filled by low-income community members (Community Action Partnership, 2002).

Today, 54% of the over one thousand CAAs in this country serve rural areas. Another 36% of the CAAs serve both rural and urban areas, and only 10% specifically target urban areas (Community Action Partnership, 2002). These community-based entities, primarily funded through the federal Community Services Block Grant, continue to provide coordination and economic development services to their targeted population, including microenterprise development, housing, transportation, and adult education programs.

CAAs and the Cooperative Extension System are only two of a multitude of publicly created entities that share a focus on rural economic development. Reorganized in 1994 by the Federal Crop Insurance Reform and Agriculture Reorganization Act, the USDA realigned many of its agencies and missions and created the USDA's Rural Development Mission Area (Reeder, 1998). Title V of the 1996 Federal Agriculture Improvement and Reform Act created a Rural Community Advancement Program, which provides funding flexibility to State Rural Development Directors in order to strategically address specific rural needs. The proposed 2003 USDA budget for rural community development totals $11.6 billion, $10.6 billion of which is available for grants, loans, and community development initiatives (USDA, 2002).

GROWING ORGANIZATIONAL COMPLEXITY

It is difficult to identify all of the resources that the United States directs toward and generates within rural communities for economic development. Federal funding programs complement federal and state tax credit programs (e.g., the federal Enterprise Zone program), which offer tax credits to businesses and other entities that contribute to economic and workforce development in a designated area. States and federal agencies create funding initiatives that target specific types of communities and communities with high poverty rates, such as the numerous funding streams that address the needs of Texas *colonias*.

Added to this growing complexity are matching funds requirements, which require states and localities to identify matching funds in order to draw down federal grant monies. Many federal funding laws still prohibit state and local entities from using funds from one federal grant source to meet match requirements for federal funding from another source. Therefore state and local projects are often faced with the daunting task of raising multiple sets of matching funds in the private sector and securing general revenue funds that are appropriated through state legislatures in order to be eligible for different federal initiatives.

For poor, rural areas, which often have lower tax receipts and revenues, meeting local matching requirements can become problematic. Competition for the same discrete set of private funds and state general revenues can become fierce, creating turf battles that engender several different initiatives providing similar services and having similar goals (National Academy of Public Administration, 1996). The result is a complex environment within which economic development activities compete for funding, resources, and participants. Moreover, the increasing globalization of the economy influences the creation of policies that affect the progression of economic development efforts. Labor agreements (such as the North American Free Trade Agreement), international farm price controls, land use and land development policies, immigration reforms, and supports for multinational companies also affect how local economic development strategies are implemented. This creates an organizational environment that is far more complex than the organizational structure of a small, rural community.

THINKING INSTITUTIONALLY

One way to manage the complexity of factors affecting rural economic development is to view the organizational environment with an institutional perspective. When an organizational environment becomes too complex for one organization to manage, it requires an interorganizational collaborative approach that changes the perspective from the single organizational level to the "domain" level (Trist, 1983, p. 270). Once viewed at the domain level, the organization can identify the areas of "interconnectedness" and reduce the uncertainty that derives from environmental complexity (Trist, 1983). Earlier in this article, it was noted that uncertainty, or a lack of information, causes perceptions of increased risk. In much the same way that banks reduce risk in financial transactions by acquiring information, organizations can reduce the effects of turbulent and complex environments through a domain-level perspective. This perspective is also known as an institutional perspective or a macro perspective.

When viewed with a macro perspective, the institutions that shape social and community organization are more clearly seen. These are the social, political, economic, and cultural constraints (both formal and informal) that gradually change through time and that govern our behavior (North, 1994). Institutions change gradually (North, 1991); for example, the political environment through policymaking (Rochefort, 1986). Economic institutions change gradually as well to address growing complexity in the institutional environment.

North (1991) discussed how the economic institutions developed to address the growing complexity of economies. What was once long ago a simple bartering system in a single town became town-to-town trade, which eventually grew into the globalized economy we have today. To deal with this complex economic environment, mediating entities assisted with the standardization of currency, and the creation and enforcement of the rules of economic interaction (see Figure 17.1).

In Figure 17.1, the environment is contained by a complex set of individual actors, including the potential mediators, each operating under a separate set of assumptions. Through the gradual development of institutions (A), mediating entities reduce this complexity by developing institutional norms and rules for interaction. Similarly, in the transition depicted in (B), mediating entities further reduce the growing complexity through the development of institutional norms for interaction.

Rapid changes in the uses of technology, growing diversity, urban expansion, and a globalized economy mean a surge in change for rural areas in the United States (Drabenstott, 2001). Although many rural areas still depend on agriculture and natural resources for their economic base, the service industry, which is strongly affected by changes in the national economy, now accounts for the majority of the jobs in rural areas (Henderson, 2002). *Colonias* regions are characterized by migrant labor opportunities in construction and agriculture, which are also severely affected by fluctuations in the economy. The complexities of a world economy, population migration patterns, urban sprawl, and other socioeconomic factors have led these communi-

ties to rethink their relationships to urbanized areas of the United States. However, this complexity is often hidden by geographic isolation and a lack of community assets on the local level, a characteristic of rural poverty worldwide (IFAD, 2001). Moreover, the factors related to rural poverty are diverse and often regionally specific (Shaw, 1997; Sheaff, 2001). This diversity requires a flexible approach to rural community development that can manage the complex resources and relationships among rural communities; economic, political, and social institutions; and different organizational entities that exist within and outside the community. Strategic bridging provides one way to manage multisector factors for the comprehensive and sustainable development of rural areas.

MANAGING COMPLEX ENVIRONMENTS THROUGH STRATEGIC BRIDGING ORGANIZATIONS

Strategic bridging theory uses an institutional perspective to visualize community and organizational assets, including the development and dissemination of information. In strategic bridging collaborations, the perspectives of the organizational and community stakeholders that represent each institution are strategically identified to be included in an overall economic development strategy. In his studies of local economic development strategies in lesser developed countries, Brown (1987) identified the need for multisector approaches that were managed by a central organizing entity: a Strategic Bridging Organization (SBO).

Strategic bridging assumes either a lack of resources on the local level or a need for organizational capacity that cannot be met by one organization (Kalegaonkar & Brown, 2000; Westley & Vredenburg, 1991). It also assumes that the solution requires and merits resources from

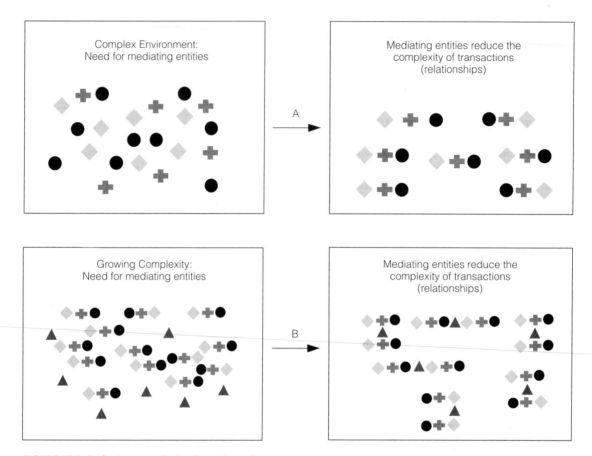

FIGURE 17.1 Reducing Complexity through Mediating Entities

multiple institutional sectors (Westley & Vredenburg, 1991).

Recent work in developing strengths–based policy approaches discusses the need to turn away from problems and deficits and develop policy by identifying the common needs and barriers of the stakeholders (Chapin, 1995). This is particularly useful when designing an asset-based development approach, which focuses on the development of assets and resources within a community (Kretzmann & McKnight, 1996). Figure 17.2 reflects the multiple uses of strategic bridging approaches by naming the SBO institutional environment as the opportunity domain.

In general, the SBO defines the opportunity domain so that it encompasses (bridges) both the needs and resources of each institutional stakeholder in the effort (Brown, 1987). Figure 17.2 depicts an SBO that bridges two institutional sectors through interorganizational relationships with Partners A and B. The SBO bridges the sectors by defining the opportunity domain in such a way that the problem and its solutions are relevant to the needs and resources of both partners. However, because the SBO includes itself in the opportunity domain, it does not serve as neutral mediator, and it has a stake in the overall success of the collaboration (Westley & Vredenburg, 1991).

As a stakeholder, the SBO's role can be problem-focused or self-serving (Westley & Vredenburg, 1991). SBOs may choose to facilitate such relationships to maintain or enhance their

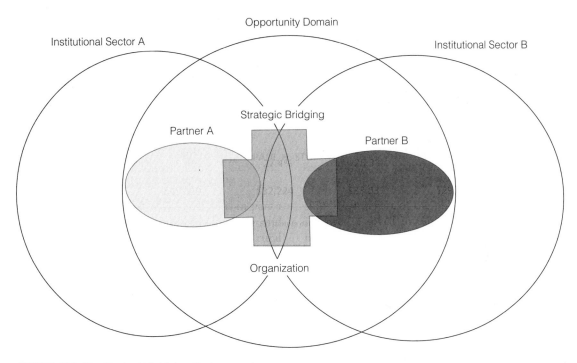

FIGURE 17.2 The Strategic Bridging Environment

place in the organizational environment or to change and influence current and future institutions (Westley & Vredenburg, 1991), such as forging new types of partnerships between the private and public sectors. On an organizational level, the Colonias IDA Program of Proyecto Azteca's community loan fund may be seen as a strategic bridging partnership, which links communities to financial intermediaries, housing initiatives, workforce and self-employment programs, and other economic development strategies.

The SBO facilitates the definition of collaborative opportunities to encompass the resources and goals of each potential collaborative partner and to provide each with access to the collaborative endeavor (Nyman & Moore, 2002; Westley & Vredenburg, 1991). Partner inclusion also mitigates the uncertainty that can emerge during problem/opportunity definitions when a stakeholder's perspective is not represented (Sharma, Vredenburg, & Westley, 1994). One of the primary ways that the SBO mitigates this uncertainty is to serve as a repository for, and disseminator of, information and to develop capacity-building efforts (Brown & Ashman, 1999).

Information-sharing activities are critical to successful bridging efforts throughout the collaborative process and affect success rates at each level of the collaboration. The strength of the strategic bridging approach is its focus on capacity-building and information dissemination as methods to bring about interorganizational and multi-institutional collaboration. Key areas for capacity-building and informational asset development are discussed in the next section.

The SBO Level—
Internal Capacity-Building

In order for an SBO to be an effective facilitator of multisector collaborations, the various partners must perceive it as a legitimate leader (Kalegaonkar & Brown, 2000; Westley & Vredenburg, 1991; Brown, 1987). The strength of its influence will also depend on the length of time it has been considered an institutionally legitimate stakeholder (McCann & Gray, 1986). The SBO must also demonstrate an internal commitment to the facilitator role and a commitment by its own stakeholders for this purpose (Brown & Ashman, 1999; Westley & Vredenburg, 1991). Commitment to the effort is determined by the formal and informal relationships of the SBO leadership, staff, and constituency, and their knowledge of both cooperative and competitive strategies to influence collaboration activities (Brown, 1993). For rural areas, this means that economic development strategies must include participation by community residents and the organizations that represent and serve them. This allows rural areas to retain their culture (Ray, 1999) and serve as a resource in the overall development effort (Brown & Ashman, 1999).

The SBO's bridging responsibilities must also align with the organization's mission and goals, which the SBO must be willing and able to change according to reorientation needs in the institutional environment (Brown, 1993). Such flexibility stems from an institutional orientation, an understanding of the larger societal context, and an ability to take advantage of new movements (Brown, 1993). SBOs typically have well-defined management structures, which are not necessarily hierarchical, but are geared toward information-sharing and cultivation of new leadership within the organization, providing an infrastructure to deal with internal conflicts (Brown, 1987; Brown, 1993). Because the SBO must have the capacity to understand each of its institutional partners, SBO staff can at times mirror the conflicts in perspectives that are present in the institutional environment. Therefore, short- and long-term goals are an important part of defining the mission of the SBOs strategic bridging activities (Brown, 1993). Information asset building, therefore, begins within the SBO, to ensure that it has the capacity to serve as the strategic bridging entity.

An SBO Example: Proyecto Azteca

Proyecto Azteca works on a number of levels to bridge the needs and resources of its partners. As a housing entity, it manages several state- and federal-level grants aimed to increase affordable housing in the area. Volunteer architects design the homes, which are then built by minority-owned subcontractors (Fannie Mae Foundation, 1998). The organization partners with the United Farm Workers to provide access to social services and other support services. Free legal advice is provided through the South Texas Civil Rights Project. The organization's Board of Directors is composed of *colonia* residents and migrant workers, many of whom have built their own home through the program (Fannie Mae Foundation, 1998).

Because members of the United Farm Workers created the organization, it has institutional legitimacy within the *colonias* communities. United Farm Workers also provides legitimacy on the organizational level, and helps the organization to take a more institutional perspective of its economic development strategies. Proyecto Azteca is also a strong partner in the Border Low-Income Housing Coalition, which links to other community and public resources. Partnerships with the Azteca Community Loan Fund, and other financial intermediaries, such as First National Bank, further link participants of the IDA program to formal financial resources beyond those available through publicly subsidized loan programs. Proyecto Azteca also partners with the Housing Assistance Council (HAC), a nonprofit corporation headquartered in Washington, DC to provide loans, technical assistance, training, and capacity building for the self-help home building projects. The HAC's role is integral to the overall capacity-building strategies for the *colonias* communities.

The Organizational Level— Developing Capacity within Partner Organizations

An SBO seeks and identifies mutual influence among its potential organizational partners (Brown, 1993). By doing so, it reveals the legitimacy of each of the partners (Westley &

Vredenburg, 1991; Brown, 1993). The SBO creates and/or identifies a common language that bridges the perspectives of all partners, and thereby allows the shared opportunity domain to encompass the resources and needs of the strategic partners (Kalegaonkar & Brown, 2000; Westley & Vredenburg, 1991). This is no easy task. Multisector collaborations are characterized by a diverse set of organizational partners who operate within vastly differing paradigms. Recent examples of these kinds of multisector collaborations are the partnerships forming between the high-tech industry and local economic development entities in order to expand access to telecommunication services and to bring about new industry growth (e.g., Lentz & Oden, 2001; Hare, 2001; and Youtie, 2000). However, such projects have met with varying degrees of success, partly due to a lack of networking among organizational and institutional users in these areas (Lentz & Oden, 2001).

Although the collaboration's purpose must be relevant to its stakeholders, it is more important that the stakeholder members have the capacity to take advantage of internal and external resources (Brown & Ashman, 1999). One way to access a set of resources is to approach the task jointly, as many rural communities are now doing in multicommunity development organizations (Borich, 1994). The Iowa cooperative extension entities, and public agencies in collaboration with Iowa State University, discovered these multiple-town, interorganizational relationships helped residents to gain access to resources that may not be available to a single small community (Borich, 1994). For rural areas, which may not have enough political or economic influence, such joint action is key to enabling access to new resources. SBOs play a critical role in this effort.

Organizational capacity to participate in the collaboration is an important factor for a potential multisector partner (Brown, 1993). Its organizational capacity will weigh heavily on its perceived incentives for participating (Brown & Ashman, 1999), and whether the organization believes a solution is viable without participation in a multisector initiative (Brown, 1987). In these cases, the SBO's role is to identify incentives for participation and/or provide capacity-building opportunities to the partnering organization.

Such capacity-building efforts are critical to effective participation by smaller, grassroots organizations, which are key stakeholders in the process but often do not hold as much political power initially as other partnering entities (Uvin, Jain, & Brown, 2000; Brown & Ashman, 1999). SBOs leverage the differing types of political power of the participating organizations by identifying the specific strengths of each stakeholder entity (Brown & Ashman, 1999).

An example of grassroots strength is the unique ties these organizations have to local stakeholder populations, which provide important perspectives on the likelihood of local economic development strategies to succeed or fail. Proyecto Azteca's grassroots origins tie the organization to the *colonias* it seeks to develop. Despite their economic and geographic isolation, poor, rural communities have opportunities to voice their needs. SBOs can help to amplify this voice so that it factors into policy decisions and program implementation. Because public bureaucracies, as well as private sector entities, seek only praise—and not criticism—within the media, local stakeholders can leverage this information as they do any other asset. These assets can then be developed with capacity-building activities, such as training in collaboration strategies, evaluation and research, information dissemination, and identification of new sources of funding (Uvin, Jain, & Brown, 2000).

The Interorganizational Level—
Capacity Building
for Multisector Partnerships

Capacity building at the interorganizational level pertains to the capacity of the partners to collaborate. It is at this level that information sharing becomes a crucial part of the strategic bridging approach. Communication norms must be identified in order to sustain interorganizational relationships (Westley & Vredenburg, 1991; Brown & Ashman, 1999). Identification of shared goals becomes an important activity, one that is supported throughout the literature on collaboration (e.g., Gray, 1989; Wood & Gray, 1991; Bruner, 1991; Kagan, 1991; Melaville & Blank, 1991; Mattessich, & Monsey, 1992; National Assembly, 1997; Taylor-Powell, Rossing, & Geran, 1998).

Formation of these goals is a challenging task for organizations that share similar intervention approaches due to power differences, levels of institutional legitimacy, and other external and internal factors (McCann & Gray, 1986). However, even when general goals of organizations are similar, the approaches used to provide a certain service may be very different (Schreiner, 1999). In multisector collaborations, where partner goals and service structure can differ tremendously (e.g., a rural bank and a community nonprofit organization), identifying commonalities is a greater challenge (Westley & Vredenburg, 1991; Brown, 1993; Brown & Ashman, 1999).

The SBO must be able to balance the goals for the collaboration with those of each participating entity in order to ensure that the needs of the organizations are met (Brown, 1993). Negotiating these power differences and the differences in levels of social capital (information and resources) among the participating organizations are important parts of strategic bridging goal formation (Brown & Ashman, 1999).

Common definitions of the problem/opportunity domain and identification of shared values are facilitated through a deeper understanding of the issues to be addressed (Pasquero, 1991). This is another challenging task because changes in the institutional environment can bring about changes in the issue, and it can make the definition of the problem/opportunity difficult. Given the importance of the institutional environment in developing legitimacy, creating capacity for collaboration and change, and in forming common goals, the SBO must also address issues on an institutional level.

The Institutional Level—Building Capacity for Changing Institutions

The SBO plays an important role in how institutions affect and influence the collaborative effort (Nyman & Moore, 2002). The SBO strategically identifies its partners with an institutional perspective. Resources (and challenges to accessing resources) are viewed not only as what is available locally, but also in terms of what is available within an organization's institution. For example, on the local level, the public sector is represented by local government entities such as city councils, county judges, county commissioners, chambers of commerce, and other locally based and publicly funded resources. However, these entities share an institutional sector with state and federal entities, which can make policies and support mandates that may not necessarily benefit local communities (Rakodi, 1999). Therefore, it is important that in the collaboration, their state and national counterparts complement the local representative organizations and entities, and that the multisector collaboration includes multiple levels of partners within each represented institution.

In the private sector, local employers and businesses are important collaborative partners because these entities create the environment in which small- and medium-sized businesses develop (North & Smallbone, 2000). However, they can also provide ties to markets outside the local community, and thereby provide resources (such as information and connections to larger networks) beyond the local economy. For example, community development banks are often players in asset development strategies in rural areas. These types of financial intermediaries, which typically hold assets of less than $100 million, play an important roles for the financial sector in serving smaller communities because they are keenly aware of local area needs (Padgett, 1998). However, these financial intermediaries (as well as community development corporations (CDCs), community development financial institutions

(CDFIs), community development credit unions (CDCUs), and small business development centers (SBDCs)) often belong to or have ties to national- and regional-level associations and agencies, which either administer programs (e.g., the Small Business Administration in the case of SBDCs) or lobby for changes in policy (e.g., the National Credit Union Association in the case of CDCUs). Partnerships formed with local and regional entities can also provide access to much larger sources of information, funding, and political support.

Another major institutional sector in rural economic development activity is represented by higher education entities (i.e., community colleges and universities, junior colleges, and technical colleges). In addition to the activities of the Land Grant Universities and Cooperative Extension System, distance learning initiatives (Skerik, Gilbertson, & Kiley, 2000), vocational education and workforce training programs (Warren, 2000), and Tech Prep initiatives through two-year and four-year higher education entities provide specific development activities to local areas.

The faith-based sector is also an important player in the local economic development of rural areas. President Bush's establishment of the White House Office of Faith-Based and Community Initiatives in 2001, as well as new changes to funding policies (e.g., Charitable Choice), provides a new legitimacy to faith-based organizations that for decades have participated in local economic development strategies (Kimball, 2001; Belden, 2001).

A multisector collaborative approach brings together partners from multiple institutional sectors and forges interorganizational relationships among entities that often have not operated collaboratively. As these partnerships become more successful, they lead the way for new collaborative relationships to develop. The growing frequency of collaborative relationships among community development corporations (CDCs) and community-based organizations (CBOs) is one example of the growth in the diversity of multisector relationships (Waddell, 1997). Since the passage of the Community Reinvestment Act of 1977, which requires banks to be responsive to their local communities, locally operated financial institutions have increasingly developed relationships with CBOs that provide mutually beneficial outcomes. Although early relationships targeted housing initiatives, these partnerships have expanded to include development of small businesses and increasing the social capital, or networking capacity, of their communities (Waddell, 1997).

Implications for Policy

Strategic bridging theory provides a framework in which to bring together multisector resources and organizations for collaborative, community development projects. Use of the framework and the strategic bridging methodology also has implications for change in policymaking institutions. This article has focused on information-sharing and capacity-building activities, which assist organizations, communities, and institutions to share in the development of community assets. The diversity that exists on each of these levels is an important strength that can bring about potent and sustainable development activities.

Mediating entities, such as strategic bridging organizations, play important roles in bridging the differences that exist between institutional sectors and their representative organizations and communities. Figure 17.3 summarizes some of the important capacity-building tasks and strategic bridging resources discussed in this article, which are critical factors in the successful bridging of multiple institutional sectors. Admittedly, comprehensive economic development requires more than capacity-building and information activities to achieve successful outcomes. However, these activities help to build strong partnerships that can respond to the opportunities that arise from institutional change. More

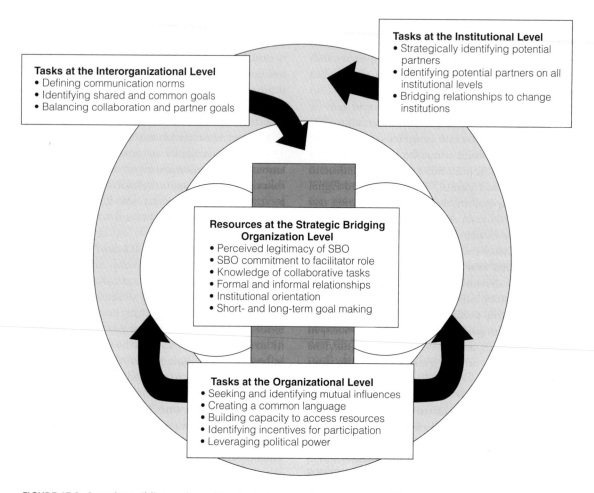

Tasks at the Interorganizational Level
- Defining communication norms
- Identifying shared and common goals
- Balancing collaboration and partner goals

Tasks at the Institutional Level
- Strategically identifying potential partners
- Identifying potential partners on all institutional levels
- Bridging relationships to change institutions

Resources at the Strategic Bridging Organization Level
- Perceived legitimacy of SBO
- SBO commitment to facilitator role
- Knowledge of collaborative tasks
- Formal and informal relationships
- Institutional orientation
- Short- and long-term goal making

Tasks at the Organizational Level
- Seeking and identifying mutual influences
- Creating a common language
- Building capacity to access resources
- Identifying incentives for participation
- Leveraging political power

FIGURE 17.3 Capacity-Building Tasks and Strategic Bridging Resources for Collaboration

importantly, strategic bridging provides the means for local communities to effect change on the institutions. The responses and resulting innovations of rural communities to global change will reveal new ways to incorporate global information assets into local community perspectives and will provide models for retaining a diversity of cultural assets in a global society. Strategically defined, these innovations are powerful tools to empower the lives of the rural poor.

In the case of the *colonias* housing initiative, the Border Low-Income Housing Coalition (BLIHC) has brought together the resources of housing organizations, community development financial institutions, policymakers and other

public entities, and community residents. However, the BLIHC is just one of many interorganizational efforts to bring about economic development in the region. Texas A&M University has also organized a set of economic development and human service agencies to address the needs of border residents. An entire division in the Texas Department of Housing and Community Affairs works with local and state agencies to build resources and community assets in the area. Workforce development efforts are guided by Local Workforce Development Boards, which oversee multicounty workforce initiatives in the border region, as well as participate in state-level workforce initiatives. In effect, a number of strategic partnerships exist along the Texas–Mexico border to address the needs of *colonias* residents. It is likely that any illustration of the organizational environment would resemble the examples in B of Figure 17.1.

If there is no central organizing entity, but several collaborative partnerships operate in a very complex environment, it may seem that the SBO model may not apply. However, despite the lack of an overarching strategic bridging structure to the border region's initiatives, one can still identify a bridging entity—the community itself. The community may not meet the organizational requirements of a strategic bridging organization, but it is a stakeholder in the collaborative strategy, and it does bring together multiple resources for a shared purpose. The concept of communities serving as strategic bridging entities is a very powerful argument for citizen and community participation in local economic development approaches. The multiorganizational networks serving the *colonias* regions build community capital and assets, which strengthen communities from within. For disinvested, rural communities this can mean sustainable and meaningful community development, which can turn temporarily funded projects into enduring economic development strategies.

This direction of institutional change has many implications for policy. Public policymakers must begin to understand how each source of funding and other resources play a role in comprehensive economic development strategies. Human service organizations play as great a part in the economic development of low-income rural areas as do financial intermediaries, educational entities, businesses and employers, and economic development organizations. The key is not to parcel development strategies into funding streams and demonstration projects; but rather to build networks, community capital, and community assets for sustainable development. Public policymakers must also endeavor to mitigate the effects of policies that reduce cooperation and collaboration among these entities.

More importantly, however, is the role of community residents as strategic partners in all economic development initiatives. Because community residents have the best knowledge of what their communities need, more attention should be focused on how to build these linkages and provide information to residents so that they have the capacity to serve as strategic bridging entities. In this way, individual asset development will become community asset development—a sustainable opportunity for all.

DISCUSSION QUESTIONS

1. Community assets represent common, public resources, as well as the businesses and organizations that make up a community's infrastructure. *Colonias* are characterized by a lack of these kinds of resources. However, rural areas, such as the Texas *colonias* discussed in the article, also have certain community assets that counteract this disinvestment. How do these community assets differ from those in your own community?

2. According to Douglass North, institutions change gradually and govern our behavior through formal and informal mechanisms. Institutions affect how organizations

collaborate in a complex environment. Proyecto Azteca bridges economic and political institutions to provide asset-development strategies in rural areas of South Texas. What are some other examples of bridged institutions identified in the article? What organizations or other entities help to bridge these institutions?

3. Strategic bridging collaborations can provide a framework for rural economic development. Of particular importance is the role of the strategic bridging organization in capacity-building efforts. What challenges do these organizations face when building

capacity in rural areas? How can strategic bridging organizations create opportunity domains in rural areas?

4. Communities are important stakeholders in economic development efforts. In rural areas, grassroots participation is especially critical to the success of economic development strategies. *Colonias* residents in Texas created Proyecto Azteca in order to improve the housing opportunities of the community's residents. How does their stakeholder participation improve their chances for increasing the political power of the community? What other gains might their participation provide to the community?

5. Policy choices can both improve and impede the chances of successful economic development in rural areas. However, because policy making is inherently incremental, the effects of those choices may not be realized immediately. How can a strategic bridging collaboration mitigate the institutional complexity that is brought about by a constantly changing political environment? How might this institutional complexity be advantageous to the collaboration and the overall economic development effort?

CLASSROOM ACTIVITIES AND ASSIGNMENTS

1. Hector Galán's film, *Forgotten Americans* (1 hour, produced in association with Southwest Texas State University and the W. K. Kellogg Foundation), provides a stark picture of the *colonias* of South Texas over a one-year period. (The video may be purchased from the Galan, Inc. Web site at http://catalog.galaninc.com.) After watching the video in class, discuss the following questions: What is the most striking aspect of the film? In which ways do the *colonias* residents participate in the region's economic development strategies? What is the significance of water in the film? What role or influence does public policy have to the economic development of *colonias* in Texas? Do any of the identified organizations perform a strategic bridging role? Which resources were most important to the success of the economic development strategies depicted in the film? Which resources did you identify in the film that might apply to other poor, rural areas?

2. Capacity-building strategies are an integral part of successful strategic bridging efforts.

Information sharing serves as a primary method for building the capacity of partnering organizations. Vast quantities of information can be found on the Internet, which disseminates information to policymakers, stakeholders, organizations, and other important entities. However, the Internet is only as representative of stakeholder diversity as the strength of Internet access. That is to say, without access to electronic media, some stakeholder groups may not be represented in electronic resources.

Prior to class, spend at least three hours researching the experiences of *colonias* residents using only electronic resources (for example, public information Web sites, e-publications, chat rooms, and discussion groups specifically related to *colonias* communities, and electronically available articles). Record the Web sites you visit by organizing them by four subject areas:

- Public policy (e.g., public information sites);

- Target stakeholder populations (e.g., Web sites run by or regarding stakeholders);
- Organizational resources (e.g., agency/business Web sites); and
- Information and education resources (additional information sites).

Record at least six different resources for each subject area. Then identify at least four areas of information that you would have expected to find but either were unable to find or unable to retrieve (e.g., the Web site was down, required membership fee or password, etc.). An aggregate list of visited Web sites will be created for distribution to the class following the in-class activities.

3. (In Class) Small Group Discussions (20 minutes)—Assemble in groups of 4–5 students each, and designate one person to record and one person to report the results of the group discussion. Discuss the following topics:

- After each group member has shared their Internet resources, identify the information resources that were well-represented.
- Discuss the common missing sources of information.
- Identify the stakeholder groups that lacked electronic representation.
- Identify the stakeholder groups that were represented the best.

4. (In Class) Large Group Discussion (35–40 minutes)—After small group discussions are completed, assemble into the large group. After each group reports briefly on the above four items, the large group should discuss the following topics:

- In which ways could missing stakeholder populations be better represented in the electronic media?
- Do these missing stakeholder populations have access to electronic information? If not, how could access be improved?

- If stakeholders are represented in the electronic media, do they represent themselves, or are they represented by another entity (e.g., migrant farmworkers do not have their own Web site, but a Web site for labor unions does discuss migrant farmworker issues).

5. People who work in strategic bridging organizations often need the ability to view an issue from multiple perspectives in order to adequately represent and meet the needs of a collaboration's different organizational partners. In an in-class role play, imagine that you work for a strategic bridging organization that is bringing together banks and other financial entities, policymakers, community-based organizations, and other community stakeholders for a rural economic development project. In small groups that represent members of these stakeholder groups, list the factors that influence these stakeholder groups' perspectives. The following questions may be used as guides to these discussions. Reconvene in a large group to discuss how staff in a strategic bridging organization may be able to bridge the differences between the stakeholder groups.

Political institutions: What are the political factors that influence how their stakeholder group perceives economic development? How does their stakeholder group express political power? How have the other participating groups expressed political power? Which local, county, state, and federal policies are most important to the stakeholder group? If the group is to collaborate with the other represented groups, what strengths does it have to bring to the collaboration? What needs does the group expect to be met and what are its goals for participating?

Social institutions: What are the social institutions that contribute to the perspectives of their stakeholder group?

Factors within social institutions include: demographics, migration patterns, cultural history, educational access, community assets, education and training resources, community capital, social and organizational networks, and so on.

Economic institutions: What are the economic institutions affecting the decisions and perspectives of their particular stakeholder groups? Factors derived from economic institutions include: chronic unemployment; community disinvestment; the existence or lack of financial capital; the existence or lack of financial and trade markets; the state of the local, state, and national economies; the availability of funding and funding policies; macroeconomic and fiscal policy.

Other institutional factors: What other institutional factors influence the choices made by their stakeholder groups? Institutional factors include existing relationships among the different stakeholder groups, historical interactions and conflicts, interorganizational frameworks, societal norms and belief systems, and assumed "ways of doing things." Students may also identify other factors, such as potential and untapped community resources, public infrastructure needs, environmental concerns, or innovative empowerment strategies used in other U.S. communities.

REFERENCES

Belden, J. (2001). Faith-based legislation advances in Congress. *Rural Voices: The Magazine of the Housing Assistance Council, 6*(2), 21. Retrieved May 2, 2002, from http://www.ruralhome.org/pubs/ruralvoc.htm.

Borich, T. O. (1994). Collaboration: A different strategy for rural economic development. *Economic Development Review, 12*(1), 18–21.

Brown, L. D. (1987). Development partnerships: Problem-solving at institutional interfaces. In *Where development policies, programs and projects meet: Managing the interfaces.* Panel paper presented at the American Society for Public Administration, Boston.

Brown, L. D. (1993). Development bridging organizations and strategic management for social change. *Institute for Development Research Reports, 10* (IDR Report No. 3). Retrieved March 24, 2001, from http://www.jsi.com/idr/IDRreports.htm.

Brown, L. D., & Ashman, D. (1999). Social capital, mutual influence, and social learning in intersectoral problem solving in Africa and Asia. In D. L. Cooperrider & J. E. Dutton (Eds.), *Organizational dimensions of global change: No limits to cooperation* (pp. 139–167). Thousand Oaks, CA: Sage Publications.

Bruner, C. (1991). *Thinking collaboratively: Ten questions to help policy makers improve children's services.* Washington, DC: Education and Human Services Consortium.

Center for Housing and Urban Development. (1998). *Status report of the Center for Housing and Urban Development College of Architecture—Texas A&M University.* College Station, TX: Author. Retrieved May 2, 2002, from http://chud.tamu.edu/files/status.pdf.

Chapin, R. K. (1995). Social policy development: The strengths perspective. *Social Work, 40*(4), 506–514.

Chen, D. (2001). Smart growth: More choices for rural development. *Rural Voices: The Magazine of the Housing Assistance Council, 7*(1), 8–9. Retrieved May 2, 2002, from http://www.ruralhome.org/pubs/ruralvoc.htm.

Cisneros, A. (2001, June). *Texas colonias: Housing and infrastructure issues.* Dallas, TX: Federal Reserve Bank of Dallas. Retrieved May 2, 2002, from http://www.dallasfed.org/htm/pubs/border/cisneros.htm.

Community Action Partnership. (2002). About Community Action Agencies (CAAs). Retrieved May 2, 2002 from http://www.communityactionpartnership.com/about/about_caas/default.asp.

Cooperative State Research, Education, and Extension Service of the USDA. (2002a). 1890 Land Grant Web site. Retrieved May 2, 2002 from http://www.reeusda.gov/1890/.

Cooperative State Research, Education, and Extension Service of the USDA. (2002b). *Hatch Act of 1887.* Retrieved May 2, 2002 from http://www.reeusda.gov/1700/legis/hatch.htm.

Davidson, R. H. (1969). The War on Poverty: Experiment in federalism. *The Annals of the American Academy of Political and Social Science, 385,* 1–13.

Drabenstott, M. (2001). New policies for a rural America. *International Regional Science Review, 24*(1), 3–15.

Fannie Mae Foundation (1998). *Maxwell Awards of Excellence Program: Round Ten casebook.* Washington, DC: Author. Retrieved May 2, 2002, from http://www.fanniemaefoundation.org/grants/casebook10/index.shtml.

Federal Deposit Insurance Corporation. (2002). *Money Smart: An adult education program: Building: knowledge, security, confidence.* Brochure. Washington, DC: Author.

Federal Reserve Bank of Dallas. (1996). *Texas Colonias: A thumbnail sketch of the conditions, issues, challenges and opportunities.* Retrieved May 2, 2002, from http://www.dallasfed.org/htm/pubs/ca/colonias.html.

Flacke, T., Grossman, B., Dailey, C., & Jennings, S. (1999). *Individual Development Account program design handbook: A step by step guide to designing an IDA program* (4th ed.). Washington, DC: Corporation for Enterprise Development.

Gray, B. (1989). *Collaborating: Finding common ground for multiparty problems.* San Francisco: Jossey-Bass.

Hare, W. (2001). Rural telecommunications: Partnerships that bridge the digital divide. *Public Management, 83*(6), 12–14.

Henderson, J. R. (2002, January). Will the rural economy rebound with the rest of the nation? *The Main Street economist: Commentary on the rural economy.* Kansas City, MO: Center for the Study of Rural America, Federal Reserve Bank. Retrieved May 2, 2002, from http://www.kc.frb.org/RuralCenter/mainstreet/MainStMain.htm.

International Fund for Agriculture Development. (2001). *Rural poverty report 2001: The challenge of ending rural poverty.* New York: Oxford University Press. Retrieved May 2, 2002, from http://www.ifad.org/poverty/index.htm.

Kagan, S. L. (1991). *United we stand: Collaboration for child care and early education services.* New York: Teachers College Press.

Kalegaonkar, A., & Brown, L. D. (2000). *Intersectoral cooperation: Lessons for practice. Institute for Development Research Reports, 16* (IDR Report No. 2). Retrieved May 21, 2001, from http://www.jsi.com/idr/IDRreports.htm.

Kimball, F. C. (2001). Concerns about the President's faith-based initiative: Opening public coffers to religious organizations. *Rural Voices: The Magazine of the Housing Assistance Council, 6*(2), 4–6. Retrieved May 2, 2002, from http://www.ruralhome.org/pubs/ruralvoc.htm.

Kretzmann, J., & McKnight, J. P. (1996). Assets-based community development. *National Civic Review, 85*(4), 23–29.

Lentz, R. G., & Oden, M. D. (2001). Digital divide or digital opportunity in the Mississippi Delta region of the U.S. *Telecommunications Policy, 25,* 291–313.

Mattessich, P. W., & Monsey, B. R. (1992). *Collaboration: What makes it work: A review of research literature on factors influencing successful collaboration.* St. Paul, MN: Amherst H. Wilder Foundation.

Melaville, A. I., & Blank, M. J. (1991). *What it takes: Structuring interagency partnerships to connect children and families with comprehensive services.* Washington, DC: Education and Human Services Consortium.

McCann, J. E., & Gray, B. (1986). Power and collaboration in human service domains. *The International Journal of Sociology and Social Policy, 6*(3), 58–67.

Naples, N. A. (1998). From maximum feasible participation to disenfranchisement. *Social Justice, 25*(1), 47–66.

National Academy of Public Administration. (1996). *A path to smarter economic development: Reassessing the federal role.* Washington, DC: Author.

National Assembly of National Voluntary Health and Social Welfare Organizations (1997). *The new community collaboration manual.* Washington, DC: Author.

North, D. C. (1991). Institutions. *Journal of Economic Perspectives, 5*(1), 97–112.

North, D. C. (1994). Economic performance through time. *The American Economic Review, 84*(3), 359–368.

North, D. C., & Smallbone, D. (2000). Innovative activity in SMEs and rural economic development: Some evidence from England. *European Planning Studies, 8*(1), 87–107.

Nyman, K., & Moore, A. (2002). *Intersecting strategic bridging theory and institutional analysis for understanding multi-sector collaborations.* Paper presented at the annual program of the Council on Social Work Education, Nashville, TN.

Padgett, T. (1998). Community bank deals expected to slow this year. *American Banker, 163*(19), 3A–3B.

Pasquero, J. (1991). Supraorganizational collaboration: The Canadian environmental experiment. *Journal of Applied Behavioral Science, 27*(1), 38–64.

Putnam, R. D. (2000). *Bowling alone: The collapse and revival of American community.* New York: Simon & Schuster.

Rakodi, C. (1999). A capital assets framework for analysing household livelihood strategies:

Implications for policy. *Development Policy Review,*
17(2), 315–343.

Ray, C. (1999). Towards a meta-framework of endoge-
nous development: Repertoires, paths, democracy,
and rights. *Sociologia Ruralis, 39*(4), 521–537.

Reeder, R. (1998). The changing face of rural development assistance in USDA. *Rural Conditions and*
Trends, 9(1), 37–47. Retrieved from the Economic
Research Service, USDA, May 2, 2002, from http://
www.ers.usda.gov/Publications/RCAT/Archives/.

Rochefort, D. A. (1986). *American social welfare policy:*
Dynamics of formulation and change. Boulder, CO:
Westview Press.

Schreiner, M. (1999). *Aspects of outreach: A framework for*
the discussion of the social benefits of microfinance
(Working Paper Series No. 99-33). St. Louis, MO:
Washington University, Center for Social
Development. Retrieved May 2, 2002, from http://
gwbweb.wustl.edu/csd/Publications/wp99-3.pdf.

Schreiner, M., Sherraden, M., Clancy, M., Johnson, L.,
Curley, J., Grinstein-Weiss, M., Zhan, M., & Beverly,
S. (2001). *Savings and asset accumulation in Individual*
Development Accounts: Downpayments on the American
Dream Policy Demonstration: A national demonstration of
Individual Development Accounts. St. Louis, MO:
Center for Social Development, Washington
University in St. Louis.

Servon, L. J. (1998). *Microenterprise development as an eco-*
nomic adjustment strategy. Washington, DC: Economic
Development Administration, U.S. Department of
Commerce.

Sharma, S., Vredenburg, H., & Westley, F. (1994).
Strategic bridging: A role for the multinational cor-
poration in Third World development. *Journal of*
Applied Behavioral Science, 30(4), 458–476.

Shaw, W. (1997). Regionally specific strategies to alleviate rural poverty. *Economic Development Review, 15*(1),
52–58.

Sheaff, K. (2001, October). The 2000 Census and
growth patterns in rural America. *The Main Street*
economist: Commentary on the rural economy. Kansas
City, MO: Center for the Study of Rural America,
Federal Reserve Bank. Retrieved May 2, 2002, from
http://www.kc.frb.org/RuralCenter/mainstreet
/MainStMain.htm.

Sherraden, M. (1991). *Assets and the poor: A new American*
welfare policy. Armonk, NY: M. E. Sharpe.

Sherraden, M., Schreiner, M., & Beverly, S. (2002).
Income, institutions, and savings performance in individual
development accounts. Working Paper 02-3, Center for
Social Development. Retrieved May 2, 2002, from
http://gwbweb.wustl.edu/csd/Publications
/wp02-3.pdf.

Skerik, J., Gilbertson, P., & Kiley, J. (2000). Collaboration
in education: Business and education partnership in
Northern Wisconsin. *T.H.E. Journal, 27*(8), 98–100.

Taylor-Powell, E., Rossing, B., & Geran, J. (1998).
Evaluating collaboratives: Reaching the potential.
Madison: University of Wisconsin-System Board of
Regents and University of Wisconsin-Extension,
Cooperative Extension.

Texas C-Bar (2001, August). *The faces of Texas C-Bar.*
Texas C-Bar Bulletin: Community Building with
Attorney Resources. Austin, TX: Author. Retrieved
May 2, 2002, from
http://www.texascbar.org/news/BulletinAug.pdf.

Trist, E. (1983). Referent organizations and the development of inter-organizational domains. *Human*
Relations, 36(3), 269–284.

U.S. Department of Agriculture. (2002). Federal year
2003 proposed budget summary. Retrieved May 2,
2002, from http://www.usda.gov/agency/obpa
/Budget-Summary/2003/2003budsum.htm#rd.

U.S. Department of Health and Human Services.
(2002). *Grantee listing for the Assets for Independence Act*
Demonstration. Retrieved May 2, 2002, from http://
www.acf.dhhs.gov/programs/ocs/demo/ida/grantees
/northeast.html.

Uvin, P., Jain, P. S., & Brown, L. D. (2000). Scaling of
NGO programs in India: Strategies and debates.
Institute for Development Research Reports, 16 (IDR
Report No. 6). Retrieved May 21, 2001, from
http://www.jsi.com/idr/IDRreports.htm.

Waddell, S. (1997). Outcomes of social capital strategies
of banks and community-based organizations in the
United States: The four pros: property, profit,
processes, and products. *Institute for Development*
Research Reports, 13 (IDR Report No. 1). Retrieved
May 21, 2001, from http://www.jsi.com/idr
/IDRreports.htm.

Warren, J. (2000). Collaboration between a small rural
community college and a large industrial corporation for customized training. *Community College*
Journal of Research and Practice, 24, 667–679.

Westley, F., & Vredenburg, H. (1991). Strategic bridging:
The collaboration between environmentalists and
business in the marketing of green products. *The*
Journal of Applied Behavioral Science, 27(1), 65–90.

Wood, D. J., & Gray, B. (1991). Toward a comprehensive
theory of collaboration. *Journal of Applied Behavioral*
Science, 27(2), 139–162.

Youtie, J. (2000). Field of dreams revisited: Economic
development and telecommunications in La Grange,
Georgia. *Economic Development Quarterly, 14*(2),
146–153.

INFOTRAC COLLEGE EDITION

capacity building
collaboration
colonias
disinvestments

rural economic development
strategic bridging
sustainability

18

Charitable Choice, Social Workers, and Rural Congregations

Partnering to Build Community Assets

ROGER AKER

T. LAINE SCALES

Kretzmann and McKnight (1993) have challenged social workers to recognize the richness of rural communities. They encourage us to look upon the strengths and assets of rural life and discover a community's capacity that can be developed and enhanced. Using this asset-building framework, social workers begin to see that people can deliver, as well as utilize, services to improve community life.

Asset-building frameworks are designed to allow rural citizens to determine their own directions, set their own priorities, and utilize their own strengths to improve their communities. Some of the assets typically found in rural communities include natural resources, strong social networks, durable traditions, voluntary associations, and institutions such as schools and religious congregations.

Social workers serving in rural communities have sometimes looked to rural churches as a resource in social service provision. Rural congregations help mold and shape rural communities. From frontier days to the present, people in rural communities have established and rigorously sustained regular religious gatherings. In rural life, where people are connected to nature for livelihood and recreation, there is an abiding appreciation and reverence for both divine order and supernatural intervention. A rural congregation is a conduit for invoking divine blessings and comforting those afflicted with hardship.

Congregations have much to offer rural communities and can contribute assets of human and social capital. Their potential for community aid is often unrecognized and usually underutilized. As our nation focuses attention on facilitating coalitions between faith-based organizations and government, professional social workers have tremendous opportunities to broker creative partnerships. Recent legislation, known as Charitable Choice, aims to increase involvement of the private sector, including faith-based organizations, in the delivery of government-funded social services. Charitable Choice was designed to facilitate partnerships. We contend that by forging stronger partnerships with rural congregations, social workers can tap into a wealth of assets for social services in rural communities. A professional social worker can provide knowledge and skills essential for coalition building, such as networking, referring, and brokering to bring groups together, negotiating agreements and contracts, assisting with technical aspects of service delivery, aiding in grant writing and fund-raising, and demonstrating problem-solving skills that address barriers that hinder a coalition.

Professional social work has recognized a category of *church social workers,* who are employed specifically to work with churches or church-related agencies (Garland, 1995). In this article we are addressing not only those who have chosen to specialize as church social workers, rather we address any professional social worker in a rural context who is interested in collaborating with rural congregations.

Rural social workers working in any context, public or private, religious or nonsectarian, can benefit from knowing how to collaborate with churches. As social workers who have worked with congregations that are rural and Christian, our discussion and examples will be limited to this context. However, we recognize that many of these principles can be applied to other rural religious bodies.

In order to facilitate partnerships with churches, social workers need information about: (1) characteristics of rural congregations, (2) effectively communicating with rural congregations, and (3) locating resources for rural congregations. To more fully understand congregations as assets in a rural community, it is necessary to consider their capacity, potential, and limitations. It is worthwhile to consider the essence of rural congregations and how they function within their communities.

CHARACTERISTICS OF RURAL CONGREGATIONS

Each rural congregation is unique and there are differences among religious traditions and denominations represented in rural communities. However, there are identifiable characteristics that shape the culture of rural congregations. Expanding upon a set of ten characteristics proposed by Farley (1988) for the small church, and drawing from our own experiences in rural congregational social work (Scales & Aker, 1998, 1999), we will sketch a portrait of a rural congregation. Because some of these characteristics are related to the small size of the church, rather than its rural context, they may apply to a small urban or suburban church as well. The characteristics are organized into four categories: organization, leadership, relationships, and methods. Each cate-

gory presents both a potential asset and a potential challenge for the congregation and for the social worker who is considering the kinds of collaborations necessary for maximizing services within a rural community.

Organization

Rural congregations are typically single cell, rather than complex, organizations. The hierarchy is clear and simple. If a social worker were to draw and analyze an organizational chart, he or she would see that the chain of command and the assignment of responsibilities would not be complicated. In addition, rural congregations are often small organizations that have not evolved into complex bureaucratic structures characteristic of large urban churches or suburban "megachurches."

Providing worship services one day each week is seen as the primary function of a rural church, in contrast to a larger urban church, which may operate a variety of programs throughout the week. In fact, social workers hoping to facilitate social service programs may find that programs not directly related to worship may be viewed by the small rural congregation or its leaders as extraneous to the main business of the congregation. Finally, small rural congregations are limited in terms of resources. They typically have fewer members, fewer staff, fewer volunteers, and fewer dollars than urban and suburban churches. Therefore, social workers who facilitate cooperation among congregations, between congregations, and with local agencies will help enable rural congregations to make the most of their limited resources.

Leadership

Rural congregations are typically led by one full-time or part-time clergy person, with part-time personnel or volunteers assisting. There are few people to whom the clergy can delegate responsibility, so leaders tend to be very "hands-on" and operate as generalists. Leaders are expected to be available to address a wide variety of needs in their congregation and in the larger community.

In addition, leadership is localized, with clergy and other leaders making their own decisions. Rural church leaders may sometimes ignore directives initiated through denominational structures or other organizations that have structural authority or influence over the local congregation. Exercising tremendous autonomy in decision making, rural churches often ignore denominational directives, believing programs designed for urban or suburban churches are irrelevant, or because leaders seldom notice noncompliance of a remote, often disconnected congregation.

Relationships

Rural congregations have a particular relationship style that may be noticeable to outsiders. First of all, the rural church is a people-centered place where "everyone knows everyone else's name." Rural congregants depend on one another in times of crisis and celebrate with one another in times of joy, such as the birth of a child. They value the person-to-person relationships found both within the church and in the larger community. However, the closeness of this "clan" can be a barrier to outsiders, as one does not become a member simply by officially joining the church. Regardless of official church membership, one must be "adopted" into the church family to be a true member of the congregation. Church members typically have multiple connections with one another. For example, church elder Jose Gonzalez may be the uncle of his Sunday School teacher, Marco, as well as the father of the church secretary, Maria, while employing ten other church members in his factory.

Methods of Helping

Members and leaders of the rural church use less structured methods to plan and execute programs and activities. Rural congregations do very little long-range planning. Instead, programs are developed along two principle lines of action. First, congregations react quickly to needs and issues as

they become known. Observers are often amazed at how quickly a rural church can collect food, clothing, furniture, or appliances simply by spreading the word, or manage to buy a new furnace by passing the plate.

External projects are often designed on the spot when the need is identified. For example, one church in the Texas Hill Country town of Utopia learned of a family whose home had been destroyed by fire. The congregation worked quickly to mobilize the whole community in providing shelter, food, clothing, and cash donations. In the same way that a project is quickly created, it is quickly put away with little follow-up or afterthought. The old time revivals of the rural church tradition are an example of short-term events that come quickly and are swept away as soon as the revival tent is torn down. Although this tendency to respond quickly is an asset, abrupt terminations make it difficult to sustain interest in long-term projects and partnerships.

The second way that rural congregations help is through special interests. Responses are more related to the passion of a congregant than particular circumstances. This special interest is often the result of a personal experience or observation and a spiritually driven motivation to take action. If the congregant can communicate the need, stimulate interest in others, and organize action, the whole church may get involved. For example, a social worker contacted a home economics teacher about a rural family who was in danger of being evicted from their home because of perceived "unsanitary housekeeping conditions." The teacher quickly established a corps of volunteers within her congregation to help her with training and mentoring the family so that they could meet the requirements and avoid being evicted. Soon, the teacher established an entire program with volunteers from several different congregations offering this service to other families in similar circumstances. A social worker could help establish collaborations between churches and other community partners (like 4-H and County Extension) for projects like this. Once the social worker has cultivated an understanding of how the rural congregation functions, he or she can begin to prepare for communication with the congregation and other organizations about community issues. To build partnerships with a variety of agencies, social workers must communicate well with other social workers, government agencies, and congregations.

COMMUNICATING WITH RURAL CONGREGATIONS

In all types of social work practice, good communication skills are essential. We have identified six communication essentials for social workers to consider as they develop working relationships with rural congregations.

1. Communicate with Cultural Sensitivity

Social workers who have never been part of a rural congregation before may find themselves in a cross-cultural context. Both the rural setting and the church context have their own languages and cultural patterns that must be learned. Garland and Conrad (1990) note that in the church context, "the Bible, theology, and Christian values and lifestyle become resources for practice." Language that includes concepts such as forgiveness, the family of God, and Christian hospitality motivate church volunteers to participate in social service programs (p. 80).

2. Communicate in Ways that Respect This Group's Theology of Helping

Social workers and congregants agree that social services (or physical ministries) are important, but may disagree on the level of importance. Congregations may sometimes view physical assistance as temporal and therefore subordinate in importance to eternal things. In order to communicate with congregations, it is crucial to understand that, for some congregations, temporal issues are filtered through eternal values.

Social workers may not agree with the congregation's theology or priorities, in the same way that social workers often disagree with the values and priorities of other partners. However, when each partner respects the other and focuses on the common desire to be an asset to the community, then the partnership can be successful.

3. Communicate a Connection to the Congregation's Mission

Congregations are more willing to respond to opportunities in the community outside the congregation when they can relate community projects to their own mission. What is the history of this group of congregants (particularly their history of helping)? What do they value most? What service activities are they already doing? Has their denomination identified particular social concerns to address? Rural congregations may tend to cling to their traditions and may be resistant to change. Though some traditions are clearly immutable, congregations with extensive traditions may be encouraged to subtly recast some traditions by changing the focus or adding new elements. For example, a rural congregation that has had a gift exchange among members for many years has now added an option to simultaneously provide a gift for a struggling family in the community. Building upon structures and programs that are already in place, particularly those that have been around for a long time, may be viewed by the congregation as less threatening. Social workers with good communication skills will use creative thinking to connect current needs with established responses.

4. Communicate in Ways that Respect the Congregation's Decision-Making Style

Learning how decisions are made is critical. The decision-making path may vary greatly from one congregation to another. Often the polity of the larger denomination indicates the style likely to be used by a congregation. But assumptions should be avoided, because local adaptations often occur in rural communities. A recent study of congregations in a rural community suggested differences in how congregations make the decision to begin a new program (Aker, 2001). The following list suggests styles ranging from less to more autocratic in organizational decision-making style:

1. Members see a need and budget funds or raise financial support.

2. Members see a need and recruit others to get involved.

3. Staff members or congregants identify a group of members who seem to be passionate about a certain cause.

4. Committees go through a visioning process to thinking about what is possible.

5. A missions committee may develop an idea and study its potential.

6. Members present ideas to Board of Trustees and Church Council.

7. A governing board has a Missions Committee to screen all ideas.

8. A governing board decides what the church will do.

9. The pastor or another staff member takes initiative.

What seems to be missing from the list is a perspective that focuses on assets. From this paradigm, the congregation is looking for needs to address, rather than examining their assets and what they have to offer to the community. In addition, Kretzman and McKnight (1993) recommend that churches examine what partnerships already exist in the community and see where they can join in, thus bringing their unique assets.

5. Communicate Information about Policies and Social Services

Professional social workers can provide much-needed information to congregations about policies and existing services. Social workers may provide technical assistance or information to prepare a congregation for building partnerships. They may help congregations locate resources to operate and further develop social service programs. The expertise of social workers may be needed to broker and negotiate working agreements, perhaps resulting in contracts between agencies and congregations. For example, one rural African-American congregation consulted with a social worker as they applied for grant funding to sustain a program that began as a natural part of their congregational life. An astounding number of children (76) had been placed with families in the church through the state system of foster care and adoption. Social workers were involved in the process and one social work consultant served as a resource broker, grant writing consultant, and program evaluator for a program that would benefit the entire community.

6. Communicate Your Patience and Persistence

Any partnership with a rural congregation requires patience. As a volunteer organization, congregations proceed with tasks according to their own priorities. To honor the timing and limited resources of a congregation is to patiently persist during the period from an idea's inception to a program's implementation. Follow-up for assigned tasks should be done with friendliness and understanding. The same congregation that moves swiftly to meet some needs may carefully debate over a different issue, particularly if it involves new collaborations with other organizations. A social worker must realize that in a rural community, trust and credibility are necessary for partnerships. This trust is not immediately given to the worker, but is earned over time.

RURAL CONGREGATIONS AS COMMUNITY PARTNERS

Proactive and Reactive Efforts

Congregations can be valuable partners in coalitions of organizations in rural communities. Congregations may unite with coalitions whose members may be other congregations (both interfaith and intrafaith), private agencies (including faith-based organizations), civic organizations, public agencies, local businesses, and charitable foundations (Kretzman & McKnight, 1993).

Coalitions may be *proactive,* establishing visible, permanent, services driven by special interests of the congregation. Proactive coalitions sometimes form with unlikely partners who share a special interest for differing reasons. For example, religious bodies, community organizations, and state agencies may form partnerships to work with prisoners and their families. Interest in the welfare of clients outweighs differences for the sake of delivering services effectively in a continuous coalition.

Another type of coalition that congregations may join are *reactive* coalitions. These coalitions tend to be more spontaneous, driven by particular needs, and partners of the coalition are often determined by the nature of the need. These coalitions are often more time-limited. For example, an agency social worker providing services to a foster grandparent formed a temporary coalition involving a state agency, a community organization, a utility company, and a small congregation to assist her client who had lost her job and electrical service at her home. The community organization negotiated with the utility company, which forgave part of the debt and allowed installments for another portion of the bill to help her become current with payments. The social worker contacted a congregation that, although they did not know the client, rallied to pay the remaining $190 on the past due electric bill, as well as $100 on her upcoming bill. Other members of the congregation installed a new wall gas furnace to replace several small electric space heaters in her home. Then several members hired her to clean their homes and helped her establish a housecleaning business that permitted her to work flexible hours and earn more income than in her previous job. By working together, the partners and the family were able to continue the placement of the foster children and avoid another disruption in their lives.

Barriers to Partnership

With patience, social workers can help churches to participate in community asset building by tapping into a congregation's resources, but several obstacles may hinder these partnerships. In a recent study, clergy in a rural community in Texas identified several barriers that prevented their churches from providing service programs that would benefit residents of their town. They noted as primary barriers a combination of overwhelming need combined with the limited resources of their congregations. Another barrier identified was congregants' lack of sensitivity to situations of those in need. Congregations may hold particular attitudes about helping that cause them to question the legitimacy of a client's requests for assistance. Other barriers mentioned from the clergy perspective were a lack of understanding of the community's needs, lack of training and education to provide programs, and lack of time and commitment of congregants (Aker, 2001). The priorities, values, and dynamics of a particular congregation may create barriers that frustrate the social worker. However, identifying these barriers is the first step in overcoming them, and the skilled social worker can address many of these obstacles through education of clergy and congregants.

RESOURCES FOR PARTNERSHIPS IN RURAL COMMUNITIES

The assets rural congregations provide to their communities vary according to their individual resources. The tangible resources of a congregation can be easily assessed. Their willingness to utilize them for purposes beyond the congregation, however, are not so easily determined. By tangible resources, we refer to the observable items under the ownership of the congregation such as real estate, a building, equipment, staff, volunteers, money, and vehicles. A congregation, at its discretion, may avail the community of these resources to accomplish certain service goals. However, a congregation is certainly more than its real assets. There are intangible resources as well, such as expertise (or access to it), power (or access to it), sanction (blessing or credibility), informal helping networks, and religious motivation (Scales & Aker, 1998). Welfare reform has dramatically expanded the potential resources of rural congregations. By making additional funds available to congregations, Charitable Choice legislation helps supplement and magnify existing congregational resources by infusing added funding. Unfortunately, research suggests that many religious leaders are unfamiliar, or even uncomfortable, with Charitable Choice. In a recent study of clergy leaders of congregations in one rural community, only 22% of the clergy surveyed expressed knowledge about Charitable Choice and interest in seeking external funds through its provisions (Aker, 2001). In a national study, Chaves (1999) found that 76% of clergy interviewed were unfamiliar with Charitable Choice. When asked if they thought their congregations would apply for government money to support human services programs, only 36% of clergy respondents replied that they would.

Not only can social workers help clergy understand Charitable Choice and safeguards for their congregation, but they can also lead clergy to envision new programs that would utilize new funding. The following section relates information about the background and issues of Charitable Choice. It is important that social workers understand the legislation and be able to communicate its provisions to congregations interested in expanding their services.

Background of Charitable Choice

The United States Congress passed into law legislation that changed significantly how the poor receive assistance. The law, The Personal Responsibility and Work Opportunity Reconciliation Act of 1996 (PRWORA), had the purpose of changing the role of the federal government in providing aid to the poor, effectively reducing the bureaucratic structure needed to

provide benefits. States were allowed more freedom in structuring their own welfare programs to distribute federal funds. Eligibility requirements for benefits to families were stiffened and time-limited, and financial benefits were reduced to provide greater incentive for them to seek employment.

The law signaled the devolution of government involvement in social welfare programs. Among the cost-cutting features of the legislation was a reduction of the bureaucratic workforce needed to administer the programs and provide needed services. Some of the welfare infrastructure was passed on to state governance, while part of it was simply lost. Legislators anticipated the vacuum of missing services and included a compensatory section, which authorized and directed states to seek the delivery of services from the private sector. Known as the Charitable Choice provision, Section 104 allowed states to:

> . . . Administer and provide services under the programs . . . through contracts with charitable, religious, or private organizations and provide beneficiaries of assistance under the programs with certificates, vouchers, or other forms or disbursement which are redeemable with such organizations (PRWORA, 1996, Section 104).

Though the states' implementation of the law varied according to their own social service structures and priorities, the interpretation of the Charitable Choice section was fairly uniform, and is represented by this excerpt from the Texas Department of Human Services:

> Charitable Choice encourages states to utilize community and faith-based social service providers, by contracting or voucher arrangements or both, in delivering welfare-related care to the needy (Charitable Choice Report, TDHS, 1998).

The goal of Section 104 of PRWORA was to expand the involvement of the independent sector, including faith-based organizations, in the delivery of government-supported social services. Some noted that religious charities were among the most effective providers of help and were often "willing to serve even the most distressed families and neighborhoods" (Center for Public Justice & Center for Law and Religious Freedom, 1997, p. 14). Some saw the new law as a momentous opportunity the congregations and other faith-based organizations. These supporters noted that religious charities tend to be flexible, take a personal approach, and are deeply committed to the needy. Others were encouraged that congregations could provide help that is guided by a moral code that evokes personal responsibility. They believed that such assistance would be particularly important when individuals, families, and communities are experiencing long-term poverty and self-destructive patterns of behavior.

However, some religious leaders were concerned about the new legislation because they feared being cast as the community safety net for the needy. (Center for Public Justice & Center for Law and Religious Freedom, 1997).

Faith-based organizations have been a small segment of the service delivery environment. Statistics from one state agency with a mandate to implement Charitable Choice provisions also indicate that a small percentage of service providers were faith-based. In 1998, the Texas Department of Human Services reported that, of its 6,000 contracts with providers of services to clients, 49% were with private and public non-profits, 41% were with for-profit organizations, and only 10% were with faith-based organizations. Enlarging the role of faith-based organizations is the goal of Charitable Choice.

In January 2001, President Bush signed an executive order establishing the White House Office of Faith-based and Community Initiatives (known as Faith-Based Initiatives, or FBI). He then signed a second order establishing parallel offices in five federal agencies—Departments of Health and Human Services, Justice, Labor, Education, and Housing and Urban Development. The goal of this new action was to adjust federal policy to support new and existing faith-based programs providing social services.

The White House document *Rallying the Armies of Compassion* (Bush, 2001) outlined the goals of this new initiative, which were to:

1. Identify and eliminate improper federal barriers to effective faith-based and community-serving programs through legislative, regulatory, and programmatic reforms;

2. Stimulate an outpouring of private giving to nonprofits, faith-based programs, and community groups by expanding tax deductions and through other initiatives;

3. Pioneer a new model of cooperation through federal initiatives that expand the involvement of faith-based and community groups in after-school and literacy services, help the children of prisoners, and support other citizens in need.

The purpose of this legislation was to "level the playing field" between local congregations (and other local faith-based organizations) and the large faith-based organizations that garnered much of the funding available through federal grants and contracts. This initiative attempted to identify and remove any statutory, regulatory, and bureaucratic barriers preventing the funding of effective faith-based and community social programs.

Among the inequities to be corrected was the practice of large organizations utilizing their considerable organizational resources to secure new funding. Specialists are retained for the purpose of seeking new federal programs and writing program proposals most likely to be funded. In an unprecedented move, the 2001 initiative mandated that federal staff would be available to assist small organizations that lack expertise in grant writing to write effective proposals.

Why has government turned to the option of soliciting help from congregations to resolve social problems? In part, it is out of frustration. Senator Daniel P. Moynihan has commented in *Miles to Go* (1996): "No one has a clue as to what it would take for public policy to be sufficient" (p. 225). Another factor, as Wineburg (2001) notes, is the conservative rhetoric that has grown in our country beginning with the Reagan

Administration. Religious fervor and idealism translated from constituents to politicians suggested the real possibility of having all social services delivered locally and voluntarily. However, many social analysts agree that such a utopian state of interpersonal compassion and mutual responsibility is not likely in our generation.

The Debates over Charitable Choice

Describing recent debates over faith-based initiatives, Koopman (2002) notes that the complex process of policy making often combines straightforward analysis of data, controversial views over personal issues such as religion, political calculation, and uncontrollable events. All of these factors are reflected in the debates over Charitable Choice. Lively discussions of Charitable Choice legislation have produced many unanswered questions: Can religious organizations replace the millions spent funding welfare? Will evangelizing the poor become the new work of congregations? How can well-intentioned but untrained volunteers replace professionally trained staff?

When discussing Charitable Choice issues, it is important to clarify what a faith-based organization (FBO) actually is. The term is commonly misunderstood. These organizations are local entities that serve the needs of particular neighborhoods. Unlike other community organizations, faith-based organizations have as part of their mission to extend their religious values through their charitable activities.

There are two kinds of FBOs. Some organizations are "pervasively religious" enterprises where religious activities are inextricably bound to any other activities. Other FBOs are "religiously affiliated" and offer services independent of religious activities (Baptist Joint Committee on Public Affairs and The Interfaith Alliance, 2001). An example of the first FBO may be a daycare center managed completely by a local congregation. An example of the second FBO is a privately incorporated, tax-exempt nursing home that was established by a religious body and continues to be partially funded by it.

The aims of Charitable Choice are better suited to the second kind of FBO, and states prefer contracting with an FBO affiliated with, but independent of a particular congregation, rather than the congregation itself. Some states, such as Ohio, will contract only with FBOs that are thus organized as tax-exempt organizations. Many religious bodies have printed documents to guide houses of worship wishing to contract for providing services funded by the state. Most suggest caution and recommend much forethought and even the advice of an attorney.

Although Charitable Choice is but one step in a twenty-year progression toward political and economic conservatism, it is a demarcation that established a new scheme for welfare, the effectiveness of which is still being evaluated. It is important to consider a few of the major issues in order to gain a realistic expectation of the extent to which a congregation is, or can become, an asset for services in a rural community. The remaining paragraphs in this section will briefly sketch out the debates spawned by Charitable Choice. This simple overview should serve only as a primer and guide to further study on a topic that has received and will continue to draw much attention in scholarly literature.

Legal Concerns   Opponents of Charitable Choice contest the constitutionality of Charitable Choice on the grounds that it endangers the Establishment Clause of the First Amendment, endangering the protected freedoms of both the "beneficiaries of assistance" and "the mission of religious faiths" (Katz & Segal, 1996). Many find objectionable any use of tax policy, administrative regulations, or distribution of government funds to support organized religion in any manner (NASW, 2001). Others note the lack of specificity in Section 104 creating such regulatory loopholes as would allow religious discrimination in publicly funded programs and a lack of provision for licensing and accreditation policies for pervasively religious organizations.

Some religious leaders, though, dismiss the new concerns of constitutionality of Section 104 as a "red herring" because the First Amendment prohibits the government disbursements that have the purpose and primary effect of aiding in the establishment of religion. It does not prevent faith-based groups from receiving tax dollars for social welfare and health programs. In fact, many FBO programs have depended on government funding for decades (Brownstein, 1999, Ellerbrake & Greenshaw, 2001).

Professional Issues   Another issue of concern is the capacity of FBOs to provide the caliber of expertise that has developed within the human service network. It is noteworthy that professional and capital-intensive services were the types of services least frequently provided by congregations prior to PRWORA. More frequently provided by congregations were emergency goods or financial aid, counseling, clothing, child care, and senior services (Yates, 1998). Some professional associations have expressed concern over some of the points related to professional services. They are uneasy about how Section 104 will affect accessibility to service without discrimination, emphasis on activity reporting and accountability, staff expertise to manage complex issues and problems, and maintenance of a strategic, coordinated network of social services (NASW, 2001). The role that government will take in creating interfaces between volunteers and professionals, as well as in distinguishing their separate services has not yet completely unfolded.

Public/Private Partnerships   Some social service analysts note that a paradox in capitalism has occurred in Charitable Choice. Reform is clearly spurred on by incentives to reduce government spending and inefficiency. And yet the delicate system of interdependency between social services and religion at the local level that has evolved through free enterprise is being altered. Wineburg (2001) suggests we would be better served "to study ways of refining the real partnerships that have evolved, sustaining the emerging ones, and creating conditions for the development of new partnerships that really work" (p. 74). He suggests that it is questionable

policy to upset this equilibrium without a clear understanding of the capacity of FBOs.

A corollary concern is the uncertainty of the effects of the new competition. Some of the questions often arising in the literature may be summarized as follows: What will be the effect of local religious groups competing for the same funds? Will coalitions based on social service interests be unnatural and troublesome? Will some religions be favored above others? Conversely, some are worried that government dollars may be claimed by "doers of the lesser good" (Ellerbrake & Greenshaw, 2001).

Many of the questions are based on apprehensions about allowing government, in part, to determine the impact of a house of worship on its community. But competition is not outside the scope of religion. If religious bodies compete on a level playing field, argue supporters, then free-market capitalism will ensure that beneficiaries are better served. Consumers can decide if Muslims or Methodists, Baptists or Bahá'is can deliver the best services.

Effects on FBOs and Congregations   Some religious leaders are opposed to the involvement of pervasively religious bodies in contractual agreements with the government. They caution houses of worship to consider carefully a course in which, eventually if not immediately, those external entities with the "power of the purse" may control programs they fund. Surrendering absolute control may dilute or distort the unity, resolve, or mission of a religious body.

On a different scale, there is a wariness of how the reforms will affect the role of religion in the United States. As an institution of social conscience, the prophetic voice of religion in the United States is part of the genius of a system of disestablished religion. And yet, it will be more difficult for a congregation to critique a culture in which it has been made a partner. Evidence of excesses resulting from the fusion of religion and government pervade history in both Eastern and Western cultures. Will Charitable Choice threaten our social conscience on a national level? Will government overregulate or control faith-based programs? We must acknowledge that the government's role is to regulate; any provider's role is to resist inappropriate regulation and petition for modification. The genius of the American system is in the negotiation (Ellerbrake & Greenshaw, 2001).

Concerns over the financial impact of Charitable Choice are voiced differently by various groups. Religious communities fear becoming dependent on external financial support from the government and worry that the integrity and responsibility for their local programs may diminish once they no longer depend on their own volunteer service and monetary donations. Local religious leaders hesitate to take on a financial "partner" whose values differ from their own, especially government. Ownership, enthusiasm, and satisfaction of FBO programs will be "shared" with an outside partner—the government. Many social analysts wonder about the long-term impact on volunteerism. As a significant resource for volunteers, will new faith-based initiatives alter the largest reservoir of community volunteers?

Practical consequences of reapportioned funds are that there is less money for established programs and the competition will be keen between established and emerging programs, both nonsectarian and religious. Another product of funding changes is that established social service programs, recognizing that faith-based initiatives are being funded by reallocated rather than additional money, wonder if welfare programs are being "deprofessionalized" on an unprecedented scale.

To balance the above concerns, we must acknowledge that there are leaders in government, service delivery, and religious organizations who are optimistic about the possibilities of Charitable Choice. It is seen as a unique window of opportunity for American religious bodies to recover charitable services lost in the twentieth century. In *The Newer Deal* (1999), Cnaan, Wineburg, and Boddie are interested in the possibilities provided by Charitable Choice, yet advise that we proceed with caution. In summary, they suggest:

1. Welfare reform that includes religious bodies as a significant partner in service delivery signals a new attempt by both political parties at a new solution to welfare problems that persist after years of effort. "In an era of public entrenchment, the religious community holds an important asset [tangible and intangible resources] for the health of both local citizens and the community as a whole" (Cnaan, 1999, p. 15).

2. "Religious communities in the United States are already providing services to a degree unimagined and unrecognized in social work literature" (Cnaan, 1999, p. 157). Even small religious organizations have highly effective local programs, though they lack the resources of larger entities.

3. Public and government alike sense that "our social problems have both socioeconomic and moral/religious roots," Sider concludes (2001, p. 84). To include religion as a part of a problem-solving approach to social problems is to acknowledge the possibility of a more holistic and balanced solution.

4. In a 1994 survey, Independent Sector found that people who attend religious services regularly are about twice as likely to volunteer, and volunteer twice as much in terms of hours as people who do not attend (Hodgkinson, Weitzman, Noga, and Knauft, 1994). This study demonstrates a close relationship between religion and good citizenship.

Deanna Carlson summed up the potential of Charitable Choice and the value of religious organizations to our social service system by quoting social work pioneer Mary Richmond, who said in 1899:

After all has been said in objection to past and present methods of charity, we must realize that, if the poor are to be effectually helped by charity, the inspiration must come from the church. The church has always been, and will continue to be, the chief source of charitable energy. (cited by Carlson, 1999, p. 2).

Social Workers, Charitable Choice, and Rural Congregations

In the wake of welfare reform, religious groups are faced with an opportunity and challenge unparalleled in United States history—collaborating with government to build stronger communities and help others. These cultural changes pose questions not fully answered yet. Will the faith-based organizations accept the challenge in time? Will the effect of welfare reform be to revitalize congregations through this new opportunity? Can the religious community recover the "relevance" that some say it has lost? Specifically, will a local congregation risk its limited resources—the time and money of members—to work with those who, under new policies are no longer entitled to public support?

Rural social workers are well-advised (and well-equipped) to work with congregations. Together, workers and congregations may overcome barriers to service provision and tap into the church's assets. Not only are members of rural congregations compelled by religious beliefs to help relieve the suffering of others, they are often capable of supplying the resources needed. Successful rural social workers will find win-win strategies in which congregations fulfill their desire to address both spiritual and physical needs, and develop trust and credibility in the process. By understanding and participating in the local informal helping networks, congregational members are close to the needs of people in the community, in both proactive and reactive situations. With the proper approach, congregations can willingly partner with others to improve their rural communities with the faith that they can be successful even if they have limited material resources. Charitable Choice, with all its possibilities and problems, can provide an avenue for these partnerships.

DISCUSSION QUESTIONS

1. The idea of building assets to sustain rural communities encourages groups to enter into partnerships with one another. Study the section "Characteristics of Rural Congregations." What assets of rural churches may make building partnerships with others feasible? What limitations may make it difficult? Can you think of examples in your community (rural, urban, or suburban) where churches are addressing social concerns? Do you think they could be more effective or efficient by partnering in new and different ways?

2. Review the section "Resources for Partnerships in Rural Communities." There are many reasons given in support of and opposition to the main goals of Charitable Choice. Looking through each subsection as a class, list on the board as many arguments for and against the legislation as you can find. Can you think of any more arguments

not discussed in the article? Continue discussing the legislation in small groups or as a class. Do you have a good diversity of opinions with the class or small group? If not, consider appointing some members to play "devil's advocate" and argue a different side. What areas of common ground can you agree upon?

3. In the section "Background of Charitable Choice," the authors note that the purpose of the Faith-Based Initiatives plan was to "level the playing field" between small congregations and other faith-based organizations and the large faith-based organizations that garnered much of the funding available through federal grants and contracts. In your opinion does this goal seem realistic? What obstacles might prevent rural churches from playing on this "level playing field"? What assets might assist them to "play the game"?

CLASSROOM ACTIVITIES
AND ASSIGNMENTS

1. The authors note that many characteristics of rural congregations can function as both assets and limitations. Review each characteristic in the section, "Characteristics of Rural Congregations." Divide into small groups, assigning each group a characteristic. Considering that characteristic, imagine two scenarios in which that characteristic would serve as an asset. Now imagine two scenarios in which that characteristic would serve as a limitation. What can social workers in the community do to encourage the congregation to understand and use that characteristic as an asset?

2. The Hudson Institute's Faith in Communities Initiative researches the work of congregations that are partnering with their states for social services. Review their Web site at http://www .hudsonfaithincommunities.org and access the Fifteen State Study of Charitable Choice Implementation. You may choose to read about partnerships in your own state, or a state you would like to learn more about. Review the various projects and the amounts of money granted. What differences do you see between the projects in rural areas and those in urban areas? Use the contact information provided to contact a rural congregation by phone or e-mail. Find out more about their project and report to the class.

3. Interview a religious leader in a rural congregation. Ideally, class members would interview leaders from a variety of different religious traditions. Find out what partnerships this religious group has established with other community groups. If few (or none) have been established, what are the obstacles that prevent such partnerships? Find out what the religious leader sees as the assets in the religious organization. Is the organization willing to offer those to the community to address concerns? What does the religious leader see as the assets of the community? Is the religious leader aware of Charitable Choice? (If not, be prepared to give a brief description of it.) Would the religious organization be likely to partner with government entities? If not, why not?

REFERENCES

Aker, R. (2001, October). *American Christianity: Will the bones come together for ministry?* Paper presented at the Fifty-first Convention and Training Conference of the North American Association of Christians in Social Work, San Antonio, TX.

Baptist Joint Committee on Public Affairs and The Interfaith Alliance Foundation. (2001). *Keeping the faith.* Retrieved October 7, 2001, from http://www.interfaithalliance.org/Initiatives/ktf.pdf.

Brownstein, A. (1999). Constitutional questions about charitable choice. In D. Davis & B. Hankins (Eds.), *Welfare reform and faith-based organization* (pp. 219–265). Waco, TX: Baylor University Press.

Bush, G. W. (2001). *Rallying the armies of compassion.* Washington, DC: The White House.

Carlson, D. L. (1999, June). *Our churches can make a change in our neighbors' welfare.* Address to Western New York State Article of the North American Association of Christians in Social Work, New York.

Center for Public Justice & Center for Law and Religious Freedom. (1997). *A guide to charitable choice: The rules of section 104 of the 1996 federal welfare law governing state cooperation with faith based social service providers.* Washington, DC and Annandale, VA: Author.

Chaves, M. (1999). Religious congregations and welfare reform: Who will take advantage of "Charitable Choice"? *American Sociological Review, 64,* 836–846.

Cnaan, R. A. (with Wineburg, R. J., & Boddie, S. C.). (1999). *The newer deal: Social work and religion in partnership.* New York: Columbia University Press.

Ellerbrake, R. P., & Greenshaw, L. H. (2001). *Quit demonizing Bush's "faith-based initiative."* United Church of Christ. Retrieved October 12, 2001, from http://www.ucc.org/ucnews/aug01/asiseeit.htm.

Farley, G. (1988). *Ten Characteristics of the Small Church.* Atlanta, GA: Home Mission Board, Southern Baptist Convention.

Garland, D. S. R. (1995). Church social work. *Encyclopedia of Social Work.* Washington, DC: National Association of Social Workers.

Garland, D. S. R., & Conrad A. P. (1990) The Church as a Context for Professional Practice. In D. Garland & A. P. Conrad, *The Church's Ministry with Families* (pp. 71–84). Dallas, TX: Word.

Hodgkinson, V. A., Weitzman, M. S., Noga, S. M., & Knauft, E. B. (1994). *Giving and volunteering in the United States, 1994.* Washington, DC: Independent Sector.

Katz, D. E., & Segal, J. A. (1996). *Constitutional and policy problems with Senator Ashcroft's "Charitable Choice" provisions.* American Civil Liberties Union. Retrieved October 1996, from http://www.aclu.org/congress/ashcrft.html.

Koopman, D. L. (2002). Faith-based initiatives: An essay on the politics of social service change. In B. Hugen & T. L. Scales (Eds.), *Christianity and social work: Readings on the integration of Christian faith and social work practice* (pp. 339–360). Botsford, CT: North American Association of Christians in Social Work.

Kretzmann, J. P., & McKnight, J. L (1993). *Building communities from the inside out: A path toward finding and mobilizing a community's assets.* Chicago: ACTA Publications.

Moynihan, D. P. (1996). *Miles to go: A personal history of social policy.* Cambridge, MA: Harvard University Press.

National Association of Social Workers. (2001, February 14). *NASW cautious about Bush's faith-based initiative.* Retrieved October 7, 2001, from http://www.naswdc.org/nasw/press_release/021401.htm.

Scales, T. L., & Aker, R. (1998, November). *Utilizing churches and other religious organizations for service delivery in rural areas.* Paper presented at the Twenty-second Annual Conference of NASW/Texas, Austin, TX.

Scales, T. L., & Aker, R. (1999, October). *Building networks of natural helpers among rural congregations.* Paper, Annual Meeting, North American Association of Christians in Social Work, St. Louis, MO.

Sider, R. J. (2001, June 11). Revisiting Mt. Carmel through charitable choice. *Christianity Today 45,* 8.

Texas Department of Human Services. (1998). *Charitable choice report.* Retrieved October 12, 2001, from http://www.dhs.state.tx.us/regops/charitable/char4.htm.

Wineburg, R. J. (2001). A limited partnership: The politics of religion, welfare, and social service. New York: Columbia University Press.

Yates, J. (1998). *Partnerships with the faith community in welfare reform.* Welfare Information Network. Retrieved April 5, 1998, from http://www.welfareinfo.org/faith.htm.

INFOTRAC COLLEGE EDITION

Charitable Choice
church
faith-based organizations

religious organizations
rural congregations

19

Living in Limbo

Homeless Families in Rural Communities

JIM WINSHIP

When you think of someone who is homeless, what's the first image that comes to mind? (Close your eyes and wait for the image to appear.) Where is the person and what does he or she look like?

For most students (and most North Americans), the image is likely to be that of an older man in shabby clothes, drinking from a bottle in a long paper bag, or a woman dressed in seven layers of clothing, pushing all her belongings in a shopping cart, mumbling to herself. The scene or locale for both of these figures is likely to be in a city. If you were familiar with homelessness in rural areas of the United States, these images might have occurred to you:

1. A family living in an abandoned farmhouse on the Great Plains, without running water or electricity;

2. A fifteen-year-old boy unable to stay with his mom and younger sister in a family shelter, because no males over thirteen are allowed to stay there; he "couch surfs," staying a few days or a week with a succession of relatives, friends, and acquaintances in his small town;

3. A family living in a camper all year around (in Wisconsin as well as Florida);

4. A family living for a month in a hotel paid for by vouchers by the Salvation Army, then "doubled up" living with relatives for two weeks, and finally living in their van for a week until they get vouchers to go back to a cheap motel.

Widespread homelessness in the United States is a recent phenomenon, and for a variety of reasons has been seen as an urban phenomenon affecting single adults. This article will explore reasons for the increase in homelessness for families in rural communities. The term *rural* will be used to designate areas described by the U.S. Census as "nonmetropolitan"; a nonmetropolitan county is one outside an urban area with a population of less than 100,000 and with no city having a population of 50,000 or more. The connections between rural poverty and rural homelessness will be discussed, with particular emphasis on the impacts of limited public transportation and limited housing availability in rural areas, along with cutbacks in federal housing programs. The ways that the federal government and some state governments have addressed homelessness will be examined, with particular attention to how they consider assets.

UNDERSTANDING AND COUNTING HOMELESSNESS IN RURAL AREAS

Categories of those who are homeless include:

1. *Single-parent households,* typically headed by women who have their children with them. They may be leaving (or have left) relationships; or have been evicted for failure to pay

rent, removed on vacate orders (ordered by a Health Department for unsafe habitation where they were living), burned out, or turned out by family or friends with whom they had been doubling up;

2. *Single men,* either indigenous or on the road, who are out of work, are increasingly of ethnic minority status, and often have rudimentary or obsolete job skills, the younger men tending to have job histories concentrated in the peripheral job market;

3. *Single women* of all ages, who have lost husbands or mates, have been turned out by friends or family, or simply cannot keep up with rising rents (many of whom have children who are either staying with family members, in foster care, or grown);

4. *Individuals with serious disabilities, severe and persistent mental illness, or long-standing substance abuse problems*—some of them having been hospitalized, and all have lost whatever precarious accommodations they once had and are now at a severe disadvantage in competing for the affordable housing that remains;

5. *Ex-offenders* released from jail or prison to fall back on their own meager resources, who face discrimination in securing jobs;

6. *Homeless youths,* who are especially vulnerable to the depredations of the street—some having been ejected from households unwilling or unable to support them any longer, and some having been victims of abuse or graduates of foster care;

7. *A host of smaller groups,* including the displaced elderly, victims of domestic violence, and legal and undocumented immigrants (Hopper, 1997, pp. 22–23).

There are a number of problems in estimating the number of people who are homeless. This is typified by the bumper sticker put out by the National Coalition for the Homeless: "If you lived here, you'd be home now." H. C. Covington (2002), who provides technical assistance for pro-grams serving homeless in rural areas, states that he has been collecting local and statewide reports for ten years, and has yet to see two reports based on the exact same methodology.

The rural context makes estimates even more difficult. "We have no national database to track the rural homeless, in part because it is so difficult," says Gene Summers, a professor in the Department of Rural Sociology at the University of Wisconsin in Madison. "Most small communities do not have homeless shelters, and a lot of the families are finding temporary shelter with friends and kin rather than living in a pickup truck down by the river. The rural environment helps to disguise the hardship" (Wilkinson, 1999, p. 2).

DEFINING HOMELESSNESS IN RURAL AREAS

"How many people are homeless?" The initial answer to that question is that "it all depends." First, it depends on the time period under consideration. Most people experiencing homelessness are homeless for a period of time; it's a temporary, not a permanent condition. Therefore, one gets different numbers if one looks for how many people experience homelessness on April 3, 2003, how many experience homelessness during the month of April 2003, or how many experience homelessness at some point during 2003.

Second, there is no universally agreed-upon definition of homelessness. Most everyone would agree that a family living in their van is homeless, as is a person sleeping under the bridge or in the woods. However, one also needs to include persons living in situations on acute housing distress not generally associated with homelessness—the family "doubled up" who stays in the living room of the sister's apartment for two weeks, the person living in the abandoned farmhouse without plumbing or electricity, the family who spends the summer at a campground.

Yvonne Vissing, author of *Out of Sight, Out of Mind: Homeless Children and Families in Small-*

town America, defines rural homelessness as "lack of a consistent, safe physical structure and the emotional deprivation that occurs as a result" (1996, p. 8). According to Vissing, this includes housing displacement and housing distress (a habitation with safety concerns and/or the lack of electricity, heating, and water/sewage).

This article considers an individual or family to be homeless if they:

1. Sleep in limited or no shelter for any length of time (e.g., outdoors, in one's car).

2. Sleep in shelters or missions operated by religious organizations or public agencies that serve homeless people and charge either no fee or a minimal fee.

3. Sleep in inexpensive hotels or motels where the actual length of stay or intent to stay is 45 days or fewer.

4. Sleep in other unique situations where the actual length of stay or intent to stay is 45 days or fewer, including staying with family or friends for short periods of time for other than economic reasons (doubled-up).

5. Sleep in housing conditions considered to be unsafe.

Complicating the distinction between homelessness and housed, particularly in rural areas, is the emergence of *colonias* along the border between the United States and Texas. Since the passage of the North American Free Trade Agreement (NAFTA) in 1994, there has been a growth of small unplanned communities. Many Mexicans and other Latin Americans who move to this country for jobs find themselves too poor to afford regular housing. Tens of thousands live in makeshift homes, build community outhouses, and bring their water in by truck.

Hidden among the cornfields of Hidalgo County, Texas, down dirt paths and along riverbanks, live tens of thousands of people. These *colonias,* or shantytowns are home to one of every five residents of the fourteen Texas counties along the U.S.–Mexico border, counties whose populations have surged by almost one-third since 1990 (Axtman, 2001).

In addition to the period of homelessness considered and the definition of homelessness used, the methodology for counting the homeless—including whether or not one only counts on one day or tries to look for an unduplicated count over several days or weeks—will also have an influence on the numbers counted.

It is easier to count those experiencing homelessness in urban than in rural settings. Far fewer of those experiencing homelessness in rural areas reside in shelters compared to urban areas. It is also easier to locate those sleeping outside in urban areas—in parks, under bridges—than in rural areas, where those sleeping outside are usually much less visible. Additionally, homeless families in campgrounds are difficult to distinguish from other families in campgrounds.

REASONS FOR THE GROWTH IN HOMELESSNESS

The growth in rural homelessness can be traced both to national trends over the last twenty-plus years, as well as several factors specific to rural areas. The trends that are most significant are poverty, transportation for the rural poor, the rise in housing costs, the availability of affordable housing, and cutbacks in federal government funding for housing programs.

Poverty and Rural Poverty

One cannot understand homelessness in rural areas without first understanding rural poverty. Think of being poor as *living on the edge,* having barely enough money to meet basic needs. For a low-income working single parent, for example, income may meet expenses if everything works out just right. However, any number of circumstances may push that family over the edge—a sick child which forces the parent to miss several days at work (at a job with no sick pay), an unusually cold winter that pushes up utility payments, unexpected car repairs. In choosing between paying bills, sometimes rent payments are not the most critical priority, and if the rent gets too far behind, the family may get evicted.

Most people who are poor are not poor most of the time. According to a recent study, nearly two-thirds of all Americans and more than 90% of African-Americans will experience at least one year of living below the poverty line during their lifetimes. According to the authors, "For the majority of Americans, the question is not if they will experience poverty, but when. Rather than an isolated event that occurs only to what has been labeled the 'underclass,' the reality is that the majority of Americans will encounter poverty firsthand during their adult lifetimes." (Rank & Hirschl, 2001, p. 739). And some of those who are poor will become homeless.

Poverty rates in rural areas are higher than in urban areas as a whole, with only central cities having higher poverty rates. In 2000, the national poverty rate dropped to 11.3%, the lowest rate since 1979. However, the poverty rate for those in rural areas was 13.4%; in central cities it was 16.1%. This pattern has been described as an "inverse doughnut, where poverty is high in the middle hole, low in the suburban ring, and high in the outside ring" (Hirschl & Rank, 1999, pp. 155–156).

According to Janet Fitchen (1996), lack of awareness of the extent of poverty in rural areas is due to the dispersed nature of poverty. Rural areas are more economically mixed settings than urban areas. For example, I live in a town with 6,000 permanent residents. Our children attended an elementary school in the countryside, where family income of the most affluent children in a classroom was at least ten times that of the least affluent children. Looking at the children, it was often difficult to tell who were the children of a dentist or doctor, and who were the children whose parent(s) were marginally in the workplace. The rural poor are hidden from outsiders because they are not concentrated like the poor in central cities.

Although the social and economic integration in rural areas is often greater than in urban areas, the job market and other factors are often problematic for low-income rural residents. The availability of jobs, especially well-paying jobs, continues to be an issue in rural communities. Rural unemployment rates were at their lowest level in three decades in 2000, although they have risen somewhat since then. However, finding well-paying jobs is more difficult. Average weekly earnings for those in rural areas were 20% lower than their urban counterparts in 1999. Only half of that difference can be explained by the lower cost of living in rural areas (Gibbs, 2001).

Homeless women interviewed in the most extensive statewide study of homelessness cited economic reasons as the predominant reasons for their homelessness. This is consistent with national data that show that since the late 1970s, the percentage of rural wage earners able to lift their families out of poverty has declined compared to urban workers (Cummins, First, & Toomey, 1998).

Jobs are not equally available in all rural areas. Persistently poor counties constitute 23% of all rural counties, as 20% or more of the population in these counties has been living in poverty for the last three decades. A disproportionate number of these counties are in the deep South (Rural Policy Research Institute, 1999a).

Transportation Issues for Rural Poor

Jobs are not equally available in all rural areas, and rural residents often need to travel distances within rural counties and from county to county to find employment. Perhaps the biggest difference between being poor in rural areas, as compared to being poor in central cities, is the lack of public transportation. Nearly 80% of rural counties have no public bus service, compared to 2% of urban counties. It is difficult to have public transportation in sparsely settled areas, since the routes to remote parts of counties are long, and the ridership is not large enough to make these routes cost-effective. Only 43% of the rural poor were found in one study to have a car, and only 4% of public assistance recipients owned a vehicle (Rural Policy Research Institute, 1999b).

Public assistance recipients are not likely to own vehicles because of the cost, and also because of provisions in the old Aid to Families with Dependent Children (AFDC) and current Temporary Assistance to Needy Families (TANF) programs that limit the amount of assets a family can have in order to keep receiving benefits. In most states, people who have assets worth more than $2,000 or $1,000 (depending on the state) are ineligible for benefits. Automobiles worth $4,650 or less are excluded from the asset calculation. As will be discussed later, programs for the homeless also do not have an orientation toward maintaining and enhancing assets.

The connection between car ownership and homelessness was clear to me on my first trip to a homeless shelter in a rural area fifteen years ago, as part of a church group that was serving a meal at the shelter. Sitting down with the residents at the meal, I listened to one young couple describe how they became homeless and ended up at the shelter. They were both working at low-paying jobs at a nursing home over twenty miles from their house. Their old car broke down, they couldn't get to work for over a week, and so they lost their jobs, which led to their inability to pay rent and the loss of housing.

Housing Availability

Without sufficient income, people can become homeless. The availability of decent and affordable housing also has much to do with whether or not individuals living on the edge can find housing. When determining housing availability, social workers must consider three questions: Is there any housing available? Is the housing in decent shape? Is it affordable? For the rural poor, the answer to these questions is often "no." The percentage of housing in rural areas that is renter occupied is smaller than in urban areas (26.5% to 37.3%). The amount of new housing in rural areas has grown at a slower rate than in urban areas, and most of this is owner occupied. What housing is available may be substandard; housing in rural areas is more likely to have problems with plumbing, wiring, and structural problems than in urban areas (Whitener, 1997). Rural homelessness is often precipitated by families having to leave their housing due to a structural, health, or safety concern. When families relocate to safer housing, the higher rent is often too much to manage (Fitchen, 1992).

The inability to afford housing affects more than those who are homeless and on the brink of homelessness in rural areas. One in every five rural households, and 70% of poor rural households, pay more than 30% of their income for housing costs; households paying more than 30% are considered *cost-burdened* according to the federal government. Ten percent pay over half of their income on housing (Housing Assistance Council, 2000; Whitener, 1997). Families that have to pay so much for rent are particularly vulnerable when their income faces a reduction for any reason.

Decreased Government Support for Housing

For many low-income individuals, government support for housing can allow them to get into housing and stay housed. To understand government support for housing (or any program) over time, it is important to take inflation into account. A program that had a $100 million allocation in 1969 and a $150 million allocation now has suffered an actual reduction in inflation-adjusted dollars. My family bought a new Volvo for $3300 in 1969; new Volvos now start at more than six times that amount.

Funds for subsidized housing programs reached their peak in 1978, with over $75 billion (using the value of the dollar in 2002). When Ronald Reagan became president in 1980, he vowed to cut spending for social programs. He was not successful in cutting spending in many areas, but did cut spending on housing programs substantially, to $17 billion (inflation-adjusted dollars) in 1983. Support for subsidized housing has never approached the 1970s levels.

DIFFERENCES BETWEEN THOSE WHO ARE HOMELESS IN RURAL AND URBAN AREAS

Although there are many reasons for being homeless—such as poverty, the gap between wages and housing costs, and lack of affordable housing—studies of homelessness in rural and urban areas reveal several differences.

The most recent national study of homelessness revealed that, in general, rural homeless clients have experienced fewer and shorter episodes of homelessness during their lifetimes. Fifty-five percent of rural clients have been homeless for three months or less, compared with 22–27% of central city and suburban homeless clients. In addition, only 27% have been homeless for more than a year, compared with 48% of central city and 49% of suburban clients (Interagency Council on the Homeless, 1999).

Families make up a larger percentage of those who are homeless in rural areas as compared to urban areas. The largest statewide study of the rural homeless was conducted in Ohio in 1993. Findings from this study indicate that homeless people in rural areas are younger, more likely to be single women or mothers with children, more highly educated, and less likely to be disabled. Economic factors are more likely to lead to homelessness in rural areas than are mental illness or drug and alcohol abuse (First, Rife, & Toomey, 1994). The rural women in this study identified family conflict and dissolution as the primary contributor to their homelessness nearly 38% of the time (Cummins, First, & Toomey, 1998).

A 2001 study of homelessness in Virginia found that over half of the homeless (53%) were women. Lack of affordable housing was described as the paramount reason for homelessness, closely followed by domestic violence, family break-up, and mental illness (Koebel, Murphy, & Brown, 2001). These findings parallel an earlier study in Kentucky), which showed a higher percentage of homeless women and families in rural areas than in urban areas, and demonstrated that domestic violence was more of a factor in leading to homelessness in rural parts of the state (Kentucky Housing Cooperation, 1994). Over half of the homeless in rural Colorado are families with children (Colorado Coalition for the Homeless, 2000).

Rural areas differ widely from one to another. Communities with economies based on tourism, such as those in Colorado with ski resort areas and gateways to National Parks, Forests, and Monuments, have experienced extreme shortages of affordable housing; homelessness has been on the rise in these places. These areas often have an abundance of low-wage, seasonal jobs. Service-industry workers, who cannot afford housing in the communities where they are employed, frequently must live in neighboring communities and face long commutes. Those without transportation or resources are at great risk of homelessness. Eagle County, Colorado, with a tourism-based economy, had a 0.1% multifamily rental vacancy rate in 1999, the lowest in the state. The average rent for an apartment was $948 a month.

RESPONSES TO HOMELESSNESS ON THE NATIONAL LEVEL

In the early 1980s, when homelessness was becoming more visible in the United States, most programs to address problems associated with homelessness were created, funded, and administered at the grassroots level. The administration of Ronald Reagan believed that states and local jurisdictions were best equipped to handle their own housing problems, and not the federal government (remember that Reagan cut funds for subsidized housing almost 80% in his first years as President).

As the number of homeless people grew during the mid-1980s, pressure grew to address the problems of homelessness in a tangible way from the top down, with the federal government as an active participant in addressing the needs of homeless people. In 1986, Congress passed a few small parts of the Homeless Persons' Survival Act. Later that same year, legislation containing Title I of the Homeless Persons' Survival Act—emergency relief provisions for shelter, food, mobile health care, and transitional housing—was introduced as the Urgent Relief for the Homeless Act. After an intensive advocacy campaign, the legislation was passed by large bipartisan majorities in both houses of Congress in 1987. After the death of its chief Republican sponsor, Representative Stewart B. McKinney of Connecticut, the act was renamed the McKinney Homeless Assistance Act. It was signed into law by President Reagan on July 22, 1987. The bill was renamed the McKinney-Vento Homeless Assistance Act in 2001 to honor the late Bruce Vento, a Minnesota Congressman who was an advocate for services for those in homeless situations. The programs that most directly support families in homeless situations, through the U.S. Department of Housing and Urban Development, are:

Emergency Shelter Grants (ESG) Funds are granted on a formula basis to states and communities to finance renovation, major rehabilitation, or conversion of buildings for use as emergency shelter or transitional housing for people experiencing homelessness; essential services; payment of operating costs of facilities for people experiencing homelessness; and homelessness prevention.

Supportive Housing Program (SHP) New and renewal funds are awarded on a competitive basis to states, communities, and nonprofit organizations to finance transitional housing, permanent supportive housing, supportive services, innovative and alternative housing, and safe havens.

There is also funding under the McKinney-Vento Act for Section 8 Moderate Rehabilitation for Single Room Occupancy (SRO) Dwellings for Homeless Individuals, and Shelter Plus Care funding for homeless people with disabilities.

Funding under the McKinney-Vento Act is categorical funding, and the distinction between categorical programs and entitlement programs is important. Entitlement programs are ones where if a person meets the qualifications (poor enough or disabled enough, for example), they automatically qualify for services or benefits, which have to be provided by that government. Supplemental Security Income (SSI), the program for those with disabilities who do not qualify for Social Security Disability and the poor aged, is an entitlement program. Student financial aid programs such as Pell Grants and Work Study programs are also federally funded entitlement programs.

Categorical programs are ones in which the federal government makes available a specific funding amount to the states, which then decide how to divide them up to communities or programs throughout the state. Often, there are some criteria as to how the money imposed from the federal level can be spent, and the states can also add other criteria. In the case of homeless assistance programs, like many other categorical programs, nonprofit organizations (and occasionally local governments) submit applications to the state, and the state chooses among the applications and determines how much each funded program will receive. This differs from Food Stamps, for example, in which each county in the nation has staff who can determine eligibility and provide Food Stamps to eligible individuals and families.

Funding from the federal government can be considered inadequate in several respects. Funding for all Housing and Urban Development programs for the homeless totaled one billion dollars in fiscal year 2002, $150 million of which was for Emergency Shelter Grants. In Wisconsin, $1.8 million was available for Emergency Shelter Grants in Fiscal Year 2002. Seventy-seven organizations submitted requests for $3.8 million that year. Only fifty-five of those were funded, at levels generally below what the organizations had requested.

Funding for programs addressing homelessness can also be considered inadequate in terms of meeting the demands for shelter. It is difficult to obtain figures on the degree to which homeless families are unable to find shelter in rural areas. Examples from statewide organizations and urban areas indicate a serious problem with unmet needs for those in homeless situations. In Minnesota, almost 6,000 individuals are sheltered across the state during a typical day, with children and unaccompanied youth making up nearly half of this population. On a typical night, 816 individuals are turned away from shelters. The U.S. Conference of Mayors, in its 2001 survey of hunger and homelessness in twenty-seven cities, found that in one year the number of homeless families seeking shelter had increased by 23%, and that 52% of the shelter requests by homeless families were not met in the cities surveyed (U.S. Conference of Mayors, 2001).

The categorical funding from the federal government to the states is then distributed to organizations, most of them small, not-for-profit organizations. Over 90% of homeless shelters in Wisconsin, for example, are local nonprofit organizations unassociated with a larger organization (such as Catholic Charities or The Salvation Army). This categorical funding is never sufficient to fully fund an emergency shelter, so emergency shelters in rural counties exist only where there is a nonprofit organization with enough commitment and fund-raising capability to begin and maintain services.

In North Carolina, half of the rural counties have no shelters for those experiencing homelessness (Brown, 2002). In Wisconsin, only about a third of the rural counties have shelters, although most have some funding for motel vouchers and other services. However, in three rural counties in the southwest area of the state, no nonprofit organization has applied for emergency shelter funds, so there are no services in that part of the state (Wilcox, 2002).

Starting a shelter in rural America is not easy. In Jefferson County, Wisconsin, which has a population of 75,000, a group of citizens raised enough money to start a homeless shelter in the early 1990s, but could not get zoning approval from local governments for any of the sites that they found.

In Danville, Virginia, a minister noted that the emergency room was full of people who were homeless, hoping to get into the hospital and off the street. Borrowing $5,000 from a local bank, he started a shelter in the basement of this church. Since 1994, the shelter has served more than 10,000 homeless persons. The effort did not come without cost to the minister. Many of his church members thought he was wasting his time, and almost a quarter of his congregation of 100 members left the church after he started the shelter.

STATEWIDE APPROACHES TO ADDRESS FAMILY HOMELESSNESS

Minnesota is a state that has taken a proactive approach to family homelessness. The 1993 Minnesota Legislature established the Family Homeless Prevention and Assistance Program (FHPAP) to assist families with children, youth, and single adults who are homeless or are imminently at risk of homelessness. The goal of the program is to help families remain in their homes, rehouse those who become homeless, shorten the length of time families spend in shelters, and reduce the number of families who experience episodic homelessness.

Dakota County, Minnesota, which participates in the FHPAP, estimates that a homeless episode for a family of three costs $12,000 (emergency shelter costs, county staff time, and housing subsidies). Preventing that homeless episode costs only $1,600 (payment of back rent, other miscellaneous expenses, and staff time).

In conjunction with the Family Homeless Prevention and Assistance Program, Minnesota is also embracing a "Housing First" philosophy, in which as many families as possible are moved into permanent housing rather than into transitional housing units. In contrast to emergency shelters, transitional housing programs typically provide families with apartments for up to two years. Most apartments have a bedroom, living area, and a kitchen. Transitional housing programs typically offer "life skills" training, which may include teaching families parenting skills, as well as how to budget money and manage a home. In addition, these programs may provide job training programs, educational programs for parents and children, substance abuse programs, and assistance in finding employment and permanent housing. Even after a homeless family has found permanent housing, it is not uncommon for the family to continue participating in activities and counseling offered by the transitional housing program (McChesney, 1990).

Especially in areas of tight housing markets, transitional housing has at times become a "waiting area" for families until affordable permanent housing becomes available. In rural Crow Wing and Morrison counties in Minnesota, a nonprofit organization has partnered with the local housing authority to use a "housing first" approach to move homeless families who otherwise would not qualify for public housing (because of bad credit or other issues) into housing units, with case management support. Volunteers are also enlisted to provide support to the families. Formal services are provided for a year, and families have been able to maintain housing after that period. Of the 134 households that received aid by the program in its first year, 89.5% had not been homeless at any time during the next twelve months (Vanderwall, 2002).

Transitional housing in rural areas, although invaluable in many instances, can be implemented in ways that deplete, rather than enhance, the assets of those served by the programs. Gerstel, Borgard, McConnell, and Schwartz (1996) describe one service-intensive transitional housing facility in New York State where residents were required to attend a number of activities designed to enhance residents' housing stability, including life-skill classes, parenting classes, and psychological counseling sessions. Many of the residents had moved from nearby small towns or other rural areas to the shelter. Although the women coming to the transitional housing facility had not made enough money to be stably housed, many of them worked. The combination of the distance from employment and the required activities meant that most of the residents were unable to work. Additionally, because of the distance and time constraints, they were less able to maintain contact with their social networks.

In order to minimize the disruption of social networks for rural families in transitional housing, transitional housing programs in Minnesota utilize "scattered sites," housing families in apartments in their home communities instead of forcing them to move to other community.

PAYING ATTENTION TO ASSETS IN POLICIES AND PROGRAMS

There is a need to adopt asset-building policies that ensure that all Americans are equipped with the individual resources essential to gaining meaningful opportunities. One means for achieving that is to provide universal access to those assets that foster independence and growth, not distinguishing between those that are "truly needy" and those "not quite needy enough." A second characteristic of asset-based policies is that they not only supply remedies to correct deficiencies, but also provide the assets necessary to realize individual capacities. Finally, policies would enhance the infrastructure of opportunity (Beefermen, 2001).

Many of the policies and programs designed to help those experiencing homelessness have not been designed or implemented from the perspective of maintaining and enhancing the assets of those in homeless situations. However, there are a few promising approaches.

Programs that ideally prevent homelessness and at least minimize moving out of the locality not only keep the social network of homeless adults intact, they also minimize the impact of dislocation on adults and children. The title of this article comes from a statement that one homeless woman made to me while I was conducting a parent support group at a rural shelter: "I feel like I'm living in limbo." Programs that prevent homelessness and moving also acknowledge the sense of place for the children involved. In the *Power of Place,* Galagher (1993) describes how children learn state-appropriate behavior during childhood. Children learn how to match emotional states and behavior (e.g., sleep, excitement, and concentration) to specific places: home, playground, or school. This is an essential part of establishing one's identity and, in familiar settings, can be a more powerful determinant of children's behavior than their personalities. Homelessness disrupts this sense of identity with the loss of predictable places where the child has learned what she or he can and cannot do (Locke, Garrison, & Winship, 1998).

"Housing first" policies are not deficit-centered. Working with families who ordinarily might not be able to secure permanent housing, they place the family in housing and concurrently add the services and support. Housing First policies start with the assumption that people in homeless situations need to be housed; they may not need counseling or other supporting services.

Policies, like the transportation program described previously, can be oriented to more than helping persons escape homelessness. Earlier in this article, being in poverty is described as "living on the edge." If one is poor and has a couple of bad breaks, maybe makes a bad decision, one can fall off the edge into homelessness. Programs that only help individuals escape the worst case situation in essence help them back onto that precarious edge.

Homelessness in rural areas must be considered from the larger perspective of the lack of housing and lack of economic opportunities in rural areas. Universal policies that strengthen the economic, housing, and transportation infrastructure of rural areas will make it easier for those who are homeless, on the brink of homelessness, and all low-income rural residents to obtain and maintain economic security.

Finally, when more programs and policies are designed to help families and individuals develop the competencies and assets so that there is greater stability and success in their lives, the nation will have made real progress. Then there will be fewer people "living in limbo."

DISCUSSION QUESTIONS

1. What are three barriers to stable housing impending homeless families who are homeless in rural areas of the United States that are generally not major obstacles for homeless families in urban settings? Are there barriers for urban homeless families not found in rural areas?

2. "Housing First" policies were discussed in the article as examples of policies that are not deficit-based. However, they do not enhance the economic or housing infrastructure of rural areas. What is one policy that would bolster the economic or housing infrastructure in rural areas?

CLASSROOM ACTIVITIES
AND ASSIGNMENTS

1. Select a rural county with which you are familiar. In talking with social service providers, try to understand both the extent

of family homelessness and the nature of the services provided to those in homeless situations. If there appears to be considerable need that is unmet, what are two factors that would contribute to the needs not being fully met?

2. The Fair Market Rent measures the monthly rental cost for a two-bedroom apartment in good condition. The National Low Income Housing Coalition's Web site (http://www .nlihc.org) has the Fair Market Rent for every county in the United States (go to the section under "Out of Reach"). Find the Fair Market Rent for a county for which you are familiar. In your opinion, how difficult would it be for low-wage earning families to make enough money to be able to pay housing and other costs and stay out of homelessness?

REFERENCES

Axtman, K. (2001). In Texas, free trade puts border colonias in spotlight. *Christian Science Monitor, 93*(116), 3.

Beefermen, L. W. (2001). *Asset develoment policy: The new opportunity.* Waltham, MA: Brandeis University Center on Hunger and Policy.

Brown, L. (2002, April 17). The rural homeless: Nowhere to go. *Greensboro News and Record,* p. 7.

Colorado Coalition for the Homeless (2000). *Rural Homelessness.* Retrieved April 12, 2002, from http:// www.coloradocoalition.org/info/homerur.htm.

Covington, H. C. (2002). Private conversation, April 4, 2002.

Cummins, L. K., First, R. J., & Toomey, B. G. (1998). Comparisons of rural and urban homeless women. *Affilia: Journal of Women & Social Work, 13*(4), 435–454.

First, R. J., Rife, J. C., & Toomey, B. G. (1994). Homelessness in rural areas: Causes, patterns, and trends. *Social Work, 39*(1), 97–109.

Fitchen, J. (1992). On the edge of homelessness: Rural poverty and housing insecurity. *Rural Sociology 57*(2), 173–193.

Fitchen, J. (1996). Rural poverty and rural social work. In L. Ginsberg (Ed.), *Social work practice in rural areas* (3rd ed., pp. 115–134). Alexandria, VA: Council on Social Work Education.

Galagher, W. (1993). *The power of place.* New York: Poseidon Press.

Gerstel, N., Borgard, C. J., McConnell, J. J., & Schwartz, M. (1996). The therapeutic incarceration of homeless families. *Social Service Review, 70*(4), 544–572.

Gibbs, R. (2001). Nonmetro labor markets in the era of welfare reform. *Rural America, 16*(3), 11–22.

Hirschl, T., & Rank, M. (1999). Community effects on welfare participation. *Sociological Forum, 14*(1), 155–174.

Hopper, K. (1997). Homelessness old and new: The matter of definition. In D. P. Culhane, & S. M.

Hornburg (Eds.), *Understanding homelessness: New policy and research perspectives* (pp. 9–67). Washington, DC: Fannie Mae Foundation.

Housing Assistance Council. (2000). *Why housing matters: HAC's 2000 report on the state of the nation's rural housing.* Washington, DC: Author.

Interagency Council on Homelessness. (1999). *Homelessness: Programs and the people they serve.* Washington, DC: Author.

Kentucky Housing Corporation (1994). *Kentucky homeless survey: Preliminary findings.* Lexington, KY: Author.

Koebel, C. T., Murphy, M., & Brown, A. (2001). *The 2001 Virginia rural homeless study.* Blacksburg, VA: Center for Housing Research, Virginia Polytechnic Institute and State University.

Locke, B., Garrison, R., & Winship, J. (1998). *Generalist social work practice: Context, story and partnership.* Thousand Oaks, CA: Brooks/Cole.

McChesney, K. Y. (1990). Family homelessness: A systemic problem. *Journal of Social Issues, 46*(4), 191–205.

Rank, M. R., & Thomas A. Hirschl. (2001). The occurrence of poverty across the life cycle: Evidence from the PSID. *Journal of Policy Analysis & Management, 20*(4), 737–755.

Rural Policy Research Institute (1999a). *Rural policy context: Income characteristics in rural America.* Retrieved April 8, 2002, from http://www.rupri.org.

Rural Policy Research Institute (1999b). *Rural by the Numbers: Transportation.* Retrieved April 8, 2002, from http://www.rupri.org.

State of Minnesota. (2000). *Family Homeless Prevention and Assistance Program Annual Report, 1999.* Minneapolis: Author.

U.S. Conference of Mayors. (2001). *A status report on hunger and homelessness in America's cities, 2001.* Retrieved April 12, 2002, from http://www

.usmayors.org/uscm/news/press_releases
/documents/hunger_121101.asp.

Vanderwall, B. (2002). Private conversation with Mr.
Vanderwall, Director of Housing Services, Lutheran
Social Service of Minnesota, April 12.

Vissing, Y. M. (1996). *Out of sight, out of mind: Homeless
children and families in small-town America.* Lexington:
University Press of Kentucky.

Whitener, L. (1997). Rural housing conditions improve
but affordability continues to be a problem. *Rural
Conditions and Trends, 8*(2), 70–74.

Wilcox, J. (2002). Private conversation, April 9, 2002.

Wilkinson, T. (1999). How small-town America handles
rural homelessness. *Christian Science Monitor, 91*(7),
5–7.

INFOTRAC COLLEGE EDITION

assets
homeless
housing

poverty
rural
transportation

20

Transportation to Work*

Policy Implications for Welfare Reform in Rural Areas

KENNETH R. WEDEL

FRAN C. BUTLER

Lulene Allen is a single parent with two children, aged 3 and 6. She lives in a small town of 800 residents in eastern Oklahoma where she was raised. When her husband left last year, he took his possessions and the family car, but left her with the debts they had outstanding. Lulene is 22-years-old and believes she is a self-starter. Recognizing that life would be tough without a high school education, she completed a GED program last year. Lulene just completed the job readiness course required of participants in the public assistance program, Temporary Assistance for Needy Families (TANF). She is anxious to find a job that will provide financial security for herself and the children. The work options are not very promising, though hiring is underway at a garment factory 20 miles away in a larger community. The plant offers a starting salary above minimum wage, along with fringe benefits. The problem is that Lulene has no vehicle, bad credit, and no means to get back and forth to work. Car pooling doesn't appear to be an option since no one near her residence works at the plant. However, there is a potential for community and regional asset building to make rural transportation available. Lulene's caseworker is exploring whether other TANF recipients in the county are working (or could work) at the garment factory, and whether rural public transit might be a possibility for transportation. As soon as the caseworker gathers a little more information, perhaps she and her supervisor can meet with the public transit operator who administers the transit system in this rural county.

This case scenario reveals the sad fact that lack of transportation can pose a major barrier to self-sufficiency and quality of life for welfare populations in small towns and rural areas. Social workers and other human service professionals are challenged to the task of asset building in order to make these services available locally, and beyond, to meet what Green and Haines (2002) refer to as "the challenges of regionalism" in community development (p. 7). This article explores policy implications arising from study data on rural public transit services for welfare recipients and other low-income workers to access work, educational, and job-training sites in order to make these services available. Utilizing the basic principles of Kretzmann and McKnight's (1993) asset mapping approach, we gathered information on four rural public transit systems in Oklahoma and collected primary data from transit riders. Our purpose was to gain a better understanding of transportation availability and the potential for asset building through alternative policies that can be advocated by social workers in collaboration with rural transit operators and other community and regional service providers. We

*The study was funded by a grant from Mack-Blackwell Rural Transportation Center, University of Arkansas, Fayetteville.

collected primary data from transit riders on four rural public transit systems in Oklahoma in order to better understand transportation availability and to explore alternative policies that can be advocated by social workers in collaboration with rural transit operators and other community service providers.

RURAL TRANSPORTATION REALITIES

Compared to nonrural settings, rural communities often have greater dispersion, fewer public transportation options, and poorer road conditions (Marks, Dewees, Ouellette, & Koralek, 1999). This is particularly burdensome for individuals receiving public assistance. About one in four families receiving public assistance live in rural areas and a disproportionate number reside in poverty-level households (Department of Transportation, 1998). Although automobile ownership among welfare recipients in urban areas has been the subject of researchers (Ong, 1996, 2002), very little research has focused on rural employment commuting patterns (Maggied, 1982).

Private vehicle ownership is believed to be slightly higher in rural areas than in urban areas, but nearly 57 percent of the rural poor do not own a vehicle (Rucker, 1994). One strategy to make transportation available for rural Temporary Assistance for Needy Families (TANF) participants is to make vehicle ownership or accessibility more feasible (Dewees, 2000). Some possibilities are the following: donation of vehicles to selected recipients by various organizations or social programs; purchase of surplus state and county vehicles by welfare agencies for recipients to lease, purchase, or use to travel to work; and the repair of vehicles which could be utilized (Kaplan, 1998).

Other approaches that policy makers have considered in making transportation available for TANF recipients include: taxi services; van pooling arrangements to make use of school busses and other vehicles operated by programs such as senior centers, churches, and other faith-based organizations; and encouragement for employers to provide transportation services.

Another important strategy, and the subject of this study, is to examine the role of rural public transit in providing transportation services for small town and rural welfare recipients and the working poor. Although rural public transit is not available throughout all of the rural United States, the potential of this transportation mode for serving a welfare population is worth exploring (Goldenberg, Zhang, & Dickson, 1998; Butler & Jacob, 1997; Miller, 1997).

Local social welfare departments, rural public transportation operators, and other community and regional service providers often lack asset mapping information upon which to develop policies and programs to assist welfare households. In order to explore the potential of rural public transit for welfare populations, we raised a number of questions to inquire about the nature and extent of rural public transit services, assets, and resources available; potential for advocacy in asset building; and characteristics of transit riders and their experience as riders. Questions to guide policy analysis are the following:

1. How is welfare reform likely to change demand for rural transportation?

2. What are the characteristics of rural public transit systems?

3. What are the characteristics of rural public transit riders?

4. How accommodating is rural public transit to welfare populations?

5. How can public welfare personnel and rural public transit operators work together to provide transportation services for TANF recipients and the working poor?

We set out to address these questions by first examining the mandates for work and training imposed by welfare reform legislation. Next, we collected primary data from rural transit riders and individuals who used other transportation modes for the commute to work or vocational training. Interviews were also conducted with transit operators. Data were examined to assess their utility for planning and organizing services for rural individuals affected by welfare reform. Finally, we assessed the potential for public welfare and rural transit personnel to work together in shaping policies that would address asset building for rural transportation services.

Mandates for Work

Welfare reform, as embodied in The Personal Responsibility and Work Opportunity Reconciliation Act of 1996 (PRWORA) (P.L. 104-193), contains a number of mandates for public social welfare programs to increase welfare recipients' job training and work activities. Included are work requirements and time limits for receiving TANF and food stamps. Parents, or relative care givers, in TANF cases are required to participate in work activities after receiving assistance for a maximum of two years. Also required is participation in community service within two months of receiving benefits if adult recipients are not working. A phased minimum number of work hours began with 20 hours per week for Fiscal Year 1997–98, graduating to 30 hours per week in FY 2000 and beyond. For two-parent families, the cumulative work hour requirement (both able-bodied parents) is 35 hours per week, and 20 hours for the caretaker spouse. The limit of federal financial assistance to a family under TANF is a cumulative total of five years, though states may set a shorter time frame. Able-bodied food stamp recipients ages 18 to 50 with no dependents are also required to participate in a work program for 20 hours or more a week, and they may receive benefits for only three months in every 36-month period, unless they are engaged in work or work programs. Given the TANF and Food Stamp program mandates and transportation funding opportunities, it is not surprising that there is a growing interest in rural

public transit (Community Transportation Association of America, 1999).

Description of Study Sites

Oklahoma has 16 rural public transit systems. These transit systems are designed to provide public transportation for rural areas and communities with populations of 50,000 or less. No restrictions regarding age or physical disability are placed on those who may want to use these transportation services (Oklahoma Department of Transportation, 1996). In addition, the Oklahoma Department of Human Services administers an Elderly and Persons with Disabilities program to make transportation services available for those categorical groups in both urban and rural settings.

Eligible sponsors of the rural public transit programs include local public bodies and their agencies, nonprofit organizations, and Native American tribes. Support for the rural transit systems comes primarily through grants from federal, state, and local governments. Funding is also received through contributions from local businesses, civic groups, and other government organizations (Oklahoma Department of Transportation, 1996). These rural public transit systems provide transportation to meet a wide range of transportation needs. Each system provides transportation routes specific to the area served. Typical services include travel to and from medical facilities, Head Start programs, educational facilities, and work site locations. Some transit systems also use their vehicles to deliver meals to homebound individuals and provide transportation to human service facilities.

Descriptive data for our study were drawn from four of the 16 rural public transit systems within the state. Study sites were chosen on the basis of size of operation (small to large), geographic area (regional locations in the state), diversity of populations served (gender and ethnic differences), and service characteristics (scheduled and demand response transportation, funding approaches). The work routes included three in

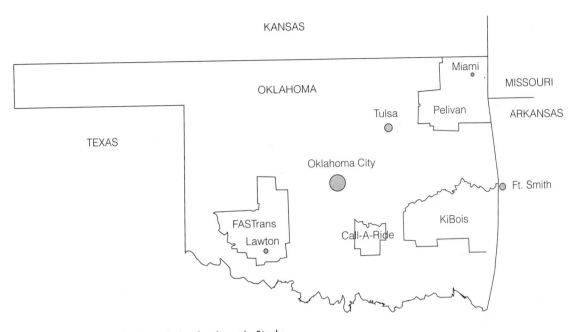

KANSAS

OKLAHOMA

Miami

MISSOURI

ARKANSAS

Tulsa

Pelivan

TEXAS

Oklahoma City

Ft. Smith

FASTrans

KiBois

Lawton

Call-A-Ride

FIGURE 20.1 Rural Public Transit Service Areas in Study

eastern Oklahoma, one work route in southwest Oklahoma, and the public transit system in east-central Oklahoma. The service areas for the four public transit systems where we collected data are graphically displayed in Figure 20.1.

The KiBois Area Transit System (KATS) began in 1983, and provides transportation in a four-county area of 109,000 residents in south-eastern Oklahoma. With a fleet of more than 35 vehicles, it is one of the larger rural transit systems in Oklahoma. The program offers both scheduled and demand response transportation (Oklahoma Department of Transportation, 1996). The authors interviewed riders on two of three KATS work routes originating in Talihina, Oklahoma, a rural crossroads community of 1,297 residents. One of the work routes chosen for study serves a garment factory 34 miles away in Wilburton, Oklahoma. Cost for this work route at the time of our study was $3.00 one-way.

The other work route drops workers at a food processing plant in Fort Smith, Arkansas, and terminates at a food processing plant in Van Buren, Arkansas, some 75 miles from origination. This work route takes approximately two hours and ten minutes travel time one-way in good weather. Cost for this route was $4.00 one-way. On each of these work routes riders gather at the origination site or are picked up at points along the route.

The Pelivan transit began in 1985, and serves a five-county area in the northeastern corner of Oklahoma with more than 160,000 residents. With a fleet of 18 vehicles it is a midsized transit system. Demand and response routes are available within the city limits of several larger cities within the area served, and special contract routes are established in other nearby cities (Oklahoma Department of Transportation, 1996). The Pelivan work route we studied originates in Miami, Oklahoma (population 13,142), and terminates in Noel, Missouri, at a food processing plant. Pelivan riders from areas outlying Miami either drive or are transported to designated pick-up locations or are picked up along the way. The route is 51 miles one way and takes approximately one hour and ten minutes of travel time. Cost for this route was $3.00 one way.

FASTrans transit system was established by the Kiowa Indian tribe, and serves over 84,000 residents in the three southwest counties of Oklahoma. With a fleet of five vehicles it is a small transit system. The FASTrans route we studied originates in Carnegie, Oklahoma (population 1,593), and terminates in Lawton, Oklahoma. The regularly scheduled route carries riders who work in Lawton as well as individuals who receive health care at the Indian Health Services clinic in Apache, Oklahoma. One-way fare ranged from $.75 to a maximum of $2.00, depending on where the rider is picked up and dropped off.

Call-A-Ride Public Transit in Ada, Oklahoma (population 16,010) began in 1974 as a transportation service for senior citizens, and expanded services to persons with disabilities and the general public. The program places an emphasis on target groups of low-income families in Pontotoc County, Oklahoma. Services are also provided to students at East Central University in Ada. The transit services we studied involve transportation for TANF recipients traveling to and from work sites and a vocational training site. TANF recipients are provided round-trip transportation from their homes in Ada, Oklahoma, and surrounding communities (as well as rural addresses). Stops are made at child-care facilities. Call-A-Ride provides the transportation service through a "fixed-fee" TANF contract from the Oklahoma Department of Human Services.

Who Rides Rural Public Transit to Work?

To find out about the characteristics of transit riders, we rode along on work routes and administered a brief survey questionnaire to transit riders on their way to work or training. A structured interview guide covered the following areas: (1) household composition, including the age and gender of head of household, (2) ages and genders of other household members, (3) data on commute patterns, (4) auto availability, and (5) welfare experience. This interview guide was also used in conducting on-site employee interviews with individuals at work sites who had used other modes of transportation to get to and from work, by driving separately, carpooling, or getting a ride from a friend or relative. Data gathering occurred in April and May of 1998 and 1999 while primary and secondary schools were in session.

We administered survey questionnaires to a total of 86 subjects, with 43% representing transit riders. A majority of transit riders were 40 years of age or less, and the greater proportion (65%) were female. Although there were similarities between transit riders and individuals who used other modes of travel, there were also several differences between the two groups worth examination. Of particular interest is a comparison between the two groups regarding household size, vehicle status, time of commute, and welfare experience.

Transit rider households were more evenly distributed in size than those who utilized other transportation modes to get to work or training (see Figure 20.2). However, transit rider households revealed a greater number containing more than four persons living in the household. We also found that in transit rider households, a greater proportion of children (60%) were 18 or younger. Close to one-fourth (24%) of transit rider households included a child less than six years of age.

Transit riders reported fewer licensed vehicles in their household, and the ones in their possession were generally older. Figure 20.3 gives a comparison of vehicle ownership per household by mode of travel. Over 43% of transit riders reported not having any licensed vehicle in the household. Even though some individuals among the other mode subjects carpooled to work or training, none reported not having a vehicle in their household. As a relative measure of vehicle value, respondents were asked to provide model and year of licensed vehicles in their household. Only 14% of transit riders had a vehicle five years old or newer in the household. By contrast, 35% of nontransit riders reported models that were five years old or newer.

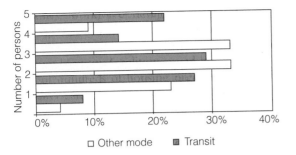

FIGURE 20.2 Household Size by Mode of Travel

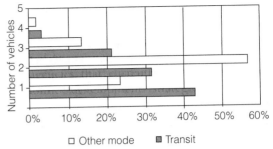

FIGURE 20.3 Vehicle Ownership per Household by Mode of Travel

Commute Distance and Time away from Home The distance a worker lived from the work site was similar for transit and other mode riders since the study controlled this variable by matching zip codes for both transit riders and the other mode group interviewed at work and training sites. Nevertheless, transit riders spent a longer time period between leaving home and returning home. This was particularly true for those working in the large food processing plants that have staggered starting and ending times for several work shifts. The transit van arrived for the first increment of a shift, but although some workers started at 4:30 P.M., other riders started at 4:45 p.m., 5:00 P.M., and 5:15 P.M. The transit van began the return trip home only after the last workers got off work. In addition, a number of the riders lived in remote areas up to 20 miles from route origin or pick up points along the way, adding to their transportation time. In most cases, for the transit riders an 8-hour work day turns out to be 10.5 to 11 hours when transportation time is added.

Welfare Experience Of the 86 subjects we interviewed, 31% reported they were currently receiving TANF, or had received benefits from the predecessor program Aid to Families with Dependent Children (AFDC), at some time during the past five years. All of those currently receiving TANF were transit riders. A total of 36% of study subjects reported they had received TANF, or had received AFDC or other benefits at some time in past. As noted in the description of

study sample, 31% currently received TANF or had received AFDC or TANF in the past five years. All of those currently receiving TANF were transit riders, primarily riding the FASTrans and Call-A-Ride transit routes. All of the seven tribal van commuters attending Vo-Tech received TANF.

What Was Learned from Transit Riders

Welfare Reform and Transportation Welfare reform, as embodied in the TANF and Food Stamp programs, places increased pressures on recipients of these programs to obtain and maintain jobs. Though other options are available to provide needed transportation for work and job training, findings from our study indicate that rural public transit can be a viable alternative. A high proportion (38%) of current TANF recipients and those who had received AFDC/TANF in the past five years currently had no vehicle in the household, and those that did have vehicles reported older vehicles than other study subjects. In Oklahoma, eligibility for TANF at the time of our study allowed an applicant to have a vehicle valued at no more than $5,000. Some states are more generous, but the fact remains that access to a dependable vehicle is a problem for many TANF or food stamp recipients. Based on these criteria, it appears that the rural transit riders we interviewed generally reveal characteristics of vehicular ownership similar to persons who fit the requirements of eligibility for TANF or food stamps, whether or not they currently received welfare at the time of our study.

Child Care and Gender Issues Study data provide information on the characteristics of rural transit riders, and also raise some important questions for potential users of the service. Almost one-fourth of the transit riders lived in households with a child less than six years of age. All of the transit riders in the study served by the Call-A-Ride transit system were TANF recipients and received transportation service to and from child care providers when required. Generally these were relatively short trips within a small town region. By contrast, the long commute to work from Talihina to Fort Smith and Van Buren, Arkansas was a night shift, and all the riders on the KATS van were males. Also, as reported, there was a longer time span for transit riders between leaving home for work and returning home after work. Moreover, child care was not available at employment sites for any of the three longer commute work sites involved in this study. Although not transportation issues per se, long commute time, lack of provisions for child care, and night or odd-hour work shifts can be imposing obstacles for TANF recipients in terms of arranging child care and other family responsibilities.

An interesting pattern emerged on the basis of gender for the three different work routes. The riders on the KATS (Talihina to Wilburton) route to the garment factory were all females. Although the Talihina to Fort Smith and Van Buren, Arkansas route to food processing plants were all male, the Pelivan route from Miami to Noel, Missouri, consisted of five males and two females. On the basis of our observations, riding the van can involve a significant opportunity for social interaction. The female riders were observed to interact with each other, particularly about family matters. On the all-male route there was little social interaction. Many factors such as time of day and the lack of commonalities between riders, may influence this social context. The attraction to riding on rural public transit may be

determined in part by the environmental factor of social interaction; this may be a worthwhile topic for further study.

Collaboration of Agencies Intuitively, welfare reform should open new possibilities for asset building through collaboration between rural public transit operators and local public welfare agencies, a belief confirmed through direct observation. Rural public transportation systems serve TANF recipients engaged in meeting work and training requirements. Passengers on regularly scheduled rural transit routes also included riders who had received welfare benefits at some time in the past but who now hold regular full-time jobs. Rural public transportation reaches more TANF recipients when the state welfare agency subsidizes the service. Our study included an example of a rural transit operator (Call-A-Ride) collaborating with a county welfare agency to receive grant funding to help TANF recipients reach work and training sites. Crain and Associates, Inc. (1999) note that transportation and social service agencies at the local level "lack an understanding of each other's goals and fear that their programs will suffer if they share scarce resources" (p. 2). Putting added resources into the equation appears to have overcome such fear in this case, and a strong working relationship developed.

The study revealed three general types of work route patterns, each representing somewhat different collaborative interactions between transit operators and potential transit riders, welfare agency personnel, employers, and others. One type of work route, represented by the KATS and Pelivan routes, consisted of transit riders gathering at a central location (and several riders picked up along the route) with a specific work destination. The FASTrans route included transit riders heading to different work sites, as well as riders traveling for reasons other than work. The Call-A-Ride trips represented current TANF welfare recipients traveling to various work sites, a vocational educational facility, and in one case a job interview site. Interviews with transit operators revealed that the roles of operators differed some-what in terms of addressing services to a welfare population.

The Call-A-Ride transit operator was the most integrally involved in providing services to TANF welfare recipients. A contractual arrange-ment with the state welfare department struc-tured the interactions among transit riders, county welfare department personnel, and employers. The transit operator and county wel-fare department were in regular contact (on a daily basis if needed) in order to provide the transportation service needed by identified TANF recipients to access work and training sites. Interaction between the transit operator and employers (and potential employers) was shared with county welfare personnel, which linked welfare recipients with needed/required jobs. In this example, welfare reform has clearly increased the demand for small town and rural transit ser-vices (particularly for TANF recipients who reside in households where no dependable vehicle is available). The other transit operators collaborate in informal ways with welfare department per-sonnel and community residents who receive welfare. Given the small size of the rural commu-nity served, one transit operator knows virtually all families in the community. When one of the four work sites served by a work route seeks to add employees, the transit operator acts as a link-ing person to notify county welfare personnel and individual welfare recipients about job open-ings. Some personnel in transit offices have pre-viously received welfare assistance, and/or employment experience at selected work sites. They are particularly active in informally recruit-ing transit riders for work sites they consider being good employment opportunities.

Funding Rural Public Transit Services

Unfortunately, in rural Oklahoma, as in the rural United States generally, public transportation services are not available in all rural areas of the state. General funding for rural public transit comes from the U.S. Department of Transportation. The Transportation Equity Act for the 21st Century (TEA 21) funds the Federal Transit Administration's Formula Grant Program for Areas Other than Urbanized Areas (Section 5311 of Title 49 of the U.S. Code). Even though this federal funding source is available, only about one-half of the nonurbanized counties in the country are served by rural public transit systems (Burkhardt, Hedrick, & McGavock, 1998). Since welfare reform began in 1996, a greater diversity of federal, state, and local resources earmarked for assisting welfare participants to work and training have emerged (Wedel & Butler, 1999). Many of these resources are linked to a competitive grant process. At the time of our study, Oklahoma rural transit operators—the operator of the KATS service in particular—were looking into the pos-sibility of expanding service areas through such funding opportunities. Conditions for collabora-tion with public welfare agencies, employers, and other interested entities in several rural counties appeared favorable.

RURAL PUBLIC TRANSIT: IMPLICATIONS FOR POLICY

The rural public transit systems addressed in this article are in themselves examples of asset build-ing within communities and regions. Citizens within these participating communities and regions united to establish transportation venues for rural residents. Their abilities to effectively collaborate, acquire recommendations from their neighbors, and explore and develop ideas have led to successful implementation of individualized plans. Citizens used their assets, both formal and informal, to offer transportation services to enhance the unique needs of their communities and regions. Informal collaboration among tran-sit operators, employers, county welfare depart-ment personnel, and potential transit riders led to asset building in areas where rural public transit systems currently exist. Rural transit operators identify strongly with their communities and regions, some having lived most or all their lives in a small town or rural setting. Several have experienced first hand the economic and social challenges faced by many individuals who decide to remain in their hometown settings. Formal collaboration is enhanced when earmarked resources are available to provide transportation services for TANF recipients. Although we did not address transportation options available in rural areas that lack public transit services, the topic should be considered a prime issue for study and asset building in communities and regions throughout the country.

We found that personal and social characteristics can influence rural public transit patronage. An example is gender and mode choice. Rural transit commuter trips may take more than an hour one-way, offering a significant opportunity for social interaction. A mixed-gender environment can be intimidating for a female rider in an otherwise male group, and vice versa. Although TANF recipients are overwhelmingly female, only one fixed-site work route in this study involved only female transit riders. Transportation to child care services was observed. Survey data

on rural public transit riders and persons using other transportation modes to work and vocational training sites revealed similarities and differences between the two groups. Most prominent were the findings that transit riders represent larger households, but have fewer and older vehicles in their households.

If TANF and other welfare programs that require recipients to work are to succeed, then program recipients must achieve the success of financial security. Program success should be measured by the personal successes of program recipients, not simply by numbers of those who leave welfare. In order for program recipients to succeed, it is critical that supporting services such as transportation be made available, accessible, and environmentally friendly to those who need them. Social workers are called upon to advocate and participate in the community and regional asset-building process as required in small town and rural areas to make this support service of transportation available. Rural public transit services for TANF and other low-income populations should not be overlooked as an opportunity for advocacy through asset building.

DISCUSSION QUESTIONS

1. Describe the rural public transit system in your community (or a rural setting identified by the group). Does it provide transportation services to work sites? Are TANF recipients encouraged to access public transportation?

2. Describe the transportation problems in a rural area with which you are familiar. Are there major barriers to transportation such as poor road conditions, limited or no public transportation options, or lack of personal vehicle ownership?

3. Select students to volunteer for role play. One student is the administrator for the

local Public Welfare Department. Another is the operator of the rural public transit system for your area. Discuss advantages and barriers to expanding services to serve TANF and low-income working poor in your rural county.

4. If you were a planner for TANF services in a regional office of the Department of Human Services, how would you go about exploring funding opportunities for rural public transportation?

CLASSROOM ACTIVITIES
AND ASSIGNMENTS

1. Imagine you are social workers at the Department of Human Services in a predominantly rural county. Each of you can identify TANF recipients similar to Lulene Allen, described in the beginning of the article. Several recipients may be able to work at a factory 20 miles away. A few of the recipients have cars, but they are not reliable and they are shared with other family members. The public transit system does not currently have a work route going to the town where the factory is located. Other jobs for which the recipients qualify do not pay enough to move them off welfare. How do you help the recipients obtain jobs and required transportation? Where would you start? Who would you contact?

2. Form groups composed of four or five students to complete any number of the following activities:

   - Arrange to visit with the appropriate administrator in your area public welfare office. The purpose of the visit is to gather information about the transportation needs of TANF recipients and the various ways the need is being met.

   - Visit the local public transit operator (if one is available). The purpose of the visit is to gather information about public transportation in your area. For example, are there any special work routes for TANF recipients?

   - Interview a professional public administrator (city manager, county administrator, or other public administrator involved with public transportation) or elected official (city councilperson, county commissioner, etc.) to learn about planning and decision making regarding public transportation.

   - Visit a business community representative, such as the local Chamber of Commerce director, to learn his or her philosophy about public transportation.

3. Research and identify the funding sources available (or potentially available) to your community for financing rural public transit in your area for TANF recipients and the working poor.

4. Design a plan to address transportation for your rural community. Consider how you would determine transportation needs. Who would you involve in the planning? What resources would be required for planning?

5. In groups of six to eight students, form coalitions to address barriers to transportation for TANF recipients and the working poor in a rural area. Determine what organizations coalition members represent, what will be the lead organization, and what resources each coalition member might commit to the asset-building process.

REFERENCES

Burkhardt, J. E., Hedrick, J. L., & McGavock, A. T. (1998). *Assessment of the economic impacts of rural public transportation*. Transportation Cooperative Research Program Report 34, Transportation Research Board. Washington, DC: National Research Council.

Butler, D., & Jacob, M. (1997). *Evaluating the role of public transportation in welfare reform*. Mack-Blackwell Transportation Center, MBTC FR-1026. University of Arkansas, Fayetteville, AR.

Community Transportation Association of America. (1999). *Access to jobs: A guide to innovative practices in welfare to work transportation.* Washington, DC: Author. Retrieved May 14, 2000, from http://www.ctaa.ntrc/atj/pubs/innovative.

Crain & Associates, Inc. (1999). *Using public transportation to reduce the economic, social and human costs of personal immobility.* Transportation Cooperative Research Program Report 49. Washington, DC: Transportation Research Board, National Research Council.

Department of Transportation, Federal Transit Administration (1998). *Access to jobs and training.* Washington, DC: Author. Retrieved March 11, 1998, from http://www.fta.dot.gov/library/legal/reauthissues/issurs4.html.

Dewees, S. (2000). *Transportation in rural communities: Strategies for serving welfare participants and low-income individuals.* Calverton, MD: Macro International, Inc.

Goldenberg, L., Zhang, J., & Dickson, C. (1998). Assessment of JOBLINKS demonstration projects: Connecting people to the workplace and implications for welfare reform. In National Research Council (Ed.), *Transportation Research Record 1618* (pp. 3–13). Washington, DC: Transportation Research Board, National Research Council.

Green, G. P., & Haines, A. (2002). *Asset building & community development.* Thousand Oaks, CA: Sage Publications.

Kaplan, A. (1998, June). Transportation: The essential need to address the "to" in welfare-to-work. *Welfare Information Network Issue Notes, 2* (10). Retrieved August 15, 1998, from http://www.welfareinfo.org/transita.html.

Kretzmann, J. P., & McKnight, J. L. (1993). *Building communities from the inside out: A path toward finding and mobilizing a community's assets.* Chicago: ACTA Publications.

Maggied, H. S. (1982). *Transportation for the poor: Research in rural mobility.* Boston: Kluwer Nijhoff Publishing.

Marks, E. L., Dewees, S., Ouellette, T., & Koralek, R. (1999). *Rural welfare to work strategies: Research synthesis.* Calverton, MD: Macro International, Inc.

Miller, J. (1997). *Welfare reform in rural areas: A special community transportation report.* Washington, DC: Community Transportation Center of America. Retrieved August 12, 1998, from http://www.ctaa.org/ct/sepoct97/rural-welfare.shml.

Oklahoma Department of Transportation. (1996). *1996 directory of public transportation in Oklahoma.* Oklahoma City, OK: Author.

Ong, P. M. (1996). Work and automobile ownership among welfare recipients. *Social Work Research, 20*(4), 255–262.

Ong, P. M. (2002). Car ownership and welfare-to-work. *Journal of Policy Analysis and Management, 21*(2), 239–252.

Personal Responsibility and Work Opportunity Reconciliation Act of 1996. Pub. L. No. 104-193, 110 Stat. 2105 (1996).

Rucker, G. (1994). *Status report on public transportation in rural America, 1994.* Rural Transit Assistance Program, Federal Transit Administration. Washington, DC: Department of Transportation. Also available from the Community Transportation Center of America. Retrieved June 15, 2000, from http://www.ctaa.org/ntrc/rtap/pubs/statns/.

Transportation Equity Act for the 21st Century. Pub. L. No. 105-178, 112 Stat. 107 (1998).

Wedel, K. R., & Butler, F. C. (1999). Welfare reform and demand for rural public transportation. In I. B. Carlton-LaNey, R. L. Edwards, & P. N. Reid (Eds.), *Preserving and strengthening small towns and rural communities.* Washington, DC: NASW Press.

INFOTRAC COLLEGE EDITION

job access
rural public transit

transportation
welfare reform

21

Voices from the Mountains

Living on and Past Welfare

BARRY L. LOCKE

LUCINDA A. POTTER

Public Law 104-93, the Personal Responsibility and Work Opportunity Reconciliation Act of 1996—better known as welfare reform—brought forth a major shift in how the United States would care for its most vulnerable families. This law shifted the nature of the government's contract to care for these families away from its original basis as an entitlement program. Under entitlement, families who met specified criteria (e.g., their income was below a certain level) automatically qualified for benefits. Now, under welfare reform, programs are based on charity and dependent upon the willingness of the society to support those less able to function in the economy. The very adoption of this law demonstrates that the society is less willing to meet this obligation for care. The reform set in place time limits, spending caps via the Temporary Assistance for Needy Families (TANF) block grant, and a "work first" mentality that downplayed education. Such a policy ignores the value of asset building, especially as it concerns the building of social capital through education. Social capital according to Putnam (2000) is the "social networks and the associated norms of reciprocity" that provide the bridging and bonding capital that supports both the need for internal identity and the external links to a range of assets (pp. 21–22). It is in the development of social capital that individuals and rural communities will likely find success.

This policy also runs counter to the hopes and behaviors of many adults recently associated with the program. For example, between 20–30% of the respondents studied in West Virginia indicated that they had volunteered in their community. A majority also indicated they desired a better future for their children. These client behaviors and dreams run counter to a public perception that they are lazy and unmotivated. Popular views supported a process of welfare reform designed to change people's behavior, while ignoring systemic barriers to success.

One of the more positive developments in welfare reform has been the degree of research associated with it. Several national and state studies have been conducted that attempt to determine how the people being served by this program, as well as those leaving it, have fared. Two such studies have taken place in West Virginia and provided the data for this article (Dilger, et al., 2000; and Dilger, et al., 2001). The first study was conducted by an interdisciplinary research team at West Virginia University, in partnership with the West Virginia Department of Health and Human Services (WV DHHR). This study investigated the circumstances of former clients who had left the TANF program, also known as WV WORKS, during 1998. The same research team conducted this second study and investigated the circumstances of current clients who remained on the program in 2000.

METHODOLOGY

The two studies utilized a consistent strategy of mailing a survey to a randomly drawn and scientifically valid sample. To encourage participation in the 10-page survey, a participation fee of $15.00 was paid to those who completed the survey and returned a fee request that was separated from the data, so that identification of specific respondents would not be possible. One follow-up mailing was done for each survey.

Study One, of former recipients, was conducted during the summer of 1999 and used only closed cases that included former adult recipients (child-only cases were excluded). The sample size was 1,920 former recipients out of a universe of 18,254 and the response rate was 50.1% (N = 962). The second study, of current recipients, was conducted during the summer of 2000 and used only open cases with at lease one adult recipient in them (child-only cases were excluded). The sample size for this study was 2,100 out of a universe of 8,307, with a response rate of 57.4% (N = 1,206). The samples drawn were representative of the universe within the state. A review of fee requests suggests that the respondents matched closely the universe from which they were drawn.

The survey instrument itself was a series of both closed and open-ended questions. For example, respondents were asked to check lists of activities they engaged in and rate the effectiveness of some of their experiences, and were given the opportunity to respond to open-ended questions. Although analyzing the open-ended questions was a challenge, the degree to which respondents chose to answer them provides a richer understanding of how TANF clients, both former and current, see their role and opportunities for working toward building a better life for themselves and their children.

In the remainder of this article we will describe the first review of this data and build some links to the policy issues that must be addressed as policymakers move into the second round of welfare reform. Given the fact that West Virginia is a very rural state, with a history of persistent rural poverty, the voices of these respondents may provide much needed insight into the challenges policymakers face as we move toward the next stages of welfare reform.

WEST VIRGINIA

To assist the reader with understanding the findings, it is necessary to place West Virginia in context. West Virginia, located in the Mid-Atlantic region, is the only state whose entire borders are found within the Appalachian region. During the decade of the 1990s, the state experienced very modest growth (1.8 million new residents). Its largest city and the state capitol, Charleston, has 54,598 residents. By comparison, Houston, the largest city in the state of Texas, has more residents than the entire state of West Virginia. In terms of educational attainment, West Virginia ranks last in the United States in the percentage of residents 25 years and older who have completed high school (77.1%) and 48th in the percentage of those same residents who hold a Bachelor's degree or higher (17.9%) (U.S. Census Bureau, 2002). Not surprisingly West Virginia ranks last in income (median family income of $29,052) and has a high poverty rate (16.8%) (U.S. Census Bureau, 2002). Finally, the Appalachian Regional Commission has declared almost one-half of the states' 55 counties (26) ARC Distressed Counties. Such counties are so designated because of their high unemployment and poverty rates over time. The unemployment rate over a three-year period has to be at least 1.5 times the U.S. average, as does the poverty rate (Distressed designation and county economic status classification system, 2002).

As welfare reform moved forward in West Virginia a rather unique asset emerged in the voluntary sector. This asset, know as the West Virginia Welfare Reform Coalition, was created to educate, study, and advocate around emerging policy issues associated with welfare reform implementation. This private membership coalition included individuals and organizational groups across the private and public spectrum. Groups such as American Friends Service Committee, National Association of Social Workers, West Virginia Department of Health and Human Resources (DHHR), legal services, women's organizations, private business, faculty from higher education, as well as a wide range of interested individuals, came together to better understand the new policy. From that effort came an education campaign created for current clients and others likely to apply to the TANF program about the likely consequences of welfare reform. Information was disseminated to the business and local government sectors, as well as a major newspaper. The coalition, in some respects acting like a Strategic Bridging Collaborative, was instrumental in bringing a major conference to the State Capitol. They also worked with the legislature on some needed policy changes in the second year of the program. This coalition helped to keep a dialogue open between policy advocates, clients, and the policymakers in the public agency.

Families in Poverty

The two studies (Dilger, et al., 2000, 2001) bring into sharp relief the realities of poverty in a rural state. The respondents to the first study (former recipients) reported that although they were for the most part employed (54.4% reported receiving wages or a salary) they remained in poverty, with 82.9% of the respondents reporting annual household incomes of less than $10,000 per year. Additionally, 19.6% of former recipients reported that the reason their TANF benefits were discontinued was because they received funds from nonemployment sources (like Social Security or child support), while only 6.1% reported losing benefits because of some form of program sanction. Program sanctions ranged from grant reduction to case closure for noncompliance, with the personal responsibility contract developed for each applicant. The contract is a written plan specifying client behaviors regarding the search for work, childcare, and child support; and the responsibility of the client to attain self-sufficiency.

Current recipients reported similar or even more challenging data, with 91.1% of the respondents reporting annual household incomes of less than $10,000 and placement on the TANF program more than once (78.3%). Although 69.6% of the former recipients indicated that they had at least attained the GED, only 60.4% of those remaining on TANF reported that they had done so. Family size, often a concern among the public, was similar for both study cohorts. Seventy-two percent of former recipients had one or two children in their households, as did 70.2% of current recipients. One important difference between the two cohorts, especially when one thinks of assets that may be necessary for moving toward self-sufficiency, was access to a telephone. Former recipients had much greater access to this resource (92%) than did current recipients (only 57%). When families do not have phone access, it is much more challenging to contact or provide information, such as work opportunities, to them.

Financial and Personal Well-Being

Although the questions are not identical, which makes comparative analysis more difficult, both cohorts were asked questions that addressed how they saw their financial and personal well-being. Former recipients appeared more optimistic about their current well-being, with 43% reporting they feel better off financially and 47% reporting they felt better off personally as compared to when they were on TANF. Only 26% felt worse off financially, and 20% indicated that they were worse off personally. Although such a question would not be appropriate for current recipients, they were asked to speculate about their future. From a financial viewpoint, 49% of the current recipients rated their financial future as poor, with only 16% seeing it as good. At the personal level, 36% of the current recipients rated it as poor, with 26% seeing it as good. Respondents were asked to give their views about how they saw their children's future. Sixty-four percent of former recipients felt their children's future was good, with only 9% rating it as poor. Current recipients were less positive, with

50% rating their childrens' future as good, and 19% rating it as poor. This data is somewhat disturbing, as those currently receiving welfare appeared less hopeful. This tendency continued with the question that asked both cohorts to rate how confident they were in their ability to provide for their family in the future. Given the social pressure to be good parents and breadwinners that still inform the family structure in West Virginia, the results here were somewhat surprising. West Virginia has long embraced family responsibility, yet only 65% of former recipients agreed that they were confident they could provide for their families. This falls to a level of 56% for current recipients. Often, a person's negative perception of their abilities serves to create the feared outcome. Unfortunately, these predictions suggest that many children who have been part of the new welfare system may not face a positive future.

Respondents were also asked about the kinds of personal or family emergencies they may have experienced from time to time. Those no longer on TANF indicated that they have experienced some events more frequently than when they had been receiving cash assistance. For example, there was a sharp increase in the percentage who reported they had experienced times when they lacked money to purchase food, glasses, or medicine, or go to the dentist, or doctor. The average percentage who indicated these kind of problems while on TANF ranged from 15.3% to 32.2%. Since leaving TANF these respondents reported experiencing these problems in a range from 39.8% to 59.3%. Consistent with the overall finding that those remaining on TANF are more vulnerable, the range for respondents still on TANF who experienced these kind of programs went from 34.5% to 55.6%.

The two groups of respondents turned to different places for assistance. Current recipients were much more involved in other public programs like Food Stamps, Medicaid, school lunches, and school clothing vouchers. Former recipients were less likely to continue to use these programs, even though their financial circumstances might suggest potential eligibility to use

them. Rather, former recipients tended to increase their use of private sector programs like food pantries (13.9%) and assistance from churches (7.7%).

Respondents were provided with an opportunity to respond to several open-ended questions that sought their perceptions about actions they could take to improve their personal and family well-being, and changes they would like to see to the TANF program. Each of these questions received several hundred responses; with the range being a low of 581 and the highest being 982.

Improving Recipient's Well-Being

Two of the questions addressed each former recipient's sense of the one thing that could be done to improve their personal well-being, as well as the one thing that could improve their family's well-being. Regarding their personal well-being, the 803 former recipients tended to cluster their responses around the following:

1. Get a job or better paying job (29.4%)
2. Get more education (16.3%)
3. Get more money (9.6%)
4. Get medical insurance (9.0%)
5. Get healthy (6.6%)
6. Improve self-confidence (5.2%)

A very selective sample of the actual statements of the former recipients is provided to illustrate the range of the actual comments provided by them.

"Less stress from working two jobs trying to provide for my family and live comfortably."

"Find a good paying job that will not totally screw me up about receiving help paying rent, utilities. It is a setup, if you make just a little over allowable they take away your food stamps, and what you make over will not make up for loss of food stamps, or they have you pay 3/4 rent and still you are not any further ahead, only out of food stamps and money and still in debt with no way out."

"To someday own my own business."

"Nothing. I am proud of my accomplishments. Since 1998, I have bought a home, acquired health and dental insurance and a steady job."

"Find a secure job."

"Win the lottery."

"I would like to find a job in the field of my degree, which is a social work B. A. degree, in the area in which I live. I would like to be able to provide health insurance for my family. I would like to have [help] up until I could afford food with money."

"I need a miracle."

"For my children to be well and happy. To be able to care for my family more financially. Not having to worry from day to day, month to month, what bill to put off and take a chance on a cut-off notice. To know my children will be able to further their education after high school if they choose."

Improving Family Well-Being

A second question asked the former recipients to identify the one thing that could be done to improve their family's well-being. Their responses, 753 of them, clustered around the following:

1 Get a job or better paying job (29.1%)
2. Get more money (11.3%)
3. Get better housing (10.1%)
4. Get more education (8.1%)
5. Get healthy (5.8%)
6. Move (4.4%)

Although the responses are quite similar to those of the personal well-being question, there is one important difference. Better housing and the possibility of moving made the final list of clustered responses. This would suggest that the respondents are well-grounded in the issues faced within West Virginia. Although West Virginia has one of the highest, possibly the highest, rate of home-

ownership in the nation, much of that housing is substandard, suggesting that quality housing is a challenge for these low-income families, especially those in smaller towns. The West Virginia economy has struggled for many decades and the recognition of this reality is found in the expressed desire to relocate, often outside the state, as well as the recognition that better paying jobs are necessary to improve the circumstances of the respondents.

Improving Well-Being of Recipients and Their Families

In the second study current recipients were asked a combined version of these questions. This was done based on the fact that many respondents remarked on how they saw the personal well-being and family well-being questions as basically the same thing. This change limits the ability to do direct comparisons but the combined question did result in very similar responses. The most frequent responses, among the 982 provided, clustered around:

1. Find a good or better paying job (33.0%)
2. Get more education or training (12.5%)
3. Get healthy (10.2%)
4. Nothing (6.9%)
5. Get more money (6.6%)
6. Find reliable transportation (6.4%)
7.   Get better housing (5.7%)
8. Resolve child care/child support issues (5.4%)

Although these responses mirror to some degree those of the former recipients, two differences become apparent. Current recipients appear to be less hopeful about the possibility that something could be done to improve their circumstances. The fourth-highest ranking was for the idea that nothing could be done. This was expressed by the use of words like "nothing, none, n/a, unknown" and phrases like "A miracle! Do you provide those?" Almost 7% of the respondents made this choice. Facing a 60-month time limit, this reality suggests that the public agency, not to mention the families themselves, may be facing an important barrier here. The other important issue is the concern about childcare and child support needs. Those who listed this concern often expressed the need as "better child care" or "if their father would pay child support." If we get better at collecting such support, it may be possible to give families more money as well as reduce the stigma of being part of the welfare system.

Health Care Needs

Both study cohorts raise the issue of health. Many of the responses noted the need for health care for debilitating illness, as well as rehabilitation services to return to employment. When looking at public health data, West Virginia is a leader in most negative health categories. This is reflected in the low-income families as well. A much-mentioned solution to getting more money was to qualify for disability benefits. In fact, at a recent meeting on welfare reform in West Virginia, it was noted that the West Virginia Department of Health and Human Resources looked into establishing a contract with the state Legal Services Plan to work with current TANF clients to establish their eligibility for disability benefits like SSI (Boothe, 2002). With the call for increasing work participation rates to 70% under TANF, reauthorization states like West Virginia will be at increased risk of meeting that standard with large numbers of clients who may not be able to enter into the workforce.

Improving WV WORKS

Former recipients gave rather surprising answers to the question of what would be the one thing that they would change about the WV WORKS program. The most frequent responses were:

1. Improve the sensitivity of DHHR employees (17.1%)

2. Provide additional help finding work (13.9%)

3. Provide transitional benefits (10.1%)

4. Ease eligibility standards (8.1%)

5. Provide more money (7.0%)

6. Provide more assistance for education/college (6.9%)

A sampling of specific illustrative comments for this question were:

> "For them to start getting on dead beat dads (such as my ex-husband) to start paying child support. In my case WORKS did nothing about it."

> "Change some people's attitude that works for them, because some of them stinks!!"

> "Everything! They just do not understand. They have not been where I am but they can still sit back and not give a [expletive] what happens to me and may [sic] family."

> "Get people off of WV WORKS that do not really need it."

> "That they would not count SSI as earned income."

> "In WV WORKS people are not as stupid as they are treating them. Stop! Thinking and acting smarter and better than your clients."

> "Do not cut people off of assistance as soon as they find a job. Give them 2-3 months to get financially settled in their new job."

> "More jobs in WV for WV people to work and out of state people not to come in and take them away from us."

> "I just would like to never see it or hear of it again."

> "I would not change anything."

> "I would not change WV WORKS. I would change the employers at DHHR. They are hateful and should not treat people like bum and other things I shouldn't say."

> "Start investigating more people in the housing projects. There is more fraud going on than you think."

"Fire all those workers and hire those that care. That is saying it as kind as possible."

"More help for those who want to help themselves. Instead of the lazy ones. It is just not right for the working person."

Current recipients were also invited to identify the one thing that they would change about WV WORKS. The most frequent responses were:

1. Nothing (18.0%)
2. Provide more help finding a job or a better paying job (11.0%)
3. Eliminate or extend time limit (10.7%)
4. Increase benefits (8.7%)
5. Improve information/flexibility (8.3%)
6. Improve their workers' demeanor (6.5%)
7. Provide more education or training (4.9%)
8. Provide more help with transportation (3.7%)

These responses differ from former recipients in several ways. The first difference is the level of concern expressed about the workers they encountered. Current recipients were a full 10% under the level expressed by former recipients. It is worth recalling that this was an open-ended question with no prompts. For the former recipients, the sensitivity of workers was seen as the area needing the greatest change. Given the rapid implementation of welfare reform it is entirely possible that many states, like West Virginia, asked eligibility workers to assume a more direct practice role with the clients. In their new role as Family Support Specialists, staff was expected to have expanded knowledge of employment systems and apply professional judgment to client circumstances. Often this was done with little or no professional development. This study suggests an on-going need for professional training.

The fact that the largest response from current recipients was that they had no recommendation, or that they saw nothing to be changed, is more difficult to interpret. It is possible that those who chose this response (some 18%) may in fact be satisfied with how the program works for them. It is also possible that even though the researchers went to great lengths to set the research apart from the WV DHHR, some current recipients did not feel comfortable offering what may be seen as criticism of the state agency. Equally plausible, given the greater appearance of hopelessness in the current recipients, is that they do not see any way to make things better.

Current recipients were also asked what they thought the best thing was about WV WORKS. The most frequent responses were:

1. Help in finding a job (16.7%)
2. Help in general (15.0%)
3. Food stamps and/or Medicaid (12.5%)
4. Education/training (11.3%)
5. Nothing (11.3%)

As a works-first program, the focus on getting a job is not surprising and it has worked for some of the respondents. The other items reflect tangible resources that help people meet basic needs for food, medical care, and so on. The 11% who said "nothing" may continue to reflect those who do not see much improvement within their lives. Although a relatively small group, there is concern that they may have multiple barriers to self-sufficiency. Given the very deep cuts in the active caseload within West Virginia, it is possible that those who remain on the rolls may be those that present many more barriers to leaving than the system can manage. This is particularly true for rural areas where survey respondents were less optimistic about the future and were more likely to be unemployed and lack access to transportation and childcare services (Dilger, et al., 2001, p. 17).

Volunteerism

Both of the welfare reform studies in West Virginia asked respondents about their level of volunteer activity. The interest in this activity was associated with the belief that volunteering was another way to be integrated within one's community, as well as a means to further develop social capital as a valued asset for the goal of self-sufficiency. Not unlike the findings of Putnam (2000), the majority of the respondents were not active volunteers. However, 30% of the current recipients did indicate some level of volunteer activity, with the largest number, again approximately 43%, linked with schools or Head Start. At the community level, the largest number of those responding (11%) indicated that they volunteered with programs serving the elderly. Former recipients tended to be less active; this could reflect the fact that volunteering may on occasion be used as a TANF-related work activity, making it something less than a pure choice by the client, with only 19.6% indicating they were active volunteers. Again volunteering with schools or Head Start (26%) lead the way, with volunteering with children activities (13.3%) the leading community activity. Finally, consistent with the findings of Putnam (2000), very few of the volunteers were associated with volunteer fire departments. Between 2–3% of all respondents noted this as a volunteer activity, which is somewhat surprising given the importance such institutions play in many of the small towns and rural areas that exist within the state.

Volunteerism is an important way to develop and add to one's assets, in addition to giving back to the community. The respondents in both studies named several assets they thought they possessed for employment; those same assets could be further refined through their volunteer experiences. Volunteering expands the network they have access to, as well as supports their integration into the community. The fact that the respondents are engaged in service to their communities at about the same level as the society in general suggests that low-income families do connect with community. Social workers will want to help their clients take advantage of this expanding network in seeking expanded economic opportunities, along the lines discussed by Wedel and Butler (see Article 20) about rural transit drivers being a source of information for low-income persons seeking jobs.

CONCLUSIONS

Many of these findings are consistent with the historical findings associated with the "voices" of recipients in the "welfare system" (Schein, 1995; Rank, 1994; and Chisman, 1992). The system appears to be one that asks the participant to pay a very high psychological cost in terms of self-esteem. Although we may have ended welfare as we knew it in 1996, that high cost appears to continue to be part of the current reform effort. This interpretation is reinforced by the fact that the workers' lack of sensitivity was so very important to former recipients, and that they were likely to forego other benefits for which they remained eligible, such as Food Stamps. Once away from the system, even when current economic circumstances appear to be less than adequate, former recipients thought that they were "better off." We should not jump to the conclusion that this is a reason to do away with programs; rather we need to listen carefully to what is being said and seek ways to nurture a sense of personal worth as we offer assistance to those living in difficult places and spaces.

Although not its intent, welfare reform policy may end up helping those in the public human services discover the value of asset thinking. To be successful, clients and those who help them must move away from just seeing the deficits associated with their situation and actively name the assets—an individual asset map if you will—upon which the goal of employment can be built. This use of strengths, while common to the social work profession, is often lacking in program policy. Social workers are in a rather unique position to use this knowledge to shape program policy. To illustrate, the possible contract with legal services to assist clients who appear to meet the disability requirements of the Supplemental Security Income (SSI) program mentioned earlier in this article reflects the goal of finding the best program fit between the client's need and available resources. Asset thinking leads both the client and the worker in this direction. As clients build their asset base, they are then better positioned to further engage their social contexts with increased confidence and power.

Additionally, these studies reinforce the value of quality research in the public policy process. Shortly after the initial effort was done and its results found their way into the public debates about welfare reform taking place within the state, policy advocates associated with the West Virginia Welfare Reform Coalition began to use the findings to push policy modifications. For example, the advocates, including NASW and the American Friends Service Committee project in West Virginia, were successful in convincing the state legislature to require the public agency to stop counting SSI benefits as an asset in determining TANF eligibility (about one-third of the original case closures had been a result of the decision to count them). Additionally, the data were used to build a case for allowing education, including college participation, to count as a work activity. The research team had been very careful to remain neutral in the presentation of the findings and the ensuing policy debates. This was important in demonstrating to the state agency that the interest was on quality research, and not the pursuit of a political agenda. This resulted in the second study of current recipients that only added to the level of understanding about how welfare reform was being experienced within the state. Finally, it is worth noting the value of interdisciplinary research in an effort such as this one. The research team was composed of faculty from the disciplines of Political Science, Public Administration, Sociology, and Social Work. Although at times frustrating and challenging, the effort was also rewarding, in that a better product emerged from the various viewpoints as the work was done.

As with any good research, more questions need to be addressed by future projects. A few important questions are: How can programs and services better address the multiple barriers many current recipients appear to face? Have we created a delivery system where we have both victimized workers and victimized clients? Has the social work profession contributed to this by basically abandoning poverty as a focus issue for its efforts? Can persistent rural poverty effectively be addressed within the context of weakening economic structures? Given the income levels associated with work in a persistently rural state, can there be a viable discussion about a "living wage" and a minimally acceptable standard of living for all of our citizens?

There is value in asking those influenced by policy choices just what took place and how to improve upon their experiences. While this lesson should be obvious, it is often ignored in the policy process. Anna Quindlen (2002) wrote about the need for lawmakers and other elites to work to bridge the gaps in their understanding of how people live with the consequences of their policy decisions. Several respondents took time to thank the research team for inviting them to participate in the survey and for the opportunity to tell their story. One legitimate concern with the recent TANF reauthorization debates may very well be that policymakers will continue to focus attention on work first, think about the fact that the minimum wage has not increased in six years, and miss the opportunity to think more carefully about ways to support poverty reduction.

It appears clear that the respondents, in the best sense of this phrase, are "just plain folks." They share their time and talents volunteering and they desire to provide a better future for their children, as well as express a desire for self-sufficiency through work. The degree to which social welfare policy continues to be predicated on the assumptions that the recipients are somehow very different, and in need of some form of behavior change and management, is likely to result in continuing failure. This failure will keep many families living in hard spaces and places.

DISCUSSION QUESTIONS

1. Why do you think the ex-clients say they are better off now than when on welfare?

2. In what ways do you think the rural context was influential in the views expressed by the clients in the two studies reported on in this article?

3. Based on your reading of this article, what two policy changes might you advocate for in the next round of TANF reauthorization? Why? How can we support and facilitate low-income people to have greater access to legislative decisionmakers?

4. What may the concerns about their workers' attitudes tell us about the way that we offer services?

5. What does the clients voice in this article say about how this society sees social welfare and its obligation to care for the poor? What actions might you take as a citizen to better support low-income working families?

6. Given that most of the clients say they want to work, what might be done in our society to better support work? How would you better ensure a living wage for those who work? What about our society would make adopting your recommendation difficult?

CLASSROOM ASSIGNMENTS AND ACTIVITIES

1. Visit a local food pantry or homeless shelter and spend some time talking with persons who use its service. Your goal is to try and learn about their story and how they experience life. You are not to solve their problems, but get to know them as people.

2. In small groups, share with one another your own help-seeking experiences. Listen for how those experiences were or were not empowering. Did your experiences feel like those of the clients in the welfare reform studies? What does this suggest for how we should extend the offer of help to another person?

3. In teams of two, visit the local public welfare agency. Sit in the waiting room and observe what takes place there. What did you see that could help you understand how policy is designed to send certain messages to the clients about who they are and what they should be doing.

REFERENCES

Boothe, F. (2002, April). WV DHHR TANF Update: Remarks to the 2002 Spring Conference of WV-NASW, Charleston, WV.

Chisman, F. P. (1992). *It's not like they say: Welfare recipients talk about welfare, work, and education.* Washington, DC: The Southpoint Institute for Policy Analysis.

Dilger, R. J., Blakely, E., Dorton, K. V. H., Latimer, M., Locke, B., Mencken, C., Plein, L. C., Potter, L. M., Williams, D., & Yoon, D. P. (2000). West Virginia case closure study. *The West Virginia Public Affairs Reporter, 17*(1), 2–15.

Dilger, R. J., Blakely, E., Latimer, M., Locke, B., Mencken, C., Plein, L. C., Potter, L. M., & Williams,

D. (2001). WV WORKS: The recipients perspective. *The West Virginia Public Affairs Reporter. 18*(3), 2–19.

Distressed designation and county economic status classification system. (2002). Retrieved July 23, 2002, from http//www.arc.gov.

Putnam, R. D. (2000). *Bowling alone: The collapse and revival of American community.* New York: Simon & Schuster.

Quindlen, A. (2002, July 1). Staring across a great divide. *Newsweek,* 64.

Rank, M. R. (1994). *Living on the edge: The realities of welfare in America.* New York: Columbia University Press.

Schein, V. E. (1995). *Working from the margins: Voices of mothers in poverty.* Ithaca, NY: Cornell University Press.

U.S. Census Bureau (2002). *2001 Statistical abstract of the United States.* Retrieved July 31, 2002, from http://www.census.gov/prod/2002pubs/01statab /stat-ab01.html.

INFOTRAC COLLEGE EDITION

Appalachia
TANF

welfare reform
West Virginia

PART V

✳

Using Research
to Evaluate Practice
in Rural Settings

DENNIS L. POOLE

Asset building and research go hand in hand. Knowledge generated through research informs asset-building processes, heightens sensitivity to local perspectives, improves the accuracy of assessments, and enhances the potential to achieve desired outcomes in policies and programs. Research is not the only source of knowledge. But unlike intuition, tradition, and experience, research generates knowledge through systematic observations and scientific methods.

Social workers have contributed significantly to research in rural communities. Still, we owe a great historical debt to rural sociologists, the first social scientists to study rural community as a shared way of life. They contributed as well to decades of research on rural community development processes, laying the early conceptual foundations of asset-based development.

Professional education equips social workers with knowledge and skills in research. Many excellent textbooks are available to us. Here we need to emphasize, however, that the chief purpose of research in asset building is to be a catalyst for community action. Our primary role is not to conduct research for rural communities, but to facilitate processes that generate knowledge for asset-building purposes. The findings should cry out for community attention and action.

Research begins by asking the right questions. Typically the questions we ask relate to accountability: What services do people need? How should a program be designed? Do people benefit more from one program than another? Are outcomes achieved efficiently? Community leaders usually ask broader questions, however. We must respond to these questions even though they do not fit neatly within our particular service domain. In asset building the rural social worker is a jack of all trades.

Our research questions usually flow from problem statements. This is not surprising. Many of us have been taught that the purpose of social work research is to help people solve complex and difficult problems. But putting human problems at the starting point of research reinforces a tendency in professional circles to view rural communities from a perspective of deficiencies and weaknesses. To counter the tendency, we begin this part with Murty's article on asset mapping. Asset-building research normally begins with an inventory of the assets and strengths of local institutions, associations, networks, people, and patterns of helping.

It is also easy for professionals to focus too much on methods rather than processes at this stage of research. The operative term to recall is participatory ownership. Our role is to facilitate processes to ensure that community members assume a leadership position in decision making. Thomas, Albaugh, and Albaugh demonstrate how to involve community members in all components of a research project: topic identification, design, data collection, analysis, interpretation, and policy formulation.

Once the assets of a community are identified, and processes are in place to involve local people in the study, the next challenge is to generate valid and reliable information. Qualitative and quantitative research methods are at our disposal. Qualitative research methods emphasize depth of understanding through rich observation, usually with a small number of cases. Words rather than numbers are generally used to describe the findings and to discern the patterns in relationships. Conway and her coauthors demonstrate the use of qualitative methods in their article. In-depth personal interviews were conducted with six adults who lived in out-of-home care as adolescents. Their reflections on the experience helped child welfare planners identify better ways to achieve federally mandated outcomes through family-centered, community-based services.

Quantitative research methods emphasize numerical explanations of phenomena. Production of statistical findings from a large number of cases, or representative sample, characterizes most quantitative studies. The article contributed by Shields and colleagues, for example, reports findings from a random sample of 3,000 residents in southeast Ohio. The purpose of the study was to evaluate media campaigns to increase public awareness of domestic violence. Survey data revealed that these campaigns had little discernable effect on public awareness. Community groups were forced to reexamine the strategies they use to disseminate information on domestic violence in rural areas.

Some studies utilize both quantitative and qualitative research methods. Grinstein-Weiss and Curley's article on the individual development account (IDA) program in rural Minnesota is one example. This program allowed low-income participants to use accumulated assets for home purchases, home improvements, microenterprise, and education. Quantitative data explained the effects of IDAs on the savings of program participants; and qualitative data gathered from administrators and staff identified advantages and challenges for implementing IDA programs in rural communities.

Frequently rural communities need external assistance to generate valid and reliable information. We must help outside experts understand that their main role in asset-building research is to assist community members, not to control or experiment on them. Thus, we close this part on community-university partnerships, contributed by Cooper and Morales. University-based researchers must win the trust of the community, and the community must appreciate their need to share findings with a larger audience.

22

Mapping Community Assets

The Key to Effective Rural Social Work

SUSAN MURTY

*Rural communities are like nuts. It takes time and work to break the shell,
but once you break in, you are rewarded for your effort!*

Have you ever driven through a small town and wondered, "What do people *do* here?", or said to yourself, "This town does not seem to have much of anything!", or "This is Nowheresville!" These are perceptions based on expectations of urban life. Rural residents probably have different perceptions. Some people say that if you drive through a rural community, there is nothing to do. But if you live there, you never have an evening free! If you have lived in a rural community, you know that they are very busy places with many things to do and strong community assets.

An essential step in assessing a rural community is mapping its assets. The goal is to find out what are the strengths of that particular community. Who are the strong community leaders? What organizations get things done there? Where do people go to discuss things and get help with problems? What resources are available and where are they? This approach is an application of the strengths approach recommended by Saleebey (2002) applied at the community level. The idea is that communities have the capacity to deal with their own problems and to assist individuals and families who live there when they need help.

In an urban community, how would you locate community assets? Maybe you would study the phone book, or a directory of social services. For example, the United Way often publishes a list of the social services that they fund. Or you might go to an organization that provides infor-

mation and referral and ask them about the resources and organizations.

In a rural community it is not so easy. There are fewer formal organizations. There may be a lot of resources and assets, but they are likely to be informal and there may not be lists you can refer to. You will have to work a little more to find the assets. If you take on the challenge, it is kind of like a treasure hunt to search for the assets of a rural community.

One of the things that makes rural community asset mapping a challenge is that each rural community is a little different. Urban communities tend to have a fairly predictable set of formal resources. But each rural community is somewhat unique. In this article, you will learn how to identify some of the assets of a rural community. But to apply what you learn, you will have to spend some time in a particular rural community to discover its assets.

PURPOSE OF ASSET MAPPING IN RURAL SOCIAL WORK

Asset mapping is part of assessing a community. This is a little different than the typical "needs assessment" because you assess the strengths, assets, and resources of the community. It is a strengths approach to community assessment; rather than focusing only on needs and problems, you look for the strengths a community has. You find out the resources it has to offer and the ways it solves problems and assists its residents when they need help. Saleebey (2002) states that "the first steps in the development process do not focus on the problems, deficits, and conflicts of the community. Rather, the emphasis is on first discovering the assets of the community" (p. 231).

Mapping the assets of a rural community will help you in many ways as a social worker in the community. When you know these assets, you can link clients and families to them so they can get their needs met. You can also collaborate with strong community leaders and community organizations to integrate families into the activities of the community. This will help to reduce their isolation and provide opportunities for them to contribute in positive ways to the life of the community and get positive recognition. You can also work with local groups to develop a partnership to address community issues. At an organizational level, you can help link formal social and health services with the local organizations and informal networks of the community. You can also work with local groups and with organizations from outside the community to integrate programs and services with local informal resources, and draw on the leaders and assets that are already there.

AN OVERVIEW OF ASSET MAPPING FOR COMMUNITY-BASED SOCIAL WORK

Community-based social work has recently regained its position in the literature of the social work profession. In reaction to problems created by overly professionalized and bureaucratic social service programs and organizations, numerous authors have recommended more community-based and localized approaches (McKnight, 1995; Specht & Courtney, 1994). Schorr (1997) notes

that "[s]uccessful programs deal with families as parts of neighborhoods and communities" (p. 7). The Search Institute encourages communities to become more supportive of youth by focusing their efforts on forty developmental assets (Search Institute Web site; see the Internet References list). In both urban and rural settings, social workers receive encouragement to form partnerships with local community organizations and leaders, and to draw on informal helpers to supplement professional services. Saleebey (2002) states that "none of this happens without the full involvement and direction of residents" (p. 237). Mattessich and Monsey (1997) stress the importance of involving what they call "existing indigenous organizations"; and that "[s]uccessful community building efforts tend to occur most often in situations where community organizations of long tenure and solid reputation become involved early" (p. 39).

The community-based approach has recently been recommended as innovative, but it is a familiar one to rural social workers. The rural social work literature has always emphasized assessing and mobilizing and collaborating with local community resources, especially informal ones (Martinez-Brawley, 1998).

Some of the principles of community-based social work are:

1. Getting to know the local community within a small geographical area.

2. Taking time to develop personal relationships before suggesting or making changes.

3. Valuing the help and support provided by local informal organizations and individuals.

4. Adjusting practice to local conditions rather than always following standard procedures.

5. Creating partnerships with local community organizations and leaders. Involving local leaders in developing solutions to community problems.

6. Interweaving formal and informal resources and assets to meet needs.

(Martinez-Brawley, 1998; Ginsberg, 1998)

It is obvious that in order to apply these principles, you must identify local community leaders, informal organizations, and resources. It is now common to call this a process of "mapping community assets." Kretzmann and McKnight (1993) provide specific instructions for mapping community assets in their book *Building Communities from the Inside Out*. Their suggestions are based on research carried out in a low income Chicago neighborhood of 85,000 people. Some of their methods—such as a formal telephone survey with a structured interview schedule and the use of published directories of organizations—are more appropriate for urban settings. More personalized and informal methods will be more successful in rural areas, as this article delineates. However, the basic approach recommended by Kretzmann and McKnight is compatible with rural community social work. The idea is to identify local associations and institutions by talking to local citizens, leaders, and residents. In this way you can get in touch with the network of connections that underlies a neighborhood (Kretzmann & McKnight, 1993). In this way you can uncover what Wilkinson (1991) calls the interactional community.

A wide variety of local associations can be identified such as churches, neighborhood associations, sports leagues, study groups, collectors' groups, business organizations, and self-help groups. Kretzmann and McKnight (1993) emphasize that valuable assets may be informal: "[T]here are many associations that are informal groups without officers or even a name. However, they do vital community work. The fact that these associations don't have a formal name should not keep us from recognizing what a powerful community force they are" (p. 112).

THE VARIETY OF RURAL COMMUNITIES

The recommendations that follow are for mapping assets of rural communities. Of course, communities are not 100% urban or rural. Rurality is

a relative concept. If you live in New York City, you would think that Springfield, Missouri or Portland, Maine is very rural. If you grew up in an Alaskan village or on a ranch in Montana, you might consider Springfield, Missouri and Portland, Maine to be pretty urban. Many communities have rural characteristics as well as urban ones. Some communities are moderately rural and others are extremely rural. This article discusses asset mapping in communities that have very rural characteristics. If the community you learn about is only moderately rural, you can use some of the ideas in this article along with other more formal, urban methods.

Remember also that communities are often changing over time. A rural community that becomes a boom town for mining or oil may rapidly gain a population of newcomers. The characteristics of such a community may undergo rapid change. It may become polarized between old-timers and new arrivals. The social network may be overstressed and may even disintegrate under such conditions. Informal support may no longer be available. A boom is often followed by a bust, and the sudden exodus of the population may leave the town almost destroyed. Even without the "boom and bust" pattern, rural towns frequently experience loss of population and loss of critical businesses. Towns affected by the farm and rural crisis are examples. Many of these towns now have boarded up businesses on the main street. Residents are increasingly isolated from services and products they need to survive. Even if they were once sources of vibrant community activity, such "dying towns" may have few resources left at present for the rural social worker to assess.

APPLYING ASSET MAPPING TO RURAL COMMUNITIES

The assets in a rural community can be mapped using a series of steps. It is often helpful to begin with a local newspaper. Most rural communities have a weekly newspaper that contains local community news that will help identify informal leaders and groups. A telephone book can also be helpful, although the current trend to include rural communities in large regional telephone books makes this resource less easy to use for this purpose. Also, it is important to note that many organizations are not listed in the phone book. Look for local businesses and employers. Look for local city and county services such as a police station or sheriff's department, public library, senior center, the volunteer fire department, and the local schools. Look for community organizations and service clubs such as the Rotary Club, the Lions, and the Elks. Note if there is a community center. Determine how many churches there are and where they are located. Try to identify informal groups that announce meetings and events ahead of time or report afterwards in the newspaper. Names of leaders will often be mentioned.

Follow this initial assessment with visits to the community. Locate the sites that are to be found in most rural communities such as the post office, library, city hall, firehouse, the churches, grocery stores, community center, restaurants, taverns, laundromat, bank, medical clinic, school buildings, cemetery, mobile home park, and area of newly constructed housing. Identify any historical buildings. Find out if there is a museum. Visit the Chamber of Commerce and pick up any local information they have there. Look for a bulletin board where local people post notices and information. These are general suggestions, but be sure to search out the unique things that this particular community has to offer. Get into conversation with some residents and talk about the town, emphasizing the positive things you have noticed.

Table 22.1 provides an asset matrix that will be useful to you as you map the assets of a rural community. Fill in as many cells as you can with the name and location. If you locate several resources of the same type, list each one in the cell. For example, if there are six churches, list each one. If there are six taverns, list each one. Try to figure out how they are different and what segment of the population they serve. Over time you may be able to complete more and more of the matrix for a particular rural community. You can also use Table 22.2 to help you identify services that are provided by visiting service providers from outside the community on some kind of regular schedule.

It is a good idea to expand your asset assessment by attending community events such as the annual parade, the county fair, and any community festivals, celebrations, and open houses. Better still, volunteer to help with some of these events. Over time, you may be able to become acquainted with local community leaders who will serve as your "key informant" or "cultural guide" as you learn more about the community. As you become trusted and valued, it will become easier for you to learn about the assets of the community.

CHALLENGES OF ASSET MAPPING IN RURAL COMMUNITIES

Although the community asset assessment is now being recommended for urban and suburban communities too, this approach is *essential* for successful rural social work. That is because there are some characteristics of rural communities that create barriers to approaches to community assessment that focus on formal services and service providers, professional expertise, and data documenting community problems and deficits.

1. Residents of rural communities tend to be suspicious and distrustful of "outsiders," "experts," and "professionals."

The residents of rural communities are well-known. Outsiders are noticed immediately and everyone wonders who they are and what they are doing in town. In most cases, only after they get to know an outsider over a period of time do rural residents begin to open up and share information. It is important to invest time in getting to know members of the community, letting them get to know you, and forming partnerships *before* making suggestions or mobilizing for change.

Table 22.1 Rural Community Asset Matrix

Business/Commercial	Private and Semiprivately Funded Formal Services	Government-Funded Formal Services	Formal County and Regional Services	Informal Resources
Gasoline for sale	Veterinarian	Senior Center with regular schedule of congregate meals	County Court House	Churches (Name each and identify pastor)
				Ministerial Association
Convenience store	After-school program	Home-delivered meals	County Sheriff's Office	Fraternal orders and clubs (i.e., Rotary, Lions, Elks, Moose, Knights of Columbus, Grange)
Fast food store	Preschool program	Schools: Elementary	County Jail	
Grocery store, supermarket	Veterinarian	Schools: Middle or Junior High	County Government Building	American Legion Hall
Café or diner	Bank	Schools: High School	County Road Department	Women's clubs
Pizza parlor		Park	County Fairgrounds	Children's activities groups (scouts, 4-H, youth sports, etc.)
				Adult sports (i.e., softball, soccer, etc.)
Tavern	Basketball courts	Fire Department (indicate if volunteer)	Public Health Services	Chamber of Commerce
Restaurant	Medical clinic or doctor's office	City Hall	County Extension Services	Parent Teacher's Organization (PTO, PTA)
Thrift store, resale store	Chiropractor's office	Police Department	Area Agency on Aging Office	Arts Council
Laundromat	Massage therapist	Public Library	U.S. Dept. of Agriculture Service Center	Museum
Drug Store	Physical therapist	Recreation Center, Recreation Program	Other	Historical Society
Bowling alley	Eye doctor	Subsidized housing for elderly and disabled		Informal services for elderly (transport, meals, etc.)
Beauty parlor	Nursing home	GED Classes		Food Pantry
Barber shop	Assisted living facility	ESL Classes for adults		

Table 22.1 *continued*

Business/Commercial	Private and Semiprivately Funded Formal ServicesH	Government-Funded Formal Services	Formal County and Regional Services	Informal Resources
Hardware store	Hospital	Alternative School		Clothes Closet
Local weekly newspaper	Exercise and health facility	Group Home		Other
Video rental store	Private school	Other		Other
Bakery	Other	Other		
Country club	Other			
Auto repair, tire store				
Feed and seed store				
Agricultural equipment store				
Grain elevator				
Manufacturing business, factory				
Movie theater				
Flower shop, gift shop				
Liquor store				
Pet grooming business				
Lawyer's office				
Real estate office				
Insurance representative				
Funeral home				
Mobile home park				
Discount department store (i.e., WalMart)				
Motel				
Tourist attraction				

Note: Write in the name and location of each of the assets in the community that you identify; include all the assets you identify that fit into a particular cell. For example, if you identify several convenience stores, list each of them.

SOURCE: Bureau of the Census (1975), Series A 57–72

Table 22.2 Service Providers Visiting on a Regular Schedule from Outside the Community

Organization	Location of Main Office Outside the Community	Services Provided	Regular Schedule	Local Facility Used
Mental Health Services				
Child Welfare Services (i.e., child protection services, foster care, adoptions, etc.)				
Government Financial Assistance (Welfare, Food Stamps, Medicaid)				
Visiting hospital and clinic services				
Immunizations				
Well-child and Prenatal Services				
Blood pressure check for elderly				
Bookmobile				
Mobile health services				
Eye doctor				
Dentist				
Other				

2. Rural communities have fewer formal services and service providers than urban and suburban communities.

Formal professional services are scarce in rural communities. Some formal services are provided at nearby towns or at the county seat and are difficult to access. Others are provided by professionals who travel into town once a week or twice a month. For example, there may be an eye doctor who comes to town once a week or once a month. It is important to identify the sources of support and caring that are provided in rural communities where formal services do not exist.

3. Rural communities tend to focus their "community spirit" on a relatively small geographic area.

Most formal services and service providers are provided over large areas that do not correspond to the local community as it is perceived by the residents. In order to know the local community, you must spend time in that small geographical area. One way large regional organizations can make this possible is to assign staff to particular

rural communities within the service region and encourage them to become "experts" on the informal resources located there.

4. Rural residents often are loyal to their communities and hesitate to discuss needs, problems, and deficits with outsiders.

Denial of problems and conflict can make it challenging to address needs and mobilize resources. A rural community will often assert that there is no child abuse in their area, for example, or that they do not have anyone with AIDS. Such attitudes make it difficult for people to acknowledge their own or others' problems and address them. When a trusting relationship has been formed, rural residents are more likely to discuss issues and problems of concern to them.

5. Rural communities often neglect or ignore groups of residents who are different from the dominant culture of the community.

Rural residents may exclude members of minority groups from the social networks of the community, or even deny that such groups exist in their community. European ethnic groups frequently dominate rural community life in large areas of the United States (Ginsberg, 1998). In some communities, people in poverty, people of color, and recent immigrants are not encouraged to participate in community activities. Gay, lesbian, bisexual, and transgendered persons are often completely ignored; homophobia in many rural communities makes it unsafe to be openly gay or lesbian (Smith, 1997; Lindhorst, 1997). In order to find out about *all* the residents of the community, you will need to spend some time observing subgroups and noting which groups are not included in local organizations and activities. Mattessich and Monsey (1997) list questions to guide successful community-building efforts. These include: "Do the people participating in the community building initiative represent the population? Are some groups of community members not involved? What options exist to reach out to groups not already involved?" (p. 29).

Often, excluded minority groups have assets and resources that go unnoticed and unappreciated by other members of the community. The asset approach will help you to find them and increase awareness and respect for them. Kretzmann and McKnight (1993) acknowledge that communities create walls that exclude some groups: "The response to these walls may be to use laws to breach them, education to influence their members, or traditions that emphasize hospitality rather than exclusion. The effort to create open communities has been, and will be, a never-ending struggle" (p. 375).

6. Certain individuals and groups who exert power over a rural community may constrain your assessment.

Power imbalances exist in rural communities and can make it difficult to carry out your assessment. Residents may hesitate to voice their concerns or to collaborate with you because they are concerned that powerful members of the community might disapprove or might hold it against them. Individuals with power may include elected officials and openly recognized community leaders. However, sometimes the power structure

of a rural community is hidden. Someone who owns a lot of property or whose family has lived in the area for a long time may exert control from behind the scenes. There may be opposing factions among those with power in the community. Certain individuals may want to protect the status quo in the community and to maintain patterns that exclude certain groups from community decision making. Your informants may hesitate to let you know about their concerns until they know what attitude these influential power have toward you and your assessment project.

It takes some time to learn about the power dynamics of the community. Hardcastle, Wenocur, and Powers (1997) suggest methods to identify community figures who have local power. Reputational methods require the researcher to ask others who are known to have community power (p. 133) and locate sources of information that can lead a person to the "old, monied, or revered families in the area" (p. 135). Network analysis methods can also be used to identify central members of the community (Murty, 1998). It is worthwhile to make the effort to assess the power structure of the community. Once you have identified the individuals with power, try to get to know them and, if possible, build trust and form alliances with these powerful individuals. If you can "win them over," your assessment and your interventions will become much more effective. With these leaders as partners, you will have the power to begin to unlock the assets of the community.

STRENGTHS OF RURAL COMMUNITIES

Although there are challenges to mapping assets in rural communities, there are also positive characteristics that are typical of rural communities and that make the asset-mapping approach ideal. The more commonly used "needs assessment" approach, might miss these important community strengths.

1. Rural communities often have tightly knit dense social networks in which people know each other in multiple ways.

In rural communities people tend to know each other personally (Ginsberg, 1998). There is usually a high level of mutual acquaintanceship in a rural community. Your neighbor may cut your hair at the beauty parlor and her husband may service your car. One of her children may be in the same grade as your child and you may both attend the same church. In rural communities, most people know each other by name. "This sense of interconnection makes the community-oriented approach an appropriate avenue for exploration" (Martinez-Brawley, 1998, p. 109). Also, once a new idea is accepted by a few rural residents, it may rapidly spread through the dense social network of the community.

2. Many rural communities have a tradition and perception of communal responsibility (Martinez-Brawley, 1998).

Many rural communities advocate the motto "We take care of our own." Rather than send people to specialists and counselors, rural residents often help each other out in informal ways. Although this can have disadvantages when a person urgently needs highly skilled care from an expert, it represents an ethic of caring for one another that is a very positive community characteristic.

3. Many rural communities have strong local organizations and institutions.

Churches play a central role in most rural communities. Traditional farming and agriculture institutions pervade many of these communities. For example, the County Extension Services are respected and used as a source of information on a variety of subjects including farming, gardening, canning, child rearing, and budgeting. The 4-H youth groups and Future Farmers of America provide positive experiences for young people throughout rural America. The Grange and the Farm Bureau are active in many areas. County fairs provide opportunities for community participation and recognition to countless rural children and adults. Active fraternal and community service organizations in rural communities

range from the Rotary Club, Lions, and Elks to the Chamber of Commerce, the Boy and Girl Scouts, and organizations particular to specific communities.

4. Informal groups provide valuable support and influence over residents of rural communities.

Most small towns have places where specific groups of local people gather regularly. Men and women often have separate informal organizations. A group of men might meet about seven or nine in the morning at the local diner to drink coffee and talk. A group of women may meet to play cards, discuss books, study the Bible, or just visit. Groups of elders may gather to play cards and may travel together to shows or casinos. These are active informal organizations that strengthen the community. They can also be valuable informal resources for a rural social worker who learns to use them respectfully and appropriately.

5. Most rural communities have a few easily identified active community leaders.

These leaders spearhead many of the community's activities and projects. They usually have multiple roles in the community, holding both formal offices and informal leadership roles in clubs and organizations. If the rural social worker can identify them and establish a relationship with them, these leaders can be valuable community partners. They can influence community members to consider new ideas, participate in new projects, and integrate members of diverse groups into their activities.

CONCLUSION

Mapping rural community assets takes time. It cannot be done from your arm chair or your computer. It requires local visits, observation, and interaction over a period of time. However, you will find that it is fascinating, enjoyable, and rewarding. Social workers who can map rural community assets are very valuable assets themselves. They will be valued and appreciated for their work!

DISCUSSION QUESTIONS

1. What type of research does this article recommend to map assets in rural communities? Is it primarily qualitative or quantitative? What can you learn about assets of rural communities from quantitative data? Give some examples. What can you learn from qualitative data? What are the advantages and disadvantages of each?

2. Give examples of informal resources and assets you might find in a rural community. It is usually more difficult to identify these informal resources and assets than the formal ones. Why is that? Why do rural social workers need to know about these informal resources and assets? What are some good strategies for finding them?

3. Which assets and resources on the asset matrix will you find in smallest rural communities? Which ones will you find only in larger rural towns and cities? Which ones

are you more likely to find in a county seat? If a rural community is close to a large city, is it less likely to have some of these assets or more likely to have them?

4. How can a rural social worker make good use of local assets and resources? Develop a plan for services for an individual, family, or community that depends on local assets and resources.

5. What kinds of services are provided on a "circuit rider" basis in rural communities? Such services are brought to the community on a regular schedule and may be provided at a local building or using a mobile van or vehicle. Where do the service providers come from who provide these services? What are the advantages of such services brought in from outside the community? What are the disadvantages? How can the disadvantages be minimized?

CLASSROOM ACTIVITIES AND ASSIGNMENTS

1. What does "rural" mean? List four communities that you know. Pick one that is very urban and one that is only moderately urban. Then pick another that is very rural and one that is moderately rural. Next to each one, write a sentence identifying at least one characteristic that makes it either rural or urban from your point of view. After you have completed your list, find a partner in your class and compare your lists. Discuss your perceptions. Do you perceive "rural" and "urban" in different ways? What kinds of experiences have you had that may have affected your perceptions? In a large group or class discussion, compare your perceptions with other members of your class. See if you can develop a definition of "rural" or "urban" that you will all be able to agree on.

2. Class project: Initial Assessment Using the Local Newspaper and Phone Book. Divide the class into groups to assess different rural communities. Using local newspapers and phone books provided by the instructor, identify as many of the formal and informal resources in the community as you can. Be sure to read the local news and "gossip columns" to make sure you do not miss anything. Compare your asset matrix with the ones completed by the other groups. Discuss why they are different.

3. Class Group Project: Initial Community Asset Mapping. Visit a rural community. Divide the class into small groups. Spend at least three or four hours and see what resources and assets you can identify just by driving or walking around, noticing things.

Try to locate a bulletin board where people post local notices. Try a laundromat or bank. What kinds of local assets can you spot on the bulletin board?

Buy a copy of the local newspaper. It may be a weekly paper. Go through the newspaper and identify clubs and groups that meet in the community. Note what community activities are scheduled.

Based on what you learn, complete as much of the Table 22.1 Asset Matrix as you can, as well as the Table 22.2 list of visiting service providers. Also try to find answers to some of the following questions:

a. Where do people work? Are there any large businesses that employ people locally?

b. Where do people gather to chat?

c. What kind of housing do you see? Are there new housing developments? Trailer parks? Older homes? What is the condition of the housing? Are there better houses in one part of town and worse housing in another part of town?

d. Where can people shop in the town?

e. Are there school buildings located in the community? Or do children travel to a consolidated school outside the local community? Is there one school or separate elementary, middle, and high schools?

f. What can people do for fun in town? Is there a community hall that can be used for groups to meet and have celebrations?

g. Are there formal social or health services provided locally? What are they? Can you figure out whether the service providers have only a local office or whether they travel into town on a regular schedule to provide services weekly or monthly?

After you have spent three or four hours in the community, meet with your classmates and compare notes on what you have learned. Later on, as a class you can compile your asset matrices into a single matrix. Discuss how these assets would be useful to a social worker serving this community.

Note: During your visit, see if you can get into conversation with anyone who lives in the community. You can be certain that they have noticed you by now! They are probably wondering who you are and what you are doing in their town. Explain in a way that will help to establish a positive relationship and that shows respect for the residents and the strengths of their community.

4. Individual or Group Research Project: Mapping the Boundaries of the "Perceived" Rural Community. Choose a rural community and find out what the local government boundaries are. These might be the city limits or in some cases, the limits of several cities located near each other. Also find out what the geographical limits of the school district are. Then ask residents of that area about their community. Where do they live? What is the name of the community where they live? How big an area does it cover? What are its boundaries? Does it include or exclude small towns in the surrounding area? Has the geographic area of the community changed over time? If so, why and how? After you have gathered resident perceptions, make a map of the "perceived community" and its geographic area. If there are differences of opinion among your respondents, you may need to make more than one map!

REFERENCES

Ginsberg, L. H. (1998). Introduction: An overview of rural social work. In L. H. Ginsberg (Ed.), *Social work in rural communities* (3rd ed., pp. 3–22). Alexandria, VA: Council on Social Work Education.

Hardcastle, D. A., Wenocur, S., & Powers, P. R. (1997). *Community practice: Theories and skills for social workers.* New York: Oxford University Press.

Kretzmann, J. P., & McKnight, J. L. (1993). *Building communities from the inside out: A path toward finding and mobilizing a community's assets.* Chicago: ACTA Publications.

Lindhorst, T. (1997). Lesbians and gay men in the country: Practice implications for rural social workers. In J. D. Smith & R. J. Mancoske (Eds.), *Rural gays and lesbians: Building on the strengths of communities* (pp. 1–11). Binghamton, NY: Harrington Park Press.

Martinez-Brawley, E. E. (1998). Community-oriented practice in rural social work. In L. H. Ginsberg (Ed.), *Social work in rural communities* (3rd ed., pp. 99–113). Alexandria, VA: Council on Social Work Education.

Mattessich, P., & Monsey, B. (1997). *Community building: A review of factors influencing successful community building.* St. Paul, MN: Amherst Wilder Foundation.

McKnight, J. (1995). *The careless society: Community and its counterfeits.* New York: Basic Books.

Murty, S. A. (1998). Network analysis as a research methodology for community practice. In R. H. MacNair (Ed.), *Research strategies for community practice* (pp. 21–46). New York: Haworth Press.

Saleebey, D. (2002). Community development, neighborhood empowerment, and individual resilience. In D. Saleebey (Ed.), *The strengths perspective in social work practice* (3rd ed., pp. 228–246). Boston: Allyn and Bacon.

Schorr, L. B. (1997). *Common purpose: Strengthening families and neighborhoods to rebuild America.* New York: Anchor Books.

Smith, J. D. (1997). Working with larger systems: Rural lesbians and gays. In J. D. Smith & R. J. Mancoske (Eds.), *Rural gays and lesbians: Building on the strengths of communities* (pp. 13–21). Binghamton, NY: Harrington Park Press.

Specht, H., & Courtney, M. (1994). *Unfaithful angels: How social work has abandoned its mission.* New York: Free Press.

Wilkinson, K. P. (1991). *The community in rural America.* New York: Greenwood Press.

INTERNET RESOURCES

Asset-Based Community Development Institute
http://www.northwestern.edu/ipr/abcd.html

The Asset-Based Community Development Institute (ABCD), established by the Community Development Program at Northwestern University's Institute for Policy Research, spreads its findings on capacity-building community development in two ways: (1) through extensive and substantial interactions with community builders, and (2) by producing practical resources and tools for community builders to identify, nurture, and mobilize neighborhood assets.

Search Institute:
http://www.search-institute.org/

The Search Institute has developed a framework of forty developmental assets, which include positive experiences, relationships, opportunities, and personal qualities that young people need to grow up healthy, caring, and responsible.

 **INFOTRAC COLLEGE EDITION**

assessment
asset mapping
research

rural
strengths

23

Asset Building in Rural Communities through Participatory Research

LEELA THOMAS
PATRICIA ALBAUGH
BERNARD ALBAUGH

Participatory research is an asset-based approach to community development. The purpose of participatory research is to build knowledge for action that will lead to community development. In doing so, such research places a community's greatest asset, its people, in control of the knowledge-building work. This article devotes itself to the method of participatory research. It begins with a review of the history of participatory research. Then a description of the framework of participatory research is presented in which the underlying principles are elaborated. Next, it details new assets that can be built in rural communities through participatory research. This is followed by a discussion of the limitations of participatory research. The article concludes with a description of participatory research in action as a means of addressing the problem of alcoholism in a American Indian community.

HISTORY OF PARTICIPATORY RESEARCH

The beginnings of participatory research date back to the early 1970s. Community development activists and researchers, working in several developing countries, were dissatisfied with the classical model or positivist model of research. They felt it failed to grasp the reality of the poor, the oppressed, and the exploited (Hall, 1984, 1992). Developed in North America and Europe, the positivist model of research was, and continues to be, the most prevalent model of research used by investigators around the world. Rooted in the scientific method, it is systematic, controlled, and very structured. Its focus is on precision and objectivity, discounting intuitive and subjective knowledge. Its primary purpose is to discover general laws and to construct theory, not to build communities. Any action resulting from the research, such as community building, is secondary.

Much of the research in rural communities of developing countries was conducted by investigators from urban communities trained in the positivist model of research. Such researchers initiated the study, defined the needs and problems of the community as the investigators perceived them, used instruments containing a predetermined set of questions, and collected data using interviewers from outside the community. Once collected, the data were analyzed, and the results were used either by researchers to disseminate information through publications and presentations or by dominant groups to determine priorities and allocate resources for rural residents (Rahman, 1978; Hall, 1984, 1992). Rarely did these investigators seek input from those who lived and worked in the community and who would be affected by the outcome of the study; nor was any attempt made to seek out people in the community who could participate in the research process. Rural people were perceived to lack the knowledge and sophistication to take part in the research process. The research was based on what Kretzmann and McKnight (1993) would call the "deficiency-model" of community development.

Disillusionment with the positivist model started to rise in the 1970s. Researchers in developing countries saw it as an example of Western dominance and colonialism (Hall, 1992; Smith, Willms, & Johnson, 1997). From India, Tandon (1981) contended that researchers using the positivist model were not only taught the research skills but were also indoctrinated into the values and way of thinking of the West. In addition to these concerns, researchers and social activists who worked with the disadvantaged were influenced by the writings of Paulo Freire, an educator and social thinker from Brazil (Hall, 1992; Freire, 1973, 1982, 2000).

Freire was the coordinator for the National Literacy Program in Brazil (Freire, 1973) until he was exiled after the Military Coup in 1964 (Shaull, 2000; Goulet, 1973). Freire argued in his writings that the traditional model of community development was paternalistic and elitist. In the traditional model outside experts observe the struggles of rural peasants from a distance and prescribe steps for the peasants to follow. The relationship between the experts and the people of the community is vertical. Such a top-down relationship, according to Freire, is "arrogant" and "self-sufficient" (Freire, 2000, p. 90; Freire, 1973, p. 46). It is without love, faith, and respect for those who are being helped. It cannot lead to real community development because it will transform the people of the community.

Real community development can only occur through dialogue between outside experts and the people of the community. Dialogue implies a relationship that is horizontal. A horizontal relationship is based on the ideology of equality and reciprocity. The outside experts and the people of the community accept each other as peers and learn from each other. The relationship is based on "love," "humility," "mutual trust," and "faith" (Freire, 2000, pp. 89–91; Freire, 1973, p. 45) in the potential of those who are being helped. Through dialogue, as people in the community change, they begin to transform their community. Thus development occurs not from top-down but rather from inside-out. Community people are recognized by experts as "subjects" who design their own futures instead of "objects" that are of interest to outside experts (Freire, 1973, 2000).

The concept of "participatory research" was developed as a challenge to the positivist model by a group of researchers in Tanzania. Marja Lissa Swantz of Finland, who worked with the group in Tanzania, conceived the name "participatory research" (Hall, 1997). The concept was used and further developed by Budd Hall and his associates in Tanzania, where he began working in 1970. In 1977, Hall and his associates started an international network of participatory research with contacts in Canada, Chile, India, the Netherlands, Tanzania, and the West Indies. Thus, although the concept of participatory research was under development in Tanzania, work along similar lines progressed in several countries around the world and participatory research gained substantially from this international perspective (Hall, 1981; 1992; Smith, et al., 1997).

In the 1970s, Orlando Fals-Borda worked in Colombia and other Latin American countries to involve people in building knowledge for social action. He called his work "action research." Later he began a collaboration with Francisco Vio Grossi, who had worked in Venezuela and Chile, and changed the term to "participatory action research." The terms *participatory research, action research*, and *participatory action research* each describe the same activity: a method of research in which ordinary people participate as researchers to create knowledge that will lead to social action (Hall, 1992).

The United Nations and the World Bank also recognized the effectiveness of participation in rural development (Rahman, 1978; Ansley & Gaventa, 1997). After several years of unsuccessfully attempting to build rural communities, the International Labour Organization (ILO), a special agency of the United Nations, concluded that participation was essential for development (Rahman, 1978). People must take the initiative for their own development and be actively involved in improving their lives. It was only by taking control of the development process and by actively participating in the development strategy that the poor in rural communities would develop their human potential. In fact, Rahman (1978), a senior research officer from Bangladesh at the time for Rural Employment Policies, ILO, describes participation as being vital for the survival of humans. He explains that development does not merely mean satisfying the fundamental needs of life but also the building of mental faculties and creative potential which are essential for growth as humans. Rahman notes that in his own developmental work with peasants, they expressed a desire to be included in the research process. They told him that they would have benefited much more from the research done on their developmental efforts if they had been allowed to participate in the study.

PARTICIPATORY RESEARCH FRAMEWORK

Participatory research is an asset-based method of research. It capitalizes on the assets of the community to create knowledge. Unlike positivist research, participatory research is less structured. It has no systematic methodology, and it is context specific (Hall, 1992). Research questions evolve depending on the common needs and collective deliberations of the community members; research methodology develops depending on the circumstances of the community and input of its members. However, there are some underlying principles of participatory research.

A community's greatest resource is its people. Participatory research requires that the people of the community be involved in the entire research process (Hall, 1984). They should be included in defining the problem, planning the study, collecting and analyzing the data, and interpreting the results. People who live and work in the community have unique experiences, perceptions, and understandings of their community. For example, a rural person's view of "privacy" may be different from that of an urban-dwelling researcher. Thus, people who live in the rural community are familiar with their community's needs and assets, customs and traditions, values and mores, spiritual beliefs and age-old wisdom. Unless this knowledge is considered, an outside researcher's perception of the reality of the community will be incorrect. Therefore, participatory research requires that this knowledge be incorporated into the research process. Unlike positivist research, which discounts intuitive knowledge and experience, participatory research considers it indispensable to the research process.

Including community people in the research process and using their experiences, perceptions, and understandings makes the knowledge that is generated relevant to the reality of their lives. Participatory research requires that the study be directly useful to the people in the community on whom the study is based (Hall, 1984). Thus, if the problems that are defined, the data that are collected, the results that are interpreted, and the solutions that are recommended are done in partnership with the people of the community, the actions that will result will be directly useful to the people of the community.

A variety of procedures have been used to generate knowledge for action that would fall under the rubric of participatory research (Hall, 1992). Some of these include knowledge that has been produced by community members without the assistance of professionally trained researchers from outside the community. In fact, Hall (1984) notes that participatory research is a method of producing knowledge with or without the cooperation of outside researchers. However, involving outside researchers is beneficial to both the people of the community as well as the outside researchers. Trained researchers can conceptualize ideas and validate the knowledge produced by participatory research (Couto, 1987). Members of the community can bring knowledge about the reality of their lives into the research process. To produce development strategies that are culturally sensitive and effective, outside researchers must be able to understand this reality. They must be able to see the oppression, struggle, needs, and resources within the community from the community members' points of view. This requires gathering information through conversations with community members, participation at community meetings, and discussions at focus groups, along with collecting data through conventional methods of research.

Rahman (1978) and Ornelas, a social activist from Mexico (see Debbink & Ornelas, 1997), recommend living in the rural community: sharing their lives, tasting their soup (as Ornelas puts it), and integrating with the people of the community so that they see the outside researcher as one of them and not as an agent of the government or some member of an oppressive group. Outside researchers must be humble and willing to learn. They must treat the members of the community, who may be poor and illiterate, as intelligent, equal partners who are knowledgeable about the community and are capable of devising their own community development strategies. In other words, outside researchers must be able to see the assets of the people in the community. However, it must be noted that although outside researchers must acknowledge the perceptions of the community members, they are free to draw their own conclusions.

PARTICIPATORY RESEARCH AND NEW ASSETS

Participatory research builds new assets; scientific research is a systematic process of reflective thinking (Dewey, 1933; Kerlinger, 1986). When people in a rural community become engaged in the process of research, they develop the ability to think reflectively. Community members develop reflective thinking ability when they struggle collectively to define the problems of their community, when issues that were once felt intuitively by the people begin to take shape intellectually, and when community members use their knowledge and experience to deduce causes, to design survey instruments, to gather empirical evidence, and to interpret behavior.

Participatory research develops critical consciousness. Freire (1973, 2000) defines critical consciousness as the ability of the oppressed to comprehend the economic, political, and social realities that led to their oppression. During participatory research, when people in rural communities examine a problem, identify its causes, and subject these causes to analysis, critical consciousness is developed. This, according to Freire (1973), differs from magic consciousness. When people have magic consciousness, they attribute the cause of their problems to supernatural powers. Belief in supernatural causes leads people to accept their fate, and it results in inaction. People adapt to the conditions. Critical consciousness gives people a deeper understanding of the causes of their problems and motivates them to take action that will change their condition and solve their problems.

Participatory research reduces the sense of mental dependence. Some poor in rural communities have historically been dependent on the government or outside sources for sustenance. These outside sources define the problems of the community, determine their needs, set priorities for them, and provide aid. Over time, such aid leads to a sense of mental dependence and passivity from which the people find it difficult to disassociate (Rahman, 1978). Participatory research reduces such mental dependence by enabling the rural people to take control of their own lives. Through the process of knowledge building, members of the rural community become aware of the assets within the community, as well as their own human potential to become self-reliant.

Participatory research creates new associations or informal organizations. Unlike the positivist model of research, which is individualistic in nature, participatory research is a collective process. When people in the community gather to share common concerns and define common problems, deliberate over the strategies to resolve their problems, struggle together through the various stages of the research process, and collectively take action to address their problems, they develop a common bond. Over a period of time these bonds among community members develop into associations or informal organizations which continue to work for the development of the community. This was found to be the case in several rural parts of Asia (Tandon, 1981).

Finally, participatory research empowers people. In fact, the goal of participatory research is to empower the powerless. Knowledge has always been a means of achieving and holding power. Be they the landlords in a traditional agrarian society, as in India, or the executives in large corporations, as in the United States, people with greater knowledge have control over those with lesser knowledge. Such imbalance in power has often been a source of abuse and manipulation. The power to create knowledge has traditionally been considered the exclusive privilege of highly trained intellectuals from universities. On the other hand, participatory research is a method that shares such exclusive power with ordinary people (Tandon, 1981). When people engage in the knowledge creation process with outside researchers and use their own abilities, knowledge, wisdom, and creative faculties to do so, they acquire the power to control their destinies. They gain confidence to assert their own ideas and needs as well as faith in their ability to solve their own problems. They grow in self-worth and become self-reliant. The increase in self-worth that comes with the ability to create knowledge is reflected in a remark made by a participant from Brazil, quoted by Freire, "I make shoes, and now I see that I am worth as much as the Ph.D. who writes books" (Freire, 1973, p. 47).

LIMITATIONS OF PARTICIPATORY RESEARCH

A major limitation of participatory research is that it can take considerable time, patience, and money to conduct (Hall, 1984; Smith, et al., 1997). It takes time to build relationships with the people in the community. If people are to confide in an outside researcher, as noted earlier, they must view the outside researcher as "one of them." A relationship of trust is built over time, particularly in rural communities which tend to be less trusting of outsiders.

The process of participatory research involves sharing of knowledge among people of the rural community and outside researchers. Community members educate outside researchers about the community, while outside researchers educate the community members about the techniques of research. This may appear inefficient and time consuming. But Freire (1973) argues that any time spent in facilitating people's ability to solve their problems is time well spent. He notes that the goal of community development is to transform people; any development that merely changes the structures of the community but does not empower its people is superficial and time ill-spent.

In addition to the time it takes to educate the members of the community, time and patience are also needed to organize community meetings and focus groups. It takes time to obtain the permission of rural community leaders and the cooperation of formal and informal organizations. Disagreements and misunderstandings can derail the research process.

Participatory research can also be expensive. Methods of data collection can involve conventional methods as well as extensive dialogue with community members. This may require investigators to travel considerable distances to meet community members. Moreover, some people may be illiterate, which would make mailed surveys inappropriate for data collection. Local interviewers would have to be hired and trained to conduct interviews, which can be costly.

PARTICIPATORY RESEARCH IN ACTION

For several years, American Indian communities have been concerned about members' health. In Oklahoma, the elected tribal government and chiefs decided to initiate their own Health and Human Service programs to address the needs of their tribes. Studies were conducted by the tribes to understand the demographic profiles of tribal members. As the demographic research began to reveal the needs of tribal members and gaps in existing services, other agencies, including the National Institute of Health, asked to be included in specific aspects of this research concerning the etiology of some of the tribal members' physical and mental health problems. The tribes agreed, and since 1984, several studies have been completed by the tribes in partnership with the National Institute of Health.

The following pages describe how participatory research was used to address the problems of alcoholism, as well as other psychiatric disorders in an American Indian tribe that had a low prevalence rate of alcoholism. This project was part of an ongoing study by the National Institute of Health and the tribes to understand the genetic and environmental causes of alcoholism. Due to its low prevalence rate, the tribe offered a unique opportunity to examine the genetic and environmental causes from a strengths perspective. Moreover, the asset-based approach to community development capitalizes on the potential of individuals, associations, and institutions within the community (Kretzmann & McKnight, 1993). Consequently, this study depended on the participation of community institutions, including a

tribal organization, associations such as the tribal research advisory council, and individual local residents who were members of the tribe for its implementation.

Problem

American Indians have had a sordid relationship with alcohol since the introduction of liquor to North America. In fact, alcoholism and other psychiatric disorders appear to have a higher prevalence rate in many American Indian populations than in other minority and nonminority populations. A number of studies have been devoted to understanding the genetic and environmental causes of alcoholism among American Indians (e.g., Robin, Long, Rasmussen, Albaugh, & Goldman, 1998; Goldman, et al., 1993; Newmann, Mason, Chase, & Albaugh, 1991).

Although most studies have focused on American Indian tribes with very high rates of alcoholism, not all tribes share this history. A number of tribes in Oklahoma historically have demonstrated a very low rate of alcoholism (University of Oklahoma American Indian Institute, 1987). One of these tribes, which participated in this project with the understanding that it would not be identified, lived in the Southern coastal section of North America prior to European colonization. They were farmers and hunters, and many owned large plantations and farms. But their land was taken away from them by the U.S. government during national development, and they were forced to move to a section of what is now the state of Oklahoma. In Oklahoma, the tribe suffered some of the most insidious forms of mental oppression. Tribal members were forced to accept the idea that the U.S. government knew what was best for them. If they refused to cooperate, they were denied food rations and shelter. Tribal children were forced to attend government boarding schools where they were forbidden to speak their native language, dress in native clothes, eat native food, or practice native ceremonies and customs. At the start of the American Civil War, this tribal nation signed treaties with the Confederate states and fought against the United States.

Prior to 1880, this tribe had open access to alcoholic beverages and had used alcohol since their contact with non-Indians in the mid 1500s. Since 1880, this tribe has lived under the same federal and state laws regarding the use of alcohol as all other American Indians and has had the same access to alcohol. Despite this history, they have one of the lowest rates of alcoholism among American Indian tribes.

This tribe has approximately 25,000 members living within its vast geographical boundaries, which span numerous counties. They live in the more rural and isolated areas of the state. Unemployment and underemployment are very high. One-third of the population receives some kind of public assistance. Via the tribal Nation Health Services Authority, the tribe has administered its own health services for over a decade through a PL 93-638 contract with the Indian Health Service. The tribe has a hospital and a number of clinics accredited by the Joint Commission on Accreditation of Health Care Organizations. The hospital and clinics keep records on the health of the community, including the number of ambulatory and in-patient visits for substance abuse and mental health problems.

Methodology

Major work for this project was implemented by the Center for Human Behavior Studies (CHBS). Located in a federally designated rural area, the CHBS is a research and education organization controlled by American Indians. It is directed by Bernard Albaugh, a clinical social worker with over 30 years of clinical and research experience with American Indian and other cultures. All but one of the CHBS staff members is American Indian.

The goal of the CHBS is to develop scientific knowledge about alcohol abuse and alcoholism. It also endeavors to put that knowledge

to use and to enhance the quality of life for American Indians. For over thirteen years, the CHBS has worked in close collaboration with the National Institute on Alcohol Abuse and Alcoholism Intramural Program. It has conducted both pedigree studies concerning psychiatric transmission and linkage studies on alcoholism vulnerability. The CHBS helped to assemble the largest existing database of American Indian pedigrees for psychiatric transmission and linkage studies on alcoholism vulnerability. The CHBS has successfully conducted research and clinically related activities in a number of diverse, American Indian communities. Among other research, the CHBS has investigated the comorbidity of alcoholism and other psychiatric disorders in three tribes, and assessed the mental health needs of on- and off-reservation American Indians, encompassing numerous tribes.

The CHBS's success in conducting participatory research with American Indian populations that are often closed to outsiders has largely been due to Albaugh's efforts. His relationship with the American Indian community was built during his work as a clinical social worker with the Indian Health Service for 25 years. During the early years of his tenure at the Indian Health Service, he noticed that clients referred to him for counseling would not confide in him. He was advised by elderly American Indian women to develop a relationship with the community members because people would not confide in a stranger. Accordingly, he visited the clients in their homes, participated in tribal dances, and shared meals with them. As many American Indians live in rural and isolated areas of the state, transportation was a problem. Consequently, Albaugh would drive to the homes of clients and conduct counseling sessions in their homes. Throughout his tenure, he expressed a desire to learn from the tribes and share in their lives. So strong was the relationship he had built over the years that, although white, he was made a member of a tribal clan and given an American Indian name. During this time, the elected tribal government and the chiefs decided to develop their own

Health and Human Service Programs. They asked Albaugh to work with them on this project. In order to achieve this extensive goal, Albaugh conducted research with the tribe to describe the tribal population demographics, both past and present.

A relationship of trust was critical to the completion of the study on the genetic and environmental causes of alcoholism. Much of the work depended on the manner in which relationships had been formed with tribal leaders and social services delivery professionals. These relationships were crucial for: (1) eliciting the cooperation and active participation of the tribe in the research process, including formal approval of this study, (2) initially forming and then facilitating focus groups and thereby acquiring local perspectives and knowledge pertaining to the prevalence of disorders and underlying or associated conditions, (3) recruiting subjects for the study, and (4) effectively disseminating study outcomes to tribal leaders and the communities at-large.

A Memorandum of Understanding and Protection of Human Subjects

When the National Institute of Health approached the tribes and asked to be included in the tribes' research efforts, the tribes agreed. But the tribes, the CHBS, and the National Institute of Health investigators designed elaborate controls for their inclusion in the research process. The controls were necessary to protect the tribes from harm by outside researchers. These gateway controls included the following actions:

- A Memorandum of Understanding that set the terms for participating in the research activity was drawn up between the CHBS, the National Institute of Health, and the tribal government. As a result of the close working relationship that the CHBS staff had with the staff of the tribal government and the confidence the leadership of the Tribal Nation had in CHBS, the CHBS played a critical role in framing the Memorandum. At the time the CHBS

applied for funding from the National Institute of Health to conduct this research, the Tribal Nation had already indicated its willingness to assist with the contract. In addition, the Tribal Nation had opened their demographic database to staff from the CHBS in order to provide the preliminary data necessary for the application.

- The Memorandum of Understanding clearly delineated the conditions under which the tribes would participate in the study. Tribes could not be identified by name, and researchers could not disclose any information that would help identify the tribes. Because in the past researchers have presented American Indians in a poor light, the Memorandum of Understanding clearly stated that before publication, all manuscripts would have to be submitted to a Tribal Research Advisory Council for review. In addition, manuscript would have to be accompanied by a written explanation in terms that could be understood by someone who was not a researcher. The Tribal Research Advisory Council would offer suggestions wherever it saw inaccuracies or misrepresentations in the manuscript. If the National Institute of Health disagreed with the suggestions, then the National Institute of Health and the tribal research advisory council would meet to discuss and resolve the disagreements. If the disagreements could not be resolved, then the National Institute of Health would assist the tribal research advisory council in its communication with the journal editor. This communication would include a request from the tribal council that the council's disagreement with the manuscript or its alternative interpretation be published along with the manuscript. The final decision would rest with the journal editor. The Memorandum of Understanding also included terms for the protection of human subjects. It required that the study be submitted to the Tribal Research Advisory Council Committee for Human Subjects Review.

Thus, the study had to be approved by three human subjects review boards: the National Institute of Health Internal Institutional Review Board, which provided the funds for this study; the National Institute of Health Office for the Protection of Research Risks (OPRR); and the Tribal Research Advisory Council Committee for Human Subjects Review Board.

Several steps were taken to address the informed consent and subject protection conditions of the agreement with the tribe. Written informed consent was obtained from all subjects. Research interviewers from the community were carefully selected and trained. There was ongoing rigorous formal training for interviewers conducted by the director of CHBS. Training included didactic presentations; a training manual that provided background on trauma, alcoholism, and other psychiatric disorders; step-by-step explanation of procedures for conducting the interview and handling problems; structured exercises; and practice interviews. All test instruments and questionnaires used in the study were reviewed, when completed by each subject, by the CHBS director, who was the principal investigator for the field portion of the research. The site coordinator and interviewers held monthly meetings to ensure that they continued to interview in accordance with research protocol. To minimize any discomfort participants might experience, interviewers were personally trained to communicate the value that participant welfare superseded research concerns, and formal procedures were documented in the training manual to recognize signs of anxiety. To protect the confidentiality of the subjects, code numbers identified all subjects. In addition, all research assistants were instructed and trained about the expectations for their behavior, including restrictions on discussing case material outside of work.

- Finally, the Memorandum of Understanding required that the CHBS project staff keep the Tribal Research Advisory Council informed about the progress of the project. Accordingly, the CHBS project staff met with the Tribal Research Advisory Council periodically, provided them with progress reports, and sought feedback from them regarding community response to the research. As a result of this input, the CHBS made appropriate changes to the research process.

Focus Groups

One of the greatest assets of a community is the experience and knowledge of the people who live in the community. Only people living in the community can provide information about family kinship patterns and family history, which are essential for the study of alcoholism. Community members also know about opportunities for, and access to, employment. These are knowledge and experiences that are unique to each American Indian community and are necessary to gain an understanding of the sociocultural and economic context in which human behavior is expressed.

Focus groups were created to obtain input from the community. These groups were composed of local residents who were active in, and familiar with, the sociocultural life of their communities. More specifically, focus groups provided a broad range of community representation by including elders, educators, health service providers, parents, and homemakers. It also included tribal leaders, spiritual leaders, and women who were familiar with traditional language and customs.

The CHBS staff spent significant amounts of time working with focus groups at each field site. The sessions were conducted in a semistructured and open-ended manner intended to elicit the greatest degree of input from the focus group participants. Four members of the CHBS team, who were familiar with the tribal culture, facilitated focus group discussions. The project team members developed a set of structured probes or questions designed to elicit information in each thematic area. Confidentiality was assured for all focus group participants.

Focus groups helped to develop materials and procedures that promoted subjects' understanding of the purpose, aims, and objectives of the study. Focus groups also assisted in the construction of test instruments. Few test instruments have been normed and validated for American Indian populations. Therefore, the National Institute of Health investigators and collaborators found it necessary to develop new test instruments specifically for American Indian tribes.

Most notably, an acculturation scale that measured whether tribal members were traditional or acculturated was developed. It included questions about tribal language (such as, "Do you speak the [Native] language everyday?"), culture (such as, "Do you wear your hair in a traditional way?"), ethnic identity (such as, "How much of your life have you spent living on the [tribal] reservation/ancestral homelands?"), religion (such as, "Have you participated in the [traditional] ceremony [performed when a child]?"), and perceived discrimination (such as, "Do non-Indian people treat you differently because you are Native?"). The questions for the scale were developed with input from focus group members.

In addition to acculturation, the CHBS, in collaboration with the National Institute of Health, also field-tested instruments for psychopathology with help from members of various tribal communities. Measuring instruments and tests used to obtain knowledge and data are influenced by cultural factors. Whereas all human cultures and societies have been found to have persons affected by the psychopathologies of depression and psychoses (Day, Nielsen, & Korten, 1985; Draguns, 1980), differences can occur in the context, frequency, and expression of specific disorders. Inherent within efforts to develop instruments with cross-cultural validity is the recognition that assessments using unmodified Western-based testing instruments can be problematic. Cultural diversity and differences in education, language, and cognition have been recognized as impeding factors (Rhodes, 1989; Guilmet, 1983; Browne, 1984; Common & Frost, 1988; Kinzie & Manson, 1987). Similarly, deficiencies in unmodified structured interviews for affective disorders have resulted in flawed diagnoses for depression (Baron, Manson, Ackerson, & Brenneman, 1990; Shore & Manson, 1981), personality disorder (Pollack & Shore, 1980), and alcoholism (Albaugh & Washa, 1987).

Data Collection

Subjects for this study were selected through sampling of the Native populations, living in the Tribal Nation in a region of Oklahoma, based on the tribal rolls. Because it was a random sample, both genders and all adult age groups (21 years and older) were included in proportion to their representation in the community. Although only 300 subjects were needed for the study, a random sample of 500 was drawn to prevent the need to return to the tribal rolls to draw new names should identified potential subjects decline or be unable to participate.

To recruit subjects for the study, the CHBS sought the help of community leaders and the community media. The CHBS staff believed that the initial point of contact with the potential subjects was the most important, and every effort was made to establish good communication and understanding with potential subjects. Furthermore, the CHBS knew that much of each potential subject's decision to take part in the study was influenced by word-of-mouth knowledge from the general community. Therefore, the manner in which individuals were initially approached would greatly impact CHBS's ability to recruit study participants. To increase the response rate, CHBS proceeded in partnership with tribal leaders, local health service providers, and community members. In addition, the CHBS published an article in the tribal newsletter describing the study, what the CHBS was doing, what would be expected of the subjects, and why the subjects were needed.

Participatory research enables ordinary people to participate in the research process. This was nowhere more evident in the research process than during the data collection phase of the study. The skill, knowledge, and ability of the people were invaluable assets during this phase.

Researchers have noted American Indian interviewees' discomfort and distrust of white interviewers, factors that may result in underreporting (Rozynko & Ferguson, 1978; Ryan, 1979). Conversely, other disorders, such as depression and schizophrenia, may be overdiagnosed due to unfamiliarity with culture-specific mourning and grieving patterns and practices among American Indian populations (Shen, 1986; Manson, Shore, & Bloom, 1985; Peltz, et al., 1981; Sue, 1977; Miller & Schoenfeld, 1973; Matchett, 1972). Researchers, therefore, have called for the participation of "culturally experienced clinicians" (McCubbin, Thompson, Thompson, McCubbin, & Kaston, 1993; Manson, et al., 1987a) and local interviewers (Westermeyer, 1985; Beltrame & McQueen, 1979) in studies of American Indians.

The active involvement of local researchers had been suggested to be of critical importance in conducting research within American Indian communities (Uecker, Boutlier, & Richardson, 1981; Beltrame & McQueen, 1979, Rozynko & Ferguson, 1978). The CHBS, therefore, recruited and trained local Indian interviewers from this low-prevalence rate tribe who were then responsible for recruiting subjects and subsequent administration of questionnaires and interviews. As a result of its extensive working relationship with the low-prevalence rate tribe, the CHBS had knowledge of individuals within the tribe who have been employed in the past as interviewers and site coordinators for other research projects very similar to this study. These trained individuals were recruited to work on this project. Also, the low-prevalence rate tribe offered the project free office space in six different community buildings scattered through the tribal country for the interview.

The CHBS designed a timetable for conducting interviews that would not interfere with tribal activities and tribal holidays. Maximum emphasis was placed on interviewers establishing good communication with subjects before beginning the interview. Total interview time was estimated to be six hours. All instruments were administered to subjects in face-to-face sessions by trained interviewers. Interviews were conducted in environments most comfortable to the subject, as well as where privacy and confidentiality could best be maintained. Due to geographical distances in the tribal country, some interviews occurred in subjects' homes. The interviewer checked all questionnaires and forms before the subject left each assessment. The questionnaires and diagnostic instruments were examined for completion by the site coordinator before data entry was done.

The site coordinator/data manager at the CHBS was a member of the low-prevalence rate tribe which was involved in this research. She had a detailed understanding of her culture and history and had wide acceptance in her tribal communities. She coordinated the study with the tribe and supervised the interviewers in the field. She received the data from the interviewers, reviewed the data for accuracy and completeness, performed data entry, and referred incomplete data sets back to the interviewers for correction. She also maintained complete files of all interview data until it was turned over to the National Institute of Health for analysis.

CONCLUSION

Participatory research was developed as an alternative to the conventional method of research. In the conventional method, outside urban researchers would study rural communities and determine for them their courses of action. This made the people in rural communities the "objects" of an urban researcher's study and, hence, dependent on the urban researcher's knowledge for their own development. Participatory research was designed to invest ordinary people with the power to create knowledge by using their own assets and participating as researchers. In doing so, control of community building is transferred from the hands of urban experts to the people of the rural community. This article discussed the concept of participatory research and demonstrated its application in the study of alcoholism in an American Indian tribe that is located in one of the most rural areas of Oklahoma. By participating in the research project as equal partners with researchers from the National Institute of Health, the tribal members became not "objects" of the study but rather "subjects," as envisioned by Paulo Freire. The participatory process gave them greater control over their destiny and empowered them to develop new assets that can be used by them in further research and development of their own tribal community.

DISCUSSION QUESTIONS

1. Briefly discuss the contrasting roles between researchers and subjects in the participatory research model and the traditional model.

2. Partnership, education, and empowerment are key terms for the outcome expected for any community involved in participatory research. Discuss these three key terms in relation to asset/capacity building in rural communities.

3. Discuss how cross-cultural variables can impact the findings of participatory community-based research.

4. Discuss why focus groups are a necessary aspect of participatory community-based research.

5. Discuss the ethical issues involved in developing a memorandum of understanding (MOU) with the community that is to be the subject of research.

6. Many traditional scientists are concerned that involving the community in the development of the process of research, within the community, can impact the validity of the research outcome. Discuss how involving the community can impact the outcome validity of the research.

CLASSROOM ACTIVITIES AND ASSIGNMENTS

1. Break into groups of eight "ethnic group members," with one "researcher" group leader to identify and discuss hypothetical issues of "mental dependency" for that ethnic group.

2. Break into small groups to act out being members of an ethnic focus group discussing the diagnostic criteria of the DSMV for depression and how the different classifications fit within the normal symptoms expressed by their ethnic group.

3. Form small groups and discuss how you would explain the benefits of participatory research to a tribal council (or any ethnic community council). How would you explain "informed consent" to such a council?

REFERENCES

Albaugh, B. J., & Washa, J. (1987). *Cheyenne alcoholism from a Cheyenne perspective.* Report to the USPHS Indian Health Research Center, Tucson, AZ.

Ansley, F., & Gaventa, J. (1997). Researching for Democracy and Democratizing research. *Change, 29*(1), 46–53.

Baron, A., Manson, S., Ackerson, M., & Brenneman, D. (1990). Depressive symptomology in older American Indians with chronic disease: Some psychometric conservations. In C. Attkisson & J. Zich (Eds.), *Depression in primary care: Screening and detection* (pp. 217–231). New York: Routledge.

Beltrame, T., & McQueen, D. V. (1979). Urban and rural Indian drinking patterns: The special case of the Lumbee. *International Journal of the Addictions 14,* 533–548.

Browne, D. B. (1984). WISC-R scoring patterns among Native Americans of the Northern Plains. *White Cloud Journal, 3,* 15–22.

Common, R. W., & Frost, L. G. (1988). The implications of mismeasurement of Native Student intelligence through the use of standardized intelligence tests. *Canadian Journal of Native Education, 15,* 1.

Couto, R. A. (1987). Participatory research: Metho-dology and critique. *Clinical Sociology Review, 5,* 83–90.

Day, R., Nielsen, J. A., & Korten, A. (1985). Stressful life events preceding the acute onset of schizophrenia: A cross-national study from the WHO. *Culture, Medicine, and Psychiatry, 11,*123–205.

Debbink, G., & Ornelas, A. (1997). Cows for campesinos. In S. E. Smith, D.G. Willms, & N.A. Johnson (Eds.). *Nurtured by knowledge: Learning to do participatory action-research,* (pp. 13–33). New York: Apex Press.

Dewey, J. (1933). *How we think: A restatement of the relation of reflective thinking to the educative process.* Boston: Heath.

Draguns, J. G. (1980). Psychological disorders of clinical severity. In H. C. Triandis & J. G. Draguns (Eds.), *Handbook of cross-cultural psychology* (pp. 178–206). Boston: Allyn and Bacon.

Freire, P. (1973). *Education for critical consciousness.* New York: Seabury Press.

Freire, P. (1982). Creating alternative research methods: Learning to do it by doing it. In B. Hall, A. Gillette, & R. Tandon (Eds.), *Creating knowledge: A monopoly?* (pp. 29–37). New Delhi: Society for Participatory Research in Asia.

Freire, P. (2000). *Pedagogy of the oppressed.* New York: Continuum.

Goldman, D., Brown, G. L., Albaugh, B., Robin, R., Goodson, S., Trunzo, M., Akhtar, L., Waynne, D. K., Lucas-Derse, S., Limmoila, M., & Dean, M. (1993). DRD2 dopamine receptor genotype linkage disequilibrium and alcoholism in American Indians and other populations. *Journal of Clinical and Experimental Research, 17,* 199–204.

Goulet, D. (1973). Introduction. In P. Freire (Ed.), *Education for critical consciousness* (pp. vii–xiv). New York: Seabury Press.

Guilmet, G. M. (1983). The inappropriateness of standardized testing in a culturally heterogeneous milieu: A Navajo example. Research report for the National Institute of Child Health and Human Development, No. ED 261 830, Bethesda, MD.

Hall, B. L. (1981). Participatory research, popular knowledge and power: A personal reflection. *Convergence, 14,* 6–19.

Hall, B. L. (1984). Research, commitment and action: The role of participatory research. *International Review of Education, 30,* 289–299.

Hall, B. L. (1992). From margins to center? The development and purpose of participatory research. *The American Sociologist, 23,* 15–28.

Hall, B. L. (1997). Preface. In S. E. Smith, D.G. Willms, & N. A. Johnson (Eds.), *Nurtured by knowledge: Learning to do participatory action-research* (pp. xiii–xv). New York: Apex Press.

Kerlinger, F. N. (1986). *Foundations of behavioral research.* Orlando, FL: Holt, Rinehart and Winston.

Kinzie, J. D., & Manson, S. M. (1987). The use of self-rating scales in cross-cultural psychiatry. *Hospital and Community Psychiatry, 38,* 190–196.

Kretzmann, J. P., & McKnight, J. L. (1993). *Building communities from the inside out: A path toward finding and mobilizing a community's assets.* Evanston, IL: Institute for Policy Research.

Manson, S. M., Shore, J. H., & Bloom, J. (1985). The depression experience in American Indian communities: A challenge for psychiatric theory and diagnosis. In A. Kleinman & B. Good (Eds.), *Culture and depression* (pp. 331–368). Berkeley: University of California Press.

Manson, S. M., Shore, J. H., Bloom, J. D., Keepers, G., & Neligh, G. (1987). Alcohol abuse and major affective disorders: Advances in epidemiologic research among American Indians. In D. L. Spiegler, D. A. Tate, S. S. Aitken, & C. M. Christian (Eds.), *Alcohol use among U.S. ethnic minorities,* NIAAA Research Monograph No. 18, Department of Health and Human Services

Publication No. (ADM) 87-1435. Washington, DC: U.S. Government Printing Office.

Matchett, W. F. (1972). Repeated hallucinatory experiences as a part of the mourning process among Indian women. *Psychiatry, 35,* 185–194.

McCubbin, H. I., Thompson, E. A., Thompson, A. I., McCubbin, M. A., & Kaston, A. J. (1993). Culture, ethnicity, and the family: Critical factors in childhood chronic illnesses and disabilities. *Pediatrics, 9*(5), 1063–1070.

Miller, S. L., & Schoenfeld, L. S. (1973). Grief in the Navajo: Psychodynamics and culture. *Internet Journal of Social Psychiatry, 19,* 187–191.

Newmann, A. K., Mason, V., Chase, E., & Albaugh, B. (1991). Factors associated with success among Southern Cheyenne and Arapaho Indians. *Journal of Community Health, 16,* 103–115.

Peltz, M., Merskey, H., Brant, C., Patterson, P. G., & Heseltine, G. G. (1981). Clinical data from a psychiatric service to a group of Native people. *Canadian Journal of Psychiatry, 26,* 345–348.

Pollack, D., & Shore, J. H. (1980). Validity of the MMPI with Native Americans. *American Journal of Psychiatry, 137,* 946–950.

Rahman, A. (1978). A methodology for participatory research with the rural poor. *Les Carnets de l'enfance/Assignment Children, 41,* 110–124.

Rhodes, R. W. (1989). Standardized testing of minority students: Navajo and Hopi examples. *Journal of Navajo Education, 6,* 29–35.

Robin, R. W., Long, J. C., Rasmussen, J. K., Albaugh, B., & Goldman, D. (1998). Relationship of binge drinking to alcohol dependence, other psychiatric disorders, and behavioral problems in an American Indian tribe. *Alcoholism: Clinical and Experimental Research, 22,* 518–523.

Rozynko, V., & Ferguson, L. C. (1978). Admission characteristics of Indian and White alcoholic patients in a rural mental hospital. *Internet Journal of the Addictions, 13,* 591–604.

Ryan, R. A. (1979). *American Indian/Alaska Native mental health research: A community perspective.* Paper presented at the Society for the Study of Social Problems, May 1979, Boston.

Shaull, R. (2000). Forward. In P. Freire (Ed.), *Pedagogy of the oppressed* (pp. 29–34). New York: Continuum.

Shen, W. (1986). Single case study. The Hopi Indian's mourning hallucinations. *Journal of Nervous and Mental Disorders, 174,* 365–367.

Shore, J. H., & Manson, S. M. (1981). Cross-cultural studies of depression among American Indians and Alaska Natives. *White Cloud Journal, 2,* 5–12.

Smith, S. E. (1997). Deepening participatory action-research. In S. E. Smith, D. G. Willms, & N. A. Johnson (Eds.), *Nurtured by knowledge: Learning to do participatory action-research.* New York: The Apex Press.

Smith, S. E., Willms, D. G., & Johnson, N. A. (1997). *Nurtured by knowledge: Learning to do participatory action-research.* New York: The Apex Press.

Sue, D. (1977). Barriers to effective cross-cultural counseling. *Journal of Counseling Psychology, 24,* 420–429.

Tandon, R. (1981). Participatory research in the empowerment of people. *Convergence, 14,* 20–29.

Uecker, A. E., Boutlier, L. R., & Richardson, E. H. (1981). Indianism and the Richardson Indian Culturalization Test: A reply to Walker et al. *Journal of Studies on Alcohol, 42,* 168–171.

University of Oklahoma American Indian Institute (1987). *Differential alcohol-implicated mortality among Oklahoma Indians, a tribal comparison of the magnitude of alcohol problems.* A substudy of the Oklahoma Medicare Alcoholism Services Demonstration Project. Monograph no. 00115.

Westermeyer, J. (1985). Psychiatric diagnosis across cultural boundaries. *American Journal of Psychiatry, 142,* 798–805.

INFOTRAC COLLEGE EDITION

alcoholism
American Indians
asset building

community development
Native Americans
participatory research

24

Adults Who Lived
in Out-of-Home Care as Adolescents

A Qualitative Study

PAT CONWAY
TOSHA APODACA
SEAN M. BORZEA
CHAD SHAVER
NANCY TODD

Learning more about the outcomes of adults who lived in out-of-home care as adolescents can provide information to guide organizational change and program development. It allows the identification of strengths existing within programs, communities, families, and children that contribute to positive outcomes, and provides indicators for the most opportune times to intervene. The stories of adults who lived in out-of-home care as adolescents in rural communities also highlight resiliency factors in the lives of adolescents that may have contributed to positive outcomes as adults. In rural, sparsely populated states, the numbers of children in out-of-home care may be smaller than in more urban areas, but the impact on individual lives is just as great.

Out-of-home care includes foster care by relatives; foster care by nonrelatives, either traditional or therapeutic; and placement in group homes, institutions, and independent living apartments (Bates, English, & Kouidou-Giles, 1997; Courtney & Barth, 1996; McDonald, Allen, Westerfelt, & Piliavin 1997; Reddy & Pfeiffer, 1997). The most common reason that children enter out-of-home care is neglect: the failure of caretakers to provide safe, dry, and warm housing; meet basic physical needs, including clean and appropriate clothing and personal hygiene items; and ensure adequate and competent supervision (Briere, Berliner, Bulkley, Jenny, & Reid, 1996). The second most common reason a child enters out-of-home care is physical abuse, the nonaccidental injury to a child under the age of 18 by a parent or caretaker (Briere, et al., 1996). Sexual abuse, the exploitation of a child for the sexual gratification of another person, is the third most common reason (Barth, 1990; Brown & Cohen, 1998; Duramet, Coppel-Batsch, & Couraud 1997; Kendall-Tackett & Simon, 1988; Kendall-Tackett, Williams, & Finkelhor, 1993; Takayama, Wolfe, & Coulter, 1998).

RESILIENCY AND DEVELOPMENTAL STAGE

Outcomes for children in the child welfare system are better understood when placed in the context of knowledge about developmental stages and the interaction between genetic make-up and environment (Shonkoff & Phillips, 2000), the impact of child abuse and neglect at different developmental stages (Howing, Wodarski, Kurtz, & Gaudin, 1993; Thomlison, 1997), and the development of resiliency in adverse conditions. Early childhood development has a critical impact on later outcomes. Events occurring during the period from conception through early childhood can increase a child's chance of successful development (Shonkoff & Phillips, 2000; Siefert, Hoffnung, & Hoffnung, 2000). The importance of enhancing a rural community's capacity to better meet each individual child's needs, rather than just preventing trauma, is vital when thinking of creating the best outcomes for children (Fraser & Galinsky, 1997). Previous research has identified key components for enhancing young children's outcomes, including contact with supportive adults outside the family and a warm mother (Farber & Egeland, 1987). The presence of supportive adults outside the home is an important asset for enhancing resiliency in adolescents (Seifert, et al., 2000).

Understanding "normal" adolescent development contributes to a better understanding of the impact of out-of-home care on adolescents. Adolescence, the developmental stage between the ages of 10 and 22, is characterized by narcissism, exploration, and the development of identity (Bates, et al., 1997; Browne, 1998; Mech, 1994; Seifert, et al., 2000). In addition to discovering and accepting one's identity and separating from primary caregivers, adolescents must confront another major challenge, that of leaving home and becoming a self-sufficient, independent person (Seifert, et al., 2000).

Persons in out-of-home care have more complicated issues during adolescence. Colca and Colca (1996) stated, "Many adolescents leaving their parent's home find the transition difficult. Foster adolescents naturally find it more difficult because of the dysfunctional circumstances related to their entering foster care and the lack of resources and back-up supports available when they leave foster care" (p. 7). McDermott (1987) stated that the development of identity for children in out-of-home care is characterized by three questions: "Who am I? How did I get separated from my birth family? What will become of me?" (p. 101).

METHODOLOGY

A qualitative approach is particularly well suited for gaining in-depth insight into the lives of adults who lived in out-of-home care as children, and their current situations. Six stories from young adults are presented. This qualitative study provides rich information from experts—people who themselves recently left out-of-home care—regarding the experience of living in out-of-home care as adolescents. Their poignant stories highlight the experiences prior to out-of-home care, during care, and after leaving care that contribute to current outcomes, providing much needed insight into the difficulties faced, and inherent strengths necessary to confront the challenges associated with the experience of living in out-of-home care.

The six young adults interviewed consisted of three males and three females, ranging in age from 18 and 20. Each had experienced neglect, physical abuse, emotional abuse, and/or sexual abuse as a child. All six had a parent and other relatives with a mental disorder, which included depression, schizophrenia, alcohol and drug use, and/or anti-social personality disorder. Two had parents that committed suicide. Their experience with public education varied. Two were still in high school, three had graduated from high school, two were attending a community college, and one dropped out of school in junior high school.

The six young adults were first contacted by the child welfare agency. Each volunteered to participate in the study and received $20 following completion of the interview. Tapes of the interviews and their written responses to a structured interview provided the data used to identify and cluster common themes.

Common themes that emerged from these stories include: (1) harm by parents and guardians, (2) a lack of successful prevention and early intervention services, (3) struggles obtaining education, (4) criminal behaviors, (5) multiple moves prior to out-of-home care, (6) multiple moves during out-of-home care, (7) a parent with a mental disorder, (8) diagnosis with a mental disorder,

(9) an agency promoting family reunification, (10) difficulties with employment, (11) financial instability, (12) problematic relationships, and (13) resiliency. Stories from the participants' lives provide examples of each of these themes. The stories are presented for each child, in order by age, so that a comprehensive picture emerges.

RESULTS

Harm by Parents and Guardians

All reported harm inflicted by parents or guardians, including exposure to substances while in utero, abandonment and neglect at a young age by parents, exposure to substances at a young age, educational neglect, physical abuse, sexual abuse, emotional abuse, viewing violence between others in the family, lack of meeting basic needs, and frequent moves. Caregivers, birth parents, grandparents, uncles, and foster parents inflicted the harm. In the following discussion the names of research subjects have been changed to protect their privacy.

Katherine, a 20-year-old female college student, is the older of two children. As a young child, she witnessed her father physically abuse her mother prior to their divorce. Her parent's divorced when Katherine was four years old. Katherine currently has a restraining order to ensure that her father and his parents do not harass her. Katherine described her mother as emotionally abusive. "She would say really, really hurtful things." When Katherine was 10, her mother entered another abusive relationship. As an adolescent, Katherine said that her "family situation was really hard. I raised myself and my brother, I took care of the house, I cooked and cleaned, balanced the checkbook and had to pay the bills. Somebody who is still developing; it is just not something you should have to put a kid through." When Katherine was 16, her mother filed a "child in need of supervision" petition on Katherine because "she didn't want me." Katherine said the petition was "full of lies," because Katherine was

not using drugs or any other illegal activities and she was successful at school at the time.

Tyler, a 20-year-old unemployed male who is currently living with his mother and stepfather, was exposed to alcohol in utero. His mother was drunk when he was born. His parents divorced when he was three months old. Tyler and his older sister lived primarily with their mother, and then with her mother and stepfather when she remarried. Tyler was physically abused by his mother, father, and stepfather. "I used to get beat on from my mom and real dad. My mom would get drunk and come home and I was the target. I was kicked, beat, hit with stuff, there was nothing I could do. There were times that I didn't go to school because I was hit so bad." When Tyler was 10, he was admitted to a psychiatric hospital after attempting to kill his sister. Tyler returned to a foster home, where his foster father would box with him and "beat me up." In the second foster home Tyler was beaten with a belt buckle.

John is a 19-year-old unemployed male who currently lives with his pregnant girlfriend. He and his older sister lived with their father as young children. Their mother, described as an alcoholic and a "pothead," left when John was 13 months old. John was then sent to live with other family members until he was five. Back with his father at five, John remembers alcohol, pot, and heroin parties, lack of supervision, and his own access to the substances at a young age. The two children changed elementary schools frequently, were unsupervised, and did not receive medical or dental care. When their father married a second woman who also used drugs, John and his sister were emotionally abused by their father and stepmother, and John was physically abused. Additionally, they observed violence between their father and stepmother. John stated he had received mental health treatment for depression, ADHD, and abuse. In spite of this outside intervention, the abuse continued until, at age 11, John's father beat John severely. His father used his fists, giving John black eyes with red spots on the eyes, a swollen nose and lips, and knocking out teeth.

Karina, 18, the oldest of five children, lives with John. When Karina was two, her uncle sexually abused her. When she was six, Karina's parents began using drugs and became physically abusive. "They were hitting, kicking, biting, and punching. My parents physically abused my brother and my sisters. I saw my dad batter my mom." They were also left alone "for hours, sometimes for days." Karina also felt emotionally abused. "My parents were mean. They would call me fat and stuff like that, constantly." She also was affected by watching her parents' friends neglect their children. At age 9, Karina was again sexually abused by her uncle. When Karina was 10, she and her siblings were placed together in foster care because her father bit her brother. They were returned home, and the physical and emotional abuse and neglect continued for five years. Karina's parents divorced when she was 14. All of the children were sent to live with their maternal grandparents, because her father was in prison and her mother was unable to cope. From there, Karina was placed in a group home, after stealing from her grandparents. A year and a half later, Karina moved to a foster home. She was there for seven months. The day she left, her foster father threw her against a wall.

Roberta, 18, was sexually abused by nonrelatives when she was two (at a day care center) and when she was seven (by her mother's boyfriend). Roberta was angry that her mother did not protect her from the boyfriend. Roberta said her mother did not have any rules or structure within the home. All of Roberta's brothers used drugs. She thought she was removed from the home because she was a "bad kid," doing alcohol and drugs. Roberta witnessed violence between her parents, and was the object of ridicule within her family.

Jeremy, 18, currently lives with his adoptive family. After his mother disappeared, Jeremy and two older sisters lived with their father and paternal grandparents when Jeremy was one-year-old, he did not see his mother again until he was 13. As a child, Jeremy lived in a "trashy" trailer house in the country. His father, the only person who worked outside the home, was a mechanic. Jeremy stated that he and his sisters could not depend on adults for help with school or rides. His father called him "dumb" and yelled at him. Jeremy's paternal grandmother was "rude" and "mean." When Jeremy was in early elementary school, he and his father and sisters left their grandparents' home, because the paternal grandfather was sexually abusing the girls. They moved from one friend's home to another, sometimes sleeping in their truck. Jeremy entered out-of-home care while he was in junior high school due to "physical abuse, neglect, parental substance abuse and family violence."

A Lack of Successful Prevention and Intervention Services

Even though the six young adults had experienced neglect and abuse throughout their lives, none were aware of receiving successful prevention or intervention services that ameliorated their abuse or neglect. For instance, one stated that he was an "alkie baby" and that his mother drank when she was pregnant with him. He was neglected and physically abused throughout his early life, yet nothing occurred to change his life experiences. All participants in this study reported abuse or neglect occurring years before they were aware of receiving services. Either communities were unaware of the need, communities didn't respond to their needs, or the responses were not successful.

All of the interviewees received interventions after coming to the attention of the child welfare agency and entering out-of-home care, and received some form of counseling while in out-of-home care. Katherine received counseling as a young teenager. She received individual and family counseling at the group home but saw it as ineffective. Katherine also took several different psychotropic medications. John received counseling at school, as a part of his placement in a classroom for children with emotional and behavioral disorders. He received medication for ADHD. Tyler received counseling while hospitalized and at school, in the same type of classroom that John attended. He also took psychotropic medications. Rebecca remembered the investigation regarding the sexual abuse, when she was two, as an intrusive event. She did not view the abuse itself as damaging. She received counseling regarding the second sexual abuse episode when she was at a group home in late adolescence. Karina participated in counseling while in the group home and currently attends Narcotics Anonymous (NA). She said the most helpful intervention was a group for girls who had been sexually abused. Karina took antidepressants. Jeremy said he benefited from an AA-type group while at the boys school.

Struggles Obtaining Education

All had negative educational experiences. One participant struggled due to being more academically advanced than the class as a whole. Three of the participants reported having difficulty learning. One has Fetal Alcohol Syndrome (FAS), the second ADHD; both were in classrooms for children with emotional and behavioral disorders. The third appeared to have cognitive complications, but she did not identify their cause. Five had received counseling through their school setting, the sixth was in counseling in the community. One had struggled with school, perhaps due to frequent moves, depression, and missing a year of school after an accident. All of them experienced multiple moves and therefore attended more than one school before entering out-of-home care.

Katherine, currently attending a community college, moved several times during elementary school. She liked school and felt successful. She was allowed to work at her own pace. Junior high school was difficult, but Katherine said this was due to a move to another school and the beginning of her own depression. Katherine liked high school, where she was able to participate in advanced and honor classes. She did experience stress from academic pressures and complications with her home life. She received her diploma two days after exiting out-of-home care.

Tyler, the 20-year-old unemployed male with FAS, attended special education classrooms for children with behavioral disorders and received counseling and was repeatedly in trouble because of his behavior. "I would hit people, and get kicked out of class. I was a troublemaker." Tyler completed high school through a special education program before exiting out-of-home care.

John has not yet completed high school. He moved frequently throughout elementary school and high school, attended classes for children with emotional disabilities, was explosive at school, was suspended frequently, and eventually quit school. He said he was treated for depression and ADHD. He did attend a variety of special education programs while in public school. John attended Job Corps but was asked to leave. He hopes to complete his GED at some point, but has taken no steps toward completing this goal.

Karina attended five elementary schools. She has little memory of what school was like for her until the fourth grade. At that time, "the teachers were prejudiced against me. And I didn't really learn a lot. I was in trouble and I didn't have friends." Karina also remembers junior high school as unpleasant. She missed most of the seventh grade due to a serious auto accident. Although Karina attended only one month of the seventh grade, she was passed to the eighth grade. Karina missed a good deal of the eighth grade, also. "In the eighth grade, I didn't go but I still passed. I just didn't want to go so I didn't." She had few friends. Her family life was chaotic. Karina completed her GED. She is currently attending an alternative high school; she hopes to graduate soon, although she has missed school due to complications of pregnancy. Karina plans to attend college, so that she can be an elementary school teacher.

Roberta, 18, remembers elementary school as positive, even though she attended three different schools. In elementary school, Roberta attended a special class with six children on a part-time basis, but she does not know why. Junior high was easy for her, but in high school she was in trouble during her freshman and sophomore years, primarily for drug use and rebellious behavior at school. She was suspended and then "put away." Roberta attended a typical high school, school at the group home, and the alternative high school. She missed school and failed courses during her freshman and sophomore year, but was successful in her junior and senior year while attending the alternative high school. She took some courses for college credit during that period. Roberta currently has a 3.7 grade point average at community college.

Jeremy is currently in high school. He hopes to graduate this year and attend the state's four-year college. Jeremy's adoptive parents have agreed to assist him financially. He also hopes to find funding through his sports interest, baseball.

Criminal Behaviors

In all cases, either the participant or the participant's family, or both, had interactions with the legal system. Katherine's father threatened her life. Her brother is in the state boy's school. Tyler's mother's drug use brought her into contact with the law. John's father was imprisoned for stealing, drugs, and beating John. John was in a correctional facility. Karina's mother was on probation for two years for drug-related charges. Her father was sent to prison for drug-related charges. He also had charges in another state. Karina was removed from her grandparents' home for stealing. She was on probation for assault while at the group home. Karina's brother is currently at the state boy's school. Roberta stated that she and her brothers all had participated in illegal activities regarding drugs and alcohol. She "got three tickets for possession in one week." Jeremy's father was in prison for stealing. Jeremy's mother was in a halfway house. Jeremy was in correctional facilities and jail several times.

Multiple Moves Prior to Out-of-Home Care

All of the children moved frequently prior to out-of-home care and expressed concern about the impact moving had on them. Katherine, who experienced many moves, stated that the move in

junior high school contributed to her educational problems at that point. John lived initially with his mother and father, then his father and paternal grandparents. The family moved frequently, living with friends and sometimes sleeping in their vehicle. They moved back to their paternal grandmother's home, and then to a home with their father and stepmother. Tyler lived with his mother and father initially, then with his grandparents. He then moved back with his mother, who moved frequently as she changed intimate relationships. Karina and her family moved often, and a variety of people lived with them, such as grandparents, stepparents, and friends who used drugs. Roberta moved three times while in elementary school. Jeremy lived with his mother and father first, then his father, then his father and stepmother, then his mother. A maternal aunt cared for Jeremy during crisis periods.

Multiple Placements in Care

All of the children moved at least two times while in out-of-home care. Katherine was in the group home and an independent living situation. John had multiple moves, including a crisis home, several foster homes, jail, the boy's school, an episode of running away and staying with friends, and a group home. Tyler was hospitalized several times at private psychiatric settings and the state hospital, and was in foster homes and a crisis center. Karina was in a foster home for two weeks while in the fourth grade. When she reentered care as an adolescent, she was in a group home and a foster home. While in out-of-home care, Roberta moved five times. She was at a drug treatment program, two group homes, and three foster homes. Jeremy was in foster homes, group homes, jail (several times), boys' schools in two states, and crisis centers.

Diagnoses of Mental Disorders: Parents and Guardians

Katherine's mother has depression. Her father had a mental disorder. She described him as dangerous, beating her mother when Katherine was young and recently threatening Katherine's life. Tyler's mother used alcohol throughout Tyler's life. John's mother used substances (alcohol and marijuana) and committed suicide; his father used substances (alcohol, marijuana, and heroin) and was imprisoned. Karina's mother has depression, suicidal tendencies, issues with substance abuse, and criminal behaviors. Her father has paranoid schizophrenia, suicidal tendencies, substance abuse, and criminal behaviors. Roberta's uncle had schizophrenia. She does not know her father. Roberta did not seem to know what might have been going on with her mother's disorganization. Both of Jeremy's parents evidenced mental disorders. His father used alcohol, marijuana, and cocaine and seemed to have antisocial personality disorder. He had been caught stealing, and was described by Jeremy as "short tempered, tearing things up, hitting people, turning tables over, every week or so." His mother committed suicide sometime after Jeremy lived with her when he was 13 years old.

Diagnoses of Mental Disorders: Young Adult

Three participants identified that at one time they were diagnosed with manic depression. One participant was diagnosed with FAS. All but one reported having used substances.

Katherine was diagnosed with bipolar disorder while in out-of-home care. She did not respect the treatment she received, though "the easiest way to keep me unopinionated and just quiet basically was to medicate." Katherine is currently on antidepressants. Tyler has FAS, and reports occasional depression and drinking when he has a chance; his biological father provides Tyler with beer. John stated he is currently in recovery from drug use, but he appeared to be using currently. John stated he has depression, in addition to ADHD. Karina, 18, received counseling in elementary school. She began using drugs at age 13. Karina received antipsychotic medication and antidepressants while in group home care. Roberta has been in NA, completed a two-

and-one-half-year community drug treatment program, and uses marijuana daily and drinks to the point of intoxication at least two times a week. She said she was not depressed, but indicated repeatedly that she was unhappy and dissatisfied with her life. Jeremy currently uses marijuana four times a week, chews tobacco daily, and uses alcohol two times a week.

Family Reunification

The young adults thought that the child welfare agency's goal for all but one of the participants was family reunification. All of the respondents attended family counseling to attempt to reach this goal at some point while they were in out-of-home care. All indicated that they did not feel that returning home was the best goal for them, even though four of the six are currently in close contact with their birth family.

Katherine entered out-of-home care at 16 as the result of a "child in need of supervision" petition filed by her mother. She was adamant that the pressure from the social worker to reunite her with her mother was inappropriate. "They pushed so much, especially with family counseling. They just pushed for family transition, when it was just obvious it wasn't going to work. It was just like beating a dead horse, it was just such a waste. I never really had her as a parent, anyway."

Tyler returned to his mother's home several times as a young adolescent. He repeatedly left because of his and other family members' violent behavior, and was placed in a variety of out-of-home placements. Tyler currently lives with his mother, but stated that they fight frequently and has questioned the wisdom of their living together.

John left out-of-home care to live with his father. He and his father did drugs together. They separated when his father was incarcerated. John has little contact with his father's family now. John's mother committed suicide. He has no contact with his mother's family.

Karina entered foster care first when she was in the fourth grade; the goal of reunification occurred quickly. She and her siblings were only in care for two weeks. The abuse and neglect in her birth home continued. Although Karina was in the group home and the foster home, she participated in family therapy twice monthly, with the goal of reunification. At age 17, Karina left her foster home, after her foster father physically assaulted her. She was in a crisis shelter for two weeks, and then went to live with her birth father. "We fought constantly, because it was a battle of wills. I wanted to do what I wanted and he wouldn't have any say-so."

Roberta, the only person for whom reunification was not a goal, reported that the child welfare agency did not want her to return to her mother's home, and they would not let Roberta spend over nights with her mother for several years. It was Roberta's choice to return to her mother's home. Roberta was evasive regarding why others thought living with her mother was not a good plan for her.

Jeremy and his sisters remained with their father in spite of his drug use, lack of supervision, sexual abuse by the paternal grandfather, and physical violence between adults and against Jeremy. Jeremy then was reunited with his birth mother by the agency when he was in junior high school. They "did not get along very good. She was gone all the time. I never saw her." Finally, reunification with his biological parents was abandoned as a plan and Jeremy was adopted by a family that he identified and introduced to the child welfare agency.

Difficulties with Employment

Only one participant was satisfied with her work experience; she currently has two part-time jobs. One had just obtained a full-time job but it was precarious. Another had just obtained a part-time job and it too was precarious. Two of the respondents were unemployed.

Katherine has two part-time jobs and works a total of 40 hours a week. She is also a full-time student at a community college. She is satisfied with her current employment and anticipates a

positive change in employment as she gains further education.

Tyler is unemployed and receives SSI. Although he has attempted to work, Tyler said he is unable to hold a job longer than a month. John is unemployed. He stated that he cannot hold a job for long. John attended Job Corps for a while but was asked to leave. He hopes to obtain a GED at some point and increase his opportunities for employment but had no concrete plans.

Karina had started a full-time benefited job with a cleaning company, although she was worried that she was going to lose the job. Karina had missed a week of work due to complications of pregnancy. "I pretty much worry about if I am going to lose my job or not. I was sick for a week and I missed all but one day last week. Which is why I don't have to work until Wednesday. They cut my hours." She had attended Job Corps for three months, but left when her boyfriend was asked to leave.

Roberta stated she had a good job, but she hated it, therefore she quit. She found a new part-time job in the previous week, interviewing at the mall on the weekends. Roberta did not think she would return to the job or that it would work out. Jeremy's funding comes from his adoptive parents, who Jeremy views to be well off financially. He has a part-time job at school, but it is not important to him. At this point, completing high school is a top priority for Jeremy.

Financial Issues

All depended on others for financial assistance. Three had been living with birth/adoptive parents in young adulthood. One participant was receiving assistance with rent and groceries from a biological parent. Three participants were receiving medical assistance from a state program, one was receiving benefits from a parent's job, and one received medical benefits from an adoptive family. Another participant relied on SSI for support. One of the people in the study relied on student financial aid. Katherine, as a college student, earns approximately $1,000 per month from educational financial assistance and two part-time jobs. She is satisfied with her capacity to pay rent for her apartment, which she shares with a male friend, and to cover living expenses. Katherine is covered by her mother's health insurance. Tyler receives SSI and is eligible for Medicaid.

John has not had a consistent income or home since leaving out-of-home care. He has lived with his father, paternal grandfather, a friend, the Job Corps, and his girlfriend. At one point, he was homeless. John is only able to maintain a job for a short period of time before being fired; he stated that he was "extremely bothered by employment problems." He has no health insurance. Karina currently has a full-time job with a cleaning company. It also provides benefits. She receives WIC assistance because of her pregnancy. She stated that her mother paid the rent for the trailer in which she lives; her boyfriend stated that HUD subsidized their housing. The trailer is in poor repair, and they are currently seeking another place to live. Karina receives a small SSI check ($68), Medicaid, food stamps and money from her mother. Karina is worried about being pregnant. "I wanted to be more prepared to take care of my kids. I wanted to have my career started. And I wanted to have a set down place where we wouldn't have to move."

Roberta's only secure source of funding is her educational support through grants and scholarships. She works sporadically. Roberta asks her mother for money often, and thinks she probably receives about $20 monthly in spending money from her mother. Roberta's source of funds for drugs was not apparent. Jeremy's funding comes from his adoptive parents; as a result, he views his finances as stable. He earns a small income from a part-time job and receives an allowance from his adoptive parents.

Problematic Relationships

All reported having difficulty in their relationships with biological parents/birth family. Two participants were having difficulty maintaining relationships with friends. Two participants reported having very few friends. One has struggled to fit in with peers.

Katherine was satisfied with her social support system. She currently has a good relationship with her mother, although "when I left the system I was so upset that if I never talked to my mother again, it wouldn't have made any difference to me." Katherine's mother has returned to college, and they eat lunch weekly. During lunch, Katherine tutors her mother. Katherine has no contact with her father or his family, at her choice. She has a close relationship with her brother. She hopes he will live with her when he leaves "the system." Katherine is close to her mother's parents, who live in another state. She has five male friends that she considers best friends. She does not have a close, intimate relationship or any female friends.

Tyler described himself as a loner. His relationship with his mother and stepfather is physically violent. Tyler drinks with his birth father. Tyler expressed concern about his lack of friends. He said he is close with his sister, but hasn't seen her for at least five years. She lives in another state. Tyler's girlfriend is not allowed to see him.

John lives with his pregnant girlfriend, who is his primary support. He expressed concern about a lack of friends. Karina perceives her support system as strong, including John, her parents, and her grandparents. Her father attends NA meetings with her. Her mother provides some financial support and takes Karina to doctors' appointments. Although she sees her parents as part of her support system, Karina says they are not reliable. "They are constantly fighting back and forth so I get stuck in the middle." Karina is particularly close with her brother who lives at the boys' school. Karina also maintains supportive contact with the members of her sexual abuse group from the group home.

Roberta depends on her mother to listen to her, but her mother usually cannot help financially or practically. Roberta's maternal grandmother also listens, but she has had a serious stroke recently. Roberta's boyfriend lives in California. She rated her other friends as less supportive. Jeremy is very close to his adoptive mother and seems attached to the entire family. "We are close. She always comes to my basketball games." He considers his adoptive father a "cool guy." Jeremy spoke fondly of both his maternal and paternal grandparents, although they live in other states and he does not see them often.

Resiliency

All participants have survived and continue to live their lives despite the adversity they have endured. Katherine demonstrates great potential for success, given her current independence and academic achievements. In spite of exposure to alcohol while in utero, and a very chaotic early life, Tyler managed to survive to adulthood without being institutionalized. He has stable income through SSI. John, who was neglected and abused from a young age, abandoned by his mother, encouraged to use drugs by his father, and who was seriously injured in two automobile accidents, continues to struggle in most areas. He has an important intimate relationship with someone who cares about him. Karina, currently pregnant, completed her GED and hopes to graduate from high school in spite of earlier negative educational experiences and a history of frequently missing school. She aspires to attend college, is able to think critically concerning her situation, and cares for others. Roberta is friendly, outgoing, and energetic. She continues to struggle with family relationships and drug use, but her engaging nature increases her potential for getting through this transition period and finding a more successful adulthood. Jeremy appeared very intelligent; he is a problem solver, able to look to the future. For instance, he said he told his adoptive parents not to adopt him until he reached 18 so that they could continue to receive foster care funds. He has an excellent memory and is a capable storyteller. Jeremy is able to learn from his experiences: "The Boy's School helped me quit being an idiot."

DISCUSSION

The outcomes of the young adults whose stories are presented here are varied, depending on their genetic heritage, events during fetal development, their family experiences during early childhood, and the impact of the broader community environment. Identifying strengths within the young adults has the potential to improve their adult lives. Identifying assets within the rural communities in which the child and their family lives can prevent the factors that reduce a child's resilience and increase his or her opportunity for success.

Areas of resiliency within the child and their family include strong family ties. All but one of the adults has reconnected with their birth family. Each has strong relationship ties to family members and friends. Communities had, at points in the children's early lives, attempted to intervene and protect them in dangerous situations. Each of the young adults had an opportunity at some point to participate in therapy, and they identified some kinds of interventions that they perceived to be more successful.

The predominant theme emerging from these stories is that, as children, the storytellers' resiliency has been compromised by early life experiences. The combination of their potential for genetic predispositions to mental disorders and the many assaults they experienced during childhood predicts poorer outcomes in adulthood. Rural communities are placed in the position of finding ways to ameliorate the risk factors for children subject to abuse and neglect; for instance, ensuring that children' development is protected in utero, that they have adults present from birth who encourage secure attachment, and that the family has their basic needs met. Increasing social support and reducing poverty would directly address these concerns. These interventions require community collaboration in prevention, identification, and intervention.

Recommendations for community models for serving children exist in the fields of health, public health, mental health, school social work, juvenile justice, developmental disability, as well as child welfare. Given that the concepts of communities working together to serve children are not new, why are children still unprotected? This question must be answered in order to solve the problem of allowing children to be harmed, thus compromising their potential for success in adulthood.

Strategies for improving outcomes of adults who lived in out-of-home care in a rural community as adolescents include early prevention and intervention to increase resiliency and reduce risk factors. Some possible strategies include:

1. Pursuing aggressive early identification of children and families at risk (perhaps easier in small communities where everyone knows everyone else);

2. Building on the community's commitment to caring for and about children, increasing the community's capacity to ensure each child's safety;

3. Increasing knowledge about the destructive impact of child neglect and child psychological abuse and methods for preventing them;

4. Creating a broader permission for communities to intervene to protect children (sometimes more difficult in a rural community where personal freedom and independence are highly valued);

5. Increasing the number of safe out-of-home care settings that can serve a range of levels of care (another challenge in a sparsely populated area when one values the "least restrictive" setting as close to the child's home as possible);

6. Ensuring that interventions during out-of-home care enhance the presence of consistent, warm, reliable adults who respect children and have hope for their future;

7. Considering the ties that children and families have, and creating family interventions, assuming that the young adult child will reunite with his or her birth family; and

8. Preparing children for an adulthood that includes support into young adulthood that mimics that of a birth family.

Because studies rarely include people who live in rural, sparsely populated states, or the geographic characteristics of the sample are not included, it is difficult to identify the characteristics of out-of-home care that are unique to a rural, sparsely populated area and their impact. These stories set the stage for further exploration into a way to identify the assets in rural, sparsely populated communities, families in those communities, and children in the child welfare system. Learning from a larger sample of children, families, and communities in varied rural settings will add to this knowledge and improve the community's capacity to provide the most beneficial climate for children to grow and succeed.

DISCUSSION QUESTIONS

1. What are the pros and cons of the existing research regarding outcomes of out-of-home care?

2. What are some of the strengths and limitations of qualitative research methods, such as the use of life stories?

3. What strengths did the adults interviewed in this study present?

4. What characteristics of rural communities can be considered assets when thinking about creating a nurturing environment for children and families?

5. How might living in a rural, sparsely populated area improve outcomes for people in out-of-home care? What might be the concerns?

CLASSROOM ACTIVITIES
AND ASSIGNMENTS

1. Working in a small group, create an imaginary rural community that would provide safety for children. How large would the community be? What would be the income level of people in the community and their sources of income? What is the economic base for the community? What kind of formal and informal supports exist (especially those that impact on families and children)? How would services such as education and health care be provided? Financed? What is the role of social work in this community?

2. Develop a plan for the "rest of the story." How could one conduct the next step in this research project, learning about outcomes of children in out-of-home care from a sample that is generalizable to a larger population? Considering the characteristics of qualitative and quantitative research, what research design would you choose? How would the concept of "level of rurality" impact on what would be considered the larger population? What characteristics of rural communities need to be considered when determining the feasibility of your planned data collection procedures?

REFERENCES

Barth, R. P. (1990). On their own: The experience of youth after foster care. *Child and Adolescent Social Work, 7*(5), 419–440.

Bates, B. C., English, D. J., & Kouidou-Giles, S. (1997). Residential treatment and its alternatives: A review of literature. *Child and Youth Forum, 26*(1), 7–51.

Briere, J., Berliner, L., Bulkley, J. A., Jenny, C., & Reid, T. (Eds.). (1996). *The APSAC handbook on child maltreatment.* Thousand Oaks, CA: Sage.

Brown, J., & Cohen, P. (1998). A longitudinal analysis of risk factors for child maltreatment: Findings of a 17-year prospective study of officially recorded and self-reported child abuse and neglect. *Child Abuse & Neglect, 22*(11), 1065–1078.

Browne, D. C. (1998). The relationship between problem disclosure, coping strategies and placement outcome in foster adolescents. *Journal of Adolescence, 21,* 585–597.

Colca, L. A., & Colca, C. (1996). Transitional independent living foster homes: A step toward independence (a program for foster adolescents). *Children Today, 24*(1), 7–11.

Courtney, M. E., & Barth, R. P. (1996). Pathways of older adolescents out of foster care: Implications for independent living services. *Social Work, 41*(1), 75–83.

Duramet, A., Coppel-Batsch, M., & Courad, S. (1997). Adult outcome of children reared for long-term periods in foster families. *Child Abuse and Neglect, 21* (10), 911–927.

Farber, E. A., & Egeland, B. (1987). Invulnerability among abused and neglected children. In E. J. Anthony & B. J. Cohler (Eds.), *The Invulnerable Child* (pp. 253–287). New York: Milford Press.

Fraser, M. W., & Galinsky, M. J. (1997). Toward a resilience-based model of practice. In M. W. Fraser (Ed.), *Risk and resilience in childhood: An ecological perspective* (pp. 265–275). Washington, DC: National Association of Social Workers.

Howing, P. T., Wodarski, J. S., Kurtz, P. D., & Gaudin, J. M. (1993). *Maltreatment and the school-age child: Developmental outcomes and system issues.* New York: The Haworth Press.

Kendall-Tackett, K. A., & Simon, A. F. (1988). Molestation and the onset of puberty: Data from 365 adults molested as children. *Child Abuse & Neglect, 12*(1), 73–81.

Kendall-Tackett, K. A., Williams, L. M., & Finkelhor, D. (1993). Impact of sexual abuse on children: A review and synthesis of recent empirical studies. *Psychological Bulletin, 113*(1), 164–180.

McDermott, V. A. (1987). Life planning services: Helping older children with their identity. *Child and Adolescent Social Work, 4*(3/4), 97–115.

McDonald, T. P., Allen, R. I., Westerfelt, A., & Piliavin, I. (1997). *Assessing the long-term effects of foster care.* Washington, DC: Child Welfare League of America.

Mech, E. V. (1994). Foster youths in transition: Research perspectives for independent living. *Journal of Child Welfare League of America, 73*(5), 603–623.

Reddy, L. A., & Pfeiffer, S. I. (1997). Effectiveness of treatment foster care with children and adolescents: A review of outcome studies. *Journal of American Academy of Child and Adolescent Psychiatry, 36*(5), 581–588.

Seifert, K. L., Hoffnung, R. J., & Hoffnung, M. (2000). *Lifespan development* (2nd ed.). Boston: Houghton Mifflin.

Shonkoff, J. P., & Phillips, D. A. (Eds.). (2000). National Research Council and Institute of Medicine Committee on Integrating the Science of Early Childhood Development. *From neurons to neighborhoods: The science of early childhood development.* Washington, DC: National Academy Press.

Takayama, J. I., Wolfe, E., & Coulter, K. P. (1998). Relationship between reason for placement and medical findings among children in foster care. *Pediatrics, 101*(2), 201–208.

Thomlison, B. (1997). Risk and protective factors in child maltreatment. In M. W. Fraser (Ed.), *Risk and resilience in childhood: An ecological perspective* (pp. 50–72). Washington, DC: National Association of Social Workers.

INFOTRAC COLLEGE EDITION

child welfare
early intervention
out-of-home care

prevention
qualitative
resiliency

25

Evaluating Media Strategies in Rural Communities

The Appalachian Domestic Violence Project

GLENN SHIELDS

WILLIAM KING

MARIAN WILLIAMS

SARAH CHARD

STEVEN LAB

The physical abuse of women and children is a major social problem that can be found in every community, whether urban or rural. Domestic violence knows no boundaries. It cuts across race, ethnicity, and socioeconomic status. However, there is disagreement in the literature as to whether domestic violence is more or less prevalent in rural areas (Feyen, 2001). Social workers who respond to domestic violence in rural communities face an unusual set of demands, often much different than those in urban areas.

According to Gumpert, Saltman, and Sauer-Jones (2000), rural social workers must contend with a "rural life style." This includes the prevalence of natural or informal helping networks, cultural norms of a slower pace of life, the importance of informal communications, suspicion of governmental control and outsiders, and the value of independence. Each of these factors must be considered by social workers in rural communities.

Hamlin (1991) argues that combating domestic violence is best done through a community-based systems approach that involves a coalition of law enforcement, medical services, shelter, and social and mental health services. Martinez-Brawley (1990) suggests that distinctive physical and economic features, face-to-face social rela-tionships, and the integral roles of local organizations such as schools and churches characterize rural communities and can inhibit coalition building.

The Duluth Model (Shepard & Pence, 1999), adopted in the Appalachia region of Ohio in 1998, is such a community-based approach to domestic violence. This psychoeducational model is based on a nationally recognized curriculum for treating men who batter. Its main premise is that domestic violence is a choice and perpetrators must be held accountable. The treatment approach involves group discussions, role-playing exercises, video vignettes, and homework assignments. The overall goal is to help perpetrators of domestic violence learn appropriate nonviolent alternatives and develop healthier patterns of conflict resolution.

During implementation of the Duluth Model in the Appalachia region of southeast Ohio, crisis response teams, service providers, and community members attempted to build community coalitions to respond to victim needs and prevent domestic violence. Each coalition used a different style of publicity campaign—consisting of radio ads, billboards, and newspaper ads—to inform the general public and victims about domestic violence and available services.

This article evaluates the success of these publicity campaigns. Evaluating social work practice is an important part of helping communities to combat social ills. Evaluation is based on the simple premise that our efforts to cure social problems must be checked to ensure they are effective. If our attempts are unsuccessful, we should try another solution. Furthermore, our evaluations must be systematic. Although it is easy to rely on anecdotal data to document success, it is better to ensure that our efforts were successful by vigorously evaluating the impact of our efforts. This article details an evaluation of the Appalachian Domestic Violence Project publicity campaign, by systematically questioning service providers and the public, to see if they noticed an increase in publicity concerning domestic violence.

DEFINING THE REGION

To concisely define Ohio's region of Appalachia is a complex task. The most geographically inclusive delineations, such as the one used by the Appalachian Regional Committee (ARC) in 1965, include a swath of the Eastern States stretching from southern New York State to northern Mississippi, Georgia, and Alabama (see Drake, 2001, p. 176). In addition to the 27 counties in southeast Ohio classified by the ARC as Appalachian, three counties contiguous to these were included in the domestic violence coalition.

There is considerably less agreement about what unique cultural attributes distinguish Appalachia from the rest of the United States and the causes of this alleged uniqueness. For example, Drake (2001) contends that Appalachia is distinguished by five characteristics: (1) a unique place inhabited by unique people, (2) a region which relies on outside cash sources, (3) a region which relies heavily upon farming, (4) an area characterized as wilderness, and (5) an area diverse enough to provide examples of just about any stereotype. Weller (1966) posits that Appalachian people are fearless, independent traditionalists who are person–oriented. In addi-

tion he argues they have a fatalistic outlook on life and prefer unique events instead of routines. Other scholars, however, have criticized Appalachian stereotypes (Billings, Norman, & Ledford, 1999), and suggested that the "belief in a distinct, regionwide Appalachian subculture resistant to economic development was shaped by a large body of literature that accepted uncritically a fictional Appalachia invented by local color writers of the late nineteenth century" (Lewis, 1999, p. 38).

It appears that much of this recent debate is not whether a unique Appalachian culture exists, but rather what this culture embodies and what factors have contributed to its development. For example, some contend that Appalachia has developed a culture that disdains social advancement and perpetuates helplessness and the victimization of the people of Appalachia (Weller, 1966). The competing view claims that outsiders have exploited Appalachia as a resource-rich "colony." Some scholars even state that Appalachian people have been victimized by social and economic forces that are beyond their control (Bean & Jackley, 2001; Billings, et al., 1999; Drake, 2001; Harper, 2000).

DOMESTIC VIOLENCE
IN APPALACHIA

There is ample evidence that two factors make combating domestic violence in Appalachian areas troublesome. First, the role of women in Appalachian culture makes combating domestic violence particularly difficult. This is not to say that domestic violence is more prevalent among Appalachians, or that everyone who lives in an Appalachian area is "really" Appalachian. Rather, a number of scholars contend that certain aspects of Appalachian culture serve to isolate and thus result in disempowerment of women (Seitz 1995; Smith 1999). Harper (2000) states that "Appalachian girls learn to be dependent, caring, mothering and socially responsive to relatives and acquaintances"

(p. 76). Second, it appears that victims of domestic violence have trouble finding accessible, responsive help from existing organizations. In her study of Appalachian women, Seitz (1995) notes, "The institutions of community have failed the people of South-West Virginia: churches, schools, community organizations, the union (UMWA), local government, law enforcement, the courts, health care providers, and social service agencies have been described by the women in this study as inaccessible, degrading, oppressive, or, at best, irrelevant to their daily lives and struggles" (p. 102). In sum, combating domestic violence in rural Appalachia is a daunting task.

Adding to this body of literature, several researchers have noted isolation in rural areas as a major factor that complicates an effective response to domestic violence. Victims who live in rural communities were described as unable to leave abusive relationships (Pagelow, Straus, & Gelles, 1990; Dobash & Dobash, 1979). Feyen (2001) posits that battered women in rural communities tend to be disconnected from their social networks, which further compounds the issue of isolation. She argues that because physical abuse is a source of shame and fear victims are unlikely to connect with services. This is especially troublesome in rural communities where programs and services can fail their clients because of fragmentation and a lack of coordination within and among agencies (Hamlin, 1991).

Faced with this considerable task, social workers and other human service providers launched the Duluth Model in a communitywide approach to preventing domestic violence in Ohio's Appalachian region. This community response approach involved the efforts of local community domestic violence prevention groups, criminal justice agencies such as police and sheriff's officers, prosecutors and judges, and social service agencies. The goal was to produce a broad-based response to domestic violence by coordinating the efforts of these disparate agencies.

One of the first problems the leaders encountered, however, was finding and enlisting the aid of existing service providers. Most of the communities had existing programs and services to assist children and families experiencing family violence. The main question was how to organize an effort that would result in a coordinated and conceptually clear community-based response in order to support victims and respond in an effective manner to perpetrators. Professionals that made up the crisis response teams determined that an initial key element in this process was trying to educate local residents about domestic violence and providing victims with information about shelters, medical, legal, and social services. In sum, the community response approach should also benefit from an increased awareness of domestic violence (and domestic violence service providers) among the general population.

INFORMING THE PUBLIC

Many studies have attempted to ascertain the impact of public awareness campaigns on attitudes and behaviors. Much of the previous research has focused on health-related issues such as AIDS awareness, smoking, and drug use in order to examine the extent to which the public has become knowledgeable about pressing health concerns. Zucker (1978) asserts that because of the pervasiveness of the media, public awareness campaigns can reach those who do not see or hear them. Regardless, research is mixed with regard to the effectiveness of these campaigns.

In a study of AIDS awareness, Hardy (1990) selected a nationally representative sample of over 40,000 adults to determine knowledge about AIDS after a publicity campaign featuring radio, television, and brochures. The study was aimed at examining knowledge of AIDS within particular demographic subgroups. Results indicated that awareness in general was high, but that certain subgroups had more limited knowledge. In particular, racial–ethnic minorities and those who were less educated than the general population had less knowledge about AIDS than others in the sample. This is troubling because most HIV-infected persons—about two-thirds—are African American or Latino. This includes an increasing number of African American females who are infected. In addition, AIDS education has been difficult for high-risk populations (e.g., the homeless, high school dropouts, etc.), a disproportionate number of which are African American or Latino (Rosenberg & Biggar, 1998). This suggests that although public awareness campaigns have the *potential* to reach wide audiences, they are not as effective in reaching certain *target* audiences who would benefit from the information.

Other studies have assessed the impact of public awareness campaigns on attitudes and behaviors. A study by Popham, Potter, Bal, Johnson, Duerr, and Quinn (1993) examined whether antismoking media campaigns help smokers quit. The authors evaluated a campaign in California that appeared in 1990–1991 through the use of radio, television, and billboards. Results indicated that the campaign did in fact influence a substantial number of smokers to quit. These results are tempered, however, by a study conducted by Murray, Prokhorov, and Harty (1994) that found mass media campaigns certainly increase exposure to the issue, but have little impact on beliefs and behaviors.

Relevant to the current study and supporting the research by Murray, Prokhorov, and Harty (1994), a study by Kolasa, Horner, Wilson, Irons, Black, and Causby (1995) assessed adult attitudes regarding school-based health services in a rural community. Assessing a public service announcement campaign that involved radio, television, newspapers, posters, and booths, results indicated that the media campaign did not modify attitudes and behaviors.

In sum, there are mixed results regarding the effectiveness of public awareness campaigns. What can be said, however, is that public awareness campaigns do not necessarily reach the target population; even if they can, they do not necessarily alter attitudes or behaviors about the particular issue. This is troubling, considering the perceived need for coalition building in

Appalachian areas. Rural and isolated populations may be hard to reach with public awareness campaigns and, if it is true that this type of population does not seek to empower women, it could be said that even a saturated public awareness campaign may not be effective in helping to create coalitions that attempt to alter perceptions of domestic violence in these areas.

THE DOMESTIC VIOLENCE MEDIA CAMPAIGNS

Three different groups, modeled on the Duluth community domestic violence prevention model, were created during 1999 in southeast Ohio. Each utilized a different media campaign. We will refer to these three groups as West, Central, and East, based on their section of the 27 counties that make up Appalachian Ohio, along with the three contiguous counties referred to earlier. One group served a 9-county region; one served 10 counties; the third served 11 counties. All three groups used brochures or pamphlets to educate the public, victims, and other service providers about the services available for victims. Furthermore, each group relied on both formal and informal contacts with the print and/or broadcast media to advertise their existence, the domestic violence issues they hoped to raise awareness of, and their activities.

These three groups differed, however, in their primary effort to reach the public and other service agencies. The most formal of the initiatives, used by the East region, was to rent 23 billboards (in 9 of their 10 counties) for at least one month. The billboards were located along well-traveled roads in each county and provided the phone number of a local domestic violence hotline. This region also distributed 50 antidomestic violence posters to local service providers. The Central region utilized public service announcements (PSAs) that ran on local radio stations, sponsored a poster competition in the local schools, and conducted a candlelight vigil. The media campaign in the West region tended to be the most informal, and concentrated on publicizing local events and activities via newspapers and radio shows. The West region also conducted a march for domestic violence, and staffed an information booth during Lilith Fair (a popular, all-female music festival). Overall, however, the bulk of money was directed toward purchasing billboards in the East region, purchasing radio advertisements in the Central region, and less-formal contacts with the media in the West region. This variation in publicity campaigns permits us to assess the effectiveness of each of these techniques in reaching the public and other service providers.

ASSESSING THE EFFECTIVENESS OF THE MEDIA CAMPAIGNS

During 2000 we surveyed a sample of the population of these three regions, as well as local service providers, to assess the effectiveness of these three different media campaigns. This section will describe the methodology, data analysis, and findings of this assessment.

The Public Survey

A survey was mailed to a random sample of 3,000 residents (1,000 from each of the three regions) 18 years or older during 2000. One wave of this survey, with a postcard follow-up of nonrespondents, netted 792 completed, usable surveys (response rate = 27.5%). One hundred and nineteen surveys were returned as undeliverable. The survey asked respondents whether they had noticed an increase in the amount of media information about three topics (domestic violence, gangs, and drug use). Respondents who claimed they had noticed an increase in information over the past year concerning domestic violence were also asked to identify the media source of this increased information (TV, newspapers, bill-

boards, radio, magazines, or fliers/brochures). Almost 28% of the respondents in all three areas reported seeing an increase in the amount of information about domestic violence. A decrease was noticed by 4%, and the majority (68%) observed no change. A 28% increase is not outstanding; however, this suggests that the change in public perceptions were in the expected and desired direction.

To better assess the effectiveness of each group's media campaign, researchers asked those who saw an increase in information to identify the media outlet through which they noticed this increase. Respondents could identify more than one media source. It was expected that respondents from each region would be more likely to identify that particular group's media campaign as the source of the increased information. For example, respondents from the East group should have perceived greater information attributable to billboards than respondents from the other two groups.

For the East group (which concentrated on billboards), only 18% of respondents who noted an increase in information attributed it to billboards, and 19% attributed it to fliers/brochures (see Table 25.1). Most of the respondents in the East region attributed the increase to newspapers (72%) and television (57%). In the Central region, which relied heavily on radio, only 22% reported radio as the source of increased information, while 80% attributed it to newspapers and 78% to television. Finally, respondents in the West region reported seeing increased information in newspapers (74%) and television (68%), with fewer seeing an increase in information on the radio (31%).

These results suggest that the media efforts had little impact on the public's knowledge of domestic violence. In each area respondents reported increased domestic violence information on television, even though no group specifically utilized that media. Only for newspaper coverage, which all three groups used, did the results show some impact. It is questionable, however, whether the increased perceptions for the newspaper coverage

Table 25.1 Media Campaigns, Public Perceptions, and Service Provider Perceptions, by Group

Region	Primary Media Use	Public Perception of Source of Increase		Service Provider of Sources of Increase	
East	Billboards	Newspaper	(72%)	Pamphlets	(64%)
	Posters	TV	(57%)	Newspaper	(60%)
		Billboards	(18%)	Radio	(56%)
Central	Radio PSAs	Newspaper	(80%)	Radio	(83%)
	Vigil	TV	(78%)	Pamphlet	(67%)
		Radio	(22%)	Newspaper	(50%)
				Poster	(50%)
West	Newspaper	Newspaper	(74%)	Newspaper	(62%)
	Radio	TV	(68%)	Pamphlet	(46%)
	March	Radio	(31%)	Radio	(46%)
	Info Booth			Television	(31%)
				Posters	(31%)

were due to the groups' efforts. Based on the data about the other media forms, the changes in domestic violence information are most likely due to general changes in media coverage, independent from the groups' efforts.

The Service Provider's Survey

Community coalition building requires the collaboration of local community groups; in this case, agencies that provide services to victims of domestic violence. This coalition-building activity can benefit from the media campaigns. To assess the impact of the three media campaigns, local providers of domestic violence services were surveyed.

A list of domestic violence service providers in each group's region was collected. Each group provided a list of local service providers, and this list was supplemented with statewide lists of agencies providing social services in each county (e.g., drug and alcohol, and mental health agencies) and with agencies known to the local social service umbrella agencies. These three sources produced a list of 191 local agencies. Sixty-five usable surveys were returned (response rate 34%). Many of the nonrespondents may have refrained from responding because domestic violence is

only a small portion of their overall agency workload. The survey asked the agencies about their perceptions of media changes in coverage of domestic violence, if that coverage had changed, and, if they reported an increase in information, the source of the increased information.

Only 8 agencies responded from the Central region, and 16 from the West region. Overall, the majority (69%) of respondents in all three areas reported that they had noticed an increase in media attention to domestic violence over the past year. When asked to identify the source of this increased media attention, service providers in the East region attributed it mostly to pamphlets/fliers (64%), newspapers (60%), and radio (56%) (see Table 25.1). Only 36% of respondents noticed increased domestic violence information from billboards, the media technique most used in the East region. In the Central region, where radio was the primary media outlet used, service providers attributed the increase in information to radio (83%), pamphlets/fliers (67%), and newspapers and posters (both 50%). It appears that service providers were more cognizant of this area's attempts to employ radio to inform the public. Finally, in the West region, service providers reported that newspapers (62%), pamphlets/fliers and radio (both 46%), and television and posters (both 31%) were responsible for the increased information.

These results suggest that service agencies observed an increase in public information concerning domestic violence, although it was not always due to each group's efforts. For example, in the East region, only about one-third of agencies noticed the billboards. The efforts of the radio campaign; in the Central region appeared more effective, however, the low number of responses makes this a tentative conclusion. The various approaches employed in the West region appear to be reflected in the responses. Overall, it is difficult to find clear evidence that any of these media campaigns, conducted over a 12-month period, were effective. It is possible that the groups added to a more generalized trend toward more domestic violence coverage in the media, although the work of the individual groups is not evident. Also, it may be that the groups have contributed to a generalized feeling (among service providers) of increased media attention, but that this feeling did not accrue to the specific forms used by each group.

CONSIDERING
THE RESULTS

There is little evidence that the media campaigns succeeded at informing either the general public or domestic violence providers in a significant manner. Results indicate that the specific media outlets targeted by each group were usually not the most influential media sources noted by the public and service providers.

The findings detailed here may be attributed to three issues: dosage, the use of written materials, and saliency. First, interventions such as media campaigns can be considered in terms of their strength or intensity (called dosage) and the time over which they intervene. Insufficient dosages will not have the desired effect. For example, in medicine small dosages of antibiotics may breed

more virulent strains of bacteria and virus. Antibiotics must be administered in sufficient quantities to achieve the desired result. Likewise, each media campaign should have used sufficient and repeated efforts in order to inform the public and other service providers. We suspect that these media campaigns were unsuccessful because they were not sufficiently strong, and were short-term. Measuring the dosage of each media campaign detailed here was problematic. Except for the billboards of the East group, it was not possible to count the number of radio PSAs that were run, how many people heard them, or how many other people received information from the other media initiatives. Simply put, we cannot assess the dosage of these campaigns accurately. This is not to say that these groups did not try hard enough, nor that success is only a matter of trying harder. Rather, these three groups did the best they could with the limited resources they had. Spreading these resources over the entire Appalachian region probably meant that their efforts were spread too thin. Conducting a campaign for 12 months was probably not long enough. Media campaigns must be sufficiently funded, must have good resources, and must run long enough to have an impact. In other words, both dosage and time of intervention are important.

Second, the provision of written information (i.e., brochures, pamphlets, newspapers articles, etc.) may not effectively reach large segments of the Appalachian population targeted. The illiteracy rate in these Appalachian counties is quite high. Illiteracy in any population prevents potential readers from receiving the message, regardless of dosage. Estimates of illiteracy in Appalachia vary, depending on what criteria of "illiteracy" are employed. However, two studies of Appalachian areas estimate illiteracy rates ranging between 15% (in one Ohio county) and 30% (in Appalachian counties in Kentucky).

Third, the degree to which people respond to important issues, such as domestic violence, becomes tied to the saliency of the issues presented. Websdale (1997) found that domestic violence is likely to be considered a private matter among Appalachian people, with physical violence between family members often viewed as an accepted practice. Using the media as a major method to inform Appalachian citizens about the importance of the need to develop a public response to domestic violence is simply not effective because the issue has low saliency.

A final consideration related to the media campaign is the nature of the condition. Simply advertising a specific condition may not in itself produce a desired result. Given the location of the population studied, rural Appalachia, there is evidence that intergenerational abuse observed and experienced is likely to be repeated as one matures from childhood through adulthood (Straus & Stienmetz, 1980; Finkelhor, Gelles, Hotaling, & Straus, 1983). There is also the issue of isolation, discussed earlier, in which services offered by police officers and support services may not be as easily accessible. This may act to deter people from reporting their victimization. In instances where there is need for shelter, great geographical distances must be negotiated. This complicates matters such as continued schooling, especially for younger children. In areas where poverty is present, conveniences such as a phone may not be available. Perhaps an even deeper issue about the violence is that telling a helping professional, such as a social worker or health practitioner, about the violence may be outside the cultural norms.

IMPLICATIONS FOR PRACTICE

Ginsberg (1998) indicates one of the paradoxes of social work in rural areas, as well as smaller communities, is that while there are both shortages and difficulties attracting professionals, those who accept the challenge of rural practice do not gain immediate acceptance simply because services are needed. Citizens in areas like Appalachia operate on a highly personalized basis and rely heavily on church, family, and peer group for decisions and values. Therefore, effective rural practice requires social workers to spend time learning about the community in order to be effective. To advertise and promote the necessity and availability of services for things like domestic violence may be met with resistance and suspicion.

The implications for practice based on findings from this study help validate that the methods of publicizing domestic violence services were not as effective as intended. It would be difficult to assess whether the number of cases increased or decreased in the Appalachian region as a result of a media campaign. If the intent is to increase awareness and promote knowledge about domestic violence in Appalachia, more information about domestic violence, its consequences, and available services may reach an intended audience when publicized on television and newspapers. If monies are available, publicity of the effects of domestic violence and available services should be directed to victims and not based on marketing research.

Finally, the media campaign should be developed as one method in an overall approach to addressing the issue of domestic violence. According to Ginsberg (1998), in smaller communities social workers should be: advocates for services to community members through leadership in social agencies; cautious about expressing one's views, which may be dramatically different than the communities; and proactive in community activities such as religious services, popular festivals, and social functions.

DISCUSSION QUESTIONS

1. Domestic violence is found in both urban and rural communities, yet resources and assets are more readily accessible in urban areas. Discuss the factors that you think might account for this and make suggestions for creating a "systems" approach to remedy this apparent disparity in resources and assets in rural communities.

2. There is little qualitative or quantitative research to examine how the social fabric of a battered woman's rural community affects her experiences and life chances. Discuss what you might expect to find if more qualitative and quantitative research was done to investigate this phenomenon.

3. Assuming that community assets were available to aid victims, recommend how you would make them known (in terms of publicity). Do you believe battered women in rural communities would make themselves available to receive services? Why or why not?

4. Consider the following. You are part of a team at a rural family service agency. The county commissioners have expressed some interest in funding a program that will aid victims of domestic abuse to become "self-sufficient" and less dependent on local welfare services. Given your knowledge of human behavior, define "self-sufficient" and "less dependent." Discuss how you would design *a community assessment* that would provide information to the commissioners regarding community assets such as transportation, job training, education, and counseling. Recommend how these and other assets would be integrated to optimize service delivery? Do you believe the commissioners would be more interested in quantitative data (numbers) or qualitative data (subjective experiences) in deciding what kinds of programs to fund? Why? What would you envision as major obstacles to service delivery?

CLASSROOM ACTIVITIES
AND ASSIGNMENTS

1. Connect yourself to an agency in the community that services either victims or perpetrators of domestic violence. Commit to 10 hours of service learning at one of the following types of agencies: health or mental health, social services, law enforcement, or the courts. Within that structure, develop a research proposal that addresses an area of need. This may be in the form of a needs assessment or program evaluation. Working with someone in the agency, identify a researchable topic, complete an appropriate literature review, define and operationalize variables including dependent and independent variables, describe a method for conducting the research, identify a sample and data collection method, and describe methods of analysis, including qualitative and quantitative data. Present this proposal in class and, if appropriate, to the agency.

2. Write a 10–12 page research paper that examines critical factors in developing a community response to domestic violence in rural communities. Consider such things as isolation, the changing structure of the rural family, availability (or lack of) resources, community attitudes, overall knowledge of domestic violence, and technology including computers. Answer the question of how these elements either collectively or individually impact the community.

3. Investigate your community's response patterns to domestic abuse. Is there an arrest policy when police are called to a domestic abuse situation? How do the courts view domestic abuse? Are perpetrators more likely to be diverted to a counseling program or sent to jail? Can you discern a difference in the health care system's response to victims of abuse compared to others who present for emergency care? What is the prevailing attitude within the community itself about domestic abuse? Could you argue that assets for victims are combined into a consistent and integrated approach that seeks to reduce domestic abuse? Why, or why not, does an integrated approach exist?

REFERENCES

Bean, H., & Jackley, A. (2001). *Women, music and faith in Central Appalachia.* Lewiston, NY: The Edwin Mellen Press.

Billings, D. B., Norman, G., & Ledford, K. (Eds.). (1999). *Confronting Appalachian stereotypes: Back talk from an American region.* Lexington, KY: The University Press of Kentucky.

Dobash, R., & Dobash, E. (1979). *Violence against wives: A case against patriarchy.* Albany: State University Press of New York.

Drake, R. B. (2001). *A history of Appalachia.* Lexington: University of Kentucky Press.

Feyen, C. K. (2001). Isolated acts: Domestic violence in a rural community. In R. Moore (Ed.), *The Hidden America: Social problems for the twenty-first century* (pp. 101–127). Cranbury, NJ: Associated Press.

Finkelhor, D., Gelles, R., Hotaling, G., & Straus, M. (1983). *The dark side of families.* Beverly Hills, CA: Sage.

Ginsberg, L. H. (1998). An overview of rural social work. In L. H. Ginsberg, (Ed.), *Social work in rural communities* (3rd ed., pp. 3–22). Alexandria, VA: Council on Social Work Education.

Gumpert, J., Saltman, J., & Sauer-Jones, D. (2000). Toward identifying the unique characteristics of social work practice in rural areas: From the voices of practitioners. *Journal of Baccalaureate Social Work, 6*(1), 19–35.

Hamlin, E. (1991). Community-based spouse abuse protection and family based preservation team. *Social Work, 36*(5), 402–419.

Hardy, A. (1990). National health interview survey data on adult knowledge of AIDS in the United States. *Public Health Reports, 105,* 630–634.

Harper, K. V. (2000). Appalachian women's ways of living: Within and beyond their cultural heritage. In M. Julia (Ed.), *Constructing gender: Multicultural perspectives in working with women* (pp. 69–88). Belmont, CA: Wadsworth.

Kolasa, K., Horner, R., Wilson, K., Irons, T., Black, C., & Causby, V. (1995). Community perceptions of adolescent health and sexuality: Results from a Southern, community-based project. *Archives of Pediatrics and Adolescent Medicine, 149,* 611–164.

Lewis, R. L. (1999). Beyond isolation and homogeneity: Diversity and the history of Appalachia. In D. Billings, G. Norman, & K. Ledford (Eds.), *Confronting Appalachian stereotypes: Back talk from an American region* (pp. 21–43). Lexington: The University Press of Kentucky.

Martinez-Brawley, E. (1990). *Perspectives on the small community: Humanistic views for practitioners.* Washington, DC: National Association of Social Work Press.

Murray, D., Prokhorov, A., & Harty, K. (1994). Effects of a statewide anti-smoking campaign on mass-media messages and smoking beliefs. *Preventive Medicine, 23,* 54–60.

Pagelow, M., Straus, M., & Gelles, R. (1990). *Physical violence in American families.* New Brunswick, NJ: Transition Books.

Popham, W., Potter, L., Bal, D., Johnson, M., Duerr, J., & Quinn, V. (1993). Do anti-smoking media campaigns help smokers quit? *Public Health Reports, 108,* 510–513.

Rosenberg, P., & Biggar, R. (1998). Trends in HIV incidence among young adults in the United States. *Journal of the American Medical Association, 279,* 1894–1899.

Seitz, V. R. (1995). *Women, development, and communities of empowerment in Appalachia.* Albany: State University of New York Press.

Shepard, M., & Pence, E. (Eds.). (1999). *Coordinating community response to domestic violence: Lessons from Duluth and beyond.* Beverly Hills, CA: Sage.

Smith, B. E. (1999). Beyond the mountains: The paradox of women's place in Appalachian history. *NWSA Journal (National Women's Studies Association Journal), 11*(3), 1–17.

Straus, M., & Steinmetz, S. (1980). *Behind closed doors: Violence in the America family.* New York: Anchor.

Websdale, N. (1997). *Rural women battering and the justice system.* Beverly Hills, CA: Sage.

Weller, J. E. (1966). *Yesterday's people: Life in contemporary Appalachia.* Lexington: University of Kentucky Press.

Zucker, H. (1978). The variable nature of news media influence. In B. Ruben (Ed.), *Communication yearbook, vol. 1* (pp. 225–240). New Brunswick, NJ: Transaction Books.

INFOTRAC COLLEGE EDITION

Appalachia
domestic violence
Duluth Model

media campaign
rural

26

Individual Development Accounts in Rural Communities*

Implications for Research

MICHAL GRINSTEIN-WEISS
JAMI CURLEY

As the American economy becomes more global, the source of its economic health and security changes. In the frontier era, rural areas in the United States were the source of health and security, promising economic growth, new opportunities, and an abundance of jobs. As the economy changed and cities grew, other sources of economic stability emerged, leaving rural communities behind. Today, rural areas suffer from a decrease in job creation, outmigration of young and skilled workers, and a decrease in the demand for many rural products (Henderson, 2002; Pezzini, 2000). As a result, rural areas are in need of sustainable development to help improve their local industries and compete in the new global market. Current discussions emphasize the lack of economic assets in rural communities—as not only a symptom but also as a cause of poverty. These discussions suggest that it might be valuable to include asset building as an approach to reducing poverty in rural areas (Dorward, Anderson, Clark, Keane, & Moguel, 2001).

In the last few years, the value and potential of assets in the form of wealth accumulation—and their positive effects on individuals, families, communities, and the society as a whole—are gaining ground in both academic and policy settings (Scanlon & Page-Adams, 2001). Traditionally, the

major indicator of well-being used by economists, sociologists, and other social scientific researchers was income. Accumulated wealth was a neglected aspect, and scientists were much more engaged in describing and analyzing occupational, educational, and income distributions (Shapiro, 2001). However, recently researchers have recognized the importance of measuring family wealth independently from income.

Although income and assets (wealth) are strongly related, they are different concepts with different meanings (Sherraden, 1991). Income refers to the flow of resources in the household over time (i.e., salaries, wages, government transfer). Families use income to provide the household with daily necessities such as shelter, food, and clothing. The concept of income is usually associated with the consumption of goods and services and the standard of living (Shapiro, 2001; Sherraden, 1991). Contrary to this, wealth is a stock variable. Wealth refers to the total amount of an individual's accumulated assets at a given time. Wealth is measured as the net value of assets minus debt held at a given time (Oliver & Shapiro, 1995). Shapiro (2001) notes: "Wealth is what families own, a storehouse of resources . . . not usually used to purchase milk and shoes or other life necessities. More often it is used to cre-

---

*"In a global economy, your economic health and security is measured by what you own in addition to what you earn" (Senator Bob Kerrey, as cited in Stegman, 1999, p. 10).

ate opportunities, secure a desired stature and standard of living, or pass advantages and class status along to one's children" (p. 12).

Gittleman and Wolff (2000) argue that the economic position of two households earning the same income but having widely different wealth accumulation clearly cannot be regarded as identical. The wealthier family is likely to be living in a better neighborhood that can offer more amenities and lower crime rates, send their children to better schools, provide them with better health care, and have greater resources that the family can draw on in a time of need.

WELFARE BASED ON ASSETS THEORY

The idea of the potential and benefits of asset accumulation as antipoverty policy developed in the seminal work of Sherraden (1991), in which he proposes a theory of welfare based on assets. Sherraden argues that the traditional, income-based welfare policy, which assumed that the consumption capacity of the household as an indicator of the welfare or well-being of that household, is inadequate, and that asset holdings generate positive outcomes that are beyond consumption. Sherraden introduces two primary attributes of his theory. First, according to his theory, household financial welfare should be viewed as a long-term and dynamic process as opposed to a cross-sectional financial position at a specific time. Because assets represent lifetime financial accumulation, they reflect this long-term process much better than income does. Second, the household financial welfare status encompasses more than just consumption, and holding assets generates many positive outcomes.

Asset holdings, according to this theory, yield many economical, psychological, and sociological positive outcomes. As Sherraden (1991) puts it, "people think and behave differently when they are accumulating assets, and the world responds to them differently as well. More specifically, assets

improve economic stability; connect people with a viable, hopeful future; stimulate development of human and other capital; enable people to focus and specialize; provide a foundation for risk taking; yield personal, social, and political dividends; and enhance the welfare of offspring" (p. 148).

ASSETS EFFECTS ON THE COMMUNITY

Most of the research that examines the effects of assets on the community tends to focus on homeownership (Scanlon & Page-Adams, 2001). Results from these studies consistently indicate that homeownership is strongly correlated with a wide range of variables that indicate good citizenship and investment in the community. There is a long-held belief that "compared with renters, homeowners are better citizens, better neighbors, and even better persons" (Rohe & Stewart, 1996, p. 38). Individuals who are homeowners are more likely to participate in volunteer work, be involved in local government, be more aware about their political leaders, become a member in nonprofessional organizations in their community, maintain their properties at a higher standard, and even garden more than nonhomeowners (DiPasquale & Glaeser, 1999; Rohe & Stewart, 1996). In addition, it was found that cities and counties with higher rates of homeownership were characterized by lower levels of government spending. In these areas, a larger share of the government budget was used for education and the improvement of highways (DiPasquale & Glaeser, 1999). Additional support for the belief in the benefits of homeownership can be seen in the increase in government-supported homeownership programs, which have been justified with the arguments that these programs benefit the society as well as the individual (Rohe & Stewart, 1996).

Scanlon and Page-Adams (2001), in their review of the literature on the effects of asset holdings, present four major themes that appear as the effects of homeownership on the community. The first effect is property value. They present many economic studies indicating that homeownership is a good investment for households in the United States. The second effect is the decrease of residential mobility. Homeowners are a major predictor of residential stability; when compared with renters, homeowners tend to stay longer in one location. Residential stability is an important quality, especially due to the fact that residential instability is correlated with negative psychosocial functioning, particularly among youth. Third, homeowners are more likely to invest in property maintenance, such as painting their houses, repairing roofs, and replacing broken or worn out fixtures. Finally, homeownership seems to increase social and civic involvement.

DiPasquale and Glaeser (1999) maintain that homeownership may increase positive community behaviors for two primary reasons. First, being a homeowner provides incentive for the individual to improve his or her immediate community. Second, home ownership leads to longer residence and better property condition because residents are less likely to move frequently. Others suggest that homeowners have a large financial stake in their community and, as a result, they have higher incentives to protect their property values through investment in their neighborhood, school capital, and their community that will generate positive future returns for them and for their children (Aaronson, 2000; Saunders, 1990; Sherraden, 1991).

Beyond the direct effect of assets on the community, holding assets was found to have a profound impact on members of the community. Individuals, children, and families were all found to benefit significantly from holding assets. These benefits included increased well-being, life satisfaction, self-efficacy, positive expectations toward the future, and reduced depression and alcohol use (Page-Adams & Sherraden, 1996; Page-Adams & Vosler, 1996; Rohe & Stegman, 1994; Yadama & Sherraden, 1996). In the family, asset holdings seem to have an effect on entering into first marriages, marital stability, family well-being, and economic security (Scanlon & Page-Adams,

2001). Moreover, parental assets consistently have been found to be related to positive educational outcomes in children (Green & White, 1997; Hill & Duncan, 1987) and better health (Joshi & Macran, 1991).

TOWARD AN ASSET-BASED POLICY

Although the recognition of the potential benefits of asset accumulation for the poor has accelerated in recent years, many governments and institutions still largely use traditional policies in their efforts to alleviate poverty. These traditional policies usually promote and emphasize income transfers (e.g., income support, safety nets, rental assistance or other types of consumption) (Carney & Gale, 2001). Although the policies have succeeded in temporarily easing hardship for many families, it seems that in most cases they have failed to consistently remove people from poverty.

Consequently, the challenge policymakers face today is to create inclusive policies that promote asset building among low-income households. Without asset-building policies that specifically focus on providing equal saving opportunities to everyone, only a few low-income families will have the ability, incentive, and institutional support to save, accumulate assets, and begin the journey to escape poverty (Edwards & Rist, 2001).

ASSET BUILDING IN RURAL COMMUNITIES

Background

Asset building in rural areas of the United States is not a new idea. Government policies dating back to the late 1700s, when the United States gained much of its territory, deal with the distribution of land to the nation's citizens; the Homestead Act of 1862 was a major piece of these policies. Providing they did not bear arms against the United States, any citizen over the age of 21, the head of a household, or a military veteran was entitled to 160 acres of unappropriated land (Dick, 1970). The only requirements were that an interested party had to file an application at the appropriate land office, guarantee the land was for personal use, and begin making improvements on it within six months. After five years, if these conditions were met, an applicant could take final possession of the land at a minimum cost. If these conditions were not met, or the applicant vacated the property before the five years, the land reverted back to the government. The Homestead Act officially came to an end in 1934 when President Roosevelt withdrew all remaining land from public domain (Dick, 1970).

Throughout its duration, the Homestead Act gave 1.5 million households parcels of land totaling 246 million acres (Williams, 2000). According to estimates calculated by Williams (2000), as many as 92 million ancestors of homesteaders could have benefited from the asset effects of the initial investments. In essence, this statute was profitable to everyone. By using national resources to provide property to citizens at a minimal cost, the government allowed anyone who was willing to go West and work the land to build assets that could be passed on to future generations. Homesteading also aided the government in expanding the Western frontier by encouraging population and economic growth in the new territory. As a result of this policy initiative, rural areas of the United States grew and began to prosper.

Rural Communities Today

Since that time, however, rural communities have experienced some dramatic changes. As the economic base shifted from agriculture to manufacturing, cities grew and many people moved from farms to cities to be closer to better jobs and other opportunities not offered by farm communities. As time went on, other changes occurred, causing rural areas to weaken. Because of resource depletion and the high cost of extraction, mines began to close down; technological

changes brought in new machinery and new crop varieties that allowed fewer farmers to feed more people; globalization brought in more competition at lower prices for rural areas that supported businesses such as textile and steel mills; and yet another economic shift from manufacturing to service increased the number of businesses in cities, but decreased the number of businesses in rural communities where the customer base was not as strong (Freshwater, 2000).

Today, some rural communities are struggling to stay alive. Employment opportunities have declined. Young people have migrated out to gain better access to educational facilities, leisure activities, and better employment possibilities. As younger community members move out, they leave behind many of the older population displaced by the changing economy. Furthermore, retirees migrating to some rural areas have created a new demographic composition. Older citizens need a variety of public services that their communities cannot afford to maintain (Pezzini, 2000). In spite of these difficulties, however, many of these rural communities do have certain strengths that could be and have been used to make improvements that benefit everyone. The availability of more land at cheaper prices entices manufacturing and service industries to relocate to these areas, bringing jobs and other businesses. Because of transportation improvements, more urban dwellers are looking at rural areas as a safer and more natural environment in which to live, and some rural areas have capitalized on the tourism industry to increase their vitality (Pezzini, 2000).

In an effort to help improve rural areas, recent government policy has concentrated on individual sectors, such as providing subsidies to farmers without looking at the communities as a whole. Using the Homestead Act as an example, the government could establish policy that aims directly at investing in the people and the infrastructure. Instead of concentrating on their limitations, rural communities can use their strengths to build assets and become more competitive. Individual Development Accounts (IDAs), a current policy initiative that encourages savings and asset accumulation by matching funds in savings accounts for the low-income, are a means by which rural communities could begin to grow again. Depending on the particular program a person is participating in and his or her individual goals, IDAs could be established for a variety of asset-building purposes, including education, homeownership, home improvement, microenterprise, and retirement.

Individual Development Accounts (IDAs) Research

A national policy demonstration, the American Dream Demonstration (ADD) was designed and implemented to evaluate the effects of Individual Development Accounts (IDAs) on asset building. IDAs are matched savings accounts. Unlike savings accounts such as Individual Retirement Accounts (IRAs) or 401(k) plans, IDAs are targeted to the poor and provide subsidies through matches rather than through tax breaks. ADD was the first large-scale test of IDAs as a social and economic development tool for low-wealth households and communities.

Beginning in 1997, the evaluation followed over 2,000 participants at 14 community-based program sites (including four rural sites) across the United States for 6 years. The 14 sites operated their programs for four years with an additional two years used for postprogram evaluation. Participants were allowed to use their accumulated assets for home purchases, home improvements, microenterprise, and education. ADD used an extensive multimethod research design to gather as much information as possible concerning the effectiveness of the programs in terms of the communities, participants, designs, and administrations in order to inform IDA policy and program development outside of ADD (Sherraden, et al., 2000).

Research results from ADD data showed that poor people can indeed save with an average monthly deposit of $25.42. Furthermore, the study reported that financial education, at least up to 12 hours, mattered in terms of higher saving

outcomes, as did asset ownership. The rate at which their own deposits were matched made no difference in terms of how much money participants saved. No significant differences were found between rural and urban participants (Scheirner, et al., 2001).

IDAs IN RURAL COMMUNITIES

Quantitative Results

Data from the Family Assets for Independence in Minnesota (FAIM) project was used to examine the effects of IDAs in rural communities. In the 1998 state legislative session, the Minnesota Community Action Agencies Association initiated IDA legislation. Through inclusion in the Children and Families omnibus legislation, the Minnesota Legislature passed FAIM for IDAs into law. The purpose of the FAIM Pilot Project was to help working poor Minnesotans build wealth and achieve long-term economic self-sufficiency. FAIM was scheduled to run for four years (2000–2003) as a demonstration project; however, it has been currently renewed as an ongoing program subject to yearly funding availability. As of March 31, 2001, 513 IDA participants were enrolled in the program. All participants were considered working poor with an income of 200% or less of the poverty line (Grinstein-Weiss, Schreiner, Clancy, & Sherraden, 2001). Thirty-five percent ($n = 173$) of the participants in the collected data came from rural communities. This sample is the data set used for the following analysis. The purpose of the analysis is to determine what variables explain savings among this population. The results of this examination will have important policy and practice implications for the design of programs such as IDAs, which target low-income people in rural communities.

The dependent variable in this study is Average Monthly Net Deposits (AMND), and is defined as net deposits divided by months of participation. AMND is the key outcome, because greater AMND implies greater savings and asset accumulation in IDAs. The independent variables used included a wide range of participant demographic, financial, and program characteristics (see Figure 26.1).

Descriptives

Eighty-three percent of the participants were female. Ages ranged from 17 to 66 years, with a mean age of 36 years. Approximately 92% of participants were between 20 and 49 years of age. Seventy-one percent of the sample were Caucasian, 24% were Native American, and the remaining 5% were other races. The majority (47%) of the participants were never married, 25% were married, and 27% were divorced or separated, or widowed (1%).

Homes were owned by 38% of the participants and cars were owned by 90%. Thirteen percent of the rural sample had direct deposit while 46% owned a passbook savings account other than their IDA account, and 72% owned checking accounts. Eighty-two percent had either one or the other. The most reported intended use for IDA accounts was home purchase (56%); second was microenterprise (26%); and last was postsecondary education (18%).

As of March 31, 2001, four (2.3%) rural participants had made a matched withdrawal (a withdrawal from their IDA account which included eligible matching funds), and 34 (19%) participants had made unmatched withdrawals (withdrawals from their IDA accounts which were ineligible for matching funds) from matchable balances (balances that were eligible for matching fund withdrawals). Average net deposits per participant were $245 with AMND at $24.43. The average participant made a deposit 9 out of 12 months, saving 86% of their monthly savings target. The average savings rate was 2%.

Multivariate Analysis

In order to assess the unique experiences of rural participants in savings and asset accumulation, Ordinary Least Squares (OLS) regression analysis was used to explore what predicts higher AMND among IDA participants. The unstandardized regression coefficients estimated by this technique give the estimated changes in AMND (in units of dollars of net deposits per month) given a unit increase in a given characteristic, holding all the other independent variables constant (see Table 26.1).

The results of the multiple OLS regression analysis indicated that the model was significant [$F_{(39, 109)} = 5.773$, $p = .000$], and explained approximately 67% of the variance in AMND ($R^2 = .674$). The adjusted R^2, which attempts to correct R^2 to more closely reflect the goodness of fit of the model in the population by taking into account the number of independent variables and sample size, has a value of .557.

A closer examination of the results revealed that the following independent variables were significantly related to the AMND. These variables included: current TANF recipient, dependency ratio, health insurance, direct deposit, the frequency of deposits into IDA accounts, and hours of financial education attended.

Being a current TANF recipient was associated with $7.25 less AMND ($p = 0.048$) implying that participants currently receiving TANF have a more difficult time saving than those who are not receiving assistance. In addition, having health insurance is associated with $5.18 higher AMND ($p = 0.029$), possibly suggesting that those participants who do not have health insurance may have less money to save because of out-of-pocket health expenditures.

The dependency ratio or the number of household members per adult was linked with an increase in AMND of $2.85 ($p = 0.036$). Families with more dependents may feel the pressure of future expenses more heavily than families with fewer dependents, and, therefore, try and save more.

Direct deposit was found to be significantly related to AMND, and participants who had direct deposit were associated with $5.49 higher AMND ($p = 0.035$) than those participants who did not have direct deposit. This result is congruent with

Participant Characteristics	**Gender** Female or male. This variable was dummy coded with female set to one (yes/no). **Age** The age of the participant. Two variables make up this category in the regression: age 40, participants 40 years and younger; and age 41, participants 41 years and older. **Race/ethnicity** Whether the participant identified himself as Caucasian, African American, Asian American or Pacific Islander, Latino or Hispanic, Native American, or Other. In the regression each category was set up as a dummy variable (yes/no). **Education** Whether the highest grade completed corresponded to less than a high school diploma, a high-school diploma, some college but no degree, a two-year college degree, or a four-year college degree or more. In the regression each category was set up as a dummy variable (yes/no). **Employment** Whether the participant was employed full-time, part-time, unemployed, student, not employed, or student, employed. In the regression each category was set up as a dummy variable (yes/no). **Marital status** Whether the participant was married, never married, separated or divorced, or widowed. In the regression each category was set up as a dummy variable (yes/no). **Household size** The number of adults and children living in the household. **Dependency ratio** This variable was calculated by adding the number of children to the number of adults in the household and then dividing it by the number of adults in the household.
Financial Characteristics	**Income total** The sum of the participant's reported household income for a year. **Income/poverty level** The participant's reported household income divided by the family-size-adjusted poverty guideline. **Welfare status** The welfare status of the participant. Two variables make up this category: tanf_now, is participant currently on TANF (yes/no); and tanfnvr, whether participant has never received TANF or not (yes/no). **Foodstamps** Whether the participant received foodstamps (yes/no). **SSI** Whether the participant received SSI (yes/no). **Health insurance** Whether the participant had health insurance (yes/no). **Life insurance** Whether the participant had life insurance (yes/no). **Own car** Whether the participant owns a car (yes/no). **Own home** Whether the participant owns a home (yes/no). **Own business** Whether the participant owns his/her own business (yes/no).
Program Characteristics	**Passbook savings or checking account** Whether the participant owns either a passbook savings or a checking account (yes/no). **Direct deposit** Whether the participant participates in direct deposit (yes/no). **Deposit frequency** How frequent did the participant make deposits. **General financial education** How many hours of general financial education the participant attended. This variable was divided into four categories. The first variable, finged0, was a dummy-coded variable with no education set to one. Finged6 represented participants with up to 6 hours of general financial education; Finged12 represented participants with between 7 and 12 hours; Finged18 represented participants with more than 12 hours.

FIGURE 26.1 Variable List

the proposition suggested by the institutional theory on saving that argues that individuals who are receiving some kind of saving facilitation that makes saving more manageable, simpler to understand, and more convenient will increase their willingness to save (Beverly & Sherraden, 1999).

Direct deposit is a simple and efficient method of facilitation. By taking out the savings directly from one account and putting it into another, it decreases the chance that an individual will use the money for consumption (Beverly & Sherraden, 1999).

Table 26.1 Regression Results

Independent Variables	Standardized Beta Coefficient	t-Value	p-Value	Independent Variables	Standardized Beta Coefficient	t-Value	p-Value
Participant Characteristics				**Financial Characteristics**			
General				*Income*			
Female	−0.075	−1.13	0.26	Total income	−0.32	−1.96	0.06
Age: 40 or under	0.010	0.12	0.91	Poverty level	0.20	1.42	0.16
Age: over 40	−0.023	−0.31	0.76	*Receipt of Public Assistance*			
Race/Ethnicity				Currently on TANF	−0.16	−2.00	0.05
Caucasian				Never on TANF	0.01	0.14	0.89
African American	−0.088	−1.43	0.16	Food stamps	−0.06	−0.70	0.49
Asian American or Pacific Islander	−0.007	−0.12	0.91	Receiving SSI	0.10	1.38	0.17
Hispanic or Latino	−0.101	−1.46	0.15	*Insurance*			
Native American	0.089	1.00	0.32	Health	0.15	2.21	0.03
Other ethnicity	0.008	0.13	0.90	Life	0.05	0.66	0.51
Education				*Assets*			
Completed 4-year degree or more				Own car	−0.09	−1.50	0.14
Completed 2-year degree	−0.100	−1.31	0.19	Own home	−0.09	−1.21	0.23
Attended college	−0.035	−0.41	0.68	Own business	0.03	0.43	0.67
Completed high achool or GED	−0.017	−0.20	0.84	**Program Characteristics**			
Did not complete high achool	−0.035	−0.50	0.62	*Account Structure*			
Employment				Checking or savings account	−0.04	−0.53	0.60
Employed full-time				Direct deposit	0.14	2.14	0.04
Employed part-time	−0.012	−0.15	0.88	Deposit frequency	0.63	8.43	0.00
Unemployed	0.041	0.60	0.55	*Financial Education*			
Student, not working	−0.028	−0.47	0.64	No financial education	−0.64	−2.28	0.03
Student, also working	0.089	1.26	0.21	1 to 6 education hours	−0.66	−2.00	0.05
Marital				7 to 12 education hours	0.37	2.53	0.01
Never married				13 to 18 education hours	−0.21	−2.19	0.03
Married	0.043	0.39	0.70				
Divorced or separated	0.016	0.21	0.83				
Widowed	0.13	1.83	0.07				
Household Composition							
Household size	−0.02	−0.11	0.92				
Dependency ratio	0.22	2.13	0.04				

Deposit frequency is the share of months with a deposit divided by the months of participation. It is expected that as one deposits more often, one will have higher AMND. And indeed the results indicate a statistically significant relationship between deposit frequency and AMND; a unit increase in deposit frequency is associated with a $30.33 increase in AMND. Schreiner and colleagues (2001) suggest several reasons why high deposit frequency, or frequent savings, leads to high savings. First, when facing difficulties to save in some months, a participant who seeks to be a more frequent depositor is more likely to try harder and make more efforts to save, even in the difficult months. Second, a more frequent depositor may develop techniques and habits to put money aside for savings. And third, high savings can lead to more frequent savings because making a deposit has a transaction cost, and for a higher saver with a higher deposit, this transaction cost will be more worthwhile.

Finally, hours of financial education attended by participants were also statistically related to AMND. Participants who have attended financial education were associated with $18.26 higher AMND ($p = 0.025$) than participants who did not attend any financial education. More specifically, between the ranges of 1 to 6 hours, each additional hour was linked with a $3.25 decrease in AMND. Beginning with the 7th hour of financial education and until the 12th hour, each additional hour was associated with a $2.03 increase in AMND. Then, from 13 hours to 18 hours, each additional hour was associated with a $1.33 decrease of AMND. These results, however, should be interpreted with caution, since the majority of the sample at the time of the study had not yet attended financial education. And out of the people who did attend, the majority had between 7 to 12 hours. In general, financial education does appear to be an important predictor of AMND, particularly between the 7th and 12th hours.

Qualitative Results

In a survey of rural IDA programs, administrators and staff were asked to identify the advantages and challenges associated with implementing and managing IDA programs in their particular regions. The strongest theme to emerge in the area of advantages was that of trust. An IDA participant's trust in his or her sponsoring organization is an important issue regardless of the program location. The rural programs felt that they had a distinct advantage in this area over urban sites because in smaller communities most people are familiar with the organization and often are acquainted with the employees, allowing participants to feel more comfortable and safe. Moreover, because of their size, rural programs are better able to provide one-on-one contact to participants, which again reinforces the feelings of trust. As the trust grows, participants become eager to share their experiences with their neighbors, thus exposing other people to the program. As one program administrator commented, "If the financial institution, or the IDA sponsoring agency, are known and trusted in the community, it will go a long way in helping the program succeed, in recruitment, facilitation, and overcoming resistance."

Two central challenges emerged from the study. First, whereas the small size of a community is a benefit in terms of trust building, it becomes a barrier when trying to secure local funding. Rural areas tend to have fewer resources available that can provide adequate funding amounts, causing fewer people to be able to participate. The second problem that arose regarded distance. It is often hard for participants to attend classes when they do not live close to the facility. Either lack of transportation was a problem or participants did not have enough time to get to classes after work because of the location. This problem is not as severe in urban areas, where there is public transportation and the participants live in a more concentrated region.

In addition, a few issues arose that were not necessarily advantages or challenges, but were important in respect to rural IDA programs. Several programs emphasized the need to be more flexible in terms of IDA uses. Many current programs do not allow IDAs for uses such as car purchases or home repairs, but for rural residents both of these uses are important. Cars are needed to get to and from work and to run necessary errands. Having a car loan can also provide a much needed credit history for a future home loan. In rural areas, many participants already have homes through inheritance and are, therefore, in much greater need of home repairs than of home purchases. Finally, because rural communities do not have a large pool of consumption sources as opposed to urban areas, more emphasis is placed on increasing income (e.g., microenterprise) rather than controlling spending. Rural participants still discuss spending choices, but do not discuss at length topics such as resisting advertisements and consumer education.

DISCUSSION

Many rural communities today are suffering from high poverty and are in need of revitalization. The building of assets is a realistic and progressive policy initiative to fight poverty. As was suggested earlier, savings and asset accumulation are crucial in escaping poverty. Assets lead to positive outcomes for individuals, families, and communities; they create opportunities for advancement and can enable the poor to expand their economic, political, and social positions. History has demonstrated that providing an institutional mechanism that fosters asset building among residents is a practical approach that can benefit individuals as well as communities. According to research, IDAs can be that mechanism. ADD found that IDAs do indeed help people save money and build assets. Furthermore, using data from rural IDA programs, this study identified several key variables specific

to rural areas that predict savings and asset accumulation in rural communities. Finally, the qualitative research provided insight on how to operate rural programs more effectively by taking advantage of their particular strengths while still recognizing their weaknesses.

Knowledge gained from these studies can be used by policymakers and program administrators to shape IDA programs specifically for rural communities. Upon examination, it seems likely that some program characteristics may have large effects on saving outcomes. First, having a mechanism for direct deposit seems to facilitate increased savings. Therefore, it is suggested that program administrators should encourage participants to use direct deposit and provide them with the means to do so. Second, direct deposit was also found to be an important factor in higher savings. Participants who were more frequent depositors saved at a higher rate than those who were less frequent depositors. Programs can use these findings and develop guidelines regarding deposit consistency, even if it is a small amount. Third, financial education also seems to matter. It is suggested that financial education be an initial program requirement, with between 7 to 12 hours being the most beneficial. Fourth, program administrators should be aware of participants with special needs who are at a disadvantage in terms of being TANF recipients or having no health insurance and may face greater difficulties in terms of trying to save. Links to other organizations could be provided so that participants may access additional economic resources.

Furthermore, the quantitative findings identify certain rural-specific issues that need to be addressed to ensure program effectiveness. Particular attention should be paid to funding sources. At the policy level, lawmakers need to create new initiatives that will influence funding efforts at the local level, such as providing tax incentives to organizations and institutions that fund IDA programs. At the local level, program administrators need to educate local funders on the advantages of IDA programs such as how funding IDAs can not only help build community trust in their organizations and institutions, but also improve the community as a whole. Transportation is another rural challenge. Program administrators should be mindful of the transportation needs of program participants when deciding location of training, access to facilities, and timing of training offered.

Finally, program administrators should be aware of local needs when establishing allowable uses for IDAs. In rural communities, IDAs could specifically be used for microenterprise, allowing residents to start their own businesses and contribute to their town's assets as well as their own; they could be used for educational purposes to train displaced workers for other jobs; or IDAs could allow some residences to repair and restore their existing homes and allow others to establish homeownership to help strengthen and build the community. Also, IDAs could be used for car purchases to assure reliable transportation for participants to get to their jobs. In conclusion, IDAs alone cannot create sustainable rural communities, but they can be an important proactive piece in an investment-oriented strategy.

LIMITATIONS

Some limitations of this study are important to note. Participants in IDA programs in ADD and FAIM are not a random sample of people eligible for IDAs. They are both program-selected because of eligibility criteria, and self-selected because they volunteer to participate in the program. Moreover, compared with the U.S. low-income population, participants in ADD and FAIM are better educated, more likely to be employed, and more likely to have some form of bank account prior to the program. This is probably due to the fact that the program targets the "working poor." Participants in ADD and FAIM are more likely to be female and never married. This pattern reflects the population that is served by community programs that offer IDAs. Therefore, our results reflect this segment of the population. We can argue, based on our research, that poor people in rural communities with these characteristics can save, but this does not mean that low-income people with different characteristics can or cannot save (Grinstein-Weiss, et al., 2001; Schreiner, et al., 2001).

DISCUSSION QUESTIONS

1. The American government has supported the idea of individual asset accumulation for several centuries. A major policy enacted by legislation, The Homestead Act of 1862, provided the opportunity for thousands of Americans to purchase land at a very low cost with minimum requirements. How did this Act affect the idea of asset accumulation in rural areas at the time of its enactment? What is its impact on asset accumulation today?

2. Changes in technology as well as economic sources have altered the face of rural United States. Due to these changes, many rural residents have had to reevaluate their situations and adjust their lives to the new

economic conditions. Do you think IDAs can be a successful antipoverty measure for rural communities? Why or why not?

3. Qualitative research found that communities that were small in size were at an advantage in terms of building trust among IDA participants and sponsoring organizations. However, smaller communities were at a disadvantage when it came to funding because of fewer monetary resources. What kind of initiatives can legislators enact to encourage organizations and funders to participate in IDA programs in rural communities? Explain why you think your responses would be effective.

CLASSROOM ACTIVITIES
AND ASSIGNMENTS

1. Design an IDA program for a rural community.

   a. Search the Internet to find out as much information as possible about IDAs, such as: Who can be a sponsoring organization? Who funds the programs? What are some of the eligibility requirements for participants? How long does the program last? What are the allowable uses? What are the match rates? How much savings can be matched?

   b. Next, get into groups and discuss what features you found and which ones would be the best for a rural IDA program.

2. Working in groups, design a marketing plan to present to local rural funders to encourage them to participate in IDA programs. Then present your plan to the class.

REFERENCES

Aaronson, D. (2000). A note on the benefits of home-ownership. *Journal of Urban Economics, 47*(3), 356–369.

Beverly, S., & Sherraden, M. (1999). Institutional determinants of saving: Implications for low-income households and public policy. *Journal of Socio-Economics, 28,* 457–473.

Carney, S., & Gale, W. (2001). Asset accumulation among low-income households. In T. M. Shapiro & E. N. Wolff (Eds.), *Benefits and mechanisms for spreading asset ownership in the United States* (pp. 165–205). New York: Ford Foundation.

Dick, E. N. (1970). *The lure of the land: A social history of the public lands from the Articles of Confederation to the New Deal.* Lincoln: University of Nebraska Press.

DiPasquale, D., & Glaeser, E. (1999). Incentives and social capital: Are homeowners better citizens? *Journal of Urban Economics, 45*(2), 354–384.

Dorward, A. R., Anderson, S., Clark, S., Keane, B., & Moguel, J. (2001). *Asset functions and livelihood strategies: A framework for pro-poor analysis, policy and practice.* Paper presented at the 74th EAAE Seminar on Livelihoods and Rural Poverty, Imperial College at Wye, United Kingdom, September 2001.

Edwards, K., & Rist, C. (2001). *IDA state policy guide.* Center for Social Development (St. Louis: Washington University) and Corporation for Enterprise Development (Washington DC).

Freshwater, D. (2000). Rural America at the turn of the century: One analyst's perspective. *Rural America, 15,* 2–7.

Gittleman, M., & Wolff, E. N. (2000). *Racial wealth disparities: Is the gap closing?* (Working Paper no. 311).

New York: Bureau of Labor Statistics, New York University.

Green, R. K., & White, M. J. (1997). Measuring the benefits of homeowning: Effects on children. *Journal of Urban Economics, 41,* 441–461.

Grinstein-Weiss, M., Schreiner, M., Clancy, M., & Sherraden, M. (2001). *Family assets for independence in Minnesota research report.* St. Louis, MO: Washington University in St. Louis, Center for Social Development.

Henderson, J. R. (2002, January). Will the rural economy rebound with the rest of the nation? *The Main Street Economist, Commentary on the Rural Economy* (Brochure). Center for the Study of Rural America, Federal Reserve Bank of Kansas.

Hill, M. S., & Duncan, G. J. (1987). Parental family income and the socioeconomic attainment of children. *Social Science Research, 6,* 39–73.

Joshi, H., & Macran, S. (1991). Work, gender and health. *Work, Employment and Society, 5,* 451–469.

Oliver, M., & Shapiro, T. (1995). *Black wealth/White wealth.* New York: Routledge.

Page-Adams, D., & Sherraden, M. (1996). *What we know about effects of asset holding: Implications for research on asset-based anti poverty initiatives* (Working Paper no. 96-1). St. Louis, MO: Washington University in St. Louis, Center for Social Development.

Page-Adams, D., & Vosler, N. (1996). Predictors of depression among workers at the time of a plant closing. *Journal of Sociology and Social Welfare, 23*(4), 25–42.

Pezzini, M. (2000). Rural policy lessons from OECD countries. *Economic Review* (Federal Reserve Bank of Kansas City), Third Quarter, 47–57.

Rohe, W., & Stegman, M. (1994). The effects of home-ownership on the self-esteem, perceived control and life satisfaction of low-income people. *Journal of the American Planning Association, 60*(2), 173–184.

Rohe, W., & Stewart, L. (1996). Home ownership and neighborhood stability. *Housing Policy Debate, 9*(1), 37–81.

Saunders, P. (1990). *A nation of homeowners.* London: Unwin Hyman.

Scanlon, E., & Page-Adams, D. (2001). Effects of asset holding on neighborhoods, families and children. In R. Boshara (Ed.), *Building Assets* (pp. 3.025–3.049). Washington, DC: Corporation for Enterprise Development.

Schreiner, M., Sherraden, M., Clancy, M., Johnson, L., Curley, J., Grinstein-Weiss, M., Zhan, M., & Beverly, S. (2001). *Savings and asset accumulation in Individual Development Accounts: Downpayments on the American Dream Policy Demonstration; A national demonstration of Individual Development Accounts.* St. Louis, MO:

Center for Social Development, Washington University. February.

Shapiro, T. M. (2001). The importance of assets. In T. M. Shapiro & E. N. Wolff (Eds.), *Benefits and mechanisms for spreading asset ownership in the United States* (pp. 11–33). New York: Ford Foundation.

Sherraden, M. (1991). *Assets and the poor. A new American welfare policy.* Armonk, NY: M.E. Sharpe.

Sherraden, M., Johnson, L., Clancy, M., Beverly, S., Schreiner, M., Zhan, M., & Curley, J. (2000). *Saving patterns in IDA programs.* St. Louis, MO: Washington University in St. Louis, Center for Social Development.

Stegman, M. (1999). *Savings and the poor: The hidden benefits of electronic banking.* Washington, DC: The Brookings Institution.

Williams, T. (2000). *The Homestead Act: A major asset-building policy in American history* (Working Paper no. 00-9). St. Louis, MO: Washington University in St. Louis, Center for Social Development.

Yadama, G., & Sherraden, M. (1996). Effects of assets on attitudes and behaviors: Advance test of social policy proposal. *Social Work Research, 20,* 3–11.

INFOTRAC COLLEGE EDITION

asset building
IDAs
policy

poverty
rural

27

If We Build It, Will They Come?*

A Case for Practice-Based Research

H. STEPHEN COOPER
LINDA MORALES

Students in field practicum are scarcely into their first practice experiences when they encounter those "thorny questions" for which there are no precise answers. They hear their field instructors and supervisors say "that is a good question, but . . . we just don't know," "we have yet to discover the causes of," and "at this time our understanding is just so limited." Typically, field students and new professionals hold the happy but false notion that they have left "research methods" far behind in the classroom. Yet those thorny questions that impede professional practice can and must be addressed not just by researchers but by professionals as they seek to improve the quality of services to clients and enhance the knowledge base of the profession.

The purpose of this article is to demonstrate the importance of research in practice settings. Directors of the Hope Center Wilderness Programs, a therapeutic residential treatment program for adolescent males and females located in rural East Texas, recognized the potential need for a strengths-based program for adolescent female sex offenders. Developing a practitioner–academic partnership led to a further refined conceptualization of the problem for research; a literature review on adolescent female sex offenders, patterns of offending, and outcome-based programming; a survey of Texas juvenile probation departments that often encounter the population;

and the use of those data for program building. The recurring themes of this project are:

1. Partnerships between practitioners and representatives of a school of social work;

2. The evolution of important research questions from the "thorny question" commonly encountered in practice settings;

3. The importance of research to program planning for practice; and

4. A focus on assets and strengths: the assets of the rural setting for residential treatment programs, the assets of rural partnering, and implications of a strengths-focused approach for treatment of adolescent female sex offenders.

WHEN IS RESEARCH NEEDED?

Social work students, practitioners, and educators must acknowledge that research is a necessary part of successful field practice. Research is not reserved for researchers and educators. Duehn (1985) states that "the basic proposition is well within the realm of possibility for a social worker to be both a practitioner *and* a researcher or a practitioner/researcher" (as cited in Grinnell, 1985,

*Hope Center Youth and Family Services supported the survey phase of this project. The authors would like to thank Scott Spaw, Gary Blackburn, and Hector Garcia for their assistance.

p.19). However, it is more complicated than simply acknowledging the connection between practice and research. One must know when it is appropriate to conduct practice-based research, what method(s) to use, and when to use them.

According to Weinbach (1985), social work research is "applied research undertaken by social workers to advance practice theory and methods for our profession" (p. 66). In this context, research is anything that increases the understanding of social phenomena and their causes, as well as improving social work interventions.

Most research is conducted in the format of a problem-solving process that consists of: (1) problem identification, definition, and specification, (2) generation of alternatives and selection of strategies for problem solution, (3) implementation, and (4) evaluation and dissemination of findings (Duehn, 1985). This process supports the concept that an increase in understanding raises more questions, or simply put, the more we know, the less we know.

One of the keys to success is to know when it is appropriate to engage in research and if a topic is researchable. Creswell (1994) outlined these parameters for determining whether a question or topic is researchable:

1. Is the topic researchable, given time, resources, and availability of data?

2. Is there a personal interest in the topic in order to sustain attention?

3. Will the results from the study be of interest to others (e.g., in the state, region, or nation)?

4. Is the topic likely to be publishable in a scholarly journal (or attractive to a doctoral committee)?

5. Does the study fill a void; or replicate, extend, or develop new ideas in the scholarly literature?

6. Will the project contribute to career goals? (p. 3)

Once a topic is deemed researchable, the researchers must plan the process, including but not limited to how the data will be gathered and analyzed, how it will be disseminated, and how the project will be funded.

THE IDEA

In the case of Hope Center, the program was searching for ways to diversify its services through a wilderness program. The question was how could the existing program serve a different population of adolescents in a way that is on the cutting edge of children's services? A possible answer came when the outreach coordinator returned from a statewide juvenile probation conference and reported that probation departments wanted a program for adolescent female sex offenders. The Executive Management and Directors knew that this could prove to be "our niche" and the recurring questions began to crystallize. Is there a need for a specialized treatment program for adolescent female sex offenders in Texas? What kind of a program would facilitate the strongest treatment outcomes? Would therapeutic wilderness programming provide an appropriate treatment setting for such a population? What would a strengths-based program for female sex offenders look like? Without the answers to these questions, any efforts to design and fund such a program would most likely be disastrous. At this point, it was clearly time for research.

Time for a Consultant

The Directors began the research process with inquiries about the various aspects of sex offender treatment and a literature review. It quickly became obvious that additional help would be of beneficial and a decision was made to consult a social work educator with expertise in the field of sexual offender treatment. The Directors partnered with a professor from the School of Social Work at Stephen F. Austin State University (SFASU), a school with a strong rural focus.

The partnership proved to be advantageous to all of the participants. Since the consultant's doctoral dissertation focused on the treatment of adolescent sex offenders, countless hours of literature review were saved. The Directors provided the hands-on knowledge of therapeutic wilderness programs and had already shifted the program's treatment philosophy to that of a strengths perspective. Access to SFASU enhanced the available resources in terms of library and technological support for the project. The only significant barrier was the remoteness of the wilderness camp, which was located approximately 10 miles from paved roads and approximately 75 miles from SFASU. To overcome this barrier, the Directors arranged weekly project planning meetings at SFASU's library. In addition, the consultant visited the wilderness site on several occasions.

The initial meetings were dedicated to further refining the research questions, updating the literature review to include specific information about adolescent female sex offenders, and identification of current programs to treat the population. This process led to the final research questions:

1. Is there a need in Texas for a program to treat adolescent females who are classified as sex offenders?

2. If there is a need for such a program, what is the profile of the referral population?

3. Are there examples of programs for adolescent female sex offenders that utilize a strengths perspective?

4. Would therapeutic wilderness programming be appropriate for this specific population?

These questions were examined in terms of Creswell's criteria for researchability. Clearly the topic was researchable within the given time frame and agency resources. The topic held strong interest for all parties in the partnership; as the literature was searched, it became evident that knowledge about adolescent female sex offenders is limited, as is knowledge about the efficacy of treatment of this population via therapeutic wilderness programming. The study would also fill a void, adding to the scant body of literature about treatment interventions with this population.

To determine if there was a need for such a program in Texas, the team designed a survey to assess the level of need for a program and the possible treatment issues. Specifically, the survey sought to answer the following questions:

1. What behaviors are considered sexually inappropriate?

2. How many adolescent female sex offenders have been encountered within the last six years? Females who molest others? Females who engage in sexually inappropriate behaviors?

3. How many referrals per year to a specialized program for adolescent female sex offenders are anticipated? Barriers to such referrals?

4. How often is each of the seven types of sex offenders encountered (see Table 27.1)?

5. What are the most common residential situations for adolescent female sex offenders?

Since Hope Center served the entire state, the surveys were distributed to all juvenile probation departments in Texas. Although juvenile probation departments are operated on the county level, some departments serve multiple counties through a judicial district probation department. Thus, there are 161 juvenile probation departments to serve 254 Texas counties. The 161 juvenile probation departments were separated into 11 regions to assist with data analysis. The regions coincide with the service regions of the Texas Department of Protective and Regulatory Services (TDPRS), which allows for comparison with data collected from TDPRS. Each of the 161 juvenile probation departments was mailed a survey and a self-addressed stamped envelope. The departments were not required to participate and they were not compensated. All responses were anonymous.

Results

Of the 161 juvenile probation departments, 54 responded to the survey. Fourteen of the respondents were located in an urban area defined by a population of 50,000 or more. Twenty-five of them were located in a small town, which is defined as an incorporated city or town with a

Table 27.1 Seven Types of Sex Offenders

Type I	**Naïve Experimenter/Abuser:** This describes a girl with little history of acting out, good social skills, but gets in trouble because of being naïve sexually. Usually experimenting, and has engaged in a few isolated situations often playful behaviors, but with a victim.
Type II	**The Undersocialized Child Molester:** This girl is severely socially isolated, not accepted by peers, internal feelings of inadequacy and insecurity. Seems to be drawn to younger children who look up to and admire her. Lacks social skills to relate to peers.
Type III	**The Pseudosocialized Child Molester:** Often an older girl with good social skills but not intimate with peers. Often was herself a victim of childhood abuse of some kind. Probably can rationalize and justify her behaviors, and feels little guilt or remorse for sexual behaviors.
Type IV	**Sexual Aggressor:** This girl has usually come from a disorganized, confused, and abusive family. Often she is charming and gregarious. She uses physical force and threats to victimize younger children or even peers. An inner rage is often present and sex is used as an expression of anger or personal power.
Type V	**Sexually Compulsive:** Usually this girl has emerged from a family of very rigid boundaries, rule bound, but often with emotionally disengaged parents. She is confused and unable to express her feelings in a clear direct way. She engages in repetitive, sexually arousing behaviors in a compulsive driven way. Usually she is caught in a repetitive cycle of abuse followed by temporary elation and then remorse.
Type VI	**Disturbed Impulsive:** This girl has a history of serious problems, severe family problems, substance abuse problems and/or learning difficulties. Her behaviors are usually impulsive and unpredictable. There may be brain damage or serious thought disturbance present. Behaviors are highly erratic and unpredictable.
Type VII	**Group Influenced:** This girl is usually a younger girl with no previous history in the juvenile system. Her abuse occurs within a peer group and she usually knows her victim. The motivation for the abuse often relates to peer pressure. She is often a follower and is trying to gain approval of her peers.

Based on a scale developed by O'Brien and Bera (1986).

population of 5,000 to 50,000 that is not part of a metropolitan area. Fifteen of the departments were located in a rural town with a population of 5,000 or less.

Responses indicate the following averages for the past six-year period: 2.05 sex offenders were encountered per department, 1.42 females who molest others were encountered, and 11.73 females who engage in sexually inappropriate behaviors. However, when examined as rural versus urban, the averages are as follows (respectively): 1.15 vs. 3.71 sex offenders encountered, .11 vs. 3.50 females who molest others, and 9.04 vs. 19.00 females who engage in sexually inappropriate behaviors. Since the concept of "sexually inappropriate behaviors" varies by gender and age of the child and the personal beliefs of the person completing the survey, respondents were asked to identify specific inappropriate behaviors. The following behaviors were the most commonly iden-

tified: sexual promiscuity, prostitution for drugs, dating men over 18 years of age, multiple sexual partners, engaging in sexual acts at an early age, and lack of personal boundaries.

Since one of the main reasons for the survey was to determine if referrals would support a specialized program, it was encouraging that the anticipated number of yearly referrals would be 99 (26 from rural agencies and 73 from urban agencies). Although barriers to placement, such as cost, distance, parental cooperation, family involvement, and segregation of offender types were mentioned, none of them were unexpected. Furthermore, none of them are impossible to overcome and could be addressed via program planning.

The respondents were asked to identify the types of offenders encountered using criteria provided in the survey. The criteria, based on a scale developed by O'Brien and Bera (1986), are presented in Table 27.1. The respondents indicated that Type I was the most common offender encountered, followed by Type II and Type III. Type V was the least commonly encountered offender. Fifty seven percent of the respondents reported having never encountered Type IV. Furthermore, 12 (22.2%) of the agencies reported never having contact with a female sex offender, 11 of which were rural departments. However, 4 of those 12 did report formal contact with females who engaged in inappropriate sexual behavior.

Respondents were also asked to identify the most common type of residence for adolescent females with serious sexual behaviors. The most common residence was that of the biological parents (50% of the respondents), followed by residential treatment centers, and juvenile correctional facilities.

DESIGNING THE PROGRAM

Since the survey results supported the development of a specialized treatment program, the next logical step was to refine the literature review and focus on the treatment of the chosen population. Specifically, there was an obvious need for a program to treat adolescent females who meet the criteria for Type I, II, and III sex offenders. Although the researchers were able to find numerous studies on male adolescent sex offenders, specific studies on the characteristics and treatment of female adolescent sex offenders were not as plentiful. Travin, Cullen, and Potter (1990) suggest the research is limited due to a general reluctance to acknowledge girls are capable of committing sex offenses. It is also possible that the general reluctance is responsible for the low rate of female adolescents formally identified and treated as sex offenders. Furthermore, Righthand and Welch (2001) found the existing research on the population to be limited by methodological drawbacks, such as "small sample sizes and retrospective analysis of selected populations that may not be representative of the general population" (p. 16).

Despite the identified limitations, the authors were able to formulate a general profile of the client population. The Type I, II, and III offenders are typically identified early in their patterns of sexual offending or "acting out," including "sexually inappropriate behaviors." Research and practice experience supports the assumption that many of these clients have been prematurely "sexualized" and may be victims of sexual abuse (Gil & Johnson, 1993; Ray & English, 1995; Bumby & Bumby, 1997; Matthews, Hunter, & Vuz, 1997). However, there is a general tendency to ignore and/or informally address the behaviors until they have manifested to the point of interfering with the client's ability to function. Therefore, it is common for these clients to present with a variety of emotional, psychological, and behavioral issues in addition to sexual offending.

Treatment Approach

Once the client profile was developed, the next step was to identify an appropriate treatment approach. Due to the presence of multiple treatment issues, the program should be capable of providing a variety of interventions, including trauma resolution, social skills, sex education, and behavior modification. Such an approach is supported by Marshall and Barbaree (1990) and Ryan and Lane (1991), who found that a wide treatment array has greater success in the treatment of adolescent male sex offenders, as opposed to one that focuses on one specific treatment approach or technique. Furthermore, it was decided that the treatment interventions should be based on the strengths perspective, a combination clearly supported by Righthand and Welch (2001). Specifically, they identify the most successful interventions as "those that address the needs underlying a juvenile's behavior and make the most of the juvenile's existing strengths and positive supports" (Righthand & Welch, 2001, p. xxii).

The decision to utilize the strengths perspective is important and somewhat unique. Most sex offender programs are based on a therapeutic model, but tend to be at least mildly punitive in nature. Although punitive interventions are commonly accepted methods of addressing delinquent behavior, they tend to inhibit the therapeutic process and lead to a negative view of the client. On the other hand, the strengths perspective fosters a positive view of the client through:

1. Identification of the client's individual strengths and use of those strengths as the foundation for treatment planning and interventions.

2. Incorporation of the assets associated with wilderness programming in the treatment plan; for example, activities that build self-esteem and self-reliance, as well as a sense of community and environmental consciousness.

3. Recognition and utilization of assets associated with the rural community and maintenance of those ties between the program, clients, and community (including faith-based organizations, civic groups, schools, businesses, and county government).

4. Integration of the assets associated with a rural location, such as geographic isolation, limited influence by mass media, strong support networks, and traditional values.

Such an approach is important to the maintenance of social work values, such as empowerment, self-determination, dignity, and self-worth. The strengths perspective also encourages the client to view himself or herself in a positive manner, which increases his or her involvement in treatment and subsequent chances of success.

Assessment

Successful implementation of the identified treatment approach requires a clearly defined assessment process, which according to Ross and Loss (1991) must be thorough and multi-faceted. According to Kraemer, Spielman, and Salisbury (1995), the assessment process should include four foci: (1) intellectual and neurological, (2) personality functioning and psychopathology, (3) behavioral, and (4) sexual deviance. The use of a thorough assessment is supported by the relationship between accurate identification of the cause or "root" of the problem behavior(s) and successful treatment. The assessment must also identify client strengths related to each of the treatment areas, which would be used to develop treatment goals and interventions. Specifically, the assessment component would include the following:

1. A thorough psychosocial assessment completed by a program social worker, including family structure and dynamics, patterns of abuse, and criminal history, as well as other pertinent psychological, sociological, biological, and spiritual aspects.

2. A brief measure of general sexual knowledge (Salter, 1988).

3. A psychophysiological measure of deviant sexual arousal, The Abel Assessment for Interest in Paraphilias (Righthand & Welch, 2001).

4. A measure of the client's understanding and degree of perceived responsibility for offending behaviors, such as The Juvenile Culpability Assessment (Hindman, 1992).

5. A measure for locus of control, to assess a client's degree of taking responsibility for her own thoughts and behaviors (Nowicki & Duke, 1974).

6. A detailed assessment of the cognitive-behavioral offense chain, which examines the thoughts and events leading up to the sexual offense (Laws, 1989).

7. Standardized psychological testing, including an IQ test (full scale, verbal, and performance) to assess the client's ability to understand the treatment process.

Treatment Interventions

As previously mentioned, the treatment component consists of specialized interventions to address sexual offending, as well as a variety of behavioral, emotional, and psychological needs. The use of a broad treatment array is supported by the tendency of inappropriate or sexual offending to be accompanied by other issues, such as truancy, academic difficulties, abuse, substance abuse, runaway, theft, suicidal ideation, and mental health disorders (Ray & English, 1995; Bumby & Bumby, 1997; Matthews, et al., 1997; Righthand & Welch, 2001). Based on these issues, development of strengths—such as self-esteem, self-reliance, teamwork, and acceptance of responsibility for actions—are vital for treatment success with sex offenders (Staudt, Howard, & Drake, 2001; Righthand & Welch, 2001). The program also used basic sex education classes and social skills–based interventions, such as anger management (Salter, 1988; Righthand & Welch, 2001), and specialized therapeutic interventions based on a cognitive behavioral framework (Jenkins-Hall, 1989). The desired outcome is to replace maladaptive thought processes with ones that are adaptive (Jenkins-Hall, 1989). The cognitive behavioral techniques include four techniques:

Behavioral rehearsal is a type of behavioral technique in which a client rehearses a behavioral response to a specific anticipated problem situation. The goal is to develop the client's ability to appropriately respond when in a situation that places them at risk of reoffending (Hall, 1989).

Cognitive restructuring "is the process of modifying thinking, both its premises and its assumptions" (Jenkins-Hall, 1989, p. 207).

Covert sensitization is a therapeutic technique "that teaches juveniles to interrupt thoughts associated with sex offending by thinking of negative consequences associated with abusive behavior" (Righthand & Welch, 2001, p. xix). For example, a juvenile may imagine participating in a sexual offense and then imagine being shamed publicly. Other interruptive thoughts could be used such as being attacked by spiders or snakes. The therapist leads this guided imagery technique.

Vicarious sensitization involves exposing juveniles to audiotaped crime scenarios designed to stimulate arousal and then immediately having audio/video that portrays negative consequences of sexually abusive behavior (Righthand & Welch, 2001).

The treatment array would also provide trauma resolution groups to address sexual abuse victimization and other traumatic events. Finally, relapse prevention, teaching clients to self-monitor, would be included as an end stage approach (Laws, 1989).

Program Evaluation

Relevant outcome studies of treatment programs for sex offenders, both for adults and adolescents, have proved problematic (Marshall & Barbaree, 1990). Chiefly this is true because of the problems in establishing an accurate tracking system for released offenders (Ryan & Lane, 1991) and difficulty in obtaining accurate measures of recidivism (Furby, Weinrott, & Blackshaw, 1989). For example, scores on posttests at release have not been considered strong predictors of reoffense (Furby, et al., 1989). Furthermore, measures tend to be relatively rare among treatment programs for juvenile sex offenders (Marshall & Barbaree, 1990; Ryan & Lane, 1991).

It is recognized that recidivism measures are imperative to the establishment of feasible and meaningful outcome studies (Furby, et al., 1989). The drawbacks to this approach are the tendency of sexual offenses to go unreported, inadequate follow-up periods, and lack of information on the client after release (Rightand & Welch, 2001). In order to address these drawbacks, the program used a follow-up system to track program graduates for three years from program completion. A case manager was assigned solely to this duty and gathered data from multiple sources, including the client (self-report measure), TDPRS, and juvenile probation departments. Finally, an overall satisfaction survey was distributed to referring agencies, participants, and their families, which provided a broad measure of program efficacy. The data were also used to identify and resolve program deficits.

IMPLEMENTING THE PROGRAM

Since the Directors intended to design and implement a strengths-based treatment program for adolescent female sex offenders utilizing therapeutic wilderness programming, the next step in the process was to address the final research question: Is therapeutic wilderness programming an appropriate foundation for the treatment of female adolescent sex offenders? The process of determining compatibility included a comparison of the treatment approach, assessment process, treatment interventions, and program evaluation methods of both programs. The following description of Hope Center's therapeutic wilderness program demonstrates the appropriateness of wilderness programming as a foundation for the proposed program.

Program Overview

One of the unique aspects of wilderness programming is the use of the wilderness and rural areas as therapeutic tools. In other words, characteristics such as geographical location, lack of transportation, slower pace of life, weak links with mass society, and lack of public utilities are viewed as strengths, not deficits. Since the girls' wilderness program had ten miles of dirt roads with two low water bridges between it and any paved road, runaways were naturally discouraged. Other than electricity and phone service, the facility was completely self-contained. The clients did not have access to television, and radios were limited. The clients lived in campsites consisting of structures they planned and built. The building process included cutting, skinning, and notching the pine trees, as well as assembly of the final product. Campsite utilities were limited to running water and meals were cooked on wood fires. The primitive nature of the program facilitated the development of self-reliance, confidence, and cohesion that could not be achieved in any other way. Furthermore, the process was one that urban clients would not be exposed to otherwise.

Hope Center's treatment approach was firmly based in the strengths perspective, which takes a positive holistic view of the client. The goal was to mobilize client strengths as a method of empowering them to achieve their goals, visions, and a better quality of life. Furthermore, it was dependent upon a collaborative effort between the clients, staff, and program, which served to benefit all involved individuals. The strengths perspective was exemplified via the philosophical tenets of the program:

1. All individuals are capable of change.
2. All individuals possess strengths that can be built upon and utilized to overcome personal and environmental barriers.
3. All individuals both influence and are influenced by environmental factors: biological, emotional, familial, cultural, spiritual, and intellectual.
4. When placed in a nurturing and safe environment, all individuals are capable of positive growth, empowerment, and change.
5. All individuals have dignity and worth.
6. Consistency is the key factor of treatment.
7. Everyone has the right to self-determination.
8. All individuals have the right to ethical, fair, and equal treatment that is free of personal and agency bias.

Implementation of the strengths perspective occurred through the program groups (for daily activities and living), therapeutic recreation (daily activities, sports, trips, construction, etc.), group interventions/therapy, individual therapy, family therapy, psychiatric services, and educational interventions.

Clients were assigned to one of several small program groups based on age, size, and maturity level. Each program group was assigned four group facilitators, who were adult staff members responsible for supervising all aspects of daily activities. The program groups were assigned to a wilderness campsite consisting of semipermanent living shelters and other structures necessary for daily activities. The groups slept together, ate together, attended school together, maintained the campsite, built new structures, and prepared meals. Such a format fostered an understanding of cooperation, interdependence, and the need for social and life skills. Clients learned how to share common goals with a group and a larger community, the camp, the end result being the understanding that each individual is an important part of the larger community and that the community benefits from individual growth.

Assessment and Treatment Planning

Although Hope Center's assessment process was not as thorough as the one identified for the sex offender program, the basic components were similar. The assessment process began at intake with receipt of a psychological evaluation conducted by a licensed psychologist or psychiatrist that included the following:

1. Standardized IQ test including verbal, performance, and full scale IQ scores,

2. Complete *DSM-IV* diagnosis, and

3. Academic achievement scores.

Once the psychological assessment was received the intake case manager and the clinical director determined eligibility. If the client was accepted for services, the intake case manager conducted a full biopsychosocial assessment, including interviews with the client and parents, as well as other relevant resources, such as juvenile probation, TDPRS, and mental health service providers. The assessment also included the client's initial plan of service, which was updated no later than the 30th day in the program.

In order to develop a full treatment plan by the 30th day, the client was assigned a case manager prior to arrival at the program. During the first ten days at the facility, the client's case manager gathered information from various staff members regarding the client's behavior, including strengths and weaknesses. A Licensed Chemical Dependency Counselor also assessed the client within the first seven days. Prior to the

client's 14th day at the facility, the clinical director and case manager would meet with the client to conduct a diagnostic evaluation. The purpose of the interview was to include the client in the identification of strengths and weaknesses, as well as treatment goals and objectives. The case manager would then use the information to develop a comprehensive treatment plan containing goals, objectives, and tasks for each of the following areas: educational, familial, physical, social, and emotional/psychological/behavioral.

Once the treatment plan was developed, the treatment team, client, parents, and other relevant parties—such as juvenile probation officers or TDPRS case managers—reviewed and approved it. After implementation, the case manager monitored progress through a variety of methods built into the program, such as Daily Client Activity Forms (DECAFs) and weekly treatment team meetings with clinical and direct care staff. The treatment plans were formally reviewed 60 days after implementation (90 days from admission to the facility) and every 90 days after the first review. However, the treatment plan could be reviewed at anytime deemed appropriate by the clinical staff and/or requested by those involved in the treatment process.

Treatment Interventions

Therapeutic recreation, a unique combination of individual and group therapy, was the primary treatment intervention. It was implemented via the planning and construction of campsite structures, planning and preparation of weekend meals, and planning/completion of experiential activities and trips. The process provided numerous opportunities to learn and utilize a variety of social skills, such as anger management, impulse control, conflict resolution, and stronger communication. Furthermore, it encouraged clients to cope with issues as they arose and to acknowledge the consequences of their actions. Success was ensured through a variety of supports designed to assist clients in the development of the necessary strengths and interpersonal skills.

The end result was an increase in one's ability to interact in a variety of social situations and cope with general life issues. Additional outcomes were an overall improvement in self-concept, self-esteem, and resiliency.

Since the clients spent the majority of their time participating in group activities and interacting with their peers, there were numerous opportunities for conflict. The clients and groups typically dealt with conflict through a group problem solving session referred to as a "circle-up." Each time a problem occurred, the group would stop its activity and address the situation. The session could be initiated by a client or staff member and allowed the group to process the behaviors of one or more individuals. The session also provided a forum for the expression of feelings and receipt of constructive feedback from the other group members. The desired result was to teach the client to address and resolve problems as they occur instead of avoiding them.

The program also offered additional interventions designed to assist clients with the process of therapeutic recreation. For example, it was recognized that personal issues, such as symptoms of depression, conduct disorder, or posttraumatic stress disorder, could interfere with social interaction. These interventions were developed as components of the client's treatment plan and monitored by the case manager. One of the most common types were group interventions, which targeted a variety of issues, such as substance abuse education, abandonment, self-expression, trauma resolution, communication, anger management, conflict resolution, and socialization. Other interventions were individual therapy, family therapy, medical and psychiatric services, and educational services.

Educational services were provided by on-site schools staffed with certified teachers and supervised by the Houston-Trinity County Special Education Cooperative. Since all of the clients met the Texas Education Agency (TEA) guidelines for emotionally disturbed (ED), they qualified for special education services. As a result, a variety of special education services were provided, including: (1) all students had an Individual Education Plan (IEP) that was developed by an Admission, Review, and Dismissal (ARD) Committee and contained specific educational objectives and remediation strategies, (2) behavior intervention plans and instructional modifications as needed, and (3) a transition plan and a graduation plan for high school students. The clients attended classes with their program group five days per week on a standard academic calendar. The school program also provided summer school, which offered electives and a variety of opportunities for course make-up. One of the greatest benefits to the on-site school program was the ability to coordinate treatment and educational goals, leading to a stable and supportive environment.

Program Evaluation

Hope Center's program evaluation was primarily based on the number of successful discharges, which were defined as the demonstration of progress in at least three of the five treatment areas. Furthermore the client must have spent at least 60 days in the program unless he or she was removed by an outside agency for a reason unrelated to his or her behavior. Client progress after discharge was monitored for six months through the aftercare program. The intensity of aftercare services was based on individual needs and could range from monthly monitoring to supportive interventions, such as assistance with accessing local resources. Aftercare services also allowed the program to monitor the number of successful discharges that were not rereferred for a Class B Misdemeanor or above within 6 months of discharge. Although the existing aftercare program did not meet the proposed program's requirements for intensity and duration, it could have been easily modified.

IMPLICATIONS
FOR PRACTICE

As previously stated, the purpose of this article is to demonstrate the importance of research in social work practice settings and to provide a comprehensive example of practice-based research. In review, the process typically begins with a "thorny question" and a desire for further exploration. The next step is to decide whether the topic is researchable and to design the project. Implementation of the project follows, including a literature review, data collection, data analysis, and application of the findings to address the question. Although some make the mistake of ending the process here, there must be a system to determine the effectiveness of the improvements. Then data from the evaluation process is fed back into the "loop" and the process starts over.

Practice-based research is an ongoing process. That process is proactive in nature and reduces the number of trips "back to the drawing board." More importantly, practice-based research ensures that clients receive the best quality treatment and furthers the knowledge base of the profession.

DISCUSSION QUESTIONS

1. Each student should answer the questions individually. Then divide the class into groups of three and have students discuss their answers with the group.

   a. Why is it important to choose a topic for research that:

      1. has enough personal interest to sustain attention?

      2. will contribute to your career goals?

   b. Identify a research topic that would meet both of these criteria.

   c. Identify a personal career goal and a related research question/topic to share with the group.

2. The instructor leads a class discussion related to the connection between practice and research. The discussion should include real life examples from the local community. After the discussion, divide the class into small groups of four or five. The groups should discuss the following questions and be prepared to present their answers to the class.

   a. How does social work practice guide/ influence research?

   b. How does research guide/influence social work practice?

   c. Can practice and research occur independent of one another? Why or why not?

3. Divide the class into groups of four or five. Each group will chose a discussion leader. Discuss the following questions and present their answers during a class discussion.

   a. What barriers would make it difficult to implement and maintain a program for sex offenders that is based on the strengths perspective? Identify at least two.

   b. What strengths would have to exist for the program to be successful? Identify at least two strengths for the client, family, program group, organization, and community.

   c. How could one utilize those strengths to overcome the identified barriers?

4. If you were part of a wilderness program that was in the process of designing an innovative and critically needed program for female sex offenders, and suddenly your program lost funding, what would you do?

CLASSROOM ACTIVITIES
AND ASSIGNMENTS

1. What does Creswell (1994) mean by these terms in his criteria for researchability?

    a. Filling a void

    b. Replication

    c. Extend

    d. Development of new ideas

2. Table 27.1 outlines seven types of sexual offenders. Which type(s) of offenders do you think would be most amenable to wilderness programming and which type(s) would be the most difficult to manage in a wilderness program? Why?

3. Identify two other methods of gathering the necessary data to determine whether the need for a specialized sex offender program existed. Identify at least two pros and two

cons for each. Use a research text for assistance.

4. Provide students with an article on practice-based research or have the students locate an article outside of class. The student will describe the relationship between practice-based research and social work values and ethics within the context of the chosen article. Identify at least one example/issue for each of the following levels of practice: individual, family, group, organization, and community. Possible issues include, but are not limited to, use of human subjects, informed consent, control groups, etc. The students should refer to *Social Work Speaks*, the NASW Code of Ethics, and the state Code of Ethics for this assignment.

REFERENCES

Bumby, K. M., & Bumby, N. H. (1997). Adolescent female sex offenders. In B. K. Schwartz & H. R. Cellini (Eds.), *The sex offender: Vol. 2. New insights, treatment innovations, and legal developments* (pp. 10.1–10.16). Kingston, NJ: Civic Research Institute.

Creswell, J. W. (1994). *Research design: Qualitative and quantitative approaches.* Thousand Oaks, CA: Sage Publications.

Duehn, W. D. (1985). Practice and research. In R. M. Grinnell (Ed.), *Social work research and evaluation* (2nd ed., pp. 19–48). Itasca, IL: F. E. Peacock.

Furby, L., Weinrott, M. R., & Blackshaw, L. (1989). Sex offender recidivism: A review. *Psychological Bulletin, 105,* 3–30.

Gil, E., & Johnson, T. C. (1993). *Sexualized children: Assessment and treatment of sexualized children and children who molest.* Rockville, MD: Launch Press.

Grinnell, R. M. (1985). *Social work research and evaluation* (2nd ed.). Itasca, IL: F. E. Peacock.

Hall, R. L. (1989). Relapse rehearsal. In D. R. Laws (Ed.), *Relapse prevention with sex offenders* (pp. 197–206). New York: Guilford Press.

Hindman, J. (1992). *The juvenile culpability assessment.* Baker City, OR: AlexAndria Associates.

Jenkins-Hall, K. D. (1989). Cognitive restructuring in relapse prevention with sex offenders. In D.R. Laws (Ed.), *Relapse prevention with sex offenders* (pp. 207–215). New York: Guilford Press.

Kraemer, B. D., Spielman, C. R., & Salisbury, S. B. (1995). Juvenile sex offending psychometric assessment. In B. K. Schwartz & H. R. Cellini (Eds.), *The sex offender: Vol. 1. Corrections, treatment, and legal practice* (pp. 11.1–11.3). Kingston, NJ: Civic Research Institute.

Laws, D. R. (1989). *Relapse prevention with sex offenders.* New York: Guilford Press.

Marshall, W. L., & Barbaree, H. E. (1990). Outcomes of comprehensive cognitive-behavioral treatment programs. In W. L. Marshall, D. R. Laws, & H. E. Barbaree (Eds.), *Handbook of sexual assault* (pp. 363–385). New York: Plenum Press.

Matthews, R., Hunter, J. A., Jr., & Vuz, J. (1997). Juvenile female sex offenders: Clinical characteristics and treatment issues. *Sexual Abuse: A Journal of Research and Treatment, 9*(3), 187–200.

Nowicki, S., & Duke, M. P. (1974). A locus of control scale for college as well as non-college adults. *Journal of Personality Assessment, 38,* 136–137.

O'Brien, M. J., & Bera W. (1986). Adolescent sex offenders: A descriptive typology. *Preventing Sexual Abuse, 1,* 3–4.

Ray, J. A., & English, D. J. (1995). Comparison of female and male children with sexual behavior problems. *Journal of Youth and Adolescence, 24*(4), 439–451.

Righthand, S., & Welch, C. (2001). *Juveniles who have sexually offended: A review of the professional literature.* Washington, DC: Office of Juvenile Justice and Delinquency Prevention.

Ross, J., & Loss, P. (1991). Assessment of juvenile sex offenders. In G. D. Ryan & S. L. Lane (Eds.), *Sexual offending: Causes, consequences and correction* (pp. 199–251). Lexington, MA: Lexington Books.

Ryan, G. D., & Lane, S. L. (1997). Integrating theory and method. In G. D. Ryan & S. L. Lane (Eds.),

Juvenile sexual offending: Causes, consequences and correction (pp. 255–297). San Francisco: Jossey-Bass.

Salter, A. C. (1988). *Treating child sex offenders and victims: A practical guide.* Newbury Park, CA: Sage Publications.

Staudt, M., Howard, M. O., & Drake, B. (2001). The operationalization, implementation, and effectiveness of the strengths perspective: A review of empirical studies. *Journal of Social Service Research, 27,* 1–21.

Travin, S., Cullen, K., & Potter, B. (1990). Female sex offenders: Severe victims and victimizers. *Journal of Forensic Sciences, 35*(1), 140–150.

Weinbach, R. W. (1985). The agency and professional contexts of research. In R. M. Grinnell (Ed.), *Social work research and evaluation* (2nd ed., pp. 66–82). Itasca, IL: F. E. Peacock.

INFOTRAC COLLEGE EDITION

adolescents

females

juvenile delinquents

practice-based research

sex offenders

Therapeutic Wilderness Program

Appendix

NASW Professional Policy Statement in Rural Social Work

This Statement was approved by the Delegate Assembly of National Association of Social Workers, August 17, 2002. A team of eleven members of the Rural Social Work Caucus wrote the statement which was supported by the following state chapters of NASW:

Writing Team Coordinator:
  Samuel A. Hickman

Statement Authors:	Chapter Support:
Freddie Avant	Iowa Chapter
Michael Daley	Ohio Chapter
Susan Murty	Maine Chapter
Richard Osburn	Michigan Chapter
Varsha Pandya	Texas Chapter
Lucinda Potter	Utah Chapter
Susan Sarnoff	West Virginia Chapter
T. Laine Scales	
Scott Sorenson	
Sharon Templeman	

RATIONALE

The 1996 NASW Delegate Assembly approved action to establish a timetable to identify and eliminate "outdated" policy statements. The 1999 Delegate Assembly voted to eliminate the professional policy statement "Social Work in Rural Areas," thereby eliminating it from the NASW Press publication *Social Work Speaks*. The members of the Rural Social Work Caucus, at its 25th Annual National Institute on Social Work and Human Services in Rural Areas in Presque Isle, Maine, in July 2000, voted unanimously to redraft and seek to reinstate an appropriate professional policy statement on social work in rural areas. The caucus created and instructed a policy committee to undertake this task. A progress report and plans to finalize the updated and rewritten statement "Social Work in Rural Areas" were made at the 26th Annual National Institute in Austin, Texas, in May 2001.

Adoption of this policy statement by the 2002 NASW Delegate Assembly will accomplish several tasks critical to NASW and to the social workers who live and work in rural areas:

Our profession will again formally acknowledge and support corrective action for troubling issues of equity and diversity that negatively affect rural people. Rural residents comprise one-third of the population of the United States and the majority of the world's population. Despite the many comforts and advantages of rural and small community life, rural people experience higher rates of unemployment and persistent poverty. Government, health, and social services delivery systems, chiefly based on urban models, fail to consider or adapt to rural services issues such as distance and time of travel, the absence of public transportation, and the inability to achieve urban economies of scale.

This policy statement will reconnect the profession with one of its major historical foundations—social work practice in rural areas—and acknowledge that it remains a vibrant and challenging area of practice. Rural social work practice has its roots in the application of community organization skills in coal mining regions, seeking social justice for workers and their families. It continued with community organization in cotton and textile mills, lumber towns, "dust bowl" farm communities, and during the Civil Rights movement in the rural south. Community and religious-based social services organizations were created to reach out to the rural poor—white, black, Hispanic, and Native American. Government-sponsored social and economic programs created by the New Deal administration of President Franklin Roosevelt, such as the Homestead communities championed by Eleanor Roosevelt, fostered self-sufficiency among the rural poor and encouraged the development of our profession. Social work's rural roots go back more than one hundred years.

This policy statement will correct unintended consequences that occurred when the previous statement was eliminated from *Social Work Speaks*. Many social workers working in rural areas perceived the elimination of the previous statement as an act of abandonment by the profession. This heightened the sense of professional isolation experienced by rural social workers, leading some to question whether to belong to an organization that seems to not value the unique and special challenges they face. The statement's adoption will send a clear message that NASW understands and is concerned about what is happening among isolated rural women, the hidden rural poor, new immigrants seeking a better life, and NASW members working in relative isolation.

An approved policy statement will give rural social workers and NASW chapters the support and credibility of a national professional platform from which to advocate in state legislatures and among policy makers, and from which to encourage new generations of rural practitioners.

The authors, on behalf of the Rural Social Work Caucus, invite you to read the following statement with care and to learn more about the unique considerations of social work practice in rural areas and with rural people and cultures. We

heartily endorse this statement, and ask that you give it your full consideration and approval when it comes before you during the 2002 NASW Delegate Assembly.

BACKGROUND

Social Work Values and Ethics

Rural social work practice contributes to the social work mission of advocating for social justice and extending access to services for underserved populations. Rural practice requires a sophisticated level of understanding of values and ethics and highly developed skills in applying them. Small communities pose challenges to confidentiality, particularly when relatively few professional social workers interact with providers and community members who may have limited understanding of professional ethics. Effective rural practice involves locality-based community development. It is frequently inappropriate to maintain "professional distance" from the community. Instead, it is essential to participate in community activities and establish trust among the residents.

Rural social workers interact with clients and their families in a variety of ways, such as at schools, churches, sports events, or fundraisers. Protecting clients from any negative consequences of dual relationships in rural settings has less to do with limiting social relationships and more to do with setting clear boundaries. Discussing possible conflicts and apprising clients of options is essential. However, the general lack of resources limits referral alternatives.

Residents of rural areas can be judgmental toward clients and services that reflect cultures and lifestyles different from community norms. Education of community members requires sustained effort based on trust. Empowering clients who have limited opportunities can be challenging, but some rural communities provide examples of support and commitment that enhance the services social workers can provide. The professional literature deals so little with aspects of rural practice that the preparation that all social workers should receive to work in rural communities or with clients from rural cultures is limited.

Professional Services and Education

Rural areas face a shortage of social welfare services to meet their needs. Those that do exist are further diminished by the lack of professional training among staff (Ginsberg 1993; NASW 1994; Daley & Avant, 1999). Agencies often are forced to use higher proportions of baccalaureate level and non-professional staff than is typical in non-rural areas. (Johnson 1980) It is common for workers to be isolated from direct professional supervision.

Recruitment and retention issues are, in part, by-products of a social work educational system that developed largely from urban roots and pays relatively little attention to rural populations (NASW, 1994). Most social workers receive little content on rural social work in their professional training. This general lack of preparation creates a major barrier to developing the professional social work labor force needed to address the needs of rural clients and the unique social problems of rural communities.

Most authors agree that generalist preparation is the best approach for rural practice (Ginsberg 1976, Davenport & Davenport 1995, Daley & Avant, 1999), yet graduate education tends to force students away from this approach. The appearance of new social work programs in rural areas, some with advanced generalist concentrations, is encouraging. They create an opportunity to address the shortage of professional social workers in rural areas. The educational challenge that remains is to continue to strengthen the content in rural social work and integrate it in the overall curriculum.

Rural Poverty

Great wealth has been extracted from rural America, yet it remains the site of some of the nation's most intense and persistent poverty (Rural Policy Research Institute, 1995). People in rural areas experience lower income levels, higher unemployment, and higher poverty rates than people in urban areas. However, public assistance utilization rates are lower because they lack access to program information and because of the stigma attached to public assistance in rural areas. (Rank & Hirschl, 1993)

In 1997, the poverty rate in non-metropolitan counties was 15.9 percent compared to 12.6 percent in metropolitan counties (U. S. Department of Commerce, 1998). Poverty levels in metropolitan areas have slowly decreased, but have not gone down in rural areas. (U. S. Department of Commerce, 1998) Nonmetropolitan counties have a higher percentage of children in poverty, and more rural children live in female-headed households. (U. S. Department of Commerce 1998). Twenty-three percent of people in nonmetropolitan counties are considered persistently poor. Studies indicate that the duration of poverty is a strong predictor of school attainment and early patterns of employment (Duncan, Young, Brooks-Gunn, & Smith, 1998; Caspi, Wright, Moffitt, & Silva, 1998). Children in nonmetropolitan areas who become poor or are born poor are more likely than urban children to stay in poverty; nonmetropolitan children in female-headed households are at even greater risk of persistent poverty (Sherman, 1992).

The increasingly global economy and proliferation of international corporate conglomerates has further transformed the political, social, and economic landscape of rural areas. Rural manufacturing operations relocate to places with cheap labor. Without the training to move to a technology-based economy and with under-funded school systems and limited taxation capacity, even more rural people are left out of the economic mainstream and remain in or near poverty (Dilger et al, 1999).

Some rural communities experience an in-migration of population, often made up of mid-career "baby boomers" seeking a more peaceful way of life. Ironically, the resulting increase in property values forces long-term rural residents out because they cannot afford property taxes, or to turn down the money offered for their land. Rural newcomers press and vote for city-like services—such as libraries, recreation centers, and road maintenance—that again raise taxes. Because they commute to urban jobs or keep only weekend homes in rural settings, they do not tend to make major purchases locally, participate in local events, become invested in the rural culture, or have true concern for the success or failure of neighbors. The new job opportunities they create tend to be low wage service jobs. Rural service sector wage earners drive long distances to work because increased property values and taxes make it impossible to live where they work (Dilger et al, 2001).

Rural Communities

Rural communities often retain traditional structures and faith-based service delivery systems that can be assets as well as challenges. They provide self-monitoring and vigilance, making rural communities safer than urban areas, and have a strong informal helping system. However, the same structures may be less hospitable to individuals perceived as outside the mainstream, such as people of color, women, or gay, lesbian, bisexual, and transgendered populations.

The "strip and leave" practices of extractive industries and the crisis of urban and industrial waste have left rural areas with real or potential ecological disasters and few resources to deal with them.

Service Delivery Systems

Many rural areas are part of large geographic service areas. Multi-county social and health services programs based in population centers are designated to serve rural areas. Rural communities are generally offered fewer services than their numbers in the service area justify. Services may be offered primarily at a central location. All social workers should develop knowledge and skills for effective rural social work. Regional agencies must ensure that rural communities receive accessible and appropriate services and include rural residents in planning processes. Regional agencies should train staff to provide rural services in effective ways, such as assigning responsibility for particular rural sections and making efforts to build trust with residents of rural communities.

ISSUE STATEMENT

Social work practice in rural areas historically has sought to resolve issues of equity, service availability, and isolation that adversely affect rural populations, and to support and advocate for vulnerable and at-risk people living in rural communities. Practitioners of rural social work are confronted with rural poverty that is more pervasive and hidden than urban poverty. Rural communities tend to be closed to "outsiders." The dominant rural culture may harshly judge those who are perceived to be "different." Rural communities are experiencing diminishing infrastructure systems and resources. Our colleagues in rural practice face professional and personal challenges that urban social workers may never face. The relative closeness of rural cultures, communities, and peoples greatly magnifies these concerns. Confidentiality can be an unachievable goal in rural areas, and professional distance is difficult to maintain.

Effective rural social work practice demands that the social worker have command of impressive levels of expertise, subtlety, and sophistication and practice skill-sets to match. The lack of professional preparation for rural social work practice is a concern that must be addressed. The recruitment and retention of social workers for rural practice is a major problem for the profession, leading to declassification, resistance to legal regulation, and the siphoning of social work jobs to those with little professional training.

Throughout history rural people have migrated to urban centers seeking economic security in the face of joblessness, disaster, conflict, or war, sometimes creating rural ghettos in the city. Urban social workers should develop and maintain a minimum proficiency in practice skills effective with rural individuals, families, and communities.

Rural areas are under attack from the popular culture. Worldwide, young rural residents turn away from their cultures, families, and traditions after exposure to television images and media presentations of "the good life."

Rural social workers deal with challenging issues of poverty, at-risk populations, and service delivery at the community, family, and individual intervention levels that are unique and different from urban practice. These and other factors raise crucial issues for social work practice and educational preparation for social work practice in rural areas.

POLICY STATEMENT

The understanding of rural people and cultures is a pressing issue of cultural competence in professional social work. Rural people and cultures occupy and influence the majority of the earth's landmass. Twenty-five percent of the population resides in rural areas that comprise 83 percent of the landmass of the United States. Rural people and cultures possess and foster strengths that are rapidly being lost in the cultural mainstream. Many observers decry the urban loss of that which still survives, even thrives, in rural areas: a sense of community, individual character, an awareness of place, and a sense of family and tradition.

When rural people relocate, by necessity or choice, to take advantage of urban and suburban-economic opportunity, their unique cultural values, norms, and ways of being go with them. Special skills are needed to work effectively with displaced rural people.

Social work practice in rural communities challenges the social worker to embrace and effectively use an impressive range of professional intervention and community skills. It is critical that the social worker have practice expertise in multiple areas. Like all major subcultures, rural populations must be understood to be effectively engaged. The difficulties associated with experiencing social problems are magnified in rural areas because close social and personal relationships coexist with a low population base. This and other unique features require the social worker to apply professional ethical constructs more consistently to protect confidentiality, analyze relationship issues, and otherwise behave in the best interests of clients.

Rural areas suffer disproportionately when urban-based policies are forced upon them. Corporate mergers, centralization, managed care, globalization, and similar cost-saving strategies based solely on urban models are disadvantageous to rural areas, where distance and time are the enemies of efficiency and of access to social services, health care delivery, and health maintenance.

It is known that many rural people experience economic poverty, but not well understood that they experience persistent poverty. Such lack of infrastructure, development, housing, education, and adequate health care is usually associated with blighted urban areas. The factors that foster despair, hopelessness, substance abuse, and domestic violence in our inner cities exist among the rural poor.

Ethical practice in rural areas requires special attention to dual relationship issues. Few other settings expose social workers more to the risk of violating the *NASW Code of Ethics* (2000) admonition that social workers are to ". . . take steps to protect clients and are responsible for setting clear, appropriate, and culturally sensitive boundaries" (1.06 (c)). Social Workers practicing in rural areas must have advanced understanding of ethical responsibilities, not only because dual or multiple relationships are unavoidable, but also because the setting may require that dual or multiple relationships be used and managed as an appropriate method of social work practice.

Public and social policy must take in to account the unique nature of rural areas and residents. Equitable policy formation should be the goal, so that urban and rural populations and jurisdictions are not pitted against each other over issues of livelihood, lifestyle, economy, or ecology.

Rural areas require the services of professional social workers to provide the broad range of services, including clinical and health practice, community organization, administration and management, public welfare, and community-based services.

The concept of teaching cultural competency in social work education programs must be expanded to include the understanding of rural cultures, diversity issues, and people in a contextual practice skills framework. Specialized coursework and advanced practice concentrations must be offered to prepare and encourage graduates to practice in rural areas.

The skills of professional social workers are uniquely suited to helping rural people organize their lives, families, communities, and organizations to overcome adversity, identify and develop resources, and change lives for the better. NASW should promote advocacy, legislation, and policy development that improve rural infrastructure, economic development, and availability and access to needed health care, service delivery, public services, and education. NASW must work to promote preparation for social work practice in rural areas, including developing proficiencies through professional continuing education.

REFERENCES

Daley, M., & Avant, F. (1999). Attracting and retaining professionals for social work practice in rural areas: An example from East Texas. In I. B. Carlton-Laney, R. L. Edwards, & P. N. Reid (Eds.), *Preserving and strengthening small towns and rural communities* (pp. 335–345). Washington, DC: NASW Press.

Davenport, J. A., & Davenport, J., III (1995). Rural social work overview. In R. L. Edwards (Ed.-in-Chief), *Encyclopedia of Social Work* (19th ed., Vol. 3, pp. 2076–2085). Washington, DC: NASW Press

Dilger, R. J., Blakely, E., Dorton, K.V.H., Latimer, M., Locke, B., Mencken, C., Plein, C., Potter, L., Williams, D., & Yoon, D. P. (1999). *West Virginia WORKS Case closure study* [Online]. Morgantown, WV: West Virginia University Institute for Public Affairs. Available: http://www.polsci.wvu.edu/ipa /par/Report17_1.pdf

Dilger, R. J., Blakely, E., Latimer, M., Locke, B, Mencken, C., Plein, C., Potter, L., & Williams, D. (2001). *West Virginia WORKS 2000: The recipients' perspective*. Morgantown, WV: West Virginia University Institute for Public Affairs [Online]. Available: http://www.polsci.wvu.edu/ipa/par /Report18_3.pdf

Ginsberg, L. H. (1976). An overview of social work education for rural areas. In L. H. Ginsberg (Ed.), *Social work in rural communities: A book of readings* (pp. 1–12). Alexandria, VA: Council on Social Work Education.

Ginsberg, L. H. (1993). An overview of social work education for rural areas. In L. H. Ginsberg (Ed.), *Social work in rural communities: A book of readings* (2nd ed., pp. 1–17). Alexandria, VA: Council on Social Work Education.

National Association of Social Workers (2000). *Code of Ethics of the National Association of Social Workers.* Washington, DC: Author.

National Association of Social Workers (1994). *Social work in rural areas.* In Social Work Speaks (pp. 244–248). Washington, DC: Author.

Rank, M., & Hirschl, T. (1993). The link between population density and welfare populations. *Demography, 30,* 607–623.

Rural Policy Research Institute (1995). *Opportunities for rural policy reform: Lessons learned from recent farm bills* [Online]. Columbia, MO: Author. Available: www.rupri.org/archive/old/rupolicyP95–2.html.

U. S. Department of Commerce (1998, September). *Poverty in the United States: 1997,* U. S. Bureau of the Census, Current Population Reports.

SUGGESTED READINGS

Barker, Robert L. (1995). *Social Work Dictionary* (3rd ed., p. 330). Washington, DC: NASW Press.

Carlton-LaNey, I., Edwards, R., & Reid, N. (2000). *Preserving and strengthening small towns and rural communities* (pp. 6–7). Washington, DC: NASW Press.

Caspi, A., Wright, B., Moffitt, T. & Silva, P. (1998). Early failure in the labor market: Childhood and adolescent predictors of unemployment in the transition to adulthood. *American Sociological Review, 63*, 424–451.

Congress, E. P. (2000). What social workers should know about ethics: Understanding and resolving practice dilemmas. *Advances in Social Work, 1*(1), 1–25.

Conklin, J. J. (1995). Distance learning in continuing social work education: Promise of the year 2000. *Journal of Continuing Social Work Education, 6*(3), 15–17.

Duncan, G., Young, W., Brooks-Gunn, J., and Smith, J. (1998). How much does childhood poverty affect the life chances of children? *American Sociological Review, 63*, 406–423.

Farley, O. W., Griffiths, K. A., Skidmore, R. A., & Thackeray, M. G. (1982). *Rural Social Work Practice.* New York: Free Press.

Hardcastle, D. A., Wenocur, S., & Powers, P. R. (1997). *Community practice: Theories and skills for social workers.* New York: Oxford University Press.

Hargrove, D. S. (1982). An overview of professional considerations in the rural community. In P. A. Keller & J. D. Murray (Eds.), *Handbook of Rural Community Mental Health* (pp. 169–182). New York: Human Sciences Press.

Horner, B., & O'Neil, J. F. (1981). *Child welfare practice in rural areas and small communities.* Washington DC: U. S. Department of Education (ERIC Document Reproduction Service No. ED 239 783).

Jayaratne, S., Croxton, T., & Mattison, D. (1997). Social work professional standards: An exploratory study. *Social Work, 42*, 187–199.

Johnson, L. C. (1980). Human service delivery patterns in non-metropolitan communities. In H. W. Johnson, *Rural Human Services* (p. 69). Itasca, IL: Peacock Publishers.

Lennox, N. D., & Murty, S. A. (1994). Choice, change, and challenge: Managing regional services. In B. Locke, & M. Egan (Eds.), *Fulfilling our mission: Rural social work in the 1990s* (pp. 150–159). (Proceedings of the 17th Annual National Institute on Social Work and Human Services in Rural Areas), West Virginia University, Morgantown.

Martinez-Brawley, E. E. (1980). *Pioneer efforts in rural social welfare.* University Park: Pennsylvania State University Press.

Martinez-Brawley, E. E. (1990). *Perspectives on the small community.* Silver Spring, MD: NASW Press.

Merrell, I. E., Pratt, S., Forbush, D., Jentzsch, C., Nelson, S., Odell, C., and Smith, M. (1994). Special education, school psychology, and community mental health practice in rural settings: Common problems and overlapping solutions for training. *Rural Special Education Quarterly, 13*, 28–36.

Miller, P. (1998). Dual relationships in rural practice: A dilemma of ethics and culture. In L. H. Ginsberg (Ed.), *Social Work in Rural Communities* (pp. 55–62). Alexandria, VA, Council on Social Work Education.

Murty, S. (2001) Regionalization and rural service delivery. In R. Moore (Ed.), *The hidden America: social problems in rural America in the 21st century* (pp. 199–216). Cranbury, NJ: Associated University Presses.

Oliver, S., & Haulotte, S. M. (2001). *A strategy for uncovering, accessing, and maximizing social services in rural areas.* Paper presented at the 26th National Institute on Social Work and Human Services in Rural Areas, May 30 – June 1, 2001, Austin, TX.

Rural Policy Research Institute. Various publications and resources [Online]. Columbia, MO: Rural Policy Research Institute: Available: www.rupri.org.

Ryder, R., & Hepworth, J. (1990). AAMFT ethical code: Dual relationships. *Journal of Marital and Family Therapy, 16*(2), 127–132.

Sherman, A. (1992). *Falling by the wayside: Children in rural America.* Washington, DC: Children's Defense Fund.

Southern Regional Education Board Rural Task Force Manpower Education and Training Project (1993). Education assumptions for rural social work. In L. H. Ginsberg (Ed.) *Social Work in Rural Communities: A Book of Readings* (2nd ed., pp. 18–21). Alexandria, VA: Council on Social Education.

Weber, G. K. (1980). Preparing social workers for practice in rural social systems. In H. W. Johnson, *Rural Human Services* (pp. 209–210). Itasca, IL: Peacock Publishers.

Weil, M. O. (1996). Community building: Building community practice. *Social Work, 41*, 481–497.

Index